FUNCTION AND MEANING IN CLASSIC MAYA ARCHITECTURE

FUNCTION AND MEANING IN CLASSIC MAYA ARCHITECTURE

A Symposium at Dumbarton Oaks
7TH AND 8TH OCTOBER 1994

Stephen D. Houston, *Editor*

Dumbarton Oaks Research Library and Collection
Washington, D.C.

Printed in the United States of America

Library of Congress Cataloging-in-Publication Data

Function and meaning in classic Maya architecture: a symposium at Dumbarton Oaks, 7th and 8th October 1994 / Stephen D. Houston, editor.

p. cm.

Includes index.

ISBN 0–88402–254–4

1. Maya architecture—Congresses. I. Houston, Stephen D.

F1435.3.A6F85 1998

720'.97281—dc21 98–4133

CIP

Contents

Preface

CUT AND DRESSED stone architecture holds a special fascination for those interested in ancient civilizations. Without it, one would not be able to visit "the ruins" the same way as when one walks through remnants of halls that once echoed with ancient chants or laughter. Architectural remains serve to gauge the relative importance of a place and its former inhabitants within the larger world in which they existed. Ruins also provide a special sense of place for visitors, just as the same functioning buildings once created a distinct experiential presence for those who built and used them. In the last century, both romantics and scientists gave importance to ruins, leading, on the one hand, to the construction of "follies" and the like, to create evocative places, while large-scale architecture, in particular, served as a key emblem of advanced civilization in theories of cultural evolution.

The special powers of architecture to evoke a romantic nostalgia for a lost world in which one has not participated, but which might be imagined or scientifically resurrected, have had a significant role in Maya studies. It was largely through the art of Frederick Catherwood that the attention of the Euro-American world was drawn to the "lost cities" of the Maya; his depictions were at once higly accurate in their rendering and romantic in their presentation of exotic architecture amidst tropical vegetation. A century later, Tatiana Proskouriakoff's *Album of Maya Architecture* stimulated the public and scholars alike to imagine ancient America and to investigate its past. Then, however, the goal was to retrieve the ancient Maya with the rigor of accurate recording and field investigations, though the lure of the exotic was perhaps just as enticing to Proskouriakoff's generation.

Investigations of Maya architecture have been among the chief vehicles for contemplating a great art tradition, the hieroglyphic writing system, and evaluating issues of comparative sociology. The powerful attraction of Maya architecture as an evocation of lost worlds, as a medium for the carved glyph and idol, and as a yardstick for measuring evolutionary complexity, makes it appropriate that attention be given to the buildings themselves, rather than simply treating them as media for the investigation of other issues, as valuable as these might be. The articles in this volume are of special value and importance in making architecture itself the focus of attention. At the same time that they give appropriate attention to the great architectural achievements of the Maya, they do not ignore the often evanescent residences of commoners. Rather than privileging cross-cultural comparisons or the anthropology of prehistoric peoples, however, structures remain at the forefront. In this, we reaffirm Maya architecture as one of the world's great building traditions, allow for meaningful interdisciplinary exchange between archaeology, art history, and anthropology, and provide new ways of appreciating Maya culture, from a unique perspective.

"Function and Meaning in Classic Maya Architecture," the symposium from which this book is derived, was held at Dumbarton Oaks in October 1994. At that time, Elizabeth Boone was director of Pre-Columbian Studies, and to her and Richard Diehl, former acting director of the program, goes credit for working so well and productively with Stephen Houston. It has been my great pleasure to learn from them and to assist Stephen in the latter stages of transforming the symposium papers into this volume.

The contributions presented here will surely mark a significant stage in the study of Maya architecture and the society that built it. These articles represent the advances that have been achieved in our understandings of the past, point toward avenues for further studies, and note the distance we have yet to travel in fully appreciating and understanding this ancient American culture and its material remains.

Jeffrey Quilter
Dumbarton Oaks

Introduction

STEPHEN D. HOUSTON
BRIGHAM YOUNG UNIVERSITY

IDEALLY, EVERY EDITED BOOK should have its inception in a sense that certain connections need to be made, that gaps still open need to be filled. This volume represents a collective attempt by Mayanists to establish such connections and to close such gaps. *Function and Meaning in Classic Maya Architecture* results from a meeting, held at Dumbarton Oaks on October 7 and 8, 1994, that confronted a growing problem in our research. As Mayanists, we draw upon an extraordinary accumulation of data. Few architectural traditions are as abundantly documented as the legacy of buildings left by the Classic Maya, whose immense palaces and platforms, pyramids and plazuelas amaze tourists and overwhelm archaeologists. For all the richness of information, however, there is much that is poorly understood. Why were these buildings constructed? How were they made, how were they used, and how were they regarded or perceived? What meanings did the Classic Maya attach to such structures? How did these meanings change, and why?

There are good reasons why such questions remain unanswered or only partly addressed by recent scholarship. Consider this: A compelling, internal logic commands the technical exercise of excavating architecture. Once started, excavations must undertake the tedious process of finding corners, moldings, and abutments; of attesting to changes in material and method of construction; and of documenting modifications over time through sections, plans, and projections. Most of us do not believe in shortcuts to understanding buried architecture. Some scholars may even question the whole enterprise of digging such buildings. Arguably, such work squanders thin resources of labor and money or, in a more ideological vein, expresses an elite-focused, Mayanist obsession with monumentality. The contributors to this volume would probably concur only slightly with these two points of view, perhaps rather less with the first than with the second. In my own opinion, reliance on test pits and surface survey produces marginal and inconclusive results in understanding structures. If buildings are to be studied and excavated, they must be uncovered properly and extensively, although the economic and political costs may be great.

But an unfortunate side effect attends this concentration of effort, thought, and money. Through its very difficulty, through the exigent demands it makes on research, documentation of architecture often becomes a conclusion rather than a beginning. This it should never be. I believe we must turn forcefully to the questions listed before, going beyond simple description to an assault on vexatious problems of meaning, function, and development. Our spirit must be interdisciplinary and impervious to intellectual parochialism. To paraphrase Mao, may a thousand flowers bloom, a thousand approaches, a thousand varieties of archaeology be brought to bear, without one excluding another.

This volume has another dimension. It can hardly have escaped notice—in fact, it presses on me every day as a student of Maya writing—that the Classic period also represents a time of historical record. This book not only confronts basic issues of function and meaning in buildings it also injects the detailed information that epigraphy now provides (see Stuart). In so doing, it explores the role of tradition in relation to individual needs and personalities (see Fash), sorts out native categories and their correspondences (or incongruities) with real buildings (Houston), and reconstructs aspects of architectural ritual, mythological background, and building function (see McAnany, Miller, Taube, and Schele).

What we cannot do, both for want of time and because we wish to avoid diffusion of focus, is to construe aspects of Classic Maya city planning, of how buildings fit into a larger landscape. Nor can we concentrate to any great extent on small-scale, domestic architecture, although Kevin Johnston and Nancy Gonlin help remedy this deficiency with their substantive and methodological essay. (Wendy Ashmore presented a similar paper at our fall meeting, but, under press of other commitments, found it necessary to withdraw her thoughtful discussion from this volume.) We lack a comprehensive review of all regions in the Maya lowlands and, worse, fail to include an architect or engineer's view of the technical restraints and possibilities that inform Maya architecture (although see Abrams). I personally regret that scheduling problems made it impossible for some of our fine Latin American colleagues to participate. So, despite our good intentions, the selection of topics and authors will appear to some—only a few I trust—as idiosyncratic and patchwork. At the least, the lacunae in this book will prompt the preparation of other volumes. My concluding essay points to productive areas of future research and suggests how Mayanists can participate in a wider, transregional dialogue on architecture.

The papers fall into three sections, all of which use "function" and "meaning" in the sense of "building use" and "indigenous perception of significance." To further their analysis, Johnston and Gonlin also employ a broader, more "etic" definition of these terms. The first section of the book provides orientation and background. David Webster's essay serves as the "prow of this boat" (although he may prefer some other, possibly sacrificial metaphor to describe his role). His acute observations make superfluous any windy, editorial introduction. In this first section, authors also address the antecedents of Classic architecture (Hansen) as well as its method of construction (Abrams) and correspondence with the "vernacular" tradition, if that is quite the right descriptor for it (Johnston and Gonlin). The following section focuses more closely on the historical setting of Classic architecture, including questions of patronage and design, and thematic concerns in monumental construction (Miller, Fash, and McAnany), including the matter of what goes *into* buildings (Chase and Chase). The final block of papers treats iconography and epigraphy. Here we approach a true cognitive archaeology that is, in my view, more solid and convincing than recent Europeanist efforts in this direction. The wealth of evidence and depth of reasoning deflect any accusation that this book on architecture simply responds to "a fashionable topic of theoretical discourse" (Johnson 1995: 644). For some time Mayanists have thought carefully about this topic and, with appropriate enrichment from anthropology and other disciplines (e.g., Steadman 1996), will do so for years to come. Our sincere desire is that this collection of essays will stimulate and provoke readers into exploring, from their own perspective, the complexities of "Function and Meaning in Classic Maya Architecture."

Acknowledgments The editor of a Dumbarton Oaks volume incurs many debts. *Function and Meaning* has coherence and flow because Elizabeth Boone and Richard Diehl, director and former acting director, respectively, of Pre-Columbian Studies at Dumbarton Oaks, shared with me their good sense about the practical organization of edited volumes. The current director, Jeffrey Quilter, facilitated the final preparation of the book. I must also acknowledge the great generosity of the senior fellows, who, in something of a departure from precedent, allowed me to organize, from June to August of 1994, an academic summer camp on the topic of the symposium that generated this publication. At Dumbarton Oaks, Nancy Gonlin, Patricia McAnany, Karl Taube, David Webster, and I not only had a rip-snorting time, but, more important, improved our minds with the unique fellowship that this institution offers. I learned a great deal from these friends and would be the poorer without their collegiality. This volume exists in part because of financial support from the National Endowment for the Humanities (NEH grant RO-22648-93, Collaborative Projects, with David Stuart) and Dean Clayne Pope, College of Family, Home, and Social Sciences, Brigham Young University. Of course, these generous sources bear no responsibility for the contents of this book, nor does John Clark of Brigham Young University, who contributed his editorial eye when it was needed. Finally, this book employs a system of glyphic transcription used to good effect in the Research Reports on Ancient Maya Writing (Stuart 1988). Site names follow those listed by the Corpus of Maya Hieroglyphic Inscriptions, at the Peabody Museum of Harvard University (Graham 1975: 9, 23–24).

BIBLIOGRAPHY

Graham, Ian

1975 *Corpus of Maya Hieroglyphic Inscriptions,* vol. 1: *Introduction to the Corpus.* Peabody Museum of Archaeology and Ethnology, Harvard University, Cambridge, Mass.

Johnson, Matthew

1995 Review of *Meaningful Architecture: Social Interpretations of Buildings,* by Martin Locock. *Antiquity* 69: 644–646.

Steadman, Sharon R.

1996 Recent Research in the Archaeology of Architecture: Beyond the Foundations. *Journal of Archaeological Research* 4: 51–93.

Stuart, George

1988 *Special Supplement: A Guide to the Style and Content of the Series Research Reports on Ancient Maya Writing.* Research Reports on Ancient Maya Writing, no. 15. Center for Maya Research, Washington, D.C.

Classic Maya Architecture: Implications and Comparisons

DAVID WEBSTER
THE PENNSYLVANIA STATE UNIVERSITY

IN JOHN GARDNER'S (1971) retelling of the Beowulf epic from the monster's point of view, Grendel characterizes human beings as "pattern-makers." Grendel, a philosophical monster, is both fascinated and appalled by this pattern-making propensity, because he realizes that it renders humans very powerful but also can ensnare them in destructive ways. Archaeologists, of course, are archetypical pattern seekers. We spend our careers trying to discern patterns in the material and symbolic records of ancient cultures, because we hope they will enable us to reconstruct the past and determine how and why it changed. The excitement in this enterprise is discovering useful patterns; the danger is that we can create them to suit our own intellectual needs.

For more than 150 years Maya archaeology has been heavily influenced, one might even say dominated, by a particularly obtrusive and durable set of patterns—that expressed in architecture or, more appropriately and inclusively, the "built environment." By built environment I mean, following Rapoport (1990), the sum total of all purposeful human modifications of the landscape. I personally would also include all human alterations of natural ecosystems. Rapoport, by contrast, relegates unintentional human landscape modifications, such as deforestation and erosion, to the "ecological environment." The "cultural landscape" is the product of all such purposeful and unintended human alterations. Our core concern in this volume is Classic Maya architecture per se, and I will have little to say about the ecological environment or settlement systems on the regional scale.

Specialized and innovative studies of the built environment by anthropologists, architects, landscape architects, art and architectural historians, geographers, social and economic historians, and urban planners have proliferated in the past two decades—for a recent review, see Lawrence and Low (1990). Research is often highly particularistic, but at least for some scholars the goal is identifying "universally valid principles for the social use of space . . ." (Douglas 1972: 516). The theme of this symposium is how Mayanists infer function and meaning from architecture, how our efforts relate to this larger evolving tradition of research, and what we can learn from and contribute to it.[1]

My own paper has three main goals. First, it relates the theme of the built environment to basic issues of archaeology in general and to Maya archaeology in particular. Second, it summarizes approaches to the built environment presently being explored by Mayanists, mainly as a prelude to papers that follow. Finally, it presents a brief historical overview of how Maya scholars have incorporated the built environment into their research. This overview is partly presented as a coherent section of its own, but some of it is woven into the discussions of issues and approaches. As a result, strict chronological order is not always followed.

THE CLASSIC MAYA BUILT ENVIRONMENT

The Classic Maya built environment encompasses all the familiar "built forms" of Maya centers: temples, palaces, ballcourts, patios, reservoirs, roads, and causeways as well as the tombs, caches, monuments, the formal and informal embellishments associated with them, and their ambient spaces. It logically comprises much else as well: the dwellings of common people, rural terraces and field systems, sacred caves, burial places, and landmarks of all sorts. Movable, impermanent or perishable structures, such as scaffolds, arbors, banners, and litters that have left no material traces but can be inferred from iconography and epigraphy, are also included (see Houston, this volume). All these forms constitute our database for understanding how the Maya used and conceived of the places they built and inhabited.

Purposeful constructions constitute a huge resource for investigating the past and have done so ever since the beginnings of systematic Maya scholarship. Readers hardly need to be reminded of the wonder and speculation excited in John Stephens and Frederick Catherwood by their encounter with the forest-enshrouded ruins and carved monuments of Copan in 1839. It is worth remembering, however, that Stephens reflexively tried to evaluate this experience (although not in any mode of systematic inquiry) in terms of what he knew

[1] Archaeologists usually borrow ideas and methods from other disciplines. For a gratifying portrayal of archaeologists as innovators in the historical study of built environments, see Rapoport (1990: chap. 5).

about other ancient civilizations in the Old World from his studies and travels, a comparative perspective later neglected by some Mayanists.

Seen in such comparative perspective, the built environment of the Classic Maya is especially impressive. It is sobering to realize how much remains missing or unknown in the archaeological records of other early great civilizations. One searches the literature in vain for a single excavated Uruk period house in the first cities of southern Sumer or the well-preserved and complete layout of a single Old Kingdom Egyptian town. While colleagues in the valley of Mexico struggle to estimate the sizes of ancient communities from surface scatters of potsherds, Maya archaeologists investigate thousands of individual household features still exposed on the surface of the cultural landscapes they study. Without putting a spade in the ground, Mayanists can map the basic features, and often the details, of huge royal centers, and these are not plain, unembellished, and anonymous places like Harappa and Mohenjo-Daro, the great cities of the Indus Valley. Rather, the Classic Maya left us centers filled with art and writing, rich and highly personalized in historical implication. Much of this symbolic material, moreover, remains superbly contextualized. Only in the coastal deserts of the Central Andes and in the American Southwest do the records of ancient built environments approximate in accessibility, quality, and quantity that of the Maya lowlands.

This embarrassment of architectural riches offers great opportunities as well as great responsibilities. If archaeologists anywhere can use the built environment to make sense of the past, we can. We, more than archaeologists virtually anywhere else, should be innovative in our approaches to the past environment. What follows is partly an assessment of how well we have lived up to this responsibility.

MAYA ARCHAEOLOGY AND THE BUILT ENVIRONMENT

Since the emergence of anthropology and archaeology as professional disciplines during the last half of the nineteenth century, Mayanists have traditionally used architecture, or the built environment, for the following main purposes:

(1) to define the Maya culture area and bolster theories of cultural origins, development, and evolution;

(2) as a repository of inscriptional and iconographic information;

(3) to understand Maya cognition, especially as it relates to spaces and places;

(4) as a source of stratified artifact deposits and features with implications for Maya culture history;

(5) to link the Pre-Spanish Maya to ethnohistoric accounts;

(6) as an inferential tool to address issues such as Maya population size and subsistence agriculture;

(7) to promote interest in the past as a matter of national pride and to attract tourists;

(8) to generate and test hypotheses about the nature of Maya society and culture, most particularly the manner in which political power was organized, legitimized, and exercised.

The last purpose is the most fundamental and is concerned with the social production of built form—"the social, political, and economic forces that produce the built environment, and conversely, the impact of the socially produced built environment on social action" (Lawrence and Low 1990: 482). Function and meaning, the two themes that form the core concepts of this symposium, were not widely and systematically addressed until fairly late in the development of the discipline.

HISTORICAL PERCEPTIONS AND USES OF MAYA ARCHITECTURE

The architectural achievements of the Maya immediately and powerfully impressed the earliest Spanish explorers, and their observations are often remarkably pertinent to later archaeological discoveries. One of my favorite eyewitness accounts is Hernan Cortés's description of an elite Maya house—what archaeologists call a palace:

> There are houses belonging to certain men of rank which are very cool and have many rooms, for we have seen as many as five courtyards in a single house, and the rooms around them very well laid out, each man having a private room. Inside there are also wells and water tanks and rooms for slaves and servants of which they have many. Each of these chieftains has in front of the entrance to his house a large courtyard and some two or three or four of them raised up high with steps up to them and all very well built. (Cortés 1986: 30–31)

Cortés's comment almost perfectly captures the essence of Maya elite compounds, built eight centuries earlier, that we excavated at Copan in the 1980s (Fig. 1).

After the conquest, the extent of the Maya built environment rapidly became apparent to Spanish colonists. Landa remarked that

> If Yucatan were to gain a name and reputation from the multitude, the grandeur, and the beauty of its buildings, as other regions of the Indies have obtained by gold, silver, and riches, its glory would have spread like that of Peru and New Spain. For it is true that in its buildings and the multitude of them it is the most remarkable of all things which up to this day have been discovered in the Indies; for they are so many

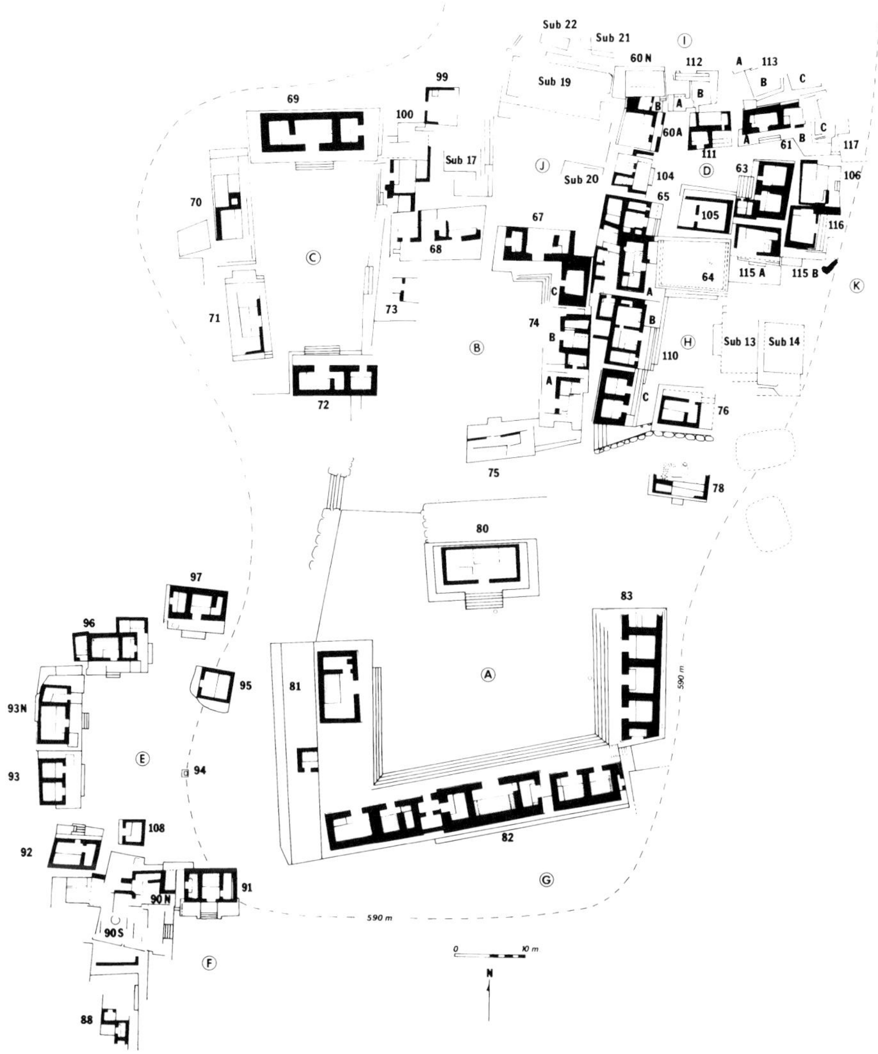

Fig. 1 Plan of Group 9N-8, an elite residential compound at Copan, Honduras.

> in number and so many are the parts of the country where they are found, and so well built are they of cut stone in their fashion, that it fills one with astonishment. (Landa 1941: 171–172)

Landa also left us some of the earliest detailed descriptions and depictions of large-scale Maya architecture, including sketches of buildings at the now destroyed center of Tiho, where Mérida presently stands, and at Chichen Itza (Fig. 2). By Landa's time, the large number of abandoned Maya centers had become apparent, and he advanced several explanations for their abundance, some of which were to echo through later Maya scholarship:

(1) that lords wanted to keep commoners occupied;

(2) that the Maya were so devoted to their deities that they compulsively built religious structures;

(3) that Maya communities were often moved and so new buildings were frequently erected;

(4) that earlier Maya were superior in size and strength to their descendants and so, by comparison, built excessively.

Interestingly, as the last explanation suggests, Landa drew what we now know to be a correct conclusion: those responsible for the abandoned architectural complexes that dotted the landscape of Yucatan were the ancestors of the sixteenth-century Maya. From the beginning the Spanish also distinguished a "little tradition" of Maya commoner architecture, mainly consisting of pole-and-thatch dwellings, from the "great tradition" of temple/elite architecture.[2] It is the latter, of course, that until very recently has most preoccupied archaeologists.

As early as the sixteenth century, growing awareness of the enormous territorial spread of the elite architectural tradition helped define the Classic Maya culture area. In 1576, Diego García de Palacio visited the ruins of Copan, 640 km southeast of the colonial capital of Mérida. Here he recorded a local legend that the city was founded and built by migrants from Yucatan, a claim that Palacio seems to have found plausible because of the similarity of the architecture in Yucatan and Honduras.

Palenque, discovered by Europeans in 1746, was the first great Classic center to capture the attention of scholars. After several other preliminary visits, a royally mandated Spanish expedition in 1787, led by Antonio del Río, collected objects and carried out excavations. Its goal "to illustrate the origins and history of the old Americans" (Hammond 1983: 9) probably qualifies this effort as the first program of problem-oriented research in the Maya lowlands.

[2] For the origins of these concepts, see Redfield (1957: chap. 3).

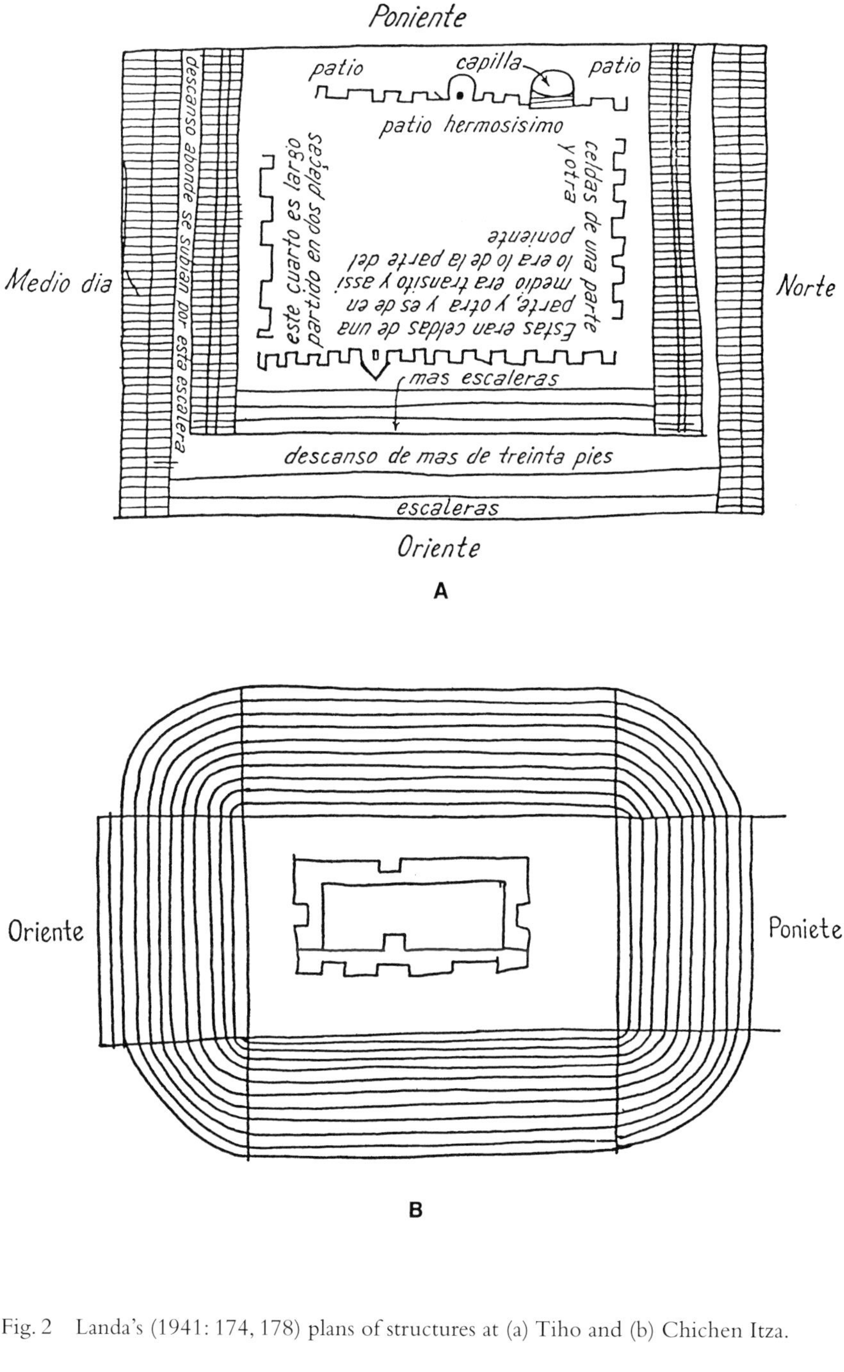

Fig. 2 Landa's (1941: 174, 178) plans of structures at (a) Tiho and (b) Chichen Itza.

Architectural drawings much more sophisticated than Landa's were made. Equally important were the illustrations and samples of sculpture and glyphs obtained (Stuart 1992: 5–6), which helped to establish Palenque and ruins like it as repositories of ancient Maya art and inscriptions. Juan Galindo's later documentation in 1834 of sculpture and glyphs at Copan that were identical to those of Palenque served to reinforce the perception of widespread Maya cultural uniformity (Graham 1963).

In the latter half of the nineteenth century, certainly in large part because of the descriptions of Stephens (1969) and Catherwood, Maya architecture played a distinctive role in the formulation of early anthropological theory, most notably in the writings of Lewis Henry Morgan. By that time, the splendors of the Mesoamerican architectural tradition were widely recognized and posed a potential embarrassment to Morgan's developing scheme of unilineal evolution, in which house form reflected social organization and, in turn, evolutionary stage.

Morgan (1965 [1881]) believed that the most highly evolved New World societies were egalitarian tribal confederations and that the most complex constructions were large communal family dwellings. Although he could dismiss Spanish accounts of the Aztec built environment because it was largely destroyed, Maya architecture presented a thornier problem. Morgan, who never traveled in Mesoamerica, knew that Maya buildings were impressive, numerous, and well preserved. He accorded the Maya high marks for stonework but confidently asserted that most major ruins had been recently abandoned and that they functioned as "communal joint-tenement houses" of essentially egalitarian people who lived together for defensive purposes. Carved stelae and associated altars at centers such as Copan were similarly dismissed as grave markers of influential men. Although this is a particularly wrongheaded example of forcing fact to fit theory—see Thompson (1892) for a spirited rejoinder—we should not be too hard on Morgan, who at least thought that people lived in Maya centers, a position rejected by some later Mayanists.

Systematic Maya archaeology began in earnest in the 1880s, and until the 1960s research focused almost exclusively in one way or another on monumental architecture (some significant exceptions are mentioned below). Only a very brief summary of this period is possible here.[3]

Until the mid-1920s archaeologists were preoccupied with exploring and mapping large sites, and large-scale excavations were few except when clearing

[3] For excellent discussions from which much of my own summary is taken, see Black (1990, n.d.).

for restoration. Centers were seen as repositories of art, dates, and written inscriptions, and it was these that archaeologists most avidly sought. During the succeeding three decades (1925–1955), approaches to Maya architecture are reflected in four Carnegie Institution projects.

Chichen Itza

At Chichen Itza (1924–1936), the most ambitious of these projects, work "focused on the excavation, restoration, and recording of the architecture and associated sculpture, inscriptions, and artwork" (Black n.d.: 83). Restoration was overtly calculated to attract tourists. Art and monuments aside, the main intent of the Chichen Itza effort was to link architectural patterns to ethnohistoric accounts of the Maya "new empire" and incursions of Nahua speakers. Attempts at large-scale mapping were largely confined to the site core after archaeologists recognized that smaller structures extended out indefinitely from the center.

Uaxactun

Because of the remoteness of Uaxactun during the years of the Carnegie project there (1924–1937), restoration and even conservation of architecture were not major issues. Uaxactun was known to have eighth-cycle dates and so was assumed to be an extremely old site. Thus, excavation there complemented research at Chichen Itza in the sense that the combined efforts bracketed most of Maya culture history as then known. One goal was to expose large architectural features; another was to trench buildings and plazas for stratified ceramic deposits to establish a basic ceramic sequence for the Peten. Built forms thus constituted the "containers" for artifacts, caches, and burials useful in reconstructing culture history.

Copan

Excavations at Copan (1935–1946), as at Chichen Itza, heavily emphasized mapping of the site core, recording of monuments and inscriptions, and restoration. One innovation was extensive tunneling for architectural stratigraphy.

Mayapan

The last of the Carnegie projects, at Mayapan (1949–1955), did produce some innovations. Compared to the other centers, Mayapan had little time depth and was not blessed with much in the way of large architecture, inscriptions, and art. What it did have was dwellings. Much more than the other projects, work at Mayapan emphasized the mapping and excavation of residences and so contributed considerably to settlement archaeology. Even so, the main goal was to supplement ethnohistoric accounts with archaeological data, although systematic ways of making this linkage remained undeveloped.

All these research efforts had in common a general lack of specific research design. As Black (1990: 261) notes for Uaxactun, "one thing led to another." For example, architectural patterns with possible astronomical implications noted during mapping prompted the excavation of Group E. Nor, reading the reports, is it easy to understand what was done: "Methodology was simply not considered the proper subject of Maya site reports" (Black 1990: 266). No project systematically investigated the functions or meanings of Maya buildings other than by loosely linking them to ethnohistoric accounts. The intellectual framework was distinctly culture historical, and work focused on large built forms at site cores. In all projects except Uaxactun, there was a strong tension between excavation and restoration.

Some of the most useful and enduring results were by-products of architectural excavations, such as the ceramic sequences created for Uaxactun and Copan. What we now see as innovations were ancillary efforts, such as the small-structure surveys and housemound excavations at Uaxactun (Ricketson and Ricketson 1937; Wauchope 1934), and were not followed up until much later.

Tikal

The University of Pennsylvania's Tikal project (1956–1969) formed a bridge between the great institutional era and more recent Maya research. In many respects, the Tikal project continued the earlier tradition of large architectural clearing and trenching based on only the most general of research designs and culture-historical goals. The enormous stratigraphic excavations in the North Acropolis, recently published by William Coe (1990), best exemplify this dimension of the project. Among many innovative approaches to architecture were the accurate mapping of a large cultural landscape, including peripheral areas, and extensive testing of many classes of buildings that contributed to the understanding of structure functions and demographic reconstructions. More than 200 monuments were recorded, repaired, and reset, and many tombs were found in architectural contexts. By the latter half of the project, new insights into epigraphy and art fostered unprecedented dynastic and historical reconstructions. Also integral to the project was restoration, done in large part to establish Tikal as a major tourist attraction.

The 1960s inaugurated the most recent era of Maya archaeology, characterized by a veritable explosion of research. Most of the resulting new information and interpretations bear directly or indirectly on architectural themes and issues. Even a cursory summary of this period is, unfortunately, far beyond the scope of this paper, although much of it is summarized in the following contributions to this volume. Readers interested in additional detail are referred to Stephen Black's (n.d.) excellent historical review of field methods in Maya archaeology and Deborah Nichols's (1996) comprehensive overview of settlement archaeology in Mesoamerica, including the Maya lowlands.

ARCHITECTURE AND THE ARCHAEOLOGICAL RECORD

We now turn our attention to some unique features of architecture that have made it such an attractive archaeological resource.

A dominant methodological theme of the past 25 years has been the transformational processes that have formed the archaeological record. One issue is place—how did something come to be where we found it? Another is association—do things found together relate to each other behaviorally and chronologically? More fundamentally, what processes formed the archaeological patterns we recovered, and are these patterns meaningful and useful in reconstructing the past? Increased awareness of the complexity of transformation processes has made archaeologists wary of facile answers to these questions, particularly with regard to portable artifacts.

One of the allures of the built environment is that it is much less affected by such transformations than other classes of material remains. One does not have to worry about how Maya temples or the stone platforms of Maya houses came to be where we find them. Such structures sit solidly and reassuringly where they are precisely because ancient people chose to build them in particular places. With proper excavation and chronological controls, the broader patterns or associations inherent in large, multistructure architectural programs are similarly recoverable. Whether on the group level or on that of individual structures, spatial configurations derive clearly from ancient intentions. Careful attention to such intentional arrangements can have enormous payoffs. Proskouriakoff's (1961: 14) insights into the meanings of glyphs at Piedras Negras, for example, were sparked as much by the arrangements and associations of built forms (stela sets and platforms) as by their symbolic content.

This is not to say that architecture is immune to the noise of transformation. Scarborough (1991: 129) characterizes Maya architecture as a *transitory* medium. What he means is that, to Maya builders, even the largest constructions, with some significant exceptions, such as ballcourts, were fair game for elimination or modification. Generations of archaeologists have remarked on this inherent plasticity of the Maya built environment and the unusual degree to which, compared to ancient builders elsewhere, the Maya destroyed, altered, or abandoned existing structures. Old buildings were frequently remodeled and used for new purposes. Temples and houses fell into disrepair and were razed for their materials or buried by later constructions (Fig. 3). The effect for archaeologists, of course (in the absence of complete destruction), is quite the opposite of transitory. Not only are buried or recycled structures preserved, but they constitute a permanent, detailed, diachronic record of how the Maya used and thought about their built environments. Such a record not only can inform us about architectural transformations and stratigraphic implications, it also reflects important aspects of the dynamics of culture history and cultural process.

Architecture also looms large in the archaeological consciousness because of the nature of the patterns it presents to us and the processes of recovery, analysis, and description that we use. Classic Maya architecture, with some exceptions, such as old, deeply buried structures, is quite easy (albeit expensive and sometimes dangerous) to excavate. After only minimal stripping, architectural configurations are often quite clear, aesthetically pleasing, and intuitively (although often deceptively) intelligible. Indeed, much detail concerning the built environment is visible without excavation and can be quickly and compellingly recorded from surface inspection (e.g., see the superb drawings of Holmes 1895). Other classes of artifacts and features are much more difficult to recover, document, and analyze properly. Architectural descriptions and analyses consequently dominated the traditional Classic Maya literature, and architectural summaries usually appeared either in the absence of information concerning other associated classes of artifacts or long before such materials were published.

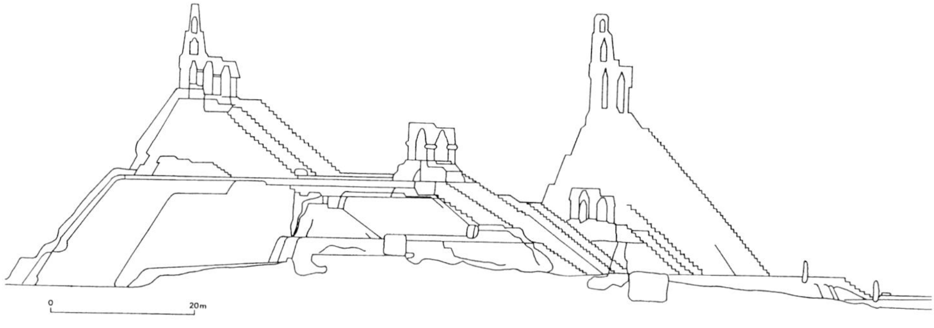

Fig. 3 Schematic and simplified north–south section of North Acropolis at Tikal, showing architectural stratigraphy (adapted from Culbert 1993: 50).

Archaeologists sometimes distinguish between *hard* deposits, of which architecture and monuments are prime examples, and *soft* deposits, such as middens, burials, or small features. Hammond (1983: 4) notes that because of the richness of the Maya archaeological record in architecture, dates, and inscriptions, Mayanists remained "immersed in facts long after those less well endowed materially had been forced to seek new ways of interpreting their material." Here he echoes much earlier criticisms by Taylor (1948) focused on the Carnegie projects.

Inferring Organization and Meaning

A fundamental hypothesis is that the relationships between humans and their built environments are dynamic and interactive. Much of the research carried out by architects, geographers, and ethnographers investigates whether, and how, the forms of the built environment are congruent with cultural, organizational, and behavioral features of the societies and people they study. Most of these efforts have one profound advantage over those of archaeologists—both sides of the equation, what Schiffer (1987) calls the "systemic context," are reasonably well known. Because research focuses on modern systems or ones documented by historical or ethnohistorical data, both the forms of the built environment and the cultural and organizational features with which they presumably interact are so well understood that conclusions are very convincing. Contrast, for example, Fairclough's (1992) spatial analysis of the changing plan and functions of a Scottish castle between A.D. 1300 and 1575, with Foster's (1989) application of the same techniques to an entirely prehistoric Scottish Iron Age enclosure.

Archaeologists, unlike architects or geographers, usually have access to only one dimension of the relationship—the built environment, which itself is imperfectly preserved, sampled, and understood. We assume that the built environment reflects ancient patterns of behavior, organization, and meaning in coherent ways, and we try to use it to reconstruct these features of past societies. Some anthropologists (e.g., Douglas 1972) have argued that in fact many important aspects of social organization are not recoverable from residues of architectural arrangements. Even if such criticism is excessively pessimistic (and I think it is), there remains an obvious risk of circularity in the archaeological enterprise: behavior, organization, and meanings reconstructed *from* ancient built environments will obviously be congruent *with* them.

Fortunately, there are three ways out of this impasse. First, we can reconstruct meaning and organization from evidence not directly tied to the forms of the built environment themselves. Certainly the Classic Maya left us abundant resources to do so. Epigraphy and iconography, for example, provide compelling details of the elite components of Maya society, as shown by other chapters in this volume. Another effective tool is ethnoarchaeology, even though in the direct historical sense we can study only modern Maya of comparatively low status. Finally, we can use methods and models derived from wider studies of historical or modern interactions between humans and their built environment to investigate past interactions, although to date these have not yielded anything like universally valid principles to understand the use and meaning of social space.

Design and the Built Environment

One concept intimately connected with analyses of built environments is design, reflecting the idea, particularly strong among some architects and planners, that such environments are the purposeful creations of human actors. Rapoport (1990), as we already saw, relegates unintentional landscape modifications to the ecological environment because they are not purposefully designed and built.

Design is an attractive notion for three reasons. First, humans unquestionably do devise and create elements of the built environment in purposeful ways. Second, to the extent that architectural components directly reflect integrated human intentions, they can be regarded as texts, preserving messages to be deciphered. Finally, existing or ancient designed environments can serve as models for social planners concerned with the design of future facilities (e.g., Fairclough 1992: 349). This notion of design must be handled very carefully, because it is a key to function and meaning, but it also can be very misleading given the processes that formed many Maya built environments.

The basic problem is that the great centers most heavily studied by Mayanists, such as Uaxactun, Tikal, Palenque, and Copan, have histories. Whole site layouts, or large portions of them, are not designed systems of architecture so much as historical accretions, with all of the noise and sloppiness that characterize evolved, as opposed to engineered, systems. Large-scale accretions consisting of many structures built at different times cannot easily be read as texts, although some Mayanists have attempted to do so (e.g., Ashmore 1992), because they are so garbled by historical contingency. Whatever freedom the original builders enjoyed to impose planned building programs on their landscapes became more and more constrained through time. Our ability to decipher such historical palimpsests depends on (among other things) adequate control over chronology of construction and use.

One reason why Maya elite architecture is durable is that it is big. The combination of durable materials and large scale means that, unlike many other kinds of artifacts, Maya elite architecture curates itself—that is, there must be very active and energy-consuming human intervention if large architecture is to be removed, altered, or covered over. Archaeologists frequently calculate the energy necessary to construct, maintain, and renovate large architectural monuments (Abrams 1994; this volume). The other side of the coin is the inertia thus created. Large architecture (and here I include "capital" investments such as agricultural terraces or drained fields) has more inertia, and hence more "drag," on human sociocultural systems than any other form of material culture. Inertia is embodied not only in masses of stone. Symbolic messages encoded in the built environment constitute another sort of constraint that increased through time, especially because they are, as we shall see, so heavily personalized and customized to historical incident.

These commonsense observations do not deny that generation after generation of Maya builders intentionally conceived, designed, and carried out ambitious building programs or that these had functions and meanings that may be accessible to us. They do suggest that if we want to talk about design and intention we had better make useful distinctions between different kinds of built forms as units of analysis. Clearly the most secure such units are individual constructions (or closely integrated sets of them) built over very short periods of time, such as the final-phase ballcourt at the Copan Main Group or the paired Temples I and II at Tikal. Such built forms offer particular potential for innovative analysis of plan and function. Scarborough (1994) has recently suggested that some carefully planned layouts are parts of elaborate water-management systems.

Good non-Maya examples are the enormous adobe enclosures at the Chimu city of Chan Chan on the north coast of Peru (Fig. 4). These were apparently the establishments of individual Chimu kings, with a new one built during each reign. Because such enclosures were highly planned and had short life spans, they lend themselves to architectural analysis as designed, functional systems. In an innovative application of access analysis (Hillier and Hanson 1984), Moore (1992) was able to test and falsify a detailed hypothesis concerning the administrative functions of one class of rooms in such enclosures. Such analyses are much less suited to complex Maya royal palaces that have long histories of accretional growth, such as the Central Acropolis at Tikal (Fig. 5). Hammond (1972) is one of the few archaeologists who have attempted to apply such analysis to Maya centers (at Lubaantun).

At long-occupied centers such as Tikal or Copan, Maya planners increasingly had to adapt their efforts to the solid realities of earlier constructional

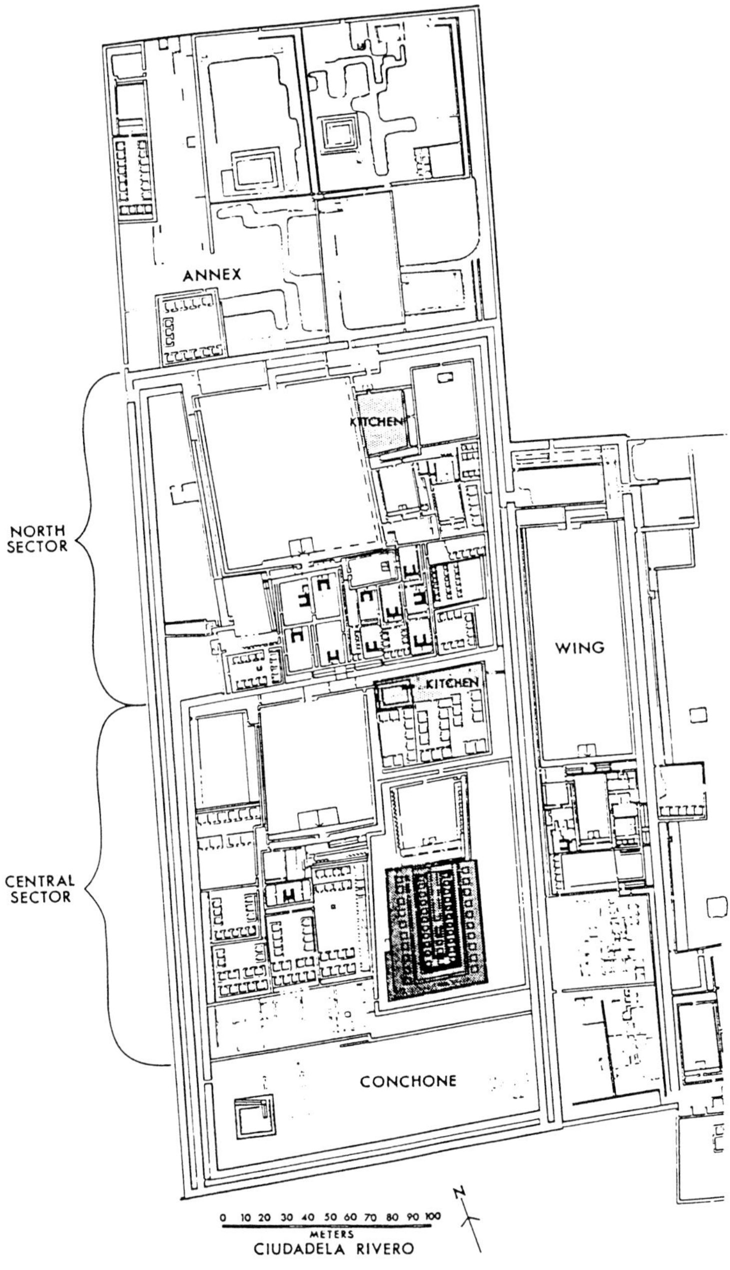

Fig. 4 Royal compound at Chan Chan. This complex of structures and rooms was presumably built at one time to a predetermined plan (after Moseley and Day 1982: fig. 3.2).

episodes, which acted as frames or containers for subsequent ones. The Late Pre-Classic fortifications of Becan, for example, "contain" later Classic constructions in a literal sense (Fig. 6). But preexisting architecture provided opportunities as well. By using earlier buildings as armatures for later ones, Maya builders could make more massive and visually imposing statements while reducing energy costs. An interesting issue is the degree to which they compromised their abstract designs to realize such advantages and hence distorted their messages.

Perhaps compromise is the wrong word, however, because there were also more positive and culturally more significant opportunities that we are only beginning to understand. Most important is the calculated integration of older built forms and their psychologically powerful associations into new building programs. For example, residential places where ancestors were venerated were sometimes transformed into more formal public or ritual places, undoubtedly retaining their original sanctity even as function changed (McAnany, this volume). Maya planners thus turned potential obstacles into symbolic resources by incorporating them into their plans, thereby producing complexes of architecture that were transgenerational repositories of information.

A great deal of variation and opportunism is evident in architectural accretions from one center to another. Tikal grew both upward, as older buildings were buried by later ones, as in the North Acropolis, and outward, as spatially distinct new complexes were completed. The Copan Main Group, by contrast, grew principally through vertical accretion, probably because neither the natural environment nor the Late Classic social environment favored lateral expansion.

Elite constructions most amenable to design analysis are logically those imposed on essentially vacant landscapes that offered wide scope for builders. Unfortunately, these tend to be either very early (especially Pre-Classic) phases of construction that are difficult to recover intact at sites with long histories or smaller, single-phase elite centers that archaeologists have tended to avoid. Here though, there are some real opportunities in some of the second-level sites in the Puuc and Río Bec regions, where late, short-lived centers proliferated. These, more clearly than the great southern centers, should preserve comprehensible design patterns.

Much of the literature on order, organization, activity, and meaning in the built environment derives from ethnographic studies of nonelite domestic units. Paradoxically, the ancient Maya who had the most latitude to arrange their built environments as they wished are those we study least. Intentional patterning should be most clear in the scattered household remains of rural Maya

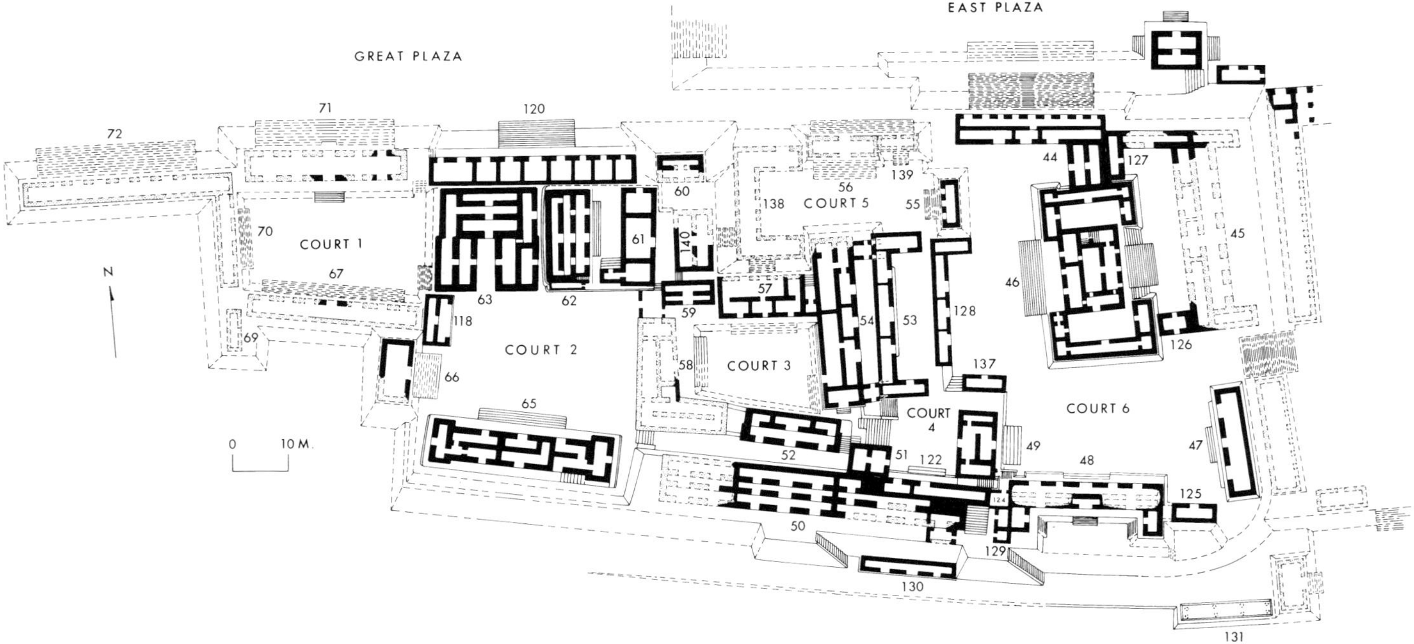

Fig. 5 Plan of the Central Acropolis palace at Tikal. Courtesy of the University Museum, University of Pennsylvania.

Fig. 6 Plan of the fortified center of Becan, showing Classic architecture inside the Pre-Classic ditch and parapet (after Marcus 1992: fig. 24).

commoners. Construction, reconstruction, or relocation of commoner household facilities was, in comparison to that at elite centers, less constrained by investment of energy and preexisting architectural features. This is not to say that rural Maya households lacked histories but rather that their histories were more attenuated than those of larger royal/elite places and their built environments had less inertia.

It follows that social organization is more likely to be reflected in small structures that have short use lives and rapid turnover, rather than large, public architecture such as temples. The latter may be used for centuries even as social organization changes. Notre Dame Cathedral is much the same as it was in the twelfth century, but those who worship in it today share few social and residential arrangements with its original builders.

Commoner Maya domestic architecture also has several practical advantages for students of built environments. Architecture used by Maya of low status is abundant and, except where deeply buried, cheap to dig. Large samples can thus be acquired, and reconstruction is unnecessary. On the other hand, details of function are difficult to determine (e.g., Webster and Gonlin 1988; Gonlin n.d.), unless sites are unusually well preserved, as at Ceren (Sheets 1992). There is also a real paucity of symbolic information compared to that present at elite sites. Here though, much more may be learned through fine-grained analysis of artifacts and subtle architectural features by using ethnoarchaeological models.[4]

Function and Contextualization

The general functions of several classes of Maya structures have long been known or assumed. These include temples, ballcourts, and some specialized features, such as sweatbaths. On the other hand, there has been considerable confusion concerning other classes of structures, such as elite residences (Satterthwaite 1935; Coe 1956; Tourtellot 1992). I believe the principal reason why archaeologists have had difficulties investigating the function and meaning of some components of the Classic Maya built environment is incomplete contextualization. By contextualization I mean two things: (1) the association of built forms with other artifacts and features, and (2) the ability to plan and carry out problem-oriented research with a reasonable knowledge of the variety, spatial distribution, and chronology of built forms on the cultural landscapes of particular Maya polities. The issue of palace architecture provides a good example.

Elite Residences

The term palace crept into the Mayanist lexicon early on to denote a variety of masonry structures (as opposed to a specific structure type) that seemed not to be temples.[5] Often ornate, vaulted, and constructed of fine masonry, palaces have low substructures compared to temples. Superstructures are long rectangular buildings with axially arranged rows of rooms often of modular configuration. Sets of palace structures, distant from monumental site cores, were often called "minor ceremonial centers." Although many such buildings were mapped, cleared, excavated, and restored, the term palace came to be a default category

[4] For a Near Eastern example, see Kamp (1993).

[5] For a good review, see Kowalski (1987: 75–86); for discussion and floor plans, see Harrison (1986).

because no clear functions were agreed upon. For example, Satterthwaite (1935: 4), who excavated two palace structures at Piedras Negras, insisted that no functional significance whatever should be attached to his use of the term.

Part of this confusion resulted from the vacant ceremonial model, according to which the rulers and nobles of contact period times (who obviously lived in elite residences as described by Cortés above) had no obvious counterparts during the Classic period. If there were no kings or nobles, what was the sense of the term palace? If Classic palaces were residences at all, they must have been more like priestly dormitories. But even as this model was being abandoned, confusion continued. Coe (1956: 387) asserted that "Structures clearly identifiable as royal residences are absent in the Classic Maya area" and went on to surmise that Maya rulers lived in perishable wooden palaces. Still later, Adams (1977: 152) claimed that no palaces were known at Copan. Most recently, Tourtellot (1993: 230) observed that we have great trouble recognizing the residences of Maya elites.

Two levels of contextualization problems are at work here. First, as we have already seen, early excavators usually did not recover or record the kind of artifacts and features necessary to demonstrate residential (or other) functions—i.e., they did not adequately recover and associate both "hard" and "soft" deposits. Fox (n.d.), for example, makes the point that ballcourts were widely investigated as core elements of the Maya built environment for many years but that artifacts and features associated with them were often unrecovered or unreported. His criticism is valid for many other classes of architecture as well.

More important, however, were the difficulties archaeologists faced in evaluating the built forms they dug (or, more importantly, proposed to dig) within the larger context of mapped regional settlement patterns. Extensive and systematic surface surveys are fairly recent innovations in Maya archaeology. Once completed, as at Copan (Fash n.d.; Freter n.d.), they allow predictions about the relationships between residence and rank based on the knowledge of a wide variety of built forms. By using one such model, several elite/royal groups that accord well with the palace definition have been chosen and excavated at Copan (Willey et al. 1994; Webster 1989; Andrews and Fash 1992). These places demonstrably had elite residential functions. Such subroyal elite places are common on the Classic Maya landscape. They may not be perfect analogs of royal residences, but they clearly help us understand the general class of "palace" architecture and, in the process, Maya sociopolitical organization.

Fortunately, both problems of contextualization are being resolved as the maturation of Maya archaeology progresses. Artifacts and features are now routinely recorded, and an impressive range of settlement data is available.

BEHAVIOR, COGNITION, AND MAYA BUILT ENVIRONMENTS: INFERENCES FROM ICONOGRAPHY AND EPIGRAPHY

Archaeologists are increasingly enjoined to investigate not only behavioral but also cognitive dimensions of past sociocultural systems (Leone 1982; Hodder 1986; Renfrew and Zubrow 1994). Unlike most prehistoric archaeologists, Mayanists are uniquely situated to reconstruct not only what people did but also some of the ways they thought. Although we cannot directly observe how people behaved in Classic built environments or directly know how they conceptualized them, we fortunately have two lines of evidence that are extremely revealing of both function and meaning. The first is the multitude of carved, woven, modeled, or painted images that the Maya created. Equally important are the inscriptions often intimately associated with such images.

Some vehicles of iconographic and written expression, such as façade sculpture, graffiti, and wall murals, form integral parts of buildings. Others, such as large stelae and altars, were strategically sited and minimally portable. In either case, they are often found in their original contexts. In addition, there are portable objects, such as figurines, small carvings, and, most importantly, painted vessels, which often lack provenience. All of these forms convey symbolic information as the Maya themselves wished to display it. I will briefly summarize a few of the extremely rich implications of this symbolism later discussed at length in other papers.

Performance

Classic Maya built environments are consistently depicted as containers for the performance of human and divine dramas, centered on sacrifice, prestation, tribute giving, and ball playing. Although many depictions appear realistic and representational, they are actually highly formulaic and structured by tightly controlled conventions (Houston, this volume). Actions are often shown associated with buildings or parts of buildings, but construction elements as frames for action are typically simplified and (from our perspective) distorted. In virtually all cases, the focus is on the actors and the relationships between them rather than on the setting, which is typically shown very schematically. Exteriors are more important than interiors. Close inspection of performance scenes does, however, reveal a great deal about the perishable accoutrement of interior and exterior spaces, such as pillows, hangings, scaffolds, arbors, and portable structures, such as litters. One such scene brought to my attention by Stephen Houston shows ball-game equipment inside a palace (Fig. 7).

Restructuring of existing built forms was done partly to improve them as

Fig. 7 Polychrome vessel showing a palace scene that includes ball-game equipment. The curved yoke (*yugo*) is shown on the right in front of what appear to be stored ball-game costume elements (after Coe 1975: pl. 14).

stages for public drama. For example, Ruz Lhuillier (1973: 228–240) illustrates three major exterior modifications of the Temple of the Inscriptions at Palenque (Fig. 8). At each stage, the superstructure temple, presumably the most sacrosanct component, was left unchanged, whereas substructure terraces and stairways were heavily altered in ways probably intended to make them more effective and dramatic stages for human actors.

Although not stressed in this volume, the Maya also built distinctive "connective" architectural features, such as causeways and roads, that bind together architectural complexes and sometimes distant centers. Although we have little information on how these were conceived or used, they undoubtedly had heavy symbolic and performance functions.

Metaphor

The Classic Maya clearly conceived of much of their built environment in metaphorical terms (Taube and Houston, this volume). The built environment

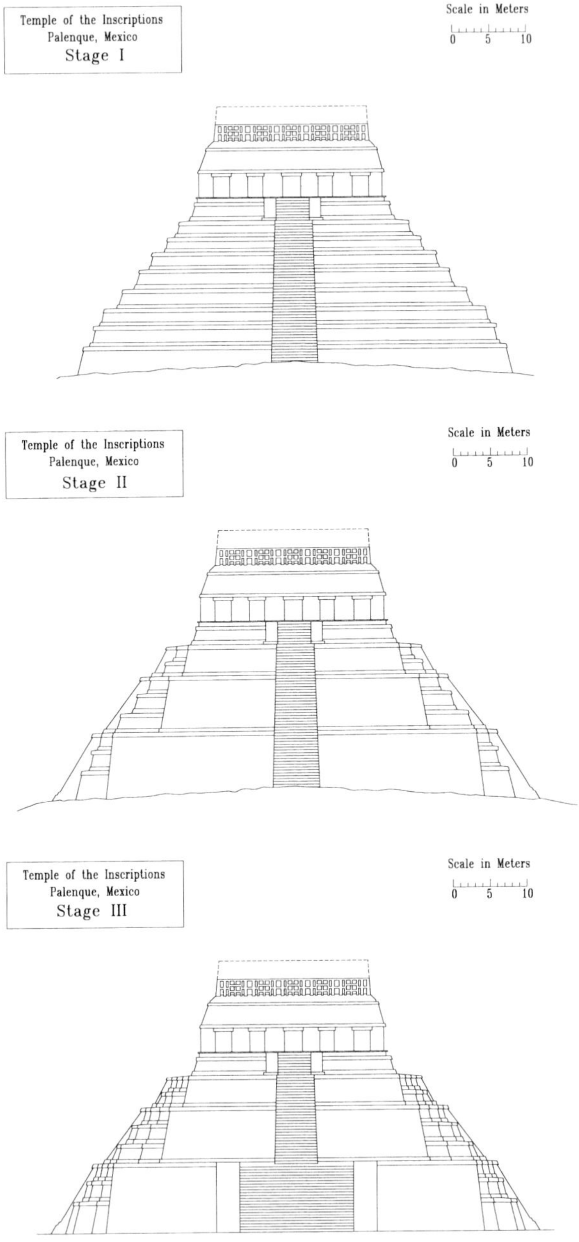

Fig. 8 Temple of the Inscriptions at Palenque, showing three stages of alteration of its substructure (computer images by Pamela Ryan, adapted from Ruz Lhuillier 1973: figs. 259–261).

itself is often characterized as a metaphor for order, in contrast with the disorder and danger symbolized by the natural environment. Karl Taube (personal communication, August 1994) points out that modern Yucatec Maya conceptualize space as "domesticated" versus "wild," a point also recently made by Stone (1995: 15–17). Maya temple and palace architecture incorporates powerful house and hearth metaphors, demonstrating the intimate developmental and symbolic connections between the great and little traditions of Maya architecture. Such metaphors also express cosmic structure and the related themes of centrality and order versus disorder.

Personification

Both epigraphic and iconographic evidence show that the Maya personified or customized their built forms to a remarkable degree (Stuart and Taube, this volume). Construction and decoration of buildings were tailored to particular historical incidents. Special dedicatory rituals animated structures and many other kinds of objects by "burning" (or censing) them and by bestowing personal names on them. Buildings may actually have been "alive" from the Maya perspective. They were also personified through identification with rulers or other notables and the traditions of dynastic power such people represented. Conversely, important people sometimes seem to have impersonated buildings, just as they impersonated deities. Other incidental symbolic information includes identification of individuals who were somehow "responsible" for a building—perhaps architects or builders. Inscriptions suggest that building projects at some centers were supervised and perhaps initiated and dedicated by overlords from elsewhere. For example, Stephen Houston (personal communication, August 1994) thinks that a Yaxchilan lord was the principal patron of events shown in the Bonampak murals, in which a Lacanha lord also figures as a protagonist.

Equally revealing is what is not shown. There are few realistic depictions of whole buildings or building elements, nor are scenes of actual construction common in Classic Maya art, although Stephen Houston has pointed out to me conventionalized images of plastering and lintel raising from the Madrid Codex (Fig. 9).

All these rich inferences drawn from Classic Maya art and writing have one obvious limitation—they refer almost entirely to the elite traditions of Maya society. Archaeologists have put small structures to rather different uses.

SMALL STRUCTURE ARCHAEOLOGY

Maya elite buildings impress us because of their scale, sophisticated con-

Fig. 9 Figures from the Madrid Codex (M15a, 21b) showing deities (a) plastering and (b) raising the lintel of a building. Drawings by Stephen Houston.

struction, and symbolic displays. Peripheral, small Maya structures are striking only because of their numbers. As we have already seen, Spanish chroniclers quickly distinguished between Maya elite and public architecture on the one hand and the residences of common people on the other, presumably because the latter were conspicuous components of the sixteenth-century cultural landscape. Archaeologists have long been aware of the ubiquity of small built forms and presumed them to be the remains of houses, but only recently have they begun to investigate systematically these humble components of the Maya built environment.

Small buildings, especially the domestic facilities of common people, are often called "vernacular structures" by architects. According to Brunskill (1978: 25–26) vernacular structures share the following characteristics: they are usually built of inexpensive local materials by amateurs (that is, nonprofessional builders) who are guided by local conventions, and function rather than design is the principal concern. He contrasts such buildings with "polite" structures—i.e., those that are more expensive and are wholly or partially planned and constructed by professionals to conform to more ideal, cosmopolitan styles in which aesthetics are as important as function. Whether these distinctions, drawn from the European architectural tradition, are valid for the Maya is questionable. Possibly the Maya saw more continuity, symbolic and otherwise, between common domestic and elite/civic architecture, as suggested by the house metaphors already discussed, and were less affected by cosmopolitan "fashion." In any case, there is a continuum between small/vernacular and large/polite forms, and here I emphasize the former.

Early, often desultory, excavations of small vernacular Maya structures (Hewitt 1912; Thompson 1892) lacked settlement context. For example, Thompson (1931) seems to have begun his investigations of small groups in British Honduras with the notion that they were residences of common people, but he quickly decided that their scale indicated they belonged to "occupants of wealth and rank" (1931: 237). In a pioneering effort, Wauchope (1934) excavated five small structures at Uaxactun within the area earlier surveyed by the Ricketsons (1937), but no one followed up his work. Apart from those reported in the unpublished work of Bronson (n.d.), the "small" structures excavated at Tikal (Haviland 1985) in fact are neither very small nor very peripheral.

Small structures have been neglected for several reasons, apart from a general fascination with Maya elite culture: (1) their general functions were not at issue; (2) they were unlikely to yield dated monuments, art, and well-stratified deposits; (3) Classic Maya commoners were thought to form a passive and comparatively homogeneous and unchanging social component little different from that described in ethnohistoric and ethnographic accounts; and (4) unlike large buildings, small structures often lacked intuitively meaningful patterns observable on the surface.

Small structures eventually engaged the attention of archaeologists not because of what they themselves could tell us but because they both posed a problem and offered the key to its solution. The problem was essentially demographic. Early surveys such as the Ricketsons' suggested that Maya sustaining populations (estimated from housemound counts) were much higher than expected—certainly higher than those supportable by the swidden systems described for the ethnohistoric Maya. If Classic populations were so high, how were they supported? The solution was to find out how many such structures were contemporaneous on the landscapes of Maya polities at various periods and use these counts to estimate population density and change. Appropriate alternative subsistence models could then be devised.

Beginning in the 1950s this goal was pursued mainly through surface survey and test excavation. Only very recently have a few small Maya sites been extensively excavated (Manzanilla 1987; Webster and Gonlin 1988; Gonlin n.d.; Johnston n.d.) (Fig. 10). Small-structure archaeology has had several effects on built-environment research apart from its implications for demographic and subsistence issues (Culbert and Rice 1990). The residential functions of small structures and the variation displayed within this category of architecture (Gonlin n.d.) have been demonstrated. Investigations of other components of the built

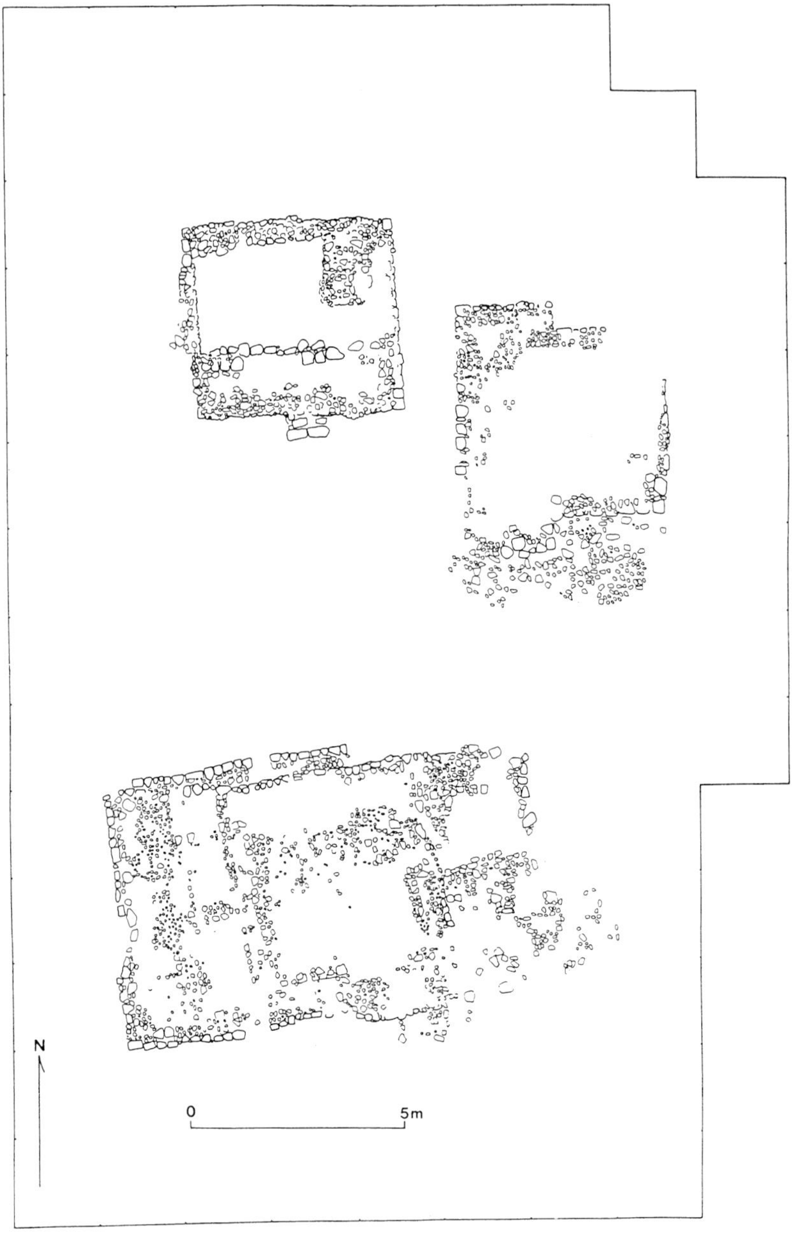

Fig. 10 Plan of small Copan rural site. All that remains are the stone and rubble platforms that supported perishable superstructures.

environment are consequently much more effectively contextualized. Another result has been to emphasize the continuity between small and large built forms and to stimulate research into how, and on what scale, labor was organized and expended (Abrams 1994; this volume).

Patterns or objects of obvious symbolic significance are very rare at fully excavated Classic Maya low-rank houses (Gonlin n.d.), although caches and other offerings do occur. Only when we have large numbers of well-excavated small sites will such scarce symbolic materials begin to make detailed sense. Fine-grained studies of activity areas and use patterns of interior and exterior spaces also might reveal cognitive aspects of past household behavior, and it will be interesting to see if these emerge from the Ceren excavations, where activity areas are very well preserved. Interestingly, the house metaphors associated with large buildings may allow us to work back to cognitive dimensions of commoner housing for which no direct evidence exists.

However we characterize the relationships between Maya little and great tradition architecture, one difference has always been clear—the latter conveys explicit messages of hierarchy and social power, themes to which we now turn.

CULTURE, ARCHITECTURE, AND POWER

Anthropologists analyzing the built environment often employ both utilitarian and symbolic perspectives (e.g., McGuire and Schiffer 1983). Writings of nonanthropologists sometimes reveal a pronounced "culture is a mental template" conception—the idea that "the built environment corresponds to ideal conceptions of social, political, and religious life" (Lawrence and Low 1990: 466). Basic adaptive or behavioral functions are often downplayed or ignored in favor of meaning: "cognitive and symbolic meaning is more important than instrumental function" (Fairclough 1992: 351).

The assumption is that humans plan and construct their built environments according primarily to culturally determined cognitive frameworks; cognition is in turn affected by the built environments. Some modern architects, such as Frank Lloyd Wright, adopted Maya design elements because they perceived universal symbolic and spiritual values in their geometric forms; these forms, it was thought, could revitalize modern society (Braun 1993: 174).

The widely shared conventions and considerable conservatism of Maya elite architecture created, in the minds of some early archaeologists, the impression of a monolithic Maya culture and society, although some thought otherwise. Merwin (n.d.: 102), for example, noted that the many small "independent groupings" of structures in the Río Bec region reflected a landscape of politically segmented ancient polities, whereas the much larger sets of integrated structures at centers such as Tikal, Palenque, Quirigua, and Copan suggested "a strong, centralized, political or politico-religious organization."

Fortunately, most Mayanists long ago rejected monolithic conceptions, and now emphasize not only regional and temporal variation among Classic Maya polities but, more importantly, their internal political complexity, factionalization, and dynamism. McGuire and Schiffer (1983: 297) note that architecture is produced by "individuals and social groups making decisions and affecting compromises to achieve various goals." In other words, ideas always intersect with quite practical considerations. Inherent in this perspective is the built environment as both arena and instrument for the pursuit, expression, and maintenance of power.

In a general comparative overview of monumental construction, Trigger (1990) observes that the built environments of the earliest civilizations include few "civic" amenities available to a wide spectrum of the populace, such as libraries, schools, theaters, or baths (infrastructural efforts such as defensive walls, reservoirs, roads, and irrigation projects are ancillary to his concerns). Instead, large constructions in central places focus on gods, ancestors, kings, and other privileged people. These early built forms may be "public" in the sense that they are constructed by collective effort, may display collective symbols, and are highly visible. They may even have practical civic purposes, such as the storage and redistributive functions of the Sumerian temple. Still, their ritual and royal dimensions are very obtrusive, and they serve most directly the interests of small segments of society rather than some wider citizenry. That emergent elites should differentiate themselves by means of distinctive built forms that serve new instrumental functions and have new meanings is understandable. What needs to be explained is why this requires monumental construction.

Trigger's answer is that conspicuous consumption of other peoples' work, including that of skilled builders, is a universal symbol of high status because it violates the laws of least effort. The evolutionary point, of course, is that the effort necessary is not expended by those who make the decisions and most directly benefit from such constructions, and hence it symbolizes concentrated social power. He thus posits a cross-cultural cognitive principle of perception: *scale = power.*

The monumentality of built forms at great Maya centers and the complex symbolism associated with them have long created profound impressions of hierarchy and social power. Landa (1941), as we saw earlier, speculated that Maya lords conscripted the labor necessary for such projects for their own political purposes. Morgan (1965 [1881]), by contrast, denied the use of "enforced labor" because it was at odds with his tribal, kin-based conception of the evolutionary status of New World peoples. Subsequent analyses of Maya cultural evolution have been heavily conditioned by the implications of a massive and sophisticated built environment. Large scale reflects the scope of communication about power: although some vehicles of information inherent in Maya built forms (e.g., painted, carved, and inscribed murals; lintels and plaques inside temples and palaces) would have been accessible only to elites, monumental constructions are never hidden; their power messages extend to everyone.

Under the old theocratic, vacant ceremonial center model of Maya society, lavish expenditures of energy on huge architectural complexes were explained in terms of collective religious devotion channeled by "bureaucratic priesthoods" (Kidder 1950: 8). The complex messages conveyed by art and inscriptions remained enigmatic because noncalendrical glyphs were not understood. Power in this model was more psychological than real.

Serious cracks in this theocratic façade of Classic society resulted from the excavation of an elaborate burial beneath the Temple of the Inscriptions at Palenque (Ruz Lhuillier 1973). This discovery stimulated Michael Coe (among others) to rethink the increasingly obvious connection between burials and building episodes (Coe 1956). Coe reasoned that if many "temples" really functioned as funerary monuments to deceased individuals, then political power of a more tangible sort must be taken into account:

> We have tended to think of the Classic Maya in terms of a stereotyped peasantry laboring in the service of a somewhat Olympian pantheon. However, if the majority of buildings in any one Classic Maya center were dedicated to the future life of certain individuals, then those persons must have possessed a great deal of political power to requisition the enormous amount of labor necessary for the erection of those monuments. In other words, authority may have been vested not only in a priestly class, but in a line of hereditary rulers who perpetuated themselves in the same manner as the Egyptian kings. (Coe 1956: 393)

Here Coe distinguishes between the psychological power of religious devotion and real "political power," by which he presumably means the power to dominate decision making, command, requisition, and, if necessary, coerce.

The fatal blow, of course, was the epigraphic revolution beginning in the late 1950s, which had two immediate effects: (1) it confirmed that the Classic Maya had dynasties of secular rulers; and (2) it placed Maya society firmly within the much larger comparative perspective of other ancient civilizations (recapitulating Stephens's sensible view more than a century before). Large Maya architecture had to be evaluated in a new way: as the product of dominant kings and elites who not only organized and controlled labor but did so by political means not wholly, or perhaps at all, consistent with religious devotion. Even more importantly, inscriptions revealed overtly political messages, which in turn caused a reevaluation of Maya art, where political themes also became obvious.

As a result, we are becoming increasingly aware of how much the personification of monumental components of the Classic Maya built environment embody assertions of power. Individual rulers such as Pacal commissioned personal mortuary monuments. These were sometimes finished or altered by successors, who thereby associated themselves with the deceased ruler. New evidence suggests that burial monuments were sometimes commemorated, and possibly built, long after the death of the honored person. Conquerors erected hieroglyphic stairways to celebrate victories, sometimes imposing them on defeated centers, as Caracol did at Naranjo. Lesser elites at Copan flaunted their titles on building façades and carved benches. Although individual assertion is evident in all this, an even stronger element is concern with continuity—rulers and other powerful people contextualized themselves within existing built environments already redolent of historical traditions of dynastic power, sanctity, and symbolism.

Most Mayanists no longer take this emphasis on continuity and order in the built environment at face value. A much more uniformitarian assumption is that "Monumental buildings mask the will to power and the arbitrariness of power beneath signs and surfaces which claim to express collective will and collective thought" (Lefebvre 1991: 143).[6] What are masked are not only the general stresses inherent in any system of hierarchy but much more subtle processes of status rivalry involving elite factions on both intra- and interpolity levels—processes that probably peaked in intensity during the Late Classic (Webster n.d.).

Building plans, the scale and timing of building events, and the images and symbols associated with them, constitute our best windows into the all-important fine texture of Maya politics. At Copan, for example, the hieroglyphic stairway seems to be constructed as compensation for some kind of interpolity loss of face, whereas the proliferation of carved monuments among lesser Copan elites signals new political assertiveness after this event. Such status rivalry is intimately related to the much greater plasticity of the exteriors of Maya elite structures rather than the interiors.

Unfortunately, our refined concepts of the messages embodied in monu-

[6] As quoted in Pearson and Richards (1994b: 3).

mental Maya buildings have not been accompanied by systematic investigations into the costs or organization of construction. Even volumetric estimates of construction components are seldom given. See William Coe's (1990) discussion of Tikal Temple I for a notable exception. Because archaeologists routinely take apart large Maya structures and often restore them by using tools and human labor in ways not dissimilar from the ancient Maya, such lack of quantification is puzzling.

Abrams (1994; this volume) has recently developed construction models for Copan based on archaeology, observations of reconstruction, and controlled experiments. Among his findings is that a range of ancient households was constructed more cheaply than we imagine. Application of his methods indicates that large temple architecture at Copan was much less costly than expected, that labor demands on commoners were low, and that such demands by themselves probably had few if any deleterious effects on the polity (Webster and Kirker 1995).

Trigger (1990: 127) repeats V. Gordon Childe's earlier suggestion that (noncivic) monumental construction was most necessary as an expression of power early on in the careers of ancient states (see also Kolb 1994: 531). If this is true, what does it say about the Maya, who appear to have built on a large (or even increasing) scale throughout the Classic period? If diminution in building efforts in other civilizations is a measure of more stable institutions and political conditions, then does the Maya trajectory reflect increasingly unstable conditions? That many dynastic "collapses" of the eighth and early ninth centuries followed close upon large-scale construction episodes is consistent with this suggestion.

Place and Power: Some Comparisons

Classic Maya polities and their attendant kings and elites were strikingly tethered to places as fundamental foci of power. Old places such as Tikal were perennial centers of political gravity, and new dynasts founded shorter-lived centers of their own. Such a pattern is hardly unique. Comparisons with southeast Asian civilizations—particularly the Khmer of Cambodia—have long been fashionable among Mayanists because of their tropical forest settings and their expansive political systems focused on regal/ritual central places that appear not to have been fully urban in terms of population.

Higham (1989) summarizes essential aspects of Khmer centers. Divine overlords built them on a grand scale not only as royal residences but as centers for cults and rituals focused on the royal person, his ancestors, his lineage, and the extensive court gathered about him. Places such as Angkor were simulacra of heaven, or "perfect" places, enlarged and improved by successive rulers. Built forms were heavily identified with important individuals, especially god-kings, some of whom styled themselves as apotheoses of the Buddha. Impressive buildings served as mausoleums for kings and their relatives. Stelae and other carvings celebrated individual kings, their accomplishments, and their families, and configurations of structures themselves were laden with symbolic significance.

Behind these façades of architectural power, however, lay comparatively weak political systems. Polities had centers, but boundaries were fluid and shifting according to the charisma and skill of individual rulers. Kings were essential to governance but by no means all-powerful in bureaucratic or coercive terms. Through royal rituals they mediated with heaven to ensure the well-being of their polities and metaphorically managed economic affairs. Force was less important than display, feasting, favors, and influence in attracting and maintaining the allegiance of retainers and other great families. Royal succession was always ambiguous, causing frequent internal power struggles. All of this should sound very familiar to Mayanists, for here again power and sanctity are tethered to monumental places.

But is this an invariable relationship in early complex societies? A little reflection suggests otherwise. A notable example to the contrary is provided by the native kingdoms of Hawai'i in the eighteenth and early nineteenth centuries (Earle 1978; Kirch 1990; Kolb 1994). Semidivine paramounts with genealogical rights to rule dominated political landscapes and populations as large as most Maya polities and surrounded themselves with retinues of lesser elites. Paramounts and associated elites were separated from commoners by a wide social gulf. They asserted the right to dispose of the products of commoners and their labor and used these for their own political purposes, which included frequent external war and internal status rivalry. Yet despite all this complexity, there was much less emphasis on durable monumental construction in Hawai'i than among the Maya or the Khmer. Appropriated labor was used to build intensive food-producing facilities and many large, scattered temples (*heiau*) that had varied functions. Some *heiau* combined ritual functions with those of elite residence, but permanent, central, royal precincts characterized by massive durable monumental architecture on the Maya or Khmer scale were not conspicuous features of the Hawaiian political landscape or ruling style. Preserved portions of the largest Hawaiian regal-ritual complex (Fig. 11), built over several centuries, have slightly more total mass than Temple I at Tikal (Kolb 1994: 524; Coe 1990, 2: 602).

Monumentality may thus convey power messages but mask internal organizational weakness and fragility. A more serious problem is that significant power

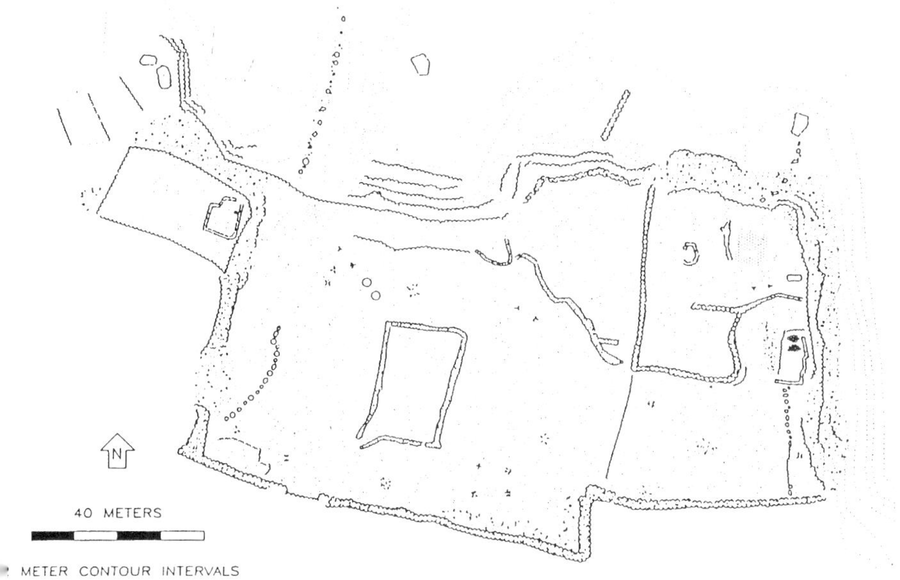

Fig. 11 Plan of the regal-ritual center of Pi'ilanihale, Maui, Hawai'i (after Kolb 1994: 525, fig. 2). This is the largest surviving Hawaiian monumental construction, built in stages over several centuries. Its mass, calculated at 21,938 m^3, is slightly greater than that of Temple I at Tikal (18,260 m^3).

and sociopolitical complexity may also be present in the absence of monumentality. If we knew about Hawaii only through its built forms, we would probably reconstruct it as much less complex than it was. Put another way, we are culturally predisposed to respond to power messages embodied in monumentality just as were the ancient Maya, but such messages may be otherwise conveyed. These comparisons serve to remind us that power, as with other aspects of sociopolitical organization, has only a loose fit with the monumental and symbolic aspects of the built environment, a set of relationships that we still do not fully understand.

SUMMARY

The enterprise of Maya archaeology, like ancient Maya elites themselves, remains strongly tethered to the built environment.

Because architecture is so abundant and well-preserved, it will continue to be a major source of information in its own right and a container for nonarchitectural data. Over the past century, we have gained considerable insights into the functions and meanings of Classic Maya built forms, although often in rather unsystematic ways. The future should be much more productive for several reasons. First, the sheer mass of data at our disposal is much larger and richer. Second, we have made considerable gains in establishing contextualization, which in turn increasingly informs research design. Finally, we have unprecedented understanding of the symbolism embodied in Maya built environments.

The last reason reminds us that the study of the Maya built environment has been and remains very much a "top-down" effort, reflecting the traditional fascination with Maya elite culture. Black (n.d.) detects a recent shift of archaeological attention back to large centers, with their temples, palaces, monuments, and tombs, reversing the trend over the past 30 years that integrated small architecture into research programs. This shift is partly justifiable because of our much more sophisticated understanding of Maya art and writing, which after all are found almost exclusively at royal centers. There remain, however, many issues that can be addressed only through small-structure research, and hopefully this shift will not be too extreme.

The tension between excavation and restoration that manifested itself as early as the Carnegie Institution's Chichen Itza project is much more pronounced today. The prohibitive cost of excavating large architecture can be justified only by the prospect of future tourist revenue, which in turn dictates restoration. Fortunately, tourists seem to have an insatiable appetite for things Maya, but inevitably archaeological research is compromised by overemphasis on restoration.

One adaptation to such restrictions is more intensive examination of small sites, where there is much less pressure for restoration. Another is to apply comparatively new methods of understanding spatial patterns to the existing universe of mapped and excavated built forms. For example, access analysis (Hillier and Hanson 1984) can be used to search for patterns within the same class of architecture, as Hopkins (1987) did for Teotihuacan apartment compounds. Although such analyses may not directly reveal function, they do point up previously unsuspected variability, some dimensions of which (e.g., greater restriction in access) may be generally correlated with increased social differentiation. So far there have been few applications of proxemics to the Maya built environment, a rather strange omission given the obvious intention of Maya builders to channel movement and create visual impressions of sanctity and power.

There is also much to be learned from traditional kinds of research that emerged early but were not followed up. Energetic studies are a prime example, but the structural details of Maya built forms also bear close attention. They have much to tell us, including, perhaps, details of the organization of work parties. So too do other classes of artifacts intimately associated with architecture, such as caches (Chase and Chase, this volume).

Although this volume is mainly concerned with Classic architecture, one of the most exciting prospects is more longitudinal perspectives on major shifts in Maya architectural and symbolic programs. Particularly fascinating are the Pre-Classic–Classic (Hansen, this volume) and Early Classic–Late Classic transitions. New patterns associated with these shifts, such as the proliferation of palace scenes in the Late Classic, should reveal a great deal about the big transformations of Maya culture history.

One thing remains constant—our archaeological propensity to seek out patterns. Our ability to detect patterns in the built environment is greater than ever. Some of these patterns reflect Maya behaviors, intentions, and meanings. Some of them reflect our own wishful thinking. As always, the archaeological problem is to tell the difference between them and to test our interpretations through rich and varied lines of research.

BIBLIOGRAPHY

ABRAMS, ELLIOT

1994 *How the Maya Built Their World.* University of Texas Press, Austin.

ADAMS, RICHARD E. W. (ED.)

1977 *Prehistoric Mesoamerica.* Little, Brown, Boston.

ANDREWS, E. WYLLYS, V, AND BARBARA FASH

1992 Continuity and Change in a Royal Maya Residential Complex at Copan. *Ancient Mesoamerica* 3: 63–87.

ASHMORE, WENDY

1992 Deciphering Maya Architectural Plans. In *New Theories on the Ancient Maya* (Elin Danien and Robert Sharer, eds.): 173–184. University Museum, University of Pennsylvania, Philadelphia.

BLACK, STEPHEN L.

1990 The Carnegie Institution Uaxactun Project and the Development of Maya Archaeology. *Ancient Mesoamerica* 1: 257–276.

n.d. Field Methods and Methodologies in Lowland Maya Archaeology. Ph.D. dissertation, Harvard University, 1990.

BRAUN, BARBARA

1993 *Pre-Columbian Art and the Post-Columbian World: Ancient American Sources of Modern Art.* Abrams, New York.

BRONSON, BENNETT

n.d. Vacant Terrain. Manuscript on file, University Museum, University of Pennsylvania, Philadelphia, 1968.

BRUNSKILL, R. W.

1978 *Illustrated Handbook of Vernacular Architecture.* Faber and Faber, London.

COE, MICHAEL

1956 The Funerary Temple among the Classic Maya. *Southwestern Journal of Anthropology* 12: 387–394.

1975 *Classic Maya Pottery at Dumbarton Oaks.* Dumbarton Oaks, Washington, D.C.

COE, WILLIAM

1967 *Tikal: A Handbook of the Ancient Maya Ruins.* University Museum, University of Pennsylvania, Philadelphia.

1990 *Excavations in the North Acropolis, North Terrace, and Great Plaza of Tikal.* Tikal Report, no. 14. University Museum, University of Pennsylvania, Philadelphia.

CORTÉS, HERNAN

1986 *Letters from Mexico* (Anthony Pagden, ed. and trans.). Yale University Press, New Haven, Conn.

CULBERT, T. PATRICK

1993 *Maya Civilization.* Smithsonian Books, Washington, D.C.

Culbert, T. Patrick, and Don Rice (eds.)
1990 *Precolumbian Population History in the Maya Lowlands.* University of New Mexico Press, Albuquerque.

Douglas, Mary
1972 Symbolic Orders in the Use of Domestic Space. In *Man, Settlement and Urbanism* (P. Ucko, R. Tringham, and G. W. Dimbleby, eds.): 513–530. Schenkman, Cambridge, Mass.

Earle, Timothy
1978 *Economic and Social Organization of a Complex Chiefdom: The Halelea District, Kaua'i, Hawaii.* Anthropological Papers 63, University of Michigan, Museum of Anthropology, Ann Arbor.

Fairclough, Graham
1992 Meaningful Constructions—Spatial and Functional Analysis of Medieval Buildings. *Antiquity* 66: 348–366.

Fash, William
n.d. Maya State Formation: A Case Study and Its Implications. Ph.D. dissertation, Harvard University, 1983.

Foster, Sally
1989 Analysis of Spatial Patterns in Buildings (Access Analysis) as an Insight into Social Structure: Examples from the Scottish Atlantic Iron Age. *Antiquity* 63: 40–50.

Fox, John G.
n.d. Putting the Heart Back in the Court: Ballcourts and Ritual Action in Mesoamerica. Ph.D. dissertation, Harvard University, 1994.

Freter, AnnCorinne
n.d. The Classic Maya Collapse at Copan, Honduras: A Regional Settlement Perspective. Ph.D. dissertation, Pennsylvania State University, 1988.

Gardner, John
1971 *Grendel.* Ballentine Books, New York.

Gonlin, Nancy
n.d. Rural Household Archaeology at Copan, Honduras. Ph.D. dissertation, Pennsylvania State University, 1993.

Graham, Ian
1963 Juan Galindo: Enthusiast. *Estudios de Cultura Maya* 3: 11–36.

Hammond, Norman
1972 The Planning of a Maya Ceremonial Center. *Scientific American* 226 (5): 82–92.
1983 Lords of the Jungle: A Prosopography of Maya Archaeology. In *Civilizations of the Ancient Americas: Essays in Honor of Gordon R. Willey* (Richard M. Leventhal and Alan L. Kolata, eds.): 3–32. University of New Mexico Press, Albuquerque.

Harrison, Peter
1986 Tikal: Selected Topics. In *City States of the Maya* (Elizabeth P. Benson, ed.): 45–71. Rocky Mountain Institute of Pre-Columbian Studies, Denver, Colo.

HAVILAND, WILLIAM
1985 *Excavations in Small Residential Groups of Tikal: Groups 14F-1 and 14F-2.* Tikal Report, no. 19. University Museum, University of Pennsylvania, Philadelphia.

HEWITT, E. L.
1912 The Excavations at Quirigua in 1912. *Archaeological Institute of America Bulletin* 3: 163–171.

HIGHAM, CHARLES
1989 *The Archaeology of Mainland Southeast Asia.* Cambridge University Press, Cambridge.

HILLIER, BILL, AND JULIENNE HANSON
1984 *The Social Logic of Space.* Cambridge University Press, Cambridge.

HODDER, IAN
1986 *Reading the Past.* Cambridge University Press, New York.

HOLMES, WILLIAM H.
1895 *Archaeological Studies among the Ancient Cities of Mexico.* Anthropological Series, Publication 8, vol. 1, no. 1. Field Columbian Museum, Chicago.

HOPKINS, MARY
1987 Network Analysis of the Plans of Some Teotihuacan Apartment Compounds. *Environment and Planning B: Planning and Design* 14: 387–406.

JOHNSTON, KEVIN
n.d. The "Invisible" Maya: Late Classic Minimally Platformed Residential Settlement at Itzan, Guatemala. Ph.D. dissertation, Yale University, 1994.

KAMP, KATHRYN E.
1993 Towards an Archaeology of Architecture: Clues from a Modern Syrian Village. *Journal of Anthropological Research* 49: 293–317.

KIDDER, ALFRED V.
1950 Introduction to *Uaxactun, Guatemala: Excavations of 1931–37,* by A. Ledyard Smith. Publication 588. Carnegie Institution, Washington, D.C.

KIRCH, PATRICK V.
1990 Monumental Architecture and Power in Polynesian Chiefdoms: A Comparison between Tonga and Hawaii. *World Archaeology* 22: 206–222.

KOLB, MICHAEL J.
1994 Monumentality and the Rise of Religious Authority in Precontact Hawai'i. *Current Anthropology* 35: 521–548.

KOWALSKI, JEFF
1987 *The House of the Governor: A Maya Palace at Uxmal, Yucatán, México.* University of Oklahoma Press, Norman.

LANDA, DIEGO DE
1941 *Landa's relación de las cosas de Yucatán* (Alfred M. Tozzer, ed. and annot.). Papers of the Peabody Museum of Archaeology and Ethnology, vol. 18. Harvard University, Cambridge, Mass.

LAWRENCE, D., AND S. LOW
1990 The Built Environment and Spatial Form. *Annual Review of Anthropology* 19: 453–505.

Lefebvre, H.
1991 *The Production of Space.* Blackwell, Oxford.

Leone, Mark
1982 Some Opinions about Recovering Mind. *American Antiquity* 47: 742–760.

Leventhal, Richard M.
1983 Household Groups and Classic Maya Religion. In *Prehistoric Settlement Patterns: Essays in Honor of Gordon R. Willey* (Evon Z. Vogt and Richard M. Leventhal, eds.): 55–76. University of New Mexico Press, Albuquerque.

Manzanilla, Linda (ed.)
1987 *Cobá, Quintana Roo: Análisis de dos unidades habitacionales mayas.* Serie Antropológica 82. Universidad Nacional Autónoma de México, México, D.F.

Marcus, Joyce
1992 Political Fluctuations in Mesoamerica. *National Geographic Research and Exploration* 8: 392–411.

McGuire, Randall H., and Michael Schiffer
1983 A Theory of Architectural Design. *Journal of Anthropological Archaeology* 2: 277–303.

Merwin, Raymond E.
n.d. The Ruins of the Southern Part of the Peninsula of Yucatan, with Special Reference to Their Place in the Maya Area. Manuscript on file describing the Peabody Museum expedition of 1912, Dumbarton Oaks Pre-Columbian Library, Washington, D.C.

Moore, Jerry D.
1992 Pattern and Meaning in Prehistoric Peruvian Architecture: The Architecture of Social Control in the Chimu State. *Latin American Antiquity* 3: 95–113.

Morgan, Lewis Henry
1965 [1881] *Houses and House Life of the American Aborigines.* University of Chicago Press, Chicago.

Moseley, Michael E., and Kent C. Day (eds.)
1982 *Chan Chan: Andean Desert City.* University of New Mexico Press, Albuquerque.

Nichols, Deborah
1996 An Overview of Regional Settlement Pattern Survey in Mesoamerica, 1960–1995. In *Arqueología mesoamericana: Homenaje á William T. Sanders* (Alba Guadalupe Mastache et al., eds.): 59–96. Instituto Nacional de Antropología e Historia, México, D.F.

Pearson, Michael Parker, and Colin Richards
1994a Ordering the World: Perceptions of Architecture, Space and Time. In *Architecture and Order: Approaches to Social Space* (Michael Parker Pearson and Colin Richards, eds.): 1–37. Routledge, New York.

Pearson, Michael Parker, and Colin Richards (eds.)
1994b *Architecture and Order: Approaches to Social Space.* Routledge, New York.

Proskouriakoff, Tatiana
1961 The Lords of the Maya Realm. *Expedition* 4 (1): 14–21.

Rapoport, Amos
1990 *History and Precedence in Environmental Design*. Plenum Press, New York.

Redfield, Robert
1957 *Peasant Society and Culture*. University of Chicago Press, Chicago.

Renfrew, Colin, and Ezra Zubrow (eds.)
1994 *The Ancient Mind: Elements of Cognitive Archaeology*. Cambridge University Press, New York.

Ricketson, Oliver G., and Edith B. Ricketson
1937 *Uaxactun Guatemala: Group E, 1926–1937*. Carnegie Institution, Publication 477. Washington, D.C.

Ruz Lhuillier, Alberto
1973 *El templo de las inscripciones, Palenque*. Coleccíon Científica Arqueología 7. Instituto Nacional de Antropología e Historia, México, D.F.

Satterthwaite, Linton
1935 *Palace Structures J-2 and J-6*. Piedras Negras Papers, no. 6. University Museum, University of Pennsylvania, Philadelphia.

Scarborough, Vernon
1991 Courting the Southern Maya Lowlands: A Study in Pre-Hispanic Ballgame Architecture. In *The Mesoamerican Ballgame* (Vernon L. Scarborough and David R. Wilcox, eds.): 129–144. University of Arizona Press, Tucson.
1994 Maya Water Management. *National Geographic Research and Exploration* 10: 185–199.

Schiffer, Michael
1987 *Formation Processes and the Archaeological Record*. University of New Mexico Press, Albuquerque.

Sheets, Payson
1992 *The Ceren Site: A Prehistoric Village Buried by Volcanic Ash in Central America*. Harcourt Brace Jovanovich, Fort Worth, Tex.

Stephens, John L.
1969 [1841] *Incidents of Travel in Central America, Chiapas, and Yucatan*. Dover Publications, New York.

Stone, Andrea
1995 *Images from the Underworld: Naj Tunich and the Tradition of Maya Cave Painting*. University of Texas Press, Austin.

Stuart, George
1992 Quest for Decipherment. In *New Theories on the Ancient Maya* (Elin Danien and Robert Sharer, eds.): 1–64. University Museum, University of Pennsylvania, Philadelphia.

Taylor, Walter W.
1948 *A Study of Archeology*. American Anthropological Association Memoir, no. 69. Menasha, Wis.

Thompson, Edward H.
1892 The Ancient Structures of Yucatan Not Communal Dwellings. *Proceedings of the American Antiquarian Society* 8: 262–269.

Thompson, J. E. S.

1931 *Archaeological Investigations in the Southern Cayo District, British Honduras.* Anthropological Series, Publication 301, vol. 27, no. 1. Field Museum of Natural History, Chicago.

Tourtellot, Gair

1993 A View of Ancient Maya Settlements in the Eighth Century. In *Lowland Maya Civilization in the Eighth Century A.D.* (Jeremy Sabloff and John Henderson, eds.): 219–242. Dumbarton Oaks, Washington, D.C.

Trigger, Bruce

1990 Monumental Architecture: A Thermodynamic Explanation of Symbolic Behavior. *World Archaeology* 22: 199–232.

Wauchope, Robert

1934 *House Mounds of Uaxactun, Guatemala.* Carnegie Institution, Publication 436. Washington, D.C.

Webster, David

1996 Review of *Die Architektur der Sepulturas-Region von Copán in Honduras,* by Hasso Hohmann. *Latin American Antiquity* 7 (4): 375–377.

n.d. Warfare and Status Rivalry: Lowland Maya and Polynesian Comparisons. In *Copan: The Rise and Fall of a Classic Maya Kingdom* (William L. Fash and E. Wyllys Andrews, V, eds.). School of American Research Press, Santa Fe. (In preparation.)

Webster, David (ed.)

1989 *The House of the Bacabs.* Studies in Pre-Columbian Art and Archaeology 29. Dumbarton Oaks, Washington, D.C.

Webster, David, and Nancy Gonlin

1988 Household Remains of the Humblest Maya. *Journal of Field Archaeology* 15: 169–190.

Webster, David, and Jennifer Kirker

1995 Too Many Maya, Too Few Buildings: Investigating Construction Potential at Copán, Honduras. *Journal of Anthropological Research* 51: 363–387.

Willey, Gordon R., Richard M. Leventhal, Arthur A. Demarest, and William L. Fash

1994 *Ceramics and Artifacts from Excavations in the Copan Residential Zone.* Papers of the Peabody Museum of Archaeology and Ethnology, vol. 80. Harvard University, Cambridge, Mass.

Continuity and Disjunction: The Pre-Classic Antecedents of Classic Maya Architecture

RICHARD D. HANSEN
UNIVERSITY OF CALIFORNIA, LOS ANGELES

SINCE THE EARLY 1960s, archaeological explorations in the Maya area have recovered remnants of Pre-Classic buildings of varying form, function, and meaning that clearly prefigure later Classic forms. The lack of hieroglyphic texts in the Pre-Classic periods, however, dictates that the function and meaning of these early buildings be demonstrated by means of detailed archaeological and technical analyses of the variations and consistencies in their sizes, forms, construction techniques, and use. My purpose in this paper is to initiate such a study and to describe the Pre-Classic antecedents of Classic Maya architecture and construction techniques. This exercise is inherently developmental and has clear implications for the evolution and early development of the institutions thought to be embodied in Classic architecture. The Middle Pre-Classic beginnings of complex architecture in the lowlands, for example, imply an equally early evolution of the complex sociopolitical institutions represented in such architecture.

Classic Maya buildings stand as mute monuments of the sociopolitical, economic, and ideological systems of their creators. Unfortunately, the antecedents of these buildings, and by implication their associated institutions, remain poorly understood. To date, information on the formal and technical antecedents of Classic Maya buildings has been limited, inaccessible, or subject to intellectual and sampling biases. Consequently, my main purpose here is to bring together the extant data on early Maya architecture and to demonstrate the connections between early developments and later architecture. New evidence of Pre-Classic architecture underscores both its novelty and uniformity vis-à-vis Classic architecture. The continuities are clear and convincing and generally much earlier than previously supposed. Considering early Maya buildings broadly in synchronic and diachronic perspective, the data presented here, I argue, suggest an autochthonous development of elaborate architecture in the Maya lowlands.

MAYA ARCHITECTURE AND EVOLUTIONARY MODELS

Traditional models for the rise of lowland Maya civilization result from decades of archaeological investigations in sites that, on the basis of architecture and associated artifacts, display what appeared to be a gradual evolutionary development. Use of terms such as "simpler," "developmental," or "formative" with respect to ceramics and architecture (i.e., Smith 1937: 3; Coe and Coe 1956: 372) had clear evolutionary implications. In 1968, Sanders and Price (1968: 140) stressed that monumental architecture accurately reflects societal complexity. But they also assumed that these patterns occurred most clearly in the great highland centers, an assertion with unfortunate, tendentious effects on regional and chronological research. According to Sanders and Price (1968) "in architecture, the contrast (between Highland states and Lowland chiefdoms) is even more striking; no Formative site is comparable in size, quality, or complexity to the great Classic and Postclassic centers."

Accordingly, Maya civilization was thought to have emerged later in Mesoamerica, and Maya accomplishments were thought to have stemmed largely from contact with their more sophisticated highland neighbors. Thompson, for example, suggested that

> such an isolated region as the Peten would hardly have witnessed the beginnings of Maya civilization, which might rather be expected in parts of the Maya area where the stimulus of contact with other cultures should have quickened development—Central Chiapas seems ideal. (Thompson 1954: 50)

Before about 1962, the relative paucity and diminutive size of known lowland Pre-Classic buildings (see Hansen 1990: 3ff), in contrast to the spectacular and abundant Classic remains, fostered a bias that Maya civilization developed by about A.D. 300. This model assumed that architectural development, as a reflection of cultural complexity, was gradual in nature, with assumptions about the antiquity and nature of formative ceremonial architecture (and related sociopolitical interactions) based on negative evidence. The initial work on the North Acropolis at Tikal was perhaps the first indication of a problem with the chronology that purported a gradual, lineal evolution from egalitarian groups to civilization. Coe and McGinn noted:

> Nevertheless, as we cut farther down, the elaborateness and Classic appearance of the discovered structures were no less apparent. Things were not getting simpler, or cruder, or increasingly formative. (Coe and McGinn 1963: 26)

Pre-Classic Maya constructions have been relatively sparse with few exceptions. Puleston found in his settlement study at Tikal that

> in comparison with areas within what later becomes the site residential area, Pre-Classic settlement is comparatively light. Sometime during Early Classic times there appears to have been a really substantial increase in population. While out of 41 tested groups, only 7 showed even possible evidence of Pre-Classic occupation, and all but 1 produced evidence of Early Classic occupation. (Puleston 1974: 308)

Haviland (1965: 19) showed that 6 of 117 housemounds surveyed at Tikal dated to Pre-Classic periods, whereas Fry (1969) noted only 14 of 102 test pits throughout the site that had Pre-Classic ceramics. Culbert (1977: 31–32) determined that little more than 13% of 267 excavation locations produced ceramic evidence of Pre-Classic occupation. Recent excavations of housemounds near Structure 5C-54 at Tikal failed to locate a single Pre-Classic residence in the 16 major groups investigated (Valdés 1985), and similar low frequencies of Pre-Classic remains are found at numerous sites throughout the Maya area (Coe and Sharer 1979: 22; Fash 1991: 71; Folan, Kintz, and Fletcher 1983: 213; Hammond 1977: 65; Pendergast 1979; Rands 1974: 54; 1977: 160; Rice 1976; A. L. Smith 1950: 71; Tourtellot 1970: 411; Valdés n.d.; Willey 1973: 22–39; Willey et al. 1965: 96, 562–564; Willey et al. 1975: 36, 40–41, 231). The various investigative strategies used at the sites suggest, in some cases, a genuine lack of Pre-Classic occupation. In other instances, however, the sample may have been biased only to superficial deposits. Of greater theoretical import is the evidence for rapid population growth and settlement concentration in some regions of the lowlands.

PRE-CLASSIC ARCHITECTURE: LOCATION AND CONTEXT

What we know today about Pre-Classic architecture comes from a variety of excavation techniques, including large- and small-scale horizontal exposures, tunnels, and deep architectural trenches. These studies permit a detailed view of Pre-Classic architectural developments as precursors of later Classic traditions (Fig. 1). It is curious that many of the great Classic centers such as Palenque, Copan, and Quirigua, situated near rich alluvial plains, were small or

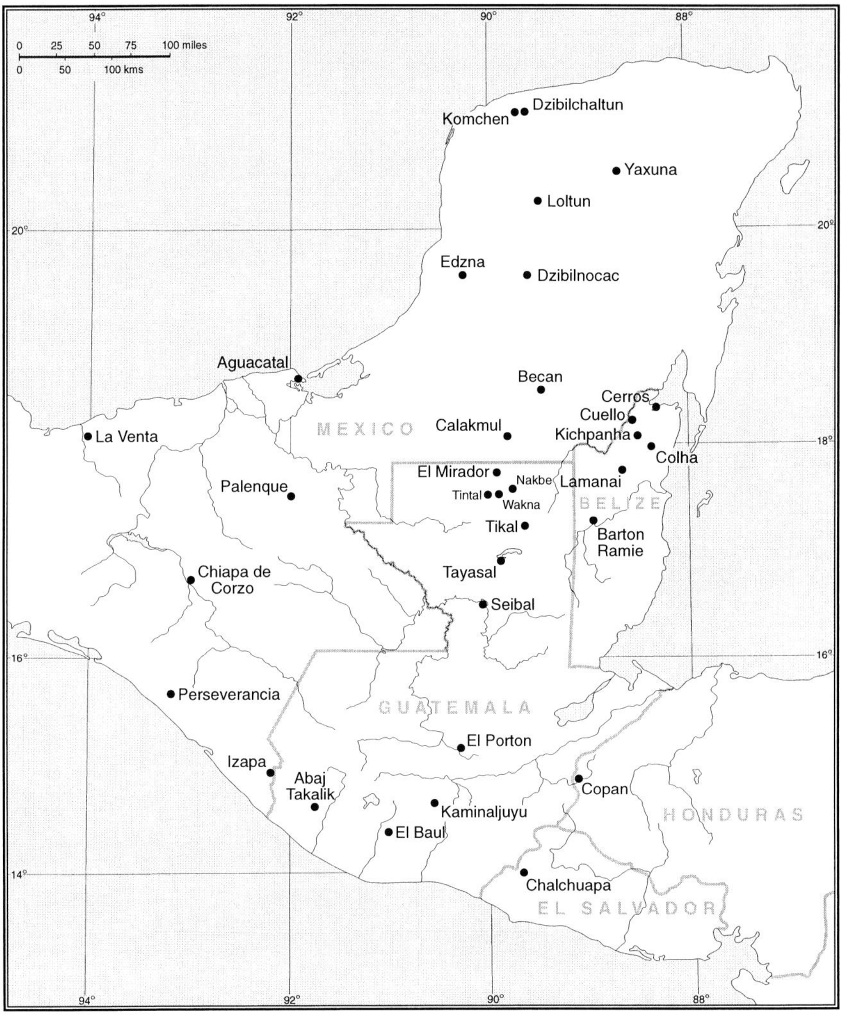

Fig. 1 Map of the Maya area showing Pre-Classic sites with known public architecture. Courtesy of the Brigham Young University Department of Geography.

nonexistent in Pre-Classic times (Rands 1977: 160; Fash 1991), suggesting that initial settlement and architectural development were not necessarily related to competition for prime agricultural soils or for other advantages such as irrigation or river transportation.

Investigations in the extreme north-central Peten reveal new information about early architectural development. This area, which we term the "Mirador

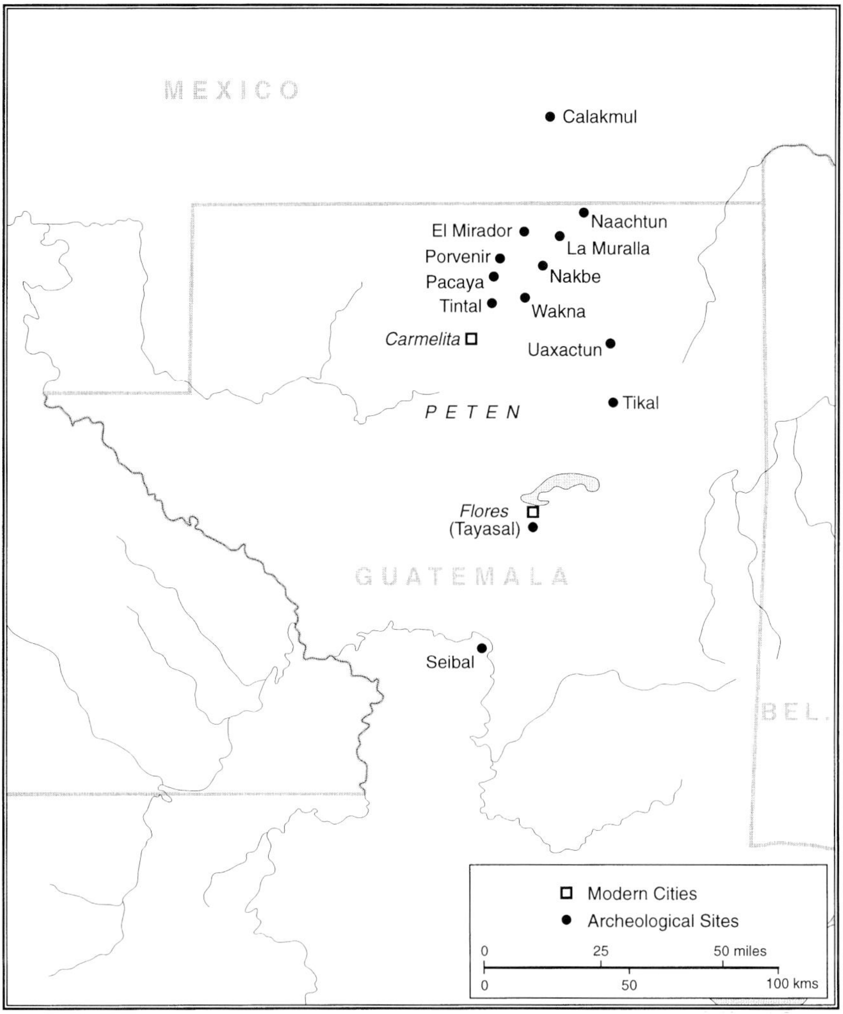

Fig. 2 Map of the northern Peten showing the concentration and density of Pre-Classic sites within the Mirador Basin. Courtesy of the Brigham Young University Department of Geography.

Basin" after the largest site in the area, is bordered by rugged karstic formations on the eastern, southern, and western flanks, forming a triangular region of approximately 1100 km^2 (Fig. 2). Extensive bajos or low-lying, seasonal swamps characterize the area. To date, excavations have revealed abundant Middle and Late Pre-Classic architectural remains and other manifestations of complex so-

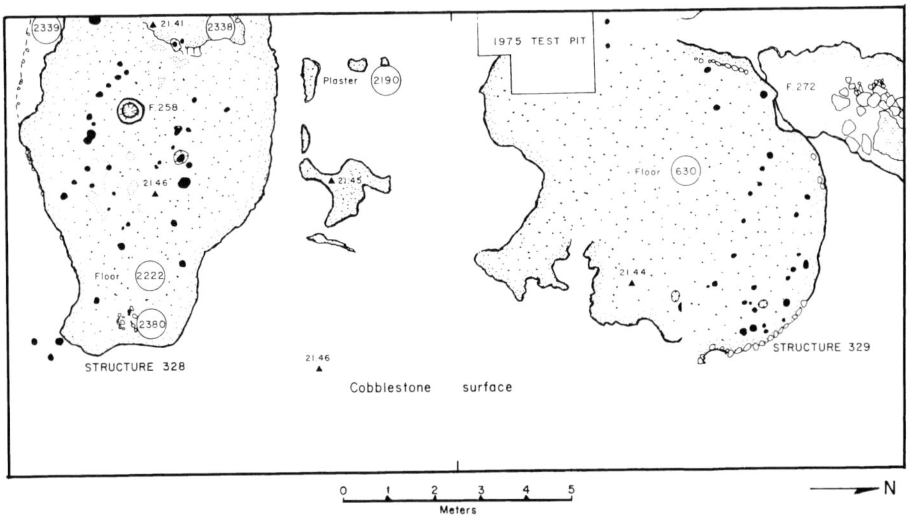

Fig. 3 Early Middle Pre-Classic architecture at Cuello, Belize (after Gerhardt 1988: 9).

ciety. The large size and scale of several sites in the basin (El Mirador, Nakbe, Wakna, Tintal) are impressive in view of their antiquity (ca. 1000 B.C. to A.D. 150) (Hansen 1992c). The presence of exposed Middle and Late Pre-Classic architecture allows easier access to early buildings than the deeply buried constructions found elsewhere (Matheny, Hansen, and Gurr 1980; Dahlin 1984; Demarest 1984; Matheny 1986, 1987; Hansen 1990, n.d.a, n.d.b; Hansen and Forsyth 1987; Howell and Copeland 1989; Forsyth 1989); but there are also problems. The preservation of these surface structures is often poor because of prolonged exposure to elements, tropical forest growth, and subsequent stone plundering. Furthermore, looters' trenches in Pre-Classic structures often result in more severe destruction than in other buildings because looters tend to place numerous trenches on the earlier structures in the mistaken belief that they missed a tomb in the initial attempts (see Hansen, Bishop, and Fahsen 1991). One advantage is that the antiquity of the surface remains allows for access to substructures of even greater antiquity with better preservation.

PRE-CLASSIC ARCHITECTURE: MIDDLE PRE-CLASSIC

From stratigraphic, ceramic, and absolute dating controls, I believe that the earliest, most securely dated architecture yet identified in the lowlands occurs at Cuello sometime around 1000 B.C. (Hammond 1977, 1991; Hammond, Clarke, and Robin 1991; Estrada 1992) (Fig. 3). The earliest constructions at Cuello, Structures 329 and 328, consisted of thin (0.05 m) plaster floors on a low platform (0.25 m high) of clay and small black stones. Associated postholes suggest a wooden superstructure that was probably apsidal in shape (Gerhardt 1988: 9–12). Subsequent fill and patio construction were surrounded by Structure 327 (rounded), Structure 326 (apsidal), and Structure 325 (Gerhardt 1988: 22). These three structures with perishable superstructures were slightly elevated above the patio floor through the accumulation of various layers of plaster floors, wash coats, and shallow construction fills. Structure 326 was apsidal, with front and back steps and a "thresholded" doorway. The apsidal forms of the earliest architectural constructions at nearby Colha (Potter et al. 1984) and other areas of Mesoamerica, such as the Pacific coast and Soconusco regions (Clark 1994; Clark and Blake 1994), indicate the antiquity and homogeneity of this form and establish a predictable pattern of early residence architecture.

Early in the Middle Pre-Classic period (ca. 900 to 600 B.C.), there are indications of an extensive, although light, occupation in several areas of the lowlands, such as at Seibal, Altar de Sacrificios, Barton Ramie, and Colha. At Altar de Sacrificios, plaster floors and small platforms, wattle-and-daub constructions (e.g., Md. 25), and postholes occur with such occupations (Willey 1973: 23, 1990: 193). The early Jenny Creek material from Barton Ramie came from 18 of the 65 mounds showing basal deposits, although only three substructure platforms were associated with this phase (Willey et al. 1965: 562). Imprints of poles in burnt mud suggested the presence of wattle-and-daub construction (Willey et al. 1965: 562). Middle Pre-Classic constructions yielding Bolay and Chiwa ceramics were found in the main plaza at Colha (Potter et al. 1984; Anthony and Black 1994). The earliest structure found there, Structure 1, was built in apsidal form on an earthen platform (Anthony and Black 1994: 56; Potter et al. 1984: 629).

Northern Peten

The earliest constructions identified so far at Nakbe in the northern Peten consist of packed, earthen floors on a buried paleosol level with postholes carved into bedrock. Carbon samples from these levels have yielded consistent calibrated radiocarbon dates of 1400 to 1000 B.C. (Table 1), but the sample of ceramics from this period is poor. Later Middle Pre-Classic deposits, primary in nature, buried these earliest levels in both the eastern and western groups at Nakbe, but we have reason to believe that remains from this period may be found closer to the *bajos* surrounding the site center. Similarly, the earliest remains at Tikal were near the Bajo Santa Fe (Harrison 1986: 49, 57), and Adams

TABLE 1. SELECTED CARBON DATES IN ASSOCIATION WITH THE EARLIEST PRIMARY DEPOSITS AT NAKBE, CALIBRATED ACCORDING TO STUIVER AND PEARSON (1986)

Provenience	Lab	B.P.	Uncalibrated	Calibrated
51C.29.12	UCLA 2834	3085 ± 50	1135 ± 50 B.C.	1433–1295 B.C.
				1278–1265 B.C.
51C.11.33	Beta 31753	2950 ± 80	1000 ± 80 B.C.	1370–1340 B.C.
				1319–1077 B.C.
				1064–1051 B.C.
53G.15.36	UCLA 2840	3110 ± 45	1160 ± 45 B.C.	1433–1373 B.C.
				1436–1318 B.C.*
				1357–1355 B.C.*
				1336–1321 B.C.*
51H.13.60	UCLA 2849 D	2980 ± 100	1030 ± 100 B.C.	1390–1080 B.C.
				1064–1051 B.C.
51G.09.43	UCLA 2836	3185 ± 55	1235 ± 55 B.C.	1519–1412 B.C.
51C.10.23	UCLA 2831	2900 ± 45	950 ± 45 B.C.	1212–1014 B.C.

*These dates are possibilities according to the Sigma ranges (Sigma 1).

(1983: 326–327) points out that population densities may be greater near swamp/marsh areas where agriculture was practiced.[1]

Sometime around 800 B.C., the occupation at Nakbe covered a 50 ha area of the site center. Architecture consisted of low, vertical stone walls forming small platforms with roughly shaped, flat, rectangular stones. These walls range from three to five courses high and about half a meter in height (Fig. 4). They apparently supported wooden superstructures, although no postholes were detected within the walls themselves. These walls contained thin *sascab* (gritty limestone marl) floors[2] and, on occasion, hard clay floors. Rich midden deposits were found on the exterior face of these walls, with sherd densities as great as 4000 sherds per m^3 (Forsyth 1993a, 1993b). Changes in the orientation and increasing size of the wall and platform constructions indicate that growth during this period was dynamic. Several clues point to changes in the society associated with the early architectural development at Nakbe, possibly in the differentia-

[1] See also Folan and Gallegos (n.d.).

[2] *Sascab,* or decomposed limestone marl, was easily mined from deposits immediately above bedrock. Unlike lime, this material did not need firing. *Sascab,* a white or yellowish material with a slightly gritty texture, was placed in the earliest floors in the Tigre plaza (Late Pre-Classic) at El Mirador and on small platforms at Nakbe (Middle Pre-Classic). Apparently lime plaster was available before the introduction of *sascab* as a widely used surfacing technique.

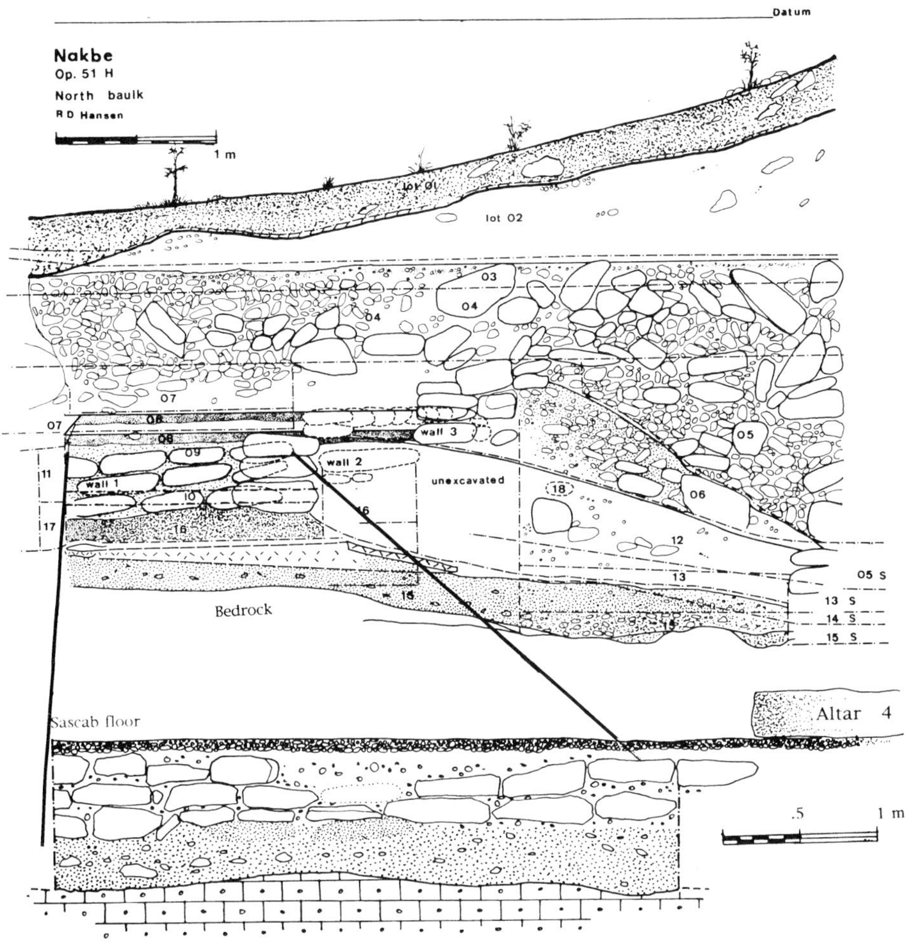

Fig. 4 Early Middle Pre-Classic walls at Nakbe, Guatemala.

tion of status, including exotic imports, symbols of rulership, and dental incrustations, which are considered markers of high status (Hansen 1992c; Mata Amado and Hansen 1992).

Evidence of wattle-and-daub constructions was recovered from a structure sealed below a Middle Pre-Classic plaster floor in the eastern group at Nakbe (Operation 51 K). This low platform had a hard clay floor flanked by large, coarse stones (Fig. 5) with imprints of parallel, narrow, wooden poles in the *mezcla* (lime and clay mortar). Similar buildings were found in Lopez Mamom contexts at Cuello with fragments of wall cladding, parallel impressions of poles,

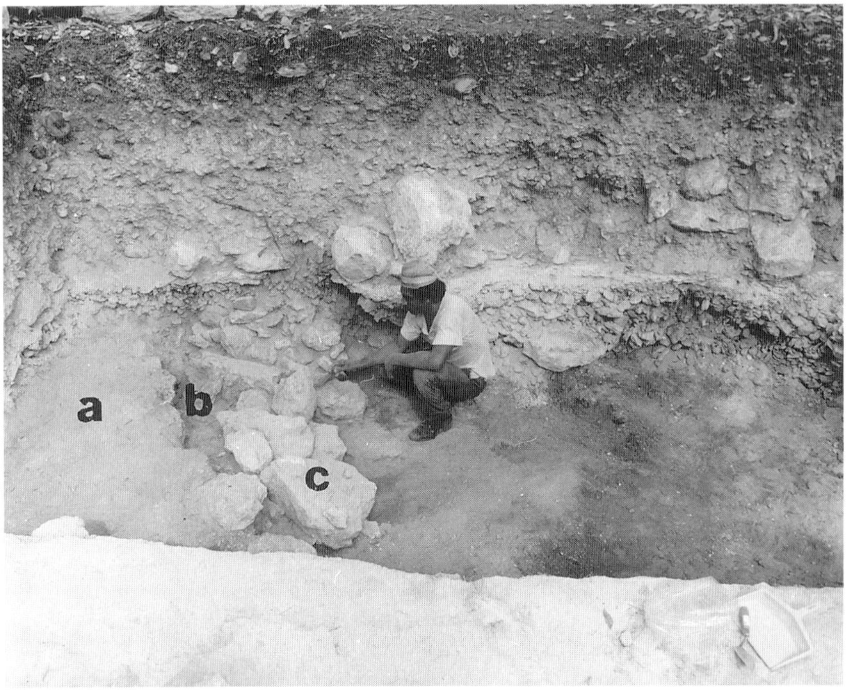

Fig. 5 Remains of an elevated platform (a) at Nakbe with a small trench (b) for vertically placed wooden poles and covered with mud (Op. 51 K). This wattle-and-daub construction was bordered on the exterior by large stones (c) stacked originally against the wall. One of the blocks had a patch of *mezcla* with imprints of poles.

marks of binder vines, and other perishable materials (Hammond, Clarke, and Robin 1991). At Colha, Middle Pre-Classic stone alignments formed the base of apsidal pole-and-thatch structures with wattle-and-daub walls (Anthony and Black 1994: 39). In the Olmec area, Coe and Diehl (1980: 388) found wattle-and-daub constructions in San Lorenzo that date to 1000 B.C. The range and dispersal of this building technique is impressive in the early Middle Pre-Classic period throughout the lowlands and deserves further study.

At Nakbe, architectural constructions during this period consist of platforms up to 2 m high with vertical walls, small, rough rectangular stones, and a crude *mezcla* surfacing (Fig. 6). The summits of these platforms were covered with thin stucco floors. Rich primary refuse middens accumulated along these platforms, indicating possible residential functions, although much of this material may also have been ritual refuse.[3]

[3] Most of the middens surrounding Middle Pre-Classic platforms contain probable do-

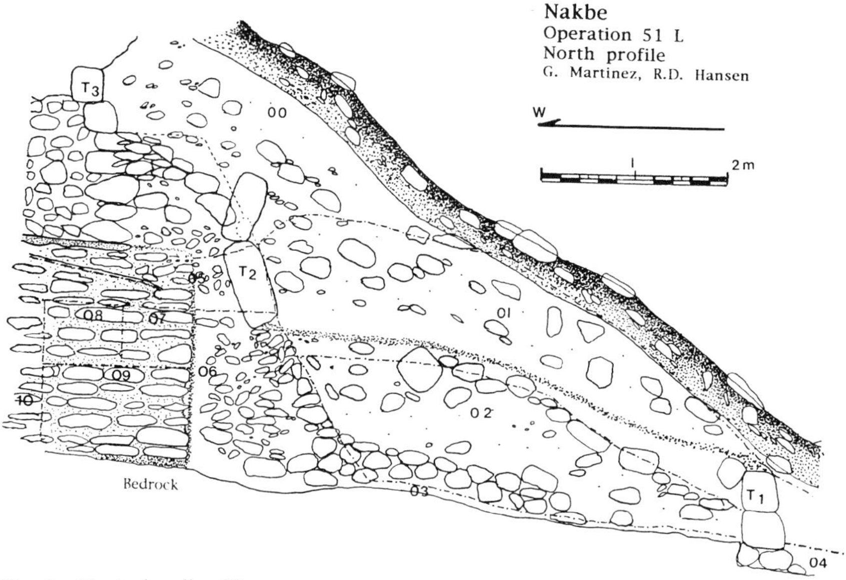

Fig. 6 Vertical walls of Structure 51 L-Sub 1. This buried structure exemplifies larger platforms of the Early Middle Pre-Classic. The vertical walls and thin, roughly shaped blocks were covered with a crude mortar/stucco *mezcla* (*right*). Drawing by Gustavo Martínez Hidalgo and Richard Hansen.

mestic refuse: broken tecomates, bowls, Palma Daub vessels associated with ash, a few bones, shells, diagnostic waste flakes from stone tool production/rejuvenation. They lack traditional diagnostic remains such as incense burners (*incensarios*). The presence of figurines, ceramics with delicate polychrome stucco applied to the slip, and the abundance of fine ceramics point to trash left by elites.

Fig. 7 Large horizontal excavations of Middle Pre-Classic deposits at the western base of Structure 51, Nakbe. Note the linear placement of stones, the thick stucco floors, and the monument, Altar 4, in the center-line axis of Structures 51 and 52. Photograph by F. R. Hillman.

The next 200 years witnessed a period of expanding platforms and the placement of thick plaster floors (Fig. 7). Platform walls continued to be vertical, although a series of unusual projecting buttress constructions were appended to them (Fig. 7). A thick, well-made plaster floor in the East Group was covered with roughly hewn stones placed in single-file rows. The stones weighed about 100 kg, requiring at least two or three individuals to move them. The increasing sizes of stones and greater labor needed to transport and place them indicate an expanding investment in the architectural landscape. The end of a platform was defined by a row of stones, whereas the top of the platform was a stone mosaic pavement covered with a thin stucco surface (Fig. 8). The construction of platforms filled with carefully placed stones in rows differs substantially from subsequent architecture with rough stone fill and mortar in cell wall

Fig. 8 Middle Pre-Classic stone pavement, which had been covered by Late Pre-Classic Structure 59 at Nakbe. Photograph by F. R. Hillman.

constructions. Nonetheless, it clearly represents a perceptible increase in the ability to muster labor by the early Middle Pre-Classic period.

Recent explorations have located a series of elevated platforms about 1 m high along the southern edge of Nakbe, with a single, elevated structure on one side of the platform. Although we have yet to excavate these structures (which are believed to date to the Middle Pre-Classic), they may be a diagnostic form of Pre-Classic residential architecture as identified at Komchen (Ringle and Andrews 1988; Andrews and Ringle 1992; Ringle n.d.a, n.d.b).

One of the enduring characteristics of Mesoamerican architecture is the association of stone monuments with specific buildings, a trait that extends to the Early and Middle Pre-Classic periods among the Olmec. During the latter part of the Middle Pre-Classic period (late Ox phase) at Nakbe, around 600 to

Fig. 9 Excavation at Nakbe showing (a) the present-day ground surface, (b) a Middle Pre-Classic platform wall, (c) a plaster floor, and (d) Early Middle Pre-Classic walls. Photograph by C. Bieber.

500 B.C., a large altar (Altar 4) was placed at the base of a platform wall (Fig. 7). This monument was situated in a center line axis immediately west of Structure 51, indicating that the linkage of architecture to freestanding monuments existed by this time.

Stonework from the early Middle Pre-Classic (Ox) period (1000 to 600 B.C.) at Nakbe consists of quarried, unfinished stones of a rough rectangular shape. These stones consisted of relatively uniform, roughly hewn, flat stones stacked vertically in walls (Fig. 9b) and in platforms. It is probable that the "meaningless rows of stones" (Ricketson and Ricketson 1937: 134, 136) and "alignments of rough stones" (Smith 1950: vi) from the earliest occupation at Uaxactun were simple Mamom platforms. The early building reported by Coe and Coe (1956) at Nohoch Ek, Belize, appears to be the same, albeit more complete. In no instance of early Middle Pre-Classic period (early Ox) building remains have finely cut blocks or evidence of complex quarry specialization been found, although these characteristics followed shortly toward the end of the Middle Pre-Classic period.

LATE MIDDLE PRE-CLASSIC ARCHITECTURE

Ceramics and absolute dates from Nakbe and Wakna indicate that between 600 and 400 B.C. the Mirador Basin experienced major changes in architectural construction styles and techniques. This period belongs to the late Middle Pre-Classic because of the continuation of ceramic types that are confined to the Mamom ceramic sphere (Palma Daub, Muxanal-Red-on-Cream). The Mamom presence is confirmed by the complete absence of types known to exist in the subsequent Chicanel phase, such as unslipped striated ceramics, mushroom vessels, and labial and medial flange bowls. In addition, vessel forms introduced during this period—large bowls with extremely wide, everted rims (up to 12 cm)—seem restricted chronologically. There is some continuity with several early Chicanel forms (incurved-rim bowls), although slip, paste, and surface treatment (incisions) appear to be more consistent with Mamom materials.

It is during this period that many of the modal attributes of later Maya architecture were introduced. The most impressive transformations included the construction of major platforms 3 to 8 m high, covering areas up to 40,000 m^2. The major platforms of the West Group at Nakbe, and nearly all the platforms of the East Group, were constructed during this time. Vast amounts of stone fill, placed in "dry" fashion (without mortar), were dumped over earlier village levels and platforms and covered with thin stucco floors. A few platforms and floors consist of a flat surface formed by a pavement of large stones (Fig. 8). In several instances, a thin *sascab* floor extended underneath Middle Pre-Classic constructions (Structure 49; Fig. 10), but in most cases the floors extended only to the edge of the buildings surrounding a plaza, indicating that the platform construction and erection of monumental architecture were planned, simultaneous events. In the East Group of architecture at Nakbe, the structures extended to heights 18 m (Structure 47) and 14 m (Structure 51) above the platform floor.

"E-Group" Complexes

The earliest consistent architectural form, the E Group, appears during the latter part of the Middle Pre-Classic period in the lowlands. This architectural pattern was first recognized as an important ritual assemblage by Blom in 1924

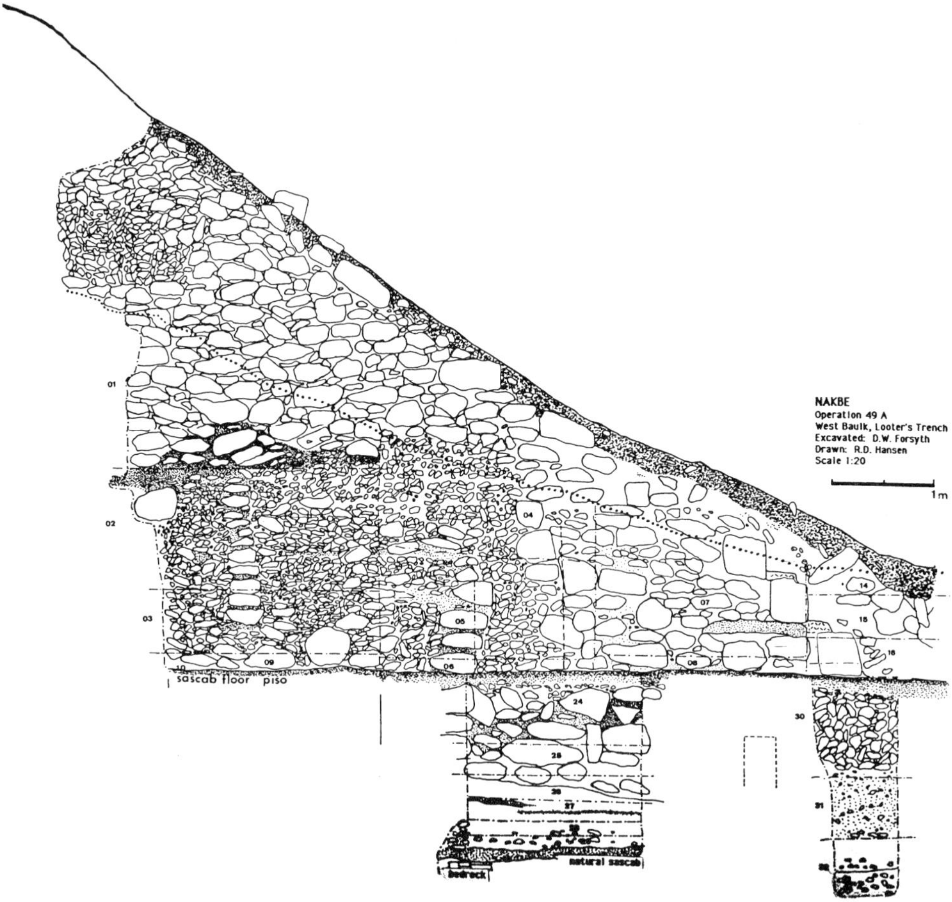

Fig. 10 Profile of Structure 49 and Middle Pre-Classic structure at Nakbe. Note the placement of cell walls and the thin *sascab* floor that extends beneath the building (after Forsyth 1993a: 141).

in the E Group at Uaxactun (Ruppert 1940: 222).[4] The pattern of this architectural assemblage consists of a large pyramidal structure on the western side of a plaza or platform; the eastern side of the plaza is dominated by an elevated, elongated structure on a north–south axis (Fig. 11). Often, there are two other

[4] See also Ricketson and Ricketson (1937), Ruppert and Denison (1943: 5–6), Cohodas (1980: 212–214), Chase (1983: 1236 ff), Fialko (1988), Hansen (1992a, 1992c), and Laporte (1993).

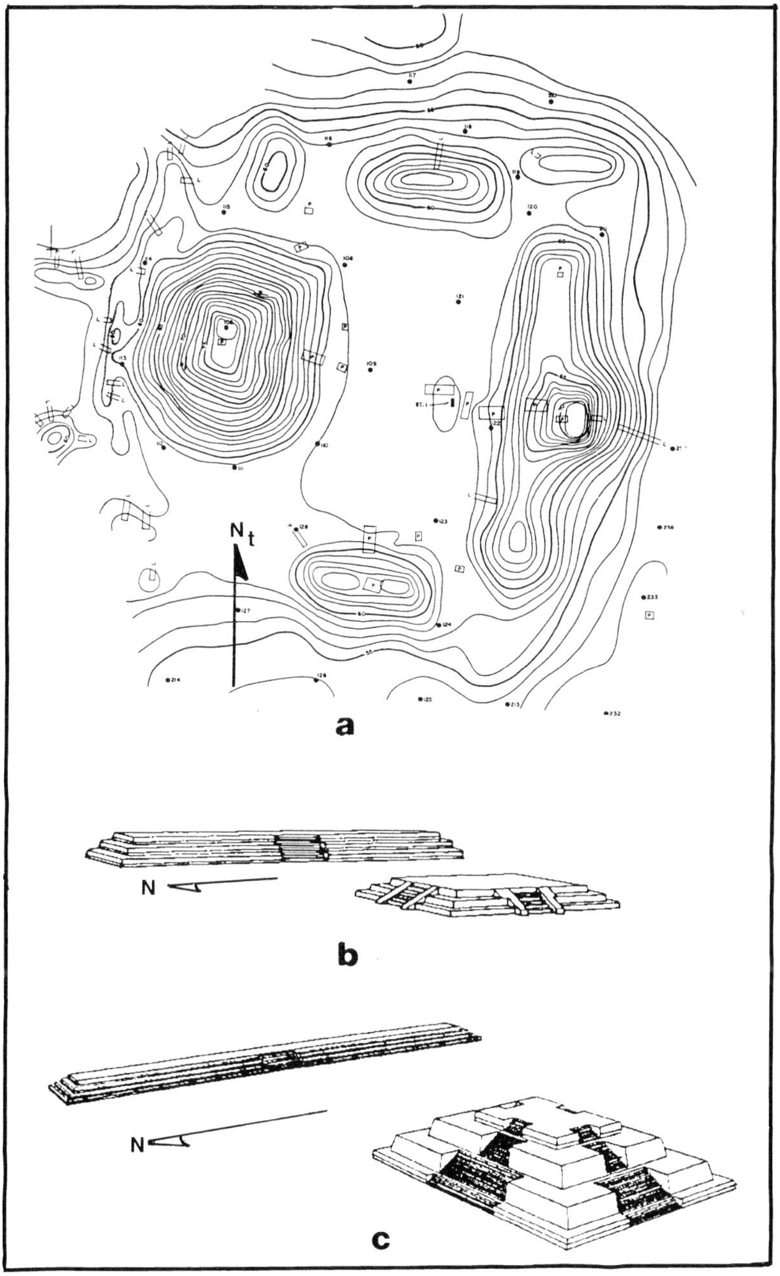

Fig. 11 E-Group complexes at (a) Nakbe, East Group (Late Middle Pre-Classic), (b) Tikal (late Eb phase), and (c) Tikal (Tzec phase) (after Laporte and Fialko 1993: 19, 20; 1995: 47, 49).

simpler and smaller buildings bordering the north and south sides of the platform to form a distinct plaza. However, it is clear that the east–west structures of the compound are the most important and most consistent in their placement and format.

The architectural group was argued by Blom (1924) to have "astronomical significance" because of perceived solar alignments of the structures (Ricketson and Ricketson 1937: 105–109). However, later evaluations of the E-Group complexes have suggested that the architectural arrangements do not appear to have had astronomical significance for solstice or equinox alignments (Aveni and Hartung 1989: 451–455). Nevertheless, further testing of possible stellar or planetary alignments may be productive, and several researchers continue to use astronomical terms—i.e., Fialko (1988); Laporte, Torres, and Hermes (1991); and Laporte and Torres (1993).

The early version of the E Group usually contains an elongated structure on the eastern side of the complex, as at Tikal (Laporte and Fialko 1995: 47–49), or the elongated eastern structure has a single, elevated building in its center, as at Tikal, Nakbe, Wakna, El Mirador, and possibly Tintal. Later forms of the eastern structure have three linearly placed structures on the platform facing toward the west (Ruppert 1940). An important distinction between the eastern platform structures of the E-Group complex and the triadic architecture format discussed below is that the end (distal) structures on the platform always face west rather than each other as do the triadic buildings. Often, the south side of the structure has another low structure, as is the case at El Mirador Structure 5D1-1 (G219) and the Cenote E-Group complex at Caracol (Chase and Chase 1995: fig. 3).

The arrangement of structures in the eastern group at Nakbe embodies an early E-Group format in the lowlands and is contemporaneous with the late Eb and Tzec E-Group constructions of the Mundo Perdido complex at Tikal (Laporte and Fialko n.d., 1993, 1995). Other groups that are believed to date to this period are at Wakna and possibly at Tintal in the Mirador Basin. In the case of Wakna,[5] the eastern structure exceeds 200 m in length and has a height of 10 m, whereas the center building extends to a height of 30 m.

The form of the western pyramidal structure of the E-Group complexes seems to vary slightly with regard to stairway construction, because the struc-

[5] Ian Graham and I changed the name of the site from Güiro (which Graham named in 1970) to Wakna because of the difficulty of spelling the name and the inconsistency of the lexical context. Graham noted that the aerial photos of the site, particularly the E-Group assemblage on the southern portion of the site, effectively formed a dot and bar, hence the number six (*wak*) when viewed from the air.

Fig. 12 E-Group complex at El Mirador with Leon pyramid. Courtesy of Bruce H. Dahlin.

ture is almost always nearly square at the base. Quadripartite stairways are commonly found on the western pyramidal structure, such as the Late Pre-Classic Structure E-VII-Sub at Uaxactun. Similar architecture is known throughout the lowlands, such as at Naachtun (of undetermined date), Tikal, and El Mirador (Fig. 12). Structure 5C-54 at Tikal had a quadrilateral stairway by the late Middle Pre-Classic Tzec phase, with four terraces (undecorated) and a height of 8 m (Laporte and Fialko 1995), whereas the eastern structure is simply an elongated, simple platform (Fig. 11). Structure 5C-54 became radically more complicated during the succeeding Late Pre-Classic Chuen and Cauac phases, when it follows closely the architectural pattern of E-VII-Sub at Uaxactun.

El Mirador Structure G212, a 34 m high building (also known as Leon

Pyramid), is identical to Uaxactun Structure E-VII-Sub with inset quadrilateral stairways, large projecting balustrades with masks and panels of architectural art (now badly damaged), and successive terraces with access to the summit only on the eastern side of the structure (Fig. 12) (Nielsen 1990: fig. 2.1). Surface ceramics, as well as information from test pits on the elongated eastern structure (Structure 5D1-1 or G219), suggest that the structure dates to the Pre-Classic, but a more accurate assessment of the antiquity of its construction will remain uncertain until more comprehensive investigations can begin. Other western pyramidal structures, such as those at Nakbe Structure 47 and Wakna Structure G31, do not appear to have quadripartite stairways. It appears that the quadripartite stairway is more common during the Late Pre-Classic.

The consistency and persistence of the E-Group form is suggested by its chronological range from the Middle Pre-Classic in the Mirador Basin to the Late Classic examples at nearby Calakmul, Uxul, Balakbal, and Naachtun (Fig. 13) and numerous other sites in the central and southern lowlands (Table 2). Ruppert and Denison (1943) and Chase (1983: table 43) note the range and distribution of the E-Group complexes within a restricted area of the southern lowlands, including areas of southern Campeche, and northern, eastern, and central Peten. In addition, there is a concentration of E-Group complexes in the southeastern Peten and southwestern Belize area (Laporte and Torres 1987; Laporte, Torres, and Hermes 1991; Laporte and Torres 1993; Laporte 1993; Chase and Chase 1995), hinting at a plausible religious unity within these areas.

The unusual predominance and antiquity of the E-Group complexes points to its central role in Maya ritual life.[6] Many early E Groups in the lowlands, including those in the Mirador Basin, are connected by a causeway to other dominant compounds. Often, but not always, the causeway extends to the northeast from the E-Group complex as observed, for example, at Ixkun (Graham 1980: 2–135; Laporte and Torres 1987: fig. 3), Ixtutz (Laporte and Torres 1987: fig. 3), and Wakna (Hansen 1992b, 1992c).

[6] There is a weak but tantalizing hint that the E-Group complex could represent a symbolic residence of First Father of Maya mythology, the "Six Sky place," the *wak chan*. The residence of First Father was the site of the first planting of three stones (Yax Ox Tun Nal) mentioned in Quirigua Stela C and the Tablet of the Cross (D5–D8). The frequent placement of three stelae, or superstructures, as on the eastern platform of Uaxactun Group E, the Mundo Perdido complex, Calakmul, and Pacbitun (Healy 1992) may allude to this mythological event. If Freidel and Schele are correct, the architectural triad on the southern side of many E-Group complexes corresponds to the three hearthstones of the fires of creation in the constellation Orion (see Taube, this volume). This important constellation is found on the southern hemisphere of the night sky.

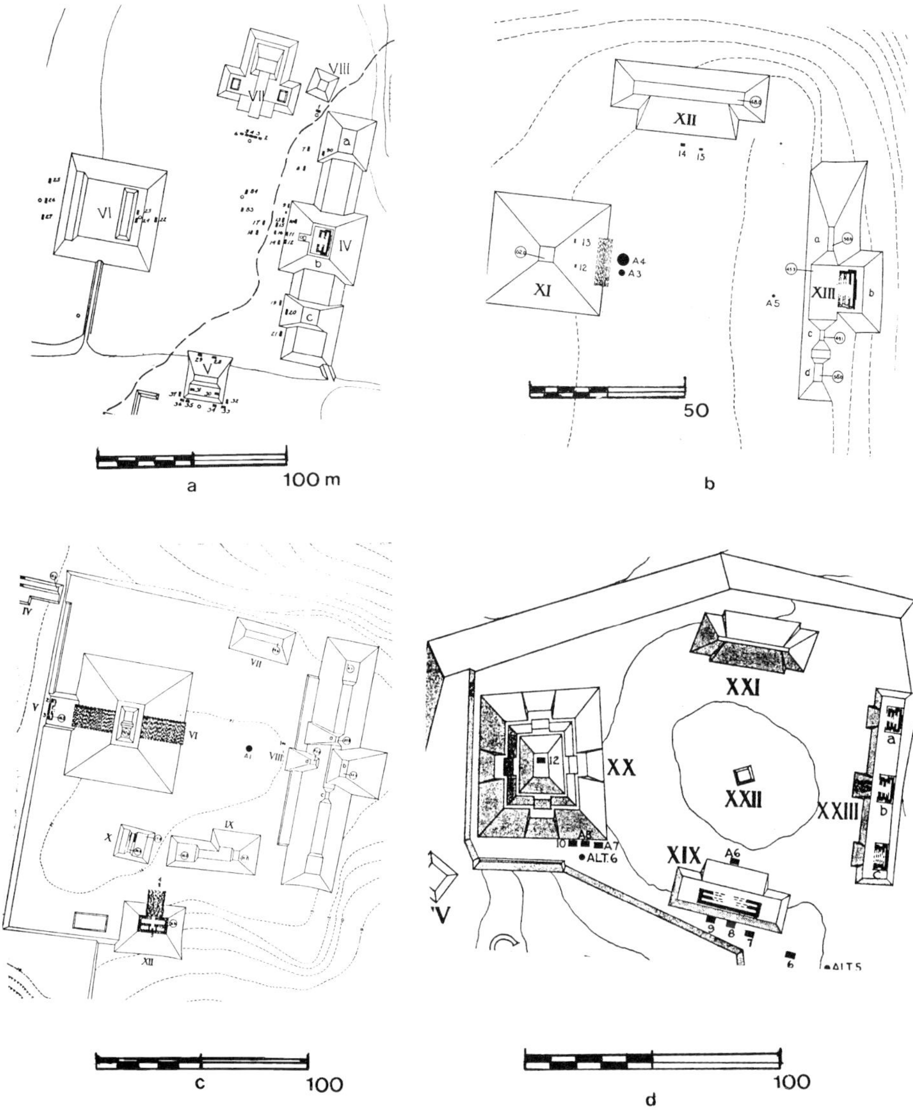

Fig. 13 E-Group complexes at (a) Calakmul, (b) Uxul, (c) Balakbal, and (d) Naachtun, all surrounding the Mirador Basin (after Ruppert and Denison 1943; pls. 61, 70, 69, 66).

Table 2. Selected Examples: E-Group Complex

Site	Structure	Phase*
Balakbal	Str. VI, VIII	?
Calakmul	Str. VI, IV	? LPC?, EC?, LC
Cahal Pichik	Str. B, D-E-L	LPC, EC, LC
Caracol	Cenote E Group	LPC?, EC, LC
	Str. A2, A5–7?	LPC?, EC, LC
Cenote (Peten)	Str. C5, C1	LC
Ixac (Peten)	Group A	LC
Ixcoxol (Peten)	Group GR-B	?
Ixkun (Peten)	Plaza A	?
Ixtonton (Peten)	Group JP1, Str. 11, 9	LPC, EC, LC
Ixtutz (Peten)	Plaza A, Str. 2, 8–10	?
Itzan (Peten)	?North Plaza, Str. 14, Str. 22–26	?
Hatzcap Ceel	Str. A, I-F-E	?LPC–EC?
El Mirador	Str. G212 Leon, 5D1-1	MPC?, LPC
Moquena (Peten)	Group PL-1	?
Naachtun	Str. XX, XXIII	?
Nakbe	Str. 47, Str. 51	MPC
Nakum	Str. C, A	LC
Sukche (Peten)	Group A, Str. 4, 2	?
Tikal	Str. 5C-54, 5D-84–88	MPC, LPC, EC, LC
Uxul	Str. XI, XIII	?
Uaxactun	E-VII-Sub, E-I–III	LPC, EC, LC
	Group D, Plaza IV, Str. 4, 2	MPC, LPC, EC, LC
Wakna (Guiro)	G31, G30	MPC?, LPC
Yaxha	Plaza F Str. LXXI, LXIX	EC?–LC
	Plaza C Str. XV, XIII	EC?–LC

*MPC = Middle Pre-Classic; LPC = Late Pre-Classic; EC = Early Classic; LC = Late Classic.

Middle Pre-Classic Architectural Variants

The variations in size between earlier small substructures and the much larger superstructures of the late Middle Pre-Classic period appear to have resulted from dramatic changes in society. Other architectural patterns also begin to appear during this time. For example, at Nakbe, large deposits of dark brown, *bajo* clay were placed in various platform constructions (Structure 31, Structure 18) in the western group during the late Middle Pre-Classic period (late Ox, 600 to 400 B.C.) (Martínez Hidalgo and Hansen 1993; Velásquez

1993). The clay deposits at Nakbe are contained by stone walls. The use of clay fill has been observed in other known Middle Pre-Classic constructions, such as those at Abaj Takalik (Schieber de Lavarreda 1994a, 1994b).

Other late Middle Pre-Classic architectural innovations include the circular structures found by Awe and Powis (Terry Powis, personal communication, 1995) in the Belize River valley. Several circular structures were found in Middle and Late Pre-Classic stratified contexts at Cuello (see below).

Late Middle Pre-Classic Masonry

During the late Middle Pre-Classic period, the size and form of quarried stone changed from the rough, simple, small stones that composed the early Middle Pre-Classic constructions to much larger blocks of consistent size and form (up to a meter long and half a meter wide). This standardization and technical expertise in production of stone blocks points to the existence of quarry and construction specialists at this time. The blocks used in late Middle Pre-Classic and early Late Pre-Classic constructions have been studied by Woods and Titmus (1994, 1996), and related investigations and experiments in the quarries at Nakbe involved horizontal excavation, detailed examinations of quarry edges, macro- and microanalyses of the stone tools recovered from quarry contexts, replication of quarrying tools, and actual quarrying of limestone blocks with stone tools to determine the energetics of architectural construction (see Abrams, this volume). This allowed the estimation of labor investment, and possible specialization, as well as identification of the methods and markers of limestone extraction along with breakage and wear patterns in tools. Woods and Titmus (1994, 1996) determined a probable minimum labor investment of approximately 34 man-hours per block for the large stones quarried during late Middle Pre-Classic and Late Pre-Classic periods.

Middle Pre-Classic: Apron Moldings

Although apron moldings at Tikal were thought to have first appeared during the Late Pre-Classic Chuen period (Coe 1965a: 1408; 1965b: 13), it is clear, on the basis of data from Mundo Perdido (5C-54-2, upper terrace) at Tikal and the architecture at Nakbe (Structures 32, 35, and 47) that such architectural manipulation began at least during the late Middle Pre-Classic period (Tzec, late Ox). The systematic production of large blocks facilitated the construction of pronounced apron moldings with stones tenoned into the structure (Fig. 14). In the case of Nakbe Structure 32, a containing wall was built on the terraces, possibly to capture and control rainwater (Hansen 1992c; López 1993; Acevedo n.d.). An identical construction, probably a hydraulic feature, was found on later Cauac phase causeways at Tikal between the Mundo Perdido complex and the Aguada del Templo (Laporte and Fialko 1995: 50, fig. 11c). The large stones were also placed in façades with a pronounced slope (or *talud*) on platforms and a combination of the talud and apron moldings with the long axis of the stones parallel with the wall. In addition, rounded corners on platforms and structures first appear during this period (Fig. 14b).

Middle Pre-Classic: Architectural Art

The façades flanking the stairways of major Middle Pre-Classic structures do not appear to have been associated with monumental architectural art. The evidence is ambiguous because of poor preservation of exposed stucco, but the façades definitely lack the relief known in subsequent Maya architectural art. Laporte and Fialko (1993) note a similar lack of artistic embellishment on the late Eb remnants and Tzec architecture within Structure 5C-54 and associated platforms at Tikal. David Freidel (personal communication, 1994) has recently discovered an 11 m high Middle Pre-Classic pyramid with no associated architectural art within a later structure at Yaxuna. However, the recent discovery by Adams and Valdez of a probable Middle Pre-Classic Mamom structure within a Late Pre-Classic structure at Río Azul shows that the façade was decorated with a large stucco J-scroll and bracket motif in very shallow relief (Valdez 1995). The pattern appears to be a general absence of monumental architectural sculpture, or at least a very limited stucco relief, in stark contrast to iconographic depictions from the subsequent Late Pre-Classic period.

Middle Pre-Classic: Internal Construction

Another characteristic of monumental Middle Pre-Classic architecture in the Maya lowlands, particularly at Tikal, Nakbe, and Wakna, is the lack of mud mortar in fill. The architectural fill consists of large stones that had been loosely dumped in the structure, making deep trenching and tunneling of the structure risky or impossible without extensive support systems. The use of cell-wall construction, however, is evident in all known monumental architecture from this period at Nakbe (see Fig. 10), occurring also in Late Pre-Classic constructions throughout the lowlands. Cell walls are crudely fashioned walls, internally constructed on various levels to contain loose fill of a building. Although the origins of the cell-wall technique are elusive, the presence of cell walls in monumental Middle Pre-Classic architecture at Nakbe indicates their great antiquity.

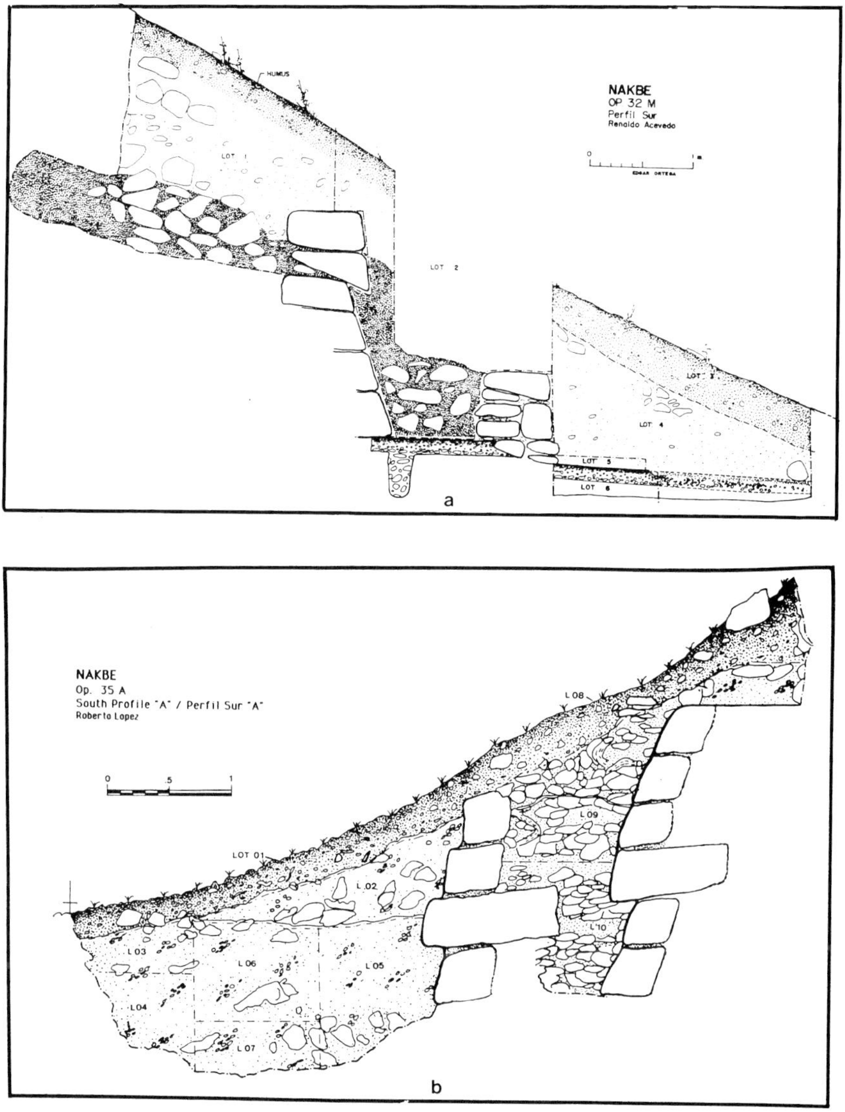

Fig. 14 Examples of late Middle Pre-Classic (ca. 630–400 B.C.) apron moldings at Nakbe: (a) Structure 32, Nakbe (note the short wall at the base of the main wall, which is believed to have captured water from the building); (b) Structure 35, platform (note how the axes of the stone are parallel with the structural line, with the apron-molding stone tenoned into the building). Drawings by Renaldo Acevedo (*top*) and Francisco R. López (*bottom*).

Ballcourts

During the latter part of the Middle Pre-Classic Ox period at Nakbe, the first phase of a ballcourt was constructed on the southern side of Structure 53 of the East Group at Nakbe (Velásquez 1992b). These structures (Structures 75, 76, and 77) were constructed in traditional form, although of a reduced size and scale consistent with known Pre-Classic ballcourts. The 2 m high ballcourt at Nakbe consists of two low parallel structures (Structures 76 and 77), separated by a narrow (5 m) playing alley, with sloping interior walls and a vertical exterior wall. Similar small Late Pre-Classic ballcourts are known at Cerros (Scarborough et al. 1982), Pacbitun (Healy 1992), Buenavista del Cayo (Ball 1993: fig. 43), Colha (Eaton and Kunstler 1980), and possibly at Tonina (Taladoire 1981). Another structure perpendicular to the axis of the alley usually borders the southern end of the ballcourts, a pattern of some duration in the lowlands. I suspect that a monument was in the alley of the ballcourt at Nakbe.[7]

The appearance of early ballcourts and related architecture places the Maya lowlands on a coeval level of development with the highlands and Pacific Coast regions, although the origins of the ball game may be foreign to the Maya area. For example, a Middle Pre-Classic ballcourt has been found at Abaj Takalik (Schieber de Lavarreda 1994a, 1994b), and Coe believes that a Middle Pre-Classic Olmec ballcourt existed at San Lorenzo (Coe and Diehl 1980: 29, 62, 388; Coe 1981: 132). Recent excavations at the Olmec site of El Manatí have located rubber balls in the muck of ancient springs (Stuart 1993: 101; Ortíz and Carmen Rodríguez 1994). In the Mexican highlands, Grove located a Middle Pre-Classic construction that resembles a ballcourt at Chalcatzingo (Grove and Cyphers Guillén 1987: 26), and evidence for what may be an early symbolic ballcourt has been found at Teopantecuanitlan, Guerrero (Martínez Donjuán 1994). The recent discovery of an Early Pre-Classic ballcourt on the Pacific Coast of Chiapas by Blake and Clark (John Clark, personal communication, 1995) may prove to be the earliest example. Parallel and elongated mounds measuring 85 m in length have been found dating to the Barra-Locona phases at the site of Paso de la Amada (John Clark, personal communication, 1995). If this complex is a ballcourt, then the ball game and the associated architectural

[7] A carved circular monument, Monument 8, was discovered at Nakbe about 70 m to the east of the ballcourt with no architectural association. The large stone was isolated and upside down, and it may have been abandoned in its present location by Late Classic Maya. The iconography of the monument represents an extremely early version of the downward-peering, dual serpent/saurian heads. The early style of the altar suggests the antiquity of such sculpture and its possible association with ballcourts.

constructions are among the most enduring cultural and architectural components of Mesoamerican societies.

Site Layout and Architectural Distribution

Architectural arrangements at various Pre-Classic sites show considerable regional variation. The Middle Pre-Classic sites of San Isidro, Finca Acapulco, and La Libertad in Chiapas (Lowe 1989, Clark 1988), for example, differ substantially in site layout from contemporaneous sites such as La Venta (González Lauck 1994) and in the valley of Oaxaca (Marcus 1976, 1989). Nakbe and Wakna also differ from all these sites in their architectural style and site layout. The differences constitute a strong case for in situ development of complex architecture in the Maya lowlands rather than borrowing from adjacent regions.

Causeways

The earliest causeway at Nakbe was probably built during the late Middle Pre-Classic period (Suasnavar 1994, n.d.). Causeways linked important platforms with other major architectural groups at this time (Fig. 15). The earliest causeway does not seem to have had a parapet, but two subsequent early Late Pre-Classic causeways had low parapets on both sides. The causeways were paved with thick layers of white *sascab* (up to a meter thick). During the Late Pre-Classic at Nakbe, causeways linked nearly all the large sites in the Mirador Basin, with an abundance of them at El Mirador (see Dahlin, Foss, and Chambers 1980). These constructions represent some of the finest engineering accomplishments of the time. Labor investment and volume of construction materials were enormous. For example, the Kan Causeway, which joins the East and West Groups at Nakbe, was built as high as 4 m above the undulating terrain and with a width of 24 m. Similar causeways join Nakbe to El Mirador (13 km) and El Mirador to Tintal (25 km). The size and extent of the causeways, their directional precision, and their number indicate an accomplished engineering program in the Pre-Classic.

LATE PRE-CLASSIC ARCHITECTURE: INITIAL CYCLE 7

Middle Pre-Classic culture in the Mirador Basin seems precocious, but it pales when compared to the cultural florescence that swept through the lowlands during the Late Pre-Classic period at the beginning of Cycle 7 (ca. 350 B.C.). Architectural innovations included a focus on monumentality, triadic building arrangements, and the introduction of monumental art on the façades of buildings. The acropolis layout characteristic of later Classic-period sites was

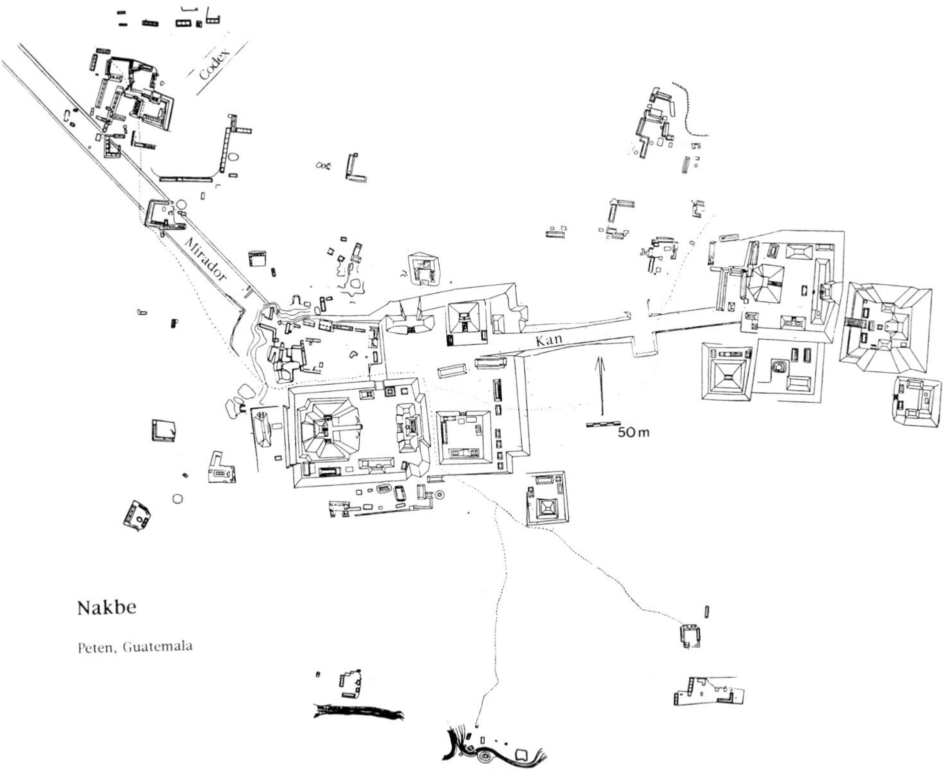

Fig. 15 Map of Nakbe, Peten.

also established during this period. The extent of the architectural transformations throughout the lowlands was paralleled by a remarkably homogeneous Chicanel ceramic sphere.

Monumentality

Massive augmentations in the size and scale of monumental architecture are evident by about 300 B.C. in the Maya lowlands. Many Late Pre-Classic structures were built, with heights ranging from 24 to 72 m. Equally impressive is the volume of materials used in construction. The explosive growth in architecture is perhaps best demonstrated at El Mirador. Tigre pyramid, which dominates the western portion of the site, was apparently built to its present height of 55 m at this time and covered an area of 19,600 m^2. When compared to Classic-era Tikal, Tigre effectively covers the entire complex of Temple I, Temple

II, the Great Plaza, and the entire North Acropolis (Hansen 1990: 215). The platforms of Danta, located on the eastern side of El Mirador, were built in the Late Pre-Classic period with the lowest platform base covering an area 500 × 350 m and rising 72 m to the summit. The masonry construction of this edifice is consistent with the long-standing Pre-Classic tradition of large, limestone tenons. Apron molding, introduced in the Middle Pre-Classic, also occurs in the building (see Fig. 26).

The variation in architectural elaboration and density of structures in the Late Pre-Classic period, ranging from major buildings on upland hills to small settlements in the *bajos,* indicates a social and economic complexity comparable to the Classic period. Demarest et al. (1984) found housemounds surrounding plazas at El Mirador, thus demonstrating that the standard Classic period format for residential architecture was established by the Late Pre-Classic. Dahlin's discovery of Late Pre-Classic rectangular and apsidal domiciles in the *bajos* is an important indicator of settlement density. Future excavation in these areas may provide more evidence of economic specialization and related differences in rank or status.

The monumentality in the Mirador Basin during the early Late Pre-Classic period also appeared in the Mundo Perdido complex at Tikal during the Chuen (ca. 400 to 200 B.C.) and Cauac (200 B.C. to A.D. 200) periods (Laporte and Fialko 1995) and in the North Acropolis (Coe 1965a, 1965b). Comparable leaps in building monumentality and sophistication are evident at Lamanai on Structures N9-56, P9-2, P9-30, P8-9, and particularly N10-43, which acquired a height of 33 m and seems to have erupted from what had earlier been a modest residential construction (Pendergast 1981: 39–42). Cerros, a nucleated village, was transformed into an impressive ceremonial center at this time (Freidel 1986: 12).[8]

Triadic Architectural Form

Accompanying the shift in the scale and elaboration of public architecture during the Late Pre-Classic period was the introduction of the triadic form (Graham 1967: 45–46; Hansen n.d.a: 411–415, 1990: 171–172, 1992a: 54–56; Cohodas 1985: 58–59). The triadic pattern consists of a dominant structure, usually on a platform, flanked by two, inward-facing smaller mounds of equal

[8] Recent excavations at Cerros suggest that the process may have been more gradual (Kathryn Reese-Taylor, personal communication, 1995). Although Freidel noted that Structure 3 at Cerros appears to have been erected in a "single episode" (Freidel 1986: 10), it appears that earlier interior structures may be inside Structure 3 (Kathryn Reese-Taylor, personal communication, 1995).

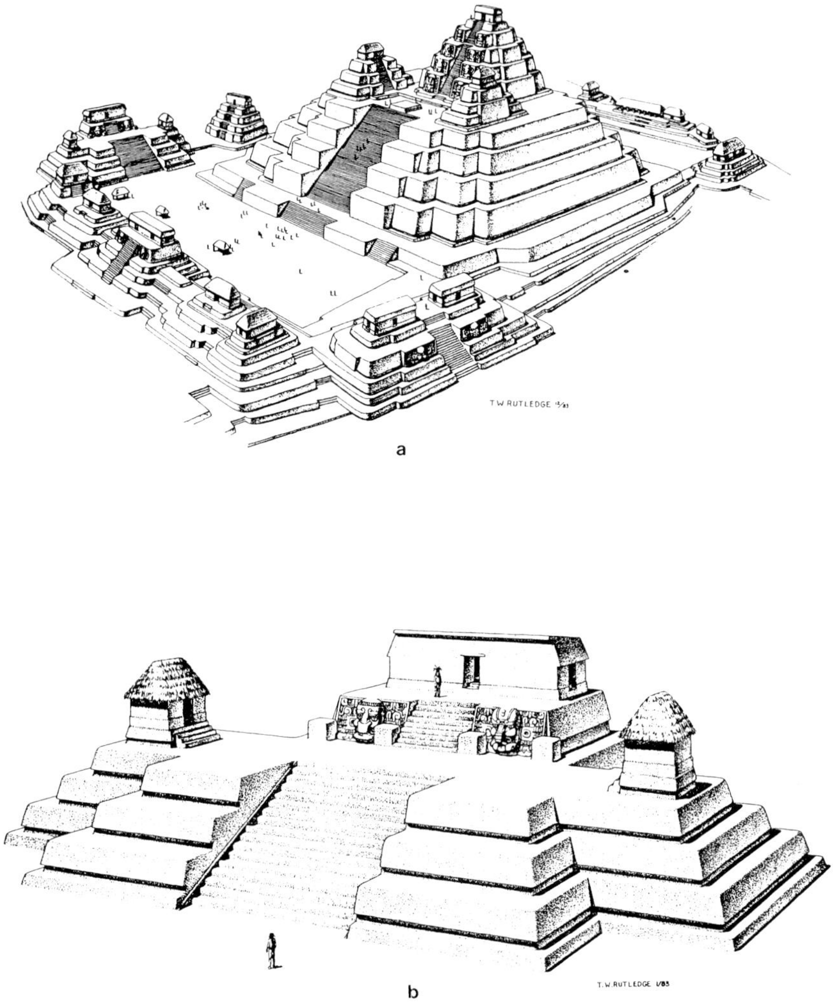

Fig. 16 Triadic platform arrangements at El Mirador: (a) Tigre complex and (b) Structure 34 (after Hansen 1990: ii and 116). Drawings by Terry Rutledge.

size (Fig. 16). Although there are no known Middle Pre-Classic antecedents, the triad may be a stylized descendant of the elongated eastern building of the E-Group complexes (Hansen 1992a: 55–56). Once the triad pattern was established, it enjoyed a special recognition for centuries. The four largest structures at Nakbe are triadic, as are more than 15 major structures at El Mirador (Graham 1967; Matheny 1986; Stutz-Landeen n.d.; Howell and Copeland 1989;

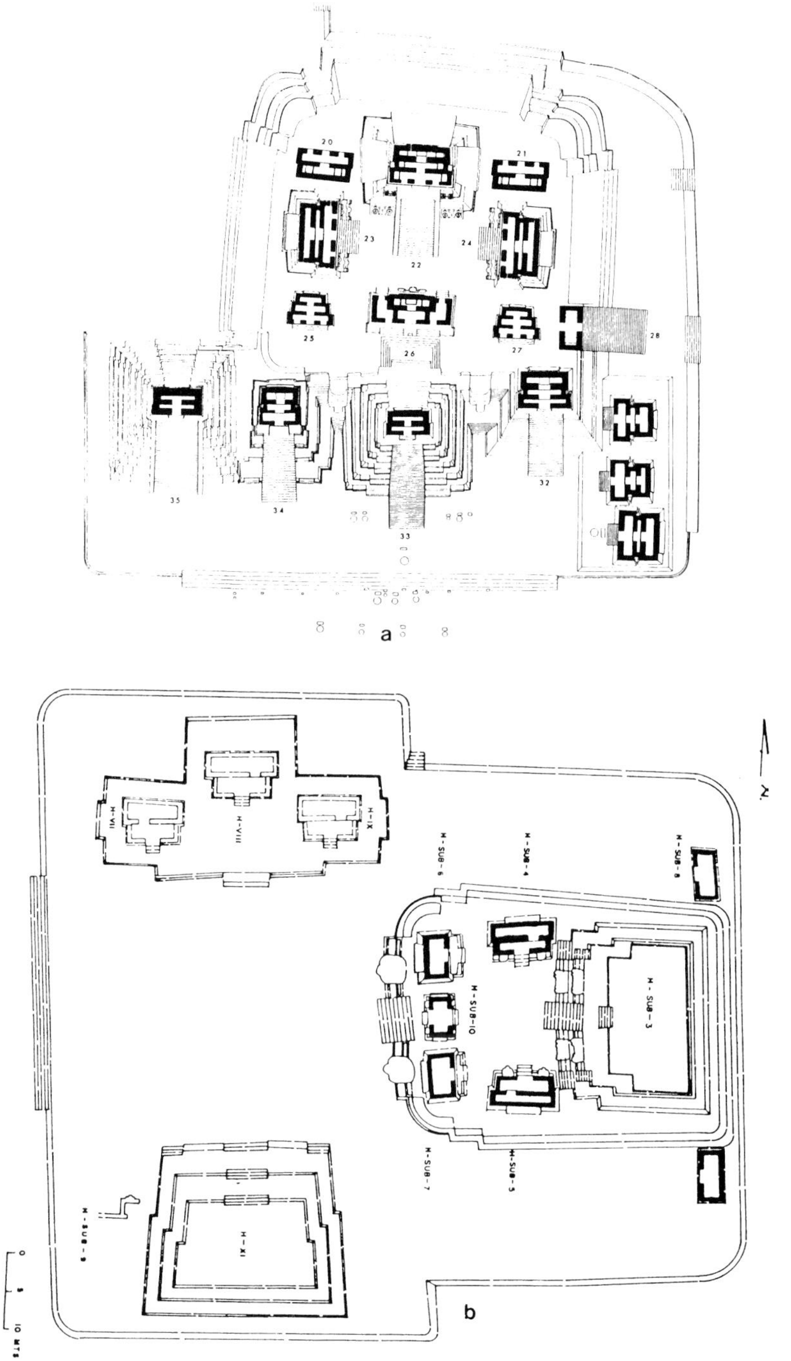

Fig. 17 Triadic platform arrangements at (a) Tikal, North Acropolis (after Coe 1967: 42), and (b) Uaxacatun, Group H (after Valdés 1992: 19).

Hansen n.d.a, 1990), the early large structures at Wakna, and two of the largest buildings at Tintal (Hansen 1992a) as well as Uaxactun Structures H-Sub-3, Sub-4, and Sub-5 (Valdés 1986, 1989a, 1992), Lamanai Structures N9-56 and N10-43 (Pendergast 1981: 39–41), Cerros Structure 29B, and possibly Structures 3 and 4 (Freidel 1981, 1986: 11), and structures at Sacnab (Rice 1976: fig. 8). The geographical extent of the triadic form is further demonstrated by its appearance at Dzibilchaltun during the Komchen phase (Andrews 1965: 29).

The continuity of the triadic arrangement is evident in the Early Classic Uaxactun complex A-V, constructed over an earlier group of three small house platforms in triadic layout (Smith 1950: 17–19), and Structures E-IV, E-V, and E-VI (Ricketson and Ricketson 1937: 60–61). The perpetuation of the triad also extends to later structures, such as Caana at Caracol and the more modest Structures D-31, 32, and 33 at Seibal. This configuration also occurred in the Late Classic on Structure N and a variant in Structure E at Nakum (Tozzer 1913: 171, 175, pl. 32; Ricketson and Ricketson 1937: 61). At Tikal, the innermost sanctum of the North Acropolis was reserved for the triad of Structures 22, 23, and 24 (Fig. 17). At Palenque, Kan Balam commissioned construction of the Temple of the Cross, the Temple of the Foliated Cross, and the Temple of the Sun in the standard triad format (Cohodas 1979, 1985), recording his accession and regal genealogy in an architectural context depicting the basic tenets of Maya ritual and mythological tradition. The identification of the three hearthstones of the mythological Maya creation as a group in the Orion constellation (Tedlock 1985: 261; Freidel, Schele, and Parker 1993: 79) may be what the ancient Maya intended to reproduce in triadic architecture (Taube, this volume). The centrality of this myth may account for the prominence of the triadic pattern. In the case of Palenque, however, the extraordinary texts themselves indicate a function for the buildings as metaphorical houses for the gods and monuments to the creation (see Schele, Stuart, Taube, and Houston, this volume). The specialized events that occurred during the accession of Kan Balam included dedication and ritual activities (Cross), bloodletting (Sun), heir designation ceremonies (Sun), and bloodletting and accession rituals (Foliated Cross). The peculiar order and placement of the events recorded at Palenque suggest the possibility that the triad may have been a standardized format for important religious and ideological rituals (see Hansen 1992a: 149 ff). The continuity of the triadic arrangement may indicate the antiquity of accession rituals and bloodletting rituals in the lowlands.

As with many fundamental aspects of Maya culture, the patterns of triadic architecture continued until historic times. Hellmuth and Estrada found an original, handwritten *relación* of Nicolás de Valenzuela regarding the Spanish

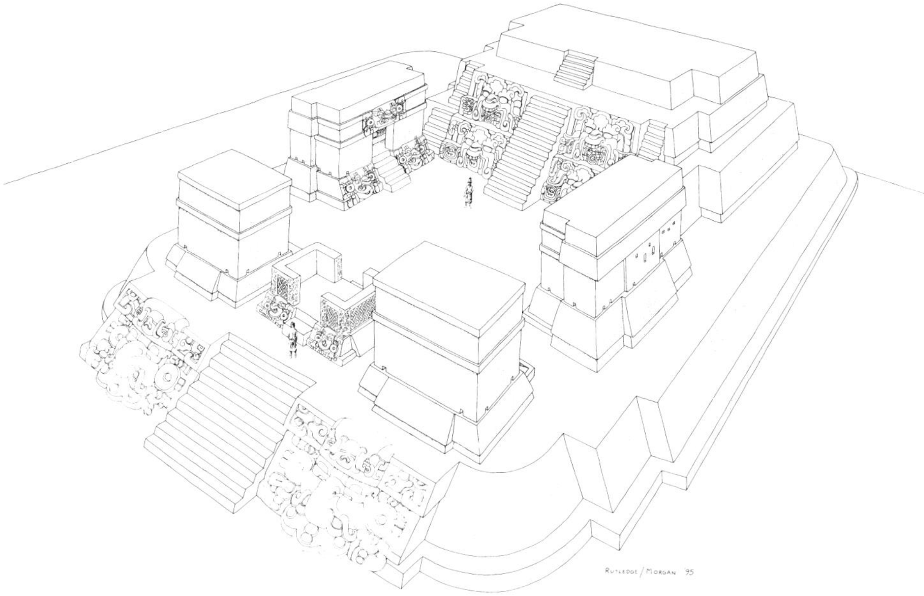

Fig. 18 Reconstruction drawing of Group H at Uaxactun. Drawing by Terry Rutledge and Dave Morgan.

conquest of the Cholti-Lacandon, which includes the following comment on building arrangement and function in the settlement of Sac Balam (Nuestra Señora de los Dolores de Lacandon):

> and there are one hundred and three houses, including three of community use. . . . In the center of this town of Sac Balam you find three community houses, one from east to west, another from north to south, and the other from east to west, each one looking out on the other, leaving in the center a spacious atrium. (Hellmuth 1977: 425)

Clearly, the layout of Sac Balam fits the triadic pattern, with the buildings ascribed to "community" or public use as opposed to private use or personal residences.

Monumental Architectural Art

With greater monumentality and introduction of the triad by ca. 300 B.C., Maya architecture adopted a new character. Architectural sculpture flanked the primary stairway of structures, although designs also adorned piers, inset panels, and cornices of Pre-Classic buildings (Fig. 18). Although the temporal range for architectural sculpture extends from the Middle Pre-Classic "Olmec" societies in Guerrero to Post-Classic and contact periods at Tayasal, the size and extent of the Late Pre-Classic architectural art differs substantially from previous or subsequent depictions. Indeed, by Cycle 7, architectural embellishment became a major means of communicating ideological expression (Freidel 1985; Freidel and Schele 1988a, 1988b) at sites such as Uaxactun (Ricketson and Ricketson 1937; Valdés 1986, 1989a, 1992, 1993), Tikal (Coe 1965a, 1990; Miller 1986), Cerros (Freidel 1979, 1981; Robertson and Freidel 1986), *Lamanai* (Pendergast 1981), El Mirador (Hansen n.d.a, 1990, 1991, 1992a), and Nakbe (Hansen 1992a, 1992b, 1992c). An unusual aspect of the sculpture is the size and extravagance of its early forms. At Nakbe, for example, the mask and panels depicting the great mythological bird of the Maya, the "Principal Bird Deity," at the base of Structure 1, were 11 m wide and 5 m high, coated with a single coat of plaster, and painted in cream, black, and red (Hansen 1992a; Martínez Hidalgo and Hansen 1992; Hansen, Hansen, and Derrick 1995). Similar immensity of architectural art was also noted on the masks of Structure H-Sub 3 at Uaxactun (Valdés 1986, 1992) (Fig. 18). As found on the masks at Nakbe, the art was primarily cream colored and outlined with red and black.

Monumental architectural art became standardized in the Late Pre-Classic and continued into the Early Classic, Late Classic, and Post-Classic periods. Architectural, sculptural façades also flanked the stairs of adobe structures at Kaminaljuyu, indicating the geographical extent of the medium and format of the religious symbols.

Group H, Uaxactun

Exemplary architecture with many diagnostics of the period was exposed in large-scale excavations in the near-complete acropolis of Group H at Uaxactun (Fig. 18). Large-scale excavations exposed a Late Pre-Classic acropolis complex that had all of the architectural characteristics known for this period (Valdés 1986, 1989a, 1989b, 1992). The construction sequence indicated that the earliest structure was a small rectangular platform upon which stood a small, circular building (H-Sub 1) (Valdés 1992, 1993). Shortly after, Structure H-Sub 2 was placed at the east side of the platform. This 5 m high rectangular structure had two corbeled vaulted chambers divided by an offset entranceway. Although the front of this structure was badly damaged during construction of the later phases of the platform, the east side of the building still had an elaborate frieze above the cornice on the sloping roof (Valdés 1989a, 1990; Hansen 1992a: 350, fig. 120). It displayed two prone supernatural figures, flanked by downward-peering heads. This structure was then covered by the dominant structure (H-Sub 3) of the entire complex as part of a triadic arrangement of Structures H-Sub 4 and H-Sub 5 (Figs. 17b and 18). The stairway of this 7 m high building was inset into the three terraces, with auxiliary stairways on the distal sides of projecting façades. Only the central stairway extended to the top of the platform. The façades contained masks and panels in excellent condition (Valdés 1986, 1989a, 1990, 1992, 1993; Hansen 1992a: 154–160). No superstructure was found on the surface of the upper platform of H-Sub 3.

The formation of the triad created an architectural landscape of profound significance. All three structures had sculptured deities bordering inset stairways. The two inward-facing buildings of the triad, Structures H-Sub 4 and H-Sub 5, were vaulted with two chambers divided by a wall with an offset entranceway. The offset entranceways, also found on Late Pre-Classic Structure 13 at Nakbe and the Early Classic triad on Group A-V at Uaxactun, vary markedly with the three-room chambers of Late Classic pyramids, which have the entranceway in the center-line axis. The interior chamber of the Group H buildings was slightly higher and narrower than the first room. The cornice on both sides of the flanking structures had a raindrip carved on the exterior basal surface of the stones, a trait that also extends clearly into the Late Classic. Also, these Late Pre-Classic structures had a mask immediately above the entranceway into the chambers (Schele, this volume). This mask, combined with the two other masks flanking the stairway, represented the three deity portraits that may have important parallels to the architectural triad. This pattern extended into the Late Classic as a common format (i.e., Tikal Temple II).

A subsequent modification of the platform of Group H created an enclosed acropolis effect. The platform with rounded corners was extended to the west to accommodate three more buildings, Structures H-Sub 6, H-Sub 10, and H-Sub 7. Both H-Sub 6 and H-Sub 7 were vaulted and faced inward toward the earlier triad. No masks were on the façades of these buildings, but remnants of a frieze were present above the cornice. The center structure, H-Sub 10, was apparently open. Masks flanked the inset stairway, and standing figures of modeled stucco were found on the walls and all corners of the superstructure. These figures bordered a woven mat design placed above the basal masks of the building (Fig. 18).

A single, inset stairway made the entire platform accessible. Large masks and panels of mythological importance adorned both sides of the stairway (see Hansen 1992a: 354, fig. 124). Group H demonstrates the continuities of individual structures as well as the overall layout of the acropolis in Maya architectural history. The same architectural sequences occurred in the Early and Late Classic ver-

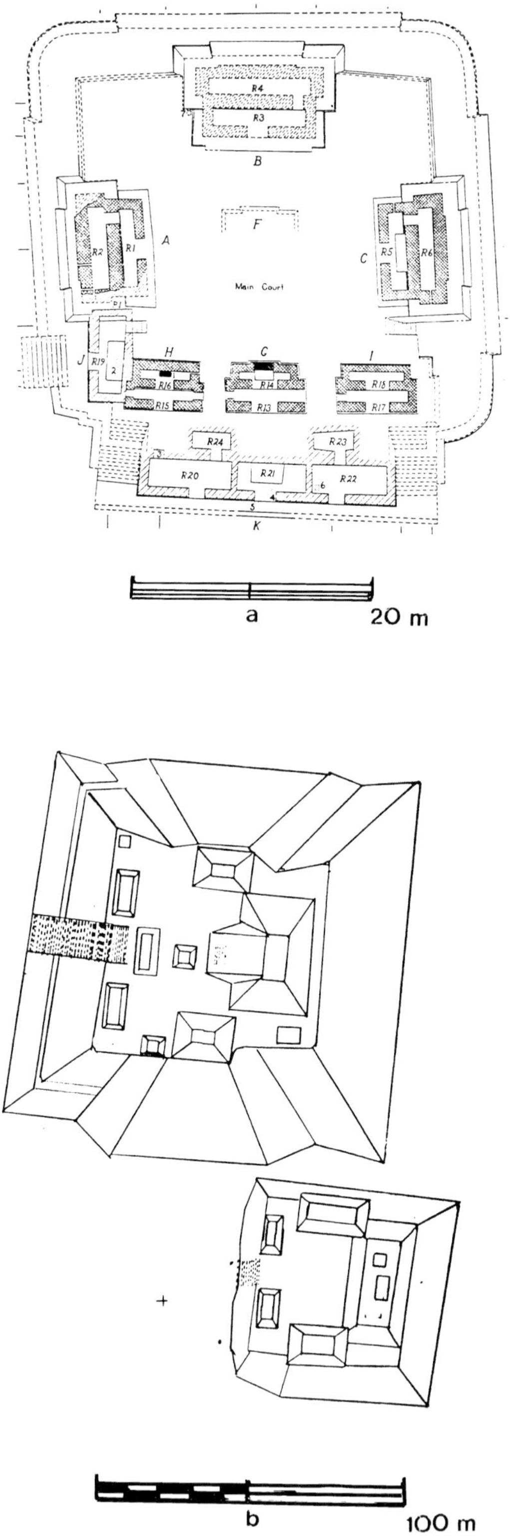

Fig. 19 Triadic architecture at (a) Uaxactun, Structure A-V (after Smith 1950: fig. 66), and (b) Nakbe, Structure 59.

sions of the North Acropolis at Tikal, Structure A-V at Uaxactun, and Structure 59 at Nakbe (Fig. 19).

The excellent preservation of Group H resulted from burial by later construction. The varied and detailed architectural sculpture, plinths, cornices, piers, friezes, stairways, corbeled vault chambers, and platforms with well-preserved stucco and intact masonry are some of the most remarkable discoveries from the period. Although there are continuities and disjunctions with both earlier and later architecture, it is clear that nearly all the known diagnostic features of Classic Maya architecture appear on this platform group in the Late Pre-Classic period.

Circular Structures

One of the lesser-known, but widely distributed forms of Pre-Classic architecture is the circular structure. These buildings may spring logically from apsidal structures of great antiquity in Mesoamerica (i.e., Clark 1994; Anthony and Black 1994). Circular structures range in date from the Middle Pre-Classic through Post-Classic periods, and their limited distribution within sites throughout Mesoamerica leads some to infer a specialized function (Pollock 1936).

Circular buildings have great antiquity in the Maya area, with the earliest appearing at Cuello as Structures 328 and 329 (Phase I-IA, early Middle Pre-Classic) and Structure 327 (Phase II) (Gerhardt 1988; Gerhardt and Hammond 1991). The constructions consist of thin plaster floors with successive timber superstructures, a low platform height (0.2 m), and diameters of 8 m (Gerhardt and Hammond 1991). The domestic function of these constructions seems evident, but it is uncertain what precipitated the difference between apsidal and circular structures. Both apsidal and circular structures are found throughout the Cuello sequence.

Circular, Middle Pre-Classic structures have recently been identified at Colha, where they were defined by carefully placed limestone blocks (Anthony and Black 1994). Middle Pre-Classic round buildings have also been found at Louisville (Haberland 1958: 128) and Cahal Pech. The largest platform at Cahal Pech, Structure 14, was situated among four small rectangular platforms erected around the perimeter of the structure (Terry Powis, personal communication, 1994). Awe and Powis found ten burials and four caches in Structure 14, indicating an emphasis on funerary and ritual behavior (Terry Powis, personal communication, 1994). The Cahal Pech example also had a rectangular "keyhole" appendage on the side, a feature noted on a round Late Pre-Classic building at Río Azul (Hendon 1989: 97); Late Pre-Classic Structures E, F, and G of E Group and the Early Classic east plaza of Group A at Uaxactun (Ricketson and

Ricketson 1937: 116; Valdés 1989b, 1992); BR-1 Structure F at Barton Ramie (Willey et al. 1965: 51–58); and the Classic–Post-Classic Structure 9 at Nohmul (Hammond 1983).

Circular structures dating to the Late Pre-Classic period appear to be more common, or at least more frequently encountered, at Nakbe (Velásquez 1992a), El Mirador (Nielson 1980: 32), Río Azul (Hendon 1989), Tikal (Coe 1965a: 1415; 1990: fig. 49), Colha (Day and Laurens 1980; Anthony and Black 1994), Ixac (Morales 1993: 312), and Chan Chen (Sidrys and Andresen 1978: 643–648; Sidrys 1983: 92–103). The earliest structure in the Group H platform (Structure H-Sub 1) at Uaxactun, described above, was also circular (Valdés 1992).

In general, these constructions are up to half a meter high and as wide as 10 m in diameter. Structure F-2 at Chan Chen is one of the larger examples (11 m wide) and has postholes placed in the edge of the 2 m high platform, demonstrating that the perishable superstructure was also circular (see Sidrys 1983: 92–103). Many of the circular structures appear to have been razed, and it is uncertain whether other levels had been constructed on the platforms. However, Late Pre-Classic Structure 70 at Nakbe consisted of a concentric series of four consecutive platforms forming a structure much like a large, 2 m high wedding cake (Velásquez 1992a). This pattern was also documented by Valdés on an Early Classic round building (Structure A-Sub 9) at Uaxactun (Valdés 1989b; Valdés and Fahsen 1992), which was called an "altar" because of the reduced size, the central location of the construction, and the fact that a small, uncarved stone monument was placed in its interior (Valdés 1989b: 34).

The longevity of circular buildings is suggested by Early Classic round edifices at Barton Ramie (Willey et al. 1965: 51–59) and Uaxactun Group A (Valdés 1989b: 34; Valdés and Fahsen 1992). Late Classic Structure C-79 at Seibal (Smith 1982: 164–172) represents the largest circular building known in the lowlands (3 m high, 18 m in diameter). Late Classic examples have also been found at Ixcol and Ixtonton (Morales 1993: 312–313), Coba (Benavides 1987), and Structure 9 at Nohmul (Hammond 1983). Circular buildings have been located in Post-Classic contexts at San Gervasio, Cozumel (Gregory 1975: 88–106).

As with most Maya constructions, paint was found on the stucco of round buildings. Round Pre-Classic examples at Río Azul and Tikal were painted red, as was Early Classic Uaxactun Altar A-Sub 9 (Valdés 1989b: 34). Late Pre-Classic Structure 70 at Nakbe was painted in red and blue (Velásquez 1992a: 38).

Modest Residence Constructions

A few Late Pre-Classic residence constructions have been found throughout the lowlands. They often consist of simple, perishable structures on packed-earth floors, low rectangular stone alignments, and low rectangular and apsidal platforms. Excavations indicate that these structures are often not detectable from the surface, a problem also noted in Late Pre-Classic sites in other areas of the Peten (e.g., Johnston, Moscoso Moller, and Schmitt 1992 and Johnston 1993). Some of the best preserved Pre-Classic examples are Structure 27 at Becan (Ball and Andrews 1978) and Structure G314 at El Mirador (Stutz-Landeen n.d.). The diversity of their architectural details suggests a wide range of construction patterns that is evident throughout all Maya periods. Structure 27 at Becan and Structure 314 at El Mirador are about the same size (1 m high), with inset stairways, walls with a *talud,* and low walls of the superstructure. But the Becan platform was topped by an apron molding, whereas the El Mirador platform sides formed a shelf at the base of the superstructure walls. Also, a bench was constructed in the rooms of Structure 314 (Stutz-Landeen n.d.: 61) that is missing from Becan Structure 27. Thick, red stucco was applied to the platforms in both cases.

Barrier Constructions/Fortifications/Canals

By the Late Pre-Classic period, the first barrier constructions or fortifications were built in the Maya lowlands. At Becan, the Maya built a moat during the latter Late Pre-Classic period (Webster 1975, 1976, 1977). This massive trench, which originally had been excavated 16 m wide and 6 m deep, completely surrounded the site center.[9] The inner edge of the construction had a 1 to 3 m high parapet or embankment formed with excavated earth upon which timbers were placed, thereby exaggerating the depth of the moat as an impressive and effective barrier. Seven causeways spanned the moat and allowed the greatest access on the northwestern and southeastern areas of the site (Webster 1976: 14–15).

Similar barriers have been found at Edzna in the form of an elaborate system of canals (Matheny et al. 1983: figs. 2, 36). The canals date to the Late Pre-Classic period and were used to provide water, aquaculture, and possibly transportation to the site. The main canal to the site was more than 12 km long. The canals were used as a wet-moat system to surround a complex of architec-

[9] The moat at Becan has long been proclaimed to have been a dry moat, but on a recent visit to Becan shortly after the hurricanes of 1995, I observed that some sections of the moat were completely filled with water, whereas other sections remained dry. I suspect that portions of the trench, particularly those on the northeastern and northern sides of the site, may have also served as *aguadas* (reservoirs).

ture known as the "Fortress" (Matheny et al. 1983: 78–79). The excavation volume of canals in the Late Pre-Classic at Edzna (1.5×10^6 m^3) represents one of the largest ancient construction programs in the Maya world (Matheny 1987) and directly reflects the complex sociopolitical and economic systems of the Late Pre-Classic.

A variant of a Late Pre-Classic barrier system is found at El Mirador; a massive wall was built on the southern, eastern, and northeastern sides of the site during the latter Late Pre-Classic period (Chambers 1982, n.d.), whereas the northern and western sides of the site were bordered by a 20 to 30 m natural escarpment. The wall is artificially elevated to a height of about 4 m. The exterior face of the wall was terraced, whereas the summit of the wall seems to have been a parapet upon which timbers may have been placed. The construction restricted access through stuccoed openings (7 m wide) at strategic locations (Chambers 1982: 8). However, by about A.D. 250 the wall had fallen into disrepair, and later inhabitants did not refurbish it (Chambers 1982: 8).

Late Pre-Classic Funerary Architecture

The nomenclature for Maya tombs and burials has long been established in the Maya lowlands (Smith 1950: 88; Satterthwaite 1954: 50; Coe 1959: 120). Although its application to remains from the Pre-Classic periods has been used in other areas of Mesoamerica (i.e., Lowe and Agrinier 1960: 39; Lowe 1962: 21; Agrinier 1964; Robles and Martínez Donjuán 1989), it could not be applied to mortuary descriptions in the Maya region because of the paucity of examples. Maya funerary constructions have been defined as tombs, crypts, cists, and simple burials, with important distinctions being made within each designated form. Simple burials consist of an "unlined hole in the ground or inclusion of a body in fill."[10] Cist burials have definite outlines[11] or consist of single, stone-lined graves with cover slabs (Satterthwaite 1954: 50). The simple, stone-lined constructions, which had been termed "crypts" by Smith,[12] have more commonly been redefined as cists, although crypt appears to refer to more complex cist burials (i.e., Sharer and Sedat 1987: pl. 4.3). Pre-Classic simple burials and cists in the lowlands have been recovered in greater frequency (for example, Tikal Burials 120–123 and 126) than tombs (and crypts).

Formal tomb constructions in Mesoamerica appear in the early Middle Pre-Classic at sites in Guerrero, such as Teopantecuanitlan (Martínez Donjuán 1994: 160) and Coovisur-Chilpancingo (Robles and Martínez Donjuán 1989). These tombs are formal masonry constructions, rectangular in form, and large (2.20 m long, 1.45 m wide, with vertical walls 1.20 m high). The chambers were covered by a corbeled vault with capstones (Robles and Martínez Donjuán 1989: 14, 16, 20). Middle Pre-Classic tombs have also been noted at La Venta, namely, Tomb A (Monument 7), Tomb B (Monument 6), and Feature A-3-a (Drucker,

[10] Smith (1950: 88) cited in Coe (1959: 120).
[11] Ibid.
[12] Ibid.

Heizer, and Squier 1959: 126–127). Both the Guerrero and the Gulf Coast tombs are noted here as a cautionary point: the corbeled vault and tomb placement in buildings may not be of Maya origin.

Pre-Classic triadic buildings consistently lack tombs.[13] One notable exception is a series of tombs in Wakna Structure 3 (Hansen 1992b, 1992c). These tombs, which undoubtedly guarded the remains of important royal figures, occur in a triadic arrangement at the base of each of the primary structures of the group (see below). Extensive tunneling and trenching of Nakbe Structure 13, which is nearly identical in size, form, and antiquity to Wakna Structure 3, however, failed to uncover any tombs or burials in comparable locations.

The differences in placement of Chicanel tombs at Wakna and other Late Pre-Classic examples are intriguing. The Wakna tombs correspond more closely to patterns in Early and Late Classic buildings. For example, a large looter's trench at Caracol found at least three major Classic-period tombs under the lower floors and in the fill of Structure B20 (see Chase and Chase, this volume). Important Classic tombs at Caracol were also placed at the base of the central building of the triad (Chase and Chase 1987). Yet, excavations in similar locations on both of the flanking structures on the Pre-Classic pyramid of Tigre at El Mirador and the central and flanking superstructures of Late Pre-Classic Structures 1, 27, and 59 at Nakbe revealed no such funerary features.

Tomb Constructions

The scarcity of known Pre-Classic tombs in the Maya lowlands may result from inadequate testing in structures. Tombs are clearly less common in Pre-Classic structures than in Classic buildings of the same size and form. Numerous looters' trenches at Tintal, Wakna, and portions of Nakbe and El Mirador failed to locate tombs or burials. As a result, additional looters' trenches were often placed in the same structures in the belief that previous trenches missed the burials (Hansen, Bishop, and Fahsen 1991: 239).

An important Middle Pre-Classic tomb or crypt with stone slab sides and

[13] Architectural excavations of triad buildings at El Mirador—Structure G34 (3D3-1, 3D3-2, 3D3-3), Tigre (4D3-1, 4D3-2, 4D3-3), Monos (2D3-1, 2D3-2, 2D3-3, 2D3-5, 2 D3-6, Structures G313 and G314), Pavos Acropolis (Structures 2A6-3 and 2A6-6)—Nakbe (Structures 1, 2, 13, 27, 59, and 60), and all triadic structures at Tintal, which have now been heavily excavated by looters, had no mortuary constructions. A similar observation was noted in the large-scale excavations of Uaxactun Group H-Sub 3, Sub 4, and Sub 5, where no Pre-Classic tombs were located in buildings. An interment known as Burial 233 was located in a sealed context under Structure H-Sub 4 (Valdés 1986: 166), but it is believed that this burial preceded construction of the building.

roof was found in a low structure at Los Mangales in the Salama Valley (Sharer and Sedat 1987: pl. 4.3). A more modest crypt, containing a male occupant with numerous vessels, was found near the summit of a Late Pre-Classic edifice (Structure A-7) at La Lagunita in the Quiche highlands (Ichon and Viel 1984: 19, fig. 15). However, extensive tunneling in the buried Pre-Classic structures in Tikal's Mundo Perdido and Group H at Uaxactun failed to locate burials in similar locations.

The best-known early tombs in the North Acropolis at Tikal are Late Pre-Classic (Fig. 20). These elite interments (chronologically ordered as Burials 164, 166, 167, 85, 117, and 125) indicate that burial of nobles did not necessarily correspond to the largest or most sophisticated buildings. Burial 85, perhaps the most elaborate Pre-Classic tomb found at Tikal (Coe and McGinn 1963), was found within the diminutive (50 cm high) Structure 5D-Sub 2-2nd. This modest, 3 m^2 platform placed at the axial base of the stairway of Structure 5D-Sub 1 contained a crude, vaulted tomb measuring 1.25 m wide and 0.9 m high. A slightly larger vaulted chamber, Burial 167 (1.80 × 1.2 × 1.6 m high), was located inside Structure 5D-Sub 10-2nd (Coe 1990: fig. 30), a modest platform only 0.9 m high, with an elaborately painted masonry superstructure.

Tikal Burial 166 was sealed by Structure 5D-Sub 11 (1.75 m high), which appeared to be situated as the center structure of a triad, but only two buildings (5D-Sub 11, 5D-Sub 12-1st) were identified by excavations. Burial 166 was a vaulted chamber (1.20 m wide and 1.35 m high) with black line paintings on the interior walls (Coe 1965a: 1410–1411; 1990: figs. 34 and 35).

The Wakna Late Pre-Classic tombs were looted in a 17 m high triadic structure, Structure 3 (Fig. 21). Structure 3 rests on a platform on the northern edge of the major architecture. This building, in the typical triad form, had been looted by large-scale trenching in all three edifices. Formal tombs had been located under all three structures of the triad, with a large chamber (Tomb 1) located in the center building at the level of the platform; the two less-elaborate tombs (Tombs 2 and 3) were found under the flanking structures at the base of the platform (Hansen 1992b). Whole Chicanel ceramic vessels were found in situ in the tomb chambers, indicating the unequivocal Late Pre-Classic date for the constructions.[14]

Wakna Tomb 1 is a chamber of pentagonal form and is 1.6 m wide, 2.3 m

[14] The Chicanel vessels at Wakna consisted of three medial-flange Sierra Red bowls, a figure-8-shaped Flor Cream bowl, and two Sapote Striated unslipped vessels. The informant, a now-deceased *chiclero* named Abraham Mejía Fajardo ("Chorro"), admitted that he had been responsible for looting the structure approximately ten years before. During excavations at El Mirador from 1980 to 1982, workers reported the existence of these tombs,

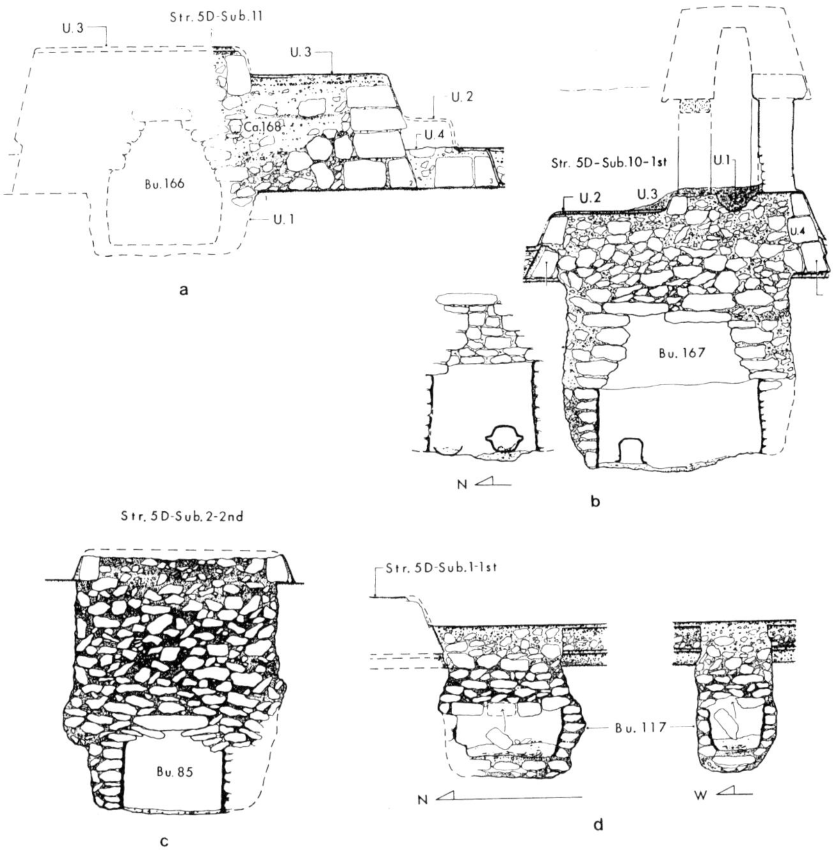

Fig. 20 Late Pre-Classic tombs at Tikal: (a) Burial 166, (b) Burial 167, (c) Burial 85, and (d) Burial 117 (after Coe 1990: figs. 33b, 30c, 27b, 26a). Reproduced by permission of the University Museum, University of Pennsylvania.

---

noting similarities with ceramics from the Tigre area (R. Hansen, El Mirador Field Notes, 1982; Hansen 1992b: 6). The informant spent considerable time searching for large Sierra Red *floreros,* which he claimed were located in the central tomb (Tomb 1) and in the eastern tomb (Tomb 2). Other artifacts purported to have come from the tombs were 17 vessels from the eastern tomb and a large quantity of jade, particularly from the center chamber of Tomb 1 (reportedly 23 pounds!), which the looter had weighed in the village of Carmelita. Intact Late Pre-Classic vessels are still in place in Tomb 2 and Tomb 3. The artifactual wealth of the tombs; the unusual, if not extravagant, architectural format; and the fact that the informant drew unsolicited drawings of three large jade plaques suggest the probable royal nature of the deceased occupant of Tomb 1.

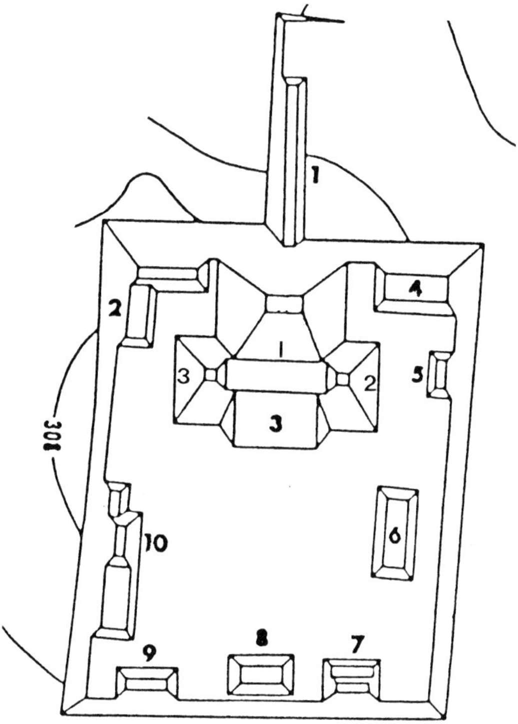

Fig. 21 Structure 3, Wakna. Courtesy of Ian Graham.

long, and 1.9 m high (Fig. 22). A springline above the floor narrows the chamber to about 0.7 m wide. Above the springline are large, finely cut blocks that had been placed on end to form an apex. Each stone rests on those from the opposite side of the chamber. There were no capstones. (This pattern perhaps best resembles the load-bearing concept of a true arch rather than a corbeled arch because the weight of each side is directly dependent on the other.) The tomb was enhanced by a façade on the southern side, thus forming a series of stepped, vertical walls or panels that receded in equal fashion on both sides of the chamber (Fig. 23). Visible portions of the walls revealed a red façade with remnants of black and blue lines and scrolls. In addition, the eastern panels revealed the faint remnants of a hieroglyphic text.

The two flanking tombs at the eastern and western distal base of the platform were not stuccoed but were crude vaults plastered with brownish-gray clay. These chambers (1.4 × 1.2 × 1.3 m high) were roughly rounded. The western chamber (Tomb 3) was not explored because of the possibility of structural collapse. The eastern chamber (Tomb 2) was located immediately inside an earlier structure (Structure 3-Sub 1) buried by the final form of Structure 3.

Fig. 22 Late Pre-Classic tomb (Tomb 1) from Wakna, showing pentagonal form and the heavy blocks that formed the vaulted roof.

This earlier building had some of the finest polychrome-painted surfaces I have seen on Maya architecture.

The architectural format of Tomb 1 in Wakna Structure 3 is not unique to the Maya area. Laporte and Fialko (1995: 52–53) note a Cimi phase burial (PNT-021) found on a north–south orientation near the center-line axis of Structure 5D-86 (Fig. 24a). The form of this vault was also pentagonal, with two large blocks forming an apex, as at Wakna. It is the earliest tomb in the Mundo Perdido complex (Laporte and Fialko 1995: 52–53).

The slab-apex tomb constructions at Wakna and Tikal are common in Zapotec tombs and other buildings in Oaxaca. A tunnel in Building J at Monte Alban has the large slab-apex construction dating to early Monte Alban II, about 200 B.C. to A.D. 250 (Fig. 24b). Large stone slabs in a later Zapotecan tomb formed the vault of Tomb 5 at Huijazoo, Oaxaca (Mendéz Martínez 1986: 79), and Tomb 7 at Monte Alban (Caso 1981: 263). It is also found in one wing of a subterranean tomb at Lambityeco (personal observation, 1990). In addition to

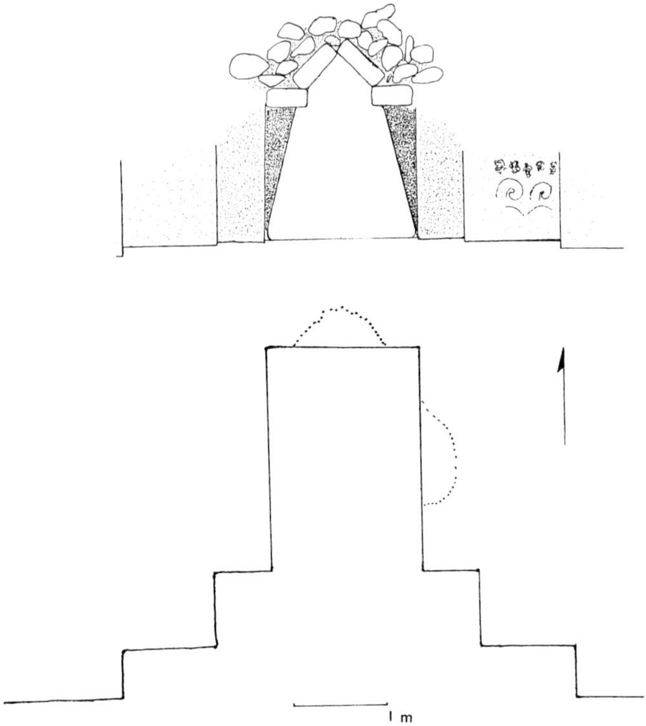

Fig. 23 Cross section and plan drawing of Tomb 1, Wakna. Note the walls that are recessed from the entrance to the back of the tomb.

the wide geographical range of this architectural form, there is considerable temporal continuity as well. Large, flat stones forming an apex were found at Hatzcap Ceel, Belize (Thompson 1931: 55), and at Chichen Itza (Holmes 1895: 5, fig. 11a; A. Smith 1940: 208–209) in Late Classic and Early Post-Classic contexts.

The varied forms of known elite Pre-Classic burials in the lowlands may suggest independent origins for tomb constructions. A good deal more information on lowland tomb architecture from the Pre-Classic periods is sorely needed to identify the variety of constructions, chronological variations, and possible sources of architectural influence.

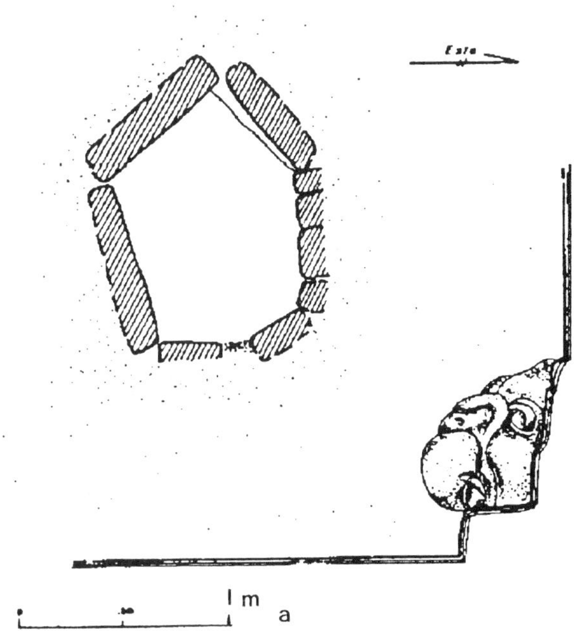

Fig. 24 Early tomb constructions: (a) Cimi phase tomb (PNT-021) in Structure 5D-86 at Tikal (after Laporte and Fialko 1993: 34), and (b) vault construction of tunnel in Building J, Monte Alban (II).

ARCHITECTURAL MASONRY

Some of the most diagnostic architectural features of the Pre-Classic are evident in masonry. The earliest stonework in the Mirador Basin, dating from 900 to 600 B.C., consists of vertical walls of small, crudely shaped stones placed in stacks up to 2 m high. The architectural transformation from these stones to finely cut megalithic blocks placed in apron moldings took place during the late Middle Pre-Classic period in the lowlands (see above). Four walls of Middle Pre-Classic terraced buildings at Nakbe (Fig. 14), and an early Late Pre-Classic terraced platform inside Structure 34 at El Mirador (Hansen 1990: 70–74), have megalithic blocks stacked parallel to the axis of the structure. During the Late Pre-Classic period at Nakbe and El Mirador, there was a slight reduction in block size from known Middle Pre-Classic antecedents, but blocks were tenoned into the fill, allowing minimal exposure of stone—see Howell and Copeland (1989: 9, fig. 5). Tenoned blocks may have provided greater architectural stability because the long axes of stones were parallel to the outward pressure of the fill of the structure. However, the labor expense of both building-stone and architectural construction was significantly greater because many more blocks were required to cover the surface area of a wall (Fig. 25). The additional manpower and materials corresponded to an emphasis on architectural monumentality during this time, which is especially notable considering the surface area of large-scale architecture, up to 72 m high, on buildings such as Danta and Tigre pyramids at El Mirador or Structures 1 and 2 at Calakmul. These edifices display sloping walls with apron moldings formed by tenoned blocks (Fig. 26).

Masonry of the Middle and Late Pre-Classic periods exhibits traits that both resemble and differ from examples of the Classic and Post-Classic periods (Fig. 27). Yet, Structure 34 in the Tigre complex at El Mirador (Hansen n.d.a, 1990) revealed a wide variation of architectural traits and masonry on a single Late Pre-Classic building, showing a greater heterogeneity of masonry types than previously thought. Whether this reflects different episodes of construction, different architects, or other variations remains unclear.

Ten varieties of modified stones have been found in architectural contexts at El Mirador and Nakbe (Hansen 1990: 156 ff), each having different functional and chronological values. The modal characteristics of the stonework are consistent with other examples of Pre-Classic and Classic architecture in the lowlands. Several of the most diagnostic shaped stones include the following forms.

1. Cornice Stones. Among the most diagnostic stones from the Late Pre-Classic, these projecting blocks were placed on the vertical walls of summit structures about 2 m above the plaster floor. Although large blocks were placed in

STONE VOLUME OF WALL CONSTRUCTION

		Average size	m³ /10 m²	m³/ 50 m²
MPC (early)	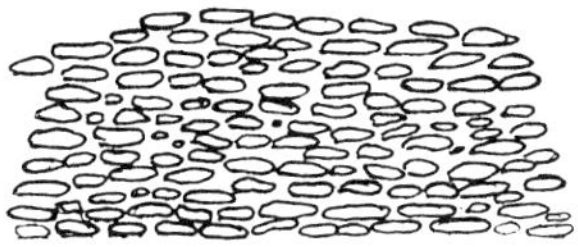	.25 x .28 x .08	2.5	12.5
MPC (late)	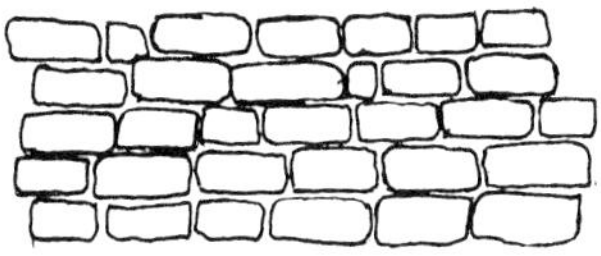	.90 x .40 x .38	3.8	19
LPC	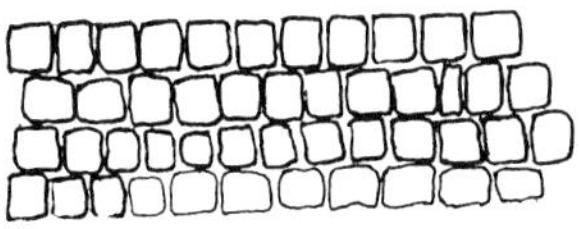	.80 x .40 x .38	8	40
Classic	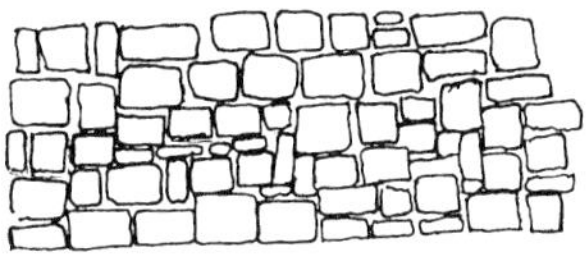	.40 x .40 x .18	1.8	9

Fig. 25 Variations in wall constructions and compositional stone volume according to time period. Volume calculations are based on similar surface areas. MPC = Middle Pre-Classic; LPC = Late Pre-Classic.

apron moldings on the platforms of Middle Pre-Classic structures at Nakbe (Structures 35A and 32) and Tikal (Structures 5C-54-2 and 5D-84-88-2), cornice stones did not appear until about 250 B.C. at El Mirador, Tikal, and Uaxactun (El Mirador: Structure 34, Danta; Tikal: Structure 5D-Sub 1-1st, Structure 5D-Sub 10-1st; Uaxactun: Structure H-Palacio Sub 2). The cornice formed a projecting, sloped roof, which often displayed sculpted panels, as shown on Uaxactun Structures H-Sub 2, H-Sub 6, and H-Sub 7 (Valdés 1986, 1987, 1989a, 1992;

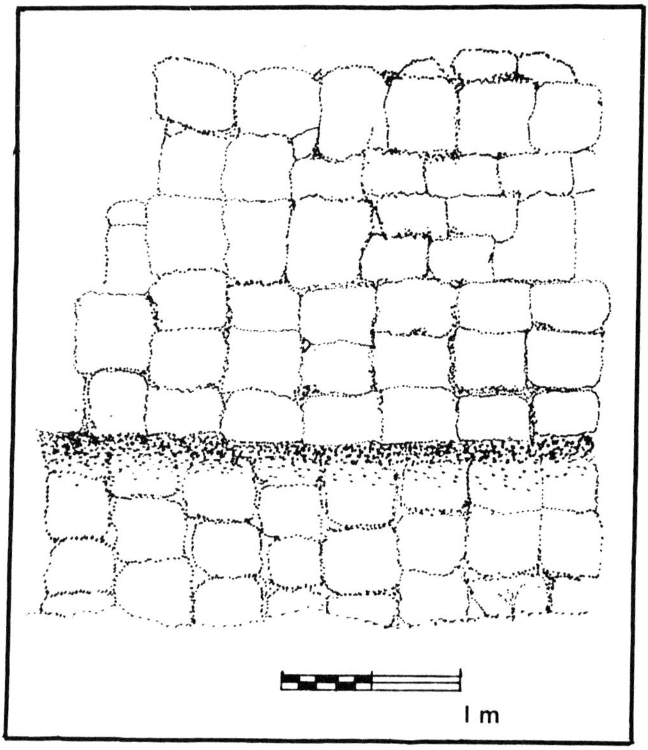

Fig. 26 South wall, Danta pyramid, El Mirador.

Laporte and Valdés 1993). The cornice usually signals the presence of a corbeled vault, although Structure 5D-Sub 1-1st at Tikal has evidence of both a vaulted chamber (with the capstone) and a room formed with flat timbers associated with the cornice. On Structure 34 at El Mirador and Structures 5D-Sub 14-1st and 5D-Sub 1-1st at Tikal, the cornice stones measured approximately 1.2 m long and 0.4 m thick and weighed approximately 460 kg at a specific gravity of 2700 kg/m^3—see Sidrys (1978: 174). In addition, the stones were carved with a raindrip, a slight overhang on the exterior lower edge of the cornice that allowed water to drip at the exterior point rather than down the face of the wall. This feature indicates the specialized function of the stones (Fig. 27)—see Coe (1990: fig. 25a).

2. Corner Stones. Another diagnostic stone is found on the corners of Late Pre-Classic buildings at the cornice level, such as on Structure 5D-Sub 1-1st at Tikal (Coe 1990: fig. 23). These stones are among the largest Late Pre-Classic

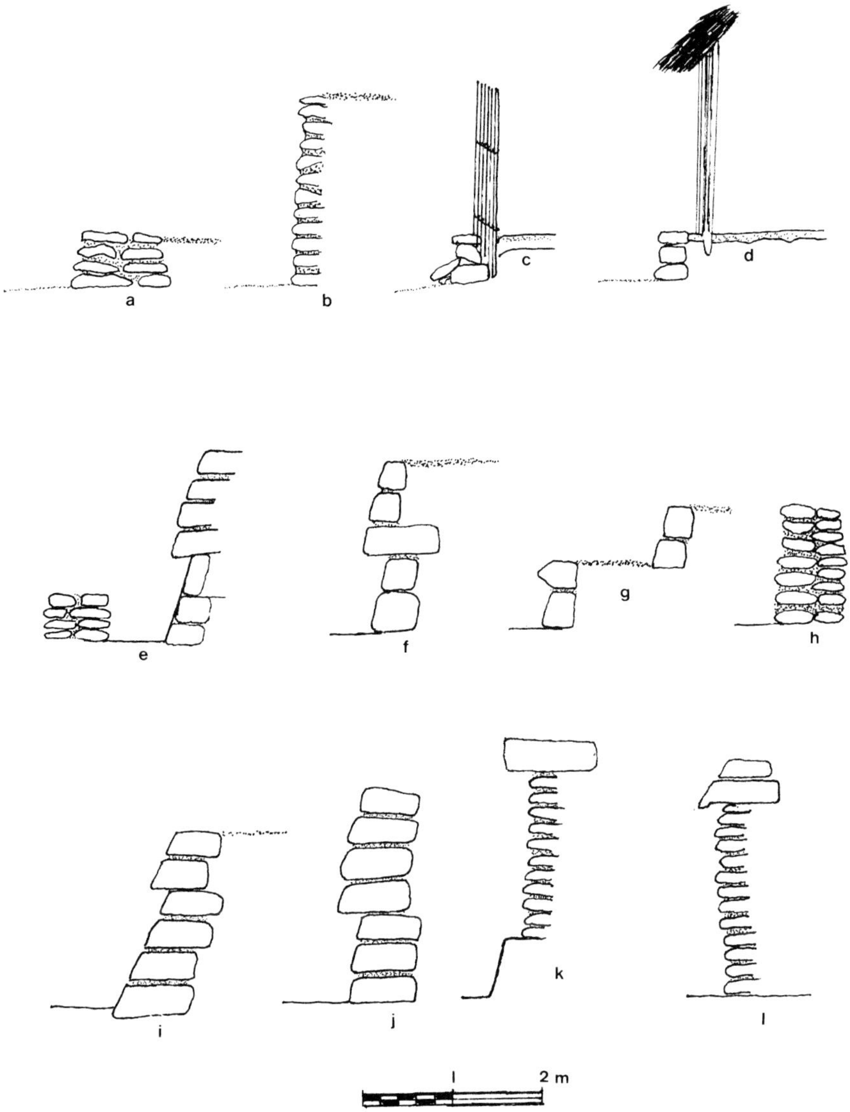

Fig. 27 Chronological chart of selected buildings and superstructures: (a–d) early Middle Pre-Classic, (e–h) late Middle Pre-Classic, (i–l) Late Pre-Classic.

blocks (up to 1.0 × 1.25 × 0.36 m thick) at El Mirador (Hansen 1990: 118–119, 157) and Nakbe.[15] These blocks are marked with a raindrip but are more square than cornice blocks and weigh up to 1400 kg.

3. Step Armatures. Pre-Classic structures also have diagnostic blocks that formed step armatures in the stairways. Although not all Pre-Classic buildings had these stones, they are rectangular, finely cut, long stones measuring up to a meter long and half a meter thick at Tikal, Uaxactun, Nakbe, Tintal, and El Mirador. They are similar to wall blocks that formed the terraced walls of Middle and Late Pre-Classic structures, except that a long side of the stone is beveled to form the exposed riser. Pre-Classic step armatures differ from Classic stairways because of their larger size, beveled sides, and lack of sharp corners.

Variant step armatures dating to the terminal Late Pre-Classic period were found on Structure 2A6-6 (La Pava) at El Mirador, where rectangular, finely cut blocks were tenoned into the building but were placed on edge so that the narrow width of the stone formed the tread (Howell and Copeland 1989: 31, fig. 14). There was also a small projection of a few centimeters at the base of each step armature, which have been termed "false steps" (Howell and Copeland 1989: 32). This feature was probably used to attach lime plaster on the tread to the riser. However, these steps are rare in the Mirador Basin.

4. Flat Wall Stones: Exterior. These stones consist of flat, rectangular blocks with rounded corners that formed the exterior walls of superstructures in the Late Pre-Classic period (Fig. 28). These flat, thin stones (0.6 × 0.3 × 0.1 m high) were stacked vertically to form the walls. These stones have been particularly noted on the superstructures of Structures 34, 313, and 4D2-1 at El Mirador (Hansen 1990; Stutz-Landeen n.d.: 33, fig. 8) and Structures 1 and 27 at Nakbe (Hansen 1992b; Forsyth and Acevedo 1994). Both exterior and interior walls were built to accommodate air ventilation apertures.

5. Slab Wall Stones. Some of the most unusual architectural stones were uncovered in the central plaza at El Mirador (Nielsen 1990) where enormous slabs of limestone, many considered by Nielsen to be reused stelae, were set in place along the edges surrounding two low platforms. These slabs were set on edge to form the walls of the structure. Associated ceramics indicate a use of the buildings in the Late Pre-Classic period.

6. Flat Wall Stones: Interior. A more common wall stone is usually buried

[15] The period of use for the large corner block on Nakbe Structure 51 is uncertain. Most of the building dates to the late Middle Pre-Classic period, with later use during the Proto-Classic period. Although we have yet to identify any portion of the building constructed during the Proto-Classic period, the upper walls of the building may have been modified at this time.

Fig. 28 Wall exterior of Structure 34, El Mirador. Note the evenly shaped stone blocks and cornice stones.

beneath stucco on interior surfaces of walls and is cruder than those on the exterior. These stones date from the early Middle Pre-Classic to the Late Pre-Classic and consist of roughly shaped, rectangular stones with no finely cut surfaces; they are not found in formal alignments (Fig. 29). These stones are usually about half the size of those on the exterior.

7. *Beveled Tenon Blocks.* Beveled tenon blocks were impressively large stones placed on the façades and flanks of structures, with the long axes tenoned into the building; the exposed area of the block was sloped. These blocks formed apron moldings and façades of both Middle Pre-Classic (Fig. 14) and Late Pre-Classic buildings (Fig. 26) and represented a maximum investment of labor. These blocks were slightly smaller in the Middle Pre-Classic; they commonly measure a meter long and half a meter thick during the Late Pre-Classic period.

8. *Wall Blocks.* These large blocks are carved in rectangular form and are approximately the same size as the tenon blocks. They lack the beveled end and the finely cut corners of the Classic period examples. They were usually placed in walls with the long axes parallel to the exterior line of the structure; this allowed maximum exposure of the stone. This is the case particularly with late Middle Pre-Classic/early Late Pre-Classic walls, such as the platform of Structure 32 at Nakbe (Fig. 14) and the interior terraced building inside Structure 34 at El Mirador (Structure 34-Sub 1).

9. *Vault Stones.* Evidence for corbeled-vault buildings dating to the Late Pre-Classic was found in Structures H-Sub 2, H-Sub 4, H-Sub 5, H-Sub 6, and H-Sub 7 at Uaxactun. Similar evidence for vaults was found on Late Pre-Classic Structures 5D-Sub 1-1st and 5D-Sub 10-1st at Tikal. Collapse patterns in the rubble-filled chambers of Structure 34 at El Mirador and Structure 27 at Nakbe indicate that the vaults were made of small, flat, roughly shaped stones.

Although some Classic vaults involved nothing more specialized than the flat interior wall stones (i.e., Structures 103 and 203 at Nakbe)—see López and Ortiz (1994) and Acevedo (1992)—many structures had specialized and diagnostic stones, such as the boot-shaped vault stones in the northern lowlands and the triangular block with the beveled edge in the central and southern lowlands. The triangular and boot-shaped blocks permitted the narrow end of the stone to be tenoned into the mortar of the structure, with the beveled face forming the interior exposed side of the vault surface.

10. *Veneer Stones.* During the Early Classic period, veneer stones were introduced; these consist of thin, finely cut blocks placed on end to cover a rubble-filled wall. Architecturally, the stones bore little or no weight, but they did provide the appearance of a finely worked wall surface. Veneer stones also

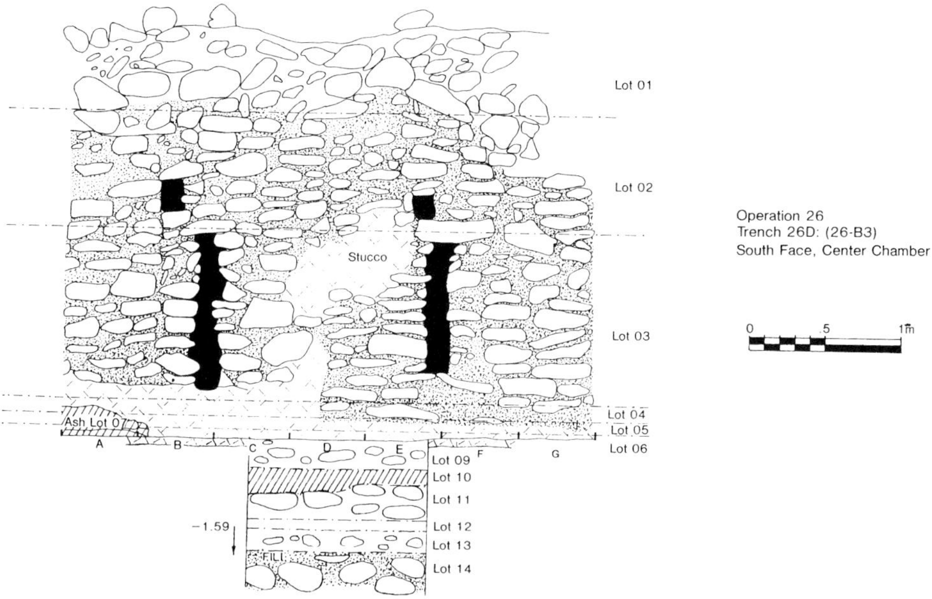

Fig. 29 Interior wall of the center chamber of Structure 34, El Mirador (after Hansen 1990: 32).

maximized the horizontal surface area of a wall with the minimal volume of stone. These exclusively Classic innovations represent a radical shift in the manufacture and use of stone, both technically and administratively. Classic masons minimized the labor per stone; Middle and Late Pre-Classic masons maximized it.

STUCCO AND COLORANT COMPOSITION

Continuities and disjunctions in the Maya built environment are further attested on a microscopic level. Preliminary studies of the chemical composition of Pre-Classic and Classic stucco and associated colorants demonstrate important differences. The red colorant from architectural contexts appears to be the same (iron oxide), but the Late Pre-Classic cream derives from an organic base with an intense autofluorescence under the ultraviolet spectrum (Hansen, Hansen, and Derrick 1995). The use of the cream color, which ranges from light cream to yellowish brown, occurs commonly on Middle Pre-Classic buildings, as in the late Eb Structure 5C-54-1 (Laporte and Fialko 1993).

The texture and composition of the stucco also differs. Late Classic stucco is harder, more gray, and denser than Late Pre-Classic samples (Hansen, Hansen, and Derrick 1995). The Classic samples analyzed to date also show a greater content of microscopic charcoal than the Pre-Classic samples, although the Pre-Classic examples had more ingredients.

Variations between the composition of architectural stucco and floor plaster indicate that floors were constructed with the addition of larger pebbles or stones but contained less aggregate overall, with a greater quantity of matrix (Hansen, Hansen, and Derrick 1995). Floor stucco from all periods displays more porosity than that used in architectural ornament. These preliminary data indicate that variations in the composition of stucco relate to architectural function.

PRE-CLASSIC/CLASSIC ARCHITECTURE: MESOAMERICAN CONTEXT

The discovery in the Maya lowlands of early architecture with its sophisticated and complex stone masonry dictates a reevaluation of the traditional models of Maya sociopolitical evolution. A review of the specific evidence concerning types of masonry, stucco composition, architectural form, and settlement distribution lends weight to the suggestion that the development of public and domestic architecture in the lowlands was indigenous to that region. These data would corroborate earlier assertions about the lack of evidence for direct external influences on Maya architecture, such as from the Olmec (Coe 1965a: 1418). The similarities of architectural development, size, and sophistication of early constructions place the lowland Maya less at odds with the developmental sequence of their cultural cousins in the highland and Pacific Coast regions. Variations in the details of construction techniques and architectural forms demonstrate more of an independent development. For example, constructions from the Charcas and Providencia phases at Kaminaljuyu differ, in form, style, and composition, from those observed on similarly early buildings in the lowlands (Gustavo Martínez, personal communication, 1995; Richard Hansen, personal observation, 1995).

SUMMARY

The sequence of architectural innovations in the Maya lowlands provides a visible record of the development of complex sociopolitical institutions that arose there during the Middle and Late Pre-Classic periods. By the Middle Pre-Classic, many of the attributes that marked the Maya as culturally distinct from their neighbors were already established. The use of stucco on floors and walls, placement of burials under floors, apsidal residences, construction of elevated platforms, and the use of limestone were developed during the earliest periods of the Middle Pre-Classic. By the late Middle Pre-Classic, architects developed the general forms of façade constructions that survived for more than a thousand years. During this time, specialist production systems for stone extraction were also established. The employment of full-time masons is evident in the archaeological record for the remainder of Maya prehistory. Ceramics also had become specialized and consistent in form, surface treatment, and use. The Middle Pre-Classic Maya conceived and constructed the E-Group architectural pattern, a major architectural format that endured for the entirety of Maya civilization. The ballcourt also appeared during this time, establishing a cultural identity with the ball game that was never to dissipate. Stone monuments were also being carved and erected in association with architecture by this time.

By the beginning of the Late Pre-Classic period, nearly all the material markers of Maya civilization were in place. It was during this time that the triadic architectural arrangement was established, and it became the dominant construction pattern in the Late Pre-Classic period. Architectural patterns utilizing the triad were replicated by Classic kings, indicating the fundamental importance of the pattern in accession ritual, ideology, cosmology, and fusion of sacred thought with secular construction programs. With the advent of major triadic buildings, monumental architectural art also became standardized, with deity masks flanking the stairways of buildings, entablatures, and walls. Such characteristics continued throughout the remainder of Maya civilization. Experimental uses of stone allowed architectural experimentation, and it was during this period that the corbeled vaults first appeared. Structures became monumental, with the largest Maya constructions being erected during this period. The establishment of true urban centers and specialized, monumental architecture demarcates the Maya as one of the world's great ancient civilizations.

Recent excavations suggest that the complexity and elaboration of architecture in the Maya lowlands were an indigenous, local development. By understanding these new data, and by evaluating them for evidence of function, meaning, and sociopolitical and ideological context, archaeologists may begin to understand what first stimulated architectural development. Along with greater knowledge of ancient ecology and other cultural factors, these understandings will sharpen our views of the beginnings of lowland civilization and reveal the foundations for the function and meaning of Maya buildings that emerged centuries later in the Classic period.

Acknowledgments Appreciation is extended to the Instituto de Antropología e Historia de Guatemala for permits and support for research in Guatemala. Funding for some of the data noted here was provided by the National Geographic Society (4984-93), Foundation for the Advancement of Mesoamerican Studies (95113), Lannan Foundation, Getty Conservation Institute, Jacob K. Javits Fellows Program–U.S. Department of Education, Explorers Club, Fulbright Hays Research Abroad Fellowships, National Graduate Fellows Program, University of California, Los Angeles (UCLA) Distinguished Scholars Program, UCLA Institute of Geophysics and Planetary Physics, Sigma Xi Scientific Research Society, Homelite, American Mobile Satellite Corporation, and UCLA–Regents of the University of California (443869-HA-40586). Previous research at El Mirador was funded by New World Archaeological Foundation, Brigham Young University, National Geographic, and National Science Foundation grants to Ray T. Matheny and Bruce H. Dahlin. I am especially grateful to Iona Benson, Herbert and Elinor Nootbaar, Steven J. Graeber, William Johnston, Elizabeth Welty, Nancy Baxter, Evelyn Stern, Mr. and Mrs. Donald E. Anderson, Keith and Pat Ballard, Kathryn Burg, Lowell and Patsy Chamberlain, Harry and Mary Cornwall, Beverly Fittipaldo, Cynthia Luce, Donald Marken, Richard Mills, Rene Motta, Amos Newton, Charles Olmstead, Sharon Belkin, Bob and Peggy Sloves, Jacqueline F. Smith, James and Sylvia Thayer, Gretchen I. Turner, Douglas and Susanne K. Upshaw, Mr. and Mrs. Victor Waithman, and Richard L. Wigle, in addition to numerous other private donors who made much of this information possible. I am thankful to the entire RAINPEG staff for the sacrifices and hardships that were necessary to bring much of these data to light. My sincere appreciation is extended to Stephen Houston and John E. Clark for reviewing and editing this manuscript. I am also appreciative to Stephen for the opportunity to participate in such a well-organized conference.

BIBLIOGRAPHY

Acevedo, Renaldo

1992 Un "domolito" clásico tardío de Nakbe. In *V simposio de investigaciones arqueológicas en Guatemala, 1991* (Juan Pedro Laporte, Héctor L. Escobedo, and Sandra V. de Brady, eds.): 129–136. Museo Nacional de Arqueología y Etnología, Ministerio de Cultura y Deportes, Instituto de Antropología e Historia de Guatemala, Asociación Tikal, Guatemala City.

n.d. Investigaciones de elementos hidraúlicos y otras excavaciones en Nakbe, Peten, Guatemala. In *Investigaciones arqueológicas en Nakbe, Peten: El resumen de la temporada de campo de 1993* (Richard D. Hansen, ed.): 178–206. Report filed with the Instituto de Antropología e Historia de Guatemala, Monumentos Prehispánicos, Guatemala, 1994.

Adams, Richard E. W.

1983 Ancient Land Use and Culture History in the Pasion River Region. In *Prehistoric Settlement Patterns: Essays in Honor of Gordon R. Willey* (Evon Z. Vogt and Richard M. Leventhal, eds.): 319–335. University of New Mexico Press, Albuquerque, and Peabody Museum of Archaeology and Ethnology, Harvard University, Cambridge, Mass.

Agrinier, Pierre

1964 *The Archaeological Burials at Chiapa de Corzo and Their Furniture.* Papers of the New World Archaeological Foundation, no. 16. Brigham Young University, Provo, Utah.

Andrews, E. Wyllys, IV

1965 *Progress Report on the 1960–1964 Field Seasons, National Geographic Society–Tulane University Dzibilchaltun Program.* Middle American Research Institute, Publication 31: 23–67. Tulane University, New Orleans.

Andrews E. Wyllys, V, and William M. Ringle

1992 Los mayas tempranos en Yucatan: Investigaciones arqueológicas en Komchen. *Mayab* 8: 5–17.

Anthony, Dana, and Stephen L. Black

1994 Operation 2031: The 1983 Main Plaza Excavations. In *Continuing Archaeology at Colha, Belize* (Thomas R. Hester, Harry L. Shafer, and Jack D. Eaton, eds.): 39–58. Studies in Archaeology. Texas Archaeological Research Laboratory, University of Texas, Austin.

Aveni, Anthony F., and Horst Hartung

1989 Uaxactun, Guatemala; Group E and Similar Assemblages: An Archaeo-astronomical Reconsideration. In *World Archaeoastronomy* (Anthony F. Aveni, ed.): 441–461. Cambridge University Press, Cambridge.

Ball, Joseph W.

1993 *Cahal Pech, the Ancient Maya, and Modern Belize: The Story of an Archaeological Park.* Ninth University Research Lecture, Graduate Division and Research. San Diego State University Press, San Diego.

Ball, Joseph W., and E. Wyllys Andrews, V
1978 *Pre-Classic Architecture at Becan, Campeche, Mexico.* Middle American Research Institute, Occasional Paper 3. Tulane University, New Orleans.

Benavides C., Antonio
1987 Arquitectura doméstica de Cobá, Quintana Roo. In *Análisis de dos unidades habitacionales mayas del horizonte clásico* (Linda Manzanilla, ed.): 26–35. Instituto de Investigaciones Antropológicas, Universidad Autónoma de México, México, D.F.

Blom, Franz
1924 Report on the Preliminary Work at Uaxactun, Guatemala. *Carnegie Institution of Washington Year Book* 23: 217–219. Washington, D.C.

Caso, Alfonso
1981 [1932] Reading the Riddle of Ancient Jewels. In *Ancient Mesoamerica: Selected Readings* (John A. Graham, ed.): 259–275. Peek Publications, Palo Alto, Calif.

Chambers, Mary Elizabeth
1982 Unusual Wall Helping Reveal Mirador Mysteries. In *BYU Project El Mirador.* Tabloid publication. Brigham Young University, Provo, Utah.
n.d. Earthwork Constructions at El Mirador, Peten, Guatemala. Ph.D. dissertation, Catholic University, Washington, D.C. (In preparation.)

Chase, Arlen Frank
1983 A *Contextual Consideration of the Tayasal-Paxcaman Zone, El Peten, Guatemala.* University Microfilms, Ann Arbor.

Chase, Arlen Frank, and Diane Z. Chase
1987 *Investigations at the Classic Maya City of Caracol, Belize: 1985–1987.* Pre-Columbian Art Research Institute Monograph 3. Pre-Columbian Art Research, San Francisco.
1995 External Impetus, Internal Synthesis, and Standardization: E Group Assemblages and the Crystallization of Classic Maya Society in the Southern Lowlands. In *The Emergence of Lowland Maya Civilization: The Transition from the Preclassic to the Early Classic* (Nikolai Grube, ed.): 87–101. Verlag Anton Saurwein, Möckmühl, Germany.

Clark, John E.
1988 *The Lithic Artifacts of La Libertad, Chiapas, Mexico: An Economic Perspective.* Papers of the New World Archaeological Foundation, no. 52. Brigham Young University, Provo, Utah.
1994 *The Development of Early Formative Rank Societies in the Soconusco, Chiapas, Mexico.* University Microfilms, Ann Arbor.

Clark, John E., and Michael Blake
1994 The Power of Prestige: Competitive Generosity and the Emergence of Rank Societies in Lowland Mesoamerica. In *Factional Competition and Political Development in the New World* (Elizabeth M. Brumfiel and John W. Fox, eds.): 17–30. Cambridge University Press, Cambridge.

Coe, Michael D.
1981 San Lorenzo Tenochtitlan. In *Handbook of Middle American Indians* (Victoria

Bricker, Jeremy A. Sabloff, and Patricia A. Andrews, eds.): 117–146. University of Texas Press, Austin.

Coe, Michael D., and Richard A. Diehl
1980 *In the Land of the Olmec: The Archaeology of San Lorenzo Tenochtitlan.* University of Texas Press, Austin.

Coe, William R.
1959 *Piedras Negras Archaeology: Artifacts, Caches, and Burials.* Museum Monographs. University Museum, University of Pennsylvania, Philadelphia.
1965a Tikal, Guatemala, and Emergent Maya Civilization. *Science* 147 (3664): 1401–1419.
1965b Tikal: Ten Years of Study of a Maya Ruin in the Lowlands of Guatemala. *Expedition* 8 (1): 5–56.
1967 *Tikal: A Handbook of the Ancient Maya Ruins.* University Museum, University of Pennsylvania, Philadelphia.
1990 *Excavations in the Great Plaza, North Terrace and North Acropolis of Tikal.* Tikal Report, no. 14. University Museum Monograph 61. University of Pennsylvania, Philadelphia.

Coe, William R., and Michael D. Coe
1956 Excavations at Nohoch Ek, British Honduras. *American Antiquity* 21: 370–382.

Coe, William R., and John J. McGinn
1963 Tikal: The North Acropolis and an Early Tomb. *Expedition* 5 (2): 24–32.

Coe, William R., and Robert J. Sharer
1979 The Quirigua Project: 1975 Season. In *Quirigua Reports* (Robert J. Sharer and Wendy Ashmore, eds.): 13–32. University Museum Monograph 37, vol. 1, no. 2. University of Pennsylvania, Philadelphia.

Cohodas, Marvin
1979 Some Unusual Aspects of Cross Group Symbolism. In *Tercera mesa redonda de Palenque,* vol. 4 (M. G. Robertson and D. C. Jeffers, eds.): 215–232. Pre-Columbian Art Research Institute, San Francisco.
1980 Radial Pyramids and Radial Associated Assemblages of the Central Maya Area. *Journal of the Society of Architectural Historians* 39 (3): 208–223.
1985 Public Architecture of the Maya Lowlands (Arquitectura pública de las tierras bajas mayas). *Cuadernos de Arquitectura Mesoamericana* 6: 51–68.

Culbert, T. Patrick
1977 Early Maya Development at Tikal, Guatemala. In *The Origins of Maya Civilization* (Richard E. W. Adams, ed.): 27–43. School of American Research, University of New Mexico Press, Albuquerque.

Dahlin, Bruce H.
1984 A Colossus in Guatemala: The Pre-Classic Maya City of El Mirador. *Archaeology* 37 (5): 18–25.

Dahlin, Bruce H., John E. Foss, and Mary Elizabeth Chambers
1980 Project Acalches: Reconstructing the Natural and Cultural History of a Seasonal Swamp at El Mirador, Guatemala: Preliminary Results. In *El Mirador,*

Peten, Guatemala: An Interim Report (Ray T. Matheny, ed.): 37–57. Papers of the New World Archaeological Foundation, no. 45. Brigham Young University, Provo, Utah.

Day, D. William, and Jane C. Laurens
1980 Excavations at Operation 2003: 1980 Season. In *The Colhá Project: Second Season, 1980 Interim Report* (Thomas R. Hester, Jack D. Eaton, and Harry J. Shafer, eds.): 71–85. Center for Archaeological Research, University of Texas, San Antonio.

Demarest, Arthur A.
1984 La cerámica de El Mirador: Resultados preliminares y análisis en curso. *Mesoamerica* 7: 53–92.

Demarest, Arthur A., Robert J. Sharer, William Fowler, Eleanor King, and Joyce Fowler
1984 Las excavaciones: El Mirador. *Mesoamerica* 7: 14–52.

Drucker, Philip, Robert F. Heizer, and Robert J. Squier
1959 *Excavations at La Venta, Tabasco, 1955.* Bureau of American Ethnology, Bulletin 170. Smithsonian Institution, Washington, D.C.

Eaton, Jack D., and B. Kunstler
1980 Excavations at Operation 2009: A Maya Ballcourt. In *The Colhá Project: Second Season, 1980 Interim Report* (Thomas R. Hester, Jack D. Eaton, and Harry J. Shafer, eds.): 121–132. Center for Archaeological Research, University of Texas, San Antonio.

Estrada Belli, Francesco
1992 Middle Preclassic Maya Buildings and Burials at Cuello, Belize. *Antiquity* 66: 955–964.

Fash, William L.
1991 *Scribes, Warriors and Kings: The City of Copán and the Ancient Maya.* Thames and Hudson, London.

Fialko, Vilma
1988 Mundo Perdido, Tikal: Un ejemplo de complejos de conmemoración astronómica. *Mayab* 4: 13–21.

Folan, William J., and Silverio Gallegos Osuna
1996 El uso del suelo del sitio arqueológico de Calakmul Campeche. *Yum Kax* 2 (3): 7–8.

Folan, William J., Ellen R. Kintz, and Laraine A. Fletcher
1983 *Coba: A Classic Maya Metropolis.* Academic Press, New York.

Forsyth, Donald W.
1989 *The Ceramics of El Mirador, Peten, Guatemala.* Papers of the New World Archaeological Foundation, no. 63. Brigham Young University, Provo, Utah.
1993a La arquitectura preclásica en Nakbe: Un estudio comparativo de dos períodos. In *VI simposio de investigaciones arqueológicas en Guatemala, 1992* (Juan Pedro Laporte, Héctor L. Escobedo, and Sandra V. de Brady, eds.): 131–142. Museo Nacional de Arqueología y Etnología, Ministerio de Cultura y Deportes, Instituto de Antropología e Historia de Guatemala, Asociación Tikal, Guatemala City.

1993b The Ceramic Sequence at Nakbe. *Ancient Mesoamerica* 4: 31–53.

Forsyth, Donald W., and Renaldo Acevedo

1994 La estructura 27 de Nakbe, Peten. In *VII simposio de investigaciones arqueológicas en Guatemala, 1993* (Juan Pedro Laporte and Héctor L. Escobedo, eds.): 299–312. Museo Nacional de Arqueología y Etnología, Ministerio de Cultura y Deportes, Instituto de Antropología e Historia de Guatemala, Asociación Tikal, Guatemala City.

Freidel, David A.

1979 Culture Areas and Interaction Spheres: Contrasting Approaches to the Emergence of Civilization in the Maya Lowlands. *American Antiquity* 44: 36–54.

1981 Civilization as a State of Mind: The Cultural Evolution of the Lowland Maya. In *The Transition to Statehood in the New World* (Grant D. Jones and Robert R. Kautz, eds.): 188–227. Cambridge University Press, Cambridge.

1985 Polychrome Façades of the Lowland Maya Pre-Classic. In *Painted Architecture and Polychrome Monumental Sculpture in Mesoamerica* (Elizabeth Boone, ed.): 5–30. Dumbarton Oaks, Washington, D.C.

1986 The Monumental Architecture. In *Archaeology at Cerros, Belize, Central America,* vol. 1: *An Interim Report* (Robin A. Robertson and David A. Freidel, eds.): 1–22. Southern Methodist University Press, Dallas.

Freidel, David A., and Linda Schele

1988a Symbol and Power: A History of the Lowland Maya Cosmogram. In *Maya Iconography* (Elizabeth Benson and Gillett Griffin, eds.): 44–93. Princeton University Press, Princeton, N.J.

1988b Kingship in the Late Pre-Classic Maya Lowlands: The Instruments and Places of Ritual Power. *American Anthropologist* 90: 547–567.

Freidel, David A., Linda Schele, and Joy Parker

1993 *Maya Cosmos: Three Thousand Years on the Shaman's Path.* William Morrow, New York.

Fry, Robert E.

1969 *Ceramics and Settlement in the Periphery of Tikal, Guatemala.* University Microfilms, Ann Arbor.

Gerhardt, Juliette Cartwright

1988 *Pre-Classic Maya Architecture at Cuello, Belize.* British Archaeological Reports, International Series 464. Oxford.

Gerhardt, Juliette Cartwright, and Norman Hammond

1991 The Community of Cuello: The Ceremonial Core. In *Cuello: An Early Maya Community in Belize* (Norman Hammond, ed.): 98–117. Cambridge University Press, Cambridge.

González Lauck, Rebecca B.

1994 La antigua ciudad olmeca en La Venta, Tabasco. In *Los olmecas en Mesoamerica* (John E. Clark, ed.): 92–111. El Equilibrista, México, D. F., and Turner Books, Madrid.

GRAHAM, IAN

1967 *Archaeological Explorations in El Peten, Guatemala.* Middle American Research Institute, Publication 33. Tulane University, New Orleans.

1980 *Corpus of Maya Hieroglyphic Inscription,* vol. 2, pt. 3: *Ixkun, Ucanal, Ixtutz, Naranjo.* Peabody Museum of Archaeology and Ethnology, Harvard University, Cambridge, Mass.

GREGORY, DAVID A.

1975 San Gervasio. In *Changing Pre-Columbian Commercial Systems: The 1972–1973 Seasons at Cozumel, Mexico* (Jeremy A. Sabloff and William L. Rathje, eds.): 88–106. Peabody Museum Monographs, no. 3. Harvard University, Cambridge, Mass.

GROVE, DAVID C., AND ANN CYPHERS GUILLÉN

1987 The Excavations. In *Ancient Chalcatzingo* (David C. Grove, ed.): 21–55. University of Texas Press, Austin.

HABERLAND, W.

1958 An Early Mound at Louisville, British Honduras. *Man* 58: 128–129.

HAMMOND, NORMAN

1977 Ex Oriente Lux: A View from Belize. In *The Origins of Maya Civilization* (Richard E. W. Adams, ed.): 45–76. University of New Mexico Press, Albuquerque.

1983 Nohmul, Belize: 1982 Investigations. *Journal of Field Archaeology* 10 (3): 245–254.

HAMMOND, NORMAN (ED.)

1991 *Cuello: An Early Maya Community in Belize.* Cambridge University Press, New York.

HAMMOND, NORMAN, AMANDA CLARKE, AND CYNTHIA ROBIN

1991 Middle Pre-Classic Buildings and Burials at Cuello, Belize: 1990 Investigations. *Latin American Antiquity* 2: 352–363.

HANSEN, ERIC F., RICHARD D. HANSEN, AND MICHELE R. DERRICK

1995 Los análisis de los estucos y pinturas arquitectónicos de Nakbe: Resultados preliminares de los estudios de los métodos y materiales de producción. In *VIII simposio de arqueología guatemalteca, 1994* (Juan Pedro Laporte and Héctor L. Escobedo, eds.): 543–560. Museo Nacional de Arqueología y Etnología, Ministerio de Cultura y Deportes, Instituto de Antropología e Historia de Guatemala, Asociación Tikal, Guatemala City.

HANSEN, RICHARD D.

1990 *Excavations in the Tigre Complex, El Mirador, Peten, Guatemala.* Papers of the New World Archaeological Foundation, no. 62. Brigham Young University, Provo, Utah.

1991 The Maya Rediscovered: The Road to Nakbe. *Natural History,* May: 8–14.

1992a *The Archaeology of Ideology: A Study of Maya Preclassic Architectural Sculpture at Nakbe, Peten, Guatemala.* University Microfilms, Ann Arbor.

1992b Proyecto regional de investigaciones arqueológicas del norte de Peten, Guatemala: Temporada 1990. In *IV simposio de arqueología guatemalteca, Julio 1990* (Juan Pedro Laporte, Héctor L. Escobedo, and Sandra V. de Brady, eds.):

1–36. Museo Nacional de Arqueología y Etnología, Ministerio de Cultura y Deportes, Instituto de Antropología e Historia de Guatemala, Asociación Tikal, Guatemala City.

1992c El proceso cultural de Nakbe y el area del Peten nor-central: Las épocas tempranas. In *V simposio de investigaciones en Guatemala* (Juan Pedro Laporte, Héctor L. Escobedo, and Sandra V. de Brady, eds.): 81–96. Museo Nacional de Arqueología y Etnología, Ministerio de Cultura y Deportes, Instituto de Antropología e Historia de Guatemala, Asociación Tikal, Guatemala City.

n.d.a Excavations on Structure 34 and the Tigre Area, El Mirador, Peten, Guatemala: A New Look at the Pre-Classic Lowland Maya. M.A. thesis, Brigham Young University, 1984.

n.d.b *Explorations at La Muerta: A Late Classic Settlement near El Mirador, Peten, Guatemala.* Papers of the New World Archaeological Foundation. Brigham Young University, Provo, Utah. (In press.)

Hansen, Richard D., Ronald L. Bishop, and Federico Fahsen

1991 Notes on Maya Codex-Style Ceramics from Nakbe, Peten, Guatemala. *Ancient Mesoamerica* 2: 225–243.

Hansen, Richard D., and Donald W. Forsyth

1987 Late Pre-Classic Development of Unslipped Pottery in the Maya Lowlands: The Evidence from El Mirador. In *Maya Ceramics: Papers of the 1985 Maya Ceramic Conference,* vol. 2 (Prudence M. Rice and Robert J. Sharer, eds.): 439–468. British Archaeological Reports, International Series 345. Oxford.

Harrison, Peter D.

1986 Tikal: Selected Topics. In *City-States of the Maya: Art and Architecture* (Elizabeth P. Benson, ed.): 45–71. Rocky Mountain Institute for Pre-Columbian Studies, Denver, Colo.

Haviland, William A.

1965 Prehistoric Settlement at Tikal, Guatemala. *Expedition* 7: 14–23.

Healy, Paul F.

1992 The Ancient Maya Ballcourt at Pacbitun, Belize. *Ancient Mesoamerica* 3: 229–239.

Hellmuth, Nicholas

1977 Cholti-Lacandon (Chiapas) and Peten-Ytzá Agriculture, Settlement Pattern, and Population. In *Social Process in Maya Prehistory: Studies in Honour of Sir Eric Thompson* (Norman Hammond, ed.): 421–448. Academic Press, London.

Hendon, Julia A.

1989 The 1986 Excavations at BA-20. In *Río Azul Reports,* no. 4: *The 1986 Season* (Richard E.W. Adams, ed.): 88–135. University of Texas, San Antonio.

Holmes, William H.

1895 *Archaeological Studies among the Ancient Cities of Mexico,* pt. 1: *Monuments of Yucatan.* Anthropological Series, Publication 8, vol. 1, no. 1. Field Columbian Museum, Chicago.

Howell, Wayne K., and Denise Ranae Evans Copeland

1989 *Excavations at El Mirador, Peten, Guatemala: The Danta and Monos Complexes.*

Papers of the New World Archaeological Foundation, nos. 60 and 61. Brigham Young University, Provo, Utah.

Ichon, Alain, and Rene Viel
1984 *La periode formative á La Lagunita et dans le Quiche Méridional, Guatemala.* Centre National de la Recherche Scientifique, Institut d'ethnologie, Paris.

Johnston, Kevin
1993 El maya oculto: Implicaciones ecológicas de estructuras habitacionales sin montículos en Itzán, Petén. In *VI simposio de investigaciones arqueológicas en Guatemala, 1992* (Juan Pedro Laporte, Héctor L. Escobedo, and Sandra V. de Brady, eds.): 209–218. Museo Nacional de Arqueología y Etnología, Ministerio de Cultura y Deportes, Instituto de Antropología e Historia de Guatemala, Asociación Tikal, Guatemala City.

Johnston, Kevin, Fernando Moscoso Moller, and Stefan Schmitt
1992 Casas no-visibles de los mayas clásicos: Estructuras residenciales sin plataformas basales en Itzán, Petén. In *V simposio de investigaciones arqueológicas en Guatemala, 1991* (Juan Pedro Laporte, Héctor L. Escobedo, and Sandra V. de Brady, eds.): 147–162. Museo Nacional de Arqueología y Etnología, Ministerio de Cultura y Deportes, Instituto de Antropología e Historia de Guatemala, Asociación Tikal, Guatemala City.

Laporte, Juan Pedro
1993 Función, arquitectura y ritual en tres plazas ceremoniales de Ixtonton, Peten. In *VI simposio de investigaciones arqueológicas en Guatemala, 1992* (Juan Pedro Laporte, Héctor L. Escobedo, and Sandra V. de Brady, eds.): 273–296. Museo Nacional de Arqueología y Etnología, Ministerio de Cultura y Deportes, Instituto de Antropologia e Historia de Guatemala, Asociación Tikal, Guatemala City.

Laporte, Juan Pedro, and Vilma Fialko
1993 El preclásico de Mundo Perdido: Algunos aportes sobre los orígines de Tikal. In *Tikal y Uaxactun en el preclásico* (Juan Pedro Laporte and Juan Antonio Valdés, eds.): 9–42. Instituto de Investigaciones Antropológicas, Universidad Nacional Autónoma de México, México, D.F.
1995 Un reencuentro con Mundo Perdido, Tikal, Guatemala. *Ancient Mesoamerica* 6: 41–94.
n.d. Una visión preliminar de Mundo Perdido, Tikal, durante el preclásico de las tierras bajas Mayas. Manuscript on file, Instituto de Antropología e Historia de Guatemala, Guatemala City, 1986.

Laporte, Juan Pedro, and Carlos Rolando Torres
1987 Los señorios del sureste de Peten. *Mayab* 3: 7–22.
1993 El proyecto sureste de Peten: Resultados del programa regional, 1985–1989. In *III simposio de arqueología guatemalteca* (Juan Pedro Laporte, Héctor L. Escobedo, and Sandra V. de Brady, eds.): 169–182. Museo Nacional de Arqueología y Etnología, Ministerio de Cultura y Deportes, Instituto de Antropología e Historia de Guatemala, Asociación Tikal, Guatemala City.

Laporte, Juan Pedro, Carlos Rolando Torres, and Bernard Hermes
1991 Ixtonton: Evolución de un asentamiento en el alto Río Mopan. In *II simposio*

de investigaciones arqueológicas en Guatemala (Juan Pedro Laporte, Héctor L. Escobedo, and Sandra V. de Brady, eds.): 206–223. Museo Nacional de Arqueología y Etnología, Ministerio de Cultura y Deportes, Instituto de Antropología e Historia de Guatemala, Asociación Tikal, Guatemala City.

LAPORTE, JUAN PEDRO, AND JUAN ANTONIO VALDÉS

1993 *Tikal y Uaxactun en el preclásico.* Instituto de Investigaciones Antropológicas, Universidad Nacional Autónoma de México, México, D.F.

LÓPEZ, ROBERTO F.

1993 Excavaciones en la estructura 32 de Nakbe, Petén. In *III simposio de investigaciones arqueológicas en Guatemala* (Juan Pedro Laporte, Héctor L. Escobedo, and Sandra V. de Brady, eds.): 99–110. Museo Nacional de Arqueología y Etnología, Ministerio de Cultura y Deportes, Instituto de Antropología e Historia de Guatemala, Asociación Tikal, Guatemala City.

LÓPEZ, ROBERTO FRANCISCO, AND ROXZANDA ORTIZ

1994 Excavaciones en un palacio residencial en el grupo códice de Nakbe, Petén. In *VII simposio de investigaciones arqueológicas en Guatemala* (Juan Pedro Laporte and Héctor L. Escobedo, eds.): 313–333. Museo Nacional de Arqueología y Etnología, Ministerio de Cultura y Deportes, Instituto de Antropología e Historía de Guatemala, Asociación Tikal, Guatemala City.

LOWE, GARETH W.

1962 *Mound 5 and Minor Excavations, Chiapa de Corzo, Chiapas, Mexico.* Papers of the New World Archaeological Foundation, no. 12. Brigham Young University, Provo, Utah.

1989 Algunas aclaraciones sobre la presencia olmeca y maya en el preclásico de Chiapas. In *El preclásico o formativo: Avances y perspectivas* (M. Carmona Macias, ed.): 363–383. Museo Nacional de Antropología, Insituto Nacional de Antropología e Historia, México, D.F.

LOWE, GARETH W., AND PIERRE AGRINIER

1960 *Mound 1, Chiapa de Corzo, Chiapas, Mexico.* Papers of the New World Archaeological Foundation, no. 8. Brigham Young University, Provo, Utah.

MARCUS, JOYCE

1976 The Size of the Early Mesoamerican Village. In *The Early Mesoamerican Village* (Kent V. Flannery, ed.): 79–90. Academic Press, New York.

1989 Zapotec Chiefdoms and the Nature of Formative Religions. In *Regional Perspectives on the Olmec* (Robert J. Sharer and David C. Grove, eds.): 148–197. Cambridge University Press, Cambridge.

MARTÍNEZ DONJUÁN, GUADALUPE

1994 Los olmecas en el estado de Guerrero. In *Los olmecas en Mesoamerica* (John E. Clark, ed.): 142–163. El Equilibrista, México, D.F., and Turner Books, Madrid.

MARTÍNEZ HIDALGO, GUSTAVO

1994 Algunos aspectos arquitectónicos respecto a la estructura 59 de Nakbe. In *VII simposio de investigaciones arqueológicas en Guatemala, 1993* (Juan Pedro Laporte and Héctor L. Escobedo, eds.): 281–289. Museo Nacional de Arqueología y Etnología, Ministerio de Cultura y Deportes, Instituto de Antropología e Historia de Guatemala, Asociación Tikal, Guatemala City.

Martínez Hidalgo, Gustavo, and Richard D. Hansen

1992 Notas adicionales respecto de la estructura 1 de Nakbe. In *V simposio de investigaciones arqueológicas en Guatemala* (Juan Pedro Laporte, Héctor L. Escobedo, and Sandra V. de Brady, eds.): 103–114. Museo Nacional de Arqueología y Etnología, Ministerio de Cultura y Deportes, Instituto de Antropología e Historia de Guatemala, Asociación Tikal, Guatemala City.

1993 Excavaciones en el complejo 59, grupo 66 y grupo 18, Nakbe, Peten. In *III simposio de arqueología guatemalteca* (Juan Pedro Laporte, Héctor L. Escobedo, and Sandra V. de Brady, eds.): 73–86. Museo Nacional de Arqueología y Etnología. Ministerio de Cultura y Deportes, Instituto de Antropología e Historia de Guatemala, Asociación Tikal, Guatemala City.

Mata Amado, Guillermo, and Richard D. Hansen

1992 El diente incrustado temprano de Nakbe. In *V simposio de investigaciones arqueológicas en Guatemala* (Juan Pedro Laporte, Héctor L. Escobedo, and Sandra V. de Brady, eds.): 115–118. Museo Nacional de Arqueología y Etnología, Ministerio de Cultura y Deportes, Instituto de Antropología e Historia de Guatemala, Asociación Tikal, Guatemala City.

Matheny, Ray T.

1986 Investigations at El Mirador, Peten, Guatemala. *National Geographic Research* 2: 332–353.

1987 Early States in the Maya Lowlands during the Late Pre-Classic Period: Edzna and El Mirador. In *City States of the Maya: Art and Architecture* (Elizabeth B. Benson, ed.): 1–44. Rocky Mountain Institute for Pre-Columbian Studies, Denver, Colo.

Matheny, Ray T., Deanne L. Gurr, Donald W. Forsyth, and R. Richard Hauck

1983 *Investigations at Edzná, Campeche, Mexico,* vol. 1, pt. 1: *The Hydraulic System.* Papers of the New World Archaeological Foundation, no. 46. Brigham Young University, Provo, Utah.

Matheny, Ray T., Richard D. Hansen, and Deanne L. Gurr

1980 Preliminary Field Report, El Mirador, 1979 Season. In *El Mirador, Peten, Guatemala: An Interim Report* (Ray T. Matheny, ed.): 1–23. Papers of the New World Archaeological Foundation, no. 45. Brigham Young Univeristy, Provo, Utah.

Mendéz Martínez, Enrique

1986 La zona arqueológica de Huijazoo y su tumba 5. *Cuadernos de Arquitectura Mesoamericana* 7: 79–81.

Miller, Arthur G.

1986 *Maya Rulers of Time: A Study of Architectural Sculpture at Tikal, Guatemala.* University Museum, University of Pennsylvania, Philadelphia.

Morales, Paulino I.

1993 Estructuras de planta circular: Nuevas referencias para las tierras bajas mayas centrales. In *VI simposio de investigaciones arqueológicas en Guatemala, 1992* (Juan Pedro Laporte, Héctor L. Escobedo, and Sandra V. de Brady, eds.): 311–319. Museo Nacional de Arqueología e Etnología, Ministerio de Cultura y Deportes, Instituto de Antropología e Historia de Guatemala, Asociación Tikal, Guatemala City.

Nielsen, Glenna

1980 Salvage of Looters' Trenches, El Mirador. In *El Mirador, Peten, Guatemala: An Interim Report* (Ray T. Matheny, ed.): 25–36. Papers of the New World Archaeological Foundation, no. 45. Brigham Young University, Provo, Utah.

1990 *Central Plaza Excavations at El Mirador, Peten, Guatemala: Operations 18 and 27.* University Microfilms, Ann Arbor.

Ortíz, Ponciano, and María del Carmen Rodríguez

1994 Los espacios sagrados olmecas: El Manatí, un caso especial. In *Los olmecas en Mesoamerica* (John E. Clark, ed.): 68–91. El Equilibrista, México, D.F., and Turner Books, Madrid.

Pendergast, David A.

1981 Lamanai, Belize: Summary of Excavation Results, 1974–1980. *Journal of Field Archaeology* 8: 29–53.

1979 *Excavations at Altun Ha, Belize, 1964–1970,* vol. 1. Royal Ontario Museum, Toronto.

Pollock, H. E. D.

1936 *Round Structures of Aboriginal Middle America.* Carnegie Institution, Publication 471. Washington, D.C.

Potter, Daniel R., Thomas R. Hester, Stephen L. Black, and Fred Valdez, Jr.

1984 Relationships between Early Pre-Classic and Early Middle Pre-Classic Phases in Northern Belize: A Comment on "Lowland Maya Archaeology at the Crossroads." *American Antiquity* 49: 628–631.

Puleston, Dennis E.

1974 Intersite Areas in the Vicinity of Tikal and Uaxactun. In *Mesoamerican Archaeology: New Approaches* (Norman Hammond, ed.): 303–311. University of Texas Press, Austin.

Rands, Robert L.

1974 The Ceramic Sequence of Palenque, Chiapas. In *Mesoamerican Archaeology: New Approaches* (Norman Hammond, ed.): 51–75. University of Texas Press, Austin.

1977 The Rise of Classic Maya Civilization in the Northwestern Zone: Isolation and Integration. In *The Origins of Maya Civilization* (Richard E. W. Adams, ed.): 159–180. University of New Mexico Press, Albuquerque.

Rice, Don S.

1976 Middle Pre-Classic Maya Settlement in the Central Maya Lowlands. *Journal of Field Archaeology* 3: 425–445.

Ricketson, Oliver G., and Edith Bayles Ricketson

1937 *Uaxactun, Guatemala: Group E, 1926–1931.* Carnegie Institution, Publication 477. Washington, D.C.

Ringle, William M.

n.d.a Preclassic Cityscapes: Ritual Politics among the Early Lowland Maya. Paper presented at the symposium "Ritual Behavior, Social Identity, and Cosmology in Pre-Classic Mesoamerica," October 1993. Dumbarton Oaks, Washington, D.C.

n.d.b The Settlement Patterns of Komchen, Yucatan, Mexico. Ph.D. dissertation, Tulane University, 1985.

Ringle, William M., and E. Wyllys Andrews V

1988 Formative Residences at Komchen, Yucatan, Mexico. In *Household and Community in the Mesoamerican Past* (Richard R. Wilk and Wendy Ashmore, eds.): 171–197. University of New Mexico Press, Albuquerque.

Robertson, Robin A., and David A. Freidel (eds.)

1986 *Archaeology at Cerros Belize, Central America*, vol. 1: *An Interim Report*. Southern Methodist University Press, Dallas.

Robles, Rosa Maria Reyna, and Guadalupe Martínez Donjuán

1989 Hallazgos funerarias de la época olmeca en Chilpancingo, Guerrero. *Arqueología* 1: 13–22.

Ruppert, Karl

1940 A Special Assemblage of Maya Structures. In *The Maya and Their Neighbors* (C. L. Hay et al., eds.): 222–231. Appleton-Century, New York.

Ruppert, Karl, and John H. Denison, Jr.

1943 *Archaeological Reconnaissance in Campeche, Quintana Roo, and Peten*. Carnegie Institution, Publication 543. Washington, D.C.

Sanders, William T., and Barbara J. Price

1968 *Mesoamerica: The Evolution of a Civilization*. Random House, New York.

Satterthwaite, Linton

1954 Unclassified Buildings and Substructures. *Piedras Negras Archaeology: Architecture*, pt. 6. University Museum, University of Pennsylvania, Philadelphia.

Scarborough, Vernon L., Beverly Mitchum, Sorraya Carr, and David Freidel

1982 Two Late Preclassic Ballcourts at the Lowland Maya Centre of Cerros, Northern Belize. *Journal of Field Archaeology* 9: 21–34.

Schieber de Lavarreda, Christa

1994a Abaj Takalik: Hallazgo de un juego de pelota del preclásico medio. In *VII simposio de investigaciones arqueológicas en Guatemala, 1993* (Juan Pedro Laporte, Héctor L. Escobedo, and Sandra V. de Brady, eds.): 95–111. Museo Nacional de Arqueologia y Etnología, Ministerio de Cultura y Deportes, Instituto de Antropología e Historia de Guatemala, Asociación Tikal, Guatemala City.

1994b A Middle Preclassic Clay Ball Court at Abaj Takalik, Guatemala. *Mexicon* 16: 77–89.

Sharer, Robert J., and David W. Sedat

1987 *Archaeological Investigations in the Northern Maya Highlands, Guatemala: Interaction and the Development of Maya Civilization*. University Museum Monograph 59. University of Pennsylvania, Philadelphia.

Sidrys, Raymond V.

1978 Megalithic Architecture and Sculpture of the Ancient Maya. In *Papers on the Economy and Architecture of the Ancient Maya* (Raymond V. Sidrys, ed.): 155–183. Institute of Archaeology Monograph 8. University of California, Los Angeles.

1983 *Archaeological Excavations in Northern Belize, Central America*. Institute of

Archaeology, Monograph 17. University of California, Los Angeles.

Sidrys, Raymond V., and J. M. Andresen

1978 A Second Round Structure from Northern Belize, Central America. *Man* 13: 638–650.

Smith, A. Ledyard

1940 The Corbeled Arch in the New World. In *The Maya and Their Neighbors* (C. L. Hays et al., eds.): 202–221. Appleton-Century, New York.

1950 *Uaxactun, Guatemala: Excavations of 1931–1937.* Carnegie Institution, Publication 588. Washington, D.C.

1982 Major Architecture and Caches. In *Excavations at Seibal, Department of Peten, Guatemala* (Gordon R. Willey, ed.): 1–263. Memoirs of the Peabody Museum of Archaeology and Ethnology, vol. 15, no. 1. Harvard University, Cambridge, Mass.

Smith, Robert E.

1937 A Study of Structure A-I Complex at Uaxactun, Peten, Guatemala. In *Contributions to American Archaeology,* no. 19, Publication 456: 189–231. Carnegie Institution, Washington, D.C.

Stuart, George E.

1993 New Light on the Olmec. *National Geographic* 184 (5): 88–115.

Stuiver, Minze, and Gordon W. Pearson

1986 High Precision Calibration of the Radiocarbon Time Scale: A.D. 1950 to 500 B.C. *Radiocarbon* 28: 805–838.

Stutz-Landeen, Ellen

n.d. Excavations on a Late Pre-Classic Plaza Unit at El Mirador, Peten, Guatemala. M.A. thesis, Brigham Young University, 1986.

Suasnavar, Jose

1994 Las calzadas de Nakbe. In *VII simposio de investigaciones arqueológicas en Guatemala, 1993* (Juan Pedro Laporte, Héctor L. Escobedo, and Sandra V. de Brady, eds.): 335–348. Museo Nacional de Arqueología y Etnología. Ministerio de Cultura y Deportes, Instituto de Antropología e Historia de Guatemala, Asociación Tikal, Guatemala City.

n.d. Las calzadas de Nakbe: Las excavaciones. In *Investigaciones arqueológicas en Nakbe, Peten: El resumen de la temporada de campo de 1993* (Richard D. Hansen, ed.): 243–261. Report filed with the Monumentos Prehispánicos, Instituto de Antropología e Historia de Guatemala, Guatemala City, 1994.

Taladoire, Eric

1981 *Les terrains de jeu de balle.* Etudes mésoaméricaines, ser. 2, no. 4. Misión Arqueológica y Etnológica Francesa, México, D.F.

Tedlock, Dennis

1985 *Popol Vuh: The Definitive Edition of the Mayan Book of the Da wn of Life and the Glories of God and Kings.* Simon and Schuster, New York.

Thompson, J. Eric

1931 *Archaeological Investigations in the Southern Cayo District, British Honduras.* Field Museum of Natural History, Publication 301, vol. 17, no. 3. Chicago.

1954 *The Rise and Fall of Maya Civilization.* University of Oklahoma Press, Norman.

Tourtellot, Gair, III

1970 The Peripheries of Seibal: An Interim Report. In *Monographs and Papers in Maya Archaeology* (William R. Bullard, Jr., ed.): 407–419. Papers of the Peabody Museum of Archaeology and Ethnology, vol. 61, pt. 4, no. 3. Harvard University, Cambridge, Mass.

Tozzer, Alfred M.

1913 *A Preliminary Study of the Prehistoric Ruins of Nakum, Guatemala: A Report of the Peabody Museum Expedition, 1909–1910.* Memoirs of the Peabody Museum of American Archaeology and Ethnology, vol. 5, no. 3. Harvard University, Cambridge, Mass.

Valdés, Juan Antonio

1985 Investigacion habitacional de los cuadrantes perdido y corriental de Tikal: Una formulacion. *Antropología e Historia de Guatemala* 7 (2): 49–65.

1986 Uaxactun: Recientes Investigaciones. *Mexicon* 7 (6): 126–128.

1987 Los mascarones preclásicos de Uaxactun: El caso del grupo H. In *Primer simposio mundial sobre epigrafía maya:* 165–181. Museo Nacional de Arqueología y Etnología, Ministerio de Cultura y Deportes, Instituto de Antropología e Historia de Guatemala, Asociación Tikal, Guatemala City.

1989a Visión evolutiva de Uaxactun a la luz de nuevas investigaciones. *Estudios: Revista de antropología, arqueología e historia* 1/89: 53–82.

1989b El grupo A de Uaxactun: Manifestaciones arquitectónicas y dinásticas durante el clásico temprano. *Mayab* 5: 30–40.

1990 Observaciones iconográficas sobre las figuras preclásicas de cuerpo completo en el área Maya. *Estudios: Revista de Antropología, Arqueología e Historia* 2/90: 23–49.

1992 El crecimiento de la civilización Maya del área central durante el preclásico tardío: una vista desde el grupo H de Uaxactun. *U tz'ib* 1 (2): 16–31.

1993 Arquitectura y escultura en la plaza sur del grupo H, Uaxactun. In *Tikal y Uaxactun en el preclásico* (Juan Pedro Laporte and Juan Antonio Valdés, eds.): 96–126. Instituto de Investigaciones Antropológicas, Universidad Nacional Autónoma de México, México, D.F.

n.d. Etude des groupes d'habitations du centre ceremonial Maya du "mundo perdido," Tikal. Ph.D. thesis, Sorbonne, 1983.

Valdés, Juan Antonio, and Federico Fahsen

1992 Gobernantes y gobernados: La sequencia dinastica de Uaxactun para el clásico temprano. In *VI Simposio de investigaciones arqueológicas en Guatemala* (Juan Pedro Laporte, Héctor L. Escobedo, and Sandra V. de Brady, eds.): 25–55. Museo Nacional de Arqueología y Etnología, Ministerio de Cultura y Deportes, Instituto de Antropología e Historia de Guatemala, Asociación Tikal, Guatemala City.

Valdez, Fred, Jr.

1995 Religion and Iconography of the Pre-Classic Maya at Río Azul, Peten, Guatemala. In *Religión y sociedad en el area Maya* (C. Varela Torrecilla, Juan L. Bonor V., and Yolanda Fernández Marquínez, eds.): 211–217. Sociedad Española de Estudios Mayas, Instituto de Cooperación Iberoamericana, Caja Madrid.

Velásquez, Juan Luis

1992a Excavaciones en el complejo 72 de Nakbe, Peten. In *IV simposio de arqueología guatemalteca, Julio 1990* (Juan Pedro Laporte, Héctor L. Escobedo, and Sandra V. de Brady, eds.): 37–44. Museo Nacional de Arqueología y Etnología, Ministerio de Cultura y Deportes, Instituto de Antropología e Historia de Guatemala, Asociación Tikal, Guatemala City.

1992b Excavaciones en el complejo 75 de Nakbe. In *V simposio de investigaciones arqueológicas en Guatemala* (Juan Pedro Laporte, Héctor L. Escobedo, and Sandra V. de Brady, eds.): 97–102. Museo Nacional de Arqueología y Etnología, Ministerio de Cultura y Deportes, Instituto de Antropología e Historia de Guatemala, Asociación Tikal, Guatemala City.

1993 Excavaciones en la estructura 31 de Nakbe, Peten. In *III simposio de arqueología guatemalteca* (Juan Pedro Laporte, Héctor L. Escobedo, and Sandra V. de Brady, eds.): 87–98. Museo Nacional de Arqueología y Etnología, Ministerio de Cultura y Deportes, Instituto de Antropología e Historia de Guatemala, Asociación Tikal, Guatemala City.

Webster, David L.

1975 The Fortifications of Becan, Campeche, Mexico. In *Archaeological Investigations on the Yucatan Peninsula* (Margaret A. L. Harrison and Robert Wauchope, eds.): 123–127. Middle American Research Institute, Publication 31. Tulane University, New Orleans.

1976 *Defensive Earthworks at Becan, Campeche, Mexico: Implications for Maya Warfare.* Middle American Research Institute, Publication 41. Tulane University, New Orleans.

1977 Warfare and the Evolution of Maya Civilization. In *The Origins of Maya Civilization* (Richard E. W. Adams, ed.): 335–371. University of New Mexico Press, Albuquerque.

Willey, Gordon R.

1973 *The Altar de Sacrificios Excavations: General Summary and Conclusions.* Papers of the Peabody Museum of Archaeology and Ethnology, vol. 64, no. 3. Harvard University, Cambridge, Mass.

1990 Excavations at Seibal: General Summary and Conclusions. In *Excavations at Seibal*, vol. 4 (Gordon R. Willey, ed.): 175–276. Peabody Museum of Archaeology and Ethnology, Harvard University, Cambridge, Mass.

Willey, Gordon R., William R. Bullard, Jr., John B. Glass, and James C. Gifford

1965 *Prehistoric Maya Settlements in the Belize Valley.* Papers of the Peabody Museum of Archaeology and Ethnology, vol. 54. Harvard University, Cambridge, Mass.

Willey, Gordon R., A. Ledyard Smith, Gair Tourtellot III, Ian Graham, and Jeremy Sabloff

1975 *Excavations at Seibal.* Memoirs of the Peabody Museum of Archaeology and Ethnology, vol. 13, nos. 1 and 2. Harvard University, Cambridge, Mass.

Woods, James C., and Gene L. Titmus

1994 Piedra en piedra: Perspectivas de la civilización maya a través de los estudios líticos. In *VII simposio de investigaciones arqueológicas en Guatemala, 1993* (Juan

Pedro Laporte and Héctor L. Escobedo, eds.): 349–368. Museo Nacional de Arqueología y Etnología, Ministerio de Cultura y Deportes, Instituto de Antropología e Historia de Guatemala, Asociación Tikal, Guatemala City.

1996 Stone on Stone: Perspectives of Maya Civilization from Lithic Studies. In *Eighth Palenque Round Table, 1993* (M. G. Robertson, Martha J. Macri, and Jon McHargue, eds.): 479–489. Pre-Columbian Art Research Institute, San Francisco.

Structures as Sites: The Construction Process and Maya Architecture

ELLIOT M. ABRAMS
OHIO UNIVERSITY

THE ARCHITECTURAL accomplishments of the Late Classic Maya embody an enormous array of collective human experience. They reflect economic prosperity, demand public attention, reify worldview, manipulate opinion, and express political relationships. As a consequence of the multiple dimensions of architecture, buildings can be studied by archaeologists through a variety of analytic and epistemological approaches. In a sense, the richness of the built environment requires that archaeologists subject architecture to the largest array of available analyses.

An important step in the study of ancient Maya architecture involves consideration of the behaviors associated with the construction, use, and abandonment of each structure. In proposing this approach, Michael Schiffer (1976) outlined what he termed "behavioral or formation processes"—those stages in the life history of an artifact that ultimately affect the archaeological record. In pursuing this analytic approach, I conceive of Maya architecture as the physical embodiment of articulated materials and behaviors involving costs, construction decisions, and human labor organization, and buildings are viewed as sites unto themselves that could be created only within a specific societal setting.

In this chapter, a sample of Late Classic Maya architecture is dissected into its constituent formation processes, essential as a precondition to deeper analysis. These various formation processes are then quantified, according to architectural energetic research conducted at Copan, Honduras (Abrams 1994), thus combining quantification with behavioral stages of construction. Together, what emerges is a more refined view of construction in terms of materials, behaviors, and sociopolitical organization.

EARLY OBSERVATIONS OF ARCHITECTURAL PROCESS

Architecture has been the focus of archaeological research in the southern Maya lowlands since the inception of Maya archaeology. The remains of Maya civilization, popularized by John Lloyd Stephens (1841), were in fact the remnants of elite architecture. The research conducted by the Peabody Museum, the Carnegie Institution, and the University of Pennsylvania placed great emphasis on large architectural works, producing some of the most comprehensive architectural studies in Maya archaeology, and in the process reinforced the association of civilization with architectural splendor (Morley 1946: 49).

Of their many contributions toward understanding Maya architecture, these earlier Maya archaeologists made three observations about construction that stand out and remain relevant to contemporary analyses. The first is the recognition that buildings were constructed in multiple and distinct episodes, with one building overlaying an earlier one. Complete excavation of Structure E-VII-Sub at Uaxactun (Smith 1950), for example, revealed the multiple stages of discrete episodes of construction as well as the evolving functions of those newly built structures.

A second important observation made by these pioneering excavators was that existing buildings were partially demolished for reuse in the construction of later, overlapping buildings—e.g., see Satterthwaite (1954); in effect, the razing of the old for the raising of the new. This suggests that spatial planning of future architecture was influenced in part by the location of existing structures to facilitate the reuse of materials.

Third, early studies were conducted on the specific engineering practices used by the ancient Maya for both elite masonry (Roys 1934) and commoner wattle-and-daub structures (Wauchope 1938). Roys (1934: 95) outlined the mathematics and mechanics of the corbeled arch, clearly illustrating the physics of stress and strain that had to be understood and controlled by the Maya architects if they were to successfully build arches and weight-bearing walls. At the same time, while excavating the Temple of the Warriors at Chichen Itza, Earl Morris and his colleagues (1931) collected data on lime plaster production; recent analyses continue to use these measurements to discern manufacturing patterns and costs (Abrams 1994). Wauchope's classic research illustrated the variability of commoner house types as well as their elements and methods of construction. Although there have been refinements in understanding the engineering of Maya structures—Littmann (1962) and Hyman (1970) have researched the chemical composition of plaster; Abrams (1994) has reevaluated the practice of breaking joints in wall construction and the sloping of roofs as a means of collecting potable water—there have to date been no significant contradictions to the insights offered by these pioneering scholars.

THE CONSTRUCTION PROCESS

The total construction process can be divided into four specific but articulated operations: (1) procurement of materials, (2) transport of materials to the construction site, (3) manufacture of finished architectural components, and (4) assembly or actual construction of the building (Fig. 1).

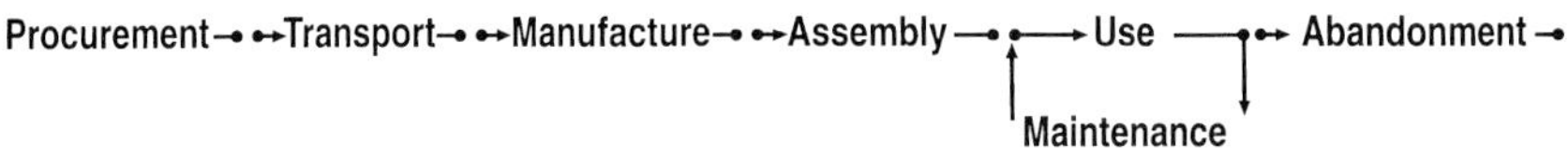

Fig. 1 Outline of the basic operations in construction.

Each of these operations can be further divided into specific tasks based on the components they are designed to provide in the structure. Thus, procurement includes quarrying stone for later manufacture into masonry blocks and cutting grass and palm for vegetal roofs. In manufacture, tasks include reduction of quarried stone into masonry blocks and sculpture as well as preparation of paints, wooden beams and lintels, and lime plaster. Depending on the specificity and appropriateness of the architectural and energetic data needed to quantify these tasks, researchers can design their own "flowchart" of construction behaviors. Researchers must also recognize the variability of these behaviors and thus their costs among sites. For example, at Copan (Abrams 1994: 44), the quarrying of tuff is a task that is distinct from facing the tuff into masonry blocks; at Nakbe (Hansen, this volume), the quarrying of limestone is largely equivalent to the manufacture of masonry blocks. The goal is not to infer some "perfect" set of behaviors for construction but rather to generate a reasonable set of formation processes that are site specific, quantifiable, and in accord with the analytic goals of the researcher.

The four operations and their subsumed tasks appear as linear stages in the construction process, but in fact many tasks were conducted simultaneously. In general, the operations were sequential in the sense that the assembly or construction of the building could not commence until some degree of procurement, transport, and manufacture had been accomplished. However, tasks must have overlapped or demanded variations in the sequence of work for both physical and organizational reasons. For example, limestone and tuff, stones used in masonry, begin to harden when exposed to the atmosphere; thus, masonry blocks had to be shaped soon after the initial quarrying and well before all of the stones necessary for construction were quarried. During the assembly of some buildings, additional masonry may have been needed, triggering the resumption of quarrying. In some cases, operations blended together, such as conclusion of transport of earth with the assembly of the earthen substructure. Ultimately, the simultaneous conduct of several tasks must have occurred if construction projects were to be completed before the rainy season.

In addition to the four operations identified above, others are relevant to the construction process (Fig. 2).

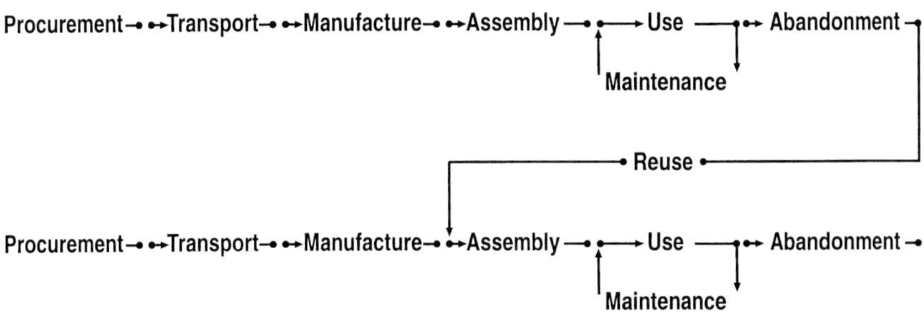

Fig. 2 Outline of the basic operations in construction with reuse of existing building materials.

The most important is reuse, which involves those processes that transform materials from one state to another within society (Schiffer 1976: 39). More specifically, "lateral cycling," a type of reuse, involves "the many processes by which used, but useable, objects circulate within a sociocultural system and persist in time" (Schiffer 1976: 39). Although there may be some repair or maintenance between episodes of use, these modifications are minimal, and the use of the material—principally masonry—is unaltered. Although other types of reuse are evident in Maya architecture (for example, stelae cut and secondarily used as masonry), lateral cycling represents the primary type of reuse in exploitation of existing materials from underlying structures.

QUANTIFYING THE CONSTRUCTION PROCESS

Dissection of a single building into its various components and consideration of behaviors responsible for each of those components must precede quantification of architecture and the building process. Quantification makes two general observations possible. First, the flow of materials identified in the formation process can be examined in greater detail. Although identification of tasks is critical to understanding Maya architecture, quantification of each task provides a basis for reconstructing labor organization and for the degree of economic specialization. Second, quantification of construction is an important means by which Maya architecture, traditionally measured on a nominal scale, can be rephrased or transformed into a more analytically valuable interval scale. That is, quantification allows the researcher to describe different architectural works not simply as "massive" or "monumental" but rather with a numeric cost, thus reducing all buildings to a single common denominator. Assuming that construction cost is related to power and/or status, the researcher can pursue quantification as an important analytic step in the comparative assessment of sociopolitical relations (Erasmus 1965; Carmean 1991; Abrams 1994).

To exemplify this quantification of buildings as dynamic sites, I consider three buildings from the site of Copan: Structures 9N-82 C, 9N-70, and 3O-28. The first two structures were masonry residences occupied by a very high ranking lord and a moderately ranked lord, respectively, during the Late Classic period. In contrast to these elite structures, the third structure is a commoner wattle-and-daub house. After each has been outlined and quantified, the organization of labor responsible for their construction is presented.

9N–82 C

Structure 9N-82 C (Fig. 3), the central building of "The House of the Bacabs," is one of the most studied elite residential structures at Copan (Webster and Abrams 1983; Webster, Fash, and Abrams 1986; Webster 1989). Its second and final episode of construction, built in A.D. 787 (Riese 1989), with its thick masonry walls and its high vaulted roof, is one of the most energetically demanding work projects in the elite residential zone of Las Sepulturas, located east of the main center. The political position represented by the occupant of this structure, as reflected in the cost of residential architecture, was that of a maximal lineage head, second in social power only to the king of Copan (Abrams 1994: 85). It was selected for this analysis because it illustrates the construction process for high-cost buildings that underwent vertical expansion and renovation.

Let us consider the costs of building this structure as though it were built as a single construction event, with no reuse of underlying materials (Table 1, column 3). The total cost of this building was estimated to be 10,686 person-days (p-d), based on the method of quantification in Abrams (1994). Each stage of construction demanded unequal labor expenditures: procurement of materials required about 9% of the total cost, transport about 49%, manufacture

Fig. 3 Structure 9N-82 C without vaulted roof in place.

about 39%, and construction about 4% (Table 2). Thus, the dominant costs of construction were not in the final assembly of the building but rather in moving raw materials and manufacturing masonry and plaster. Moreover, if all of the costs associated with masonry (excluding the actual building of walls) and plaster are summed, we see that masonry demanded 6994 p-d, or 65%, and plaster required 2568 p-d, or 24%, of the total cost of construction. Collectively, these architectural components demanded 89% of the total cost, which reconfirms that status distinctions within Maya society can be justifiably inferred from the presence and abundance of plastered and faced masonry walls and roofs. These high costs further suggest that the reuse of masonry would have been a serious consideration in the design and placement of future architecture.

This reintroduces the question of reuse. Structure 9N-82 C-2, the stage immediately beneath the final construction, consisted of a masonry substructure, but the type and quality of the earlier superstructure is currently unknown. For illustrative purposes (Fig. 4), I have quantified the evident earlier substructure as savings toward construction of the final structure (Table 1, column 1). In addition, I have quantified that known masonry substructure and a hypothetical masonry superstructure with a beam-and-mortar roof because this type of building may also have been reused for construction of Structure 9N-82 C (Table 1, column 2). If we consider only the reuse of the substructural

Table 1. Costs of Building Structure 9N-82 C (in Person-Days)

	9N-82 C-2 Substructure Savings	9N-82 C-2 Substructure and Superstructure Savings	9N-82 C If Built with No Reused Materials
Procurement	304	507	928
earth	73	73	111
cobbles	44	44	68
tuff	187	390	749
Transport	1,327	2,156	5,217
earth	101	101	204
cobbles	269	269	414
tuff	957	1,786	3,825
plaster	0	0	774
Manufacture	488	1,020	4,164
masonry	488	1,020	2,370
plaster	0	0	1,699
sculpture	0	0	95
Construction	0	0	377
walls	0	0	218
fill	0	0	47
cobbling	0	0	17
plastering	0	0	95
TOTAL COST or SAVINGS	2,119	3,683	10,686

Table 2. Comparative Percentages in Construction Process of the Three Structures, Assuming No Reuse Savings

	82 C	70 D	3O-28
Procurement	8.7	10.7	7.5
earth	1	0.4	0.6
cobbles	0.6	0.1	1.5
tuff	7	10.2	0
Transport	48.8	48.4	25.4
earth	1.9	0.5	9
cobbles	3.9	1.5	16.4
tuff	35.8	41.6	0
plaster	7.2	4.9	0
Manufacture	39	37.2	4.5
masonry	22.2	26.5	0
plaster	15.9	10.7	0
sculpture	0.9	0	0
Construction	3.5	3.7	62.7

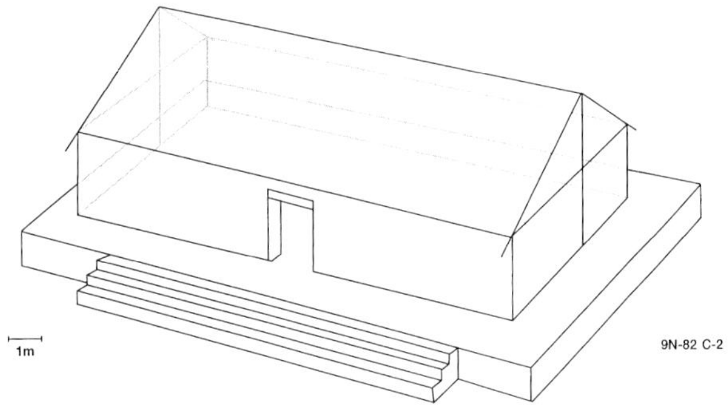

Fig. 4 Reconstruction of Structure 9N-82 C-2.
Drawing by Samuel Girton based on data from Webster, Fash, and Abrams 1986.

component, reuse would have reduced the final cost by 2119 p-d, or about 20%. This general figure does not include the cost of destruction or, more accurately, the cost of dismantling the masonry from the substructure. Most of the 2119 p-d saved are associated with masonry; in terms of manufacture savings of the masonry alone, reused masonry saved 488 p-d of a total of 2370 p-d, or about 21%. When all of the costs associated with masonry are reviewed, we see that about 24% of the masonry costs (1632/6944 p-d) are eliminated (from Table 1). If Structure 9N-82 C-2 consisted of the masonry substructure and a masonry superstructure supporting a beam-and-mortar roof and all available materials were reused to their fullest, then 3683 p-d of labor would have been saved in the ensuing construction of Structure 9N-82 C. This represents a savings of 34% on the cost of the final structure. If this earlier structure bore a vaulted roof, the savings through reuse would approximate a 45% reduction in the building of Structure 9N-82 C. The inference is that reuse of earlier materials was quite significant in reducing the cost of ensuing construction and, thus, provides a cautionary note concerning assessment of the evolution of power inferred from final-phase construction costs alone.

To build this latest structure, however, meant removing the entire superstructure, an easy task if it was composed of perishable material. However, if the superstructure was composed of masonry, then increasing the height of the substructure would involve block-by-block removal of the entire superstructure, with each block presumably placed in the courtyard. Although I have no specific costs for the dismantling process, we can presume at this stage of research that it was not particularly costly. I base this on two observations: (1) the cost of building a superstructure is itself low, comprising only 4% of the total building process; and (2) to judge from observations of workers removing walls during the restoration process at Copan, dismantling took far less time than building. Nonetheless, more research needs to be conducted on this topic.

Collectively, we see that there is a sizable reduction in cost—between 20% and 45%—by reusing underlying structures. This certainly played an important role in decisions made by architects and the elite concerning the placement of houses and the orchestration of construction projects.

Building Structure 9N–82 C. Structure 9N-82 C, if built with reused materials from the substructure of 9N-82 C-2, required an estimated 8567 p-d (10686 minus 2119 p-d). If built over a period of 60 to 100 days, then approximately 80 to 130 workers participated in this building project. Because neither the immediate courtyard unit nor the collection of courtyards in this group could have provided sufficient laborers, given demographic and status parameters, commoners from rural courtyards must have been the actual laborers. As suggested elsewhere (Abrams 1994), these laborers most likely were members of the lineage headed by the lord residing in Structure 9N-82 C, with the labor being recruited within a system of rotating obligations to the lineage administrators. This type of recruitment was part of a broader institutional framework involving festivities and redistributive returns, although it is possible that this scale of work assumed some elements of corvée or mandatory labor obligation available to the highest ranking lords of corporate units within a lineage.

The overwhelming majority of laborers were nonspecialists, some of whom probably participated in more than one task, given the differential time requirements and the overlapping scheduling of tasks. The fact that upward of 90% of the labor force were nonspecialists allows for this use of workers in multiple activities. One important exception, however, is plaster manufacturers. These producers were seasonal specialists responsible for providing lime plaster on an annual basis for various levels of the elite (Abrams and Freter 1996). Not only was the demand for, and cost of, lime plaster relatively high in the initial construction of a building, but plaster was essential in the maintenance of elite structures. In terms of the formation processes involving maintenance, plaster stands out as a critical component—one that could not be overlooked.

9N–70

Structure 9N-70 is the masonry structure of a middle-ranked elite household located on the west side in Patio C of Group 9N-8 at Copan (Hendon et al. 1990). Four features made the building desirable for study: (1) it is more modest in cost than Structure 9N-82 C; (2) it experienced several episodes of construction and reuse; (3) it provides a comparison with the costs of building substructures relative to superstructures; and (4) it illustrates the building process from the perspective of horizontal expansion.

The first form of this structure—9N-70 A—was a simple wattle-and-daub residence built on a low, 65 cm masonry substructure (Fig. 5). The cost of construction is estimated at about 125 p-d (Table 3), using the same method of quantification that was applied to all structures in this analysis. This stage itself represents a measure of status higher than commoner, being approximately twice the cost of the average commoner structure because of its masonry rather than cobble substructural retaining walls. The building was then significantly modified through horizontal expansion of the substructure, which now supports a masonry superstructure with a beam-and-mortar roof (Fig. 5). Without reuse of the previous building, this version—9N-70 B—would have cost 1413 p-d. By incorporating the reusable components of Structure 9N-70 A, the builders would have saved 58 p-d, thus reducing the cost to 1355 p-d, only a 4% savings.

The next modification, resulting in 9N-70 C, was a horizontal expansion of the substructure that provided added work surface (Fig. 6). Removing the north wall of the 70 B substructure and adding the necessary materials would have cost approximately 93 p-d, not a particularly costly project. Had no earlier material been reused, the total structure would have cost 1506 p-d.

The final modification discussed here—70 D—involved lateral expansion of both the substructure and the superstructure (Fig. 7). Adding the superstructure would have been more difficult architecturally; doing so would have required removing the superstructural north wall and supporting the roof during construction of the addition. Most of the new superstructure would have been built before removal of the north wall, and thus these stones would have been part of the new superstructural walls close to the edge of the old building. The materials removed from 70 C and incorporated into 70 D—essentially the north wall—would have saved 205 p-d, and the total cost to build the additional superstructure would have been 1031 p-d. Had Structure 9N-70 D been built with no materials from any ancestral structure, it would have cost 2537 p-d.

In terms of costs of construction, it is evident that horizontal expansion of a substructure was rather modest compared with lateral expansion of a superstructure (1031:93, or 11:1). Less obvious is that both of these types of modifications were quite limited in comparison with the vertical expansion witnessed for Structure 9N-82 C, which required more than 8000 p-d. A comparison of the percentages of labor expenditures per task for Structures 9N-82 C and 9N-70 D (Table 2), however, shows considerable similarity; thus, arguably the

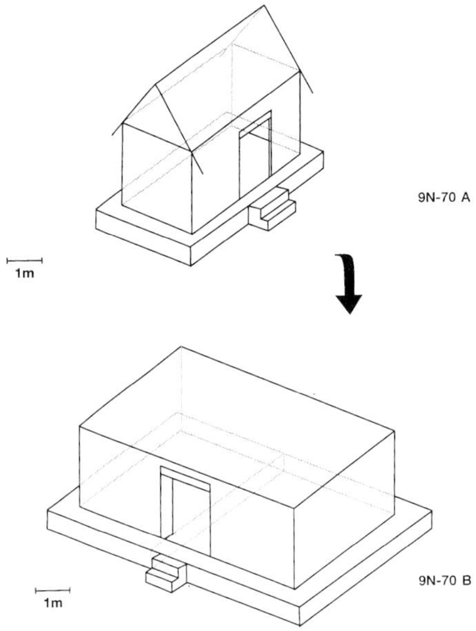

Fig. 5 Structures 9N-70 A and B.
Drawing by Samuel Girton based on data from Hendon et al. 1990.

TABLE 3. COSTS OF CONSTRUCTING STRUCTURE 9N-70 (IN PERSON-DAYS)

	70 A	70 B	70 C	70 D
Procurement	13.3	147.1	156.3	270.3
earth	1.6	5.1	8.8	9.4
cobbles	0.3	1.5	1.6	2.6
tuff	11.4	140.5	145.9	258.3
Transport	57.4	673.2	712.6	1228.9
earth	2.2	7.0	12.1	12.9
cobbles	3.7	21.0	22.5	37.8
tuff	46.5	573.8	595.6	1005
plaster	5	71.4	82.4	123.2
Manufacture	40.7	522.8	560.5	943.2
masonry	29.7	366.1	380.1	672.8
plaster	11	156.7	180.4	270.4
Construction	13.8	69.6	76.6	94.3
TOTAL	125.2	1413	1506	2537
Reuse	58	1413	1506	
Cost minus savings	125.2	1355	93	1031

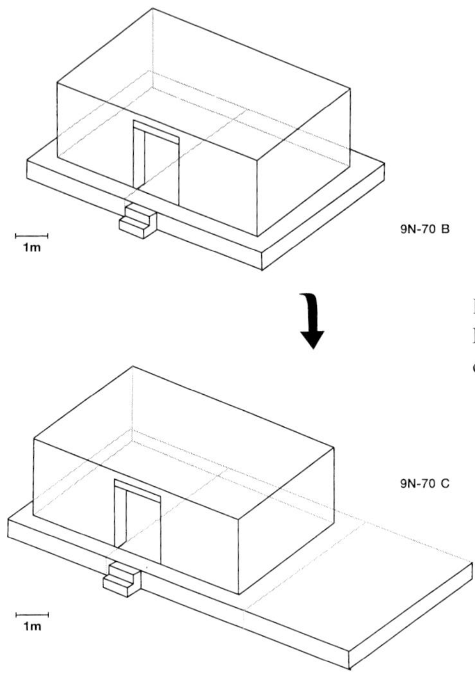

Fig. 6 Structures 9N-70 B and C. Drawing by Samuel Girton based on data from Hendon et al. 1990.

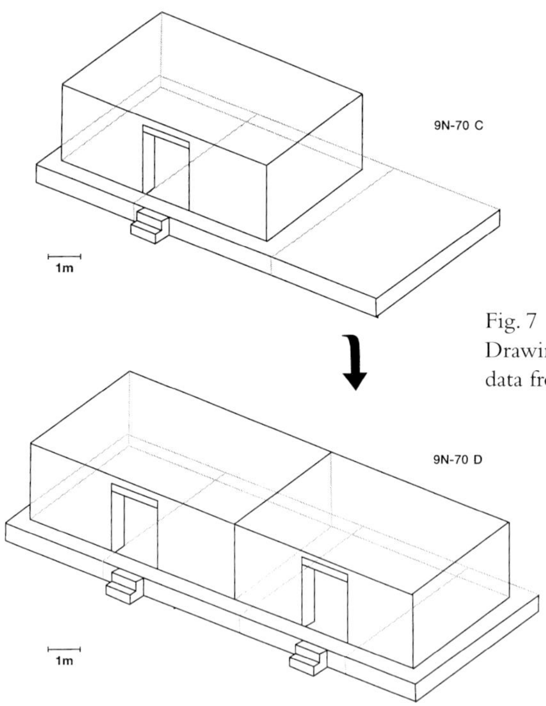

Fig. 7 Structures 9N-70 C and D. Drawing by Samuel Girton based on data from Hendon et al. 1990.

sequence of scheduling tasks and workers was similar, albeit with far fewer workers involved in the construction of Structure 9N-70.

Building Structure 9N-70. The number of laborers who participated in construction of even the most costly stage of Structure 9N-70 was likely between 15 and 20. These people were drawn from courtyards other than Patio C and were subordinate to the elite households of Patio C. The work would have been less strenuous and performed within the context of less sociopolitical distance between the lord and the laborers than existed in the construction of 9N-82 C; thus, the mood may have been more festive (Udy 1959; Abrams 1989).

There emerges an interesting pattern to constructing Structure 9N-70, assuming that the four episodes of construction were separated by time. The first and third phases required rather small expenditures of energy, whereas the second and fourth received more substantial and relatively equal outlays. These more costly building episodes involved between 10 and 20 nonspecialized commoners, whereas the first and third construction projects needed only three to five people. The first modification (70 B) may reflect then a rise in status and power—in essence, the establishment of that household within the expanding hierarchy of the elite in the context of instituting state-level power. The next modification is more a functional alteration than one relating to status, and it involved few workers. The final modification, however, did require the labor from a few sociopolitically attached commoner courtyards. This new construction may have commemorated the ascension of a new lord who celebrated his assumption of power by rebuilding and expanding his new residence or perhaps reflected some other measure of heightened social power, as expressed in a larger number of wives.

To speculate, some of the workers who participated in one building project may have contributed to that structure's subsequent modifications. For example, an adolescent who may have assisted in the substructural expansion of Structure 9N-70 C may, 10 or 20 years later, have been conscripted to build Structure 9N-70 D. Given that scribes and accountants probably monitored participation for each project, those familiar with a structure would have been the likely choice as laborers for later work. This notion of recurrent participation may ideologically reinforce the centripetal nature of homes as elements in a sacred landscape.

3O–28

Structure 3O-28 (Fig. 8), located in the Petapilla region of the foothills of the Copan pocket (Gonlin n.d.a; n.d.b), was a typical Late Classic commoner

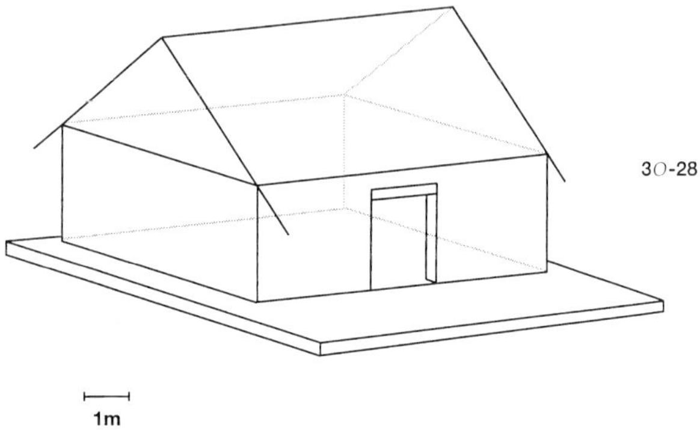

Fig. 8 Structure 3O-28.
Drawing by Samuel Girton based on Gonlin n.d.b.

residence. This wattle-and-daub structure was built in one episode, was occupied in one continuous span of occupation, and experienced no formal modifications. This pattern of short-term construction, use, and abandonment is quite typical of commoner structures in this foothill zone (Paine and Freter 1996).

The costs of construction are quite modest—only 67 p-d (Table 4)—and characteristic of most commoner structures. Far fewer components composed the structure; the absence of masonry and plaster, clearly the most costly components as well as sensitive indices of social power, accounted for the low building cost. As a consequence, the percentages of time expended in various tasks differed considerably for this structure compared with the two masonry buildings presented above (Table 2).

Building Structure 3O-28. The organization and recruitment of laborers in this work project was likely on a familial basis, involving two to five kin or peers of the household head of the residence. Whereas recruitment for construction of elite masonry structures was effected within the context of a redistributive network of obligations, recruitment for building the commoner residence was clearly within a reciprocal system; the low cost and scale of construction suggest as much.

CONCLUSION

The availability of the Maya architectural record, coupled with the cultural richness embodied by such architecture, make this category of artifacts especially well suited for archaeological inquiry. One of the key areas of study in Maya prehistory is the question of the emergence, acceptance, and use of po-

TABLE 4. COSTS OF CONSTRUCTING STRUCTURE 30-28 (IN PERSON-DAYS)

	Costs
Procurement	5
earth	4
cobbles	1
Transport	17
earth	6
cobbles	11
Manufacture	3
cobbles	3
Construction	42
substructure walls	3
superstructure	39
TOTAL COST	67

litical power, and the study of power, as created and expressed by the ancient Maya, is perhaps best approached through architectural remains.

Architectural energetics, as the means by which architecture can be quantified, is used to describe the life history of three structures from the Classic site of Copan, Honduras. These three structures represent households that held distinct positions within a six-tiered structure of social power during the Late Classic period (Abrams 1994). Rather than rely on the final cost of construction as the basis for comparison, the present analysis quantified the changes in costs through the use life of these buildings. The methodology here explicitly involved quantifying reuse (when applicable) as part of the formation processes in the evolution of architecture. It was found that reuse can result in a 40+% reduction in subsequent expenditures for the largest of masonry structures. This direction of architectural research is offered to advance our ability to observe the expression of power from generation to generation concomitant with the dynamics of state growth and decline.

The effectiveness of analytic methods, however, is a function of the quality of the archaeological data. Future research must focus on quantifying more structures at many more sites, and excavation should be conducted with energetic analysis in mind. If this approach to architecture is furthered, it can lead to a richly documented, dynamic picture of the evolution of social power on a household basis for the ancient Maya.

Acknowledgments I would like to thank the Instituto Hondureño de Antropología e Historia for permission to work in Copan. I would further like to thank Bill Sanders, Dave Webster, and Ann Freter for support and encouragement of this research as well as two anonymous reviewers for their constructive recommendations. Thanks are extended to Sam Girton for drafting the illustrations. Special thanks go to Elizabeth Boone for her courtesy and grace at the Dumbarton Oaks conference and to Steve Houston for his kind invitation to participate in the conference, his editorial insights on this chapter, and his collegiality and good spirit. Any errors in this chapter are, however, my own.

BIBLIOGRAPHY

Abrams, Elliot

1987 Economic Specialization and Construction Personnel in Classic Period Copan, Honduras. *American Antiquity* 52: 485–499.

1989 Architecture and Energy: An Evolutionary Approach. *Archaeological Method and Theory*, vol. 1 (Michael Schiffer, ed.): 47–87. University of Arizona Press, Tucson.

1994 *How the Maya Built Their World: Energetics and Ancient Architecture.* University of Texas Press, Austin.

Abrams, Elliot, and AnnCorinne Freter

1996 A Late Classic Lime Plaster Kiln from the Maya Centre of Copan, Honduras. *Antiquity* 60: 422–428.

Carmean, Kelli

1991 Architectural Labor Investment and Social Stratification at Sayil, Yucatan, Mexico. *Latin American Antiquity* 2: 151–165.

Erasmus, Charles

1965 Monumental Building: Some Field Experiments. *Southwestern Journal of Anthropology* 21: 277–301.

Gonlin, Nancy

n.d.a The Architectural Variation of Two Small Sites in the Copan Valley, Honduras: A Rural/Urban Dichotomy? M.A. thesis, Pennsylvania State University, 1985.

n.d.b Rural Household Archaeology at Copan, Honduras. Ph.D. dissertation, Pennsylvania State University, 1993.

Hendon, Julia A., Ricardo Agurcia F., William L. Fash, and Eloisa Aguilar P.

1990 Excavaciones en 9N-8, conjunto del patio C. In *Excavaciones en el área urbana de Copán,* vol. 2 (William T. Sanders, ed.): 11–109. Instituto Hondureño de Antropología e Historia, Tegucigalpa.

Hyman, David

1970 *Precolumbian Cements: A Study of the Calcareous Cements in Prehispanic Mesoamerican Building Construction.* Johns Hopkins University Press, Baltimore.

Littmann, Edwin

1962 Ancient Mesoamerican Mortars, Plasters, and Stuccos: Floor Construction at Uaxactun. *American Antiquity* 28: 100–103.

Morley, Sylvanus G.

1946 *The Ancient Maya.* Stanford University Press, Stanford, Calif.

Morris, Earl, Jean Charlot, and A. A. Morris

1931 *The Temple of the Warriors at Chichen Itza, Yucatan.* Carnegie Institution, Publication 406. Washington, D.C.

Paine, Richard, and AnnCorinne Freter

1996 Environmental Degradation and the Classic Maya Collapse at Copan, Honduras (a.d. 600–1250): Evidence from Studies of Household Survival. *Ancient Mesoamerica* 7: 37–47.

RIESE, BERTHOLD

1989 The Inscription of the Sculptured Bench of the House of the Bacabs. In *The House of the Bacabs, Copan, Honduras* (David Webster, ed.): 82–88. Dumbarton Oaks, Washington, D.C.

ROYS, LAWRENCE

1934 *The Engineering Knowledge of the Maya.* Carnegie Institution, Publication 436, no. 6: 27–105. Washington, D.C.

SATTERTHWAITE, LINTON

1954 *Piedras Negras Archaeology: Architecture,* pt. 6: *Unclassified Buildings and Substructures.* University Museum, University of Pennsylvania, Philadelphia.

SCHIFFER, MICHAEL

1976 *Behavioral Archaeology.* Academic Press, New York.

SMITH, A. L.

1950 *Uaxactún, Guatemala: Excavations of 1931–1937.* Carnegie Institution, Publication 588. Washington, D.C.

STEPHENS, JOHN L.

1841 *Incidents of Travel in Central America, Chiapas, and Yucatan,* vol. 1. Dover, New York.

UDY, STANLEY

1959 *The Organization of Work.* Human Relations Area File Press, New Haven, Conn.

WAUCHOPE, ROBERT

1938 *Modern Maya Houses: A Study of Their Archaeological Significance.* Carnegie Institution, Publication 502. Washington, D.C.

WEBSTER, DAVID (ED.)

1989 *The House of the Bacabs, Copan, Honduras.* Dumbarton Oaks, Washington, D.C.

WEBSTER, DAVID, AND ELLIOT ABRAMS

1983 An Elite Compound at Copan, Honduras. *Journal of Field Archaeology* 10: 285–296.

WEBSTER, DAVID, WILLIAM FASH, AND ELLIOT ABRAMS

1986 Excavaciones en el conjunto 9N-8, patio A (operación VIII). In *Excavaciones en el área urbana de Copán,* vol. 1 (William Sanders, ed.): 155–317. Instituto Hondureño de Antropología e Historia, Tegucigalpa.

What Do Houses Mean? Approaches to the Analysis of Classic Maya Commoner Residences

KEVIN J. JOHNSTON
OHIO STATE UNIVERSITY
AND
NANCY GONLIN
BELLEVUE COMMUNITY COLLEGE

FOR THE PAST CENTURY, Mayanists have devoted much attention to monumental public buildings, many of which are elaborately decorated with sculpture and hieroglyphs. This fascination with elite-commissioned architecture is readily understood; after all, many such buildings are prominent, aesthetically dramatic, and well preserved. Imbued with meaning by their makers, monumental structures have been the object of intense study by specialists hoping to decode these meanings, which reflect past cultural perspectives. As this volume demonstrates, archaeologists and art historians continue to develop innovative and productive approaches to monumental buildings. But do the meanings conveyed in large buildings constitute all those that Mayanists can expect to recover from ancient buildings? What meanings, if any, are implied by modest, vernacular buildings, hundreds of thousands of which dot the lowland forest floor? What do these buildings tell us about ancient Maya culture and society? Although individual Late Classic commoner houses are quite modest, collectively they outnumber public buildings, and their total architectural mass may very well be greater than that of all monumental buildings combined. The building type most frequently constructed by the Maya, in other words, was the commoner house—small, predominantly rural, and largely perishable.

Mayanists reconstruct cultural meanings—ideologies, worldviews, ontologies—through the study of architecture and art. We must ask ourselves, Whose meanings do such studies retrieve, and how representative are such meanings of Maya society as a whole? To what degree did commoners—the great, silent, and shadowy mass whose labors constituted the economic foundation of Maya society—share in the views conveyed in monumental constructions? To address such questions, archaeologists must examine the houses of the commoner Maya.

This chapter reviews the principal methodological and theoretical approaches that Mayanists can or have already taken to the recovery of meaning from Late Classic commoner houses. We discuss traditional and new approaches to architecture, examine what domestic architecture can and cannot tell us about ancient lifeways, emphasize the importance of nonstructural remains and ambient space, and review the implications of ethnoarchaeological studies of modern Maya residential patterns. We conclude that to understand the meaning of ancient houses archaeologists must, somewhat ironically, examine not just the house but the spaces and settings that surround it.

APPROACHES TO ARCHITECTURE

Typically, archaeologists adopt three principal approaches to houses and households. We describe these as a cultural approach, a social approach, and a functional approach. Not all aspects of these approaches are mutually exclusive. Indeed, there is some overlap between approaches because of intellectual cross-fertilization and because the development of some approaches is historically interrelated (e.g., the social perspective is an outgrowth of the functional one). We define these three approaches as follows.

The cultural approach focuses on the *house* to reveal culture. Rarely employed in the Maya lowlands, this approach is part of a larger theoretical paradigm that many anthropologists and archaeologists characterize as structuralist. Proponents of this approach identify houses as expressive media that communicate messages about power, gender relations, status, and humankind's relationship to the cosmos. Houses are viewed as stages where culture is enacted and reproduced through daily human action. The principal objective of this structuralist approach is identification of cultural or ideational (as opposed to architectural) "structures," defined by Bourdieu (1985: 95) as acquired systems of generative schemes and dispositions objectively adjusted to particular sociohistorical conditions. Stated more simply, such structures are the mechanisms through whose collective or individual enactment culture is produced and maintained.

The social approach, in contrast, focuses not on culture but on society. Its proponents examine not the house and its ideational load but the *household,* defined as a unit of socioeconomic organization. The social approach then has a socioeconomic emphasis that reflects explicitly materialist, rather than idealist, concerns. We describe this approach as "social," because it is concerned with household organization and economic adaptation—distinctly social phenomena.

The cultural approach and the social approach correspond to two competing archaeological philosophies. As Saunders (1990: 182) observes, the former is a structuralist, initially European approach now embraced by postprocessualists on both sides of the Atlantic; the latter is a positivist approach that underlies contemporary North American processualism. Proponents of the first approach examine the symbolic content and culture-reproducing role of material culture. Proponents of the second approach analyze the spatial disposition and formal attributes of objects (including buildings) thought to have socioeconomic significance.

The third approach, functional explanation, is the chronological antecedent to the social approach, and it enjoyed its greatest prominence in Maya archaeology from the 1950s through the mid-1980s. Devised originally as an aid to cultural historical reconstruction and settlement pattern analysis, the functional approach examines the house as an artifact endowed predominantly with social organizational (i.e., kinship) meaning. Proponents of this approach are simultaneously concerned with building use, or "function" (i.e., who did what where), as are proponents of the social approach. But the latter, unlike the former, examine not the house but the socioeconomic (as opposed to the kinship) organization of its occupants. Note that the functional approach among Mayanists should be distinguished from the "functional*ist*" school of theory (Jarvies 1973) of largely British origin once widely embraced by social anthropologists and adopted with some modification by many New Archaeologists.

The three approaches may be briefly summarized as follows:

(1) the cultural (or structuralist) approach focuses on the house as an artifact encoded with generative meaning;

(2) the functional approach focuses on the house as an artifact endowed with social organizational meaning;

(3) the social approach focuses on the house and its immediate surroundings to investigate the household (those who occupied the house), defined as a basic unit of socioeconomic adaptation.

As noted above, the partial overlap in attributes of these approaches can be understood in terms of their historical interrelations. The functional approach, deeply embedded in traditional Maya household archaeology, has been practiced predominantly by Mayanists trained before and during the era of New

Archaeology. The social approach, a new and emerging trend in Mesoamerican studies, is an outgrowth of what Schiffer (1988) terms "reconstruction theory," a modification of or reaction to New Archaeology that has gained considerable prominence among Americanists during the past ten years. Recently, Mayanists have begun to carry out projects with objectives that embrace or are consistent with the theoretical and methodological perspective of the social approach. Unlike the other two, the cultural approach is derived primarily from a European structuralist position. Widely embraced by British archaeologists, the approach has been largely ignored by Mesoamericanists, most of whom prefer a more materialist theoretical stance.

The potential of the structuralist approach for Maya architectural research remains virtually unexplored. Although widely embraced by Europeans and many North Americanists, the approach has yet to be received with enthusiasm in Mesoamerica. The reluctance of Mayanists to employ the structuralist method can be attributed to two factors: (1) the method's avowedly antimaterialist theoretical underpinning; and (2) the incompatibility of notions of culture employed by Mayanists and proponents of the structuralist approach. Although structuralist analysis promises to be highly productive when applied to well-preserved, high-status residential architecture, its usefulness for analyzing poorly preserved houses of commoners has yet to be demonstrated.

A fourth, potentially productive, approach to the problem of domestic architectural meaning is direct historical analogy. Proponents of this approach would explain archaeological patterns in ancient residences through reference to ostensibly analogous cultural patterns in modern and ethnohistoric Maya houses. There is sharp disagreement among archaeologists about the merits of this approach—cf. Gould and Watson (1982), Wylie (1985), and Stahl (1993). We do not further consider this subject here because it is highly complex and deserving of a separate, lengthy discussion.

Detailed discussions of the cultural, functional, and social approaches follow below. We begin with a review of the theoretical underpinnings of the cultural perspective and its potential contribution to the analysis of residential architecture of Maya commoners. Next we examine the accomplishments of the functional approach. We conclude by advocating an explicitly social alternative.

THE CULTURAL OR STRUCTURALIST APPROACH TO ARCHITECTURE

What we define as the cultural approach to houses derives from a structuralist paradigm (Sahlins 1976: 32) in which culture is defined as a complex system of descriptive, interpretive, and generative signs that inform behavior by being enacted. The principal proponents of this approach, Bourdieu (1985) and

Giddens (1979, 1982), view culture as an ideational screen or meaning system through which individuals conceptualize themselves, others, and the world around them. Central to this perspective is the assumption that individuals reproduce and express cultural structures by enacting them in daily practice (Hodder 1989a). Because practice transpires within the context of culturally ordered space (either the built environment or the marked or interpreted landscape), it is constrained and informed by the meanings that the space encodes.

Houses are a case in point. To the degree that they encode cultural meanings, houses become both vehicles for communication of meanings and stages for reproduction of those meanings in the context of daily household practice. In nonliterate cultures, Bourdieu (1977: 89) proposes, houses are "the principal locus for the objectification of the generative schemes" that are culture; "through the intermediary of the divisions and hierarchies [that the house] sets up between things, persons, and practices, this tangible classifying system continuously inculcates and reinforces the taxonomic principles underlying all the arbitrary provisions of this culture." Houses, in other words, are "structuring structures"—culturally loaded spaces that socialize by encouraging practices consistent with the meanings that they encode. The spatial divisions of the Saami residence, for example, reflect a specific system of values and gender relations upon which Saami society is based (Yates 1989). Saami regard these architectural divisions as transformations of ritual divisions of the universe. Such houses map in miniature a cosmos structured by specific kinds of relations (see Blier 1987). Through their objectification in architecture and reproduction in practice, these relations become naturalized. Thus, the relationship between social and spatial interactions is reflexive because production of space is linked to reproduction of social relations (Saunders 1990). Sahlins (1976: 37) describes the relationship as follows: "A 'model of' and a 'model for'—to adopt Geertz's terms—the house functions as the medium by which a system of culture is realized as an order of action."

Encoded in houses are systems of meanings that function as a kind of language or text (Hodder 1989a). These systems of meanings are generative—that is, through their enactment they re-create structure. Architecture, like all material culture, communicates as a language composed of a descriptive syntax and a generative grammar (Hanson and Hillier 1982; Hillier and Hanson 1984; Patrick 1985). The organizing principles of that language can be described schematically (Hillier and Hanson 1984) and, in some cases of prehistoric architecture, they can be reconstructed archaeologically (Sutro and Downing 1988; Sanders 1990; Blanton 1989). Hillier and Hanson (1984) offer a descriptive syntax for analyzing the relationship between built spatial organization and social organization. In all societies, they claim, principles of spatial organization are the organizing principles of social reproduction. Invoking a structuralist terminology, they propose that these principles encode the "deep structures" of culture. Analysts are encouraged to examine architecture in terms of universal principles such as "permeability" or access, the organization of which is thought to be homologous with social organization—cf. Small (1987) and Foster (1989). Intellectual antecedents are found in Hall's (1966) theory of proxemics—how a people's use of space is an aspect of culture. Proxemic codes, like the abstract codes of language, inform us about the way people think about their spatial world (Hodder 1989b: 72).

The meaning systems encoded in architecture have two aspects. First, the code of meanings can be highly abstract, preconscious, and agentless, as in pansocietal house forms that reproduce a generally accepted model of cosmological order. Blanton (1994) refers to these meanings as "canonical" messages. Yet culture is not reproduced purely through the enactment of unconscious, abstract structures that precede thought and action (Hodder 1989a, 1989b). Rather, human agency is involved in the generation of certain meanings, especially those meanings through which power is negotiated and established. This leads to the second aspect of meaning systems: some are "created and recreated in the context of specific power relations through the strategies of agents" (Hodder 1989b: 74). Indeed, dominant groups and individuals manipulate aspects of meaning systems for their own benefit. At issue is the difference between the ideational, defined as the abstract, pansocietal phenomenon of "culture," as defined above, and ideology, which might be described as the culture of power.

Social control as a mechanism of power is encoded in architecture, particularly public architecture, which serves as a stage where structures of power, privilege, and inequality are created, enacted, and re-created. The language-based system of analysis devised by Hillier and Hanson (1984) and others can be used to decipher the deliberate manipulation of meaning that architecture encodes. Access analysis, for instance, reveals strategies for social control accomplished through control of space (Moore 1992; Isbell, Brewster-Wray, and Spickard 1991). Given that hierarchy is founded on differential access to desired resources, on the stage of public architecture hierarchy may be enforced and displayed by limiting access to prestige-endowing space. In the home, the principal negotiations for power are those involving relations of gender, age, and status (Tringham 1991). Hypothetically, the symbols of negotiation or, in some cases, the structures of domination should be encoded in, and thus be recoverable from, the remnants of the house and its contents.

This synthetic aspect of the structuralist approach is attractive because it unites the idealist's concern with abstract structures and the materialist's concern with the structure of power. Unlike most materialist analyses, however, the structuralist approach focuses not on the socioeconomic or social substrata of hierarchy but on its symbolic expression in architecture. In the case of houses, the focus is not on the household that occupied the house but on the building itself in its symbolic-communicative role. What the household does—how it is constituted in terms of social organization and economy—is less important than how the household thinks about and thus creates aspects of itself through the vehicle of generative symbols. According to many proponents of structuralism, this "thinking about" activity generates behaviors and social relations that lie at the heart of domesticity. Of course, how well in ancient societies the ideal (the symbolic) actually corresponded to the real (past behavior and organization) is very difficult to determine archaeologically. Indeed, use of the approach requires an epistemological leap of faith that not all anthropologists are willing to take (Leach 1978).

The structuralist (anthropological), or postprocessualist (archaeological), approach to houses is most popular among archaeologists working in Europe and other parts of the Old World—e.g., Hodder (1990), Samson (1990), and Yates (1989). When considering the generative aspect of structure and symbol, some proponents of structuralism go so far as to suggest that the cultural meaning systems encoded in symbols determine the architectural form of the occupied house (Donley-Reid 1990). Given the materialist bias of many North American-trained archaeologists, it is perhaps not surprising that many of those working in the Maya lowlands are hesitant to endorse a perspective widely perceived to be fundamentally and avowedly antimaterialist. Although this perception oversimplifies the structuralist perspective (Hodder 1989b), some prominent structuralists, including Hodder (1989a, 1990), assert that in instances of social change the symbolic is causally antecedent to the economic—a position wholly inconsistent with materialist expectations about cultural causality—e.g., Steward (1955), Binford (1962), Sanders and Price (1968), and Sanders, Parsons, and Santley (1979).

The structuralist approach promises to reveal both culture and ideology (defined in the materialist sense as ideational structures that contribute to politicoeconomic domination and control), yet it has been little used in Latin American archaeology, including the Maya lowlands. The few attempted applications of the method have been speculative, exploratory, and highly experimental. Hammond (1975: 78–83) used the technique of access analysis to examine communication within the Lubaantun site core, but his objectives and theoretical framework were not those of structuralist archaeology. Ashmore (1989, 1991, 1992) employs a structuralist idiom in her examinations of Maya monumental architecture and ideology,[1] but her methodology and general theoretical perspective are predominantly processualist. Like Blanton (1989) and perhaps Moore (1992), Ashmore develops a position that falls midway between traditional processualism and recent structuralist theory. That is, she describes power not as a state that, because it is constituted and negotiated through practice, constantly is "coming into being" (Hodder 1989b). Rather, power in her more materialist view is a manipulated (rather than generated), preexisting entity founded in political and socioeconomic relationships, the true nature of which is disguised by religious precepts that refer to cosmological rather than mere human imperatives.

Like many anthropologists, Mayanists tend to define culture as a system of meanings embodied in symbols. These meanings describe a perceived world and the place of human beings in it. Cultural conceptions about nature and society are objectified in symbols, which can take material form in durable, publicly displayed objects. In the Maya archaeological record, symbols endure as art and iconography, which specialists analyze to reveal aspects of the imagined or conceptual universe—ancient culture—that these encode. Described as "ancient idea systems" (Ashmore 1991: 218) and "the conceptual systems of ancient civilizations" (Tate 1992: xi), culture in this highly symbolic view closely resembles Geertz's notion of worldview: a people's "picture of the way things in sheer actuality are, their concepts of nature, of self, of society . . . their most comprehensive ideas of order" (Geertz 1973: 127). Models of Maya culture developed from symbolic data emphasize the role of rules, patterns, and conceptual regularities in the elaboration of social life. Culture then is normative, inclusive, and broadly defined as how the Maya perceived their world.

Given that their conceptualization of culture differs so fundamentally from that embraced by postprocessualists, Mayanists not surprisingly resist the structuralist approach to architectural analysis. Whereas the postprocessualist perspective on culture revolves around notions of structure and is anchored in concepts like "habitus" (Bourdieu 1985) and "domus" (Hodder 1990), Mayanists and Mesoamericanists generally regard culture as equivalent to religion, cosmology, worldview, and the political ideology of a ruling elite (Willey 1973, 1976; Coe 1981; Sharer and Ashmore 1979; Demarest 1992). As far as many Mayanists are concerned, the organizing principles of culture are expressed

[1] "By Classic times, Maya builders were drawing from a standard grammar but flexible vocabulary of spatial expression" (Ashmore 1992: 173).

graphically, formally, and unambiguously in royal art, architecture, and inscriptions. Thus, Mayanists hoping to reconstruct culture tend to focus their attentions exclusively on that evocative body of data—e.g., Freidel, Schele, and Parker (1993). Why bother with houses, many would argue, when what matters most ideationally is spelled out clearly in durable graphic media? Of course, by equating the ideational aspect of culture with ideology (in the materialist sense), many Mayanists dismiss as elite-generated epiphenomena precisely those aspects of culture that are the central focus of structuralist analysis—cf. Demarest (1989).

There are also practical impediments to the application of structuralist methods of analysis to certain kinds of Maya architecture. Whereas large Maya residential structures, such as Copan Type III and IV residences or their equivalent at other sites—cf. Webster (1989)—might profitably be examined from a structuralist perspective, small, poorly preserved commoner residences probably cannot. Symbolic meanings are encoded in all houses, yet the degree to which meanings are recoverable archaeologically varies because of considerable interhousehold variation in socioeconomic factors. As McGuire and Schiffer (1983: 286) observe, residentially mobile households minimize the investment of meaning in durable architectural features as a means of minimizing the costs of new house construction that households absorb periodically. To this end, houses of the residentially mobile generally are built of wood, cane, thatch, and other inexpensive, perishable materials that do not preserve in the archaeological record. Wealthy, residentially stable households, on the other hand, are built with "expensive," highly durable materials like cut stone blocks, which, because they are imperishable, preserve the meanings they encode. Thus, preservation, itself partly governed by socioeconomic variables, determines the degree to which meaning can be recovered from ancient domestic architecture.

Aspects of culture that have not yet been explored by Mayanists include privacy and boundary construction and maintenance. Variously defined as "control of unwanted social interaction" (McGuire and Schiffer 1983: 285) and "the claim of individuals, groups, or institutions to determine . . . when, how, and to what extent information about them is to be communicated to others" (Roberts and Gregor 1971: 199), privacy is a culturally variable but presumably universal phenomenon. At Joya de Ceren (Sheets 1992, 1994), which some have argued is a Maya site (Webster, Gonlin, and Sheets 1997), benches for sleeping and sitting were placed in the innermost rooms of dwellings and in the outer rooms of communal or civic structures (Kievit 1994: 203–204). The differential placement of benches suggests that social access and information transmission varied according to social context. At many lowland Maya sites, benches were similarly placed against back or side walls, locations that provided privacy because they were least visible from the courtyards they faced. The stone walls that compartmentalized the interior spaces of wealthy houses also presumably contributed to the maintenance of privacy. Although the concept helps us to identify the existence of certain patterns of ancient behavior, it does not tell us for whom or under what conditions privacy was maintained. Privacy, in fact, is a poorly defined, highly elusive concept. As Hall (1966) and Roberts and Gregor (1971) note, even within individual societies considerable variation exists in how concepts of privacy are articulated architecturally. Moreover, privacy can be achieved in architectural settings by means (such as curtains or screens) that leave no permanent marks on architecture (Roberts and Gregor 1971: 218). Information provided by Sharer (1994: 467) reminds us that analysts must use caution when employing concepts like privacy. Describing houses along the Río Usumacinta, a seventeenth-century writer mentions the presence of crude wooden beds built to accommodate up to four people. When discussing privacy under conditions such as these we must ask ourselves, For whom did architecture establish privacy? Until archaeologists firmly establish the linkage between architectural spaces and social groupings, fundamental questions such as this cannot adequately be answered.

THE FUNCTIONAL APPROACH TO HOUSES

In contrast to the structuralists, who adopt an idealist perspective to reveal culture (i.e., houses viewed as generative structures that encode key cultural meanings), proponents of the functional approach embrace a materialist concern with socioeconomic phenomena. Underlying this theoretical contrast is an historical one: developed during the 1950s and 1960s, the functional approach incorporates tenets of American processual archaeology that the structural approach, developed more recently and principally by Europeans, rejects. Consistent with processualism (Binford 1981: 198; Hodder 1989a: 253), the functional approach asserts that the meaning of objects (including buildings) lies in their purpose or use. Function is defined in economic and social organizational terms—what a building or room is used for. For example, a small patio group is said to "house" a nuclear family. Within patio groups, some structures function as dormitories, and others function as facilities where tools and dried foods are stored. Archaeologists establish these functions by investigating the formal properties of architecture (size, form, construction materials), the presence or absence of features (hearths, caches, burials), and the composition of artifact assemblages found within houses. Based on the premise that certain features and artifact assemblages are archetypically domestic, archaeologists identify all architectural remains associated with these materials as "houses."[2] Meaning is direct and unambiguous: the presence of artifacts and features indicates function. Proponents of the functional approach typically ask, Is this structure a house, and if so what part of the house is it: dormitory, kitchen, shrine, storage chamber, or other ancillary? Among some proponents, direct historical analogy is a central component of this approach.

The popularity of the functional approach (which has dominated Maya house studies for the past four decades) can be understood in terms of the history of its development. Stung by the criticisms of Kluckhohn (1940), Taylor (1948), and others (Steward and Setzler 1938), who characterized American archaeology as nonanthropological and unscientific, Mayanists in the 1950s adopted several new and promising research methodologies, the most important of which was settlement pattern analysis (Willey et al. 1965; Bullard 1960). Settlement analysis enabled archaeologists, ecologists, and agronomists to attack with renewed vigor and creativity an outstanding problem in Maya studies: the size of the ancient population, its growth rate, and the agricultural means by which it supported itself (Culbert and Rice 1990). Mayanists had long realized that to develop scientifically sound, chronologically accurate models of population growth and size three questions had to be answered. First, which of the many mounds visible on the forest floor were houses? Second, what percentage of houses were occupied during different time periods? Third, within residential patio groups which buildings functioned as "dwellings" or sleeping structures, one of which should be associated with every family or household? Nondwelling building types might include kitchens, shrines, storage huts, and other ancillary structures.

Proponents of the functional approach generally follow a four-step procedure. After establishing a typology of building types (step 1), archaeologists excavate a sample of each building type (step 2) and determine the function of types (step 3) by studying architectural morphology (formal similarity to modern and historic houses) and associated features and artifacts. Structure types associated with "domestic" materials are identified as houses (step 4). With the architectural correlates of domesticity thus documented, archaeologists can thereafter identify houses on the basis of architectural criteria alone, usually through surface survey.

The approach appealed to Mayanists for two reasons. First and foremost, it was methodologically efficient and reasonable. Investigations focused almost

[2] See Johnston n.d. for a critical analysis of this approach.

exclusively on architecture. Buildings were exposed partially or in their entirety to determine chronology, layout, and the sequence of architectural modifications. Archaeologists frequently limited their excavations to a stratigraphic test pit or two through architecture for chronological purposes. Except for chronological probing of stratified middens, extramural space was largely ignored. Second, the approach seemingly confirmed what most archaeologists already assumed to be the case: that architectural form reflects building function (Rapoport 1990: 11), including social function.

Contributing to development of the procedure was the work of several North American archaeologists, who concluded from the publications of social anthropologists (Allen and Richardson 1971) that settlement (Steward 1937; Martin and Rinaldo 1950; Chang 1958; Turner and Lofgren 1966) and artifactual (Deetz 1968; Hill 1966; Longacre 1970) data reveal ancient patterns of family and community kinship, residence, and descent. Perhaps because its outcome was ostensibly anthropological, Mesoamericanists, e.g., Flannery and Coe (1968)—among them many Mayanists, e.g., Haviland (1968) and Fash (1983)—embraced this methodological advance enthusiastically. The function of a house, Mayanists concluded, is to accommodate a family of a particular configuration. Because the social configuration of the house changes during its "developmental cycle"—a social organizational phenomenon identified by social anthropologists during the 1950s (Fortes 1958)—so does the physical configuration of the house change. Changes in house form thus reveal the changing configurations of Maya families (Tourtellot 1988a; Haviland 1988). Studying architectural form and chronology, Mayanists drew inferences about family type and developmental cycle history.

Many Mayanists continue to embrace today, although in somewhat modified form, a functional approach to houses—e.g., Sheehy (1991), Hendon (1991, n.d.), Pyburn (1989), and Gonlin (n.d.). Like the cultural-historical approach to settlement from which it proceeds, the functional approach to houses is largely classificatory and descriptive. Buildings are categorized by "type" according to assumed functions (e.g., house, palace, temple) and details of construction are recounted chronologically. Although, as Webster (this volume) notes, some social organizational inferences can be drawn from residence construction histories, in the case of Maya commoner houses this usually entails correlating certain architectural growth patterns with specific family types. Haviland (1970, 1981, 1988), Tourtellot (1983, 1988a), and others (Fash 1983; Kintz 1983, n.d.), for instance, argue that the houses of extended families undergo diagnostic accretionary growth patterns. Idiosyncratic architectural growth patterns, on the other hand, are attributed to the vicissitudes of the family development cycle (Tourtellot 1988a; Haviland 1988). Employing the functional approach, archaeologists attribute architectural variation to one of two factors: (1) pansocietal social formations (family type) or (2) a universal social developmental cycle. What the approach cannot explain is why some Maya families were extended and others were nuclear, nor can it account for variation in family developmental cycles as evidenced by the idiosyncratic architectural histories of individual residences.

We emphasize that proponents of the functional approach have made many significant contributions to Maya archaeology—see Sharer (1993) for a review. Yet the approach is inherently problematic. Underlying the approach are a series of implicit assumptions, some of which are questionable whereas others are clearly inaccurate. These assumptions can be described as follows:

(1) Families occupy houses.

(2) House form reflects family form.

(3) Most artifacts found on house floors remain in their systemic context.

The problematic nature of the first assumption has been widely discussed by anthropologists, sociologists, and social historians (Hammel and Laslett 1974; Brown 1977; Netting, Wilk, and Arnould 1984; Ashmore and Wilk 1988; Wilk 1984, 1990; Alderson and Sanderson 1991), the majority of whom conclude that it is more accurate to say that houses are occupied by households, a unit of socioeconomic organization, rather than families, a social unit characterized by specific kinship relations. The second assumption is called into question by ethnographic and ethnoarchaeological studies (Wilk 1983; Kamp 1987) indicating that specific house forms correspond to specific family types in some but not all societies. Because this relationship is subject to considerable cross-society variation, it must be critically examined and demonstrated in each case (David 1971). Additionally, the relationship between built form and socioeconomic function is inherently unstable and ambiguous. For instance, building function can change over time (David 1971; Widmer and Sheehy n.d.) with no corresponding change in architectural form. Building functions may be heterogeneous and polyvalent (see Houston, this volume), consisting not of single activities but of multiple activity sets that shift or recombine in complex patterns over time. The simplified conceptualization of the form–function relationship offered by the functional approach potentially can mislead us. Also complicating attributions of function are socioeconomic variables. In poor households, for instance, single structures may accommodate multiple, functionally differentiated activities (sleeping, food preparation, tool manufacture, ritual) that in wealthy households transpire in two or more architecturally differentiated spaces. In cases such as this, artifact assemblages may resemble one another compositionally although individual structure functions differ (Gonlin n.d.). The relationship between built form and socioeconomic function can be more complex than the functional approach allows.

We discuss in further detail below the third assumption—that artifacts found on house floors remain in their systemic context. This assumption is characteristic of functional studies of Maya houses published before the mid-1980s, wherein residential function was determined largely on the basis of artifactual "domestic criteria": the presence of cooking pottery, grinding implements, figurines, or stone tools. Most contemporary Mayanists disavow the assumption, yet it remains implicit in much research: in the case of commoner houses constructed of perishable materials, how else can residential function be established when archaeologists excavate only the house, the architectural remains of which are typically poorly preserved, incomplete, or artifact-free? Additionally, this assumption is implied by the excavation of test pits through architecture to determine residential function. Artifacts exposed on living surfaces in test pits can be used to identify structure function only if it can be demonstrated that those artifacts remain in or near their original use location. If, on the other hand, abandonment or postabandonment processes are responsible for the distribution of living floor assemblages, they should not be used to reconstruct original room function (Schiffer 1985; Rothschild et al. 1993).

Underlying all these assumptions is a fourth that is both the most important and the most problematic: that houses reliably "signify" households. Composing this assumption are two preconceptions. First, as Smith (1993: 13) has observed, Mayanists often claim to excavate "households" when in fact they investigate houses (artifacts) to infer households (behavior and organization). This terminological imprecision betrays a flawed conceptualization. Contrary to what some Mayanists believe, houses are not equivalent to households. Closely related is the second preconception: how Mayanists of the cultural historical school perceived the notion of "function" acquired from processualism. Within the materialist formulation proposed by Binford (1962, 1981) and other processualists, function is first and foremost technological, economic, and adaptive. Function is how an artifact (whether tool or architecture) is designed to cope directly with the physical environment. Binford, for example, examines artifact function to determine what major (economic) tasks were performed at particular locations. When Mayanists embraced processualism, they adopted a concern with function, but proponents of the functional approach investigated not economic function but the functional relationship between cultural traits and social systems (Trigger 1989: 298). Thus, in the case of architectural analysis, buildings are classified according to function (house, palace, temple, etc.), but function is defined in predominantly social rather than economic terms. Houses, for example, are said to function as the dwellings of commoner families, and palaces function as the dwellings of elite families. Bypassed are questions of socioeconomic function: what economic tasks were performed at this location, and how were households constituted socioeconomically? This concern with social function, or how inferences about social organization could be drawn from the remains of dwellings, pervaded American archaeology through the early 1980s (cf. Lowell 1991: 3–6). Lawrence and Low, for example, observe that

> Archaeologists focus largely on the accuracy with which inferences about social organization can be made from the remains of dwellings. . . . In particular they ask how specific attributes of dwellings (size, number, and function of rooms, for example) correspond to features of social organization (size and composition of the domestic group). (Lawrence and Low 1990: 462)

This objective remains an important concern of Maya functional studies today.

THE SOCIAL APPROACH TO HOUSES

To more profitably evaluate the assumption that "houses reliably signify households," it is useful to restate it as a question phrased in the terms posed by this volume: "What do houses mean?" Archaeologists attribute meaning to the archaeological record on the basis of specific methodological and theoretical criteria (Patrick 1985; Sabloff, Binford, and McAnany 1987; Hodder 1989a). Meaning is not inherent in the record, nor do archaeologists simply uncover "facts" waiting to be discovered. Because attributions of meaning are only as reliable as the criteria that underlie them, it is critical that the analyst employ criteria appropriate for the problem under investigation. To investigate the household (defined socioeconomically), the analyst must shift the focus of inquiry from (1) the house to (2) the house and its surroundings as situated within the archaeological record. Rejected is the functional notion that the material condition and spatial organization of the archaeological record directly or unambiguously reflect patterns of past economic behavior and social organization. Embraced is the position advanced by Schiffer (1987, 1988) that to understand the meaning of the archaeological record we must first understand how that record was formed. Proponents of the household approach bypass the problem of building use and social function. Instead they ask, To what categories of ancient behavior do houses and their surroundings as represented in the archaeological record correspond? Theory linking the static material record to dynamic past behavior is drawn from ethnoarchaeological data. In the case of Maya house investigations, that theory examines formation processes—both cultural and environmental—that structure household sites and their artifactual contents.

Household formation processes transform a systemic record into an archaeological one, thereby interposing a filter between archaeologists and the ancient behavior that they wish to understand (Schiffer 1985, 1987, 1988). If it is true that the artifactual contents of houses are not preserved fossil-like in their systemic context, and if, as in the case of Maya commoner houses, the architectural record is both sparse and poorly preserved, then what do we establish by excavating a house beyond a crude functional classification of its architecture, a mere description of its construction history, and a foundation from which to infer commoner population size? And where in the first two of these endeavors is the anthropology?

The social approach is both an outgrowth of the functional approach and its chronological successor. Whereas the functional approach dominated Maya household archaeology through the mid-1980s and remains an important tool in certain types of settlement pattern analysis, the social trend, like the structuralist one, is new and emerging. In contrast to the functional approach, which focuses on the house and its use, the social approach examines the household, defined as the unit of socioeconomic organization that occupied the house. When applied to certain research topics the functional approach has considerable merits, but in the case of Maya commoner household investigation those merits are decidedly limited. To advance our understanding of Maya commoner households, another approach must be taken. Particularly constructive is the social approach.

The social approach examines not families but households. The distinction between these two social entities is important and fundamental (Bender 1967; Carter 1984). A family is a kinship group whose members are linked by culturally defined relations of birth, adoption, and marriage regardless of whether or not they live together or engage in any shared economic tasks. The household, in contrast, is a residence group wherein membership is defined by shared tasks of production and consumption regardless of whether its members are linked by kinship or marriage or are coresident. In many societies, households and families do not overlap: families do not always form households (Kramer 1982) and many households are not composed of families (Horne 1982; Wilk 1984; Oswald 1987). Although houses usually indicate the presence of households, the linkage between houses and families is considerably less clear. Proponents of the functional approach (Haviland 1981, 1988; Tourtellot 1983, 1988a, 1988b, 1993; Kintz 1983) embrace the thesis of Fortes (1958) and Goody (1962, 1972, 1976) that there is a close fit between dwelling form and social organizational form, but this assumption is not universally supported by comparative anthropological data (Netting, Wilk, and Arnould 1984).

The social approach then is concerned not with kinship relations but with the socioeconomic substrata that underlie those relations. Social historical research indicates that household form is largely a function of economic factors. To understand the composition of a household, one must examine the economic and ecological variables to which that composition is an attempted adaptation. The approach does not reduce archaeological inquiry to a crude base-superstructure calculation, nor does it promote a resuscitated or clandestine environmental or geographical determinism. Although recognizing the significance of cultural and social variables, the social approach asserts that these variables frequently are framed, delimited, and directed by economic necessities (Arcury 1990; Rudolph 1992).

Described by historians and sociologists as the "new household economics" (Lehning 1992: 162), the approach looks at households not just as sets of genealogically or affinally related individuals but as work groups (Laslett 1983; Viazzo 1989; Alderson and Sanderson 1991; Lehning 1992). Proponents posit that for a household to accomplish its goals, a labor force is needed whose size, composition, and organization falls within parameters consonant with and adjusted to key ecological and economic variables. As these parameters change over time, households also change. Indeed, households are dynamic, inherently flexible entities capable of adjusting to new economic opportunities and environmental circumstances (Brown 1977; Netting 1979; Hammel 1980). Ecologically adjusted labor requirements favor certain types of household form over others. In agricultural societies, there is a strong relationship between household form, labor needs (the social organization of production), land use (the mode of production), and land tenure and inheritance schemes (social conditions limiting access to land) (Netting 1965, 1993; Brown 1977; Wilk and Netting 1984; Rudolph 1992). This relationship is itself constrained by environmental variables that determine the productivity of land under given levels of agricultural technology (Mitterauer 1992). For instance, several anthropologists note that landless families frequently have simple, nuclear structures, whereas landed families (particularly those with impartible land-inheritance schemes) tend to have more complex, extended structures (Pasternak, Ember, and Ember 1976; Wilk 1983; Alderson and Sanderson 1991; Lehning 1992). The critical factors are labor availability, resource availability, and the complexity of economic tasks:

where labor requirements are incompatible with simple nuclear families, extended family households emerge (Netting 1965; Wilk and Rathje 1982). The primary determinant of household structure in these societies is a principle not of kinship but of economics.

Citing extensive comparative data, several social historians have argued that labor requirements are a powerful determinant of household form (Viazzo 1989; Mitterauer 1992; Lehning 1992; Rudolph 1992). The argument is simple, logical, and empirically verifiable: farmers occupying a specific environmental setting and having at their disposal a given agricultural technology know that some types of labor arrangements are a great deal more productive than others. How labor is organized depends on the quality and character of land holdings, their spatial distribution, and the manner in which access to land is governed by tenure and inheritance schemes. Because inheritance and tenure do not affect all individuals uniformly within a society, different household types (e.g., extended versus nuclear) often coexist. The structure of the household reflects the attempts of individuals to strike a balance between the realities of resource composition and availability (which in part is socially determined), their desire to reproduce socially, and their need to adapt economically. Yet, as noted above, economic adaptation must in an organizational sense be socially compatible with resource availability. Like land tenure organization (Adams 1981: 20), household form both reflects and is structurally consistent with the social organization of production.

By drawing from the social historical literature, two principal criticisms can be leveled against the functional approach. Paraphrasing Wilk and Netting (1984: 3), we may say, first, that what households do (economic organization) is logically prior to what they look like (kinship organization). All other things being equal, then, economic organization is more likely to structure kinship relations than vice versa. The principle at issue is self-evident: economically nonadaptive kinship relations cannot, in the long term, survive. This leads to the second criticism of the functional approach: "its tendency to treat family structure as self-levitating, thus ignoring the larger social context in which families and households exist" (Alderson and Sanderson 1991: 420). Socioeconomic context constrains household behavior, thereby limiting form. If we are to determine what causal variables (if any) determined Maya household form, we must shift our focus from the house as a spatially confined architectural entity to the larger terrain wherein socioeconomic behavior transpired and within which certain durable material residues of that behavior are likely to remain. That larger terrain is the "houselot" (Killion 1990, 1992b; Santley and Hirth 1993).

Refuse Management, Formation Processes, and the Maya Houselot

In the humid tropics, many of the productive activities that differentiate households socioeconomically from one another transpire out-of-doors. In contemporary Mesoamerican communities, courtyards and adjacent areas remain the sites of important economic, social, and ceremonial activities (Wisdom 1940; Killion 1992a; Arnold 1990). That courtyards and other extramural areas were similarly used in antiquity is evidenced by artifactual data from the sites of Copan (Gonlin n.d.; Hendon n.d.) and Ceren (Sheets 1992), and soil chemical data from Coba (Manzanilla and Barba 1990). At Ceren, where residential compounds are unusually well preserved, archaeologists have established that much of the total roofed area was devoted to *ramadas,* which shaded extramural work space (Sheets 1992). Lowland Maya architectural evidence of *ramadas*—exterior lines of posthole that parallel the front walls of houses—has been found at Itzan (Johnston n.d.). At Copan, hearths in commoner residential complexes often were placed in open courtyard space (Gonlin n.d.). Yet these areas otherwise are largely devoid of artifacts or, as we argue below, yield material scatters whose depositional context is highly problematic.

For the archaeologist, extramural productive activities are evidenced by whatever hard artifactual residues of them survive in the material record. In the case of ancient agricultural communities, these residues are likely to include the durable by-products of crop production (e.g., flakes from stone hoe manufacture) and food processing and consumption (e.g., broken pots, ash, burned bone, grinding stone fragments). According to the functional perspective, the spatial distribution of these artifactual materials directly reflects the original spatial organization of ancient productive activities; the artifacts, in other words, were dropped at their original use location and remained there until discovered by the archaeologist. Proponents of the social approach strongly disagree, arguing on the basis of extensive ethnographic and ethnoarchaeological data that residential site structure—the spatial organization of architecture and artifacts—is the outcome of three principal factors: (1) the use of space by household members, particularly their management of refuse materials; (2) household behavior at the time of abandonment; and (3) postabandonment scavenging behavior and noncultural environmental processes.

As Schiffer (1985) observes, the first of the three factors is inconsistent with a "Pompeii premise" that underlies much New Archaeology, including the functional approach to Maya houses. According to that premise, the items found in and around houses "were laid down at room abandonment as assemblages that represent, in Pompeii fashion, a systemic inventory of household artifacts, thus faithfully mirroring the activities that took place in those architectural spaces" (Schiffer 1985: 18–19). That the Pompeii premise is wrong in all but a few cases has been indicated by studies too numerous to list here.[3] Hayden and Cannon (1983) and Deal (1985) remark that in contemporary highland Maya agricultural households, the primary determinant of artifact spatial patterning is garbage disposal behavior. This observation pertains equally well to Pre-Columbian archaeological sites, including those of the Maya. The second of the three factors—abandonment behavior—complicates site interpretation further because it reorganizes the spatial distribution of artifacts in a manner that reflects not socioeconomic activity during residential occupation but storage and scavenging behavior at the time of abandonment (Cameron 1991; Cameron and Tomka 1993). Many postabandonment processes have the same blurring effect (Schiffer 1987). Thus, between the occurrence of the socioeconomic activities that we wish to investigate and the period of archaeological research, the artifacts that are the object of study in the household approach may have been moved one, two, or even three times from their original use location to their modern archaeological location (Santley and Kneebone 1993). Before archaeologists can embark on a social analysis of Maya rural residential sites they must answer two questions: (1) What behavioral processes produced the site structure found by archaeologists? and (2) How do we investigate ancient socioeconomic processes when the artifacts that constitute our database no longer remain in their systemic context?

An answer to the first question is provided by the houselot model of residential site structure developed by Killion (1990, 1992a). On the basis of his observations of contemporary farming households in Veracruz, Mexico, Killion concludes that four spatial components compose the site structure of rural residences in the American humid tropics. The first component, the *structural core,* consists of the living structures, storage buildings, and other buildings that shelter household members and their belongings. Household members regularly sweep this area clean of refuse and discarded items, particularly the hard or sharp items that potentially can cause injury. Functional analyses of houses focus exclusively on this architectural component of the houselot. The second component is a *clear area* of extramural, hard-packed earth that surrounds the household's dwelling structures. Within this area occur many of the productive socioeconomic activities that generate the hard material residues that archaeologists seek. These residue-producing activities include food processing, small-

[3] See Schiffer (1987), Deboer (1983), and Cameron and Tomka (1993) for reviews of the relevant literature.

scale craft activities, tool manufacture and repair, and some religious activities. Although most of the household debris is produced in this area, like the structural core it is carefully cleaned and maintained. Sweeping usually removes all but the smallest pieces of debris. Much of the production debris and household refuse generated within the structural core and clear area is regularly removed to an *intermediate area,* where these items are discarded. This component of the houselot frequently forms a ring that surrounds the clear area. The materials dumped in this area may become concentrated in mounded or stratified middens or they may be dispersed in thin, sheetlike scatters. Hayden and Cannon (1983) and Deal (1985) refer to this sector of the site as the toft, the area outside the dwelling and outbuildings where most productive activities occur and where trash accumulates. The final component is the garden area, where some of the produce consumed by the household is grown. Often the garden is fertilized with artifact-embedded household organic debris. High soil phosphate counts, dispersed artifact scatters, and spatial proximity to house remains are reliable archaeological signatures of ancient garden area activity (Killion et al. 1989; Dunning, Rue, and Beach 1997).

The houselot model describes not only site structure but artifactual waste flow streams within residential sites. Indeed, the model implies that the artifactual component of site structure is determined largely by the configuration of those streams. Santley, Hirth, and Kneebone (Santley and Hirth 1993; Hirth 1993; Santley and Kneebone 1993) note that the houselot model applies only to rural contexts where the space surrounding residential architecture is not sharply circumscribed. Other models of site structure pertain to Pre-Columbian households in town and urban settings. In terms of the spatial patterning of artifacts, few if any artifacts on abandoned residential sites remain in their original use location (Rothschild et al. 1993; Joyce and Johannessen 1993; Lightfoot 1993). The light living and organic debris from the structural core and the manufacturing and processing debris from the surrounding clear area are regularly swept up, collected, and transported to the intermediate area, where they are dumped and sometimes burned to reduce their bulk and odors. What remains in and around the structural core are compacted, clearly defined, but generally artifact-free living surfaces (Tourtellot 1983: 45). Small debris may become embedded in living surfaces, but it is difficult to develop an accurate picture of ancient socioeconomic adaptation on the basis of living surface data alone. How do we investigate Maya household socioeconomic activity assemblages given the intervention of transforming cultural and environmental site-formation processes?

As the houselot model suggests, most artifactual materials of interest are found in middens or along structure peripheries. Depending on topography, morphology of residential architecture, layout of settlement, length of occupation, intensity and organization of production and consumption, and management of refuse disposal, middens may consist of deep, mounded, and possibly stratified deposits of dumped refuse or they may be thin, broadcast scatters of swept or thrown trash. Most of the materials necessary for an analysis of household socioeconomic organization reside in those middens. Note that middens are here described as *all* spatially concentrated trash deposits composed of household activity by-products. Additional materials may be found in dated fill contexts, pits, burials, hearths, and on living floors, but these supplementary materials often are few in number and the conditions of their deposition can be problematic. Although some proponents of the functional approach incorporate middens into their analysis (Hendon n.d.), most tend to ignore middens, especially the thin broadcast middens typical of commoner household locations, except to the degree that middens are sampled stratigraphically with test pits to establish ceramic chronology.

Having defined some of the principal behavioral factors responsible for the site structure of Mesoamerican agricultural households, we may ask how the socioeconomic substrata of household form can be reconstructed from the contents of houselot middens. Boone (1987: 336) has coined the phrase "midden catchment" to describe "the settlement area that encompasses all the refuse-catching activities that contribute to a single midden." Boone's definition highlights an important aspect of middens: each consists of the aggregate durable detritus generated by all or some sample of the debris-producing activities once conducted within the household (Killion et al. 1989: 286; Wilson 1994). Hypothetically, if a series of ancient households engaged in a similar set of activities, this should be evident in the composition of their midden assemblages if similar practices of refuse disposal have been practiced. As Boone has stressed, "to the extent that variability exists in the spatial distribution of refuse-producing activities in a site, the contents of a particular midden will vary according to which activities are taking place within its catchment" (1987: 339). Ideally, then, the relative frequency of artifacts within a midden should reflect the mix of activities particular to the corresponding household, although, as Boone (1987) warns, this is "a function of the varying amounts of refuse each activity might produce . . . [not] the relative frequency of the activities themselves"—cf. Mills (1989) and Wilson (1994). The complete midden of a household plus the assemblages of floors, fills, and features would constitute a "systemic inventory" (Lightfoot 1993: 170), defined as the aggregate detritus of all detritus-producing socioeconomic activities conducted by household members within their houselot. From this inventory, the archaeologist should be able to reconstruct some sample of all household detritus-producing activities (Wilson 1994). Samples can be compared across households to examine socioeconomic heterogeneity and variability. At Itzan, this approach has been used to investigate variation in household socioeconomic standing and organization (Johnston n.d.).

Hammel (1980: 252) notes that households are not single events but processes that transpire, develop, and change over time. Because households go through a development cycle, they will at one point in time be different in terms of size, organization, and composition than at some other point in time. Unless that cycle is interrupted suddenly and traumatically, as in the case of natural or human-made catastrophes—e.g., Joya de Ceren (Sheets 1992; Sheets et al. 1990) and Aguateca (Inomata and Stiver n.d.; Inomata n.d.), slices of time within the household's life simply are not discernible in the archaeological record. The artifactual by-products of household processes move over time through the various spatial components of the houselot until eventually they are deposited in middens, the contents of which represent sort of a mathematical mean or average of all that has transpired socioeconomically within the household (Johnston n.d.). Just as households pool material resources to satisfy the needs and wants of their members, so the by-products of those expenditures are pooled in middens after household wants are satisfied. As the household changes in response to shifting economic or environmental circumstances or because of its developmental cycle, so its artifactual and architectural signature changes. Except when houses are very briefly occupied, the archaeologist can discern in houselot refuse only the mean or average of a household's socioeconomic activities, wealth, status, or kinship relations.

This artifactual mean within houselots corresponds to what Rapoport (1990) describes as the ideal focus of household archaeology: "systems of activities" within "systems of settings." Kent (1990a: 3) contends that archaeologists should not expect "to reconstruct anything *but* such systems from the archaeological record. Individual activities are simply not discernible. They are also probably unimportant to our understanding of the past." Binford (1981: 197) argues the same point, as does Yellen (1977: 134), who notes that what archaeologists generally find on residential sites are "the remains of many activities all jumbled together." As the studies of Killion (1992b), Santley and Kneebone (1993), Hirth (1993), and others (Kent 1990b) demonstrate, Mesoamerican household archaeology is most productive when it focuses on the long-term patterning of activities rather than reconstruction of single events or activities. Indeed, the most enduring properties of domestic sites are not discrete activity areas, which rarely remain intact, but (1) the artifactual and architectural signatures of household spatial organization and (2) the aggregated by-products of socioeconomic activities conducted by household members over time within that organized space (Killion 1990; Santley and Hirth 1993; Wilson 1994).

To approach households from a social point of view, archaeologists need to shift their frame of reference from the house viewed as a spatially isolated cultural artifact to the houselot viewed as a unitary and integrated sociocultural entity. From the houselot's spatial organization and artifactual contents, archaeologists can draw socioeconomic inferences. The authors of this paper are not the first to encourage Mesoamericanists to follow this course (Smith 1993). Hayden and Cannon (1983: 160), Killion (1990: 211), and Santley and Hirth (1993: 4) all have urged archaeologists to take as their basic unit of household analysis not single structures or even single dumps but the entire architectural compound as well as its surrounding clear areas and middens. From the social perspective, one of the most important components of the houselot is its secondary refuse deposits, or middens. As Hayden and Cannon (1983: 125) observed more than a decade ago, "the range of potential data that can be extracted from such secondary refuse deposits is probably one of the most underdeveloped and important methodological concerns in archaeology." Although challenging to decipher, middens hold the key to the socioeconomic phenomena that proponents of the household approach wish to explore (Johnston n.d.). Wilson (1994) reviews several of the socioeconomic and cultural phenomena that archaeologists can expect to investigate through midden analysis.

In the Maya lowlands, a trend toward a social analysis of commoner households has emerged in recent years. One of the earliest and most significant contributions was made in the Copan valley, where archaeologists (Webster and Gonlin 1988; Gonlin 1994, n.d.) exposed several commoner houses and houseyards through unusually large-scale horizontal excavations. Houselot investigations on a somewhat smaller scale have been carried out at Itzan (Johnston n.d.; Johnston, Moscoso, and Schmitt 1992). In both cases, archaeologists exposed what might be described as the structural core, the surrounding clear area, and in some cases the intermediate area components of ancient houselots. Of course, Mayanists need not aspire to expose complete houselots through horizontal excavations, an approach that can be extremely laborious and prohibitively expensive. As research at several sites demonstrates, comparable results can be achieved through sampling and other experimental methods. At Sayil, where soils are thin and surface visibility is high, archaeologists (Killion et al. 1989; Tourtellot and Sabloff 1989; Tourtellot et al. 1989) have carried out ambitious, innovative, and large-scale investigations of entire houselots, including houseyard garden areas, through fine-grained analyses of surface assemblages. Surface trend analysis reveals patterned uses of space, including debris management practices, daily production loci, and interresidential agricultural activity. At Sayil and in the Petexbatun region of Guatemala, Dunning and his colleagues (Dunning 1989; Dunning, Rue, and Beach 1997) have enlarged the focus of analysis by combining surface trend analysis with soil phosphate testing in studies of rural and urban houselots and associated agricultural fields. Combining soil phosphate analysis with test pit excavations, Ball and Kelsay (1992) examined off-mound residential land use, site structure, refuse discard patterning, and socioeconomic activity in the upper Belize River valley. Their archaeological model of Maya houselot structure closely complements one developed by Killion (1990, 1992a) on the basis of ethnographic observation. In both cases, the basic unit of analysis was the houselot—the dwelling, associated buildings, and the immediate surrounding area where household socioeconomic activities were carried out and where the material by-products of those activities were discarded.

Recent Examples of the Social Approach

The social approach to ancient households is exemplified by recent investigations carried out at Copan (Webster and Gonlin 1988; Gonlin n.d.), Itzan (Johnston n.d.), and Sayil (Killion et al. 1989; Tourtellot et al. 1989). Proponents of the approach focus their efforts on extramural space—the clear and intermediate areas that constitute a houselot's nonarchitectural space. Precisely how the term is defined depends on site structure and project objectives. At Copan and Itzan, for instance, archaeologists excavated rural houselots centered around minimally platformed structures, none of which was built atop basal platforms. The extramural space most frequently exposed at these sites was courtyard space and the areas at the sides and rears of buildings. At Sayil, Killion et al. (1989) and Tourtellot et al. (1989) investigated residential structures, most of which sat atop substantial basal platforms. Rather than contrasting architectural and nonarchitectural space, the Sayil archaeologists drew a distinction between "structural" space (the basal platform and its residential architecture) and the "off-platform" or "interresidential" space between basal platforms (Killion et al. 1989: 284, 288). At Copan (Webster and Gonlin 1988: table 1), approximately 80% of the total space excavated in rural houselot exposures was nonarchitectural (range, 67.6% to 94.4%). Only 19% (range, 5.6% to 32.3%) of the total excavated space exposed architectural remains. At Itzan, the percentages are roughly similar: on average 61% (range, 39% to 76%) of the total space excavated was extramural, whereas 38% (range, 7% to 42%) was

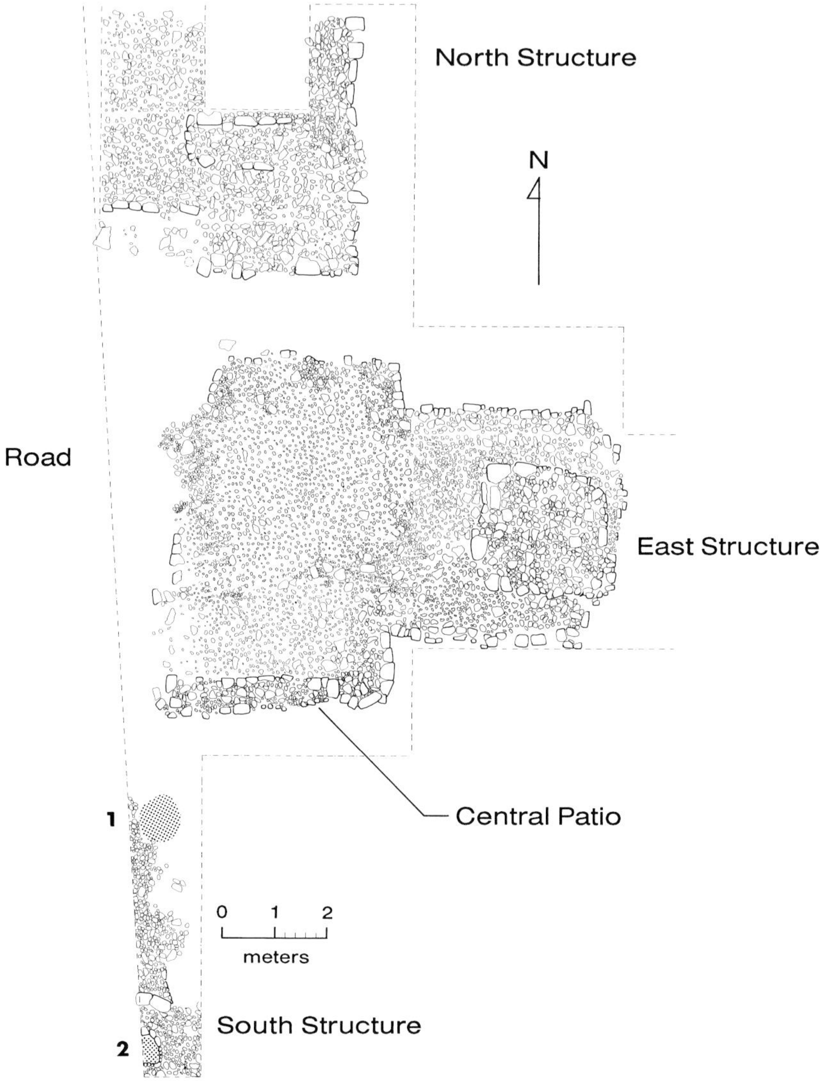

Fig. 1 Itzan IT4A group, a rural, nonmounded residential patio group. Note the presence of curated jar fragments (1) adjacent to an artesian well (2).

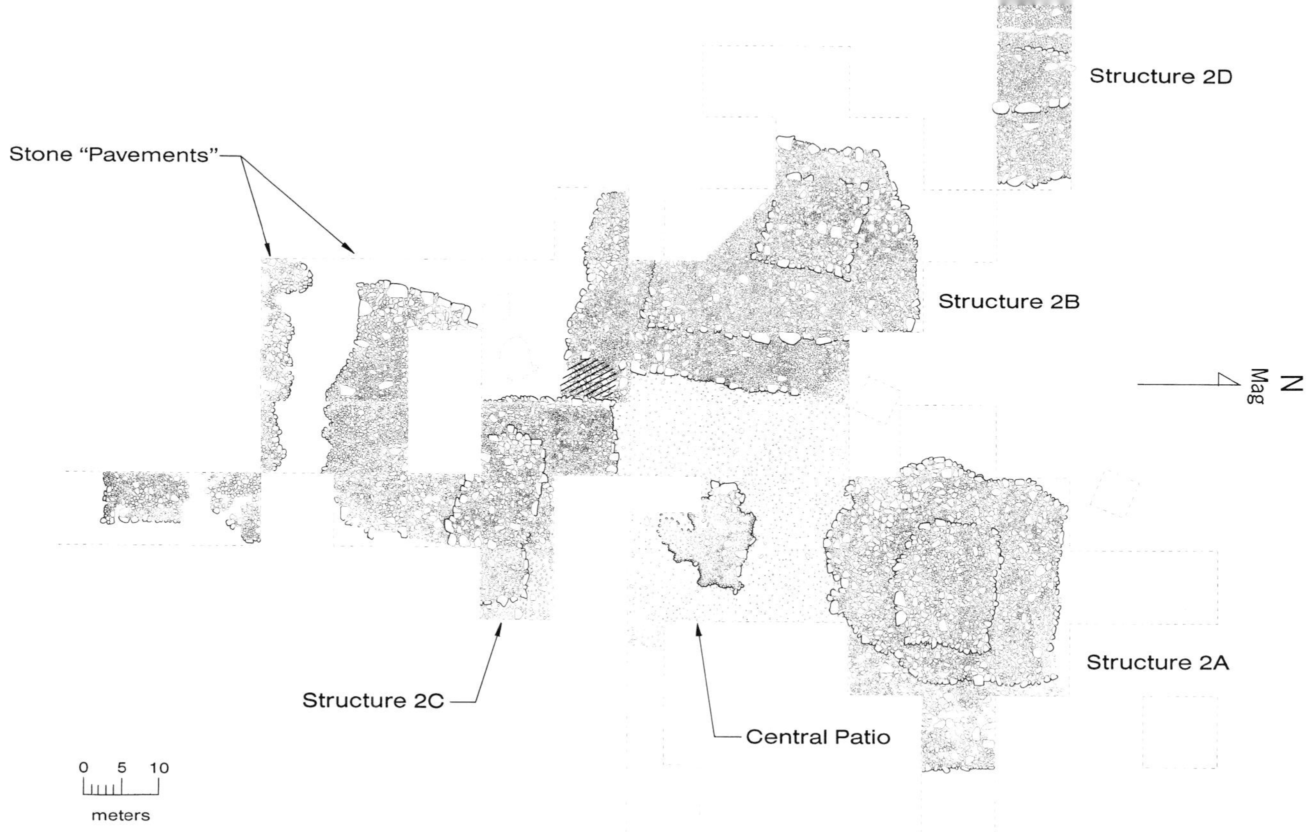

Fig. 2 Itzan IT2 group, a rural, basal-platformed residential patio group. Shaded area marks dense concentration of curated stone and ceramic artifacts between Structures 2B and 2C.

architectural (Figs. 1 and 2). At Copan and Itzan, extramural space is defined to include the patios and courtyards around which residential structures cluster. Patio space constitutes 19% of the total rural residential area excavated at Copan (range, 16% to 29%) and 14% at Itzan (range, 10% to 17%). The central courtyards of both sites yielded very few artifacts. Most of the excavated extramural space at these two sites lies to the rear of the residential structures, and it is there that most artifacts were found.

In the intensively surface-collected Miguel T quadrant at Sayil (Killion et al. 1989: table 1), 77% of the area examined was nonplatform (i.e., extramural) space and only 33% was structural space (supported by basal platforms). A mere 5% of the space examined was architectural. More than 95% of the Miguel T quadrant, in other words, was extramural space, most of it flat, open terrain evidently used for infield agriculture. Because soils are thin and surface visibility is unusually high at Sayil, the Miguel T quadrant was investigated through intensive surface collection rather than extensive horizontal excavation.

What components of the ancient Maya houselot have been exposed at Copan, Itzan, and Sayil? Let us assume for the sake of argument that Killion's (1990) model of residential site structure in the modern Sierra de los Tuxtlas region of Veracruz is roughly representative of ancient lowland Maya rural residential site structure (an assumption that cannot be proved or disproved). Judging from Killion's figure 7, we propose that on average the structural core constitutes 10% of the total houselot space, the clear area 40%, and the intermediate area 50%. (At Copan and Itzan, excavations were generally too small to expose much of the garden area component.) Returning to the Copan and Itzan data, Killion's model suggests that archaeologists at these sites have cleared all of the structural core (buildings were completely exposed in excavations at both sites) and some unknown but potentially significant percentage of the clear and intermediate areas. The Sayil project, in contrast, examined these three houselot components plus the garden area. At all three sites, then, archaeologists have examined precisely those sectors of the houselot identified by Killion's (1990, 1992b) model as the locations where the hard artifactual residues of household productive processes are most likely to be found.

Of what do these artifactual residues consist? What, in other words, do archaeologists find in extramural space? As stated elsewhere, the outside edges of a houselot's clear area are marked by a thin lens of artifacts constituting a sheet midden or broadcast scatter. Like the nonmounded residential structures excavated at Itzan, these shallow but horizontally extensive middens are frequently inconspicuous and difficult to detect. Thin but dense, they are most easily detected by the untutored eye in soil profiles. Sheet middens can contain high artifact densities: several of the Itzan sheet middens (all less than 10 cm thick), for instance, yielded an average of 210 artifacts per square meter. The artifacts composing sheet middens are those that archaeologists identify as "domestic": bits of bone, ash, and charcoal; obsidian blades and stone tools (mostly broken); sherds, most of them heavily eroded and broken into small pieces; fragments of smashed or exhausted groundstone tools; and lithic materials representing all or most phases of the lithic reduction process.

Midden location and density are largely a function of site structure, residential context (e.g., rural versus urban settings; see Santley and Kneebone 1993), and topography. At Copan, at least 65% of all artifacts recovered at rural residential sites were found scattered in bands 2 to 5 m to the rear of structures, to the sides of structures, and, in lesser densities, clustered along the front edges of structures (Fig. 3). The densest artifact scatters occur along the upper margins and slopes of the small knolls that most rural house sites occupy. At Itzan, where the terrain is considerably flatter, the great majority of artifacts were found in 3 to 10 m wide bands behind residential structures. In the Miguel T quadrant at Sayil, middens occur behind and to the sides of buildings as well as along the lower edges of basal platforms (Killion et al. 1989: 285). At all three sites, the central courtyards and the interior floors of buildings are virtually free of artifacts still in a systemic context.

Most systemic contexts are destroyed or heavily disturbed by abandonment and postabandonment formation processes. Thus, artifactual features (defined as artifact clusters indicating ancient activity locations) in the structural core and clear areas are few. Of the 57 artifact features excavated in Copan's rural residences, at least 30% consisted of dense concentrations of small lithics and ceramics clustered along the interior or exterior bases of building walls. Similar artifact clustering has been documented in the modern Maya highlands, where provisionally discarded broken or damaged materials are stored along structure walls in anticipation of future repair or reuse (Deal 1985: 253–260). Because these items have little immediate value, they are among the few articles left behind when a house site is abandoned. An artifact cluster of this sort almost certainly does not constitute evidence of an "activity area," traditionally defined as a location where a specific and identifiable economic activity transpired. The locations of these clusters reflect refuse discard rather than refuse production behaviors.

Although evidence of ancient activity areas is rarely found, Maya curate and provisional discard behaviors are occasionally represented in the archaeological record. The strongest candidate for provisional discard at Itzan occurs in the IT4A group (Fig. 1), where a very dense concentration of large pottery frag-

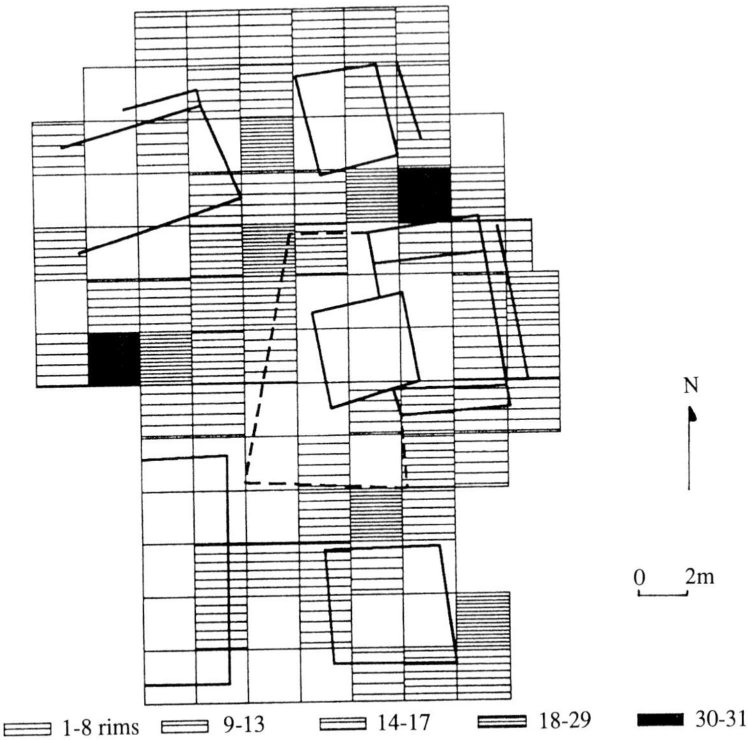

Fig. 3 Site 11D-11-2, Copan, Honduras. SAS/GRAPH map illustrating spatial distribution of ceramic rim sherds found in middens, structure peripheries, and occupation surfaces. Density of grid shading indicates artifact density. The lowest artifact densities occur on surfaces within buildings.

ments was placed in antiquity along the east edge of the patio group's southernmost structure. Six to eight broken jars had been piled, one atop the other, within the lower half of a large broken jar. Sandwiched between the nested vessels were thin, ashy layers of debris containing burned bones, shell fragments, and clay, recalling a practice of ash storage described by Hayden and Cannon (1983: 132). Eventually, the outer jar collapsed, concentrating the materials in a dense artifact cluster. This feature is functionally related to an adjacent one: an artesian well located 4 m to the south. Presumably, the water jars broke near the well and were curated for possible reuse at their present location. Curate behavior is probably represented in the IT2 group (Fig. 2), where between Structures 2B and 2C archaeologists discovered dozens of chert cores, hammerstones, tools and tool fragments, and a large chert block resting on the ancient occupation surface plus several large jar fragments leaning against the outer wall of Structure 2C. Curated artifacts (Schiffer 1987: 90–96) are valued materials set aside for possible future reuse. The occupants of the IT2 group stored in accessible but architecturally marginal space a handy supply of chert blocks and cobbles. Because chert is available along the entire Itzan escarpment, these materials were left behind when the house compound was abandoned. Artifact concentrations such as these, which remain in their systemic context, are extremely rare in Maya domestic sites.

Feature types that often survive formation processes include subterranean modifications of the ancient land surface. Among these are hearths, six of which have been found in the Copan rural residences. The Copan hearths are evidenced by shallow, ash- and charcoal-filled basins containing very few artifacts. Although hearths provide evidence of the location of cooking activities, because the surfaces surrounding them were once swept clean they do not yield the complementary artifactual data needed to identify precisely what kinds of food preparation and cooking activities occurred at these locations.

To discern commoner household organization from site structure and material patterning, then, Mayanists need to combine extensive exposures of residential architecture with intensive subsurface sampling of toft and possible garden areas. Hypothetically, such investigations should provide archaeologists with the data needed to do structuralist, functional, and social (or household) investigations. Innovative means of analyzing middens and comparing interhousehold midden assemblages are urgently needed. Midden analysis constitutes an important key to understanding household socioeconomic organization and variation. Until methodological innovation in this area progresses, the social approach will not achieve its full potential.

CONCLUSION

We return to the question posed by this paper's title: What do Classic Maya commoner houses mean? Additionally, are the meanings attributed to houses by the three theoretical perspectives described above mutually exclusive, or do they complement one another? Although we have presented the structuralist, functional, and social approaches in opposition to one another, in fact they complement one another methodologically and could easily be combined. Under conditions of sufficient architectural preservation and given a willingness among materialists to embrace the perspective for experimental purposes, the structuralist approach can be applied to architectural form and decoration to investigate generative cultural structures. Although Hodder (1990: 48) asserts that artifact patterning within houses also can be analyzed structurally, he, like his functional predecessors, does so on the basis of a "Pompeii premise," the reliability of which is highly problematic. The structuralist approach may be most productive when used to analyze large, well preserved, or decorated structures such as palaces and temple complexes.

The functional approach is most useful when the analyst wishes to determine whether a mound or building ruin is a domicile or some other structure type. The approach can also be applied productively to certain questions concerning the household developmental cycle, and it is a necessary component of population reconstruction studies (cf. Culbert and Rice 1990). Whether or not the approach can be used to determine basic family form remains to be established.

The social approach can be used to examine the socioeconomic organization of the household, the task-oriented, residentially localized group associated with the house, plus the articulation of the household with larger, including regional and pansocietal, socioeconomic processes and institutions. Recognizing the importance of site-formation processes, the household approach examines the site structure of houselots, which is the basic unit of analysis. Through its examination of artifact assemblages in secondary refuse aggregates, the approach provides a platform for cross-household comparisons of relative wealth, status, and socioeconomic organization and variation that do not simply involve comparisons of architectural morphology and materials. Now that Mayanists have documented the layout and construction histories of so many buildings, it may be useful to return to previously excavated groups and more thoroughly examine their courtyards and peripheral areas.

BIBLIOGRAPHY

ADAMS, ROBERT

1981 *Heartland of Cities.* University of Chicago Press, Chicago.

ALDERSON, ARTHUR S., AND STEPHEN K. SANDERSON

1991 Historic European Household Structures and the Capitalist World Economy. *Journal of Family History* 16: 419–432.

ALLEN, WILLIAM L., AND JAMES B. RICHARDSON

1971 The Reconstruction of Kinship from Archaeological Data: The Concepts, the Methods, and the Feasibility. *American Antiquity* 36: 41–53.

ARCURY, THOMAS A.

1990 Industrialization and Household and Family Life Course Characteristics: Appalachian Kentucky Young Adults in 1880 and 1910. *Journal of Family History* 15: 285–312.

ARNOLD, PHILIP J.

1990 The Organization of Refuse Disposal and Ceramic Production with Contemporary Mexican Houselots. *American Anthropologist* 92: 915–932.

ASHMORE, WENDY

1989 Construction and Cosmology: Politics and Ideology in Lowland Maya Settlement Patterns. In *Word and Image in Maya Culture: Explorations in Language, Writing, and Representation* (William Hanks and Don Rice, eds.): 272–286. University of Utah Press, Salt Lake City.

1991 Site-Planning Principles and Concepts of Directionality among the Ancient Maya. *Latin American Antiquity* 2: 199–226.

1992 Deciphering Maya Architectural Plans. In *New Theories on the Ancient Maya* (Elin Darien and Robert Sharer, eds.): 173–184. University Museum Monograph 77, University Museum Symposium, vol. 3. University of Pennsylvania, Philadelphia.

ASHMORE, WENDY, AND RICHARD R. WILK

1988 Household and Community in the Mesoamerican Past. In *Household and Community in the Mesoamerican Past* (Richard Wilk and Wendy Ashmore, eds.): 1–28. University of New Mexico Press, Albuquerque.

BALL, JOSEPH W., AND RICHALENE G. KELSAY

1992 Prehistoric Intrasettlement Land Use and Residual Soil Phosphate Levels in the Upper Belize Valley, Central America. In *Gardens of Prehistory: The Archaeology of Settlement Agriculture in Greater Mesoamerica* (Thomas W. Killion, ed.): 234–262. University of Alabama Press, Tuscaloosa.

BENDER, DONALD R.

1967 A Refinement of the Concept of Household: Families, Co-Residence, and Domestic Function. *American Anthropologist* 69: 493–504.

BINFORD, LEWIS R.

1962 Archaeology as Anthropology. *American Antiquity* 28: 217–225.

1981 Behavioral Archaeology and the "Pompeii Premise." *Journal of Anthropological Research* 37: 195–208.

BLANTON, RICHARD E.

1989 Continuity and Change in Public Architecture: Periods I through V of the Valley of Oaxaca, Mexico. In *Monte Alban's Hinterland,* pt. 2 (Stephen Kowalewski, Gary Feinman, Laura Finsten, Richard Blanton, and Linda Nicholas, eds.): 409–448. Memoirs, no. 23. Museum of Anthropology, University of Michigan, Ann Arbor.

1994 *Houses and Households: A Comparative Study.* Plenum Press, New York.

BLIER, SUZANNE P.

1987 *The Anatomy of Architecture: Ontology and Metaphor in Batammaliba Architectural Expression.* Cambridge University Press, Cambridge.

BOONE, JAMES L.

1987 Defining and Measuring Midden Catchment. *American Antiquity* 52: 336–345.

BOURDIEU, PIERRE

1985 *Outline of a Theory of Practice.* Cambridge University Press, Cambridge.

BROWN, SUSAN

1977 Household Composition and Variation in a Rural Dominican Village. *Journal of Comparative Family Studies* 8: 257–267.

BULLARD, WILLIAM R.

1960 Maya Settlement Patterns in Northeastern Peten, Guatemala. *American Antiquity* 25: 355–372.

CAMERON, CATHERINE M.

1991 Structure Abandonment in Villages. In *Archaeological Method and Theory,* vol. 3 (Michael B. Schiffer, ed.): 155–194. University of Arizona Press, Tucson.

CAMERON, CATHERINE M., AND STEVE TOMKA (EDS.)

1993 *Abandonment of Settlements and Regions: Ethnoarchaeological and Archaeological Studies.* Cambridge University Press, Cambridge.

CARTER, ANTHONY T.

1984 Household Histories. In *Households: Comparative and Historical Studies of the Domestic Group* (Robert McC. Netting, Richard R. Wilk, and Eric J. Arnould, eds.): 44–83. University of California Press, Berkeley.

CHANG, KWANG-CHIH

1958 Study of the Neolithic Social Grouping: Examples from the New World. *American Anthropologist* 60: 298–334.

COE, MICHAEL D.

1981 Religion and the Rise of Mesoamerican States. In *The Transition to Statehood in the New World* (Grant T. Jones and Robert Kautz, eds.): 157–171. Cambridge University Press, Cambridge.

CULBERT, T. PATRICK, AND DON S. RICE

1990 *Precolumbian Population History in the Maya Lowlands.* University of New Mexico Press, Albuquerque.

David, Nicholas
1971 The Fulani Compound and the Archaeologist. *World Archaeology* 3: 111–131.

Deal, Michael
1985 Household Pottery Disposal in the Maya Highlands: An Ethnoarchaeological Interpretation. *Journal of Anthropological Archaeology* 4: 243–291.

DeBoer, Warren R.
1983 The Archaeological Record as Preserved Death Assemblage. In *Archaeological Hammers and Theories* (Jerry Moore and A. Keene, eds.): 19–36. Academic Press, New York.

Deetz, James J.
1968 The Inference of Residence and Descent Rules from Archaeological Data. In *New Perspectives in Archaeology* (Sally Binford and Lewis R. Binford, eds.): 41–49. Aldine, Chicago.

Demarest, Arthur A.
1989 Ideology and Evolutionism in American Archaeology: Looking Beyond the Economic Base. In *Archaeological Thought in America* (C. C. Lamberg-Karlovsky, ed.): 89–102. Cambridge University Press, Cambridge.
1992 Archaeology, Ideology, and Pre-Columbian Cultural Evolution: The Search for an Approach. In *Ideology and Pre-Columbian Civilizations* (Arthur Demarest and Geoffrey Conrad, eds.): 1–14. School of American Research Press, Santa Fe.

Donley-Reid, Linda W.
1990 A Structuring Structure: The Swahili House. In *Domestic Architecture and the Use of Space* (Susan Kent, ed.): 114–126. Cambridge University Press, Cambridge.

Dunning, Nicholas P.
1989 *Archaeological Investigations at Sayil, Yucatan, Mexico: Intersite Reconnaissance and Soil Studies during the 1987 Field Season.* University of Pittsburgh Anthropological Papers, no. 2. University of Pittsburgh, Pittsburgh.

Dunning, Nicholas P., David Rue, and Timothy Beach
1997 The Paleoecology and Ancient Settlement of the Petexbatun Region of Guatemala. *Ancient Mesoamerica* 8 (2): 255–266.

Fash, William L.
1983 Deducing Social Organization from Classic Maya Settlement Patterns: A Case Study from the Copan Valley. In *Civilization in the Ancient Americas: Essays in Honor of Gordon R. Willey* (Richard Leventhal and Alan Kolata, eds.): 261–288. University of New Mexico Press, Albuquerque, and Peabody Museum of Archaeology and Ethnology, Harvard University, Cambridge, Mass.

Flannery, Kent, and Michael D. Coe
1968 Social and Economic Systems in Formative Mesoamerica. In *New Perspectives in Archaeology* (Sally R. Binford and Lewis R. Binford, eds.): 267–283. Aldine, Chicago.

Fortes, Meyer
1958 Introduction. In *The Developmental Cycle in Domestic Groups* (Jack Goody, ed.): 1–14. Cambridge University Press, Cambridge.

Foster, Sally M.

1989 Analysis of Spatial Patterns in Buildings (Access Analysis) as an Insight into Social Structure: Examples from the Scottish Atlantic Iron Age. *Antiquity* 63: 40–50.

Freidel, David, Linda Schele, and Joy Parker

1993 *Maya Cosmos: Three Thousand Years on the Shaman's Path.* William Morrow, New York.

Geertz, Clifford

1973 *The Interpretation of Cultures.* Basic Books, New York.

Giddens, Anthony

1979 *Central Problems in Social Theory: Action, Structure and Contradiction in Social Analysis.* University of California Press, Berkeley.

1982 *Profiles and Critiques in Social Theory.* Macmillan, London.

Gonlin, Nancy

1994 Rural Household Diversity in Late Classic Copan, Honduras. In *Archaeological Views from the Countryside: Village Communities in Early Complex Societies* (Glenn M. Schwartz and Steven E. Falconer, eds.): 177–197. Smithsonian Institution Press, Washington, D.C.

n.d. Rural Household Archaeology at Copan, Honduras. Ph.D. dissertation, Pennsylvania State University, 1993.

Goody, Jack

1972 The Evolution of the Family. In *Household and Family in Past Time* (Peter Laslett and Richard Wall, eds.): 103–124. Cambridge University Press, Cambridge.

1976 *Production and Reproduction: A Comparative Study of the Domestic Domain.* Cambridge University Press, Cambridge.

Goody, Jack (ed.)

1962 *The Development Cycle in Domestic Groups.* Cambridge University Press, Cambridge.

Gould, Richard, and Patty Jo Watson

1982 A Dialogue on the Meaning and Use of Analogy in Ethnoarchaeological Reasoning. *Journal of Anthropological Archaeology* 1: 355–381.

Hall, Edward T.

1966 *The Hidden Dimension.* Doubleday, Garden City, N.J.

Hammel, E. A.

1980 Household Structure in Fourteenth-Century Macedonia. *Journal of Family History* 5: 242–273.

Hammel, E. A., and Peter Laslett

1974 Comparing Household Structure Over Time and Between Cultures. *Comparative Studies in Society and History* 16: 73–109.

Hammond, Norman

1975 *Lubaantun: A Classic Maya Realm.* Peabody Museum Monographs, no. 2. Harvard University, Cambridge, Mass.

HANSON, JULIENNE, AND BILL HILLIER
1982 Domestic Space Organization. *Architecture and Behavior* 2: 5–25.

HAVILAND, WILLIAM A.
1968 *Ancient Lowland Maya Social Organization.* Middle American Research Institute, no. 29. Tulane University, New Orleans.
1970 Tikal, Guatemala, and Mesoamerican Urbanism. *World Archaeology* 2: 186–198.
1981 Dower Houses and Minor Centers at Tikal, Guatemala: An Investigation into the Identification of Valid Units in Settlement Hierarchies. In *Lowland Maya Settlement Patterns* (Wendy Ashmore, ed.): 89–117. University of New Mexico Press, Albuquerque.
1988 Musical Hammocks at Tikal: Problems of Reconstructing Household Composition. In *Household and Community in the Mesoamerican Past* (Richard R. Wilk and Wendy Ashmore, eds.): 121–134. University of New Mexico Press, Albuquerque.

HAYDEN, BRIAN, AND AUBREY CANNON
1983 Where the Garbage Goes: Refuse Disposal in the Maya Highlands. *Journal of Anthropological Archaeology* 2: 117–163.

HENDON, JULIA ANN
1991 Status and Power in Classic Maya Society: An Archaeological Study. *American Anthropologist* 93: 894–918.
n.d. The Uses of Maya Structures: A Study of Architecture and Artifact Distribution at Sepulturas, Copan, Honduras. Ph.D. dissertation, Harvard University, 1987.

HILL, JAMES N.
1966 A Prehistoric Community in Eastern Arizona. *Southwestern Journal of Anthropology* 22: 9–30.

HILLIER, BILL, AND JULIENNE HANSON
1984 *The Social Logic of Space.* Cambridge University Press, Cambridge.

HIRTH, KENNETH G.
1993 The Household as an Analytical Unit: Problems in Method and Theory. In *Prehispanic Domestic Units in Western Mesoamerica: Studies of the Household, Compound, and Residence* (Robert Santley and Kenneth Hirth, eds.): 21–36. CRC Press, Boca Raton, Fla.

HODDER, IAN
1989a This Is Not an Article About Material Culture as Text. *Journal of Anthropological Anthropology* 8: 250–269.
1989b Post-Modernism, Post-Structuralism, and Post-Processual Archaeology. In *The Meaning of Things: Material Culture and Symbolic Expression* (Ian Hodder, ed.): 64–78. Unwin Hyman, London.
1990 *The Domestication of Europe.* Basil Blackwell, Oxford.

HORNE, LEE
1982 The Household in Space: Dispersed Holdings in an Iranian Village. *American Behavioral Scientist* 25: 677–685.

Inomata, Takeshi

n.d. Archaeological Investigations at the Fortified Center of Aguateca, El Peten, Guatemala: Implications for the Study of the Classic Maya Collapse. Ph.D. dissertation, Vanderbilt University, 1995.

Inomata, Takeshi, and Laura Stiver

n.d. Floor Assemblages from Elite Households of Aguateca, Guatemala, and Their Socio-Economic Implications. Paper presented at the Ninety-Third Annual Meeting of the American Anthropological Association, Atlanta, December 1994.

Isbell, William H., Christine Brewster-Wray, and Lina E. Spickard

1991 Architecture and Spatial Organization at Huari. In *Huari Administrative Structure: Prehistoric Monumental Architecture and State Government* (William Isbell and Gordon McEwan, eds.): 19–54. Dumbarton Oaks, Washington, D.C.

Jarvies, Ian C.

1973 *Functionalism.* Burgess Publishing, Minneapolis, Minn.

Johnston, Kevin J.

n.d. The "Invisible" Maya: Late Classic Minimally-Platformed Residential Settlement at Itzán, Petén, Guatemala. Ph.D. dissertation, Yale University, 1994.

Johnston, Kevin J., Fernando Moscoso Moller, and Stefan Schmitt

1992 Casas no-visibles de los mayas clásicos: Estructuras residenciales sin plataformas basales en Itzán, Petén. In *V simposio de investigaciones arqueológicas en Guatemala* (Juan Pedro Laporte, Héctor L. Escobedo, and Sandra Villagrán de Brady, eds.): 147–162. Associación Tikal, Guatemala City.

Joyce, Arthur, and Sissel Johannessen

1993 Abandonment and the Production of Archaeological Variability at Domestic Sites. In *Abandonment of Settlements and Regions: Ethnoarchaeological and Archaeological Studies* (Catherine Cameron and Steve Tomka, eds.): 138–153. Cambridge University Press, Cambridge.

Kamp, Kathryn A.

1987 Affluence and Image: Ethnoarchaeology in a Syrian Village. *Journal of Field Archaeology* 14: 283–298.

Kent, Susan

1990a Activity Areas and Architecture: An Interdisciplinary View of the Relationship Between Use of Space and Domestic Built Environments. In *Domestic Architecture and the Use of Space* (Susan Kent, ed.): 1–8. Cambridge University Press, Cambridge.

Kent, Susan (ed.)

1990b *Domestic Architecture and the Use of Space: An Interdisciplinary Cross-Cultural Study.* Cambridge University Press, Cambridge.

Kievit, Karen A.

1994 Jewels of Ceren: Form and Function Comparison for the Earthen Structures of Joya de Ceren, El Salvador. *Ancient Mesoamerica* 5: 193–208.

Killion, Thomas W.

1990 Cultivation Intensity and Residential Site Structure: An Ethnoarchaeological

Examination of Peasant Agriculture in the Sierra de los Tuxtlas, Veracruz, Mexico. *Latin American Antiquity* 1: 191–215.

1992a Residential Ethnoarchaeology and Site Structure: Contemporary Farming and Prehistoric Settlement Agriculture at Matacapan, Veracruz, Mexico. In *Gardens of Prehistory: The Archaeology of Settlement Agriculture in Greater Mesoamerica* (Thomas Killion, ed.): 119–149. University of Alabama Press, Tuscaloosa.

Killion, Thomas W. (ed.)

1992b *Gardens of Prehistory: The Archaeology of Settlement Agriculture in Greater Mesoamerica.* University of Alabama Press, Tuscaloosa.

Killion, Thomas W., Jeremy A. Sabloff, Gair Tourtellot, and Nicholas P. Dunning

1989 Intensive Surface Collection of Residential Clusters at Terminal Classic Sayil, Yucatan, Mexico. *Journal of Field Archaeology* 16: 273–294.

Kintz, Ellen R.

1983 Household Composition: An Analysis of the Composition of Residential Compounds in Coba. In *Coba: A Classic Maya Metropolis* (William J. Folan, Ellen R. Kintz, and Laraine A. Fletcher, eds.): 133–147. Academic Press, New York.

n.d. The Social Organization of a Classic Maya City, Coba, Quintana Roo, Mexico. Ph.D. dissertation, State University of New York, Stony Brook, 1978.

Kluckhohn, Clyde

1940 The Conceptual Structure in Middle American Studies. In *The Maya and Their Neighbors* (C. L. Hay et al., eds.): 41–51. Appleton-Century, New York.

Kramer, Carol

1982 Ethnographic Households and Archaeological Interpretation. *American Behavioral Scientist* 25: 663–685.

Laslett, Peter

1983 Family and Household as Work Group and Kin Group: Areas of Traditional Europe Compared. In *Family Forms in Historic Europe* (R. Wall, J. Robin, P. Laslett, eds.): 513–563. Cambridge University Press, Cambridge.

Lawrence, Denise L., and Setha M. Low

1990 The Built Environment and Spatial Form. *Annual Review of Anthropology* 19: 453–505.

Leach, Edmund

1978 Does Space Syntax Really "Constitute the Social"? In *Social Organization and Settlement: Contributions from Anthropology* (D. Green, C. Hasselgrove, and C. Spriggs, eds.): 385–401. British Archaeological Reports, International Series 471. Oxford.

Lehning, James R.

1992 Socioeconomic Change, Peasant Household Structure and Demographic Behavior in a French Department. *Journal of Family History* 17: 161–181.

Lightfoot, Ricky R.

1993 Abandonment Processes in Prehistoric Villages. In *The Meaning of Things: Material Culture and Symbolic Expression* (Ian Hodder, ed.): 165–177. Unwin

Hyman, London.

Longacre, William A.

1970 *Archaeology as Anthropology: A Case Study.* University of Arizona Press, Tucson.

Lowell, Julie C.

1991 *Prehistoric Households at Turkey Creek Pueblo, Arizona.* Anthropological Papers of the University of Arizona, no. 54. University of Arizona Press, Tucson.

Manzanilla, Linda, and Luis Barba

1990 The Study of Activities in Classic Households: Two Case Studies from Coba and Teotihuacan. *Ancient Mesoamerica* 1: 41–49.

Martin, Paul S., and John B. Rinaldo

1950 Sites of the Reserve Phase, Pine Lawn Valley, Western New Mexico. *Fieldiana* 38: 556–573.

McGuire, Randall H., and Michael B. Schiffer

1983 A Theory of Architectural Design. *Journal of Anthropological Archaeology* 2: 277–303.

Mills, Barbara J.

1989 Integrating Functional Analyses of Vessels and Sherds through Models of Ceramic Assemblage Formation. *World Archaeology* 21: 133–147.

Mitterauer, Michael

1992 Peasant and Non-Peasant Family Forms in Relation to the Physical Environment and the Local Economy. *Journal of Family History* 17: 139–159.

Moore, Jerry D.

1992 Pattern and Meaning in Prehistoric Peruvian Architecture: The Architecture of Social Control in the Chimu State. *Latin American Antiquity* 3: 95–113.

Netting, Robert

1965 Household Organization and Intensive Cultivation: The Kofyar Case. *Africa* 35: 422–429.

1979 Household Dynamics in a Nineteenth Century Swiss Village. *Journal of Family History* 4: 39–58.

1993 *Smallholders, Householders: Farm Families and the Ecology of Intensive Sustainable Agriculture.* Stanford University Press, Stanford, Calif.

Netting, Robert, Richard R. Wilk, and Eric J. Arnould

1984 Introduction. In *Households: Comparative and Historical Studies of the Domestic Group* (Richard Netting, Richard R. Wilk, and Eric J. Arnould, eds.): xiii–xxxv. University of California Press, Berkeley.

Oswald, Dana Beth

1987 The Organization of Space in Residential Buildings: A Cross-Cultural Perspective. In *Method and Theory for Activity Area Research: An Ethnoarchaeological Approach* (Susan Kent, ed.): 295–344. Columbia University Press, New York.

Pasternak, Burton, Carol R. Ember, and Melvin Ember

1976 On the Conditions Favoring Extended Family Households. *Journal of Anthropological Research* 32: 109–123.

Patrick, Linda E.

1985 Is There an Archaeological Record? In *Advances in Archaeological Method and*

Theory, vol. 8 (Michael Schiffer, ed.): 27–62. Academic Press, New York.

Pyburn, K. Anne
1989 Maya Cuisine: Hearths and the Lowland Economy. In *Prehistoric Maya Economies of Belize* (Patricia A. McAnany and Barry L. Isaac, eds.): 325–344. Research in Economic Anthropology, suppl. 4. JAI Press, Greenwich, Conn.

Rapoport, Amos
1990 Systems of Activities and Systems of Settings. In *Domestic Architecture and the Use of Space: An Interdisciplinary Cross-Cultural Study* (Susan Kent, ed.): 9–20. Cambridge University Press, Cambridge.

Roberts, John M., and Thomas Gregor
1971 Privacy: A Cultural View. In *Privacy* (J. Roland Pennock and John Chapman, eds.): 199–225. Atherton Press, New York.

Rothschild, Nan S., Barbara J. Mills, T. J. Ferguson, and Susan Dublin
1993 Abandonment at Zuni Farming Villages. In *The Meaning of Things: Material Culture and Symbolic Expression* (Ian Hodder, ed.): 123–137. Unwin Hyman, London.

Rudolph, Richard L.
1992 The European Family and Economy: Central Themes and Issues. *Journal of Family History* 17: 119–138.

Sabloff, Jeremy S., Lewis R. Binford, and Patricia McAnany
1987 Understanding the Archaeological Record. *Antiquity* 61: 203–209.

Sahlins, Marshall
1976 *Culture and Practical Reason.* University of Chicago Press, Chicago.

Samson, Ross
1990 The Rise and Fall of Tower-Houses in Post-Reformation Scotland. In *The Social Archaeology of Houses* (Ross Samson, ed.): 197–244. Edinburgh University Press, Edinburgh.

Sanders, Donald
1990 Behavioral Conventions and Archaeology: Methods for the Analysis of Ancient Architecture. In *Domestic Architecture and the Use of Space: An Interdisciplinary Cross-Cultural Study* (Susan Kent, ed.): 43–72. Cambridge University Press, Cambridge.

Sanders, William T., and Barbara J. Price
1968 *Mesoamerica: The Evolution of a Civilization.* Random House, New York.

Sanders, William T., Jeffrey R. Parsons, and Robert S. Santley
1979 *The Basin of Mexico: Ecological Processes in the Evolution of a Civilization.* Academic Press, New York.

Santley, Robert S., and Kenneth G. Hirth
1993 Household Studies in Western Mesoamerica. In *Prehispanic Domestic Units in Western Mesoamerica: Studies of the Household, Compound, and Residence* (Robert Santley and Kenneth Hirth, eds.): 3–20. CRC Press, Boca Raton, Fla.

Santley, Robert S., and Ronald R. Kneebone
1993 Craft Specialization, Refuse Disposal, and the Creation of the Spatial Archaeological Records in Prehispanic Mesoamerica. In *Prehispanic Domestic*

Units in Western Mesoamerica: Studies of the Household, Compound, and Residence (Robert Santley and Kenneth Hirth, eds.): 37–63. CRC Press, Boca Raton, Fla.

Saunders, Tom
1990 The Feudal Construction of Space: Power and Domination in the Nucleated Village. In *The Social Archaeology of Houses* (Ross Samson, ed.): 181–196. Edinburgh University Press, Edinburgh.

Schiffer, Michael B.
1985 Is There a "Pompeii" Premise in Archaeology? *Journal of Anthropological Research* 41: 18–41.
1987 *Formation Processes of the Archaeological Record.* University of New Mexico Press, Albuquerque.
1988 The Structure of Archaeological Theory. *American Antiquity* 53: 461–485.

Sharer, Robert J.
1993 The Social Organization of the Late Classic Maya: Problems of Definition and Approaches. In *Lowland Maya Civilization in the Eighth Century A.D.* (Jeremy Sabloff and John Henderson, eds.): 91–110. Dumbarton Oaks, Washington, D.C.
1994 *The Ancient Maya.* Stanford University Press, Stanford, Calif.

Sharer, Robert J., and Wendy Ashmore
1979 *Fundamentals of Archaeology.* Benjamin Cummings, Menlo Park, Calif.

Sheehy, James J.
1991 Structure and Change in a Late Classic Maya Domestic Group at Copan, Honduras. *Ancient Mesoamerica* 2: 1–20.

Sheets, Payson D.
1992 *The Ceren Site: A Prehistoric Village Buried by Volcanic Ash in Central America.* Harcourt Brace Jovanovich, Fort Worth, Tex.
1994 Tropical Time Capsule. *Archaeology* 47: 30–33.

Sheets, Payson D., Harriet F. Beaubien, Marilyn Beaudry, Andrea Gerstle, Brian McKee, C. Dan Miller, Hartmut Spetzler, and David B. Tucker
1990 Household Archaeology at Ceren, El Salvador. *Ancient Mesoamerica* 1: 81–90.

Small, David A.
1987 Toward a Competent Structuralist Archaeology: A Contribution from Historical Studies. *Journal of Anthropological Archaeology* 6: 105–121.

Smith, Michael E.
1993 New World Complex Societies: Recent Economic, Social, and Political Studies. *Journal of Archaeological Research* 1: 5–41.

Stahl, Ann B.
1993 Concepts of Time and Approaches to Analogical Reasoning in Historical Perspective. *American Antiquity* 58: 235–260.

Steward, Julian H.
1937 Ecological Aspects of Southwestern Society. *Anthropos* 32: 87–104.
1955 *Theory of Culture Change.* University of Illinois Press, Urbana.

STEWARD, JULIAN H., AND F. M. SEZTLER
1938 Function and Configuration in Archaeology. *American Antiquity* 4: 4–10.

SUTRO, LIVINGSTON D., AND THEODORE E. DOWNING
1988 A Step towards a Grammar of Space: Domestic Space Use in Zapotec Villages. In *Household and Community in the Mesoamerican Past* (Richard Wilk and Wendy Ashmore, eds.): 29–50. University of New Mexico Press, Albuquerque.

TATE, CAROLYN E.
1992 *Yaxchilan: The Design of a Maya Ceremonial City.* University of Texas Press, Austin.

TAYLOR, WALTER W.
1948 *A Study of Archeology.* American Anthropological Association, Memoir, no. 69. Menasha, Wis.

TOURTELLOT, GAIR
1983 An Assessment of Classic Maya Household Composition. In *Prehistoric Settlement Patterns: Essays in Honor of Gordon R. Willey* (Evon Vogt and Richard Leventhal, eds.): 35–54. University of New Mexico Press, Albuquerque, and Peabody Museum of Archaeology and Ethnology, Harvard University, Cambridge, Mass.
1988a Development Cycles of Households and Houses at Seibal. In *Household and Community in the Mesoamerican Past* (Richard R. Wilk and Wendy Ashmore, eds.): 97–120. University of New Mexico Press, Albuquerque.
1988b *Excavations at Seibal, Department of Peten, Guatemala: Peripheral Survey and Excavation. Settlement and Community Patterns.* Peabody Museum of Archaeology and Ethnology, Memoir 16. Harvard University, Cambridge, Mass.
1993 A View of Ancient Maya Settlements in the Eighth Century. In *Lowland Maya Civilization in the Eighth Century* A.D. (Jeremy A. Sabloff and John S. Henderson, eds.): 219–241. Dumbarton Oaks, Washington, D.C.

TOURTELLOT, GAIR, AND JEREMY A. SABLOFF
1989 Approaches to Household and Community Structure at Sayil, Yucatan. In *Households and Communities: Proceedings of the 21st Annual Chacmool Conference* (Scott MacEachern, David J. W. Archer, and Richard D. Garvin, eds.): 363–370. Archaeological Association of the University of Calgary, Calgary.

TOURTELLOT, GAIR, JEREMY A. SABLOFF, PATRICIA A. MCANANY, THOMAS W. KILLION, KELLI CARMEAN, RAFAEL COBOS PALMA, CHRISTOPHER DORE, BERND FAHMEL BEYER, SANDRA LOPEZ VARELA, CARLOS PEREZ ALVAREZ, AND SUSAN WURTZBURG
1989 *Archaeological Investigations at Sayil, Yucatan, Mexico, Phase II: The 1987 Field Season* (Michael P. Smyth, appendix; Ronald C. Carlisle, ed.). University of Pittsburgh Anthropological Papers, no. 1. Pittsburgh.

TRIGGER, BRUCE G.
1989 *A History of Archaeological Thought.* Cambridge University Press, Cambridge.

TRINGHAM, RUTH E.
1991 Houses Without Faces: The Challenge of Gender in Prehistoric Agricultural Remains. In *Engendering Archaeology: Women and Prehistory* (Joan Gero and Margaret Conkey, eds.): 93–131. Basil Blackwell, Oxford.

TURNER, CHRISTY G., AND LAUREL LOFGREN
1966 Household Size of Prehistoric Western Pueblo Indians. *Southwestern Journal of Anthropology* 22: 117–131.

VIAZZO, PIER PAOLO
1989 *Upland Communities: Environment, Population and Social Structure in the Alps since the Sixteenth Century.* Cambridge University Press, Cambridge.

WEBSTER, DAVID (ED.)
1989 *The House of the Bacabs, Copan, Honduras.* Studies in Pre-Columbian Art and Archaeology 29. Dumbarton Oaks, Washington, D.C.

WEBSTER, DAVID, AND NANCY GONLIN
1988 Household Remains of the Humblest Maya. *Journal of Field Archaeology* 15: 169–190.

WEBSTER, DAVID, NANCY GONLIN, AND PAYSON D. SHEETS
1997 Copan and Ceren: Two Perspectives on Ancient Mesoamerican Households. *Ancient Mesoamerica* 8 (1): 43–62.

WIDMER, RANDOLPH J., AND JAMES J. SHEEHY
n.d. Archaeological Implications of Architectural Changes in a Modern Potting Compound in Teotihuacan, Mexico. Paper presented at the Fifty-Fifth Annual Meeting of the Society for American Archaeology, Las Vegas, April 1990.

WILK, RICHARD R.
1983 Little House in the Jungle: The Causes of Variation in House Size among the Kekchi Maya. *Journal of Anthropological Archaeology* 2: 99–116.
1984 Household in Process: Agricultural Change and Domestic Transformation among the Kekchi Maya of Belize. In *Households: Comparative and Historical Studies of the Domestic Group* (Robert Netting, Richard R. Wilk, and Eric J. Arnould, eds.): 217–244. University of California Press, Berkeley.
1990 The Built Environment and Consumer Decisions. In *Domestic Architecture and the Use of Space: An Interdisciplinary Cross-Cultural Study* (Susan Kent, ed.): 34–42. Cambridge University Press, Cambridge.

WILK, RICHARD R., AND ROBERT NETTING
1984 Households: Changing Forms and Functions. In *Households: Comparative and Historical Studies of the Domestic Group* (Robert Netting, Richard R. Wilk, and Eric J. Arnould, eds.): 1–28. University of California Press, Berkeley.

WILK, RICHARD R., AND WILLIAM R. RATHJE
1982 Household Archaeology. *American Behavioral Scientist* 25: 617–639.

WILLEY, GORDON R.
1973 Mesoamerican Art and Iconography and the Integrity of the Mesoamerican Ideological System. In *The Iconography of Middle American Sculpture:* 153–162. Metropolitan Museum of Art, New York.
1976 Mesoamerican Civilization and the Idea of Transcendence. *Antiquity* 50: 205–215.

WILLEY, GORDON R., WILLIAM R. BULLARD, JR., JOHN B. GLASS, AND JAMES C. GIFFORD
1965 *Prehistoric Maya Settlement in the Belize Valley.* Papers of the Peabody Museum of Archaeology and Ethnology, vol. 54. Harvard University, Cambridge, Mass.

Wilson, Douglas C.
1994 Identification and Assessment of Secondary Refuse Aggregates. *Journal of Archaeological Method and Theory* 1: 41–68.

Wisdom, Charles
1940 *The Chorti Indians of Guatemala*. University of Chicago Press, Chicago.

Wylie, Alison
1985 The Reaction against Analogy. In *Advances in Archaeological Method and Theory,* vol. 8 (Michael B. Schiffer, ed.): 63–111. Academic Press, New York.

Yates, Timothy
1989 Habitus and Social Space: Some Suggestions About Meaning in the Saami (Lapp) Tent, ca. 1700–1900. In *The Meaning of Things: Material Culture and Symbolic Expression* (Ian Hodder, ed.): 249–262. Unwin Hyman, London.

Yellen, John E.
1977 *Archaeological Approaches to the Present: Models for Reconstructing the Past*. Academic Press, New York.

A Design for Meaning in Maya Architecture

MARY MILLER
YALE UNIVERSITY

In his seminal 1961 article, "The Design of Space in Maya Architecture," George Kubler established a series of formal properties as both a basis of Maya architecture and as the basis for comparison with other Mesoamerican, and even Andean architecture. As he pointed out then,

> architecture commemorates a valuable experience by distinguishing one space from others in an ample and durable edifice. Such an edifice does not need to enclose rooms: it may suffice to cancel space by solid masses or to inscribe space. (Kubler 1961: 515)

Kubler went on to identify several key forms: among others, the road/path, the platform, the precinct, the ballcourt, and what he called the building and its various types. In recognizing the value of volume in canceling space, thus creating plazas and framing precincts ("inscribing spaces"), Kubler raised the value of Mesoamerican architecture overall, giving new prestige to the concept of "void." Often bearing a negative, "empty" connotation, the void is key to Maya architecture, the space where meaning enters, anchored by surrounding mass.

But meaning has not been easy to elicit from Maya architecture. Often informally, both Maya archaeologists and art historians have done what Gordon Willey first articulated for the Virú valley, that is, to use the images of architecture from ceramics to interpret and understand specific architectural configurations and overall settlement plan (Willey 1953). Nevertheless, such architectural analysis for the Maya remains in a nascent stage, dependent on archaeological assessment for ultimate confirmation, yet always finding the archaeological evidence wanting; by recourse to the visual and textual evidence from Bonampak, for example, archaeologists assert feather dancing on pyramids, yet no excavation will ever confirm such a practice—e.g., Houston (1984). What Kubler himself implied in the words cited above he was unable to resolve in 1961: the notion that "architecture commemorates a valuable experience by distinguishing one space from others in an ample and durable edifice." What exactly is the experience that Maya architecture is commemorating after all?

The Classic Maya infused both architectural elements and assemblages with meaning. Although Maya architecture is also often idiosyncratic and local, particular forms and assemblages do emerge as bearers of a fairly consistent message. From the assemblage, one can then move to the larger issue of city planning. Because of the greater localized presence of informative texts and iconography, examples will largely come from the Maya West, from Bonampak, Yaxchilan, Palenque, Piedras Negras, and Tonina, but not exclusively so, and important material from other regions will contribute to an understanding of the meaning.

FORMS OF MAYA ARCHITECTURE

Architecture usually solves the issue of shelter for human beings, and, in this respect, Mesoamerican architecture is like most others. But unlike, say, modern architecture, Mesoamerican architecture keenly depends for its forms on the principles of simple domestic architecture. Kubler identified three fundamental elements in Maya architecture: the platform, the hut, and the path. A fourth element, however, is also critical: steps, articulated as distinct from platform or hut. The ancient Maya then made of these elements all of their man-made elaborations, framed within the precinct. A single anomalous elaboration is the ballcourt, with its inherent, predictable geometry, nonorganic quality, and general absence from the recombinant assemblages formed of the other four.

Completed, the *sacbe* connecting Groups A and B at Uaxactun may seem more than the path across the swamp, although of course it is also nothing more on one level (Fig. 1). And the Maya palace, or what they called the *nah* of various sorts (see Stuart, this volume), is obviously just that, a structure, as compellingly addressed in the formal properties of House E at Palenque, particularly the trimmed shale edge of the mansard roof, cut to look like thatch, lest other more streamlined models make us forget the relationship between the elite Maya architecture and the humble domestic abode. Is it iconography or form that the Maya seek in the appropriation of the hut (Figs. 2 and 3)? The hut goes through many dramatic transformations, from the long galleries of Uxmal or Nakbe to the intersecting webs of the Cross Group; from the tiny space piercing dense mass at the top of Tikal Temple I to its dramatic appearance as a mere section of the whole in the Arch of Kabah. Furthermore, that very hallmark of Maya architecture and even of the Classic period itself, the

Fig. 1 Uaxactun, Groups A and B. Reconstruction by Tatiana Proskouriakoff (after Smith 1950: frontispiece).

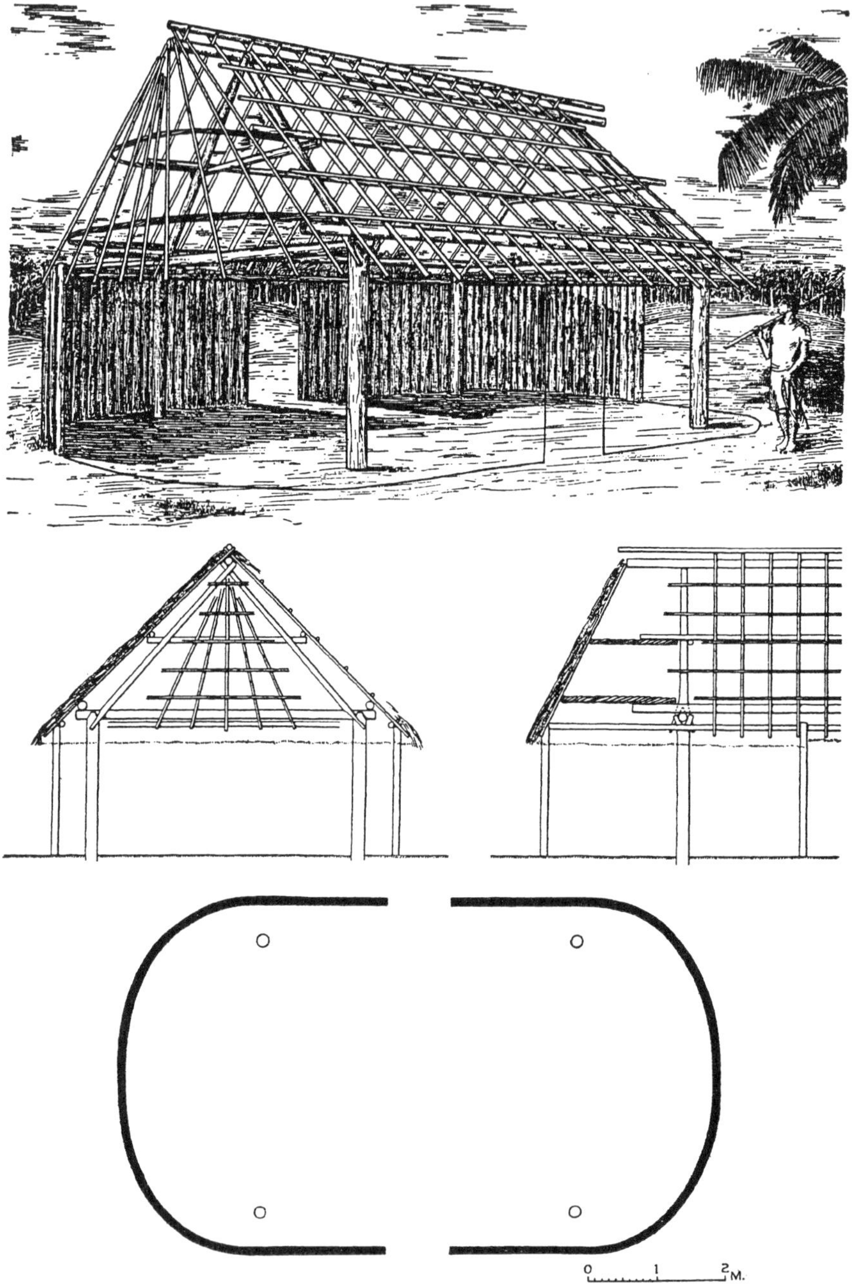

Fig. 2 A modern Maya house (after Wauchope 1938: fig. 11).

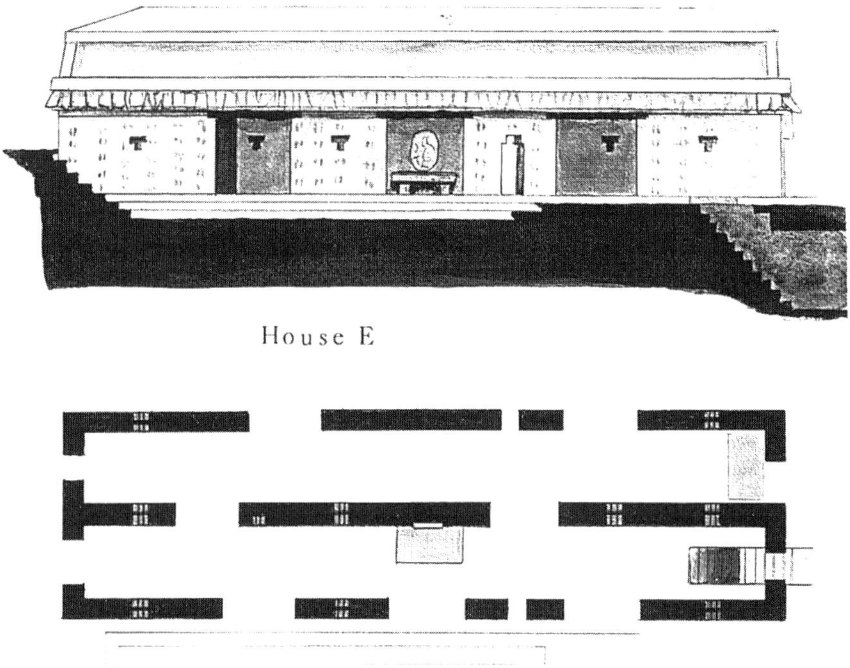

Fig. 3 View, House E. Drawing and watercolor by Gillett G. Griffin, based on Maudslay 1899–1902, 4: pl. 41.

corbel arch, a configuration described often as the "false arch" and decried as a reflection of the technological ineptitude of the New World in general, is nothing more than the transformation and confirmation of the thatch hip roof in stone. In scale, the platform eventually overtook the house itself, but its relationship to the superstructure is ancient, as is the practice of burying one's dead within its mass. The modern requirement of hallowed ground for interment has meant only that the house, too, if only symbolically, has had to move to the cemetery, and so miniature houses top modern burials. Steps may have always included roughly hewn rocks; in their ceremonial configuration, they are simply precise and finished slabs.

The silent physical spaces, the plazas and the open courts, form voids for the reception of structures and assemblages, particularly by large numbers of individuals. Exterior iconography cannot function without such components: two structures cannot enter a dialogue without the synapse created by open space.

FUNCTION

Sir Eric Thompson long thought that much of Maya architecture functioned as a sort of stage set, with feathered props to be unpacked at a moment's notice. In this, Thompson often made light of Maya imagery and, in one of his most pejorative comments, described a series of Maya architectural façades as if they were selections from Silly Symphonies (Thompson 1954: 204). Because of Thompson's irreverence for his subject in this regard, I have long resisted his larger view. But Thompson was right: Maya architecture does function as backdrop, with public iconography framing repeated public ritual. We can also go a step further, for the architecture confirms ritual and makes it present and living even when it is not being performed. Furthermore, the Maya imbued both architectural space and architectural backdrop with particular meanings, and, for them, the backdrop may well have been as significant as any grander and more labor-intensive construction. For example, Hieroglyphic Stairway 2 at Dos Pilas, set along the plaza and without superstructure, may have been considered as much a building as any funerary pyramid at the site.

Furthermore, architecture brings to life and commits to stone particular aspects of ritual as they are most appropriate to the urban setting. For example, some Maya warfare took place away from ceremonial architecture, whereas other battles surely did take place "downtown," as the Dos Pilas example confirms (Houston 1993: 51–52), and postbattle victory included the destruction of enemy monuments, as, for example, at Piedras Negras, where the great palace throne was smashed and left on the steps of J-6 at the time of that city's final defeat. Until the eighth century, however, most contests may well have taken place away from centers of population, perhaps followed by focused destruction of a few monuments. On Maya sculpture, the image of victory in warfare until the eighth century is exclusively the image of the displayed captive, or, that is, the image of victory that would be seen after the battle and within the ceremonial precinct. From the Early Classic on, the captive trampled underneath is the featured presentation. When active capture enters the visual repertory in the early eighth century, particularly at Yaxchilan and environs, the captives are rendered with conventions that indicate that they are already captured and defeated, stripped of noble attire and adorned with shredded or ripped cloth. Even in the Bonampak battle mural, where the painting might be construed to represent the battle as it took place, in fact the captives there, too, are already defeated, as signaled by attire, posture, and iconography, particularly the broken spear. In other words, the public architectural celebration of warfare celebrates not the battle as it actually took place but battle as it subsequently might be conceived and reenacted, with no doubt as to outcome. The result is the construction of images that privilege the relationship between captive and captor, rather than the event that yielded such a relationship, and, when that event is indeed featured or narrated, it nevertheless usurps any narrative by visually describing the outcome.

Although most such representations occur on stelae, they are even more graphic when rendered on other architectural features, particularly on stairs. By the Late Classic, stairs normally featured images of victory in war or triumph in ball game (Miller and Houston 1987), frequently with representations that functioned polyvalently, in text ostensibly celebrating the ball game, for example, simultaneously recalling visually both warfare and humiliation of captives. What was the purpose of such architecture? Here we have constructions where the function is clearly registered: such staircases were arenas for symbolic ball games, display, death or torture of captives, and celebration of victory in battle. The earliest examples of carved Maya steps confirm such meaning, for, although they do not carry images, their texts relate victory. Their very construction may be read as punitive: at Naranjo, in the sixth century, Caracol (and perhaps an allied Calakmul) claimed a victory and commissioned a carved staircase at the center of the Naranjo that was then inscribed by Caracol artists. Centuries later, when Naranjo had imposed its will on neighboring Ucanal, one of the slabs of this hated stair was sent to Ucanal, a token in turn of their servitude. In the seventh century, artists carved hieroglyphic stairs within the Palenque Palace, perhaps marking their record of a defeat by Calakmul (Martin and Grube 1995). Such tribute both enforced the ruling order of the day and created the spaces where subsequent warfare and the reigning hierarchies would be celebrated. In some cases, the victory is celebrated by humiliating constructions at the site of the defeated; in others, the victory swells local pride and architectural efforts by conscripting the defeated artists to work to labor in the centers of the enemy. Recognizing the specific function of stairs allows us to isolate the step as an independent architectural feature, manipulated by the Maya and frequently incorporated into larger assemblages and frequently the formal element bridging the agglutinative hut-platform-path elements and the more geometric ballcourt. Given its size, disposition, ability to elaborate hierarchies and accommodate numerous participants, the step is also the most specifically theatrical of all Maya architectural forms. Furthermore, despite the hostile implications that we may read into the making of such steps, their creation may also have indicated the end of active hostilities and a return to economic well-being—a well-being even promoted by the presence of renewed architectural and artistic commissions.

MEANING

When we turn to the subject of meaning, we find that Maya architecture has a number of distinct ends to achieve. On one level, the meaning of the Temple of Inscriptions at Palenque is to embody Pakal, buried at its base, and to stand as his sentinel throughout all time. On another level, the Temple of Inscriptions demonstrates the sheer absolute power of Pakal in his own time: he was so rich and powerful that he could martial the creation of a building to secure his posthumous memory in his own lifetime, rather than depending on his successors to take care of affairs after death, as was more typically the custom. On yet another level, the Temple of Inscriptions narrates a history in which Pakal and his achievements are inscribed, with resonance to people and events deep in a legendary past. Such a monumental narrative places Pakal at the apex of a curve in which any subsequent achievement can be read only as anticlimactic, and he himself may have believed that such a position could be captured architecturally and iconographically. Finally, once Pakal was dead, the Temple of Inscriptions memorialized a particular Maya king, and his physical presence remained a looming and dominating presence at the site, such that Kan Balam, to exercise aesthetic independence, needed to initiate his regime by defining a separate space, without much reference to the program of Pakal, resulting in what seems to be an isolated or hostile gesture. In both programs, we can see the value that the ancient builders placed on their own efforts.

One objective dominates every one of these agendas, however, and that objective is memory. The goal of Maya architecture is to promote a specific set of memories and then to enter them time and again on the mental slate through both visual images and written texts. Today, modern memories of the past in which one has lived are so imposed by repeated exposure to photographs, film, and videos that most of us develop memories of the past built around selective documentation, with increasingly less frequent amplification through review of diaries or journals. The visual memory almost always dominates the verbal one. We may think of the visual record as documentation that we have selected, but much of it has been chosen by others, with a focus largely on celebrations of one sort or another, and the near-monopolization of the mass media frames and limits the viewing of a public history that shapes our personal memories. Since the advent of mass media, human ability to frame an independent memory of either the personal or the public has been under assault. Take, for example, the celebration of the fiftieth anniversary of the Normandy invasion, or D day, in June 1994. For a generation beyond living memory of the World War II battle, the entire event was recapitulated and encapsulated in a brief series of images and films to implant the visual cues in a younger audience. And, as recent critics of revived early childhood memories of abuse have shown, repeated pictorial and verbal cues can also stimulate memories, both visual and narrative, of events that in fact did not take place or that one has not actually personally experienced.

What happens in a world without mass media? We usually look to the oral tradition to see the formation of communal memories and histories, but I suspect that something rather different happened among the Maya, where, in fact, they promulgated both the written word and the public image. Never mass produced, the figural image was nevertheless everywhere for the Maya: shaped in soft stucco on a monumental scale on the exteriors of buildings, lavishly painted on elite ceramics, carved in historical narratives presented both publicly and privately, even worn as painted designs on elite clothing. In other words, the pictorial formation necessary both to generate memories and to sustain belief was omnipresent in forms with the sorts of details and elaborations that emphasized veracity. This is usually the case with standardized religious imagery but far more unusual as a characteristic of premodern visual history. The Maya themselves initiated this practice with their religious narrative, ultimately weaving the historical into it, and finally, I believe, letting the historical dominate the story altogether by the eighth century. What also may surprise us is that despite a widely recognized vocabulary in both writing and iconography, almost no duplication ever occurs in Maya art. Over time, as static, iconic representations yielded to more active visual ones with both sequence and time depth embedded, the visual began to sustain its own integral narrative. Although the narrative capacity of the representation always lagged behind the narrative capacity of the written Maya word, the narrative quality of Maya art is nevertheless greater than that of any other Mesoamerican art. Memories are not composed of images only, or, to put it verbally, nouns, but are stories in which either the narration or the illustration may dominate but in which both are normally present. The Maya began to exploit this characteristic of memory when their art began to focus on events as well as on protagonists.

In his recent essay on Maya literacy, Houston (1994: 30) has touched briefly on the role that writing plays in stabilizing text and, by extension then, memory. Over time, the Maya image increasingly stabilizes the text and the memory by increasingly specific narrative, as it changes from the purely nominative to the increasingly verbal. Although most directly obvious in the portrayal of individual images, where the "Classic" and static motif identified by Proskouriakoff

(1950) gives way to, say, the freezing of action, the verbal is also inherent any time a series of images are juxtaposed in a particular reading order or in a reading order that requires reenactment to be seen.

Plenty of evidence confirms an active Maya interest in specific historical memories. The Tablet of 96 Glyphs at Palenque, for example, details the lineage linking its penultimate ruler, K'uk', with the great king Pakal, several generations before. Piedras Negras Panel 3 both illustrates and narrates historical events some 50 years before the stone carving was made and offers its one-sided view of the relationship between Piedras Negras and Yaxchilan. Furthermore, that relationship is spelled out in the accumulated offerings and sculptures assembled at O-13, the burial pyramid of Ruler 5, with the reuse of old monuments, and the interment of others, many of which include specifics of a 400-year relationship with Yaxchilan. The viewing of O-13, then, took one into a sort of "memory museum," where particular memories of the past were assembled and shaped onto the structure where at least one and perhaps two or three of the last kings would be buried. Here the particularistic narrative of Maya history becomes the collective, publicly promulgated from a structure that could be both "performed" and performed on.

In this essay, I examine this problem of memory and meaning through monumental architectural configuration, considering both the particulars of public display and the issue of reading order. As we shall see in various examples, configuration can function in a variety of ways, sometimes disseminating memory but at other times operating as a tool of intimidation and as a means of triggering the public display of memory. The configuration of Maya architecture, particularly in its most agglomerated constructions (e.g., Tikal Central Acropolis), often strikes the modern observer as irrational and disordered rather than as precise and ordered. As any sort of aide-mémoire, Maya architectural displays seem to offer the chaotic opposed, for example, to the specificity of linear texts. Such readings, however, devolve from plan reading and experience based on archaeological reconstruction rather than experience of buildings as demanded by the Maya themselves. To see how a complex like the Palenque Palace evolved, or how a court at either Yaxchilan or Tonina functioned, requires us to consider the construction from its approaches and function in the seventh and eighth centuries.

ARCHITECTURAL MEANING IN THE MAYA WEST

Palenque

In the mid-seventh century, King Pakal of Palenque commissioned Houses E, B, and C, in that order, atop the preexisting *subterráneos* (subterranean cham-

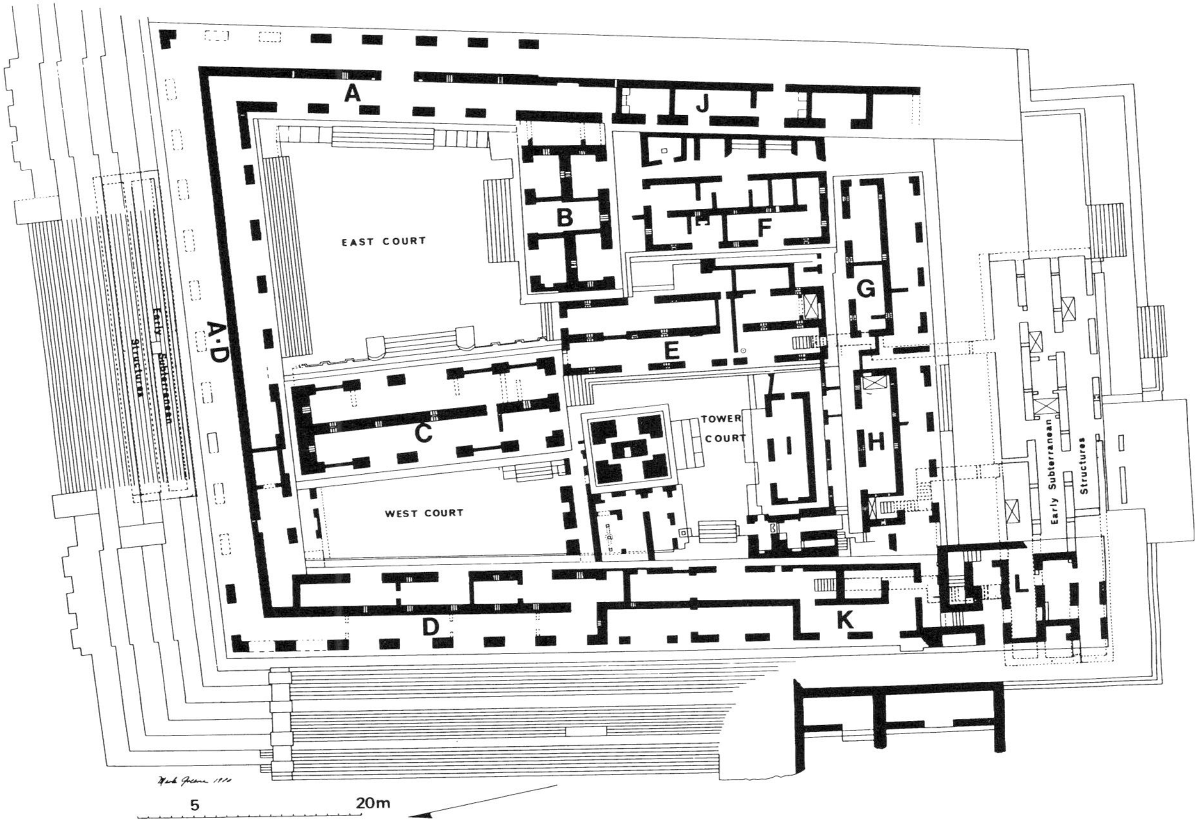

Fig. 4 Plan, Palenque Palace (after Robertson 1983–91, 2: fig. 9).

Fig. 5 The Oval Palace Tablet, with its throne (after Robertson 1983–91, 2: fig. 92).

bers) of the palace, spokes roughly radiating from an imaginary point at the northern end of House E (Fig. 4). Although House B at one time may have been a grand entrance to the court behind what is now crowded by House F (Robertson 1986: 41), the central west-facing doorway of House E, the *sak nuk nah,* or "white big house" (Stephen Houston, personal communication, 1995), was the focus of the complex, with its throne and commemorative panel of Pakal (Fig. 3). The Oval Palace Tablet not only is a throne; it also features a piece of furniture that probably predated it, a double-headed jaguar throne (Fig. 5). Pakal's picturing of this old throne probably marked its demise or rustication, just as would K'an Xul's depiction of the Oval Palace Tablet a generation later on the Palace Tablet, when he consolidated the south as the orientation of the complex.[1] Through installations of sculpture and furniture, Maya lords ensured repeated use of their buildings in a scripted fashion: through such repeated use, the buildings create in their audience a visual litany and attest to the importance of reenactment and reuse in keeping memory alive.

As Pakal and his engineers plotted the development of the palace into a rich complex, they exploited both technology and iconography. Technologically, House E is a remarkable achievement in capturing interior space, an effort most strikingly crowned at Palenque later by the intersecting corbel vaults of the Cross Group or in House A of the palace and probably begun at the Olvidado (Mathews and Robertson 1985). In any case, the parallel galleries of House E were the first step toward such interior space, but the next efforts, Houses B and C, both achieve greater interior height and span greater interior breadth, with the stability of the corbels anchored in part by the roof comb running atop the center spine. Originally conceived and used as a single open space, House B alone of any palace building offered a large but compact interior space. With its small western door to House E, it also offered the opportunity for lords, and perhaps for the king himself, to move unmonitored in and out of Houses B and E. House E, with its dramatic positioning directly over the *subterráneos,* its complex and surprising interior traffic arrangements, and its obvious emphasis on the king enthroned, celebrates the ruler in general and Pakal in particular, repeatedly re-creating framing that establishes the king as ruler and recapitulates throne events. House B does not offer these "photo opportunities" in which a framed picture is created again and again. Rather, it privileges a simple iconography of (1) what were probably lords with serpents under continuous mat motifs and (2) standing lords on exterior piers (Fig. 6). With its distinctive open plan (i.e., the original plan) and stuccoed mat exterior, this building may have been a *popol na,* or council house, of the sort that Fash and others have hypothesized as the function of Copan Structure 22a (Fash 1991: 130–134; Stomper n.d.), placed so that the king's counselors had both special access and status, similar, in fact, to the positioning of Copan Structures 22 and 22a. Subsequent alterations and interior painted additions added the themes of maize and tribute presentation to House B, appropriate subjects for those who support the kingdom economically. Once House F was constructed, additional walls were set in House B, closing access from one side of the structure to the other.

[1] This pattern of picturing thrones on the occasion of their replacement or termination also occurs with Lintel 3 and Throne 1 of Piedras Negras.

Fig. 6 House B (after Robertson 1983–91, 2: fig. 10).

The grandest element of Pakal's program for the palace, however, was House C, with its soaring vaults (Fig. 7). Whereas all doorways worked equally in House B, the center doorway of House C dominates, with the proportions of the flanking doorways taking their cue from the center but rotated 90 degrees, creating both visual and social hierarchies. The stucco piers on the west façade of House C all feature enthroned and probably masked young lords, perhaps all reiterations of Pakal, but possibly other nobles, and probably all in cutaway bird hoods. Framing and facing the central doorway, these piers seemingly invite others to come in and don elaborate costumes, their faces both revealed and hidden—and unable to be seen except at a distance.

Years later, when Houses A, D, and A-D framed and closed the palace, the Palace Tablet recapitulated the positioning of the Oval Palace Tablet, with its setting in the central doorway of House A-D. But House A-D was no House E. Rather than functioning as any sort of direct entryway to palace rituals, House A-D, with its solid internal wall running the length of the south side of the palace, provides traffic control and management, discreetly channeling visitors and participants in rituals into the two north courts, perhaps thrusting them into an arena of capture and sacrifice on the northeast or transformation on the northwest, all through a façade that seems only to celebrate the succession of a legitimate king.

Fig. 7 House C (after Robertson 1983–91, 2: fig. 198).

Yaxchilan and Bonampak

To see how memory is both the subject and ultimately the object as well of some configurations of Maya architecture, let us start by considering Yaxchilan Structure 44. No stairs appear on any map of the site, but the complex known as the West Acropolis probably featured a flight of stairs running across the isobars of the Bolles map, perhaps leading right to Structure 44. The West Acropolis buildings are oriented largely to the north and east, with Structure 51, now reduced to rubble, undoubtedly dominating the group at the end of the eighth century. Chronologically, with little published archaeology of the West Acropolis, one can feel confident only in asserting the relative priority of Structure 44 (ca. A.D. 740) and relative lateness (ca. A.D. 760) of Structure 42, the only buildings with dated monuments.[2] The presence of an Early Classic stela in front of Structure 44 may argue only for the building having superseded an earlier structure. Later monuments also took their place in front of Structure 44.

The sculptures of Structure 44 would seem to claim a number of Maya firsts:

[2] Some recent work at Yaxchilan has been published in Japan—see García Moll et al. (1990).

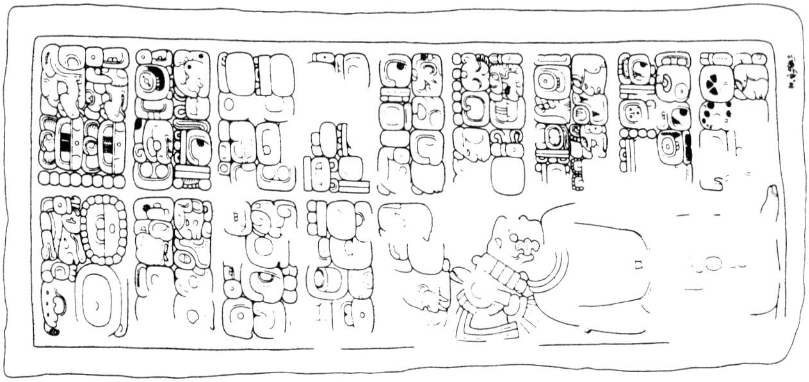

V

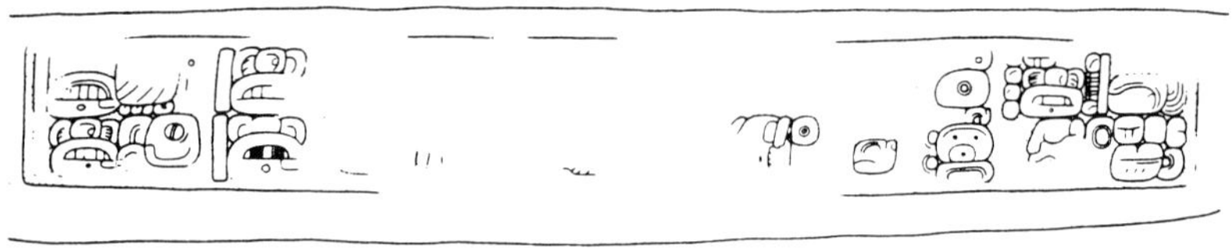

V Riser

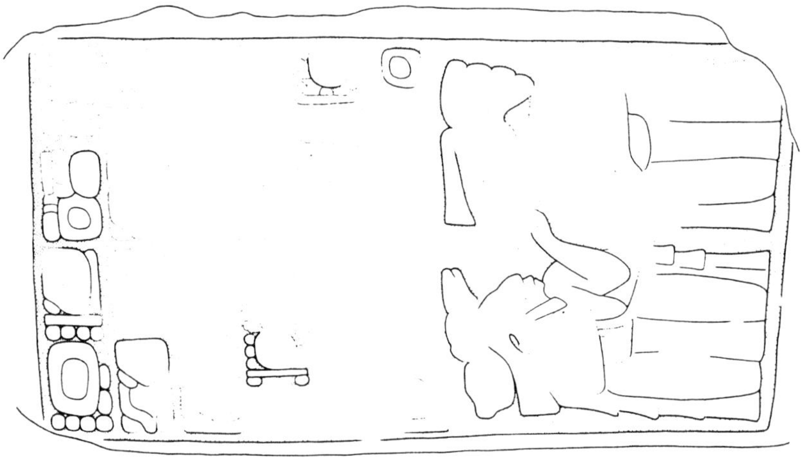

VI

Fig. 8 Structure 44, third doorway, as configured by Carolyn Tate (after Tate 1992: fig. 154). Drawing by Ian Graham (1982: 171–173), copyright 1979–82 by the President and Fellows of Harvard College.

as Proskouriakoff noted in 1950, the lintels of this structure are the first to depict capture in progress (Fig. 9). In the early eighth century, the bent posture of Shield Jaguar and the strain visible in his rear leg are both elements with few prototypes. But beyond the stylistic consideration of the lintels is the remarkable introduction of the first figural hieroglyphic stairway; even more importantly, this is the only integrated program of steps and lintels to survive at all. (Here I do not consider the lintels of Structure 33 and the risers of Hieroglyphic Stairway 2 to be programmatically integrated, although their juxtaposition certainly is meaningful.) As such, the steps and lintels work together; the central lintel, for example, depicts a capture and the step reveals its aftermath, the noble captive deployed like a doormat (Figs. 8, 9). Such a configuration animates memory by offering before-and-after images, by taking the normally terse and laconic text with, at best, one associated human representation and giving it here two, thus revealing sequence and detail that makes the memory more accessible and tangible to those who did not experience it themselves. Because the actual capture, perhaps on a battlefield or perhaps at the home of the opposition, did not take place on the West Acropolis, few could have seen it the way it ultimately came to be represented at Yaxchilan, if indeed the pictorial representation has much relationship to the events that actually transpired. Capture on the battlefield was a relatively private affair, but set at the heart of the sacred precinct it is elevated to state ritual and transmitted to the collective memory. But who could see events on the steps of Structure 44? Teobert Maler found steps that run down to a small open gallery below formed by Structures 43, 44, 45, and 46, and from such steps one would have access to a processional walkway that skirts the precinct. Seen from a point on the stairs or even from the plaza far below, a victorious king in front of Structure 44 would stand as a sort of "king of the mountain," and the entire war inventory of Yaxchilan supports such an interpretation, not only at Structure 44 but also at Structure 41, where Shield Jaguar initially presided over his victories.

As the first example of public narration, in which both the capture and its aftermath receive separate treatment, Structure 44 also can be seen as the first intimation of the sort of narrative complexity and time depth that would be revealed more privately in the battle and captive display scenes of the Bonampak murals. There, not only is capture promulgated on the south wall that one confronts on walking into Room 2, but the vast three-wall representation offers detailed time depth, with its sensitive portrayal of anticipation as well as the act accomplished and with the central representation freezing a single and obviously fleeting moment of capture. By comparison, the presentation of humiliated captives on the north wall reads lucidly and statically, but it, too, embeds time, the time registered through the captives themselves, as if they were ticks of the clock moving from the bold and resistant to the point of torture, to collapse, and to death, the termination of time altogether. Such detailed sequencing not only offers explicit memories and makes them accessible to a viewer who did not personally experience the events, but it also simplifies and sanitizes the events: Bonampak warriors triumph without a scratch; decapitation and heart sacrifice leave no visible blood, thus focusing the viewer's attention to the arcing spurts from the captives' fingers.

In Structure 44, the central lintel (Lintel 45) and step (Step III) are the most important single configurations, for they deal with the individual capture that seems to have vaulted Shield Jaguar into his position of power, a subject celebrated on much earlier Yaxchilan Stelae 19 and 15 set in front of Structure 41. The two stelae depict static, after-the-fact capture, one with both victor and victim stripped and one where they both wear luxurious war bonnets. In both instances, the depiction values equality of ceremonial regalia, elevating captive to the status of the victor and thus glorifying the victory itself. What is different about Structure 44, however, is that the strenuous postures of both Shield Jaguar and his captive infuse the lintel event with energy, whereas Step III is static, like the earlier stelae. But put the two together: the active capture yields to a passive and docile captive to be trod upon (Fig. 9). And the equality of attire yields to appropriation: yes, the captive lord wears a war bonnet on the step, but on the lintel Shield Jaguar wears it, and his captive is bareheaded, as if Shield Jaguar has stripped it off the captive and put it on himself. That is the logical progression of events, and it would seem a straightforward appropriation in an obvious chronological sequence. But now recognize what order in fact the architecture insists upon: one must first see the bound, defeated captive but still in his noble regalia before gaining access to the doorway and seeing his undoing. In other words, neither the experience nor the chronology nor the iconographic sequence is linear; rather, they are bound together and interwoven.

Such interweaving of chronology and iconography takes place with the expanded program of Structure 44 as well. The earliest date of the text, for example, occurs on Step I, with a reference to a date some 140 years before Shield Jaguar's reign, when his ancestor, Knot-eye Jaguar, took a captive named Flint Bat, from Bonampak or Lacanha.[3] Shield Jaguar brings that memory into the present, perhaps as prophecy fulfilled, and links it to his capture of a Bonampak or Lacanha king, Ah Kan. We can read across the rest of the building to wrap

[3] Here, and elsewhere, many of the names offered are "nicknames" rather than accurate translations.

back to Lintel 46, which unites this same Ah Kan's capture by Shield Jaguar to the capture of Flint Bat by Knot-eye Jaguar but turns it around, starting with an initial series that celebrates Ah Kan's capture—and probably depicting that event as well—and completing the statement by referring back to Flint Bat's demise. Step V offers what seems to be a self-contained variation on this pattern, relating the capture of a Jaguar Hill *ahau* by Bird Jaguar III, Shield Jaguar's father, to the capture of a lord from that same place by Shield Jaguar. Again, I suspect, that one of the agents at work here is the idea of prophecy fulfilled (Sullivan 1989). Only one piece of Structure 44 seems to fall outside what seems to be the stylistic program of the building, and that is Step IV, the only all-glyphic step and the bearer of the dedication of the building itself, thereby offering internal evidence that the step is not to be seen as completely anomalous.

Furthermore, the three upper steps of Structure 44 are carved on both treads and risers, unlike other carved steps, which are carved on one or the other but not both. By confining the captive depiction and capture narration to the treads, the Yaxchilan designer reserves the risers for statements of parentage and personal glorification. Accordingly, although one must step on captives, one can never step on the names of forebears, and they function as supports, elevating whoever stands above. By this configuration, Shield Jaguar both honors his parents and uses them to promote his own status.

As I have previously stated (Miller 1983), the Structure 44 program appears without any known prototype and then is not manifested in the same way again. With its emphasis on the visually expository sequence, its closest parallel would in fact be the Bonampak murals, where the sequence of active capture followed by display on a staircase is akin to Structure 44—and may in fact be the specific staircase of the captives' demise. The Bonampak murals are also in a structure where the lintels, although made 40 or 50 years after those at Yaxchilan, are the only set to recapitulate the postures of the figures on the lintels at Structure 44. The entire kinetic and interactive quality of Structure 44 is also expanded at Bonampak. In this regard, Structure 44 and the Bonampak paintings also bear a resemblance to one another, for both programs exhibit what seem to be a beginning and an end.

But here we might stop and ask a few questions: how do we get from Structure 44 to Bonampak if there are no intermediaries? Did the Bonampak artists travel around and seek out models? Even more to the point, how did Structure 44 come into being in the first place? There are earlier examples of hieroglyphic stairs, always associated with warfare and victory (e.g., Naranjo) but the entire composition of carved tread, riser, and lintel took imagination and a vision of human power encapsulated in one small building.

Lost Prototypes?

What I would like to propose is that the invention and imagination required to build Structure 44 at Yaxchilan (or Structure 23, for that matter, or even the Bonampak murals) nevertheless built on a tradition that remains only in the realm of guesswork: the lost books of the Classic Maya.

Most Maya hieroglyphic steps are carved on the risers, with only a few carved treads. The subject matter of hieroglyphic stairs is usually victory, but carved risers and treads occasionally treat other subjects, such as the comprehensive lineage history propounded on the Copan hieroglyphic stairs. The orientation of the Structure 44 treads, with their texts framing bound kneeling captives in all cases, has never been easy to interpret, such that they are usually published the way they demand to be read, that is, stelalike, rather than the way they must be experienced (that is, almost always from one side or the other).[4] Inevitably, either orientation is unsatisfactory, given the conflicting exigencies of reading the text or gaining access to the chamber. This leads me to suspect that their current positioning on stair treads is not necessarily the native one for this iconography and text. In fact, I suspect that this format may derive from the Maya screenfold manuscript, where the text of the lintel might come first, followed by depiction of the humiliated and abject captive (Fig. 9). The redundant personal genealogy of the risers might appear only once. Thus, one might well imagine that a book with screenfold leaves opposing Shield Jaguar with his many captives, as well as both historical precedent and prophecy interwoven, may have formed a real or mental prototype for Structure 44. Proclaimed on the grand scale of the building, history, prophecy, and present victory were publicly inscribed.

All history, of course, has a point of view, and the circumstances of Structure 44 offer some interesting insight into the Yaxchilan point of view. In proclaiming victory in the era of Shield Jaguar, victory of the past is recalled, even elevated—without compensatory memory of defeat, even degradation. In the generation of Shield Jaguar's father, for example, Yaxchilan and Bonampak *ahaus* appeared as liege lords of the Piedras Negras king, Ruler 2, and at least one Yaxchilan king named Knot-eye Jaguar is portrayed as a captive at Piedras Negras (on Lintel 12), perhaps the same Knot-eye Jaguar remembered at Structure 44

[4] Carolyn Tate has been the only student of Structure 44 to publish the steps horizontally (Tate 1992).

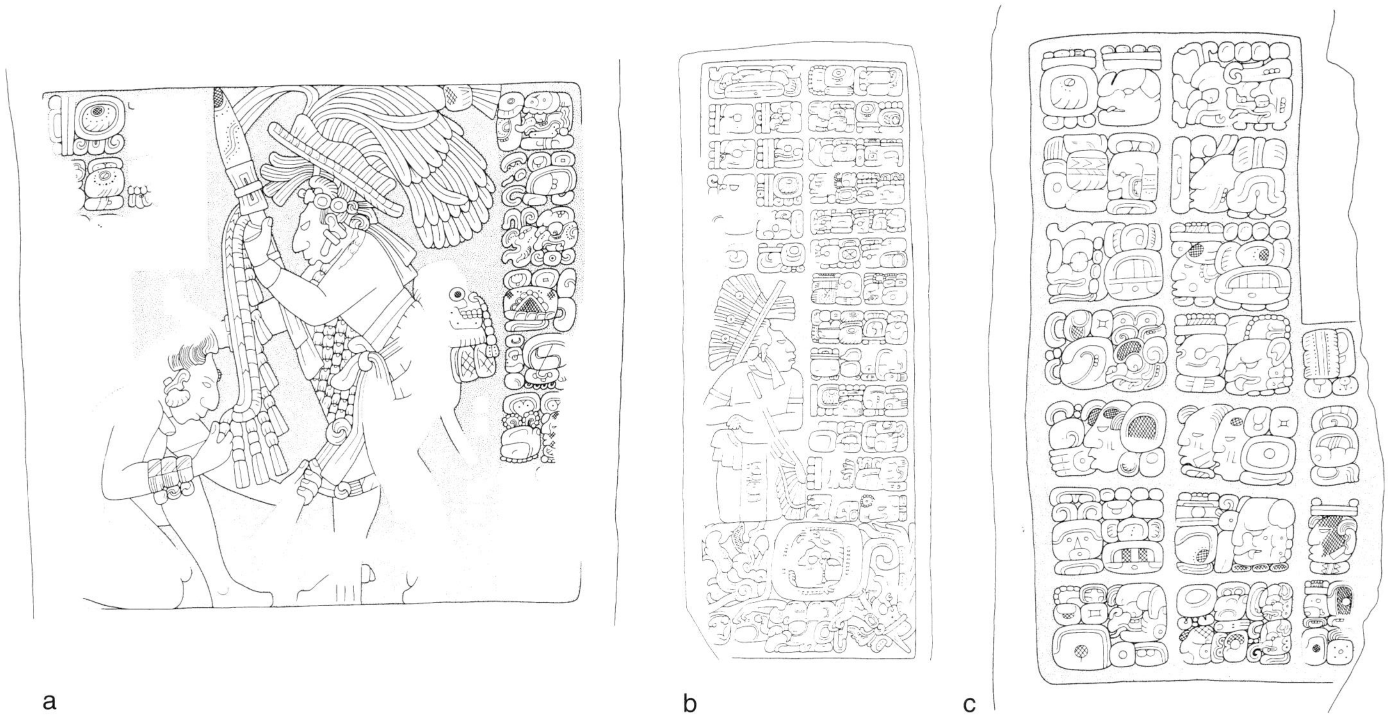

a b c

Fig. 9 Structure 44 as a book (a, after Graham 1979: 99; b–c, after Graham 1982: 169, 170). Copyright 1979–82 by the President and Fellows of Harvard College.

only in victory. Nevertheless, in these same generations, Yaxchilan may well have dominated Bonampak, and the Structure 44 statements narrate a particular history, in which Yaxchilan dominates Bonampak and without reference to ancillary events at Piedras Negras.

Furthermore, the events of Shield Jaguar's life that form the substantive narrative of Structure 44 were almost all old news by the time the structure went up: why tell the stories of Structure 40 again when surely Shield Jaguar's defeat of Ah Kan, Ah Chuen, and the *y-ahau-te* of the serpent segment place had all made his name some 40 years before the construction of Structure 44? Initially emblazoned on stelae, these proclamations had indeed been news and the definition of a new political order along the Usumacinta. At Structure 44, the same events become part of a reordered and reframed past, perhaps even publicly signaling to us that the books documenting the era had been rewritten, placing Shield Jaguar at the apex of a complex history, but one in which his role had been foretold. By narrating the complex history publicly, the Yaxchilan lords also interpreted the past for the public, establishing the new collective memory.

Tonina

We can read all this at Yaxchilan, but what goes on beyond these local political considerations? Are there Maya prescriptions for mass memory that go beyond the parochial? If we turn to Tonina, we can consider a kingdom not only deeply intertwined in Usumacinta politics but one that retained a distinctive artistic and architectural idiom while nevertheless engaged in and aware of traditions characteristic of its neighbors. The panel featuring K'an Xul of Palenque at Tonina has been recognized as evidence not only of Palencano defeat at the hands of Tonina in the early eighth century but also tributary sculpture performed by Palencano artists (Schele and Miller 1986), the linear and graceful two-dimensional rendering of the captive king contrasting with the three-dimensional format favored by Tonina's own rulers for official portraiture. If we turn back one generation, to the era of Kan Balam at Palenque, we can see an inverted artistic relationship, for the single freestanding stela at Palenque, originally set at the Temple of the Cross, would appear not only to be worked in Tonina style but even crafted of a more porous and probably foreign rock (perhaps even the sandstone of Tonina, although the stela has not been tested), in what may be evidence of tribute paid to Palenque at the end of the seventh century (Fig. 10). Furthermore, the single three-dimensional rendering of a ruler at Yaxchilan, the great three-dimensional sculpture of Bird Jaguar now kept inside Structure 33, bears eroded text that runs down its spine, a feature otherwise limited to Tonina and perhaps further evidence of artistic tribute in the mid-eighth century (Fig. 11).

Fig. 10 Stela 1, Palenque (after Stephens 1841, 2: 349).

Over the past two decades, archaeologists have been unveiling the secrets of Tonina, a site initially noted only for its late initial series date (10.4.0.0.0, in 880) and then later for its historical role in derailing Palenque's political trajectory early in the eighth century. As documented by Becquelin, Baudez, and Taladoire, however, with a few recent additions by Yadeun, the architecture of Tonina is particularly hierarchical and structured in its main ceremonial pre-

Fig. 11 Seated sculpture from Structure 33, Yaxchilan (after Maler 1901–3: 161).

cinct, a steep natural incline reshaped into seven specific terraces by Tonina lords, with some evidence of Early Classic efforts but in campaigns focused largely in the eighth century (Becquelin and Baudez 1979–82; Becquelin and Taladoire 1990; Yadeun 1992). Few other sites have had their sculptures as dispersed as Tonina has, however, and a profusion of fragments and confusion about original location, even when recovered archaeologically, have created a jigsaw puzzle that seems both to defy archaeology and to plead for more of it.

Like Yaxchilan, Tonina features victorious lords at its apex; its rare two-dimensional ruler portraits are concentrated on an unusual radial structure that may have iconographic value indicating in some way "completion" or even "apex." Other buildings on the seventh and sixth terraces enshrine rulership, surmounting the hillside like a stepped-back architectural crown. Backing in to the sixth terrace, fifth terrace structures like E5-2 present a calm and static picture of the Tonina ruler. At the base of the site lies a great plaza, or the Esplanade, as it is termed, encompassing a range of buildings featuring rulers, and including a freestanding temple pyramid that might be funerary in nature but that features two ballcourts of distinctive character.

Tonina lords constructed the large H6-2–H6-3 court on a grand scale, in an I-shape, and profusely adorned its façade with informative and enlightening architectural sculpture for the modern viewer. The small G5-1–G5-2 ballcourt sits at a near right angle to its larger mate; streamlined and slight by comparison, the G5 court is open-ended, like most Maya courts, and bears relatively little internal sculpture, as is more common at Palenque, Yaxchilan, Piedras Negras, and Tikal. In the juxtaposition of vaulting rulership and subdued ball game spread across seven terraces, the fundamental relationship between the temple pyramid and the ballcourt is revealed, the same relationship seen condensed, for example, at Tikal, with Temple I and the small ballcourt, or conflated visually, as on the carved risers of Structure 33 at Yaxchilan.

Frequently implicit but rarely explicit is the ritual and historical relationship of warfare to ball game, a subject that Stephen Houston and I have dealt with previously, particularly the issues of underrepresentation and conflation (Miller and Houston 1987). At Tonina, amid many other competing agendas, these particular connections are spelled out, with rulership at the top, victory in warfare and human sacrifice largely set in the middle ranges, particularly on the fifth terrace, and ball game and sacrifice at the base.

The small ballcourt features no surviving architectural sculpture within the court, but it is lined along the exterior of its southern structure by a series of giant *ahau* altars, a sculptural type better known through a single example at Tikal and numerous examples at Caracol, where the form may have been developed to celebrate *katuns* of conquest. The Tikal example of a giant *ahau,* along with Stela 30 the first sculpture to be made after the long wars with Caracol, is even worked in Caracol style, as is the stela itself.[5] In general, although not exclusively, the text and iconography of altars deal with sacrifice. In its round sectioned form, the stone altar may derive from a wood analogue, the stump or the sliced section of a tree, which in a natural form would have continued to weep sap for some time, perhaps the model from nature for the

[5] Clemency Coggins long ago suggested a connection to Caracol, based on the unusual presence at Tikal of a single giant *ahau* altar commemorating 9.13.0.0.0 (n.d.: 399).

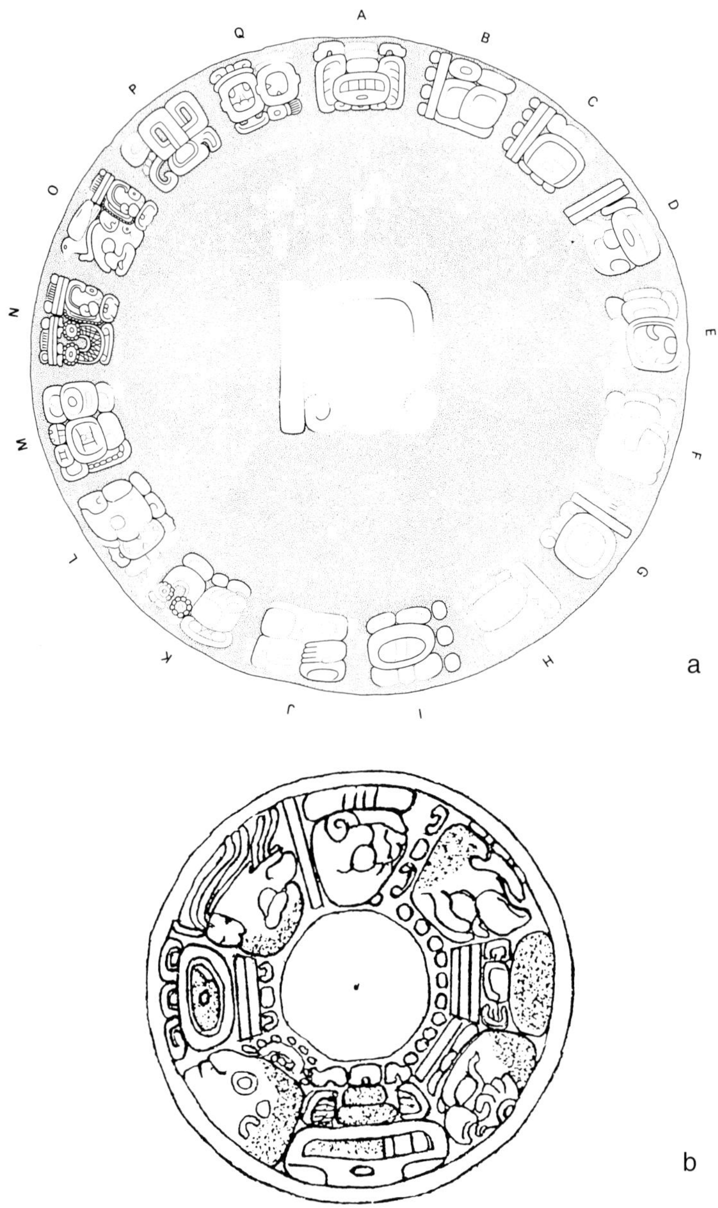

Fig. 12 (a) Giant *ahau* altar, Tonina, Monument 110. Drawing by Peter Mathews (after Becquelin and Baudez 1982, 3: fig. 135); (b) Yaxchilan Altar 10 (after Tate 1992: fig. 120).

bleeding sacrificial victim. With carved concentric text or imagery, the surface of an altar also takes on the image of tree rings, as, for example, at Yaxchilan (Fig. 12b). At the Tonina small ballcourt (G5), the giant *ahau* altars bear laconic texts that can only hint at conquest; nevertheless, aligned like stumps of severed trees these monuments may refer to the victory so specifically spelled out on the fifth terrace (Fig. 12a).

The large ballcourt eschews any such subtlety, for surely few other Mesoamerican courts—and here one might compare Chichen Itza's Great Ballcourt-Tzompantli combination—provide such a deliberate assemblage of and for humiliation. Captive bodies form protruding markers, perhaps once fitted with now lost rings where the human head would be, to indicate the bilateral axis of the court. Sculptors have compressed the captive human forms into the shape of the human phallus, to be repeatedly battered and attacked by aggressive players. Yet these human bodies are framed against massive shields, at once both objects of aggression and trophies of battle. These captive/shield configurations probably once numbered six in all and adorned the symmetrically parallel interior walls of the large court, along its highest tier (Figs. 13 and 14). Usumacinta warriors fought with shields of just this sort and, after the

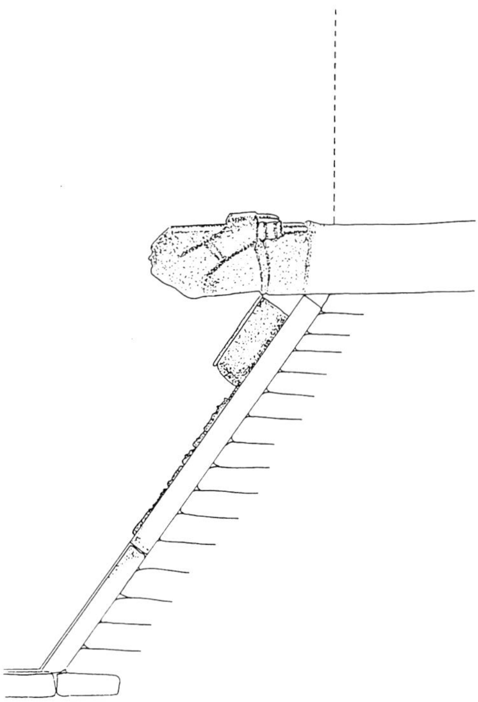

Fig. 13 Tonina Monument 31, from Ballcourt H. Drawing by Ian Graham (after Baudez and Mathews 1979: fig. 13).

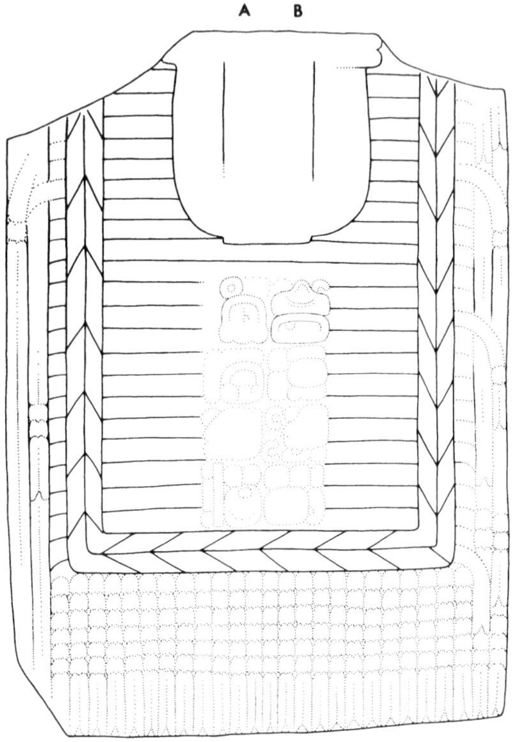

Fig. 14 Tonina Monument 31, from Ballcourt H. Drawing by Peter Mathews (after Becquelin and Baudez 1982, 3: fig. 135).

battle, they rolled them up like bedrolls and slung them from their backs before displaying them in victory, perhaps on a ballcourt. But here, the shields are the framework for now-eroded texts that relate victors and captors, with direct reference to Palenque's humiliation at the hands of Tonina. In fact, one Sac Balam named on a fifth terrace slab is named as the subject of capture on one carved shield. But beyond the text is the image on the shield, graphically depicting, despite the serious erosion, truncated human bodies, perhaps bound and trussed images of bound humans from different angles, as if representations of some bouncing ball from a flip book.

Monuments 68, 69, and 51 are ballcourt alley markers of H6, two of them plain round stones and Monument 69 featuring a seated lord with serpent bar.[6] Yet another round monument was described at the larger court by a nineteenth-century visitor. Now lost, the monument described sounds as if it were nearly

[6] According to Becquelin and Baudez (1982), even Monument 69 is not in its original setting: it was designed for a larger space than its present position.

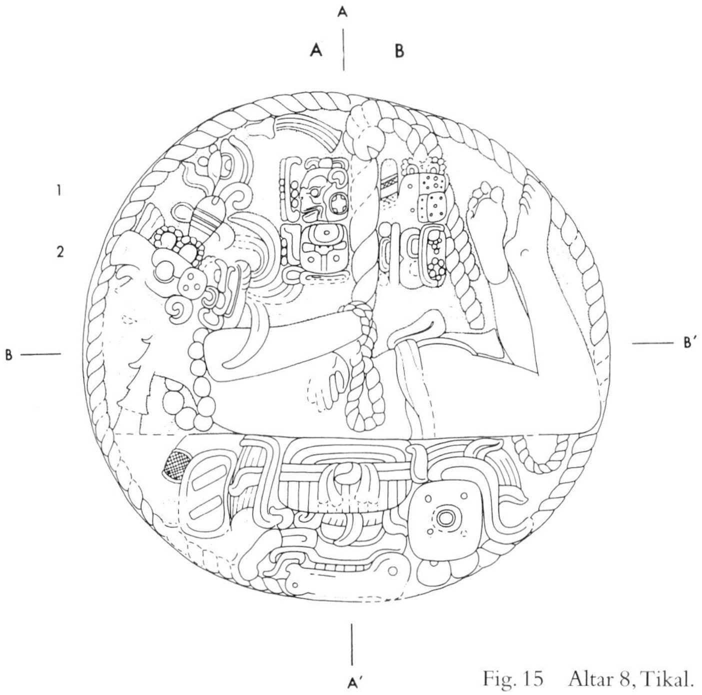

Fig. 15 Altar 8, Tikal. Drawing by William Coe (after Jones and Satterthwaite, 1982: fig. 30).

identical to Altar 8 at Tikal (Fig. 15), a monument celebrating ballcourt sacrifice (Becquelin and Baudez 1982, 2: 784–785).

The ballcourts at Tonina, then, bear a cohesive and recognizable pattern of commemorated humiliation. Where the pattern may be most innovative is on the fifth terrace, where dozens of monuments depicting captives have been recovered and where dozens of others may originally have been set, including some from distant contexts (e.g., Monument 27 in Fig. 16). Most recently excavated monuments on the fifth terrace feature captives, mostly headless. Recent discoveries have included the famous two-dimensional rendering of K'an Xul of Palenque as well as the prismatic Monument 102 and what may be the only known example of a female captive. Bearing few dates, these monuments might generally be assigned to the first half of the eighth century. Smashed in situ, or hurled down onto the Esplanade, these sculptures may be the most devastating evidence of the physical destruction Maya lords wreaked upon their foes.

Archaeologically, Becquelin and Baudez found that fifth terrace structures

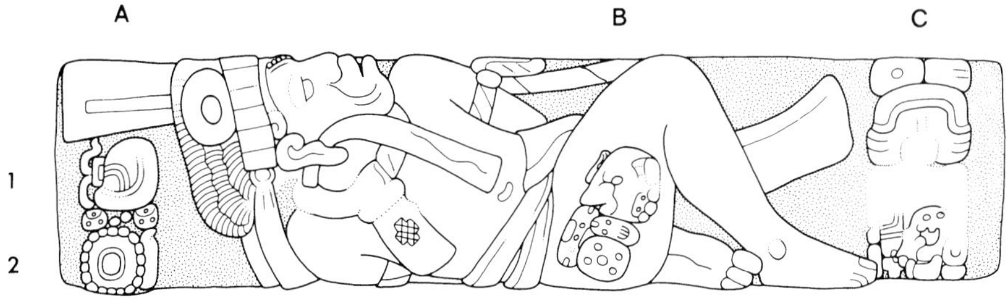

Fig. 16 Tonina Monument 27. Drawing by Peter Mathews (after Becquelin and Baudez 1982, 3: fig. 165).

included many impoverished burials, perhaps the remains of captives or perhaps merely indicative of the economic desperation in the eighth and ninth centuries (Becquelin and Baudez 1979: 45–79). Structurally, rulership at the top yields to captives, with their demise spelled out far below. Although three-dimensional captives formed part of the tableaux, generally three-dimensional ruler figures dominated two-dimensional captive representations.

Although many of the captive figures from the fifth terrace seem, upon first examination, to be unique examples of the form, they nevertheless belong to the broader tradition of rendering captives, commonly seen, for example, at Yaxchilan or Piedras Negras in this same era. Like most sophisticated artistic ateliers and developed traditions, the Maya example demonstrates that stock figures may be repeated. Although we may expect such repetition for the dominant figures, who seek to be represented in such a way as to emulate their predecessors, subsidiary figures, even ones we read as imaginative or unusual in their renderings, may also be conventional. For example, the captive depicted on La Pasadita Panel 1 finds its reversed identity in the Bonampak paintings (Figs. 17 and 18). What is more unusual than the reuse of the form per se is the geographical distance and the time lag between the two renderings, with some 75 years and at least 50 km and the Usumacinta River separating them. Furthermore, although reversing figures in the European tradition is often related to the printmaking tradition and the natural reversals thereof, among the Maya one might suspect simply the sheer common currency of certain images.

By assuming certain conventional representations, we might retrieve the assemblage that Tonina lords once configured on the fifth terrace. Just (n.d.) has recently tried to make sense of the figures by re-creating heads for them and assembling them into two parallel tiers, as facings of E5-11. We need only reverse two of them, for example, to see that they may have analogues elsewhere. Take Fig. 19a, for example, a captive in a strained and contorted seated posture.

Fig. 17 La Pasadita Panel 1. Drawing courtesy of Ian Graham.

Fig. 18 Detail, Bonampak paintings. Room 2, north wall. Photograph by Jorge Pérez de Lara © 1995 Project Bonampak/ Proyecto Bonampak.

He, as well as other figures from Tonina, can be assembled, some of them reversed, to form near identities with figures of the Bonampak captive display. A carved fragment of captive hair, thick and coiled, seems again to have been sheared from a Bonampak head (Fig. 19b). The Bonampak paintings clearly belong to the last decade of the eighth century, while the evidence at Tonina points to some 50 to 80 years earlier.

We may well suppose that the principle of "captured art" applies here and that as tributary support Tonina demanded the services of foreign artists. I think the concept of captured art may well be present, but it does not explain the entire phenomenon. Instead, what I believe these duplicated figures across a region stretching from Piedras Negras to Yaxchilan to Tonina and Palenque may also be indicating to us is the sort of training that artists may have received as well as the sort of missing books with stock imagery that we now can only guess at. Across the entire western Maya realm, artists shared some corpus of specific figural representation. Using templates, making tracings, and reversing figures, artists called on their training and their records on paper to devise new groupings or to work out individual figures. But the results were translations of the linear and the small-scale into the monumental and occasionally three-dimensional representations. The translation called for the individual artist's imagination, whether in the conception at Bonampak that makes the stages of degradation of the captives read like pages in a flip book or in the subtle recognition that the nose of the captive on Tonina Monument 27 could be wrapped around the riser onto the tread, inviting greater humiliation (Fig. 16).

CONCLUSIONS

Beyond formal considerations and, ultimately, iconography, architecture can often be read as a metaphor for a mental outlook, a period in history, or an ethnic or societal identity. In such terms, what is Maya architecture the metaphor for? In this case, the forms of domestic architecture, with their openness and egalitarian qualities, are usurped and transformed into tools of control, hierarchy, and power. Individual trappings of war and triumph may be only incidental to the larger project. By the late eighth century, when architecture itself begins appearing in works of art, as, for example at Bonampak, the particular architecture figured is the staircase and the platform. By the end of the eighth century, architecture begins to become the subject of art rather than art's armature. And even the mere suggestion of monumental stairs had become the sign for control and domination. Memory feeds on signs as well as on specific narrative.

Using a vast vocabulary in their writing and iconography, and in their art

a

Fig. 19 (a) Tonina Fragment 95 and (b) Fragment 61 (after Becquelin and Baudez 1982, 3: figs. 172b and 182b).

b

and architecture, the Maya developed endless riffs on themes. In the Maya equivalent of the Aztec *calmecac,* they practiced a vocabulary that was both universally Maya and simultaneously local. By the eighth century, in the western Maya realm, Maya architectural compositions increasingly focused on the staircase, committing to public memory a celebration of warfare and sacrifice and increasingly figuring such staircases with conventional images.

Acknowledgments Initial work for this study was supported by a senior fellowship from the National Endowment for the Humanities. Yale University students provided useful commentary on many of these ideas in a seminar on the western Maya realm during the spring of 1994. Stephen Houston provided critical insights and suggestions both before and after the October 1994 Dumbarton Oaks symposium. Preparation of the final manuscript was conducted with support from the Guggenheim Memorial Foundation.

BIBLIOGRAPHY

Baudez, Claude, and Peter Mathews

1979 Capture and Sacrifice at Palenque. In *Tercera mesa redonda de Palenque,* vol. 4 (Donnan Call Jeffers, ed.; M. G. Robertson, gen. ed.): 31–40. Pre-Columbian Art Research Center, Palenque, Chiapas, Mexico.

Becquelin, Pierre, and Claude F. Baudez

1979–82 *Toniná: une cité maya du Chiapas (Mexique).* 3 vols. Mission archéologique et ethnologique française au Mexique, México, D.F.

Becquelin, Pierre, and Eric Taladoire

1990 *Toniná: une cité maya du Chiapas (Mexique).* Centre d'études mexicaines et centraméricaines, México, D.F.

Coggins, Clemency

n.d. Painting and Drawing Styles at Tikal: An Historical and Iconographic Reconstruction. Ph.D. dissertation, Harvard University, 1975.

Fash, William L.

1991 *Scribes, Warriors and Kings: The City of Copán and the Ancient Maya.* Thames and Hudson, London.

García Moll, Roberto, et al.

1990 *La exposición de la cultura maya.* Tokyo.

Graham, Ian

1979 *Corpus of Maya Hieroglyphic Inscriptions,* vol. 3, pt. 2: *Yaxchilan.* Peabody Museum of Archaeology and Ethnology, Harvard University, Cambridge, Mass.

1982 *Corpus of Maya Hieroglyphic Inscriptions,* vol. 3, pt. 3: *Yaxchilan.* Peabody Museum of Archaeology and Ethnology, Harvard University, Cambridge, Mass.

Houston, Stephen D.

1984 A Quetzal Feather Dance at Bonampak, Chiapas, Mexico. *Journal de la Société des Américanistes* 70: 127–138.

1993 *Hieroglyphs and History at Dos Pilas: Dynastic Politics of the Classic Maya.* University of Texas Press, Austin.

1994 Literacy among the Maya. In *Writing without Words: Alternative Literacies in Mesoamerica and the Andes* (W. Mignolo and E. Boone, eds.): 27–49. Duke University Press, Durham, N.C.

Jones, Christopher, and Linton Satterthwaite

1982 *The Monuments and Inscriptions of Tikal: The Carved Monuments.* Tikal Report, no. 33a. University Museum, University of Pennsylvania, Philadelphia.

Just, Bryan

n.d. Captives at Tonina. Manuscript on file, Department of the History of Art, Yale University, 1994.

Kubler, George

1961 The Design of Space in Maya Architecture. In *Miscellanea Paul Rivet: octogenario dicata*: 515–531. Universidad Nacional Autónoma de México, México, D.F.

MALER, TEOBERT

1901–3 *Researches in the Central Portion of the Usumatsintla Valley*. Memoirs of the Peabody Museum of Archaeology and Ethnology, no. 3. Harvard University, Cambridge, Mass.

MARTIN, SIMON, AND NIKOLAI GRUBE

1995 Maya Superstates. *Archaeology* 48: 41–46.

MATHEWS, PETER, AND MERLE GREENE ROBERTSON

1985 Notes on the Olvidado, Palenque, Chiapas, Mexico. In *Fifth Palenque Round Table, 1983,* vol. 7 (V. M. Fields, ed.; M. G. Robertson, gen. ed.): 7–17. Pre-Columbian Art Research Institute, San Francisco.

MAUDSLAY, ALFRED PERCIVAL

1899–1902 *Archaeology.* Biologia centrali-americana. 5 vols. Porter and Dulau, London.

MILLER, MARY E.

1983 Some Observations on Structure 44, Yaxchilan. In *Contributions to Maya Hieroglyphic Decipherment* (Stephen D. Houston, ed.): 62–79. Human Relations Area Files, New Haven, Conn.

MILLER, MARY E., AND STEPHEN D. HOUSTON

1987 The Classic Maya Ballgame and Its Architectural Setting: A Study in Relations between Text and Image. *RES: Anthropology and Aesthetics* 14: 47–66.

PROSKOURIAKOFF, TATIANA

1950 *A Study of Classic Maya Sculpture.* Carnegie Institution, Publication 593. Washington, D.C.

ROBERTSON, MERLE GREENE

1983–91 *The Sculpture of Palenque.* 4 vols. Princeton University Press, Princeton, N.J.

SCHELE, LINDA, AND MARY ELLEN MILLER

1986 *The Blood of Kings: Ritual and Dynasty in Maya Art.* Kimbell Art Museum and George Braziller, Fort Worth and New York.

SIMPSON, JON ERIC S.

1974 The New York Relief Panel—and Some Associations with Reliefs at Palenque and Elsewhere, Part I. In *Segunda mesa redonda de Palenque,* pt. 3 (Merle Greene Robertson, ed.): 95–105. Robert Louis Stevenson School, Pebble Beach, Calif.

SMITH, A. L.

1950 *Uaxactun, Guatemala: Excavations of 1931–37.* Carnegie Institution, Publication 588. Washington, D.C.

STEPHENS, JOHN LLOYD

1841 *Incidents of Travel in Central America, Chiapas, and Yucatan.* 2 vols. Harper's, New York.

STOMPER, JEFFREY

n.d. The *Popol Na*: A Model for Ancient Maya Community Structure at Copán, Honduras. Ph.D. dissertation, Yale University, 1996.

SULLIVAN, PAUL

1989 *Unfinished Conversations: Mayas and Foreigners between Two Wars.* Knopf, New York.

TATE, CAROLYN
1992 *Yaxchilan: The Design of a Maya Ceremonial City.* University of Texas Press, Austin.

THOMPSON, J. ERIC S.
1954 *The Rise and Fall of Maya Civilization.* University of Oklahoma Press, Norman.

WAUCHOPE, ROBERT
1938 *Modern Maya Houses: A Study of Their Archaeological Significance.* Carnegie Institution, Publication 502. Washington, D.C.

WILLEY, GORDON R.
1953 *Prehistoric Settlement Patterns in the Virú Valley, Perú.* Bulletin of the Bureau of American Ethnology, no. 155. U.S. Government Printing Office, Washington, D.C.

YADEUN ANGULO, JUAN
1992 *Toniná: El laberinto del inframundo.* Gobierno del Estado de Chiapas, Mexico.

Dynastic Architectural Programs: Intention and Design in Classic Maya Buildings at Copan and Other Sites

WILLIAM L. FASH
HARVARD UNIVERSITY

MAYA ARCHAEOLOGY has always been fascinated with the elaborate temple pyramids, palaces, and stelae plazas that formed the centers of the ancient communities from its inception to the present day. Despite the intense interest in large-scale architecture, we still have a rather limited excavated sample of Maya dynastic building programs. The scale of construction of these monuments poses immense logistical problems and other challenges for conscientious investigation, stabilization, and publication. More often than not, the version of a large-scale construction visible on the surface has one or more previous structures buried inside of it. This makes the problem of complete sampling of architectural monuments even more daunting from both a practical and an interpretive point of view. Despite these rather long odds, some remarkable progress has been made. Increased understanding of the writing system and pictorial symbol systems used to adorn the buildings and the principles of organization of Maya architecture on the level of commoners and the nobility help inform our judgments about the function and meaning of the building complexes that formed the heart of the Classic Maya towns and cities. This paper represents an attempt to understand how the ruling families organized their sacred and secular spaces and what kinds of buildings and messages they erected in those environs. It also explores the degree to which one may reliably infer the political strategies, idiosyncratic concerns, and even the personality of royal Maya patrons from the architecture they left behind.

The question of the design and intent of Maya dynastic architecture is best addressed in sites where a long sequence of constructions with accompanying historical texts and pictorial imagery have been recovered. In analyzing the original contributions of individual rulers to the art and architecture of their palace compounds, Mesoamericanists often address questions of statecraft and political strategies (Fash 1988; Flannery and Marcus 1983; Gillespie 1989; Houston 1993; Marcus 1992; Schele and Freidel 1990). Some investigators try to progress even higher up the ladder of inference and get at issues of the idiosyncratic concerns and even of the personalities of particular Classic Maya rulers (Jones 1977; Schele and Freidel 1990). One potential pitfall to these approaches of course is sampling, that awful problem that is present if not necessarily properly addressed in virtually all archaeological analysis. No large Mesoamerican site has ever been excavated in its entirety, even at the level of the final-phase buildings. The earlier structures buried beneath the final phase of construction are usually sampled only by test probes or trenched if they are investigated at all. This paucity of data on the earlier buildings and the larger complexes of which they formed a part leaves us with a weak understanding of the development of particular ideas and behaviors through time and space, hardly solid footing from which to judge the architectural originality or underlying motives of the latest actors on the stage of their kingdom's history.

Extensive investigations of earlier building complexes have been carried out in a few Maya lowland epicenters, and most of them have been properly published. These studies can tell us much about the trajectory of construction and the intents of the builders through time in particular spaces. There is now a fairly complete picture of this subject at the epicenters of Tikal (Coe 1990; Laporte and Fialko 1993, 1995), Uaxactun (Proskouriakoff 1946; Smith 1950; Valdés 1988), and Copan (Andrews n.d.; Andrews and Fash 1992; W. Fash et al. 1992; Larios, Fash, and Stuart 1994; Schele and Freidel 1990: chap. 8; Sharer, Miller, and Traxler 1992; Sharer n.d.; Stuart 1992). Important excavation projects in the Copan valley directed by a number of scholars have uncovered sculpture-adorned buildings and complexes that have to some extent also been "read" as texts and compared to the works in the royal compound (Ashmore 1991; Fash 1983, 1986; Webster 1989c; Webster, Evans, and Sanders 1993; Willey, Leventhal, and Fash 1978).[1] More broadly, many of the architectural patterns and principles that have been documented in Tikal, Uaxactun, and Copan are evident in different forms at other sites in the Maya lowlands and can shed light on the issue of the ideological and political strategies put to work by different

[1] It is impossible to cite and do justice to all of the different investigators and kinds of research that they have undertaken in the Copan region over the past 20 years in a specialized article such as this one. The interested reader is referred to an upcoming volume to be published by the School of American Research (Fash and Andrews, n.d.) for a more comprehensive bibliography.

dynasties and rulers in their respective dynastic building programs.

The origin of the ruling dynasties of the Classic Maya kingdoms is likely to be a controversial topic for quite some time. In most cases, our sole source of information on the early history of a royal line is that which was recorded on stone monuments by later rulers. If uncorroborated by other sources, such textual references are of course difficult to evaluate and are presently viewed by many students with deep suspicion. In Copan, we have addressed this issue directly by designing research to document the developmental trajectory of the building complexes in the site core. In the process, we strive to systematically test the historical claims of the last rulers through archaeological excavations and epigraphic and iconographic analyses of the inscriptions and pictorial imagery found in association with the Early Classic buildings. Since the origins of the Copan Mosaics Project in 1985 and its successors, the Hieroglyphic Stairway Project and the Copan Acropolis Archaeological Project, we have scrutinized the "texts" of the final-phase buildings, imagery, and inscriptions as information to be rigorously tested and evaluated on the basis of three broad categories of data: (1) the sociopolitical context in which the later rulers were acting, based on the gamut of information available in the site core and its regional sustaining area; (2) the archaeological remains of the earlier time periods in the site core and valley, particularly the time ascribed to the "founder" of the Classic period Copan dynasty and his immediate successors; and (3) the inscribed architectural and freestanding texts buried beneath the later structures that contain contemporaneous records of the events deemed important in the early centuries of the dynasty's history (Fash 1988; Fash and Sharer 1991). Although our research is still ongoing, we can now provide some broad outlines of the continuities and changes that occurred in the dynastic building programs of many of Copan's rulers. This in turn allows us to reevaluate some of the earlier ideas about the dynasty and its strategies of statecraft, which had been based predominantly on our understanding of the Late Classic structures in the Principal Group and the valley. It is hoped that the insights derived from this research may enable scholars to make better use of their time and resources when approaching these issues at other sites and regional settings in Mesoamerica.

ORIGINS OF THE DYNASTIC BUILDING PROGRAM IN COPAN

The ruler cited as the founder of the Copan dynasty by his 15 named and numbered successors was referred to in the inscriptions as K'inich Yax K'uk' Mo' (Schele 1992; David Stuart, personal communications, 1984, 1992; Stuart and Schele 1986a). Portraits and textual references to this individual abound in the Copan dynastic monuments of all periods and are found even in ceramic burial furniture in a royal tomb (Agurcia Fasquelle and Fash 1991: 105). Initially, some of our colleagues viewed these records of a founder and a series of early kings that succeeded him with great skepticism. Even the idea that there was a polity of any magnitude in the fifth and early sixth centuries A.D. was rejected based on interpretations derived from test pitting predominantly in the rural sectors of the Copan valley. However, the archaeological evidence is now overwhelming that there was major construction in the acropolis and hieroglyphic stairway plaza areas from A.D. 420 onward (Fash and Sharer 1991; W. Fash et al. 1992; Sharer n.d.; Sharer, Miller, and Traxler 1992; Sharer et al. n.d.). Accompanying hieroglyphic inscriptions and painted texts as well as polychrome pictorial imagery in stucco and painted murals indicate that a series of individuals erected major dynastic monuments both in their own honor and in homage to their predecessors. Significantly, the individuals named in the buried texts and imagery found thus far are the same ones cited in the later texts. Both the buried and the surficial texts associate those same individuals with the same dates for royal accessions and other historical events, in the same chronological order given in the ruler succession (*ts'ah-bu*) counts and on Altar Q (W. Fash et al. 1992). Although it would be premature at this point to conclude that all later texts are historically accurate, I do think it is fair to say that there are presently no known contradictions between the dynastic records of the later (surficially accessible) and earlier (buried) stone monuments of the dynasty of K'inich Yax K'uk' Mo'. On the basis of currently available evidence, there is no documented example in the Copan corpus of rewriting of history and mindful erasing of earlier actors, at least for the dynasty immortalized in stone on the hieroglyphic stairway and on Altar Q. This makes our task of looking at building programs and their patrons' designs and intents far less complicated than it otherwise would be.[2]

The earliest extant elite constructions thus far encountered in the area of the acropolis were uncovered by Robert Sharer and his colleagues in the easternmost sector of the acropolis. These features are dated by radiocarbon assays to the fifth century A.D. and consist of three architectural groups: an elevated platform for elaborate dynastic buildings known as the "Mini-Acropolis of the South"; a palace group; and a northern group (Sharer et al. n.d.). Sharer and his

[2] It is quite possible, and should be kept open as a possibility, that an earlier dynasty resided in the area of the modern town (Morley's Group 9) or in the vicinity of the acropolis underlying Structure 10L-1 in the Principal Group. Archaeological evidence for Early Classic occupations abounds in both these loci. References to individuals antedating K'inich Yax K'uk' Mo' are found in numerous early and later texts, but short of archaeological evidence of the actual monuments of these individuals we are currently unable to evaluate the veracity of these references.

colleagues have demonstrated that the first monumental masonry architecture was built atop the elevated platform in the first quarter of the fifth century. The first structure adorned with painted and modeled stucco is presently referred to by the field name "Hunal." This building had a *talud-tablero* façade on its substructure and a superstructure adorned with vivid mural paintings. Because the superstructure was nearly completely demolished by the Maya before its burial beneath its successor, the original content of the paintings cannot presently be reconstructed from the few scattered pieces of painted plaster that have survived (Sharer n.d.). Before the termination of Hunal, a vaulted tomb was placed under its floor, which may contain the remains of the Copan dynasty's founder, K'inich Yax K'uk' Mo' (Sharer n.d.).

Hunal's successor, "Yehnal" Structure, had polychrome stucco masks depicting the Sun God K'inich Ahau on its substructure and contained a vaulted masonry tomb built integrally into the substructure along its central axis. This building was subsequently encapsulated inside the next one erected at this locus, called "Margarita" Structure, but access to the vaulted tomb of Yehnal was left open by means of a set of stairs that led to the superstructure of Margarita. The modeled stucco decoration of Margarita's substructure included a large full-figure polychrome depiction of two birds with intertwined necks that together with their "sun eyes" and "yax" signs name K'inich Yax K'uk' Mo' ("Sun-eyed Blue-green Quetzal Macaw"; Sharer n.d.). Hunal, Yehnal, and Margarita established the sacred center for the acropolis that was maintained by a succession of five more temples built atop this locus during the remainder of Copan's history, including at least two ("Rosalila" and Structure 10L-16-1st) that also prominently displayed the name of the founder K'inich Yax K'uk' Mo' (Agurcia Fasquelle n.d.; Sharer n.d.).

The birds defining the dynastic founder's name on Margarita Structure stand atop a glyph with supernatural associations that reads "9 Imix," and the whole assemblage was framed on the sides and above by a sky band. This graphic depiction of the first ruler's name was placed on the basal terrace of the substructure to the south of the central staircase on the west side of the building. In the corresponding position to the north of the stairs was another full-figure glyph that, because of its battered state, has not yet been uncovered. However, the hieroglyph at the base of it has been uncovered, and reads "7 Kan" (Sharer n.d.). These same two hieroglyphs are found beneath the feet of the two figures depicted on the Early Cycle 9 floor marker recently discovered beneath the hieroglyphic stairway (Williamson 1996; Fig. 1 here). There, the 9 Imix glyph is beneath the figure of K'inich Yax K'uk' Mo' on the left, and the 7 Kan glyph is seen on the right beneath the feet of Ruler 2, who was first identified by

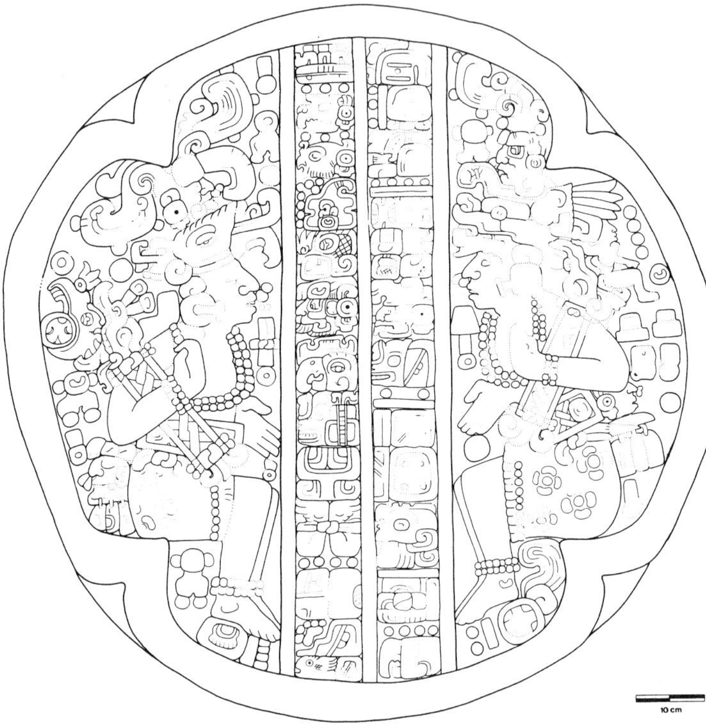

Fig. 1 The Motmot floor marker. On the left is K'inich Yax K'uk' Mo', identified by his bird headdress and his name in the left column of hieroglyphs. On the right is Ruler 2, identified by his headdress and his name in the right column of hieroglyphs. Drawing by Barbara Fash, incorporating field observations by Federico Fahsen, Nikolai Grube, Linda Schele, and David Stuart.

Stephen Houston (personal communication, 1992). This floor marker is associated with the second building constructed at that locus (field name "Motmot") and the first version of the Copan ballcourt (Fig. 2), labeled IA by Strömsvik (1952).

Thus, the first (known) hieroglyphically labeled dynastic architecture in the Copan Acropolis was commisioned by the second ruler, the successor of K'inich Yax K'uk' Mo'. The Motmot and Margarita monuments bear the names of the first two rulers of the dynasty and place them in association with the supernatural domains symbolized by the hieroglyphs 7 Kan (for Ruler 2) and 9 Imix (for Ruler 1). The Motmot marker itself stresses underworld contexts, most notably the quatrefoil in which the two rulers are depicted. The diameter and

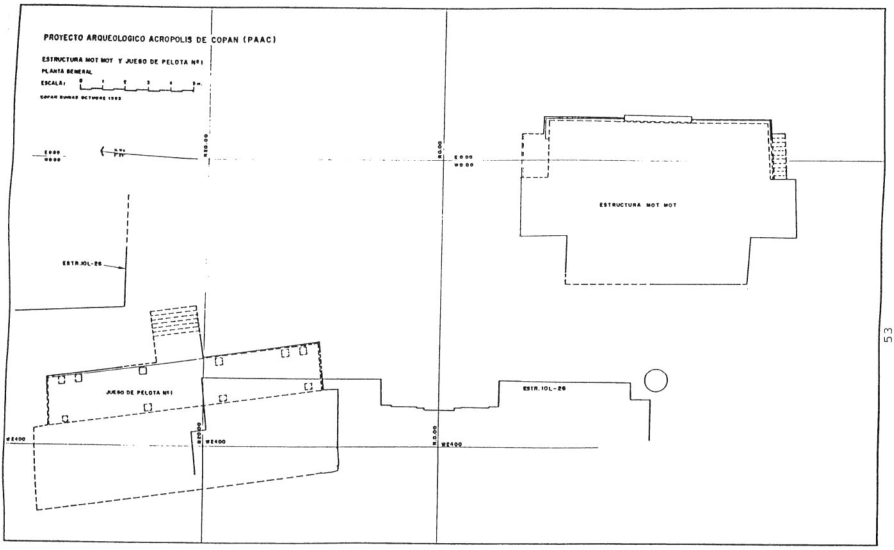

Fig. 2 Plan of Motmot structure, the Motmot floor marker, and the east building of Ballcourt I. Their location with respect to final-phase Structure 26 is shown by the outline of the latter. Plan by Richard Williamson, Fernando López, and Rudy Larios.

horizontal placement of the edges of the quatrefoil corresponded precisely to those of the cylindrical tomb (of form and size of the type most commonly used for burials at Teotihuacan; see Manzanilla 1993 and Serrano Sánchez 1993) found directly beneath the marker itself. On the substructure of Motmot there were four large sky bands and a depiction of GI (with a large bird in his headdress) on the eastern side, framing the marker and tomb in the celestial context. The Margarita substructure imagery emphasizes the celestial realm, as denoted by the elaborate sky bands that frame the large full-figure glyphs, but like Motmot the building is tied to the underworld by the tomb found in the interior of the substructure. When the superstructure of Margarita was buried, a large inscribed stone bearing the names of Rulers 1 and 2 was placed at the south end of a secondary vault built above the tomb chamber (Sharer and Sedat 1995). As of this writing, no definitive answer can be given concerning the identity in life of the adults whose remains were found in the Margarita and Motmot tombs associated with these hieroglyphic texts and pictorial images. Motmot and Margarita share a plastered floor surface and are therefore contemporaneous, with the likelihood that Margarita slightly predates Motmot.

Their stratigraphic links with each other and with other features for which radiocarbon dates have been obtained leave little room for doubt that Margarita and Motmot were designed and built by the second ruler of Copan.

Given the textual references and stratigraphic tie-ins between the Margarita and Motmot building complexes, it is considered very likely that the earlier buildings found inside of Margarita and Yehnal (Hunal) and Motmot (Yax) were designed and built by the first ruler, K'inich Yax K'uk' Mo' (Sharer n.d.; Sharer et al. n.d.; Williamson 1996). This makes the contrast between them and their successor edifices built directly above them particularly pertinent to our topic. The surviving vestiges of Hunal, Yehnal, and Yax structures do not carry texts, or modeled stucco imagery, that directly cite the name of K'inich Yax K'uk' Mo'. Yehnal bore the image of K'inich Ahau on either side of its central stairway, with a glyphic element that David Stuart (personal communication, 1995) has identified as an early form of the *way* glyph. The back side of Yax has the remains of a U-shaped bracket on its central axis. This most likely served to frame an image of GI such as the one placed in the same spot on its successor building, Motmot. Thus, although K'inich Yax K'uk Mo' may well have associated himself with supernaturals (one of which he apparently claimed as his *way*), it remained to his successor to immortalize his name in stone and stucco on the dynastic buildings of the budding civic-ceremonial center. These findings from Copan are in keeping with the broader observations made by Houston and Stuart (1996) that Maya rulers were godlike in life but became enshrined as actual deities to be revered only after their deaths. On the much later Altar Q, the first ruler sits not on his name glyph (which he bears in his headdress) but on the glyph for "lord." The example that K'inich Yax K'uk' Mo' set as a godlike being was apparently so compelling that all of his successors felt compelled to honor, to cite, and to emulate it.

The first ballcourt was also given the benefit of modeled stucco decorations on its substructures, a fact not accessible to Strömsvik because he did not dig in the two places where these were preserved (again, a problem of sampling). The east sides of the eastern structures of both Ballcourt I and Ballcourt II were uncovered in a series of trench and tunnel investigations inside the final-phase architecture of Structures 10L-10 (Ballcourt III, east structure) and 10L-26 (the basal terrace, north of the hieroglyphic stairway) by the author and Richard Williamson (Fash n.d.; Williamson 1996). The remains of two large birds were found to have decorated both Ballcourt I and its more elevated successor, Ballcourt II. The features of these birds were remarkably similar, and the one at the south end of Ballcourt I's eastern building is quite striking (Fig. 3). The bird has the head of a macaw, supernatural serpent-head feet, and a series of macaw

Fig. 3 Reconstruction drawing of the full-figure plaster bird from the south end of the east structure of Ballcourt I. Plaster conservation and refitting, and reconstruction drawing by Barbara Fash.

heads sprouting from the ends of its wing feathers. Such macaw imagery is perfectly in keeping with the macaw head markers found in association with Ballcourts II and III and with the 16 full-figure macaws that decorated the superstructure façades of the final phase Ballcourt III (Fash 1992; Fash and Fash 1990; Kowalski and Fash 1991). Much less in keeping with the Ballcourt III façade imagery is the head that emerges from the midsection of the Ballcourt I and Ballcourt II full-figure birds. This plumed reptilian would be nearly identical to the feathered serpent heads of the Temple of Quetzalcoatl in Teotihuacan were it not for the severed right forearm and hand that it holds in its jaws. The single "dot" on the forearm (for "one" or "Hun") leaves little room for doubt about the intended meaning. This is the arm of Hunahpu, tying the Copan ballcourt imagery even more firmly to the Maya myth complex later recorded by the Quiche Maya in their sixteenth-century epic, the Popol Vuh—see Baudez (1980), Kowalski and Fash (1991), Miller (1986), Schele and Miller (1986), and Schele and Freidel (1990).

The Motmot floor marker inscription ends with a reference to "4 Macaw," exactly what was seen in full-figure form on the substructures of Ballcourt I. The marker is set into the same plaster floor shared by Motmot and Ballcourt I. When the Maya conflated the Quetzalcoatl head with the macaw, the Ballcourt I full-figure birds shared both quetzal and macaw attributes, like the large-bird imagery on Margarita. Although its message is presently unclear to us,[3] there seems little doubt that these four birds were also designed to directly associate K'inich Yax K'uk' Mo' with the ballcourt and the playing of the ball game. They also associated him with supernatural forces, including in this case the Sun Imitator known to the Quiche as Vucub Caquix, and the person of Hunahpu who vanquished him just as the Copan kings were supposed to vanquish their rivals and enemies on the ball field and beyond.

The Quetzalcoatl aspect of the Ballcourt I and II full-figure stucco birds provides an entirely new and original twist to the ballcourt imagery. It also adds a provocative new element to the Teotihuacan links implied by a whole host of other archaeological features, objects, and pictorial imagery found in Early and Late Classic Copan. No longer can we dismiss the goggles over the eyes of K'inich Yax K'uk' Mo' on his depictions in the seventh-century effigy censer (Agurcia Fasquelle and Fash 1991: 105), on Altar Q (Maudslay 1889–1902, 1), or on the temple and façade of Structure 16 (Fash 1992) as the fashion-conscious designs of Late Classic kings. The cylindrical tomb beneath the Motmot floor marker, the Thin Orange and Teotihuacan-style painted pottery found in a series of Early Classic Copan tombs associated both with Motmot and with Margarita, the *talud-tablero* feature found on Yehnal Structure (Sharer et al. n.d.), and the *tablero* found on the platform that subsequently encapsulated Motmot (Williamson 1996) all point to conscious and deliberate attempts by the first two rulers of Copan to associate themselves with the great metropolis of Central Mexico. When this theme appeared in the architectural programs, pictorial imagery, and hieroglyphic inscriptions of the Late Classic it was not designed to fabricate a myth or even to present a revisiòn in the historical record of a very

[3] The assumption in previous studies of the Copan ballcourt imagery has always been that the king was associated with the Hero Twins, the conquerers of the forces of darkness and evil in Xibalba. We also thought that, as such, he stood in opposition to the macaw, who was a representation of Vucub Caquix, the evil Sun Impersonator who tore off the arm of Hunahpu in the seventeenth-century Quiche account. However, in this instance the macaw seems to be associated with—indeed, to a degree labeled as—the deified first king, who clutches the arm of Hunahpu in his serpent-head appendage. One possible solution to this dilemma is to consider that perhaps the ruler's name was derived from the supernatural one, which would certainly have inspired awe if not fear in his subjects.

"Classic Maya" city. Rather, it was a deliberate recalling of associations consciously made and reinforced in public monuments by the first rulers in the city. One implication of this is that references to linkages between the founders of Maya cities and Teotihuacan and/or the use of the latter's imagery by late Cycle 9 rulers should not be dismissed out of hand as Late Classic revisionism or fictive propaganda. The Copan and Tikal data show that such claims can productively be tested archaeologically and may have a basis that can be demonstrated in the dynastic building programs, imagery, and inscriptions. We need more comparative material from other sites, such as Piedras Negras, where David Stuart (personal communications, 1995) informs me that there is yet another reference to links between the founder of that dynasty and the Central Mexican capital.

CONTINUITY AND CHANGE IN THE COPAN DYNASTIC BUILDING PROGRAM

The evidence is clear that the layout of the dynastic center of Copan comprised an uplifted acropolis area that sustained Hunal and its successors, a residential and administrative complex directly north of it, and a more open and public dynastic temple–ballcourt–plaza complex still farther north (Fig. 4). All three of these areas saw considerable elaboration and vertical growth in the ensuing centuries.

Along with the overall continuity in imagery through time, there was a continuity in space for the ballcourt, as first noted by Strömsvik (1952). After its initial construction by Ruler 2, the main ballcourt occupied essentially the same spot thereafter. Of course, as floor levels in the plaza around it rose in keeping with the ever more grandiose temples to the south, drainage considerations mandated that the ballcourt playing surface be raised in like measure. The thirteenth ruler's additions to the adjacent Structure 26 were so ambitious that the ballcourt had to be shifted slightly to the north and east and enlarged to preserve a sense of scale with the buildings and courtyards next to it. Through it all, the court retained its original character and basic north–south orientation. In marked contrast to the dynastic temples and palatial residences and administrative buildings all around it, the ballcourt was never elevated on any sort of platform. The playing alley always sat on the lowest ground in the royal compound, perhaps in keeping with the floor markers being the most direct portals to the underworld and the Lords of Xibalba. This same vertical positioning is found for courts throughout the Maya lowlands and even at Xochicalco, Morelos.

In the case of Motmot Structure, both the building and its floor marker

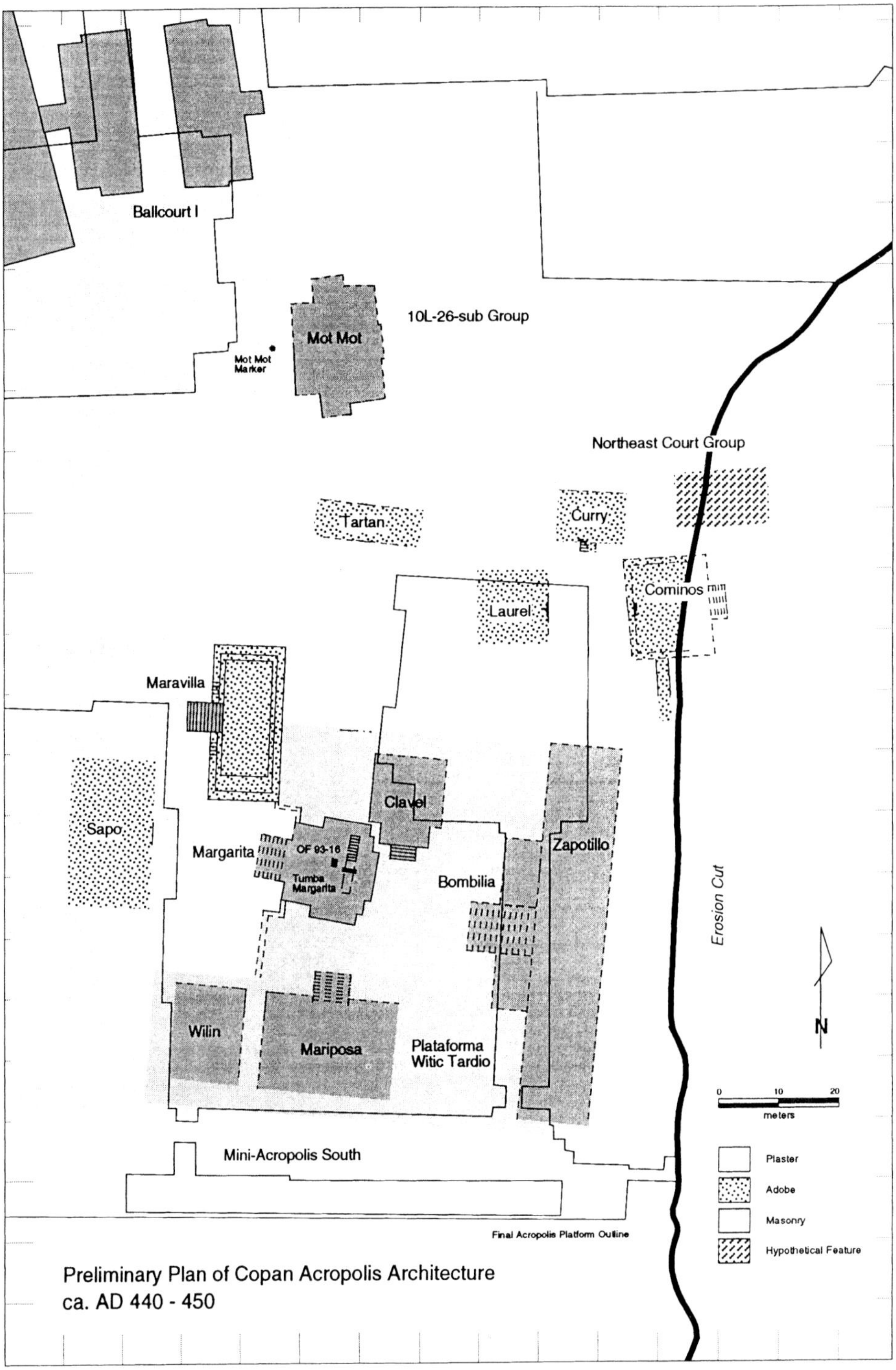

Fig. 4 Preliminary plan of Copan Acropolis architecture ca. A.D. 440–450. Produced by the Early Copan Acropolis Program under the direction of Robert Sharer (Sharer et al. n.d.). Computer-assisted map by Loa Traxler.

were covered over by a large platform within a few years of their original construction. The platform had a *tablero* on its front façade and was surmounted by a two-roomed temple (called Papagayo) and a stepped pyramid behind it (called Mascarones), which together replicated the plan of Motmot on a much larger scale. Inside the back room of Motmot stood Stela 63, which cited the 9.0.0.0.0 event first recorded on the Motmot marker and the names of K'inich Yax K'uk' Mo' and Ruler 2. The stela was subsequently abutted by a hieroglyphic step bearing the name of the fourth ruler, Cu Ix, who also placed a second floor inside the temple (Fash 1991). This temple and its inscribed stela and step were then left intact for nearly two centuries, surely an indication of their sacred nature.

Hieroglyphic steps bearing the names of rulers were also carved and used to designate the builders of subsequent versions of the dynastic buildings in other parts of the acropolis as well. These include references to the seventh ruler on an Early Classic building buried inside of Structure 11 and steps citing the tenth ruler on the structures known as "Ante" (below final phase Structure 20), and Rosalila (built above Margarita, underneath Structure 16). The spectacular modeled stucco decoration that still adorns all three stories of Rosalila's superstructure consoles us somewhat for the lack of preservation of such embellishments on the majority of the other Early Classic Copan Acropolis structures. Nearly all the structures in the acropolis had their superstructures demolished as a prerequisite step for construction of other buildings above them. This practice resulted in demolition of the pictorial imagery that adorned the exterior façades of the superstructures, possibly including named ruler portraits. As Schele notes (this volume), the entablatures of the superstructure were the part of the building most favored for this kind of embellishment during the Classic period. As a result, we are presently very limited in what we can discern about specific supernatural associations for particular buildings. Expositions of the underlying cosmological conceits and political designs of the patrons of those particular edifices are still a long way away.

In terms of the layout of the royal compound, however, Sharer and his colleagues (n.d.) have detected a rather significant change at the beginning of the sixth century A.D., which they have ascribed to the seventh ruler, Waterlily Jaguar. This took the form of a massive infilling of previously existent plazas and buildings in both the original acropolis nucleus and the royal residential and administrative complex to the north. This was the first step in a quite significant expansion of the acropolis to the north, essentially forming the direct ancestor of what we see today as the East Court. The new layout resulted in repositioning of the residential and administrative courtyards that had previously been located north of the acropolis per se, down to its southern flank. The newly built residential compound on the south side of the acropolis was the direct ancestor of Group 10L-2, the Late Classic royal residential compound whose investigation was directed by E. Wyllys Andrews V (Andrews n.d.; Andrews and Fash 1992). In uncovering and documenting this major shift, Sharer and his colleagues (n.d.) have restored Waterlily Jaguar to his rightful place as one of Copan's "Great Builders." Through the end of dynastic rule at Copan, this complex saw numerous modifications in terms of the numbers and features of the buildings that it comprised but not in terms of its essential form and intepreted functions.

One of the most important buildings of the ancestral East Court was the first (known) version of what would eventually become known to us as Temple 22. Like the ballcourts and the dynastic temples under Structures 16 and 26, the sequent versions of Temple 22 have been shown to exhibit a strong continuity through time and numerous rebuildings. The corner masks bearing the image of the personified *wits* ("hill" or "mountain") deity on the final version of this famous building have been shown to have antecedents in two of its previous incarnations. Thus, a "sacred mountain" temple identified by Freidel, Schele, and Parker (1993) as a Yaxal Wits or "First True Mountain" seems to have occupied the northern limit of the ancestral East Court from its inception. Although it is tempting to ascribe to Waterlily Jaguar either the concept or the first construction of the *wits* building itself, it seems prudent to reserve judgment on this until more of the ancestral West Court is investigated by means of tunnels. But it cannot be denied that Waterlily Jaguar did effect major changes in the design, if not the meaning, of the royal compound.

For the reign of the tenth ruler, Moon Jaguar (A.D. 553–578), we have inscriptions and surviving stucco decoration on Ante and its superstructure "Ani" (located beneath final-phase Structure 20) and on Rosalila. The human heads portrayed on the exterior façades of Ani are the same as those on the final phase of Structure 20 (Barbara Fash, personal communication, 1991), lending credence to the idea that this building also showed continuity in meaning and purpose through time. Rosalila's polychrome stucco decoration (Fig. 5) is the subject of ongoing research by Agurcia Fasquelle (n.d.) and Fash and Taube (n.d.), and no doubt many more insights will emerge as a result of their conjoined efforts. For the present purposes, we should merely note that the building contains birds combining quetzal, macaw, and K'inich Ahau elements (Ricardo Agurcia Fasquelle, Karl Taube, and Barbara Fash, personal communications, 1995), which ties it directly into the symbolism of its predecessors, Margarita and Yehnal. This once again cements the association between the

Fig. 5 West elevation of Rosalila structure. Based on the excavations of Ricardo Agurcia Fasquelle (n.d.), architectural recording by Jorge Ramos and Rudy Larios, and stucco investigations and conservation by Barbara Fash. Drawing by Barbara Fash.

deified founder and the most upraised and spectacular dynastic building in the acropolis.

THE LATE CLASSIC ROYAL COMPOUND AND ITS IMITATORS

In looking at form to infer function, the Late Classic Principal Group or epicenter of the kingdom of Copan has a number of clearly differentiated spaces (Fig. 6). Access to the center is provided by means of two roads (*sacbeob*) leading into the central open plaza area from the urban wards to the east and west. Once one had entered the largest paved area in the city, there were two basic choices: go to the north and the plaza with the stelae of the thirteenth king, or go to the south and the area of the ballcourt, hieroglyphic stairway, and the massive Structure 11. Much more restricted in access and size are the two elevated patios or courts in the acropolis, south of these great public plazas. The restricted nature of the access to the East and West Courts was noted a decade ago by Mary Miller (1986) in her classic study of the Copan Acropolis. This highly restricted nature is also reflected by the fact that the courts themselves are not even visible from anywhere below.

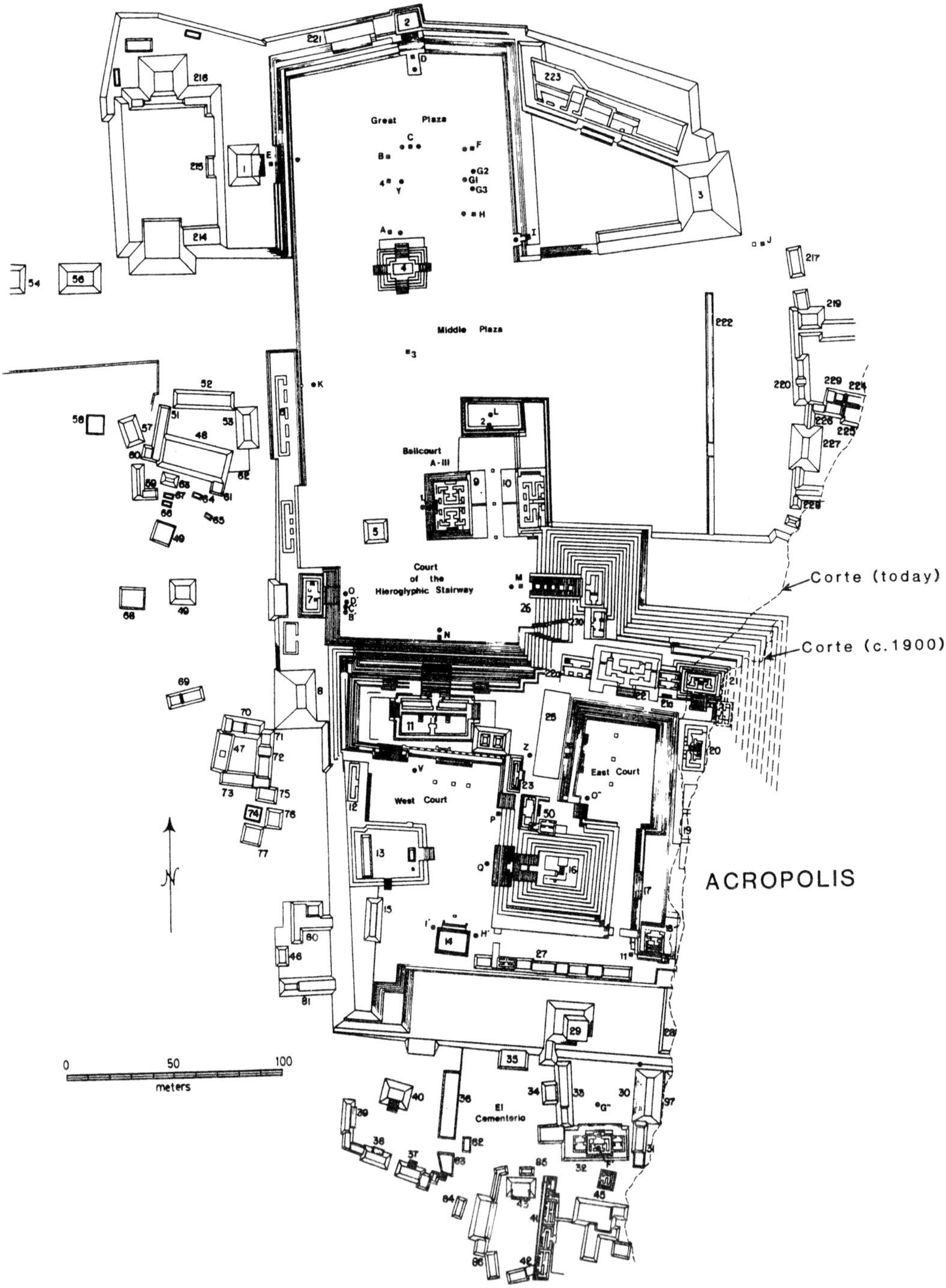

Fig. 6 Plan of the final-phase Principal Group of Copan, ca. A.D. 800 (after Fash and Sharer 1991: 168, fig. 1).

In her prescient analysis of the meaning and uses of the Copan Acropolis, Miller (1986) presented the idea that the steps of both the Reviewing Stand and the Jaguar Stairway were places where rituals were performed. She noted that, although the Reviewing Stand had long been thought to be a place for spectators, it seems more likely that it forms a half or "false" ballcourt. Miller and Houston (1987) subsequently showed that the Reviewing Stand is even glyphically labeled as a ballcourt in the accompanying inscription. The three markers in front of both the Jaguar Stairway and the Reviewing Stand were likened to the three floor markers of the main ballcourt, in further support of this important new insight. Miller then posited that the Jaguar Stairway was used for sacrifices in association with ball-game ritual and the dispatching of sacrificial victims. Remarkably, the East Court of the Palace at Palenque seems to have been the scene of similar rites, to judge from the depictions of bound prisoners and the hieroglyphic stairway that they front and flank. Miller also suggested that the adjacent north steps of the East Court were used for royal bloodletting (Miller 1986: 85).

Stephen Houston (this volume) has made another critical contribution in pointing out that the steps on Maya buildings were also used as a symbolic device for marking social status. The "palace scenes" on polychrome vases show that the relative heights of the participants on the steps correlated with aspects of dress and other indications of their social status in the scenes. If Miller is right about the use of the north steps in the East Court, and Houston's insightful analysis holds as well, a lively and revealing picture can be conjured up. The participants in the East Court rituals would have been ranked from lowest (stationed at the level of the underworld waters on the floor of the court; Freidel, Schele, and Parker 1993) to highest, who basked in their exalted station (and a much better view of the proceedings) on the steps of Temple 22 at the mouth of the temple itself.

Miller did not hazard a guess as to what the most expansive eastern set of steps in the East Court was used for. I believe that they were used, at least in part, as accommodations for people to observe both the rituals that Miller postulates and also the dances that Barbara Fash suggested were taking place above the Jaguar Stairway on the low plaster-capped platform labeled Structure 10L-25 (B. Fash n.d.a; B. Fash et al. 1992; B. Fash, personal communication, 1988). In like fashion, the steps that surround the Great Plaza were thought by Stephens (1841) to be seating accommodations for well-attended public spectacles. Fuentes y Guzmán (cited in Morley 1920) referred to this area as the "Circus Maximus," which may not be far off the mark for the kinds of awe-inspiring displays of ritual theater and pageantry that took place there.

Perhaps the clearest example of steps being designed for seating in a Classic Maya center is that afforded by the "amphitheater" at the site of Pechal (Ruppert and Denison 1943: 92 and pl. 74; Fig. 7 here). Ruppert and Denison (1943: 92) calculated that for Pechal "the seating capacity of the amphitheater, very conservatively estimated, is placed at 8,000." The amphitheater at Pechal has nearly the same dimensions ("averaging 68 by 75 meters"; Ruppert and Denison 1943: 92) as the floor and delimiting steps of the Great Plaza of Copan (cf. Fig. 6). The Pechal example seems to have been designed for all eyes to be focused on the plaza area where all of the stelae and altars of the site were situated. Likewise, the steps of the Great Plaza of Copan would have enabled all the "participant-observers"—whether seated or standing—to view the important rituals and ceremonies that made use of the altars and stelae. This certainly does not preclude that there would have been a pecking order of who got to sit or stand at particular elevations or vantage points or that the steps could also have been used for parts of the ceremonies themselves.

Richard Williamson (n.d.) estimated the seating capacity of the steps and terraces from which the Copan ball games could have been watched to be about 3000 people. The Great Plaza steps could have seated at least this many as well. If one were to allow for people standing in the plaza (as is presently practiced in the Maya highlands and is documented worldwide in such settings) and double this figure, there would have been about 6000 (or more) people present for such rituals. This would have represented about one-quarter of the total population of the kingdom during its cultural and population climax, according to the latest population estimates (Webster and Freter 1990; Webster, Sanders, and van Rossum 1992). Thus, the proportion of the population of a kingdom that could have been in attendance at public ceremonies in the Classic Maya civic-ceremonial centers was significant.

However, the East Court of the acropolis definitely did not have the capacity to accommodate as many people as did the Great Plaza or the ballcourt/hieroglyphic stairway plaza area. Taking the reduction policy even further, the West Court of the acropolis has even fewer steps and may have been reserved for activities that only a chosen few were empowered to witness. Of course, the temples themselves were the most elevated and restricted spaces of all, with the behaviors taking place there being literally the paramount example of the use of sacred space to elevate both the social hierarchy and its legitimating ideological system. The temple inside the final version of Structure 16 is the smallest and highest in the Principal Group, the most exclusive and rarefied environs in the entire city.

In comparative terms, there is a consistent design in Classic Maya dynastic

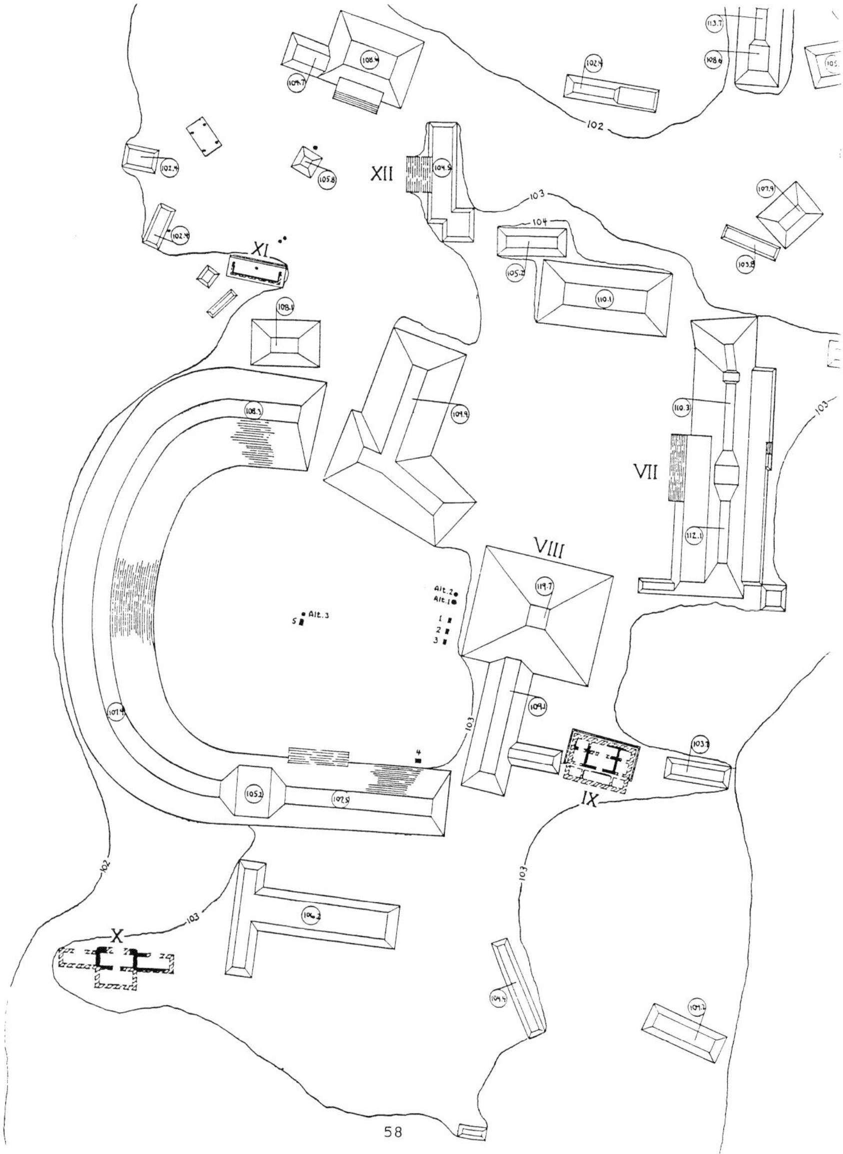

Fig. 7 Plan of the central sector of the ruins of Pechal, Campeche (after Ruppert and Denison 1943: pl. 74).

centers to make use of causeways to funnel large numbers of subjects and pilgrims into large, open plazas. One of the most often visited today is the Great Plaza at Tikal, with steps for seating accommodations and/or as "stages," forming an integral part of the assemblage on the north side (Fig. 8). Adjacent to such public squares are elevated "acropolis" areas, for example the North Acropolis at Tikal and the Palace at Palenque (Fig. 9), which were quite clearly designed for more exclusive ceremonies. Thus, the architecture can tell us something about the social hierarchy of ritual and pageantry in the royal compounds at the heart of the Maya kingdoms. In Copan, at least, it can also inform us about the social hierarchy in the residential areas that sustained the centers.

We can take this architectural layout down the social ladder in Copan, where extensive excavations of residential architecture have been conducted for the past 18 years. The largest and most imposing residential compounds in the urban wards of the Copan kingdom also had impressive architectural monuments, embellished with sculptures that portrayed the power and prestige of their owners. The hieroglyphic benches and pictorial façade sculptures that adorned the paramount structures of the elite residential groups have been the subject of considerable interest for models of status competition, political evolution, and even the nature of the Classic Maya collapse (B. Fash et al. 1992; Fash 1983, 1986, 1991; Fash and Stuart 1991; Sanders 1986, 1989; Sanders and Webster 1988; Webster 1989a; Webster, Evans, and Sanders 1993). A key to understanding the function of the buildings within their own social context and the behaviors that took place in each one of them comes in the form of the architectural spaces themselves.

Located in the Sepulturas ward less than a kilometer east of the Great Plaza, Group 9N-8's space boasted seating/stage accommodations on three of the four sides of its principal plaza and a ceremonial structure on the open end. This plan is quite similar to that of the Great Plaza in the epicenter (cf. Figs. 6 and 10) and is not unlike that of the amphitheater at Pechal (Fig. 7). Although there were no stelae set in Plaza A, Webster (1989a) has shown that Altar W was originally placed there. Also, the sculptures adorning its east and west buildings are in keeping with the themes on the east and west stairs of the East Court of the acropolis (Fash 1986). Broad stairways for seating are also found in the main plaza of Group 10L-2, the royal residential compound investigated by Andrews on the south flank of the acropolis (Fig. 11). Structures fronted entirely with stairs, such as Andrews' Structures 10L-30, -32, and -33, were uncovered at excavations of the much smaller ("Type 2") residential site, Group 9M-22 Plaza B (Webster 1989b: fig. 4). This implies a concern for rituals, or at least for ritual presentation of status, on stairways fronting plazas even for less prestigious family groups in Late Classic Copan.

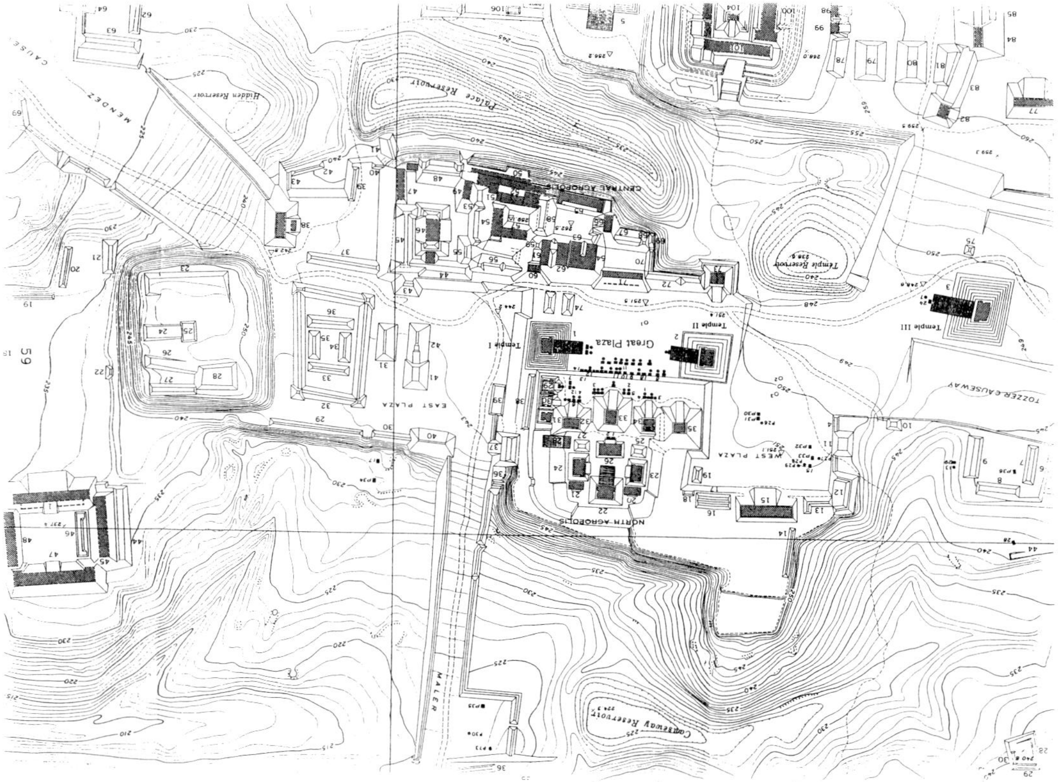

Fig. 8 Plan of the central sector of Tikal (Carr and Hazard 1961).

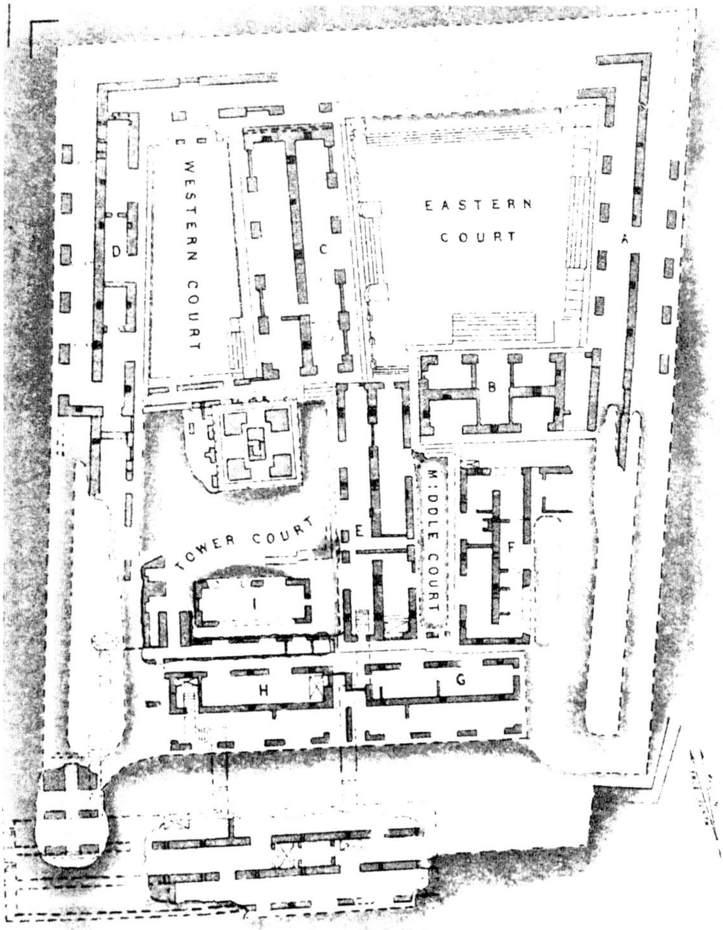

Fig. 9 The Palace at Palenque (after Maudslay 1889–1902, 4: pl. 3).

Of course, in the broader comparative study of human organization and expression, we can expect many of the manifestations of Classic Maya culture to correlate with those of other civilizations of antiquity. Grounded in considerations of ecology, social structure, and political evolution, many scholars find the theatre states of Southeast Asia and Indonesia to be productive non-Mesoamerican sources for analogy with the Classic Maya kingdoms (Webster, this volume). In his classic book on the theater state of Bali, Geertz (1980) shows the importance of pageantry and ritual in that society. All of the elaborate ceremonies, and the hundreds of palace and temple complexes that dotted

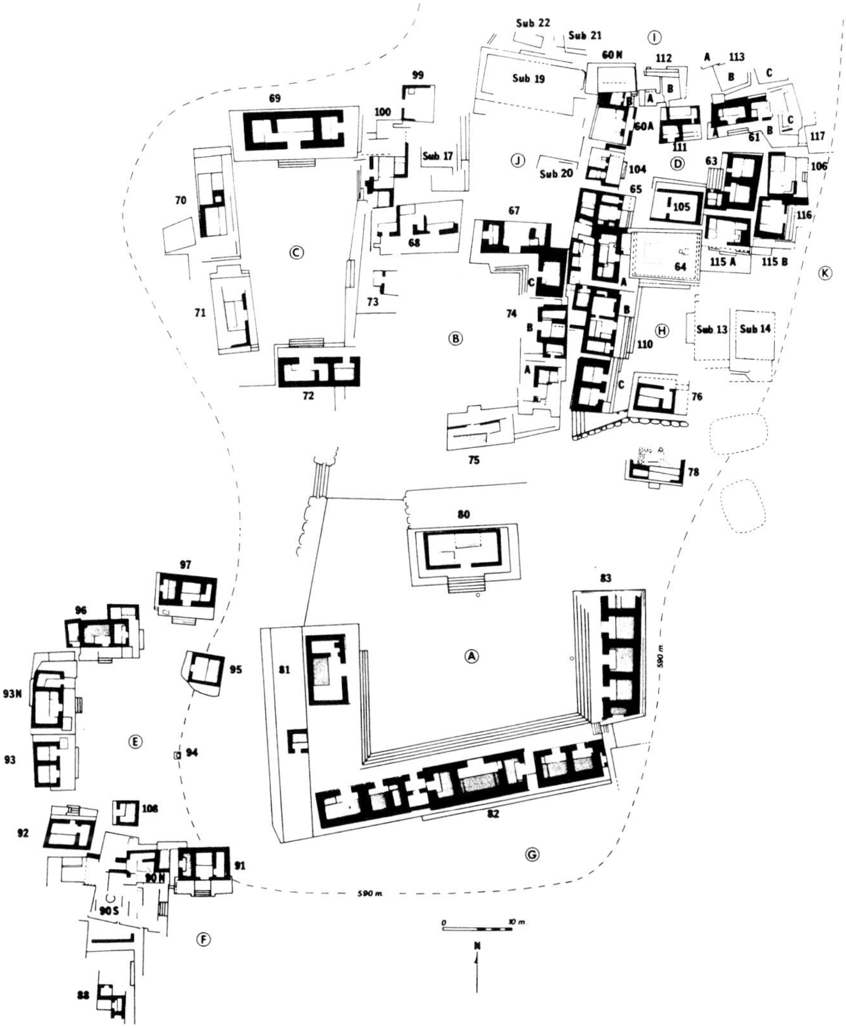

Fig. 10 Plan of Group 9N-8, Sepulturas, Copan (after Webster 1989b: 10, fig. 5).

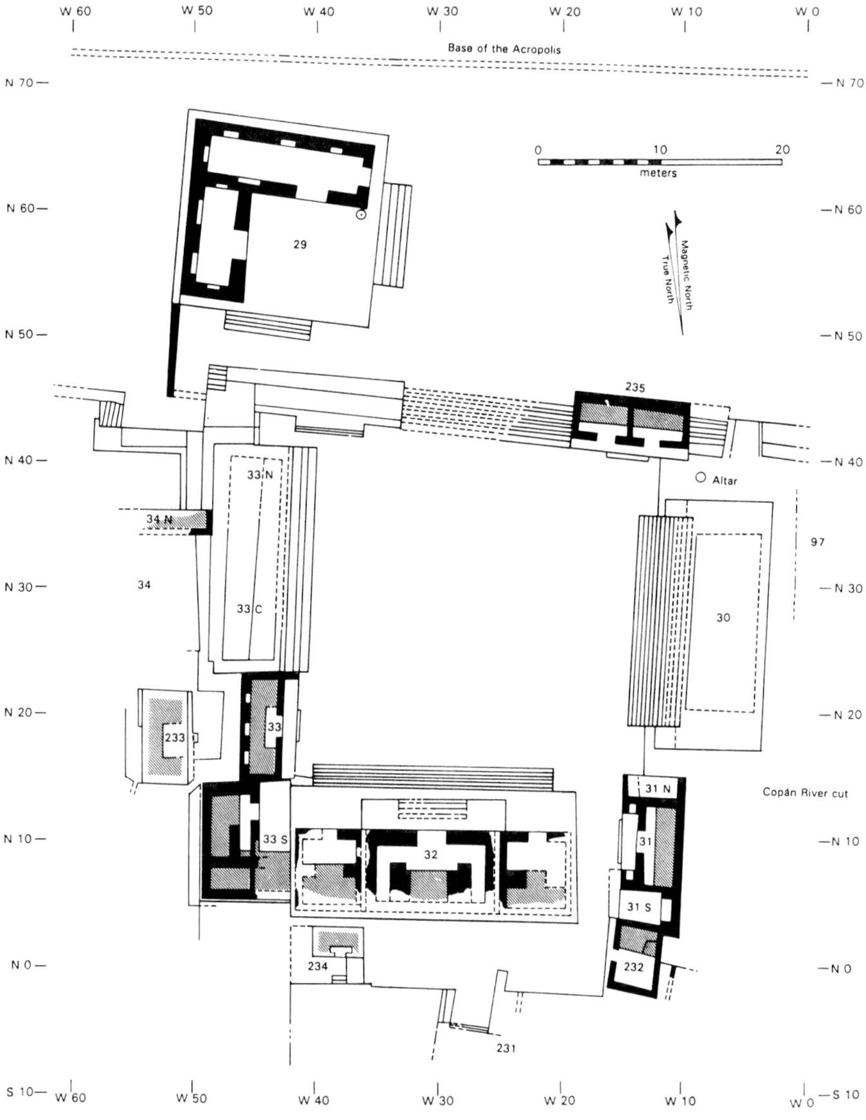

Fig. 11 Plan of Plaza A, Group 10L-2, Copan (after Andrews and Fash 1992: 66, fig. 3).

the countryside, were geared to the proposition of "making inequality enchant," as Geertz put it. This is precisely what the archaeological evidence of seating accommodations, and the epigraphic and pictorial symbolism on architecture and sculpture, point to for Copan, both at the city center and in the surrounding residential areas.

Given this concern with and social replication of the staging of public ceremony, the question then becomes what kinds of pageants and passions were played out in the Maya ritual arenas? The art and texts that embellish Classic Maya structures can lend us a hand here. I hasten to add that I am referring to the reconstruction of what it was the Maya elites were encoding in, and communicating through the edification of, their public monuments. This does not mean that I accept wholesale everything that the Maya aristocracy said about themselves and their role in their imagery and texts. My point is rather that the meanings that they designed these monuments to pass on are recoverable, albeit in varying degrees. Just as the residential architecture in the Copan valley is an explicit indicator of the relative social standing of its owners by its relative volume and complexity, so too the messages carved in stone on the steps, exterior façades and roof crests, and interior benches and jambs are explicit and very revealing of the motives, the ideals, and the pretensions of those who designed, built, and used them. Just as we all agree that the public monuments were biased and self-serving, there is also a general accord that not everyone in Classic Maya society could read the inscriptions. But I think that scholars also agree that the populace could understand and appreciate the architectural sculpture, which was designed and built to be admired and understood. Of course, the level of understanding varied with age, experience, and social standing. Thus, on a purely practical level a higher position on the steps enabled one to see more of the rituals, the architectural setting, and its attendant pictorial imagery. On a more social and intellectual level, the more elevated individuals could better understand the information and power communicated in the built environment and the pageantry that made it resonate with meaning.

BUILDINGS AND THEIR MEANING IN LATE CLASSIC COPAN

Here I summarize some of the results of our most recent work on the Late Classic Maya architecture in Copan to illustrate what kinds of meanings were encoded there, what kinds of behaviors took place in those dramatic environs, and what all of this can tell us about dynastic design and intent. The discussion will proceed chronologically from the time of the eleventh ruler to the sixteenth and final member of the K'inich Yax K'uk' Mo' dynasty in order to pursue development of the architectural program in historical sequence. Progress and pitfalls in the interpretations of idiosyncratic concerns and strategies of statecraft will be addressed for each ruler in his turn.

During the reigns of the eleventh and twelfth rulers in the seventh century A.D., change was in the air as far as dynastic monuments went. Barbara Fash (Fash n.d.b; Fash and Taube n.d.) has noted that the Copan architects and sculptors began to change the way they embellished the structures with sculpture in the reign of the eleventh ruler, Buts' Chan. Instead of using stone armatures outset from the façade to support masses of modeled stucco, the stone itself became increasingly salient and carved, and the use of stucco was correspondingly decreased. This process is best exemplified by the sculptures that adorned "Indigo" (below final-phase Temple 22) and "Oropéndula" (adjacent to Rosalila and beneath final-phase Temple 16). By the end of the reign of Ruler 12 (referred to variously as "Smoke-Jaguar" and "Smoke-Imix-God K"), this transition was complete. Some of the very finest sculptures ever carved in the Maya area were found in a context that dates to the end of the reign of Ruler 12, in a structure beneath 10L-26 first known as "Híjole" (Fash n.d.b).

Ruler 12 commissioned several buildings with the most evenly hewn dressed tuff blocks ever produced in the Maya area, on such massive structures as "Esmeralda" (beneath Structure 26) and "Púrpura" (which encapsulated the still intact Rosalila). Sadly, we are unable to even guess at what messages the adornments of the temples atop these massive renovations bore, because few of them survived the subsequent rebuilding episodes. We can take note of the fact that Ruler 12 was not just intent on large-scale renovations of the acropolis temples but on the placement of a series of inscribed stelae and altars in different parts of the Copan valley as well. Although Buts' Chan (portrayed on Stela 7), Waterlily Jaguar (memorialized on Stela 9), and other earlier dynasts (responsible for Stelae 20, 21, 23, and 24) erected monuments at the site of the modern town, Ruler 12 erected no less than six stelae and four inscribed altars in the valley at a number of different loci. This concern with leaving a literary mark on the landscape has certainly impressed the community of modern scholars working on Mesoamerica, who have interpreted these monuments in various ways.

Although I was once one of its most enthusiastic backers, I find that I no longer subscribe to the view that the outlying valley stelae delimit the boundaries of the domain of Ruler 12. The beginning of the Late Classic period corresponds with the appearance of Copador ceramics. Payson Sheets' (1992) work at the site of El Ceren shows Copador to have been in use before A.D. 600, prior to the reign of Ruler 12, who acceeded in A.D. 628. Survey and excavations conducted in the larger sustaining area demonstrate that during the reign of Ruler 12, the kingdom clearly extended far beyond the limits of the Copan pocket. In this case, our earlier assessments were in error, not because of sampling but because of the mistaken dates (A.D. 700 or even 737) then posited for the appearance of Copador polychrome. The idea that the stelae are associated with particular sacred spots on the landscape and associated ancestors (Proskouriakoff 1973), likely used in ritual pilgrimage circuits (Schele and Freidel 1990), now seems to have much more in its favor.

For the thirteenth ruler, Uaxaclahun Ubah K'awil (also known as XVIII Jog and 18 Rabbit), a whole series of architectural and freestanding monuments have been identified and subjected to all manner of scholarly interpretation. It is only with thorough investigation of earlier monuments that his considerable achievements can be put in proper perspective. Although it is true that half of the stelae (i.e., A, D, F, and 4) and one of the buildings (Structure 22) that he built have the very high relief style that made Copan famous, we know now that this style began with the work of an incredibly skilled and visionary sculptor in the reign of the previous king (B. Fash n.d.b). Although it is also true that the final version of Temple 22 was probably one of the most beautiful buildings in the New World from the time of its construction until it fell into disrepair, we know now that there were numerous antecedent versions of this artificial sacred mountain for at least a century before Uaxaclahun Ubah K'awil built the one whose ruins continue to inspire us today. Finally, the birds that adorn the façades of the ballcourt he completed in the year before his much-remarked demise were but a more plentiful version of the dramatic and powerful avians that were emblazoned on the sides of the courts of his ancestors.

On the positive side of this particular ledger, Stuart (n.d.a) has recently suggested that Uaxaclahun Ubah K'awil had not been given his due as the original patron of the hieroglyphic stairway. The lower part of the stairway carries a dedicatory date that falls fairly early in the reign of the thirteenth ruler. Because the later date higher up on the stairs had long been taken to represent the date of its completion—with a formal dedication, perhaps, when Stela M was erected at its base in A.D. 756—the earlier dedicatory date was not given its due until Stuart's recent reanalysis of this material. Thus, the idea that the hieroglyphic stairway was built after a 19-year hiatus at the site (Marcus 1976; Morley 1920; Riese 1980, 1986) is no longer tenable. The interpretations that I derived from this dating of the stairs after the death of Uaxaclahun Ubah K'awil and its purported use as a revivalist temple conceived and built to restore faith in the royal line (Fash 1988, 1991; W. Fash et al. 1992) will also have to be revised. The view now is that Uaxaclahun Ubah K'awil sought to create the most impressive hieroglyphic stairway in the Maya area to enshrine the glorious deeds of his ancestors (Stuart n.d.a). Singled out for special veneration was Ruler 12, whose portrait and exploits are found at eye level at the base of the stairs.

For the ballcourt, we have seen that the floor markers and macaws on the benches and façades of both buildings show that mythological and astrological aspects were an integral part of the symbolism and ideology of the ball game at Copan from the onset of dynastic rule through the reign of Uaxaclahun Ubah K'awil. Likewise, the Temple 22 themes of maize growing from the sacred mountain, guarded over by the figure of the king (B. Fash n.d.b) were also sacred, unchangeable propositions. This is in keeping with worldwide patterns of veneration of sacred mountains, a popular theme among the Maya in general and especially so at Copan, whose inscriptions refer to it as the "Three Mountain" place (Stuart 1992, n.d.b). The entrance to Temple 22 transformed it into the gaping mouth of a cave, which is what the interior of the temple was designed to replicate. Whatever rituals and other behaviors took place within this artificial sacred mountain, the results of them were probably communicated to the anxious public, assembled by the hundreds on the steps and the courtyard below. We are now confident that a Day or Rising Sun God originally graced the east side of the East Court, turning the entire patio into a giant cosmogram oriented on both vertical and horizontal axes (Ashmore 1991). This gives us a feel for the larger picture in which these rituals and pageants were played out, according to the design conceived by the Maya.

Barbara Fash (n.d.b) has recently demonstrated that there were numerous water birds on the façades of Temple 22, in keeping with the idea that the plaza below was a metaphor for the lagoons and reservoirs found on Maya sacred mountains. She also notes that this and the other acropolis temples and courts were designed as an integral part of a larger water capture and runoff system such as those documented for Tikal and other ancient Maya communities (Scarborough 1983, 1993). Dynastic architecture is in fact the maximal expression of the water-related concerns that faced every farmer since Formative times; the reservoirs of Tikal, Copan, and other cities are but the most sophisticated dynastic versions of that aspect of the built environment.

It is intriguing that although some were given the benefits of some refurbishment or expansion, no subsequent king sought to build over the four great architectural achievements of the ill-fated thirteenth king: the Great Plaza, the final ballcourt, the hieroglyphic stairway, and the final version of Temple 22. Perhaps the end he suffered made him a martyr of legendary, perhaps even mythical, proportions in this kingdom, making of his monuments a virtually sacrosanct legacy.

Ruler 14 ("Smoke Monkey") was long thought not to have commissioned or erected any monuments during his relatively short reign. This view has been successfully challenged by the investigation of Structure 10L-22A (B. Fash et al. 1992; Fash and Fash 1990) (Fig. 12). Just as both epigraphic and stratigraphic data support the placement of Structure 10L-22 1st in the reign of Uaxaclahun Ubah K'awil (Larios, Fash, and Stuart 1994), the textual and contextual information both place Structure 10L-22A in the reign of his successor, Ruler 14. Barbara Fash's sculpture analysis showed that this building was embellished with large mats, considered to label this as the Popol Nah, or Council or Community House (B. Fash et al. 1992). Other motifs are read as *zac nicte'il na* or "white flower house," which is another term for council house in Maya dictionaries (Stephen Houston, personal communication, 1990). Its identification as a council house thus relies on two distinct pieces of epigraphic data.

Between the oversized mat symbols were a series of niches, inset into which were human figures seated above hieroglyphs. The epigraphers recognized the hieroglyphs as place names that occur in other contexts where they may refer

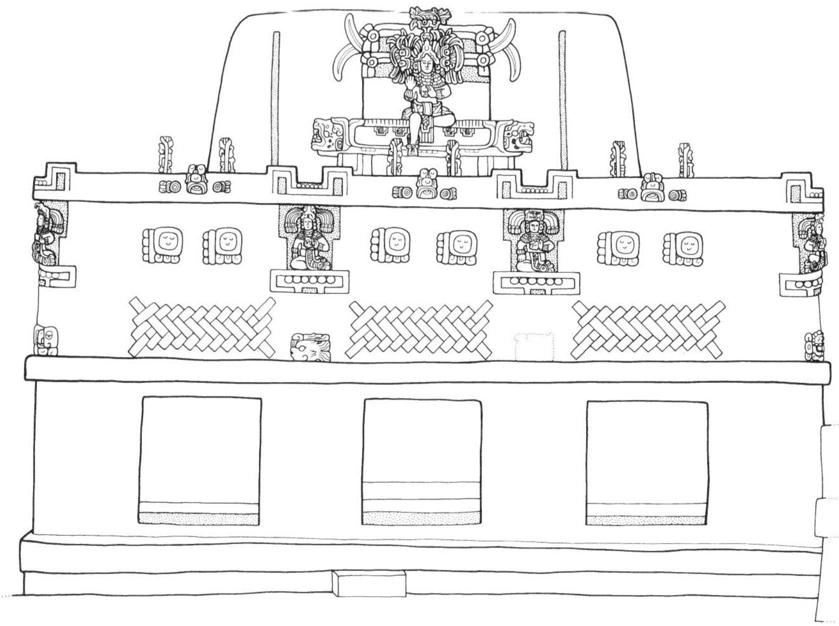

Fig. 12 Reconstruction drawing of Copan Structure 22A. Based on architectural data provided by Rudy Larios and sculpture reconstruction by Barbara Fash. Drawing by Barbara Fash.

to supernatural locales (B. Fash et al. 1992; Stuart and Houston 1994). Will Andrews found one of the place name glyphs on three different buildings in Group 10L-2, the royal residential compound that he was digging just south of the acropolis (Andrews n.d.; Andrews and Fash 1992). This provided the first archaeological evidence that the place names on the Mat House were actually associated with specific lineages and/or residential groups within the ancient kingdom of Copan. The location of Andrews' compound to the south of the acropolis is in keeping with the position of the kanal or fish glyph on the south façade of the Popol Nah. This datum leads us to wonder whether the other place names might also be placed on the façades of the building in keeping with the geographic positions of their respective lineages or communities. This hypothesis is being put to the test in new research in the valley, at Group 9J-5 (north of the Principal Group), and at the secondary center of Río Amarillo (to the east). Linda Schele (personal communication, 1992) has suggested that the "black water hole" place name on the west side of Structure 10L-22A may refer to Quirigua, which is located both west and north of Copan.

Presiding over the councillors was the portrait of the ruler, who was carved larger than life and occupied the central portion of the roof crest. Structural evidence adduced by Barbara Fash (1992) now allows us to prove that most of the major buildings of the Late Classic Copan Acropolis did sport roof crests, just as their counterparts in the Petén did and as the Early Classic temple Rosalila did (Fig. 5). As noted, the architectural stratigraphy shows that Structure 10L-22A was built after the reign of the thirteenth ruler and before that of the fifteenth ruler. The 9 Ahau glyphs that were placed prominently on the building are thought likely to refer to the 9 Ahau period ending 9.15.15.0.0, falling in A.D. 746. This building is thus thought to have been dedicated by the fourteenth king, Smoke Monkey, toward the end of his short reign and less than a decade after the humiliating death of his predecessor XVIII Jog at the hands of his former vassal from Quirigua, Cauac Sky. This historical context makes for an interesting analysis of the strategies of statecraft pursued by the short-lived fourteenth ruler, as reflected in his architectural program.

The original idea was that Structure 10L-22A and the royal council were innovations of Ruler 14 in response to the rising power of the nobles in the valley and the need to appease and engage them at a time of political crisis in the history of the dynasty (B. Fash et al. 1992; Fash and Fash 1990). The realization that Group H at Uaxactun contained a Late Pre-Classic Mat House (Fash and Fash n.d.; Freidel, Schele, and Parker 1993) and the documentation of other Late Classic buildings of this type in numerous parts of the Maya lowlands (Ringle 1990; Schele, this volume) has enlightened our thinking on this topic. So has the recent discovery that the building beneath 10L-22A does not have the form or decoration of the Mat House and appears to have had some other function (Sharer n.d.). This does not preclude the possibility that an earlier Council House might have existed in some other part of the acropolis that has not yet seen the dim light of our tunnel system. Therefore, at present we incline to the view that, although both the institution of and a building for the ruling council may well have existed before the reign of Ruler 14, public depiction of the councillors and their associated supernatural abodes was a decorative and architectural design very much in keeping with the exigencies of the times (Fash 1996, n.d.a).

In addition to showing his concern for his councillors and their people by placing the representatives' portraits and place names on the building, Smoke Monkey also created facilities for public spectacles in association with the Council House. The large platform labeled Structure 10L-25 was a low, plaster-capped surface built directly in front of the Popol Nah and was clearly never used for supporting a masonry superstructure. Again on the basis of analogy with colonial and modern Maya, Barbara Fash suggested that it was used for dance and for the public feasts that followed the council. The large size of the platform certainly would have accommodated many dancers, and the ample steps of the East Court would have been a great vantage point from which to take in the proceedings.

All of this presents a lively picture of the intent, including strategies and ideals, of the fourteenth king, in the wake of Copan's defeat at the hands of Quirigua. It could even lend itself to the pursuit of inferring aspects of his personality. But to my mind, we are still at too great a distance from these times, places, and people to do that with what a statistician would call a high degree of probability. We have postulated that the fourteenth ruler made explicit references to the representatives of the people, and the places they harked from, as a recognition of—if not an outright concession to—their political power in the years after the humiliating defeat of Uaxaclahun Ubah K'awil. On this basis, should we then claim that he was a noble visionary, a mere pragmatist, or even a quivering coward? Tempting as it may be to make a stab at this kind of inference, the information presently available does not allow us to be sure. The very existence of a council and of evidence for the importance of the competing nobles in the decision-making process opens up a number of questions about the nature and strength of the ruler's power at this and other Classic Maya kingdoms.

For Ruler 15, the monuments that have survived are Stelae M and N, and the completed hieroglyphic stairway and temple of Structure 10L-26. The immense hieroglyphic stairway was finished off by an even more elaborate and important inscription in the temple that surmounted the inscribed steps. The entire monument represents an ode to the Copan dynasty, a singular affirmation of historical continuity and divine rule, beginning with the first king in A.D. 426 and continuing up to the time of the fifteenth ruler, who dedicated the completed temple and stairs in A.D. 756 (Fash 1988; Fash and Stuart 1991; W. Fash et al. 1992; Schele and Freidel 1990; Stuart 1992, n.d.a; Stuart and Schele 1986b). The inscriptions accompany life-sized portraits of the rulers themselves, whose exploits are detailed in the text. The rulers all carry shield and lance, and many wear Tlaloc and other war imagery in keeping with the martial theme (Fash 1992). The Tlaloc imagery is, of course, consistent with surviving portraits of the first king, who is portrayed with goggles over his eyes. Thus, the ball games and most inclusive public ceremonies all took place under the watchful eyes of all of the earlier rulers, whose gaze also encompassed all of the assembled subjects.

As noted above, the investigations inside the pyramidal base of Structure 26 have shown that this building always functioned as a dynastic temple, with inscriptions relating to events that took place in the reigns of the first four rulers. Papagayo Structure's stela cited the ceremonies associated with the completion of the Great Cycle 9.0.0.0.0 and the name of the first ruler, Yax K'uk' Mo'. This temple was deliberately curated and left accessible by the Copan dynasty for some 250 years before finally succumbing to the expansive designs of Uaxaclahun Ubah K'awil. One can imagine this building serving as a kind of oracle as well as the most sacred of the dynastic temples. It is revealing that when the thirteenth ruler had this temple buried, he had its stela's text partially replicated on the mat stela (J), that symbol for divine rulership people were forced to contemplate on their way into the city from the eastern *sacbe*. Just as the ballcourt showed continuity in function and decoration through time, Structure 26 served as a dynastic shrine for the duration of Copan kingship and emphasized the sacred as well as the historical origins of divine rule.

During the reign of Ruler 16 (A.D. 763 to ca. 820), whose name is best transcribed as Yax Pasah (Stuart 1992), once again a major change was in the air as far as dynastic monument programs went. This was the complete abandonment of the medium of the stela as a vehicle for aggrandizement of the ruler. Henceforth, information was recorded primarily on buildings and secondarily on inscribed altars and the lids of portable stone *incensarios*. Of his buildings, we know that in the Main Acropolis he was responsible for the final versions of Temples 11, 16, 18, and 21A. Although Structures 18 and 21A basically represented relatively small additions to the East Court, the renovations on Structures 11 and 16 were physically imposing and visually impressive. The multiple depictions of K'inich Yax K'uk' Mo' in the sculptures that embellished and gave life to Structure 16—on its exterior temple façades, in the temple interior, and on Altar Q (Fash 1992)—are now seen as perfectly in keeping with his depiction on the earlier temples at this locus, namely Rosalila and Margarita (Agurcia Fasquelle n.d.). The emphasis on Tlaloc imagery, as noted above, is grounded in the associations made between Teotihuacan and Copan in the first three decades of the city's history. The massive renovations of Structures 16 and 11 were the most impressive part of Yax Pasah's dynastic building program; the West Court of the acropolis was virtually completely redone.

Rather than celebrating fertility, the cosmos, and dance, Mary Miller and Linda Schele have shown us that the (final phase) West Court was an underworld redoubt where, as noted, the steps for ritual participant/observer accommodations were quite limited. It is clear from the elevation and depictions of crododiles, aquatic snails, and Pawahtun musicians on adjacent buildings that Altar Q and the meeting of kings that it portrays was symbolically placed in the watery underworld. The stairs of the imposing Temple Pyramid 16 that rose just behind Altar Q contained dozens of skulls on its lower outset panel, which is also in keeping with the symbolism shown on the other buildings of the West Court. The first version of Structure 11 was one of the earliest buildings in the acropolis, and David Stuart long ago deciphered the inscription on an early buried step within it as "the lineage house of Yax K'uk' Mo'." Structure 11 faced both the most exclusive theatre space of the West Court and the most inclusive one, the great open plaza that incorporated the ballcourt, the hieroglyphic stairway, and the public entrance and Great Plaza beyond. The king could be involved with either the most inclusive or the most exclusive ceremonies simply by walking out the north or the south door. In fact, he could have supervised many pageants simultaneously, including the dances on the dance platform just outside the east door without ever having to leave the premises.

The huge Pawahtun heads found on the north side of Temple 11 (Fash 1986) formed part of two full-figure depictions of this deity that were the largest ever carved in the Maya area. Everyone entering the central plaza area by means of the *sacbeob* would have seen the imposing Temple 11 and its giant Pawahtuns and crocodilians, surely one of the most dazzling visual displays of its day. This most grandiose version of this "overarching theme" is in keeping with the virtual obsession with the Pawahtun/Bacab complex in Copan, which began (as far as we know) with the inner chamber of Temple 22 in the early eighth century. Fragments from another such Pawahtun-supported archway originally inside the temple of Structure 10L-26 were found by the Peabody

Museum expeditions of the 1890s and also in our excavations of the late 1980s, indicating that the fifteenth ruler mimicked this part of the Temple 22 imagery. During the reign of Yax Pasah, this imagery was transformed two ways: into a giant version to adorn the new king's most massive building project (Temple 11) and into a standardized smaller format used by the nobles in the valley, with Pawahtun figures (now at a smaller scale) supporting the ledge of interior benches with hieroglyphic texts. Three such benches have been uncovered in the Sepulturas ward of the city alone, and the presumption is that many more will surface as more of the elite residential compounds in the valley are dug. Perhaps the Pawahtuns/Bacabs became a special supernatural patron of the royal line in Copan, as Houston and Stuart (1989, 1996) have adduced to have been in use at various centers in the lowlands during the Classic period.

The first two Pawahtun-supported benches discovered in the Sepulturas ward of the valley led me to posit that Yax Pasah was bestowing royal gifts in the form of hieratic monuments on his most important subjects as inducements for them to remain loyal to his political order and to continue to provide him with tribute (Fash 1983, 1986, 1988). The supporting Pawahtun figures were thought to represent a metaphor for the role of the supporting nobles; both were adduced to be "pillars of the world order" during the reign of the sixteenth and last ruler in the line of K'inich Yax K'uk' Mo'. Taking matters a step further, the abundance of large elite residential compounds led me to suggest that there might have been a "nobles' revolt" at Copan or other Classic Maya sites, as push came to shove at the end of the Classic period (Fash 1988, 1991). Since then, yet another example of a Pawahtun-supported bench was uncovered by David Webster and his colleagues (Webster, Evans, and Sanders 1993) in their investigations of Structure 8N-66, the easternmost large vaulted masonry structure found at Group 8N-11, located at the terminus of the eastern *sacbe*.

The importance of the upper nobility at other Classic Maya sites was also brought to the fore by investigations at Palenque (Schele 1991) and Tikal (Haviland 1981; cf. Schele and Freidel 1990). In both cases, inscribed monuments were found in the context of long-lived elite residential compounds in close proximity to the dynastic center. Stuart (1993) has recently shown that such elites were bestowed a number of nonkingly titles in different parts of the Maya lowlands at the end of the Classic period and were a growing political force with whom the rulers were forced to contend. However, Stuart is less convinced by the idea the the Copan benches were necessarily bestowed upon the nobles by the king. He sees more independent action and political competition on the part of the aspiring elites of the Maya lowlands in the eighth century A.D. Certainly, the decipherment of genealogical information on the bench from Structure 9N-82 does indicate a desire to showcase the prestige of his family background. The inscription cites the owner of the house, his mother's name, and his "predecessor" (presumably his father). The long-term occupation sequence at Group 9N-8 included substantial Early Classic remains (Fash 1983, 1991), yet only in the Late Classic did the residents begin sculpting images of their supernatural patron (a hybrid Pawahtun/scribe), images of themselves, and hieroglyphic texts to record their story for posterity.

Future research at such elite residential groups throughout the Maya lowlands may show that many such subroyal families were creating their own monuments to exalt their genealogy, social station, political office, and supernatural affiliations. We plan such investigations at Copan and hope that others will pursue them at other sites. The work at secondary centers and subroyal elite compounds will allow us to assess continuities and change in the power politics among and between competing lineages in the middle and at the top of the political system and between those lineages and the royal family itself. It will also provide a much needed bridge between the dynastic building programs of the royal families and the more humble abodes that have traditionally been the focus of household archaeology in the Maya area. Once this is accomplished, we may be able to better address the question of who, ultimately, commissioned these monuments: the nobles themselves, bent on their own aggrandizement, or the kings who sought their continued support? We may also get a better idea of whether these "subdynastic" public monuments were purely a Late Classic development or in fact had deeper roots in the histories of the major Maya kingdoms. Finally, one can hope that we will obtain a clearer picture of whether the practice of replication in the form and functions of Maya architecture went from the top down or the bottom up.

REFLECTIONS ON THE PAST AND PORTENTS OF THE FUTURE

In the study of dynastic building programs, the researcher is confronted with a series of huge challenges, many of them owing to the scale upon which they must conduct investigations to obtain meaningful results. The present offering was designed to illustrate that the most productive way to put Maya dynastic history to the test is by uncovering it on and around the buildings that were the maximal political statements of the paramount players on the stages of the Classic period. Only by directing research to squarely address the issue of how the Maya towns and city-states were formed and how they grew in scope and complexity through time and space can we put the aspirations and achievements of the individual dynasts—from earliest to latest—in their proper historical and processual contexts. The investigations of the North Acropolis and the Mundo Perdido Complex of Tikal, as well as of the Main Acropolis of Copan, have yielded a number of revelations regarding the origins and development of complex society and the subsequent development of dynastic building programs and their accompanying ritual, pomp, and circumstance. However, even the developments at those loci cannot be evaluated in isolation but must be scrutinized in the context of the larger social system they formed the apex of before their significance in etic terms can be assessed. Likewise, results of tightly focused research on the supporting populations cannot tell us the whole story of a kingdom, as some of the more recent work in Copan has clearly shown. The dismissal of the existence of an Early Classic founder of Copan's dynasty and his pre-seventh century successors based on the results of a sample of visible mounds presents us with an object lesson in the dangers of dismissing the historical record as mere propaganda.

Obviously, the possibilities for discerning the scope and strength of dynastic rule through time are immeasurably enhanced when the data from the supporting population include information on the interest groups that are most likely to have influenced or even decided questions of policy. Certainly, the "feedback" between the rulers, lesser nobles, and commoners that J. Eric Thompson (1939) pioneered at San José and that has more recently been attempted both at Copan and elsewhere is still in its intellectual infancy. Our present attempts at this kind of analysis will likely appear crude and clumsy in the future, as a whole array of comparative ethnological and archaeological data are brought to bear on these questions.

This chapter hopefully has also served to demonstrate that analysis of the idiosyncratic concerns and strategies of statecraft of particular rulers as adjudged from their monuments can reliably be made only in the context of an understanding of their predecessors' works. Categorical statements of the innovative nature of a particular ruler's program or monuments are best reserved for cases where extensive investigations of earlier manifestations have been conducted at those loci. The "cross-cutting, self-corrective strategy" for research on sociopolitical evolution in Copan has enabled us to substantially revise a number of erroneous earlier ideas and models that we now realize were made on the basis of faulty chronology, insufficient samples (especially of earlier versions of the same phenomena before Late Classic times), or other shortcomings. A strong commitment of time and financial resources is required for even this strategy to be effective in the epicenters of ancient Maya metropoli. A willingness to constantly revise previous, sometimes cherished, interpretations and to seek answers to new questions is also a vital prerequisite for this type of work. Perhaps the most important finding, however, is that the final versions of buildings and other dynastic monument programs are often a very good basis from which to predict the forms and decoration of their predecessors.

The documentation of how an idea and a monument were transformed through time permits us to question how the exigencies of rulership may have required flexibility and change in some areas and rock-solid stability in others. The portraits of representatives on Ruler 14's version of the Mat House are thought to be an example of a change in "public broadcasting" based on political expediency to mark the ascendance and power of the nobility. Conversely, the ballcourt, Temple 22, and Temple 16 embodied and illustrated immutable themes from their first construction to their last. Nuances and styles of expression certainly changed, but the meaning and intent of these three monuments were never in doubt, either to their makers or to the public; they were designed to enthrall and engage. Structure 26 was more complex. It apparently always served as a dynastic shrine, perhaps even as an oracle, but its form and its decorative program changed dramatically more than once in its long public life. Its final version represents something of a paradox. Although its hieroglyphic stairway constitutes the longest, largest, and most explicit inscribed public record of dynastic power in the Maya world, its written message was legible only to a chosen few. Although the overall intent and meaning was made clear to all by the ruler portraits and huge Tlaloc imagery, the power of the deified rulers was at the same time rendered inaccessible by the written word itself. It was designed to inform but, more importantly, to impress and intimidate.

The question of whether Classic Maya dynastic buildings can be "read" as texts at this point in time can perhaps best be answered in some cases "yes, but to varying degrees." The most clear-cut way they can be interpreted is in terms of the volume and complexity of their construction. Elliot Abrams's studies of energetics (this volume) show us that those data can speak volumes about the power of the people who commissioned the buildings. Equally clear is that "bigger is better" meant not only "taller" but "broader" for the dynastic centers of the Classic Maya. The design and intent of vertical space is a feature of royal architecture that has largely gone uncommented on and surely holds more for us to explore. Just as the stationing of people on steps had meaning in terms of status and social standing (Houston, this volume), so the height and accommodations for people on buildings and their plazas also had meaning in terms of how many people, and which ones, were allowed to be participant observers there. The layout of the buildings themselves varies so widely from site to site that it is hard to claim there were codes that were universally agreed upon. It is clear that the earlier patterns in a particular site to a degree dictated later ones (Webster and McAnany, this volume). This makes the massive redesign of the

Copan Acropolis by Waterlily Jaguar (Sharer et al. n.d.) and the shifting of the triadic plan from the North Acropolis to the Great Plaza by Ruler A of Tikal (Coe 1990) stand out as the daring work of visionaries. But did the Maya have their own Imhoteps, or can we attribute these sweeping changes to the rulers themselves? Without the requisite textual data, at this point we can do little more than pose the question. Regarding function, it appears that certain kinds of buildings were essential components of all Classic Maya dynastic centers. The royal palace and administrative compound; funerary temples for deified ancestors; buildings and entire plaza complexes for ritual penance, sacrifice, dance, ball games, feasts, and other compelling fare; council houses; and dynastic temples, all these and more were built into the Classic Maya centers. But identifying and distinguishing them on the criteria of form and associated artifacts alone has been an uphill battle. For such identifications, the insights provided by texts and imagery are a godsend to us and worthy of the most careful scrutiny.

Certainly, the Copan dynastic architectural corpus is replete with examples of pictorial imagery that illuminated the nature of a building in clear-cut terms that the entire population could understand. The GI panel and sky bands on Motmot and Yax, the Ballcourt I full-figure macaws with their Hunahpu arms, and the K'inich Ahau and sky bands on Yehnal and Margarita show the explicitness of the imagery used to label the holy grounds from the very onset of dynastic rule. The full-figure images and associated glyphs on Margarita show that even rulers' names were literally spelled out for the viewing public on the façades of the buildings, as were the supernatural locales with which they were associated. Indeed, one cannot escape the feeling that 99% of the Maya population in Classic times understood the 7 Kan and 9 Imix references much better than we do! The *wits* masks on Temple 22, the mat designs on the Mat House, the Tlaloc imagery on Temples 16 and 26, the bats on Temple 20, and the giant Pawahtuns on Temple 11 were clear and explicit symbols that the Maya world could understand and revere.

On the other hand, the more esoteric information encoded in the longer hieroglyphic texts that adorned the steps and interior chambers of the buildings were probably designed more to lend an aura of sacred mystery to the environs than to spell things out for the person on the street. Then, as now, a specialist was needed to interpret them. Perhaps too then, as now, there were different interpretations placed on their content according to the passions of the moment and the aspirations of the reader. The point is that now, as then, they constitute an integral part of the message, especially given that in many cases the inscriptions refer as much to the monuments themselves as they do to their makers (David Stuart n.d.b; personal communication, 1995). They may still be our most direct window into the thoughts, intents, and perhaps even the personality of their patrons.

The renewal of tried and trusted religious themes and the structures that personified them is one of the most consistent patterns found to date in the study of Classic Maya dynastic architecture. This practice is entirely in keeping with the cyclical view of history shared not only by the city-states of the Classic Maya lowlands but also of the larger culture area of Mesoamerica. Curiously, this view of history seems to have an eerie counterpart in the cyclical manner in which those cultures have been interpreted by Western scholars. When Stephens published his popular books, a new window was opened to us on a wondrous and fascinating world. The initial concern with the large public monuments, and the history that Stephens knew was recorded in their glyphs, was later distorted into the dogma that the one thing the inscriptions did not record was history (Coe 1992). Fortunately, interest in housemounds (Ricketson and Ricketson 1937; Wauchope 1934), secondary centers (Thompson 1939), modern Maya people (Redfield and Villa Rojas 1934), and their material culture (Wauchope 1939) brought new avenues for exploring the human dimension of ancient Maya life at the time the denial of history was in ascendance. When the historical record finally resurfaced with the brilliant work of Tatiana Proskouriakoff and Heinrich Berlin, a new window was opened onto the workings of the ancient Maya world. But now the Post-Modern take on this is that none of it is valid, that history does not exist in the abstract, and that those who would study it do so only to upgrade or reinforce their own social position. Can it be that the investigation of housemounds, secondary centers, and the modern Maya can once again bring balance to our profession? It seems to me that there are grounds for optimism in thinking so, particularly given the progress that this volume has shown in our understanding of Classic period architecture and the many ways it can be used to open new vistas onto the lifeways and conceits of the ancient Maya. The study of their dynastic architecture can shed precious light on how the Classic Maya conceived, structured, and viewed their world during a particularly creative juncture in their history.

Acknowledgments My thanks to Stephen Houston for giving me the opportunity to participate in this important symposium and for numerous constructive criticisms on the original version of this paper. Appreciation and recognition are likewise extended to the Instituto Hondureño de Antropología e Historia for its support of all recent investigations and conservation projects in Copan, including the Copan Acropolis Archaelogical Project of which the author is director. In Copan, a number of talented people have joined forces to address a broad array of questions, including many of those addressed here. Often, their professions and interests parallel those of their ancient counterparts and as such provide a vantage upon possible meanings and motivations behind the buildings and symbols. The interest in agriculture and food production has been avidly pursued by scholars such as William T. Sanders and B. L. Turner II, whose lifeworks revolve around reconstructing the lifeways and strategies of the farmers and the agricultural economy that sustained civilized life in Mesoamerica and elsewhere. The subject of urban planning has been addressed by Sanders and David Webster from the standpoint of political evolution and by Wendy Ashmore, who reconstructed the ideological motivations that played a role in the thoughts and decisions of those who laid out the ancient city. Questions of theology have been tackled head-on by Linda Schele, who has devoted much thought to reconstructing the path of the shaman and the role of faith in moving the Maya mountains. Dynasty and political history have been tackled by epigraphers Schele, David Stuart, Nikolai Grube, Berthold Riese, Federico Fahsen, Stephen Houston, Floyd Lounsbury, and others. Stuart's insights on the different offices and specializations visible in the Late Classic inscriptions and their implications for the fall of the Classic order were the subject of a recent Dumbarton Oaks paper, and of course he has also gleaned much about the world of the Maya scribe and the many kinds of messages and meanings they succeeded in leaving behind. The Maya architecture at Copan is presently being restored by the architect Rudy Larios, whose vast experience in Maya restoration and archaeology speaks for itself. The sculptured façades that adorned those buildings are being documented, refitted, and analyzed by Barbara Fash, who brings an artist's sense of aesthetics and composition to her work and an uncanny ability to conceptualize and solve three-dimensional puzzles. The dirt archaeologists have the role of putting all of this in context. As E. Wyllys Andrews V puts it, our task is to reconstruct human behavior from the excavation of abandoned places or discarded things, especially the abandoned residential complexes that are the essential building blocks in our efforts to reconstruct social, political, and economic behavior.

My thanks to all of my students over the past ten years, for bringing fresh perspectives, tireless enthusiasm, and years of hard work to our efforts to put the Copan monuments and behavioral residues in their proper context in excavations on Structures 10L-10, -16, -22, -22A, and -26. For the earlier phases of the acropolis, the superposition of those building complexes has been the focus of five years of research by Bob Sharer and his colleagues, and Ricardo Agurcia Fasquelle has concentrated on Structure 10L-16 and its antecedents.

Their investigations have enabled us to see how the epicenter developed and what kinds of behavior took place in its buildings through time and space. E. Wyllys Andrews V and his students and colleagues have given us a magnificently comprehensive and insightful picture of the royal residential compound situated on the south flank of the acropolis as the result of four full field seasons of excavations there. Whatever success this paper and the work in Copan in general have attained owes more to their efforts than my own, although they should, of course, not be held responsible for any of the shortcomings of the present offering.

BIBLIOGRAPHY

AGURCIA FASQUELLE, RICARDO

n.d. Rosalila, Heart of the Copan Acropolis. In *Copan: The Rise and Fall of a Classic Maya Kingdom* (William L. Fash and E. Wyllys Andrews, V, eds.). School of American Research Press, Santa Fe. (In preparation.)

AGURCIA FASQUELLE, RICARDO, AND WILLIAM L. FASH

1991 Maya Artistry Unearthed. *National Geographic* 180 (3): 94–105.

ANDREWS, E. WYLLYS, V

n.d. The Organization of a Royal Maya Residential Compound at the Center of Copan. In *Copan: The Rise and Fall of a Classic Maya Kingdom* (William L. Fash and E. Wyllys Andrews, V, eds.). School of American Research Press, Santa Fe. (In preparation.)

ANDREWS, E. WYLLYS, V, AND BARBARA W. FASH

1992 Continuity and Change in a Royal Maya Residential Complex at Copan. *Ancient Mesoamerica* 3: 63–88.

ASHMORE, WENDY

1991 Site-Planning Principles and Concepts of Directionality among the Ancient Maya. *Latin American Antiquity* 2: 199–226.

BAUDEZ, CLAUDE F.

1980 Le balle, le roi, et le mais: images du jeu de balle maya. *Journal de Société des Américanistes* 70: 139–152.

CARR, ROBERT F., AND JAMES E. HAZARD

1961 *Map of the Ruins of Tikal, El Peten, Guatemala.* Tikal Report, no. 11. University Museum, University of Pennsylvania, Philadelphia.

COE, MICHAEL D.

1992 *Breaking the Maya Code.* Thames and Hudson, London.

COE, WILLIAM R.

1990 *Excavations in the Great Plaza, North Terrace, and North Acropolis of Tikal.* 6 vols. Tikal Report, no. 14. University Museum, University of Pennsylvania, Philadelphia.

FASH, BARBARA W.

1992 Late Classic Architectural Sculpture Themes at Copan. *Ancient Mesoamerica* 3: 89–102.

1996 Copan's House of Lords. *Natural History* 105 (4): 30–31.

n.d.a Copan Mosaic Sculpture: Puzzles within Puzzles. Paper presented at the 10th Maya Weekend, University Museum, University of Pennsylvania, Philadelphia, April 1992.

n.d.b Iconographic Evidence for Water Management at Copan. In *Copan: The Rise and Fall of a Classic Maya Kingdom* (William L. Fash and E. Wyllys Andrews, V, eds.). School of American Research Press, Santa Fe. (In preparation.)

Fash, Barbara W., and William L. Fash
n.d. He at the Head of the Mat: Archaeological Evidence for a Classic Maya Council House at Copan. Paper presented at the Ninetieth Annual Meeting of the American Anthropological Association, Chicago, November 1991.

Fash, Barbara W., William L. Fash, Sheree Lane, Rudy Larios, Linda Schele, Jeffrey Stomper, and David S. Stuart
1992 Investigations at a Classic Maya Council House at Copan, Honduras. *Journal of Field Archaeology* 19: 419–442.

Fash, Barbara W., and Karl A. Taube
n.d. Evolution of Dynastic Architectural Sculpture at Copan. Paper presented at the Sixty-First Annual Meeting of the Society for American Archaeology, New Orleans, April 1996.

Fash, William L.
1983 *Maya State Formation: A Case Study and Its Implications.* University Microfilms, Ann Arbor.
1986 La fachada esculpida de la estructura 9N-82: contenido, forma, iconografía. In *Excavaciones en el area urbana de Copan*, vol. 1 (William T. Sanders, ed.): 319–382. Instituto Hondureño de Antropología e Historia, Tegucigalpa.
1988 A New Look at Maya Statecraft from Copan, Honduras. *Antiquity* 62: 157–159.
1991 *Scribes, Warriors and Kings: The City of Copán and the Ancient Maya.* Thames and Hudson, London.

Fash, William L., and E. Wyllys Andrews V (eds.)
n.d. *Copan: The Rise and Fall of a Classic Maya Kingdom.* School of American Research Press, Santa Fe. (In preparation.)

Fash, William L., and Barbara W. Fash
1990 Scribes, Warriors, and Kings: Ancient Lives of the Copan Maya. *Archaeology* 45 (3): 26–35.

Fash, William L., and Robert J. Sharer
1991 Sociopolitical Developments and Methodological Issues at Copan, Honduras: A Conjunctive Perspective. *Latin American Antiquity* 2: 166–187.

Fash, William L., and David S. Stuart
1991 Dynastic History and Cultural Evolution at Copan, Honduras. In *Classic Maya Political History* (T. Patrick Culbert, ed.): 147–179. Cambridge University Press, New York.

Fash, William L., Richard V. Williamson, Carlos Rudy Larios, and Joel Palka
1992 The Hieroglyphic Stairway and Its Ancestors: Investigations of Copan Structure 10L-26. *Ancient Mesoamerica* 3: 105–116.

Flannery, Kent V., and Joyce Marcus (eds.)
1983 *The Cloud People: Divergent Evolution of the Zapotec and Mixtec Civilizations.* Academic Press, New York.

Freidel, David A., Linda Schele, and Joy Parker
1993 *Maya Cosmos: Three Thousand Years on the Shaman's Path.* William Morrow, New York.

GEERTZ, CLIFFORD

1980 *Negara: The Theatre State in Nineteenth-Century Bali.* Princeton University Press, Princeton, N.J.

GILLESPIE, SUSAN D.

1989 *The Aztec Kings: The Construction of Rulership in Mexican History.* University of Arizona Press, Tucson.

HAVILAND, WILLIAM A.

1981 Dower Houses and Minor Centers at Tikal, Guatemala: An Investigation into the Identification of Valid Units in Settlement Hierarchies. In *Lowland Maya Settlement Patterns* (Wendy Ashmore, ed.): 89–117. University of New Mexico Press, Albuquerque.

HOUSTON, STEPHEN D.

1993 *Hieroglyphs and History at Dos Pilas: Dynastic Politics of the Classic Maya.* University of Texas Press, Austin.

HOUSTON, STEPHEN D., AND DAVID S. STUART

1989 *The* Way *Glyph: Evidence for "Co-essences" among the Classic Maya.* Research Reports on Ancient Maya Writing, no. 30. Center for Maya Research, Washington, D.C.

1996 Of Gods, Glyphs, and Kings: Divinity and Rulership among the Classic Maya. *Antiquity* 70: 289–312.

JONES, CHRISTOPHER

1977 Inauguration Dates of Three Late Classic Rulers of Tikal, Guatemala. *American Antiquity* 42: 28–60.

KOWALSKI, JEFF K., AND WILLIAM L. FASH

1991 Symbolism of the Maya Ball Game at Copan: Synthesis and New Aspects. In *Sixth Palenque Round Table, 1986* (Merle Greene Robertson and Virginia M. Fields, eds.): 59–67. University of Oklahoma Press, Norman.

LAPORTE, JUAN PEDRO, AND VILMA FIALKO

1993 El preclásico de mundo perdido: Algunos aportes sobre los orígenes de Tikal. In *Tikal y Uaxactun en el preclásico* (Juan Pedro Laporte and Juan Antonio Valdés, eds.): 9–42. Instituto de Investigaciones Antropológicas, Universidad Nacional Autónoma de México, México, D.F.

1995 Reencuentro con Mundo Perdido, Tikal, Guatemala. *Ancient Mesoamerica* 6: 41–94.

LARIOS, CARLOS RUDY, WILLIAM L. FASH, AND DAVID S. STUART

1994 Architectural Stratigraphy and Epigraphic Dating of Copan Structure 10L-22: An Exercise in the Conjunctive Approach. In *Seventh Palenque Round Table, 1989* (Merle Greene Robertson and Virginia M. Fields, eds.): 69–78. The Pre-Columbian Art Research Institute, San Francisco.

MANZANILLA, LINDA

1993 Daily Life in the Teotihuacan Apartment Compounds. In *Teotihuacan: City of the Gods* (Kathleen Berrin and Esther Pasztory, eds.): 90–99. Fine Arts Museums of San Francisco, San Francisco.

MARCUS, JOYCE

1976 *Emblem and State in the Classic Maya Lowlands: An Epigraphic Approach toward Territorial Organization.* Dumbarton Oaks, Washington, D.C.

1992 *Ancient Mesoamerican Writing Systems: History, Myth, and Propaganda.* Princeton University Press, Princeton, N.J.

MAUDSLAY, ALFRED P.

1889–1902 *Archaeology.* Biologia centrali-americana. 5 vols. Porter and Dulau, London.

MILLER, MARY ELLEN

1986 Copan: Conference with a Perished City. In *City-States of the Maya: Art and Architecture* (Elizabeth Benson, ed.): 72–109. Rocky Mountain Institute for Pre-Columbian Studies, Denver, Colo.

MILLER, MARY ELLEN, AND STEPHEN D. HOUSTON

1987 The Classic Maya Ballgame and Its Architectural Setting: A Study in Relations between Text and Image. *RES: Anthropology and Aesthetics* 14: 47–66.

MORLEY, SYLVANUS G.

1920 *The Inscriptions at Copan.* Carnegie Institution, Publication 219. Washington, D.C.

PROSKOURIAKOFF, TATIANA

1946 *An Album of Maya Architecture.* Carnegie Institution, Publication 558. Washington, D.C.

1973 The Hand-Grasping-Fish and Associated Glyphs on Classic Maya Monuments. In *Mesoamerican Writing Systems* (Elizabeth Benson, ed.): 165–173. Dumbarton Oaks, Washington, D.C.

REDFIELD, ROBERT, AND ANTONIO VILLA ROJAS

1934 *Chan Kom: A Maya Village.* Carnegie Institution, Publication 448. Washington, D.C.

RICKETSON, OLIVER G, AND EDITH B. RICKETSON

1937 *Uaxactun, Guatemala: Group E, 1926–1937.* Carnegie Institution, Publication 477. Washington, D.C.

RÍESE, BERTHOLD

1980 Late Classic Relationship between Copan and Quirigua: Some Epigraphic Evidence. Paper presented at the Forty-Fifth Annual Meeting of the Sociey for American Archaeology, Philadelphia.

1986 Late Classic Relationship between Copan and Quirigua: Some Epigraphic Evidence. In *The Southeast Maya Periphery: Problems and Prospects* (Patricia Urban and Edward Schortman, eds.): 94–101. University of Texas Press, Austin.

RINGLE, WILLIAM M.

1990 Who Was Who in Ninth-Century Chichen Itza. *Ancient Mesoamerica* 1 (2): 233–243.

RUPPERT, KARL J., AND JOHN H. DENISON

1943 *Archaeological Reconnaissance in Campeche, Quintana Roo, and Peten.* Carnegie Institution, Publication 543. Washington, D.C.

SANDERS, WILLIAM T. (ED.)

1986 *Excavaciones en el área urbana de Copan,* vol. 1. Instituto Hondureño de Antropología e Historia, Tegucigalpa.

1989 Household, Lineage, and State at Eighth Century Copan, Honduras. In *The House of the Bacabs, Copan, Honduras* (David L. Webster, ed.): 89–105. Dumbarton Oaks, Washington, D.C.

Sanders, William T., and David L. Webster

1988 The Mesoamerican Urban Tradition. *American Anthropologist* 90: 521–546.

Scarborough, Vernon L.

1983 A Preclassic Maya Water System. *American Antiquity* 48: 720–744.

1993 Water Management in the Southern Maya Lowlands: An Accretive Model for the Engineered Landscape. In *Economic Aspects of Water Management in the Prehispanic New World* (Vernon Scarborough and Barry Isaac, eds.): 17–69. JAI Press, Greenwich, Conn.

Schele, Linda

1991 The Demotion of Chac-Zutz: Lineage Compounds and Subsidiary Lords at Palenque. In *Sixth Palenque Round Table, 1986* (Merle Green Robertson and Virginia M. Fields, eds.): 6–11. University of Oklahoma Press, Norman.

1992 The Founders of Lineages at Copan and Other Maya Sites. *Ancient Mesoamerica* 3: 135–144.

Schele, Linda, and David A. Freidel

1990 *A Forest of Kings.* William Morrow, New York.

Schele, Linda, and Mary Ellen Miller

1986 *The Blood of Kings: Dynasty and Ritual in Maya Art.* Kimball Art Museum, Fort Worth, Tex.

Serrano Sánchez, Carlos

1993 Funerary Practices and Human Sacrifice in Teotihuacan Burials. In *Teotihuacan: City of the Gods* (Kathleen Berrin and Esther Pasztory, eds.): 108–115. Fine Arts Museums of San Francisco, San Francisco.

Sharer, Robert J.

n.d. Patterns of Architectural Growth in the Early Classic Copan Acropolis. Paper presented at the Sixty-First Annual Meeting of the Society for American Archaeology, New Orleans, April 1996.

Sharer, Robert J., Julia C. Miller, and Loa P. Traxler

1992 Evolution of Classic Period Architecture in the Eastern Acropolis, Copan: A Progress Report. *Ancient Mesoamerica* 3: 145–160.

Sharer, Robert, and David W. Sedat

1995 *The Archaeological Context of the Margarita Stone.* Copan Note 114. Copan Mosaics Project and Instituto Hondureño de Antropología e Historia, Copan, Honduras.

Sharer, Robert, David W. Sedat, Loa P. Traxler, and Julia C. Miller

n.d. Early Classic Royal Power in Copan: The Origins and Development of the Acropolis. In *Copan: The Rise and Fall of a Classic Maya Kingdom* (William L. Fash and E. Wyllys Andrews, V, eds.). School of American Research Press, Santa Fe. (In preparation.)

Sheets, Payson D.

1992 *The Ceren Site: A Prehistoric Village Buried by Volcanic Ash in Central America.* Harcourt Brace Jovanovich, Fort Worth, Tex.

SMITH, A. LEDYARD
1950 *Uaxactun, Guatemala: Excavations of 1931–37.* Carnegie Institution, Publication 436. Washington, D.C.

STEPHENS, JOHN L.
1962 [1841] *Incidents of Travel in Central America, Chiapas, and Yucatan.* Dover, New York.

STRÖMSVIK, GUSTAV
1952 The Ball Courts at Copan. In *Contributions to American Anthropology and History* 55: 185–222. Carnegie Institution, Washington, D.C.

STUART, DAVID S.
1992 Hieroglyphs and Archaeology at Copan. *Ancient Mesoamerica* 3: 169–184.
1993 Historical Inscriptions and the Maya Collapse. In *Lowland Maya Civilization in the Eighth Century A.D.* (Jeremy A. Sabloff and John S. Henderson, eds.): 321–354. Dumbarton Oaks, Washington, D.C.
n.d.a The Texts of Temple 26: The Presentation of History at a Maya Dynastic Shrine. In *Copan: The Rise and Fall of a Classic Maya Kingdom* (William L. Fash and E. Wyllys Andrews, V, eds.). School of American Research Press, Santa Fe. (In preparation.)
n.d.b The Hills Are Alive: Sacred Mountains and Witz Monsters among the Lowland Maya. In *Maya Religion and Social Identity: Vistas from the Past and Present* (William L. Fash, ed.). David Rockefeller Center for Latin American Studies, Harvard University, Cambridge, Mass. (In preparation.)

STUART, DAVID S., AND STEPHEN D. HOUSTON
1994 *Classic Maya Place Names.* Studies in Pre-Columbian Art and Archaeology 33. Dumbarton Oaks, Washington, D.C.

STUART, DAVID, AND LINDA SCHELE
1986a *Yax K'uk' Mo', the Founder of the Lineage of Copan.* Copan Note 6. Copan Mosaics Project and Instituto Hondureño de Antropología e Historia, Copan, Honduras.
1986b *Interim Report on the Hieroglyphic Stair of Structure 26.* Copan Note 17. Copan Mosaics Project and Instituto Hondureño de Antropología e Historia, Copan, Honduras.

THOMPSON, J. ERIC S.
1939 *Excavations at San Jose, British Honduras.* Carnegie Institution, Publication 506. Washington, D.C.

VALDÉS, JUAN ANTONIO
1988 Los mascarones preclásicos de Uaxactún: El caso del grupo H. In *Primer simposio mundial sobre epigrafía maya*: 165–181. Asociación Tikal, Guatemala City.

WAUCHOPE, ROBERT
1934 *House Mounds of Uaxactun, Guatemala.* Carnegie Institution, Publication 436. Washington, D.C.
1939 *Modern Maya Houses.* Carnegie Institution, Publication 502. Washington, D.C.

WEBSTER, DAVID L.
1989a Appendix: The Original Location, Date, and Possible Implications of Altar W'. In *The House of the Bacabs, Copan, Honduras* (David L. Webster, ed.): 108–

112. Dumbarton Oaks, Washington, D.C.

1989b The House of the Bacabs: Its Social Context. In *The House of the Bacabs, Copan, Honduras* (David L. Webster, ed.): 5–40. Dumbarton Oaks, Washington, D.C.

Webster, David L. (ed.)

1989c *The House of the Bacabs, Copan, Honduras*. Studies in Pre-Columbian Art and Archaeology 29. Dumbarton Oaks, Washington, D.C.

Webster, David L., Susan Evans, and William T. Sanders

1993 *Out of the Past*. Mayfield Publishing, Mountain View, Calif.

Webster, David L., and AnnCorinne Freter

1990 The Demography of Late Classic Copan. In *Precolumbian Population History in the Maya Lowlands* (T. Patrick Culbert and Don S. Rice, eds.): 37–62. University of New Mexico Press, Albuquerque.

Webster, David L., William T. Sanders, and Peter van Rossum

1992 A Simulation of Copan Population History and Its Implications. *Ancient Mesoamerica* 3:185–198.

Willey, Gordon R., Richard M. Leventhal, and William L. Fash

1978 Maya Settlement in the Copan Valley. *Archaeology* 31: 32–43.

Williamson, Richard V.

1996 Excavations, Interpretations, and Implications of the Earliest Structures beneath Structure 10L-26 at Copan, Honduras. In *Eighth Palenque Round Table, 1993* (Merle Greene Robertson, Martha Macri, and Jan McHargue, eds.): 169–175. Pre-Columbian Art Institute, San Francisco.

n.d. Copan Ballcourt A-III: Symbol, Power, and Pilgrimage among the Classic Maya. Senior honor's thesis, University of Illinois at Urbana-Champaign.

Ancestors and the Classic Maya Built Environment

PATRICIA A. McANANY
BOSTON UNIVERSITY

Built environments are emergent phenomena that undergo constant change and transformation. They rarely form and crystallize as a singular vision or construction event but rather accrue form and meaning through a continued and dynamic interaction between people and places. This process leads to what Pred (1986: 5) has termed "place as historically contingent process" or locations at which historical events are encoded architecturally. Through ritual and performance, building activities transform places in profoundly social ways. Such a perspective on the built environment is particularly relevant to Classic Maya constructions, for which descriptive terms such as "organic, accretional, or agglutinative" often have been used, suggesting repetitive cycles of ritual performance and building activity. I suggest that this architectonic style results, in part, from the incorporation of ancestors—both their physical remains and their iconic images—into the Classic Maya built environment. Through their inclusion, ancestors facilitated a social definition of residence and augmented the political centrality of selected locales. To demonstrate this point, I first pursue a general discussion of burial ritual and the creation of ancestors; second, I examine the role of ancestors in the "ritual establishment of home" (Saile 1985: 87); third, I consider the incorporation of ancestors into monumental architecture to establish a political and ritual *axis mundi;* and, finally, I turn to a discussion of iconographic representations and textual references to ancestors and their burial places.

BURIAL RITUAL AND THE CREATION OF ANCESTORS

For Turner (1977), ritual performance was a response to a breach in the social fabric; it was a means of reintegrating society and moving through a liminal state such as that which occurs at the death of an important individual.

In contrast, Humphreys (1981) argues that death, a dangerous and chaotic rupture in the social order, also presents an opportunity for the living to reorder the system, to gain previously unforeseen advantage, or to promote themselves and their family line. In this view, protracted burial ritual, including secondary and tertiary interment as well as construction of ancestor shrines, allows time for maneuvering among the living. This method of "drawing power from the past for projection into the future" also has been emphasized by Feuchtwang (1974) in his analysis of Chinese geomancy and tomb placement. As we shall see, such attitudes seem also to have prevailed in Classic Maya society.

However one approaches it, burial ritual provides social rules for the living. Not only about the dead, such ritual helps forge linkages between the living and the dead (Pearson 1993: 227). The elaboration of burial ceremony and the extent to which the material remains of a deceased person are interred within a remembered and revered place, in turn, depend on the desire of the living to perpetuate an established order or to promulgate an unbroken chain of inheritance. For this reason, Glazier (1984: 133) used the term "domestication of death" to refer to the newly found meaning given to burial locales among the Mbeere of Kenya when the British Colonial government accorded legal status to ancestral burial grounds during tribal boundary disputes.

In a more specific sense, ancestor veneration, as it was practiced among both elites and nonelites in Classic Maya society, was a selective social practice in that ancestors were a subset of all deceased; ancestors were those who validated political power, status, and access to resources. Moreover, as facilitators of power transfers between the generations, ancestors played a particularly critical role in times of social transformation, such as the Early Classic period. Although the rituals of Classic Maya ancestor veneration no longer exist, we can study the places where ancestors were buried and their spirits were summoned for the benefit of the living.

ANCESTORS AND THE RITUAL ESTABLISHMENT OF HOME

Temple I of Tikal, the tomb of Ruler A, is a familiar monument and serves to exemplify the sense of political centrality given to a place by an ancestor interment (Jones 1977). As far back as the early part of the twentieth century, Ricketson (1925: 386) remarked on the strong association between pyramids and royal tombs. Less intuitively obvious is the creation of a sense of residence—of home—as imparted by the presence of an ancestor. From the early days of the Middle Formative, important dead were placed within the cores of structures. This pattern is a common one, whether one is examining burial data from Platform 5D-4-10th beneath the North Acropolis of Tikal (Coe 1990), the basal strata of Operation I at K'axob (Bobo n.d.), or the early structures of Cuello (Robin and Hammond 1991). From the very start, the maintenance of links with the deceased via physical proximity within a built environment is a prominent characteristic of Maya society.

Retrodicting from contemporary practices, we can speculate that burial placement may have played an important role in what Saile (1985: 87) has called the ritual establishment of home. Here I speak of home in the sense of an economic, ritual, political, and social hive of activity in nonindustrial society and not the more passive, television- and bedroom-dominated abodes of contemporary Western society. In regard to the former, the study of Davis (n.d.) on the topic of residence and land among K'anjobal Maya of Huehuetenango is particularly pertinent. Davis (n.d.: 80) describes residential units as having an unusually large or prominent structure called *yatut jichmam* ("house of the ancestor"). Within landholdings, which Davis (n.d.: 84) refers to as ancestor estates or *tx'otx jichmam*, "residents were joined together in a single religious community wherein prayer to the dead ancestors perpetuated the fertility of lands which the living gained through inheritance." Thus, among these highland Maya, home is integrally related to landholdings, and ancestors dwell metaphorically in the former and safeguard the latter. The principle of ancestors as guardians of fields and forests and occupants of residential structures is prevalent also among Quiche, who maintain lineage shrines (Bunzel 1952: 35–36; Carmack 1981: 161; Tedlock 1982: 77, 81), and among Tzotzil Maya, who venerate ancestors at shrines strategically positioned on the landscape (Vogt 1969: 391). Although ancestors are no longer physically interred within dwellings, but rather in cemeteries as prescribed by Christian practice, the residence is still considered to be an abode of the ancestors. This principle seems to have considerable antiquity and broad applicability. Both Stephen Houston and David Stuart (this volume) note that Classic-period pyramidal structures were named the *nah* or house of a specific ancestor.

Ancestral presence matters greatly in home and inheritance among contemporary Maya. Logically, then, the absence of interments in some Classic-period structures suggests that these are not homes—that is, these structures did not serve as residences. Based on the absence of burials, Harrison (n.d.: 251, 278), for instance, has argued against a residential function for much of the Central Acropolis of Tikal. The possibility exists, of course, that portions or all of the Central Acropolis were residential in function and that the esteemed inhabitants of these dwellings were buried in separate places of ritual designated for royalty, such as the large temple structures. Nevertheless, the Central Acropolis pattern presents a sharp contrast to a group such as A-V of Uaxactun, where the number of burial interments and their diversity in age and sex increase throughout the Classic period (Smith 1950: table 7). Ancestral presence, in fact, is generally coincident with the larger, temporally stable, residential complexes. Within Las Sepulturas group of Copan, Diamanti (1991: 212–225) notes that small, ancillary structures in residential compounds do not contain burials. Likewise, Gonlin (1993: table 3.16) found burials associated with only two of seven excavated rural Copan valley complexes, suggesting that rural inhabitants had strong ties to other focal residences. This evidence indicates that, although the data patterns are complex, ancestor presence played a role in defining residence (and its attendant privileges in terms of land and inheritance) within the built environment. When dealing with royal ancestors, "home" may have been defined on the much larger scale of a site rather than an individual residential complex. As discussed below, royal ancestors could also be evoked through more portable and referential media, such as personal ornamentation and sculpture.

When ancestor remains are present, longitudinal trends generally can be detected in the manner and location of interment within structures. From Middle Formative deposits at sites such as Tikal (Coe 1990), Cuello (Robin and Hammond 1991), and K'axob (Lockard n.d.), burials tend to be of single individuals of all ages and both sexes placed in an extended position. During the Late Formative and Early Classic this pattern is amplified. Burials of multiple individuals (representing a wide spectrum of ages and both sexes) were often interred within one centrally located and elaborately prepared grave. Late Formative Burial 2 from K'axob is a prime example of this pattern. It contained stratified deposits from separate burial events, which totaled nine individuals and included one child, one adolescent, five young adults, and two mature adults (Rebecca Storey, personal communication, July 1997; Fig. 1). Most of the interments were secondary, and this feature was opened and resealed several times before it was closed for the final time and capped by the construction of an Early Classic pyramid. In another example of a multiple interment, Burial 48 from Tikal, the central figure—an elderly male—was buried without head and hands and was covered with a black, organic material indicative of a textile wrapping (Coe 1990: 120). Taken together these interments suggest several things:

(1) protracted treatment of the dead, including defleshing, and selective retention of certain anatomical parts, particularly the cranium;

(2) elaborate wrapping of the corpse, sometimes into a tightly flexed and seated position and;

(3) in certain contexts—such as K'axob Burial 2—the grouping together of several individuals into what might be called a family mausoleum.

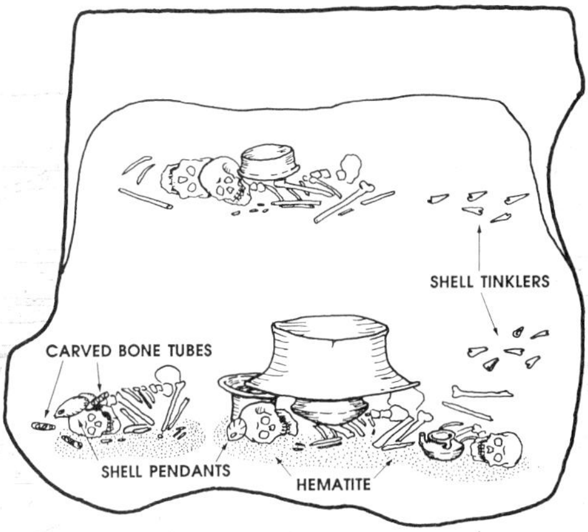

Fig. 1 Late Formative Burial 2 from K'axob, Belize, showing an example of a multiple, sequential burial interment. Drawing by J. Walkey (after McAnany 1995; reprinted courtesy of the University of Texas Press).

This pattern is elaborated at Caracol, where family tombs were used throughout the Classic period, as Chase and Chase (this volume) demonstrate. Group burial locales entail repeated opening and sealing of a tomb or pit, which serves to confirm the centrality of a locale through iterative ritual interaction between descendants and the place of their ancestors.

Merwin and Vaillant (1932) report on a particularly striking example of an Early Classic mausoleum at Holmul. Building B, located at the north end of Group II, was built in four major phases commencing in the Terminal Formative, as indicated by the fact that the burial vault under Room 9 contained mammiform tetrapodal vessels. Throughout subsequent renovations and expansions, additional interments—primarily of adults—were added to Building B. During the Early Classic, a four-room suite of vaulted rooms was constructed. This too was ultimately transformed into a mausoleum and the doorways—which once held movable wooden doors—were permanently sealed. In conjunction with the building of a pyramid capping this structure, yet another burial vault was added to the north end of Building B. The human remains described by Merwin and Vaillant (1932: 30–40) encompass considerable variability in position and completeness—extended, flexed, fully articulated, partially and completely disarticulated—and altogether comprise a total of 22 individuals. This pattern indicates that whereas some of these remains constitute primary interments, others were gathered from primary contexts and reinterred in this focal structure in a series of burial rituals that interdigitated with sequential building phases. As Karl Taube (personal communication, July 1994) notes, niches resembling cache vessels were modeled into the exterior façade of this structure—further indicating that propitiatory ritual was enacted at this locale.

ANCESTORS AND THE POLITICAL ESTABLISHMENT OF AN *AXIS MUNDI*

With the onset of the Maya Late Formative, many individuals were buried in a seated or tightly flexed position. Probably indicative of the emergence of institutionalized authority as Marcus (n.d.) has noted for San José phase figurines from Oaxaca, the seated burial position, moreover, necessitated thorough wrapping of a corpse, probably in twine and cotton. Mummy bundle depictions from Central Mexico (Fig. 2) and preserved Andean mummies from the Paracas Peninsula serve to indicate the popularity of this position. Once wrapped in this fashion, a corpse becomes much more portable and can be placed temporarily within a structure or interment and later moved to a specially prepared burial shrine or tomb. This elaboration of postmortem treatment provides "breathing space" for descendants who may need time to mobilize resources and labor to initiate a new construction that will not only house the deceased but also mark the successful passing of power between generations and the continued ability of a ruling family to mobilize support for "royal work" (Feeley-Harnik 1985: 293). Verano (1997) has documented a similar spacing between death and final interment among some of the females interred with the Lord of Sipan; apparently these "retainer burials" were transported from another holding locale. Among the Classic Maya, the time lapse between recorded death dates and shrine dedication dates for royal individuals (discussed below) suggests that construction of burial facilities and delayed transport of the dead occurred in this tropical lowland region as well. As a result, the death of an important person—soon to be an ancestor—not only triggered a series of social negotiations but also could initiate profound transformation of the built environment. The dead may have been held in temporary storage (or displayed) while their final crypt was constructed. Wrapping and preservation of a corpse ensured that the dead continued to serve the needs of the living, particularly during that liminal stage of interregnum.

A seated burial reproduces the regal position of a headman, chief, or lord seated on a stool, mat, or throne; Burial C1 of Uaxactun provides a vivid example (Fig. 3). This adult male was placed on a low throne-like platform supported by a stucco-pillow backrest. The Tzakol 3 vessels arrayed around him included an incised, individual serving bowl (originally placed in his lap), a cylindrical drinking vessel, and two larger serving bowls. His facial bones had

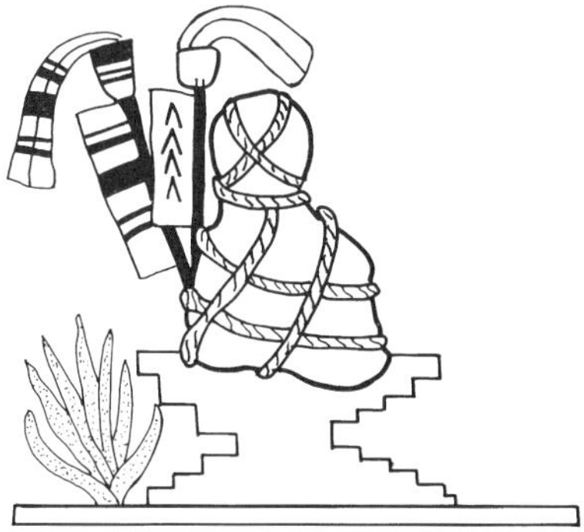

Fig. 2 Seated and tightly wrapped corpse just prior to cremation (after *Codex Magliabechiano* 1970: fol. 66).

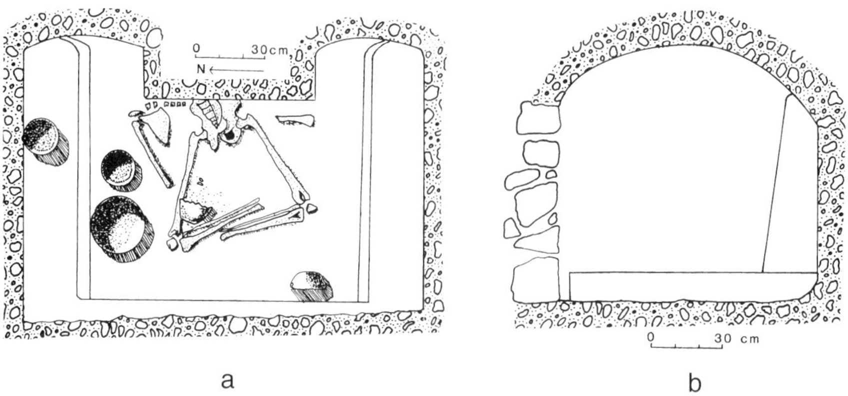

Fig. 3 Seated male burial C1 from Uaxactun shown with associated burial offerings: (a) plan and (b) side views (after Smith 1950: fig. 140).

been removed and a regal mask of jade, shell, and obsidian was substituted in their place. Not 2 m away from this throne-crypt, a simple pit had been excavated and an adult female with filed incisors was placed in a tightly flexed position. Tzakol 3 vessels with which she was interred also included an incised, individual serving bowl and a cylindrical drinking vessel. Unlike the male, however, the female ceramic accoutrements included two quintessentially Maya basal-flange Tzakol 3 bowls. Placed within the northern structure of Group C, a position suggested by Ashmore (1991) to be associated with ancestors, this ancestral couple seem to be overseers or guardians of Uaxactun. The pyramid placed over them probably served as a facility for ritual performance among descendant generations. In this way, ancestor interments encoded into the built environment a temporal dimension within a compressed spatial frame.

From the later part of the Early Classic through the Late Classic, single interments again become quite common and, in most locales, replace the family mausolea. Leventhal (1983) has discussed the coeval construction of ancestor-related shrines. Such structures, present in large residential complexes from Copan to Palenque, show pronounced variability in form, orientation, and inclusion of physical remains. They seem to have been built not so much to house the dead as to commemorate them and to celebrate the continued prosperity of the family line. During the Late Classic, burial within a house or a shrine was reserved for an increasingly selective subset of the population. Based on analysis of excavations in the elite households of Las Sepulturas, Copan, by Hendon (1991) and Diamanti (1991), there were pronounced differences in where and how individuals were interred. For instance, 19 of 20 tombs were placed in central locations within or below "alpha" structures and predominantly contained mature adults (Diamanti 1991: 214–215). More casual pit interments, on the other hand, tended to occur behind and on the side of structures and were less likely to contain the remains of middle-aged and older adults (Diamanti 1991: 214–215).

Becker (n.d.: 178–179) has labeled the repeated, separate interments within a designated shrine structure at Tikal as Plaza Plan 2. These eastern shrine structures contain distinctive mortuary assemblages as well as extensive axial burning on the plaster floors and enigmatic "problematical deposits." Such physical characteristics reinforce the linkage between ancestor interment and ritual performance. Taking a closer look at the eastern structures of Group 7F of Tikal, Haviland (1981: 94–95) draws our attention to the close articulation between burial interments and construction activity. This physical interlocking of ancestors and construction was not limited to shrines but also occurred at smaller residential complexes lacking shrines, such as Group 2G-1 of Tikal. A relatively modest complex, Group 2G-1 contained adult burials associated with sequential reconstruction of the houses, particularly the alpha Structure 2G-59, which was the largest and stratigraphically most complex (Haviland 1988: 123, 125). In more recent excavations in Late Formative structures at K'axob, McCormack (n.d.) and Henderson (n.d.) note a similar pattern, indicating a strong precedent for this practice.

Becker (1992: 189–193) has commented recently on the strong parallels between interment of burials and interment of caches. Certainly, both involve ritual performance keyed to a transformation or enhancement of the built environment. Because burial interments are often followed by structure renovation, such graves may have been viewed as indices of rebirth (see also Becker 1992: 190; Coggins 1988) and the sustained prosperity of a family line through inheritance. Parallelism in these two types of deposits is echoed in hieroglyphic texts, where references to "sealing" or "closing" (*u-mak-wa*) and to "opening" (*pas-ah*) refer interchangeably to tombs and caches (Houston 1987; Stuart, this volume).

The temporal dimension of ancestor interments provides a segue in the transformation of a place from that of a residence (firmly anchored by the corporeal presence of ancestors) to that of a shrine in which ancestral presence defined an *axis mundi* or central place in a political sense and within a grand cosmological scheme. Classic-period pyramids often are constructed over earlier residences at places such as Plaza B of K'axob (Fig. 4), the North Acropolis of Tikal (Coe 1990), and parts of Group 10L-2 at Copan (Andrews and Fash 1992). These pyramids impart a notion of sacralization of place in that the construction of an artificial hill or *wits* converts a portion of the built environment into purely ritual space. Perhaps more to the point, this transformation presages the highly political arena in which ancestors were utilized throughout

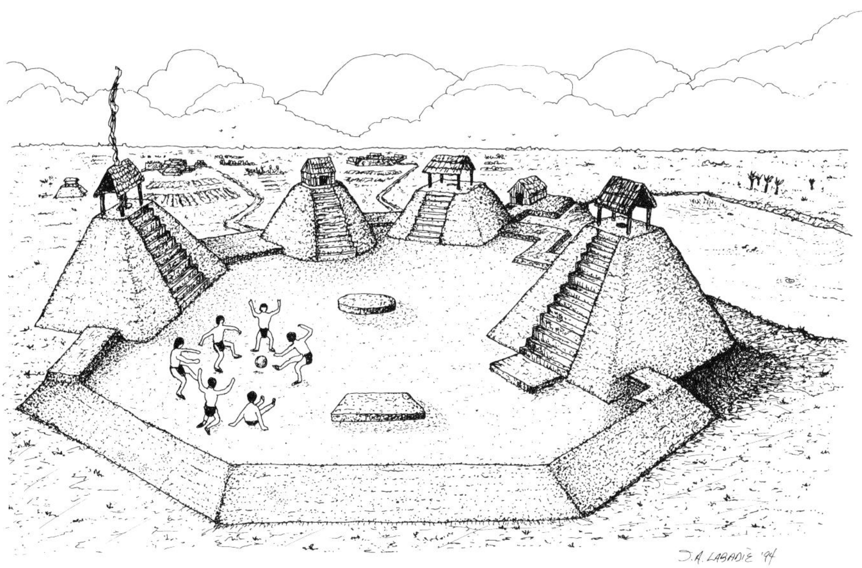

Fig. 4 Plaza B, K'axob, as it may have looked in the Late Classic. Excavated Middle Formative deposits, which include burials intruded into the floors of dwellings, are located in front of the pyramid on the right. Drawing by J. A. Labadie (after McAnany 1995; reprinted courtesy of the University of Texas Press).

the Classic period.

The mortuary pattern of elite burials at Altun Ha (Pendergast 1979, 1982) provides a clear example of the use of ancestors to define an *axis mundi.* At Altun Ha, moreover, the interments most often were linked to new construction events. Of the burials and tombs in Groups A and B, 13 were placed on the principal axis of a pyramidal structure. No subtlety here—12 of the 13 were adults and 100% (n = 8) of interments that were securely identified as to sex were male. Most significantly, the incidence of *intrusive* burials (from the surface of and into a preexisting structure) is very low—only 2 of the 13 interments. My reading of the architectural cross sections and burial descriptions suggests the following pattern. Ten of the 13 burial crypts were constructed within the core of ambitious new building programs, generally a platform, stairway, or stairblock. Unfortunately, the architectural relationship of Burial 1 of Structure B-6 could not be determined in the field and two other burials appear to be intrusive from and into preexisting structures (i.e., Tomb 1 of Structure A-1 and Burial 1 of Structure A-3). The latter seems to have been intruded into a preexisting stairway; after completion of the interment ritual, however, the old stairway was not patched, rather a new stairway was constructed over the crypt. Burial 1, therefore, is not simply intrusive but did engender construction of a new series of steps. Tomb 1 (Structure A-1) was built soon after a major renovation to Structure A-1 had just been completed. This enlargement of the structure had included the addition of a low platform at the base of a new stairway leading to the summit temple. Two burials—one of a juvenile—were sealed within this earlier construction event. The ultimate use of the low platform for an intrusive burial tomb hints at an untimely death and/or the inability of descendants to initiate another episode of construction. As one examines the plans and descriptions of osteological remains from Altun Ha, one cannot help but be struck by the highly variable state of preservation of the skeletal material. Although some of this variation undoubtedly is caused by localized atmospheric conditions and the harmful effects of building collapse, another equally important factor may be the time elapsed between date of death and date of interment. In sum, for the majority of Altun Ha axial interments in monumental architecture, new construction events had been initiated. The new stairways, platforms, and stairblocks, therefore, were built as part of the housing or frame of a burial interment and, as such, present clear evidence of the contribution of ancestor interments to the Classic Maya built environment.

ICONOGRAPHIC REPRESENTATIONS AND TEXTUAL REFERENCES TO ANCESTORS AND THEIR BURIAL PLACES

David Freidel and associates (Freidel, Schele, and Parker 1993) as well as Karl Taube (this volume) examine the central place of hearthstones in Maya cosmology. Symbolic of home and residence, hearthstones in Late Classic royal iconography became a metaphor of much more than a great place to find a fresh tamale. In a similar fashion, Classic Maya royal ancestor veneration became an overtly political institution couched within a grand cosmological scheme—see Ashmore (1991), Freidel and Schele (1989), Marcus (1992), McAnany (1995), and Schele and Miller (1986) among others. Toward the end of the Formative and through the Early Classic period, semidivine ancestors (many wearing the symbols of K'inich Ahaw, the sun deity) were depicted in a highly schematic fashion. During the Late Classic, on the other hand, emphasis shifted to realistic portraiture of immediate, ascending ancestors. In both cases, ancestors seem to provide an "anchor," as Schele and Freidel (1990: 140–141) have suggested, that ground the rule of their descendants (real or fictive) in weighty precedent. The hieroglyphic staircase of Copan, for example, is an iconographic example of royal dynastic ancestors as human ideogram (Geertz 1980: 130). Each occupies a stratum of the staircase in a manner that is similar to the layers of heaven occupied by Tzotzil ancestors (Gossen 1986: 5). As one ascended the staircase, one generally traveled both back in time and farther up into the heavens (see Houston, this volume). In hieroglyphic texts, Late Classic Maya sculptors wrote of the dedication of burial shrines (*muknal*) to house the actual remains of royal ancestors (Stuart, this volume). The political potency of ancestor remains rendered these *muknal* a target in times of hostility. For instance, Stela 23, a war monument from Naranjo, describes the plundering of the tomb of a Lord of Yaxha (David Stuart, personal communication, October 1994). Through both image and the structures built to house their remains, therefore, royal ancestors established a kind of "super-residence" and defined an *axis mundi*. Perhaps still in their role as guardians, royal ancestors helped to secure the kingdom rather than the fields and home; as always, they were available for consultation and required propitiation through offerings.

Coggins (n.d.: 186) was among the first to codify the notion that "floating" heads, facing downward and placed at the top of a composition, represent ancestors. In fact, the close juxtaposition of ancestors with living rulers, de rigueur in the iconography of Maya statecraft, occurred in many media: freestanding stone sculpture, shell pendants, pottery, and architectural façades. A small stela from El Mirador (Fig. 5) illustrates an early depiction in the lowlands, whereas

Fig. 5 Stela 18, El Mirador, showing the downward-facing head of an ancestor.

Fig. 6 Two ancestor representations as shown by downward-facing head and a single arm: *top,* Stela 2, Abaj Takalik, and *bottom,* Stela 31, Tikal (after Jones and Satterthwaite 1982: fig. 23).

Fig. 7 Shell pendant carved with image of ancestor from Tikal (after Iglesias n.d.: 539).

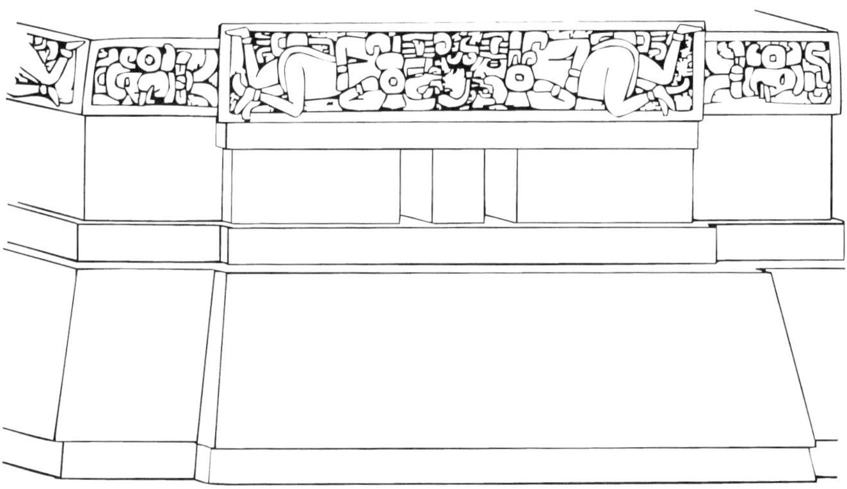

Fig. 8 Stucco frieze showing downward-facing ancestors from the south palace of Group H, Uaxactun (after Valdés 1990: fig. 10).

Late Formative Stela 2 from Abaj Takalik (Fig. 6, top) is a more ornate version of this theme, with the addition of a single arm. Variations on this composition occur on other stelae, such as the Early Classic stela of Stormy Sky from Tikal (Fig. 6, bottom). In contrast, Late Classic stelae, such as Ucanal Stela 4 and Jimbal Stela 1, show floating figures who appear to be supernatural, without any ancestral referent. Schele and Miller (1986), Houston (personal communication, 1994) and others have emphasized the heirloom-ancestry quality of Classic Maya regal ornamentation—a point strengthened by the ancestral head-and-arm images on shell pendants (Fig. 7). In the case of jewelry, the individual literally wears an image of an ancestor and absorbs the power of precedent in amulet fashion.

From Early Classic Uaxactun, Valdés (1990) reports an occurrence of downward-facing ancestors placed high on a cornice frieze on the Sub 2 structure of the south palace of Group H (Fig. 8). Here two full-bodied, prostrate figures are framed by images of two male ancestors emerging from smoke scrolls. As shown by Valdés (1990: fig. 11b), these stucco masks show differentiation in headgear; their "head-only," downward-facing demeanor marks them as specific ancestors rather than generalized supernatural beings. The structure they adorn, furthermore, may have functioned as an ancestor shrine. A similar function has been suggested for Structure 10L-29 at Copan (Andrews and Fash 1992: 63). In general, the guardian-like quality of "head" imagery is probably true to form; the following translation by Whittaker and Warkentin (1965: 88) from a Chol text confirms this interpretation: "Each one guards the boundaries of his land. When the spirit leaves (the body), the head goes with the spirit, just down to his shoulders. His strength and his head and his heart go wherever they want to."[1] Similar conceptions of the human anatomy exist among the Nahua who consider the words "head" (*tzontecomatl*) and "sky" (*ilhuicatl*) to be synonymous and note that "the head and face confer honor as well as being honored" (López Austin 1988: 171–172). The head, moreover, is "the place from which the vital force of breath issues to the outside, breath which . . . is charged with feeling and moral values" (López Austin 1988: 171). The Nahua association of head with moral values accords well with the notion of ancestors as guardians not only of land and kingdom but also of the path of life.

During the Late Classic period, ancestor imagery shifts away from schematically drawn, semidivine progenitors to portraiture of immediate ascending ancestors. The cartouches of Yaxchilan provide a well-known example. First identified by Proskouriakoff (1963, 1964), the ancestors occupy a prominent

[1] I am grateful to Karl Taube for bringing this reference to my attention.

place, generally in the upper register, of accession monuments such as Stelae 4, 6, 8, 10, 30, and 33 (Figs. 9 and 10). Often framed as couples, female as well as male ancestors take on increased significance during the Late Classic, possibly because of the importance accorded to dual, royal bloodlines in an increasingly crowded field of royal contenders. In the palace at Palenque, cartouches or medallions are fully integrated within the architectural setting and occupy a conspicuous locale in the eastern gallery of House A (Robertson 1985: 25–31). This type of portraiture is not unique to the Maya lowlands. Tomb 5 of Suchilquitongo, Oaxaca, contains a stela upon which is represented a dead lord

Fig. 9 Stela 10, Yaxchilan.

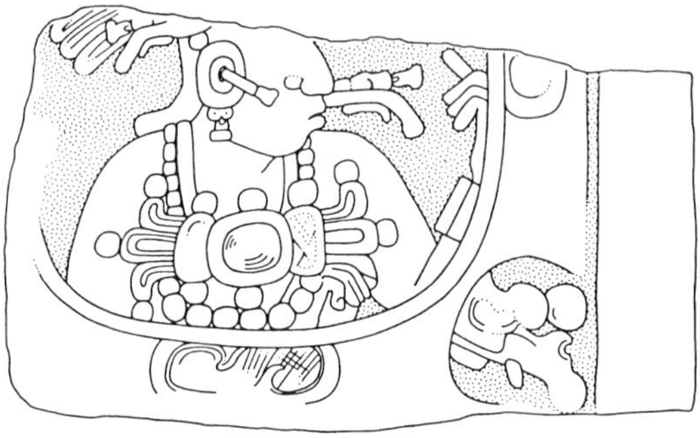

Fig. 10 Stela 30, Yaxchilan (after Tate 1992: 153, fig. 46).

"as a living ancestor" along with the year and day of his death (Miller 1991: 220). The stela is carved in the style of a later Post-Classic monument and may have been added to the Late Classic tomb during a reentry ritual (Miller 1991: 216). Miller (1991: 223) also suggests that the stela was commissioned by a descendant of the consort of Lady 12 N, possibly to strengthen the genealogical linkage to an apical ancestor.

In the Maya region, the sculptural "frame" for the ancestor image generally is a cartouche or a quatrefoil and is very similar to the *clipeata imago* of Roman Classical ancestor portraits (D'Ambra 1995: 66). For instance, the tops of Altars R and Q from Quirigua feature quatrefoils enclosing badly eroded figures, which may be ancestors. A portion of a quatrefoil is shown in the basal register of Piedras Negras Stela 40 (Fig. 11). Hammond (1981) suggested that this figure might represent an ancestor buried within a subterranean vault. Indeed, we see the familiar head-and-one-arm depiction of the lower, enthroned individual. Beneath the throne is the enigmatic glyph compound of nine plus an undeciphered glyph. Stephen Houston (personal communication, July 1994) has noted that the same compound is present on the Dumbarton Oaks white stone bowl, where it is positioned within an offering vessel held by a woman. Stela 40, however, differs from earlier stelae with ancestor imagery in a very provocative way. Specifically, the ancestor is shown below, rather than above, the central protagonist. Into this subterranean cavity, a descendant wearing a high-hat headdress performs a scattering ritual; this individual is linked directly to the ancestral world by a cord that terminates in the nose of the lower figure. To my knowledge, this is one of the few monuments that depicts the physical place of the ancestors (that is, underground) as opposed to the metaphorical place in which ancestors reside (the "heavens," north, "up"). Stela 40 also shows very

Fig. 11 Stela 40, Piedras Negras.
Drawing by John Montgomery © 1996.

clearly the lack of closure between the two worlds. The place of the ancestors (referred to as a *nah* or "home" in the accompanying text) is not represented as sealed and separate from the place of the living but rather is vitally linked through a kind of umbilical cord. This stela conveys a message on two levels; that is, the abode of the ancestors could be entered through both ritual performance and physical reentry of the burial vault.

Fig. 12 Altar 5, Tikal (after Jones and Satterthwaite 1982: fig. 23).

A dramatic example of what appears to be the opening of a tomb is shown on Altar 5 of Tikal, where two individuals in elaborate ritual regalia stand over a stack of long bones and a skull (Fig. 12). The lower band of text identifies a royal woman from Topoxte (Stuart and Houston 1994); David Stuart deciphered the glyph at position 26 as *pas-ah,* the verb "to open." It is not clear why this event would be recorded in this manner, but it clearly indicates sequential staging in the disposition of physical remains. At times, this sequence included defleshing, as Becker (1992: 189) has suggested for the headless elites in Burials 48 and 85 from Tikal (over which a shrine was later constructed). Such protracted treatment of the dead accompanied by construction of burial and shrine structures is also indicated through recent analysis of hieroglyphic texts from the western region. Specifically, David Stuart has deciphered the glyph *muknal,* translated as burial place or shrine after *muk-ah* ("is buried" or "is covered") and

Fig. 13 Panel 5 of Hieroglyphic Stairway 1, Seibal; the black triangle points to the *muknal* glyph. Drawing by James Porter (after Graham 1990: fig. 1).

the toponymic reference *nal* ("place of"). This glyph includes a telltale skull inside of what appears to be a prepared platform. Often occurring in conjunction with death dates and structure dedication dates, the *muknal* glyph has been identified on a number of texts including Panel 5 of the hieroglyphic staircase of Seibal (Fig. 13); the West Tablet of the Temple of the Inscriptions (Fig. 14); the Dumbarton Oaks panel; and Monument 69 from Tonina as well as a new disk recently published by Yadeun (Fig. 15). So far, nine occurrences of the *muknal* glyph in conjunction with death dates and later *muknal* dedication dates have been found (Table 1).[2]

Assuming that interment within a *muknal* constructed posthumously involved transport of a corpse from another locale, examination of the amount of time elapsed between the two dates gives us insight into the protracted nature of Classic Maya elite burial ritual. The median number of days elapsed between death and interment within a *muknal* was 482 days or about a year-and-a-half (Table 1). The least number of elapsed days was 260 or one revolution of the sacred calendar; this pattern occurred twice at Tonina. The longest span of time, recorded on Piedras Negras Panel 3, was 8884 days or approximately 24 years! This latter date may represent a retroactive effort by a family line to boost the status of their lineage through dedication or refurbishment of a *muknal* for a previously underrecognized but highly venerable ancestor. Such a construction may be construed as a statement by descendants of their ability to amass labor and wealth. In this regard, *muknal* construction is quite similar in rationale to the forward-looking motivations underlying Chinese geomancy and ancestor

[2] These data have been compiled by Stephen Houston, who graciously offered to share them with me.

Fig. 14 Final portion of text, West Tablet, Temple of the Inscriptions, Palenque, identifying the locale as the *muknal* of Pakal the Great; the black triangle points to the *muknal* glyph. Drawing by Linda Schele (after Robertson 1983: fig. 97).

Fig. 15 Portion of circular monument from Tonina; the black triangle points to the *muknal* glyph.
Drawing by John Montgomery.

Table 1. Sites for Which Muknal Dedication Dates Have Been Found

Site/Provenience	Monument Number	Death Date	Muknal Date	Elapsed Time (Days)
Piedras Negras	Panel 3	9.16.6.11.17 7 Caban 0 Pax, G3	9.17.11.6.1 12 Imix 19 Zip, G4	8884
Piedras Negras	Panel 4	9.10.6.2.1 15 Imix 19 Kayab, G5	9.11.6.1.8. 3 Lamat 6 Ceh, G1	7187
"Hellmuth Panel"	n/a	9.12.14.1.3 3 Akbal 1 Tzec, G5	9.12.15.12.9 4 Muluc 2 Pax, G6	586
Tonina	69	9.17.4.12.5 8 Chicchan 18 Zac, G2	9.17.5.7.5 8 Chicchan 13 Xul, G1	260
Tonina	n/a	9.18.5.10.3 12 Akbal 11 Zotz, G5	9.18.6.5.3 12 Akbal 11 Kayab, G4	260
(Dumbarton Oaks)	n/a	9.15.1.6.3 6 Akbal 11 Pax, G6	9.15.2.7.1 7 Imix 4 Kayab, G6	378
Tonina	n/a	not given	9.14.18.14.12 5 Eb 10 Yaxkin, G4	
Tamarindito	HS 2	not given	9.16.11.7.13 7 Ben 11 Yax, G9	
Seibal	HS 1	not given	9.15.16.7.17 6 Caban 10 Kankin, G4	

Data compiled by Stephen Houston, July 1994.

[n/a] Monument number not available.

tomb construction (Feuchtwang 1974). Miller (1986: 37) too has drawn a distinction between tombs of Tikal rulers—the underworld homes of the ancestors—and the aboveground structures or temples that are linked to the future of the kingdom.

What type of physical construction was a *muknal*? The glyph occurs on the Temple of the Inscriptions—apparently referring to the underlying pyramid as the *muknal* of Pakal the Great—and also is used on the circular stones of Tonina that are not in demonstrable association with a pyramidal structure. *Muknal,* therefore, probably refers to a variety of burial locales, all of which included a crypt and some kind of above-ground marker. The latter may have ranged in elaboration from a small, low platform to a nine-tiered, temple-topped pyramid. Within this small sample of *muknal* dedication dates, there also is some patterning in seasonality. That is, five of the nine dedications occurred between the middle and end of the wet season or between October and December. This period is the slack season for agricultural work in most parts of the lowlands and reinforces the notion of complementary scheduling between agrarian work and royal work.

DISCUSSION AND CONCLUSIONS

Both ideologically and physically, the boundary between the living and the ancestors was a permeable one. Powerful individuals of the Classic period, whether elite or non-elite, male or female, continued to play a role in society long after their death. At their place of interment or point of entry to the underworld, a historically contingent place emerged and a sense of residence was established. Construction of dwellings, shrines, and large temples at these locations provided staging for later ritual and commemoration. By their presence, these structures conditioned the placement and size of later alterations to the built environment (Abrams, this volume; Webster, this volume). Important parts of the Classic Maya landscape developed through an iterative process of ancestor interment and above-ground construction punctuated by ritual performance.

Imaging and placement of ancestors within the built environment of the lowland Maya changed significantly throughout the two millennia of the Formative and Classic periods. The weighty influence of the ancestors can be traced back to the Middle Formative, when their physical remains were placed under the floors of dwellings in primary interments. At this time, their presence most likely was linked to safeguarding fields and home and effecting the transmission of such property through the generations. During the Late Formative, however, burial practices diversified to include tightly wrapped and seated burials, secondary interment of defleshed bones, and burial locales with multiple, sequential interments. These practices suggest increased spacing between death and interment, possibly including the display of corpses. Increasingly, special structures were built to house the dead. Iconographically, Early Classic ancestors were represented as a fusion of supernatural and human characteristics—primarily male—and reference to ancestors was somewhat vague genealogically. During the Late Classic period, however, portraiture of both female and male progenitors of one or two ascending generations became common, particularly in the western Usumacinta region. During this time, ancestors seem to have served the very direct purpose of linking an ascendant ruler to established and revered bloodlines. When there are many elites, the ability to demonstrate a royal pedigree along both paternal and maternal lines would have been extremely beneficial (Marcus 1992: 223–260).

For early Archaic Greece, Antonaccio (1994, 1995) has discussed the role of ancestor veneration and the hero cult in mediating social change.[3] So too in the Maya lowlands, ancestor depictions and physical remains occupied a prominent place in the built environment. During the Early Classic, specifically, the concept of a ritual establishment of home through ancestor interment was amplified to provide a home for dead royalty and to impart a notion of centrality and continuity within a grand political and cosmic scheme.

[3] I thank Norman Hammond for bringing this research to my attention.

BIBLIOGRAPHY

ANDREWS, E. WYLLYS, V, AND BARBARA FASH

1992 Continuity and Change in a Royal Maya Residential Complex at Copan. *Ancient Mesoamerica* 3: 63–88.

ANTONACCIO, CARLA M.

1994 Contesting the Past: Hero Cult, Tomb Cult, and Epic in Early Greece. *American Journal of Archaeology* 98: 389–410.

1995 *An Archaeology of Ancestors: Tomb Cult and Hero Cult in Early Greece.* Rowman and Littlefield, Lanham, Md.

ASHMORE, WENDY

1991 Site-Planning Principles and Concepts of Directionality among the Ancient Maya. *Latin American Antiquity* 2: 199–226.

BECKER, MARSHALL J.

1992 Burials as Caches; Caches as Burials: A New Interpretation of the Meaning of Ritual Deposits among the Classic Period Lowland Maya. In *New Theories on the Ancient Maya* (E. C. Danien and R. J. Sharer, eds.): 185–196. University Museum, University of Pennsylvania, Philadelphia.

n.d. The Identification of a Second Plaza Plan at Tikal, Guatemala, and Its Implications for Ancient Maya Social Complexity. Ph.D. dissertation, University of Pennsylvania, 1971.

BOBO, MATTHEW R.

n.d. Operation I Excavation Report. In *K'axob Project, Interim Report, 1993 Field Season* (Patricia A. McAnany, ed.). Report on file, Departments of Archaeology, Boston University and Belmopan, Belize, 1994.

BUNZEL, RUTH

1952 *Chichicastenango: A Guatemalan Village.* University of Washington Press, Seattle.

CARMACK, ROBERT M.

1981 *The Quiche Mayas of Utatlan.* University of Oklahoma Press, Norman.

CODEX MAGLIABECHIANO

1970 *Codex Magliabechiano, CL. XIII.* 2 vols. Codices selecti phototypice impressi, vol. 23. Akademische Druck- u. Verlagsanstalt, Graz, Austria.

COE, WILLIAM R.

1990 *Excavations in the Great Plaza, North Terrace and North Acropolis of Tikal.* Tikal Report, no. 14. University Museum Monograph 61. University of Pennsylvania, Philadelphia.

COGGINS, CLEMENCY C.

1988 Classic Maya Metaphors of Death and Life. *RES: Anthropology and Aesthetics* 16: 64–84.

n.d. Painting and Drawing Styles at Tikal: An Historical and Iconographic Reconstruction. Ph.D. dissertation, Harvard University, 1975.

D'Ambra, Eve
1995 Mourning and the Making of Ancestors in the Testamentum Relief. *American Journal of Archaeology* 99: 667–681.

Davis, Shelton H.
n.d. Land of Our Ancestors: A Study of Land Tenure and Inheritance in the Highlands of Guatemala. Ph.D. dissertation, Harvard University, 1990.

Diamanti, Melissa
1991 *Domestic Organization at Copan: Reconstruction of Elite Maya Households through Ethnographic Models.* University Microfilms, Ann Arbor.

Feeley-Harnik, Gillian
1985 Issues in Divine Kingship. *Annual Review of Anthropology* 14: 273–313.

Feuchtwang, Stephan D. R.
1974 *An Anthropological Analysis of Chinese Geomancy.* Vithagna, Southern Materials Center, Taipei.

Freidel, David A., and Linda Schele
1989 Dead Kings and Living Temples: Dedication and Termination Rituals among the Ancient Maya. In *Word and Image in Maya Culture* (W. F. Hanks and D. S. Rice, eds.): 233–243. University of Utah Press, Salt Lake City.

Freidel, David A., Linda Schele, and Joy Parker
1993 *Maya Cosmos: Three Thousand Years on the Shaman's Path.* William Morrow, New York.

Geertz, Clifford
1980 *Negara: The Theatre State in Nineteenth-Century Bali.* Princeton University Press, Princeton, N.J.

Glazier, Jack
1984 Mbeere Ancestors and the Domestication of Death. *Man* (n.s.) 19: 133–148.

Gonlin, Nancy
1993 *Rural Household Archaeology at Copan, Honduras.* University Microfilms, Ann Arbor.

Gossen, Gary H.
1986 Mesoamerican Ideas as a Foundation for Regional Synthesis. In *Symbol and Meaning beyond the Closed Community: Essays in Mesoamerican Ideas* (Gary H. Gossen, ed.): 1–8. Studies on Culture and Society. Institute for Mesoamerican Studies, State University of New York, Albany.

Graham, John A.
1990 Monumental Sculpture and Hieroglyphic Inscriptions. In *Excavations at Seibal, Department of Peten, Guatemala* (Gordon R. Willey, ed.): 1–79. Peabody Museum of Archaeology and Ethnology, Harvard University, Cambridge, Mass.

Hammond, Norman
1981 Pom for the Ancestors: A Reexamination of Piedras Negras Stela 40. *Mexicon* 3 (5): 77–79.

Harrison, Peter D.
1970 *The Central Acropolis, Tikal, Guatemala: A Preliminary Study of the Functions and Its Structural Components during the Late Classic Period.* University Microfilms, Ann Arbor.

Haviland, William A.

1981 Dower Houses and Minor Centers at Tikal, Guatemala: An Investigation into the Valid Units in Settlement Hierarchies. In *Lowland Maya Settlement Patterns* (Wendy Ashmore, ed.): 89–117. University of New Mexico Press, Albuquerque.

1988 Musical Hammocks at Tikal: Problems with Reconstructing Household Composition. In *Household and Community in the Mesoamerican Past* (R. R. Wilk and Wendy Ashmore, eds.): 121–134. University of New Mexico Press, Albuquerque.

Henderson, H. Hope

n.d. Operation XII Excavation Report. In *K'axob Project, Interim Report, 1993 Field Season* (Patricia A. McAnany, ed.). Report on file, Departments of Archaeology, Boston University and Belmopan, Belize, 1994.

Hendon, Julia A.

1991 Status and Power in Classic Maya Society: An Archaeological Case Study. *American Anthropologist* 93: 894–918.

Houston, Stephen D.

1987 Notes on Caracol Epigraphy and Its Significance. In *Investigations at the Classic Maya City of Caracol, Belize, 1985–1987* (Arlen F. Chase and Diane Z. Chase, eds.): 85–100. Pre-Columbian Art Research Institute, San Francisco.

Humphreys, Sally C.

1981 Death and Time. In *Mortality and Immortality: The Anthropology and Archaeology of Death* (Sally C. Humphreys and H. King, eds.): 261–283. Academic Press, London.

Iglesias Ponce de León, María Josefa

n.d. Excavaciones en el grupo habitacional 6D-V, Tikal, Guatemala. Ph.D. dissertation, Universidad Complutense de Madrid, 1987.

Jones, Christopher

1977 Inauguration Dates of Three Late Classic Rulers of Tikal, Guatemala. *American Antiquity* 42: 28–60.

Jones, Christopher, and Linton Satterthwaite

1982 *The Monuments and Inscriptions of Tikal: The Carved Monuments.* Tikal Report, no. 33, pt. A, University Museum Monograph 44. University of Pennsylvania, Philadelphia.

Leventhal, Richard M.

1983 Household Groups and Classic Maya Religion. In *Prehistoric Settlement Patterns: Essays in Honor of Gordon R. Willey* (Evon Z. Vogt and Richard M. Leventhal, eds.): 55–76. Peabody Museum of Archaeology and Ethnology, Harvard University, Cambridge, Mass., and University of New Mexico Press, Albuquerque.

Lockard, Angela

n.d. Analysis of K'axob Burials, 1990–1993 Field Seasons. Manuscript on file, Department of Archaeology, Boston University, 1994.

López Austin, Alfredo

1988 *The Human Body and Ideology: Concepts of the Ancient Nahuas* (Thelma Ortiz de Montellano and Bernard Ortiz de Montellano, trans.). University of Utah Press, Salt Lake City.

MARCUS, JOYCE

1992 *Mesoamerican Writing Systems: Propaganda, Myth and History in Four Ancient Civilizations.* Princeton University Press, Princeton, N.J.

n.d. Men's and Women's Ritual in Formative Oaxaca. In *Social Patterns in Pre-Classic Mesoamerica* (D. C. Grove and R. A. Joyce., eds.). Dumbarton Oaks, Washington, D.C. (In press.)

MCANANY, PATRICIA A.

1995 *Living with the Ancestors: Kinship and Kingship in Ancient Maya Society.* University of Texas Press, Austin.

MCCORMACK, VALERIE

n.d. Field Report of Excavations at Operation XI. In *K'axob Project, Interim Report, 1993 Field Season* (Patricia A. McAnany, ed.). Report on file, Departments of Archaeology, Boston University and Belmopan, Belize, 1994.

MERWIN, R. E., AND G. C. VAILLANT

1932 *The Ruins of Holmul, Guatemala.* Memoirs of the Peabody Museum of Archaeology and Ethnology, vol. 3, no. 2. Harvard University, Cambridge, Mass.

MILLER, ARTHUR G.

1986 *Maya Rulers of Time.* University Museum, University of Pennsylvania, Philadelphia.

1991 The Carved Stela in Tomb 5, Suchilquitongo, Oaxaca, Mexico. *Ancient Mesoamerica* 2: 215–224.

PEARSON, MIKE P.

1993 The Powerful Dead: Archaeological Relationships between the Living and the Dead. *Cambridge Archaeological Journal* 3 (2): 203–229.

PENDERGAST, DAVID M.

1979 *Excavations at Altun Ha, Belize, 1964–1970,* vol. 1. Royal Ontario Museum, Toronto.

1982 *Excavations at Altun Ha, Belize, 1964–1970,* vol. 2. Royal Ontario Museum, Toronto.

PRED, ALLAN

1986 *Place, Practice and Structure: Social and Spatial Transformation in Southern Sweden, 1750–1850.* Polity Press, Cambridge.

PROSKOURIAKOFF, TATIANA

1963 Historical Data in the Inscriptions of Yaxchilan, Part I. *Estudios de Cultura Maya* 3: 149–167.

1964 Historical Data in the Inscriptions of Yaxchilan, Part II. *Estudios de Cultura Maya* 4: 177–201.

RICKETSON, OLIVER

1925 Burials in the Maya Area. *American Anthropologist* 27: 381–401.

ROBERTSON, MERLE GREENE

1983 *The Sculpture of Palenque,* vol. 1: *The Temple of the Inscriptions.* Princeton University Press, Princeton, N.J.

1985 *The Sculpture of Palenque,* vol. 3: *The Late Buildings of the Palace.* Princeton University Press, Princeton, N.J.

Robin, Cynthia, and Norman Hammond
1991 Burial Practices. In *Cuello: An Early Maya Community in Belize* (Norman Hammond, ed.): 204–225. Cambridge University Press, Cambridge.

Saile, D. G.
1985 The Ritual Establishment of Home. In *Home Environments* (I. Altman and C. Werner, eds.): 87–111. Plenum Press, New York.

Schele, Linda, and David Freidel
1990 *A Forest of Kings: The Untold Story of the Ancient Maya.* William Morrow, New York.

Schele, Linda, and Mary E. Miller
1986 *Blood of Kings: Dynasty and Ritual in Maya Art.* George Braziller, New York, and Kimbell Art Museum, Fort Worth, Tex.

Smith, A. Ledyard
1950 *Uaxactún, Guatemala: Excavations of 1931–1937.* Carnegie Institution, Publication 588. Washington, D.C.

Stuart, David, and Stephen Houston
1994 *Classic Maya Place Names.* Dumbarton Oaks, Washington, D.C.

Tate, Carolyn E.
1992 *Yaxchilan: The Design of a Maya Ceremonial City.* University of Texas Press, Austin.

Tedlock, Barbara
1982 *Time and the Highland Maya.* University of New Mexico Press, Albuquerque.

Turner, Victor
1977 Frame, Flow, and Reflection: Ritual and Drama as Public Liminality. In *Performances in Post Modern Culture* (M. Benamou and C. Caramello, eds.): 33–55. Coda Press, Madison, Wis.

Valdés, Juan Antonio
1990 Observaciones iconográficas sobre as figuras preclásicas de cuerpo completo en el área maya. *Estudios: Organo de Divulgación del Instituto de Investigaciones Históricas, Antropológicas y Arqueológicas* 20: 23–49.

Verano, John W.
1997 Human Skeletal Remains from Tomb 1, Sipán (Lambayeque River Valley, Peru), and Their Social Implications. *Antiquity* 71 (273): 670–682.

Vogt, Evon Z.
1969 *Zinacantan: A Maya Community in the Highlands of Chiapas.* Belknap Press for Harvard University Press, Cambridge, Mass.

Whittaker, Arabelle, and Viola Warkentin
1965 *Chol Texts on the Supernatural.* Summer Institute of Linguistics of the University of Oklahoma, Norman.

The Architectural Context of Caches, Burials, and Other Ritual Activities for the Classic Period Maya (as Reflected at Caracol, Belize)

DIANE Z. CHASE AND ARLEN F. CHASE
UNIVERSITY OF CENTRAL FLORIDA

WHAT GOES INSIDE a Maya building is just as significant in determining its function as a building's architectural plan and external appearance. Structures are not alike in their contents. Some hold interments and caches; some contain earlier buildings; others are single or multiple construction efforts with no contents other than fill. Artifacts are found littered on the floors of some buildings, whereas other buildings are found completely clean.

Careful consideration of the overall context of Maya architecture, in terms of both its siting and contents, leads to many questions about the associations of architecture and archaeological materials. For example, is there a correlation of ritual offerings with new construction? Do caches, burials, or "termination" rituals reflect the "dedication" of a new building, the final use of the previous construction, or something else altogether? Are changes in a building's function apparent archaeologically in the final treatment of a given structure? Which buildings contain ritual deposits and which do not? And what other determining factors are there besides structure form and location?

Almost by definition, many architectural forms and contents imply specific functions. Function may be manifest in the physical layout or iconographic decoration of a given building, or it may be revealed by associated ritual activity and deposits. Although the concept of temple as funerary construction is simplistic in that some temples bear multiple interments, and others contain no interments at all, certain buildings did apparently function as ancestral shrines and were used repeatedly for both interments and ritual offerings. In this context, tombs themselves may be seen as sacred spaces conjoining the world of the living and the world of the dead. Buildings that use *wits* icons (Cauac monster masks) at the base of stairs or to frame building doors reflect the concept of pyramids and buildings as portals allowing passage beyond the present world; these pyramids and buildings form not only physical entranceways for tombs but also symbolic entranceways to the underworld.

Although some correlations of architecture and ritual deposits reflect overall Maya cultural practices, others define more regionalized cultural identities or shifts in general ritual patterns over time. Data from Caracol, Belize, can be used as a springboard from which to consider both the pan-Maya and more specialized architectural context of caches (n = 133), burials (n = 183), and other ritual activities for the Classic period Maya.

THE CONTENTS OF MAYA BUILDINGS: DEFINITIONS

The contents of Maya buildings are extremely variable and may include earlier constructions as well as deposits of artifacts. Buried buildings may be relatively easy to define with substantial excavation; however, distinguishing among other activities and deposits may not be quite as simple. Activities of particular concern are deposits such as caches, human burials, and terminal offerings that have presumed ritual overtones. Caches have been defined as "one or more objects found together, but apart from burials, whose grouping and situation point to intentional interment as an offering" (Coe 1959: 77); caches may be distinguished from terminal offerings found on building floors in that, even though the latter may be encased by a new construction, caches are either intentionally intruded into earlier structures or buried within the fill of a building during construction (Fig. 1). Although perhaps the most easily recognizable caches are those found within pottery vessels, cached objects also may exist without specialized containers. The distinction between caches and burials is often clear; however, in certain cases—such as when partial human remains are concealed within a pottery container—there may be uncertainty about the nature of the offering. Instances exist when the only human skeletal remains in a covered deposit consist of a human skull or human finger bones; these are frequently, but not always, classified as caches rather than as interments; in contrast, fragmentary remains encountered in a specially constructed tomb are generally classified as interments.[1] Human remains, however, may be

[1] The reader is referred to various sources for further discussion of the identification and definition of these varied ritual deposits—e.g., Becker (1992, 1993), Chase (1988), Coe (1959), Garber (1983), and Krejci and Culbert 1995: 103.

Fig. 1 Termination deposit placed within niche in Santa Rita Corozal Structure 7-3rd and later sealed in the core of Structure 7-2nd.

interred in a number of distinctive contexts, including: (1) simple burials in fill; (2) cist burial in a simple hole; (3) crypt burial in a carefully lined grave; and (4) burial in a small open-air chamber or tomb. In addition to concealed offerings and interments, excavations sometimes reveal material remains left on floors. These items can be divided into two classes: (1) domestic or ritual materials representing the last use of a building at the time of abandonment; and (2) purposely broken and often burned material sometimes referred to as "termination offerings." The latter are not only found scattered on building surfaces but also may be associated with building defacement (see Coe 1959; Garber 1983). Later constructions usually conceal them, and the practice could be argued to form a subset of caching, in which the earlier structure served as part of the cached contents and the later structure as the container.

Postconquest descriptions of Maya ritual activities in the sixteenth and seventeenth centuries indicate that offerings, once made, were usually removed from everyday use (Tozzer 1941: 161). Items could be consumed, burned, broken, or tossed into a cenote (Tozzer 1941: 104 n. 474, 114, and 181; Edmonson 1984: 94). We presume, perhaps inappropriately, that formally cached items were more profound offerings related to the well-being of a large group of people or the entire community. It is unclear why offerings were sometimes completely destroyed by breakage or burning as opposed to being buried intact. A similar difficulty (and potential perceptional problem) attends the final treatment of buildings. In certain cases, care is taken to cover stucco façades of constructions; in other cases, stairs, walls, and decoration are cut preparatory to constructing a new building. Buildings may often see intense burning. And floors may be clean or littered with broken vessels.

The treatment of caches, burials, and buildings is, in fact, exceedingly similar, in that the contents of all may be found in differing conditions—whole, broken, or burnt. Caches contain varied numbers and kinds of offerings; however, caches also may appear to be completely empty, having once contained only perishable items that have disappeared entirely. Caches have been found intruded into floors, buried directly in a building's or platform's fill, or left in a niche. Like caches and buildings, burials also vary substantially in their content and deposition. Not only are human remains found in differing contexts, ranging from refuse deposits to tombs, but the bones themselves are found in various states, including everything from single articulated individuals to massive deposits of burnt and disarticulated remains (e.g., Caracol Special Deposit [S.D.] C7B-1). These various skeletal combinations are also accompanied by a diverse array of offerings. Similar situations exist with constructions.

Scholarly studies often reduce ritual activities to a simple (or functional) order. A major point of controversy in these works is the degree to which caches and burials may be seen as being "dedicatory" to a specific construction. Michael Coe (1956, 1975a), following Landa (Tozzer 1941), focused on the priority of funerary activities over construction; in his view, buildings frequently were erected as funerary monuments. Thus, burials were not "dedicatory," rather buildings were "commemorative." William Coe (1959: 77–79; 1965) engaged in some of the first in-depth discussions of this topic with regard to caches. Coe (1990: 920, 930), along with other archaeologists (Becker 1982, 1992: 188–189; 1993; D. Chase 1982: 555–556; 1985a, 1985b, 1988; Haviland et al. 1985: 150–152; Pendergast 1979: 198), grappled with the difficulty of differentiating the potential functions of these ritual deposits and has pointed toward the problematic polarity in seemingly simple assignations of "dedicatory" or "commemorative" ritual deposits. Schele and Freidel (1990; Freidel, Schele, and Parker 1993) have added to this predominantly archaeological discussion by using hieroglyphic materials to focus on caches as parts of complex, episodic dedication rituals.

We believe ritual offerings are more complex than current discussion recognizes. Effective typologies of burials and caches (Becker 1992) elude Mayanists, as do meaningful distinctions between dedicatory and commemorative deposits. The term dedicatory, in particular, may be an overused Western conception of ancient Maya activities (see Coe 1975b: 195; Davies 1984: 214). It is apparent from historic, ethnohistoric, and ethnographic information that the Maya of the sixteenth century and later practiced a variety of sacrifices and made many different kinds of offerings depending on the specific ritual activity taking place (Tozzer 1941: 139–145, 315–321; Edmonson 1984: 94). Some offerings may have been dedicatory in function; some were calendric (D. Chase 1985b, 1988); and others defined sacred boundaries of the community (M. Coe 1965; Garcia-Zambrano 1994: 219). William Coe (1990: 930) has suggested the "probability of multiple objectives to the act per se." Attributions of specific functions to ritual offerings is made difficult by the fact that these activities are not static but change over time. The regularities and abnormalities in distribution, chronology, numbers, and kinds of offerings may provide important clues to their ancient functions. Consideration of this variation affects interpretations not only of Maya architecture but also of the dynamic nature of Maya civilization. We believe that viewing structures within two distinct contexts—first as individual containers or repositories and second as part of a broader formal site structure—provides substantial insight into the function of both constructions and ritual deposits.

RITUAL DEPOSITS, WORLDVIEW, AND ARCHITECTURAL SPACE

Just as the placement of structures requires careful planning in terms of Maya cosmology (Ashmore 1991: 200),[2] caches and interments may provide physical representations of the Maya worldview. A number of the Caracol caches evince an ordered layout that appears to reflect the Maya view of the cosmos. Lower layers of mercury, jadeite, malachite, coral, or shells distinctly reflect the watery underworld. Distributions of groupings of four versions of the same kinds of artifacts around a central unit (usually a single jadeite ear ornament) may indicate the sacred landscape of the present world. Fragmentary beehives and depictions of a winged Itzamna located in the uppermost layers of a cache may illustrate the above world. The placement of both caches and interments within a structural location further defines them. They can be viewed as portals or

[2] See also Sugiyama (1993) for an analogous argument for Teotihuacan.

transitory points to the underworld (see Houston, this volume; Schele and Freidel 1990: 216). In fact, the hieroglyph for cache is basically a crescent of skeletal jaws, enfolding upward; the defleshed condition of the jaws indicates the underground position of such a deposit (Stephen Houston, personal communication, 1994). Building iconography can also place the interior of a given building in an underworld context; offerings placed within a construction may also indicate an underworld context. Entranceways to Caracol tombs may be seen as connecting the underworld tomb with the exterior world outside the "sacred mountain" or construction; horizontal red-painted lines on tomb walls likely delimit underworld space as do the layers of broken jadeite that may underlay a corpse. Thus, the contents and contexts of ritual offerings all combine to provide meaning.

Ritual Deposits and the Definition of Architectural Function: Tombs

The use of ritual deposits is especially critical in defining architectural space at Caana, Caracol's largest construction, and specifically in interpreting Structures B19 and B20 as an expanded version of an eastern ritual pattern prevalent elsewhere at the site. Located on the eastern side of the summit of Caana, Caracol Structure B20 provides perhaps the best example of a building that can be defined by viewing its contents (Fig. 2). It is one of the clearest examples of a funerary structure at Caracol. However, investigations here also demonstrate the difficulty in assuming that a single construction or building phase is associated with a single tomb or burial. One construction phase incorporates the creation of three chambers, but some contain no new tomb constructions. Structure B20 had a series of major modifications, the majority of which occurred within an approximately 100-year time span during the sixth and seventh centuries. Tombs with entranceways were built into two versions of Structure B20 (4th and 2nd), but not in its intermediate (3rd) or its latest (1st) version.

Structure B20-4th was built either over or in front of an earlier construction that had been placed on a different axis (Structure B20-Sub). Tomb 4 (S.D. C1H-2) was included in the core of Structure B20-4th. The entranceway to this chamber was situated within a stylized mask set into the frontal stair of the pyramid. The tomb was used before construction of Structure B20-3rd. A wall text dates the use of this chamber to A.D. 537. At this time, a single individual was interred in an extended position with the head to the north. Fifteen ceramic vessels, 1 perishable vessel and 14 stone spindle whorls, 1 jaguar paw, the bones of a bird and a reptile, and a half dozen obsidian lancets were arranged about the individual. An elaborate shell bracelet was on the left wrist; two jadeite earflares, one jadeite bead, one tubular shell bead, and one stingray spine

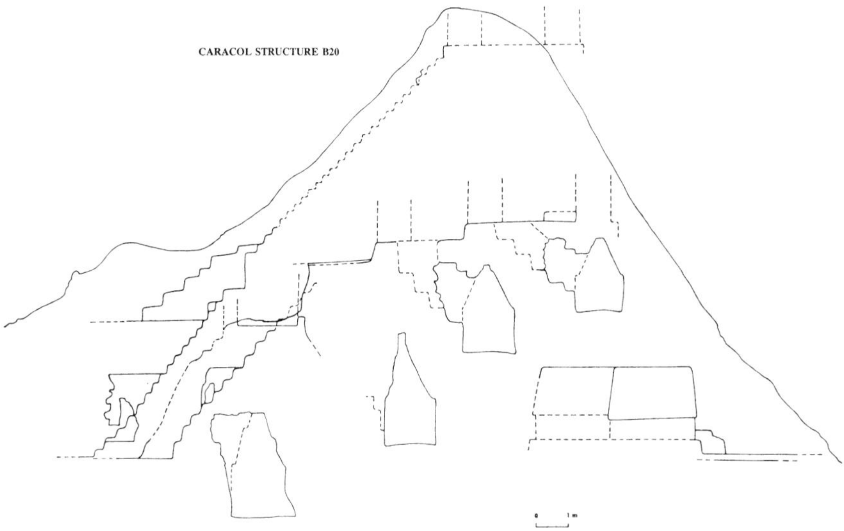

Fig. 2 Schematic section of Caracol Structure B20.

were in the vicinity of the head; three jadeite/albite balls were also associated with the body, as were two Spondylus shells, one of which covered the pelvis.

Structure B20-3rd was built over the intact lower stairs concealing Tomb 4. This construction contained no new tombs, caches, or interments but did lead to the creation of a shrine room within the central stair and directly above the preexisting Tomb 4 (S.D. C1H-2). An extensive carbon deposit covered the low "altar" in this room. Included within this carbon lens and resting directly on the room's floor was a shattered *incensario.* The preservation of this material is fortuitous, because most of Structure B20-3rd (or at least its axial part) was almost entirely dismantled to create Structure B20-2nd. Probably this portion of Structure B20-3rd was purposely left undisturbed to avoid destruction of the preexisting tomb below.

Structure B20-2nd was constructed with three formal chambers (or tombs) being built within its core. Each tomb had an entranceway for either symbolic or actual reentry. Corpses and offerings were placed inside these tombs at different times. Tomb 3 was the earliest tomb to be used. The hurried manner in which both the interior of this chamber was plastered and the text was placed on its rear wall (Houston 1987: 95) indicates that the formal finishing of the interiors of these tombs took place only upon the death of the individual selected to occupy the chamber. Although it is uncertain whether the deeply buried Tomb 3 was constructed and then reentered to place the body or whether the body was placed in this chamber during construction of Structure B20-2nd, the placement of the body apparently took place in A.D. 576 (Chase and Chase 1987a: 20). Logic and stratigraphy dictate that Tomb 1 was next used and then, finally, Tomb 2. An unplastered cut through the flooring that covers the entranceway stairs for Tomb 2 indicates that this previously constructed chamber was reentered and used before construction of Structure B20-1st; Tomb 2 thus represents the latest interment in the core of Structure B20-2nd. The area above the Tomb 2 entranceway also was heavily burned and marked by obsidian pieces. Given the intact tombs concealed within it, it is also probably significant that the building walls (interior and exterior) of Structure B20-2nd were entirely black. No terminal offerings or use-related materials were found on the floors of Structure B20-2nd; however, graffiti representing an individual being carried in a litter was found on one inner wall (Chase and Chase 1987b).

At some point after deposition of Tomb 2 in Structure B20-2nd, the Maya built Structure B20-1st-B. No additional tombs or caches were placed within its core. A critical architectural component of this version of Structure B20, however, was a large *wits* mask, forming a small room (or niche) centered in the base of the pyramid's stairway (Fig. 3). This lower mask appears to have symbolically swallowed the dead already interred within the construction (and is analogous to the earlier central mask that was on the stair of Structure B20-4th that formed the entranceway for Tomb 4). This mask was sealed in an intact condition when the plaza floor at the summit of Caana was raised about 4 m sometime after A.D. 700; at the time of its encasement, parts of a human body were placed within the room formed by the mouth of the mask. Structure B20-1st-A had extensive modifications made to the western side of its pyramid, necessitated because of the engulfment of 4 m of the original pyramid base by the new summit plaza. Two masks were placed to the lateral sides of the newly modified stairway. Initially, this modified stair contained an inset balk that mirrored the one also found on the adjacent Structure B19. In the final modification of Structure B20, however, a projecting frontal stairway encased the inset balk. Set within this final stair was a crude, stone-lined burial of several individuals with no grave offerings.

The funerary activities of Structure B20 suggest that it may have served as a prototype for the Late Classic period eastern "ancestral shrine" constructions that appear with great frequency in residential groups throughout Caracol (Chase and Chase 1994).[3] However, the eastern buildings in these residential groups

[3] See also Becker (1971) for Tikal.

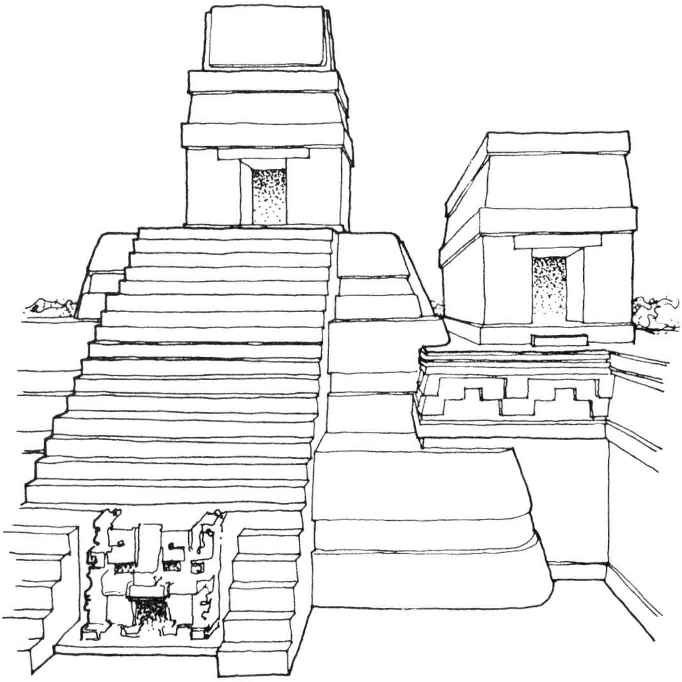

Fig. 3 Illustration of Caracol Structure B20-1st-B. Drawing by J. Ballay.

combine activities and features (specifically caches and burials) that are split between Structure B20 and B19 on the summit of Caana.

Structure B19 is the northern building at the summit of Caana. It also saw a number of rebuilding efforts and appears to have served as a locus for several caches but only one tomb. No caches or interments have been encountered in excavation of the earliest construction encountered—Structure B19-3rd. However, substantial indications exist for extensive ritual activity associated with the use of Structure B19-2nd. A major tomb was created as a modification to Structure B19-2nd. The entranceway to this chamber was concealed in a back wall of a basal niche that was centered on the lower frontal stair (Fig. 4). Similar to Structure B20-3rd, a formal building room was placed directly above this chamber, again centered in the lower pyramid stairway. This tomb was better plastered than those in Structure B20. Instead of a ritual text on its painted capstone, a black-line skull was portrayed. We doubt that the chamber was immediately occupied. Its final use was, however, almost 100 years before the impressive base of Structure B19-2nd was encased in the final raised plaza level of Caana and

Fig. 4 Illustration of Caracol Structure B19-2nd. Drawing by J. Ballay.

ultimately covered by Structure B19-1st. A text on the back wall of the tomb dates to A.D. 634 (Chase and Chase 1987a: 30). A single bundled individual was buried within the Structure B19-2nd chamber, the largest tomb yet identified at Caracol of the 80 so far investigated as of the 1994 field season. The interred individual was female and her teeth were extensively inlaid with jadeite. She also had a set of jadeite earflares and a few jadeite beads. Her only nonperishable offerings were eight ceramic vessels.

A host of ritual deposits (or caches) placed at the summit of Structure B19-2nd likely both predate and postdate reentry of the tomb. Episodic deposition is evident. All offerings were either placed on or intruded into preexisting floors and sealed by the latest floor that can be assigned to Structure B19-2nd. The latest deposit consisted of a burial of a subadult accompanied by a lidded *incensario,* which in turn was set above a lip-to-lip ceramic vessel set containing human fingers (Fig. 5). Another deposit consisted of a cache of obsidian eccentrics and stingray spines set amid a bed of jadeite chips directly on an earlier floor. Nu-

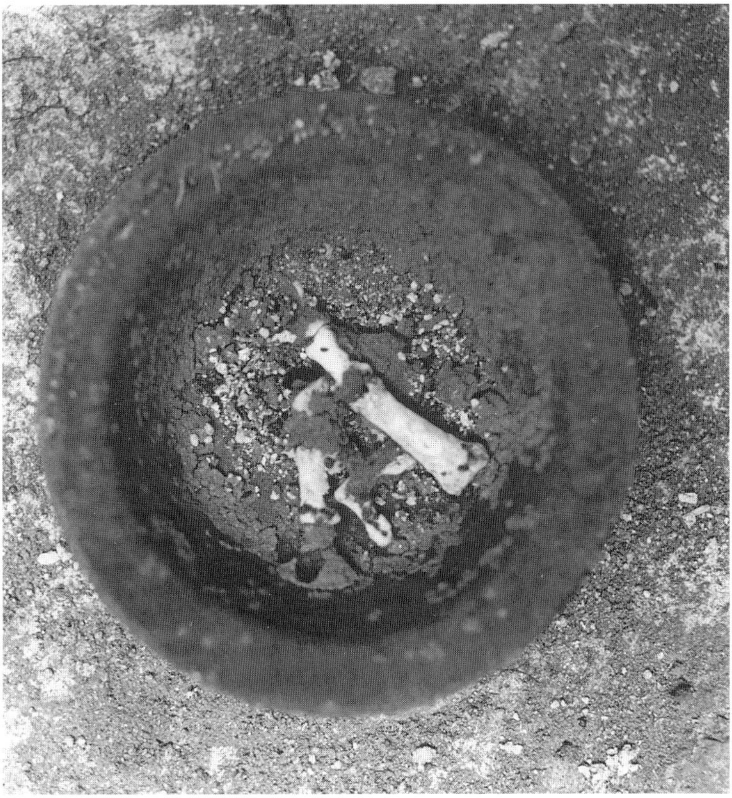

Fig. 5 Photograph of in situ finger bowl cache from Caracol Structure B19.

merous other deposits within the core of Structure B19-2nd penetrated earlier floors and consisted solely of "finger bowl" caches or single burnt jadeite beads. Before the 1993 penetration of Structure B19, caches containing human fingers in them had been associated only with eastern structures in residential group structures (Chase and Chase 1994). In this context, finger caches were primarily found in front of the eastern buildings, but they also occasionally occurred as part of tomb assemblages.

No tombs were incorporated into Structure B19-1st, the new north building created when the entire Caana summit plaza was raised over 4 m. However, a final cache was placed in the fill of Structure B19-1st directly over the northern limit of the preexisting Structure B19-2nd tomb. This cache contained paired Spondylus shells, nine eccentric obsidians, one jadeite bead, one Spondylus bead, and many small chips of jadeite, Spondylus, and pyrite. At an even later

Fig. 6 Photograph of a face cache and varieties of finger caches from Caracol.

Fig. 7 Photograph of a face cache from Caracol Structure B34 dating to the early Late Classic period.

date, an *ahau* altar was placed in a specially prepared inset stair balk directly above the buried tomb at the base of the Structure B19-1st stairs. Beneath this altar was an offering consisting of two broken incense burners, two partial ceramic vessels, a host of chert drills, and human cranial fragments; these artifacts date to or after A.D. 800. Thus, the altar correlates with the Katun 7 Ahau dating to A.D. 830. Although the locus of the altar suggests a commemoration of the death of the woman entombed far below it, we feel that this altar was meant in the sense of cyclical revitalization, invoking the earlier Katun 7 Ahau when Caracol defeated Tikal.

The predominance of caches and interments encountered in the excavations of Structures B19 and B20 are replicated in east structure excavations in residential groups throughout Caracol during the Late Classic period. This east structure pattern reflects activity related to the veneration of the dead (see Becker 1971, 1982); it has been suggested that the eastern structures of many, if not most, of the outlying residential compounds served as charnel houses (Chase and Chase 1994). At Caracol, an eastern building focus is evident in most residential groups based primarily on the ritual content of these constructions. Materials included within these eastern buildings consist of single- and multiple-individual tombs, all other classes of burials, stalagmites, finger bowl caches, and "face" caches (urns with modeled human faces; Figs. 6 and 7) that are often found in association with obsidian eccentrics and chips. Although this "veneration" pattern is found in most of the outlying residential groups at Caracol, it exists in buildings of various sizes, shapes, and plans and cannot be assumed to be present on the basis of architectural type and eastern location alone. A similar burial concentration in eastern buildings has been long noted for Tikal (Becker 1971, 1982: 120) but in a much smaller percentage of the outlying residential groups (14% recognized with ease at Tikal as opposed to more than 60% recognized with ease at Caracol) and minus both the tomb reentryway and cache components that are so important at Caracol. This eastern structure pattern is but one example of the use of ritual activity to define architectural function.

At Caracol, then, the Maya fashioned tombs in buildings long before they placed bone in them. Other data from the site demonstrate a similar pattern of chamber construction—some never received human remains—as well as multiple interments and tomb reentry over an extended time. A common practice at Caracol, in both tomb (Fig. 8) and non-tomb (Fig. 9) contexts, was the combination of primary and secondary burials as a single interment event; in these cases, the remains of several individuals were usually deposited a substantial time after death, usually in conjunction with a single primary individual

Fig. 8 Photograph of a tomb containing multiple individuals from Caracol Structure A7.

Fig. 9 Photograph of a non-tomb burial at Caracol clearly showing articulated and nonarticulated remains.

Fig. 10 Text from the Caracol Structure A34 lower tomb capstone. Drawing by N. Grube.

who had just expired. For instance, investigations into Caracol Structure A34 (Chase and Chase 1996) led to the discovery of two tombs—one located at the summit of the construction and the other located beneath the base of the frontal stair. The upper tomb illustrates the Maya practice of reentering a tomb to remove bone. Only one long bone fragment remained inside the excavated chamber; a lip-to-lip cache was left in the entrance to the chamber, presumably at the time that the original interment(s) and offerings were removed. The lower chamber shows the significance of the tomb in and of itself as well as the continued use of the tomb for more than 100 years. The lower tomb was completed and consecrated in either A.D. 577 or A.D. 582. One individual may have been interred in the chamber at this time. The closing or capping of the chamber was considered to be an event significant enough to have been witnessed by the ruler of Caracol and recorded in a hieroglyphic text that was placed in the vault of the tomb (Grube 1994; Fig. 10). The osteological and artifactual evidence indicates that the tomb was subsequently reentered on at least one occasion to place human remains and offerings. The osteological material inside the chamber represents at least four individuals (D. Chase 1994). Offerings included 13 whole and 7 partial ceramic vessels (A. Chase 1994), as well as artifacts of jadeite and shell. In addition to demonstrating the long span of time in which a tomb might be used and the significance of the tomb itself, the Structure A34 investigations indicate further problems in assuming either dedicatory functions for burials or commemorative functions for constructions. These investigations also demonstrate the difficulty in assuming a structure's function or contents without excavation, as the Structure A34 building plan and elevation are replicated in other buildings at Caracol (specifically Structure B5) that do not appear to have housed tombs.

Variation in Ritual Deposits: Caches

Caches provide an excellent view of both chronological and spatial variation in ritual deposits that can also prove to be critical in functional interpretations. It is possible to identify the existence of at least two major kinds of caches in the archaeological record of the Maya: one set helped to define a sacred domain for a broader community; the second set is more diverse and likely included a series of possible activities ranging from veneration of the dead to commemoration of historical or calendric events. Those delineating sacred space are perhaps more easily identified and are almost always associated with public architecture, but even these were likely to result from a series of different rituals.

For Late Pre-Classic to Early Classic Caracol, caches have been found predominantly in the monumental architecture of the epicenter and in nodes of monumental architecture some distance from the actual Late Classic site center. These early caches appear in only a few locations in the site and seldom in residential groups. Early caches from monumental architecture are among the most elaborate encountered at the site. Although their precise contents and layouts vary substantially, one subset of early Caracol caches is easily distinguished from the others; these have contents that are layered and/or ordered in such a way as to suggest an intentional plan or design reflecting both directional order and placement. Items within these caches are generally similar, whole, and unburnt. It is suspected that variations in numbers of artifacts—as with the "Charlie Chaplin" (Moholy-Nagy 1985: 154) or other figures—among the caches may reflect intentional differences, probably relating these offerings to specific rituals (see D. Chase 1988: 86; Landa in Tozzer 1941: 138–149; Pendergast 1979: 85).

Two excellent examples of this kind of cache were found in Caracol Structure A6 (Chase and Chase 1995).[4] Both followed the construction and use of Structure A6-2nd. Both were buried in open-air intrusive pits with capstones. The first of this kind of cache to be placed in this locus consisted of a stone box and lid. Inside this hollow geode were a series of offerings that had been wrapped together in cloth (some of the threads were still in place). The contents of the

[4] See also Thompson (1931) for other examples of this kind of cache from the Mountain Cow area.

box appeared to be intentionally organized (Fig. 11). At the bottom of the stone receptacle was a pool of liquid mercury. Uppermost in the cache was a complete jadeite earflare assemblage. A multitude of malachite pebbles overlay two lip-to-lip Spondylus shells, which held other items. Encased within the two halves of the large Spondylus shells was a solid jadeite mask covered with red hematite. A jadeite claw pendant was set at its throat and two beads (one jadeite and one shell) were set to its sides as if to form earflares.

Fig. 11 Exploded view of Caracol Structure A6 cache dating to ca. A.D. 70. Drawing by J. Ballay.

Fig. 12 Plan of interior layout of second Caracol Structure A6 cache.

Sometime shortly after the stone box was deposited, another cache was intruded on the same axial line. The container for this cache was a large urn with a lid. The urn itself rested on a series of unworked shells. The contents of the urn were layered. Uppermost inside the urn were the remains of a beehive; placed inside the base of the urn were a layer of malachite pebbles. The central area of the cache contained a series of items all located around a jadeite earflare (Fig. 12). Most noticeable were four sets of marine bivalves oriented toward the four directions and two opposing hematite mirror backs. Other artifacts included small Charlie Chaplin figures of Spondylus shell as well as items of carved shell and jadeite. Also included were bloodletting implements (stingray spines) and items most likely intended to convey underworld, and underwater

Fig. 13 Upper and lower figures from interior of cache vessel, Caracol Structure 8F8. Identifications by S. Houston, drawings by S. Houston and A. Chase.

(Hellmuth 1987), associations such as coral, sharks' teeth, fish vertebrae, and small natural shells. Pumpkin seeds and pine needles were also present.

Three other caches are similar to the one described above and can be placed within the same basic category. Two were located elsewhere in the A Group. A large urn and lid were found with much of their associated contents spilled into a pit in the core of Structure A2. Although the complete, original ordering of the objects within this cache can only be surmised, the materials associated with this deposit mimic those previously described for Structure A6. Objects from within and outside the vessel included a series of bivalve shells, coral, stingray spines, animal bone, shell Charlie Chaplin figures, a jadeite earflare, and a jadeite pendant. A similar deposit encased in a smaller urn and lid were recovered from a pit in the core of Structure A8. Among the items within this cache were bivalve shells, coral, other unworked shells, Charlie Chaplin figures of jadeite and shell, assorted shell beads, mosaic pieces, and a shell pendant. The third deposit that is within this genre was encountered in the reclearing of looter's excavations at Tulakatuhebe Structure 8F8 when an urn and its associated lid (but no remaining contents) were found. On the base of the vessel was painted a dead Maize God; on the lid of the vessel was painted a winged Itzamna or *muan* bird (Principal Bird Diety) (Fig. 13). Thus, although no interior offerings were left by the looters, the interior of the vessel itself clearly conveys the opposition (and layering) of the "heavenly" and the "underworld."

Other caches of similar date are far less simple to categorize—see also Pendergast (1979: 198) for a similar situation at Altun Ha. Not only are there no clearly defined directional layouts to these caches, but there also appear to be no prescribed universal contents. Offerings may be whole or broken, burnt or unburnt. Not all of these caches are contained within vessels; some consist solely of concentrations of objects. Examples of this kind of cache are found in epicentral Caracol and in limited occurrences elsewhere. Depositionally, these may precede layered and ordered caches in the same structure. Even though these caches do not evince the same degree of design noted for the previous group of caches, they may contain some of the same objects—such as shells, coral, animal bone, stingray spines, malachite, jadeite, or even hematite mirrors.

Examples of this second class of caches include two additional deposits placed into Structure A6-2nd during its use life. S.D. C8B-5 consisted of items placed inside a lidded vessel. In contrast to the previously described caches that had been filled with items, the offerings within this cache barely covered the base of the vessel; they included one large bivalve, one jadeite bead, one shell bead, several small pieces of cut and unworked shell, small pieces of hematite mosaics (possibly from an eroded mirror), animal bone, and stingray spines; the entire contents of the vessel appear to have been burned. A second cache into Caracol Structure A6-2nd was unusual in both its restraint and opulence. The pit for S.D. C8B-4 was bedded with hundreds of broken jadeite and greenstone beads. Above the multitude of beads, however, was an unslipped lip-to-lip vessel pair containing only one jadeite bead and one shell bead. These two earlier, use-related deposits contrast sharply with the later two set into Structure A6.

A distinctive kind of cache characterized by obsidian cores and eccentrics appears throughout Caracol—and independent of monuments—at the end of the Early Classic Period. Those in the epicenter differ from those in the core of

Caracol. Three epicentral caches in public architecture are known to contain obsidian; all are the latest special deposits in their respective structures. Two are associated with paired Spondylus shells and one is associated with large jadeite/albite balls. S.D. C70B-2 in Caracol Structure A8 consisted of a Spondylus shell pair with one large malachite ball inside it and obsidian cores, chips, and eccentrics surrounding it. The other examples of epicentral caches with obsidian have been found in Caracol Structures B19 and A2. The Structure B19 example was clearly tossed into the structure fill (Fig. 14). It consisted of nine eccentric obsidians as well as a paired set of Spondylus shells, a single jadeite bead, a single shell bead, and small flat pieces of shell, pyrite, and jadeite. The Structure A2 cache was similarly tossed into the structural fill, but consisted of only one obsidian lancet, ten obsidian eccentrics, and four jadeite/albite balls. Eccentric obsidians (Fig. 15) are also distributed with Late Classic pottery caches throughout the residential groups in the core of Caracol. Within the core area, however, the deposits usually are found in plazas at the front of structures and only rarely in the building fills.

Most common for Caracol during the Late Classic are caches identifiable by both their pottery containers and their contents; these are colloquially referred to as "face caches" and "finger bowls." Both kinds of vessels are extremely poorly fired and likely were created solely for deposition as caches. Face caches consist of pottery urns of various sizes with modeled and appliquéd faces on them; some of the individuals portrayed may be deceased, as they have their eyes closed and lips sewn. The vessels themselves are usually devoid of identifiable offerings. Finger bowls consist of small bowls and lids of various forms; if their contents are still preserved, these caches contain only the bones of human fingers. These occur in residential areas throughout the site—predominantly in or in front of eastern constructions that also house human interments. It is believed that these caches have a distinctive function as offerings to the ancestors buried in the same area. These caches are far more common and standardized than any other kind of cache at Caracol; however, caches found in presumed high-status residential groups in the Caracol epicenter are somewhat more elaborate than those found in the Caracol core area. This focus on caches in residential locations is very different from the Early Classic pattern at Caracol and is significant in that it suggests that a shift to dispersed ritual activity likely occurred during the onset of the Late Classic period rather than at the onset of the Post-Classic period.

At Santa Rita Corozal the two basic classes of caches noted for Caracol are found conjoined at the end of the Early Classic period in a single deposit placed into monumental architecture and associated with the interment of a

Fig. 14 Photograph of final cache sealed in core of Caracol Structure B19-1st.

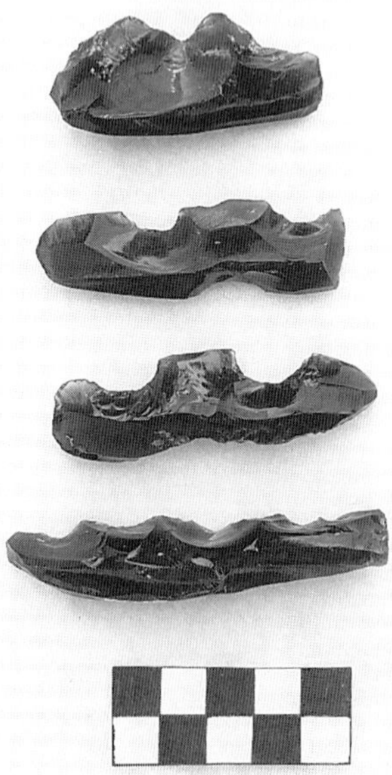

Fig. 15 Photograph of eccentric obsidians from Caracol.

Fig. 16 Hieroglyphs on outer cache vessels from Santa Rita Corozal Structure 7.

Fig. 17 Santa Rita Corozal deity heads from within Structure 7 cache vessels.

ruler of that site (A. Chase 1992: 34–36). The pairing of tombs and caches as part of the same event is recorded as early as the Late Pre-Classic period at Tikal (Coe 1990: 237–242). At Altun Ha, caches were deposited beneath the floors of tombs and also in tomb walls (Pendergast 1979, 1982, 1990: 23–42). Occasionally, pottery cache containers—e.g., Tayasal (A. Chase 1983: 405–406)—and eccentric flints—e.g., Altun Ha (Pendergast 1979: 74–78; 1982: 122; 1990: 28)—were included within the tomb itself, but more often caches and materials suitable for caches were set within the fill covering the tomb or chamber, as in the Santa Rita example. In the Santa Rita example, the contents serve to indicate both a ritual associated with the deceased—as indicated in the hieroglyphs painted on each of the three vessel sets (Fig. 16) and in the burnt stingray spines included in each of the three vessels—as well as broader cosmological or "sacred space" overtones—as indicated by the inclusion of painted deity heads on shell and jadeite (Fig. 17) and by the extensive use of shells, coral, and seaweed. This Structure 7 cache serves both to "center" Early Classic

Fig. 18 Photograph of reconstructed figurines (correctly positioned without urn) constituting Post-Classic cache within Santa Rita Corozal Structure 213.

Santa Rita and to place the dead king within a broader cosmological picture. It also presages the ritual pattern found for honored dead throughout Late Classic Caracol (although at Caracol the burial and caching activities are usually separate events in the actual archaeological record).

Post-Classic caches are not common from the Caracol area but are extensively known from Santa Rita Corozal in northern Belize. As is the case in Late Classic period Caracol, Late Post-Classic Santa Rita Corozal caches are found in residential groups throughout the site and not solely in central or monumental architecture. Although the trend is toward a continuation of residential area caching, there is an elaboration and patterning of Late Post-Classic caches that is in many ways similar to the Late Pre-Classic/Early Classic epicentral caches at Caracol. In particular, many of the Late Post-Classic caches at Santa Rita Corozal exhibit the intentional layout noted for Early Classic caches related to the concepts of settlement foundation, centering, sacred space, and a cosmological map.

Examples of this kind of cache may be seen in the offerings found in Santa Rita Corozal Structures 213 and 183. Within the core of Structure 213 was found a cache consisting of 25 figurines distributed in and around a ceramic urn with lid (Fig. 18) (Chase and Chase 1988: 48–52). Within the central en-

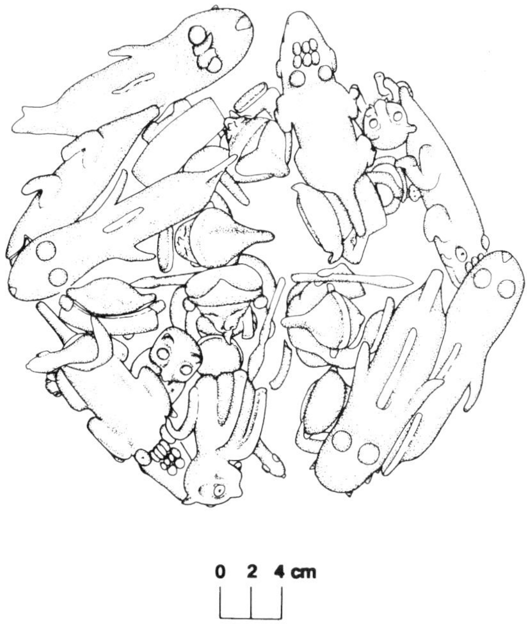

Fig. 19 Plan of Post-Classic cache within Santa Rita Corozal Structure 183.

cased unit, a single central human figure depicted blowing on a conch shell was seated on a stool located directly above a piece of jadeite and four small shells. All the other figurines were found in sets of four. This included four deities practicing self-mutilation while standing on the backs of giant sea turtles; these figures are interpreted to be the four *bacabs* holding up the four corners of the world (Chase and Chase 1986). A cache located within Structure 183 contained 28 figurines inside of a large lidded urn (Fig. 19) (Chase and Chase 1988: 56–59). There were four each of seven kinds of animal, human, and deity figurines, each oriented around a central vacant space defined by four warriors with shields. These and other Late Post-Classic caches have been interpreted as related to the *uayeb* rites as defined for the sixteenth-century Maya by Bishop Landa (Tozzer 1941: 139–145; Chase and Chase 1988: 72–75; D. Chase 1985b, 1988). Interesting because of the ideological similarities between the Late Pre-Classic and Late Post-Classic caches is the fact that an important aspect of the *uayeb* rites is the unification of sacred space correlated with the four symbolic entrances to town and the ceremonies of each of four different *uayeb* years.

INTERPRETATIONS

Maya architecture serves to define spaces, and, although ritual offerings do sanctify that space, a study of the contents of structures is clearly important in determining their functions. The construction and use sequences of tombs at Caracol indicate that both simple dedicatory functions for offerings and commemoratory functions for structures are difficult to identify archaeologically. Caracol tombs are often constructed inside buildings with entranceways for reentry at a later date. Several tombs may be placed within the same building and even building phase; several bodies may be contemporaneously or successively placed within the same tomb. And the same construction also may be rebuilt several times with varying funerary and nonfunerary functions. In addition to these considerations, the tomb chamber itself must be viewed as a sacred space. Hieroglyphic texts on tomb indicate that the creation or consecration of a given tomb chamber is an event as significant as the actual later placement of an individual within that chamber. Thus, there are occasions when neither strictly dedicatory nor commemorative functions may be assigned.

Burning of floors, buildings, and the contents of caches and burials is also a key factor in viewing ritual activities, especially as offerings and buildings are often burnt as a final act of destruction (Coe 1990: 938) or, alternatively, "activation" (Stuart, this volume). This physical act of burning, regardless of scale, has been interpreted as an important aspect of the death and rebirth cycle, as are the "earth offerings" themselves (Becker 1993).

Perhaps the most interesting consideration of ritual deposits, however, correlates them with the definition of sacred "layered" space. Caches that may play a critical role in the delineation of sacred landscape are most apparent in the Late Pre-Classic to Early Classic era and again in the Late Post-Classic period. It is important to note, however, that the architectural context of these "sacred space" or "cosmological map" caches—defined by their ordered contents—differs between these two eras. Before and in the initial part of the Maya Classic period, the elaborate caches that help to define sacred areas are found exclusively intruded into the cores of public, epicentral architecture. In their Post-Classic architectural context, these caches are found within nonepicentral residential compounds.

It has been suggested (D. Chase 1985b, 1988, 1991; Chase and Chase 1988) that a number of the Late Post-Classic caches at Santa Rita Corozal conform with the descriptions of *uayeb* (New Year's) rites detailed by Landa (Tozzer 1941: 138–149). These caches contain modeled ceramic figures that correlate with the offerings and activities described for the various *uayeb* years. As would be expected in this kind of ceremony, individual caches contain either one or four of each kind of figure; figures include humans, animals, underworld creatures, and gods. Activities within the *uayeb* rites call for integration of the four symbolic parts of the town through processions and the physical movement of items such as idols from the outskirts of the town toward the center. The ritual movements in the *uayeb* ceremonies described by Landa are very similar to the procession to town limits to define territorial space noted for foundation rituals described for sixteenth-century Mesoamerica (Garcia-Zambrano 1994: 225–229). And caches from Santa Rita Corozal Structures 183 and 213 physically depict the Maya concept of "centering" their universe (see Vogt 1976: 58; Schele and Freidel 1990: 125–131) through the orientation of groups of four figurines around a central figurine, object, or space.

Garcia-Zambrano (1994: 219) has suggested that clay *ollas* interred within pyramids may have symbolically represented sacred caves inside mountains when natural caves and mountains could not be found to center the sacred landscape of a given town—see also Freidel, Schele, and Parker (1993: 125–131). Caches in structures adjacent to the major plaza areas and causeway termini at Caracol may reflect such definitions of sacred space. Creation of Caracol's Late Pre-Classic/Early Classic epicentral precinct is associated with deposition of a series of caches. These caches (see above) contain symbolic layering (cf. Freidel et al. 1991) and numbers of units not found in other structural caches at Caracol. Most contain a central jadeite element suggestive of the centrality of the cache locus. One actually contains a layer of mercury that could be seen as corresponding to a mirror representing a map of the Caracol sacred space (cf. Garcia-Zambrano 1994: 224).

Different levels of ritual centering can be found at various sites throughout the southern lowlands. At Altun Ha, although the tombs are centered relative to constructions, the chambers themselves are both layered and centered (Pendergast 1979, 1982, 1990). Most Altun Ha tombs have one or three subfloor caches beneath the floor of the associated chamber; other deposits are sometimes found in the walls of the chamber or in the fill above the chamber. However, although the deposits may be spatially arranged according to a specific chamber (cf. Pendergast 1982: fig. 57) or building (cf. Pendergast 1990: fig. 6), no broader spatial patterns are in evidence at Altun Ha. Similar tombs, burials, caches, and ceramics were found in diverse parts of the site and "custom-built quality" homes "extended outward into the most peripheral areas" (Pendergast 1990: 243). No central focus can be clearly identified. "The heterogeneity of caches . . . is characteristic of Altun Ha, and is clearly not simply the product of different deity associations or times of construction" (Pendergast 1979: 198).

A different sort of ritual centering is found at Tikal, where an entire building complex, specifically the North Acropolis of that site, is clearly the focal point for the entire site during the Early Classic and part of the Late Classic periods. In particular, the caches placed about the northernmost plaza of Tikal's North Acropolis indicate a desire to symbolically "center" this space relative to the rest of the city. This is seen not only in the large number of caches placed within this architectural complex but also specifically in the recovered caches on the southern (Cache 120, Structure 5D-26), western (Cache 140, Structure 5D-22), and northern (Cache 86, Structure 5D-23) sides of the summit plaza. All three of these "centered" deposits included articulated crocodiles, an element central to the basic Mesoamerican worldview (see Reilly 1994; Taube 1989). It is important to note that the eastern side of this plaza was not intensively excavated; such an excavation may well have resulted in a fourth crocodile cache of Early Classic date—e.g., Muul offertory assemblage (Coe 1990: 324, 368, 427)—that would have defined the fourth side of this summit plaza. The centrality of this space is further emphasized in the inclusion of a crocodile in Burial 10 at the southwestern corner of this area and indirectly by the inclusion of numerous turtles in Burial 195 in the southeastern corner of the same space. Thus, although Tikal's North Acropolis architecturally forms the center of the site, the associated deposits and their placement confirm the importance of this public architecture in terms of a broader cosmological plan.

Offerings are not merely activities undertaken secondarily to define physical constructions. Not only do ritual offerings help to define architectural space, but they may form critical components in the definition of territorywide sacred space and may be incorporated into buildings by design and before construction. Variations in the distribution, contents, and treatment of ritual offerings relative to their architectural context are the key to interpretation of some of the most dynamic aspects of ancient Maya civilization.

CONCLUSIONS

Research at Caracol has provided a rich context for framing Maya architectural form. In particular, archaeological data illustrate that the Maya used their architecture to reflect their cosmos and active articulation of both the living and the dead. The pervasive nature of this relationship is seen not only in epicentral architecture but also in the layout and contents of residential buildings. Changing Maya views of architecture are also apparent in the archaeological record. Importantly, the architectural context of caches, burials, and other ritual activities is instructive for inferring how Maya society was both integrated and transformed during the Classic period.

There are changes in the nature of offerings at most Maya sites through time—especially during the Late Classic and Post-Classic eras. Changes occur in the caching (and burial) patterns at Caracol. Ordered epicentral Late Pre-Classic/Early Classic caches are believed to have functioned in the sanctification of ritual space related to the territorial whole. This class of caches is associated only with public architecture through the Early Classic era. Late Classic offerings were both more varied and more decentralized; these Caracol caches were also placed throughout the site in a pattern that is very different from that reported for other Late Classic Maya sites, such as Tikal, where the centering of caches in monumental architecture appears to have continued with only minor change. The shift in cache emphasis from monumental architecture to domestic architecture seen at Caracol (and possibly at Altun Ha), however, is reflective of a continuity in caching practice documented for the Post-Classic period. Whereas Late Classic caching practices placed a premium on venerating honored dead (or sanctifying personal ritual space) in many different domestic loci, by the Late Post-Classic the domestic areas were being used for sanctification of ritual space related to the larger community. This deemphasis on epicentral ritual space is also seen in a corresponding deemphasis on Post-Classic monumental architecture. Thus, the location and nature of ritual deposits serves as a mirror of societal change and organization. The shift in placement of the most important ritual deposits of the Maya ultimately from epicentral monumental architecture to domestically linked architecture located throughout the community is clearly reflective of very different, but effective, strategies for dealing with a changing Maya world.

Acknowledgments Investigations at Santa Rita Corozal were funded by the National Science Foundation (grants BNS-8318531 and BNS-8509304) as well as the Explorer's Club, Sigma Xi, various agencies at the University of Pennsylvania, and private donations. Investigations at Caracol have been funded by a variety of institutions and agencies including the Government of Belize, the Harry Frank Guggenheim Foundation, the Dart Foundation, the National Science Foundation (grants BNS-8619996 and SBR-9311773), the United States Agency for International Development, and the University of Central Florida; the Institute of Maya Studies and a host of individuals have also provided crucial donations to the project through the University of Central Florida Foundation. During the seven-year span of the Santa Rita Corozal investigations and the ten-year span of the Caracol excavations, hundreds of individuals participated in these projects or provided assistance in Belize and the United States.

Without these contributions of time and funds, the investigations reflected in this chapter would never have taken place. Wendy Giddens Teeter kindly provided faunal identifications. The authors would also like to thank Stephen Houston and an anonymous reviewer for comments on earlier versions of this paper.

BIBLIOGRAPHY

ASHMORE, WENDY

1991 Site-Planning Principles and Concepts of Directionality among the Ancient Maya. *Latin American Antiquity* 2: 199–226.

BECKER, MARSHALL J.

1971 *The Identification of a Second Plaza Plan at Tikal, Guatemala, and Its Implications for Ancient Maya Social Complexity.* University Microfilms, Ann Arbor.

1982 Ancient Maya Houses and Their Identification: An Evaluation of Architectural Groups at Tikal and Inferences Regarding Their Functions. *Revista Española de Antropología Americana* 12: 111–129.

1992 Burials as Caches; Caches as Burials: A New Interpretation of the Meaning of Ritual Deposits among the Classic Period Lowland Maya. In *New Theories on the Ancient Maya* (E. C. Danien and R. J. Sharer, eds.): 185–196. University Museum Monograph 77. University of Pennsylvania, Philadelphia.

1993 Earth Offerings among the Classic Period Lowland Maya: Burials and Caches as Ritual Deposits. In *Perspectivas antropológicas en el mundo maya* (M. J. Iglesias P. and F. Ligorred P., eds.): 45–74. Sociedad Española de Estudios Mayas, Instituto de Cooperación Iberoamericana, Madrid.

CHASE, ARLEN F.

1983 *A Contextual Consideration of the Tayasal-Paxcaman Zone, El Peten, Guatemala.* University Microfilms, Ann Arbor.

1992 Elites and the Changing Organization of Classic Maya Society. In *Mesoamerican Elites: An Archaeological Assessment* (Diane Z. Chase and Arlen F. Chase, eds.): 30–49. University of Oklahoma Press, Norman.

1994 A Contextual Approach to the Ceramics of Caracol, Belize. In *Studies in the Archaeology of Caracol, Belize* (Diane Z. Chase and Arlen F. Chase, eds.): 157–182. Monograph 7. Pre-Columbian Art Research Institute, San Francisco.

CHASE, ARLEN F., AND DIANE Z. CHASE

1987a *Investigations at the Classic Maya City of Caracol, Belize, 1985–1987.* Monograph 3. Pre-Columbian Art Research Institute, San Francisco.

1987b *Glimmers of a Forgotten Realm: Maya Archaeology at Caracol, Belize.* University of Central Florida, Orlando.

1994 Maya Veneration of the Dead at Caracol, Belize. In *Seventh Palenque Round Table, 1989* (Merle G. Robertson and Virginia M. Fields, eds.): 55–62. Pre-Columbian Art Research Institute, San Francisco.

1995 External Impetus, Internal Synthesis, and Standardization: E Group Assemblages and the Crystallization of Classic Maya Society in the Southern Lowlands. In *The Emergence of Lowland Maya Civilization* (Nikolai Grube, ed.): 87–101. Acta Mesoamericana, no. 8. Berlin.

CHASE, DIANE Z.

1982 *Spatial and Temporal Variability in Postclassic Northern Belize.* University Microfilms, Ann Arbor.

1985a Ganned But Not Forgotten: Late Postclassic Archaeology and Ritual at Santa Rita Corozal, Belize. In *The Lowland Maya Postclassic* (Arlen F. Chase and P. M. Rice, eds.): 104–125. University of Texas Press, Austin.

1985b Between Earth and Sky: Idols, Images, and Postclassic Cosmology. In *Fifth Palenque Round Table, 1983* (Merle G. Robertson and Virginia M. Fields, eds.): 223–233. Pre-Columbian Art Research Institute, San Francisco.

1988 Caches and Censerwares: Meaning from Maya Pottery. In *A Pot for All Reasons* (C. C. Kolb and L. M. Lackey, eds.): 81–104. Temple University Press, Philadelphia.

1991 Lifeline to the Gods: Ritual Bloodletting at Santa Rita Corozal. In *Sixth Palenque Round Table, 1986* (Merle G. Robertson and Virginia M. Fields, eds.): 89–96. University of Oklahoma Press, Norman.

1994 Human Osteology, Pathology, and Demography as Represented in the Burials of Caracol, Belize. In *Studies in the Archaeology of Caracol, Belize* (Diane Z. Chase and Arlen F. Chase, eds.): 123–138. Monograph 7. Pre-Columbian Art Research Institute, San Francisco.

Chase, Diane Z., and Arlen F. Chase

1986 *Offerings to the Gods: Maya Archaeology at Santa Rita Corozal.* University of Central Florida, Orlando.

1988 *A Postclassic Perspective: Excavations at the Maya Site of Santa Rita Corozal, Belize.* Monograph 4. Pre-Columbian Art Research Institute, San Francisco.

1996 Maya Multiples: Individuals, Entries, and Tombs in Structure A34 of Caracol, Belize. *Latin American Antiquity* 7 (1): 61–79.

Coe, Michael D.

1956 The Funerary Temple among the Classic Maya. *Southwestern Journal of Anthropology* 12: 387–394.

1965 A Model of Ancient Community Structure in the Maya Lowlands. *Southwestern Journal of Anthropology* 21: 97–114.

1975a Death and the Ancient Maya. In *Death and the Afterlife in Pre-Columbian America* (E. P. Benson, ed.): 87–104. Dumbarton Oaks, Washington, D.C.

1975b Death and the Afterlife in Pre-Columbian America: Closing Remarks. In *Death and the Afterlife in Pre-Columbian America* (E. P. Benson, ed.): 191–196. Dumbarton Oaks, Washington, D.C.

Coe, William R.

1959 *Piedras Negras Archaeology: Artifacts, Caches, and Burials.* University Museum Monographs. University of Pennsylvania, Philadelphia.

1965 Artifacts of the Maya Lowlands. In *Handbook of Middle American Indians,* vol. 3. (Robert Wauchope, ed.): 594–602. University of Texas Press, Austin.

1990 *Excavations in the Great Plaza, North Terrace and North Acropolis of Tikal.* University Museum Monograph 61. University of Pennsylvania, Philadelphia.

Davies, Nigel

1984 Human Sacrifice in the Old World and New: Some Similarities and Differences. In *Ritual Human Sacrifice in Mesoamerica* (E. P. Benson and E. H. Boone, eds.): 211–226. Dumbarton Oaks, Washington, D.C.

Edmonson, Munro
1984 Human Sacrifice in the Books of Chilam Balam of Tizimin and Chumayel. In *Ritual Human Sacrifice in Mesoamerica* (E. P. Benson and E. H. Boone, eds.): 91–100. Dumbarton Oaks, Washington, D.C.

Freidel, David A., M. Masucci, S. Jaeger, and R. A. Robertson
1991 The Bearer, the Burden, and the Burnt: The Stacking Principle in the Iconography of the Late Pre-Classic Maya Lowlands. In *Sixth Palenque Round Table, 1986* (Merle G. Robertson and Virginia M. Fields, eds.): 175–183. University of Oklahoma Press, Norman.

Freidel, David A., Linda Schele, and Joy Parker
1993 *Maya Cosmos: Three Thousand Years on the Shaman's Path.* William Morrow, New York.

Garber, James F.
1983 Patterns of Jade Consumption and Disposal at Cerros, Northern Belize. *American Antiquity* 48: 800–807.

Garcia-Zambrano, Angel J.
1994 Early Colonial Evidence of Pre-Columbian Rituals of Foundation. In *Seventh Palenque Round Table, 1989* (Merle G. Robertson and Virginia M. Fields, eds.): 219–229. Pre-Columbian Art Research Institute, San Francisco.

Grube, Nikolai
1994 Epigraphic Research at Caracol, Belize. In *Studies in the Archaeology of Caracol, Belize* (Diane Chase and Arlen Chase, eds.): 83–122. Monograph 7. Pre-Columbian Art Research Institute, San Francisco.

Haviland, William A., Marshall J. Becker, A. Chowning, K. A. Dixon, and K. Heider
1985 *Excavations in Small Residential Groups of Tikal: Groups 4F-1 and 4F-2.* University Museum Monograph 58. University of Pennsylvania, Philadelphia.

Hellmuth, Nicholas M.
1987 *Monster und Menschen in der Maya-Kunst.* Akademische Druck- u. Verlagsanstalt, Graz, Austria.

Houston, Stephen D.
1987 Appendix II: Notes on Caracol Epigraphy and Its Significance. In *Investigations at the Classic Maya City of Caracol, Belize, 1985–1987* (Arlen F. Chase and Diane Z. Chase, eds.): 85–100. Monograph 3. Pre-Columbian Art Research Institute, San Francisco.

Krejci, Estella, and T. Patrick Culbert
1995 Preclassic and Classic Burials and Caches in the Maya Lowlands. In *The Emergence of Lowland Maya Civilization* (Nikolai Grube, ed.): 103–116. Acta Mesoamericana, no. 8. Berlin.

Moholy-Nagy, Hattula
1985 Social and Ceremonial Uses of Marine Molluscs at Tikal. In *Prehistoric Lowland Maya Environment and Subsistence Economy* (Mary Pohl, ed.): 147–158. Papers of the Peabody Museum of Archaeology and Ethnology, vol. 77. Harvard University, Cambridge, Mass.

Pendergast, David M.

1979 *Excavations at Altun Ha, Belize, 1964–70*, vol. 1. Royal Ontario Museum, Toronto.

1982 *Excavations at Altun Ha, Belize, 1964–70*, vol. 2. Royal Ontario Museum, Toronto.

1990 *Excavations at Altun Ha, Belize, 1964–70*, vol. 3. Royal Ontario Museum, Toronto.

Reilly, F. Kent, III

1994 Enclosed Ritual Spaces and the Watery Underworld in Formative Period Architecture: New Observations on the Function of La Venta Complex A. In *Seventh Palenque Round Table, 1989* (Merle G. Robertson and Virginia M. Fields, eds.): 127–137. Pre-Columbian Art Research Institute, San Francisco.

Schele, Linda, and David A. Freidel

1990 *A Forest of Kings: The Untold Story of the Ancient Maya.* William Morrow, New York.

Sugiyama, Saburo

1993 Worldview Materialized in Teotihuacan, Mexico. *Latin American Antiquity* 4: 103–129.

Taube, Karl A.

1989 *Itzam Cab Ain: Caimans, Cosmology, and Calendrics in Postclassic Yucatan.* Research Reports on Ancient Maya Writing 26. Center for Maya Research, Washington, D.C.

Thompson, J. Eric S.

1931 *Archaeological Investigations in the Southern Cayo District, British Honduras.* Anthropological Series, vol. 17, no. 3. Publications 301. Field Museum of Natural History, Chicago.

Tozzer, Alfred M.

1941 *Landa's relación de las cosas de Yucatán: A Translation.* Papers of the Peabody Museum of Archaeology and Ethnology, vol. 18. Harvard University, Cambridge, Mass.

Vogt, Evon Z.

1976 *Tortillas for the Gods: A Symbolic Analysis of Zinacanteco Rituals.* Harvard University Press, Cambridge, Mass.

Classic Maya Depictions of the Built Environment

STEPHEN D. HOUSTON
BRIGHAM YOUNG UNIVERSITY

One of the world's richest stores of information on built environments, particularly of a monumental nature, comes from the ancient Maya civilization of the Classic period. This evidence is at once varied and plentiful. There exist (1) the buildings themselves, organized into changing, often expanding and increasingly complex groupings of plazas, pyramids with summit temples, multi-roomed structures, basal platforms, and ballcourts; (2) textual descriptions of these buildings, framed in indigenous terminology, and as recorded either in roman script at a later date or in hieroglyphic inscriptions contemporary with such constructions (see Stuart, this volume); and (3) an equally selective view of such architecture through iconographic depictions, ranging from spontaneous graffiti to more deliberate representations on painted pottery and sculpture. No single presentation can do justice to this material or to the many ways in which it can be studied. Instead, this essay focuses on one aspect of the data—what the Maya themselves chose to emphasize according to set formulas in their depictions of architecture.

If there is a theoretical portmanteau to hold such observations, then it is woven from the threads of symbolic anthropology, in which "the built environment is activated through ritual" (Lawrence and Low 1990: 446), especially through performances regulated by the conventions of courtly practice. What is beyond the scope of this paper—although increasingly of interest to scholars—is the study of "phenomenological architecture," how structures were experienced by visitors in "real time" (Foster 1989: 40–41) and how perceptions of places changed continually through "practice and recurrent usage" (Pearson and Richards 1994: 5).[1] We have precedent for this approach in the Maya re-

[1] Nonetheless, the complexity of "lived spaces" shaped by interactive experience should not be glibly underestimated by archaeologists wishing to apply such notions to prehistoric

gion: Horst Hartung (1980) pioneered work on sight lines in Classic Maya cities, an approach somewhat resembling Constantinos Doxiadis's work (1972: 5) on angles of view and site layout in Classical antiquity.[2] Nonetheless, for images of architecture such redefinitions or restructurations of meaning or spatial relationship are almost beside the point; the depictions are useful to us precisely because they show frozen vantage points and, in their details, provide a highly selective winnowing of architectural features. We are left with what the Classic Maya wanted us to see, what they found important. Classicists have been inventive in using similar data, employing architectural depictions to reconstruct lost buildings from Mediterranean civilization (Donaldson 1965; Henig 1990: 157; Price and Trell 1972), to document shifts in imagery from imaginary to real landscapes or from one architectural style to another (Pedley 1987: 77), to testify to patterns of conventionalization (Vallois 1908: 360–361), and to examine how structures were "integrated into larger complexes of buildings" (Leach 1988: 265).[3]

The Classic Maya used a considerable range of architectural depictions to represent their built environment. We can review these images in several ways—by looking at their general characteristics, the pictorial conventions used to render them, and the complex patterns of metaphor and conflation that give them shape and meaning. A final approach involves an exploration of variety in architectural images.

---

remains. William Hanks (1990: 516) describes some of the subtleties involved: "a *lived space* [is] made up of perspectival subspaces, costructured with the corporeal fields of human actors, and located within a broader sociocultural frame space." It is doubtful that archaeologists will ever possess the means to detect the nuances of "perspectival subspaces."

[2] George Andrews (1975: 81) comments more generally on "alignments or axes" in Classic Maya site layout, as do Aveni and Hartung (1986: 22–38) with regard to architectural astronomy. They pay less attention, however, to the ways in which alignments condition human movement, whether individual or processional. Earlier still, in 1833, Jean-Fréderic Waldeck drew notice to the manner in which buildings could frame and align with views of other structures, as shown, for example, in his watercolor of the Temple of the Cross, visible through a doorway in House A at Palenque (Baudez 1993: pl. 16). Regrettably, his romantic impulses, drunk with the *proportions héroïques* of the Maya, led Waldeck to invent scenes that did not exist. More recently—and far more than convincingly than Waldeck—Jeff Kowalski (1987: 132–146) has documented perceptual effects in architecture, particularly those devised by Puuc architects at Uxmal.

[3] For the time, Vallois's ideas (1908: 359–360) were surprisingly sophisticated in their sensitivity to rules of decorum and convention in architectural imagery: "Les images que nous citerons ne prétendent pas être des copies fidèles, ni même des croquis caractéristiques de monuments réels. Les modestes architectures d'un peintre de vases grecs sont . . . composées en vue du décor; ou bien, très abrégées, elles gardent tout juste la valeur d'une indication de lieu." Clearly, Vallois was disinclined to take a literal view of vase imagery.

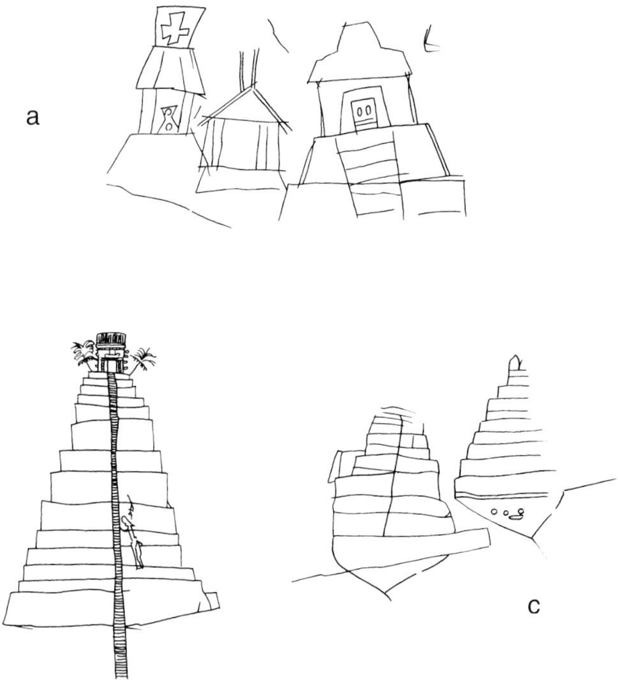

Fig. 1 Incised depictions of temples: (a) Comalcalco, Tabasco (after Pérez Campos 1992: fig. 11); (b) Chicanna, Campeche (after anonymous 1981: 90); (c) Yaxha, Peten (after Hermes and Galindo 1993: fig. 2).

GENERAL FEATURES OF ARCHITECTURAL DEPICTIONS

A basic distinction exists between depictions that include human figures (or their supernatural analogues) and those that do not. For example, images of Maya pyramids, usually shown in frontal view, are, with few exceptions, devoid of human figures.[4] This is not to say that they lack detail: inscribed bricks at Comalcalco often show braziers and anthropomorphic *incensarios* inside summit chambers (Fig. 1a; see also Andrews 1989: fig. 107), and similar images occur at the sites of Chicanna (Fig. 1b), Yaxha (Fig. 1c), and Tikal (e.g., Orrego and Larios Villalta 1983: pls. 16a, 16c, and 20; Trik and Kampen 1983: figs. 8, 34,

[4] A probable exception was documented at Río Bec by Ruppert and Denison (1943: figs. 37 and 38). A small seated figure appears within a summit temple that displays a pinched roof and an "x-ray" view of roof beams.

36, 46, and 51), where, in contrast, depictions of ballcourts abounding with human activity appear next to graffiti of pyramids. In a strikingly different pattern, court scenes, which usually focus on an enthroned lord, take their scale from the height of the human figures. Seldom do the Classic Maya sketch anything more than framing vertical supports, an open doorway, and a few broad risers leading to a room. The emphasis lies largely on communicating status differences and on illustrating certain social transactions, such as gift giving or tribute, that confirm and are mediated by such differences. Of far less importance is any attempt to represent actual details of construction, such as the ratio of doorway to roof height. The explanation for the general absence of figures on pyramids is less clear, although there is one possibility that comes to mind: the scenes reflect the general lack of human traffic on such structures. When ritual processions are shown, as in a graffiti at Yaxha, it is in the context of single lines of individuals descending over a series of platforms rather than the steps of a pyramid. The number of participants is large—cup-and-staff bearers as well as other attendants precede a plumed figure; parasol holders and a trumpeter follow (Hermes and Galindo 1993: fig. 2)—but they avoid any apparent contact with pyramid stairways.

Another distinction exists between flat images and three-dimensional views of structures (see Schávelzon 1982). Models in-the-round necessarily involve a different set of pictorial conventions; after all, a spectator can view the object from several vantage points and, in some cases, transport the object to be examined in different settings. Such models are well documented in Mexico, starting with Early Formative examples from Tlatilco, with lattice screening for walls (Fig. 2a), and continuing with anecdotal clay sculptures of about a thousand years later from Nayarit and Jalisco (Meighan 1976: 41–43, pl. 12). These sculptures show extensively painted roofing, pinched roofs, and, in comparison to Maya examples, a reduced emphasis on the human figure as a determinant of architectural scale (Lehmann 1964; von Winning and Hammer 1972: figs. 2–4, pls. 1–43). Other examples include Oaxacan temple models, almost always lacking in human figures (Hartung 1984: fig. 10), as well as stone architectural carvings in the enigmatic Mezcala style (Gay and Pratt 1992: figs. 102–116, pls. 187 and 204),[5] which typically eliminates all figures but for recumbent deities on temple roofs (Karl Taube, personal communication, 1994). Better understood archaeologically is a Mezcala-style ballcourt model found cached in what was likely the principal ballcourt at Tenochtitlan (Fig. 2b) (Solís 1982: pls. 101–103;

[5] See also Eggebrecht (1987: pl. 97) and Leyenaar and Parsons (1988: pl. 161) for ballcourt models.

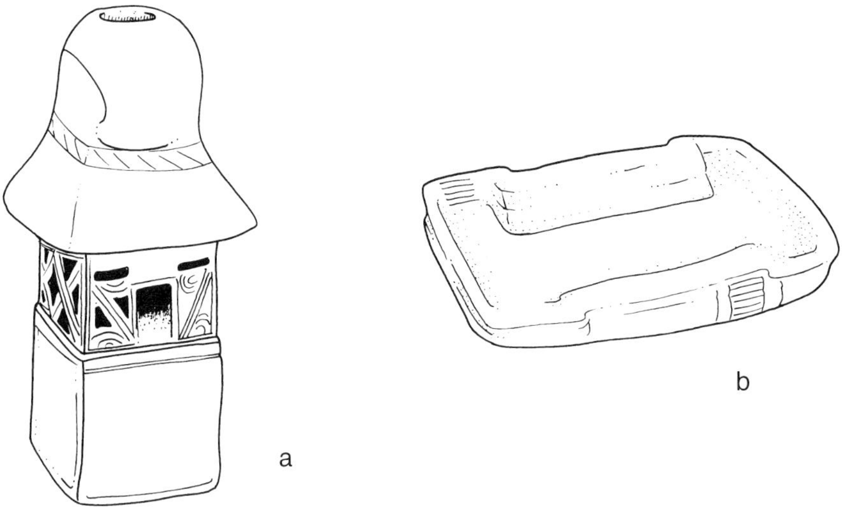

Fig. 2 Building models from Mexico: (a) house model from Tlatilco (after Coe 1965: pl. 80); (b) ballcourt model from Tenochtitlan (after Solís Olguín 1992: 149).

1992: 150–152). This minutely detailed model, which displays stairways both inside and outside the court, was accompanied by dark and white spheres—clearly intended to be representations of balls in the same relationship to rubber spheres as stone yokes are to wooden abdominal protectors (Ekholm 1946; Jones 1985: figs. 10 and 11). The best illustrations of larger, architectural landscapes are the stairways carved, probably during the Post-Classic period, into rock at Tetzcoco and Acalpixcan (Fig. 3) (Krickeberg 1969: figs. 1–3, 53). Some of these channels, depressions, and stairways—a few of which may represent agricultural terraces—could have been used to conduct fluids, either blood, as Cook (1955: 191) suggests, or more likely water, a pervasive ritual element that played a large role in, among other places, the circumferential aqueducts in the palace of Tetzcotzingo (Townsend 1992: figs. 80–83).

Maya models of houses and other buildings include stone and clay sculptures that are discussed in more detail below. What is noteworthy here is that they show a "pinched" roof, which reproduces the sheltered ventilation holes found in some modern Maya buildings (Wauchope 1938: fig. 34, pl. 13c), and, indeed, in structures elsewhere in the world, where they serve a similar func-

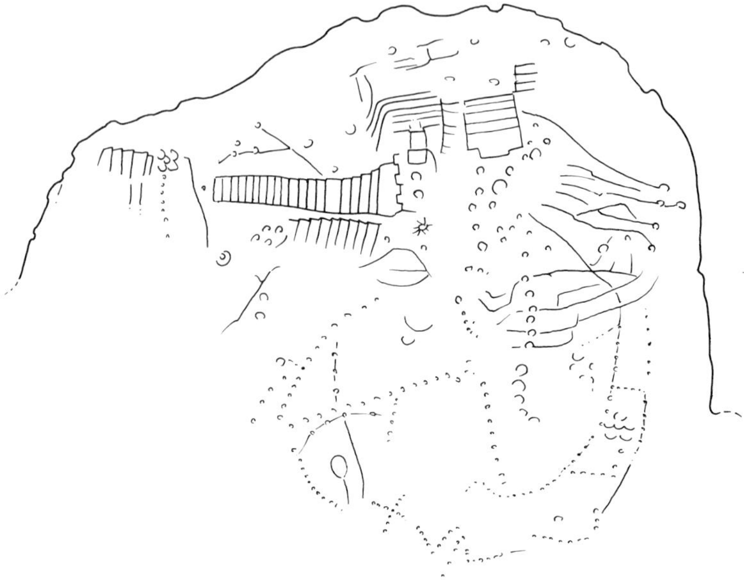

Fig. 3 Rock carving from Acalpixcan (after Cook de Leonard 1955: fig. 1).

tion (Beals, Carrasco, and McCorkle 1944: fig. 19; Hohmann 1995: 252–258).[6] Clay models are much more common, although they depart dramatically from literal representations, seeming instead to play strongly off the metaphor of a building as a metaphoric expression of a person or deity (Taube, this volume). The body and headdress of a figure become the superstructure and roof comb of a building or litter (Fig. 4). Of the flat images—and I use this term advisedly, because a scene on a cylindrical vessel or painted around the interior walls of a building cannot be seen at one glance and from one perspective—the Bonampak murals are by the far the most ambitious in their reference to architecture, depicting massed stairways and platforms only hinted at on polychrome pottery (Miller 1985). Apparently, the number of people to be shown determines the quantity and disposition of terraces and platforms.

We should mention two other distinctions that characterize Classic Maya art, the first being that between immobile and movable structures. In both the

[6] Classicists demonstrated long ago that many forms in early Greek architecture derive from wooden forms (e.g., Richter 1969: 20; cf. Carpenter 1962: 218–219). Although he does not cite this literature, Robert Wauchope (1938: fig. 22) posits a similar connection between Maya stone architecture and wooden originals.

a

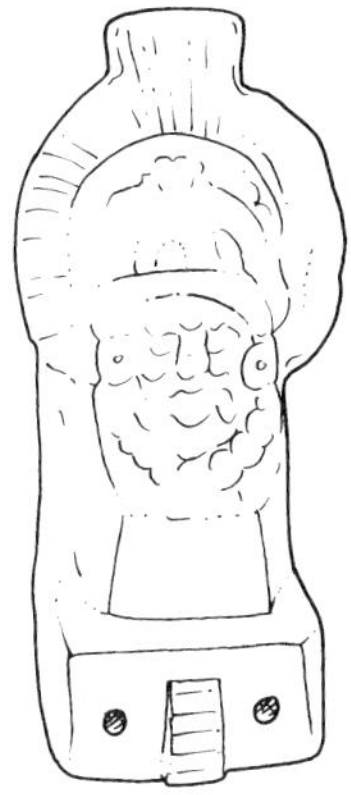
b

Fig. 4 Human figures as structures or possible litters (Karl Taube, personal communication, 1994): (a) seated ball player with Teotihuacan-style headdress as roof of building (after Goldstein 1980: fig. 5a); (b) deity effigy with stairway and holes for litter suspension (after Corson 1976: fig. 20c).

Classic and Post-Classic periods, there is ample evidence of litters, some with elaborate, thatched roofs (Fig. 5a-b; anonymous 1984: 81; Dumbarton Oaks slide archive dr. 13-LC-J4-4; Kerr 1992: 370; Trik and Kampen 1983: fig. 18, 41m, 72) and others with gigantic animal effigies standing protectively over a lord or lady (Fig. 5c) (see Stuart, this volume). A few such litters have been discovered archaeologically (Coggins n.d.: 344–347; Hall n.d.: fig. 70; Pendergast 1969: 21). A second distinction is that between perishable and imperishable structures. Ethnography, ethnohistory, and archaeology abound in references to arbors and wooden scaffolds, which bear strong sacrificial connotations (Roys 1965: xiii–xv; Taube 1988: 350–351). Many enclose underworld or supernatural beings and display wrappings of leaves or feathers and garlands of skulls or decapitated heads (Fig. 5d). The significance of both portable and perishable structures is that they compel a different view of Maya cityscapes. Instead of being empty and featureless, plazas and platforms could have been reconfigured by temporary placement of structures, banners, or parasols, whose position would change the use and meaning of ambient space.

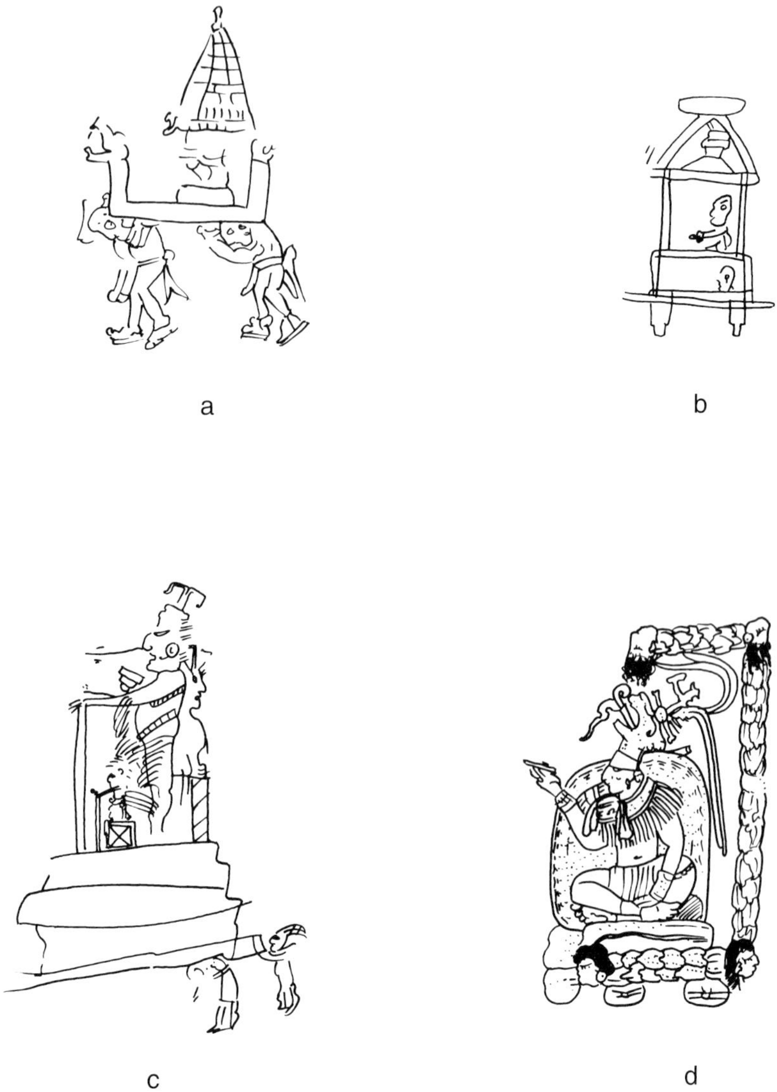

Fig. 5 Portable structures in Maya art: (a) Terminal Classic graffito from Río Bec (after anonymous 1984: fig. 2); (b) litter graffito from Tikal (after Trik and Kampen 1983: fig. 72); (c) "jaguar protector" graffito from Tikal (after Trik and Kampen 1983: fig. 72); (d) leaf-covered arbor (after Kerr 1992: 446).

PICTORIAL CONVENTIONS

Depictions of Maya architecture make little sense without an understanding of pictorial conventions, the generating principles that lie behind images of Maya structures. Attempts to itemize conventions in other parts of Mesoamerica include Donald Robertson's work (1959: 19–21) on Post-Classic Mexican depictions of architecture, Elizabeth Smith's comments (1973: 45, 49; see also Garza Tarazona 1970) on Mixtec conventions, and, in a more limited effort, Pincemin and Rosas's catalogue (1985: 90) of Post-Classic Maya representations of buildings.[7] The Classic Maya used an equal if not larger number of conventions, focusing especially on complex depictions of humans in palatial settings. Here I describe only those relevant to this paper.[8]

One dominant principle, common, in fact, to all Maya art, is that of the zone of contact—an area between the first person facing viewer's right and the first person facing viewer's left (Fig. 6). In terms of discourse, the person facing left might be described as the peak figure in the image, the cynosure of the scene. This figure usually appears on a throne. Those behind the peak figure are attendants of lesser rank, as are those to the right; typically, standing individuals hold lower rank than those who are seated. A different pattern obtains when deities are housed in buildings. Gods tend to be shown in reverse order, facing assembled figures to viewer's right (e.g., Coe 1978: pl. 11; Kerr 1989: 52, 65; 1990: 225; Robicsek and Hales 1981: 19, 20, 138, 172). Perhaps this departure from convention reflects a peculiar facet of underworld courts, such as those described in the Popol Vuh. The courts embody a mirror image of palace life in dynastic centers—in a word, they are "anti-courts," in which anomalous or even repugnant behavior is not only tolerated but expected (Karl Taube, personal communication, 1991). Such reversals and mirror images resonate with Lacandon Maya belief, in which features of one level of the universe are re-

[7] Robertson insists, though, that indigenous artists made "compromises with nature in the construction of a picture," perhaps as marks of respect for "actors in the pictures" (Robertson 1959: 20). I disagree; there is evidence of great concern with clarity of presentation, if not according to the idiom of "Renaissance realism" (Robertson 1959: 20).

[8] In a pioneering study, Mary Miller (1985: fig. 3; 1986: 66–67) discerns conventions used by the Maya to indicate the location of standing or seated individuals with respect to thrones and platforms. David Stuart (personal communication, 1993) also points out that, in visual terms, figures seated before thrones occupy a singularly complex space. Figures may fan out to either side of a throne (Piedras Negras Panel 3) or be seated in slightly overlapping positions (Bonampak Sculpted Stone 1). Despite the flattened composition, the intention is to situate the figures in double columns extending out from the throne (Panel 3) or to arrange them shoulder to shoulder (Sculpted Stone 1). This composition conveys a three-dimensional effect that is otherwise difficult to achieve in panel format.

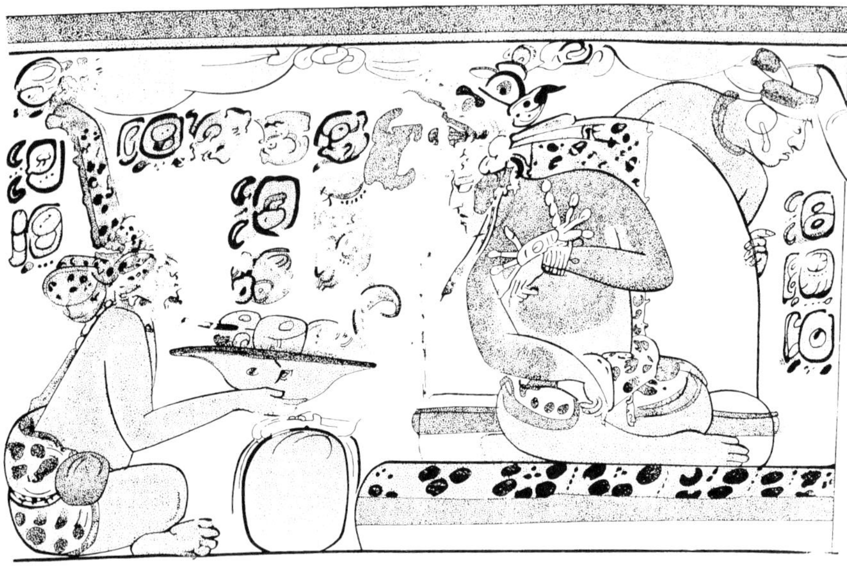

Fig. 6 Zone of contact on Classic Maya Vase (Coe 1973: pl. 29).

versed or amplified in another (Davis n.d.: 24); on a larger level, they may capture "the complexity and ambiguity of hierarchical relationships" as subtle messages in "dispraise" of rulers (Feeley-Harnik 1985: 295). The rare historical scenes that show buildings entered from the right may represent a visit to a foreign site, as shown on a Teotihuacan style vessel at Tikal (Coe 1967: 100–101) or the wall painting from Structure B-XIII at Uaxactun (Smith 1950: fig. 46).

Parenthetically, the primacy of figures to viewer's right touches on a complex point of interaction between hieroglyphic texts and images. Since the earliest days of decipherment, scholars have recognized that Maya glyphs are read from left to right; that is, in a sense, the glyphs are addressed by eye movement in which the reader approaches as a supplicant might a higher-ranking individual. This is less far-fetched than one might think: some examples of reversed texts, such as Yaxchilan Lintel 25, exist because the reader approaches through a doorway to gaze up at glyphs that have been reoriented to face the viewer (Graham and von Euw 1977: 55); the summit inscriptions of Temple 11 at Copan are another instance of glyphs oriented systematically to face a corridor entrance (Schele and Miller 1986: 122–123). In consequence, glyph reversals, especially those on lintels, can be explained partly as efforts to adjust reading order to accord with the movement of a spectator into a building. Unfortu-

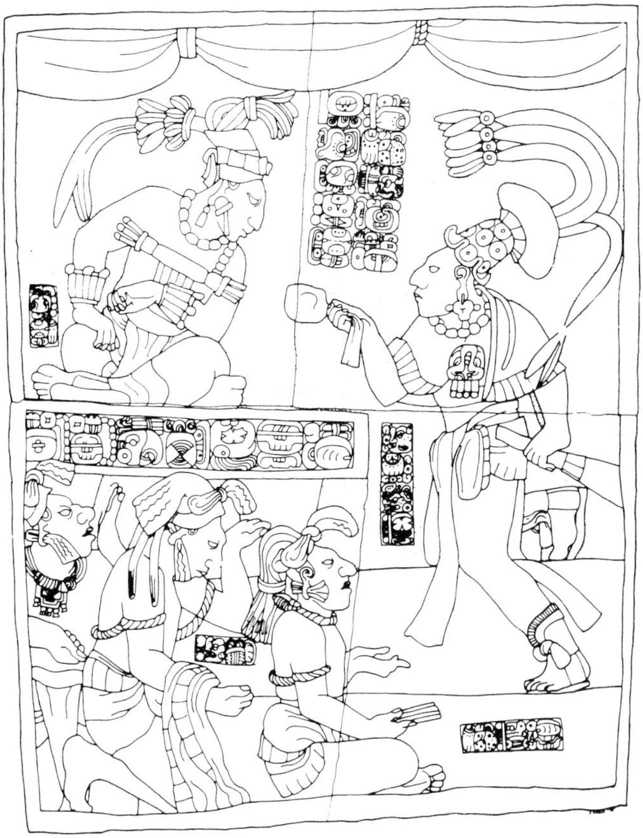

Fig. 7 Unprovenanced wall panel, Kimbell Art Museum. Drawing by Linda Schele.

nately, we cannot establish at present whether reading order determined Maya notions of courtly address or whether courtly decorum determined reading order.

Another principle is verticality—that is, the higher a seated figure in a scene, the higher the rank. This convention differs from that used in Egypt and late Classical antiquity, in which size correlated positively with social station—an emperor and his family were much larger than lesser individuals (Billig 1977: figs. 43–45). Occasionally, the Maya were compelled to reconcile rare situations in which the "peak" figure was not the highest ranking one in the image, as in a panel probably from the vicinity of La Pasadita, Guatemala (Fig. 7). Note that the highest, seated figure (an overlord from the site of Yaxchilan) appears at the

Fig. 8 Simultaneous angle of view in palace scene (after Coe 1967: 52).

top of the image, thus avoiding any problem of *lèse-majesté*. Nonetheless, the peak figure is the kneeling lord to viewer's right. He is the one who has assembled the captives, dressed them, and proffered them to his overlord. With this arrangement, hierarchical decorum is satisfied, and social relationships between individuals are made immediately apparent. Along with other visual cues, the placement of individuals in architectural space helps to establish their relative ranking and precedence, a matter of some importance to courtly society of the Classic period. Note as well that captives themselves are ranked; the individual closest to "peak" figure, yet still facing to viewer's right, is one *Ba wayib,* "top/head *wayib,*" the same captive featured in the principal text of the panel.[9]

Another way of showing architecture solves a difficult problem: How can one show the zone of contact (and all the exquisitely exact relationships of precedence it implies) and yet pinpoint the location of such zones without resorting to cumbersome three-quarter views? Apparently, this was done in the following manner (Fig. 8): the architectural support to viewer's right would do double duty as the back wall of an interior palace chamber, in which a throne abutted against the back wall and the right doorjamb delineated the entrance to the room. The resulting scene is not so much a confused jumble as a scene of maximum clarity—the exact order of relative precedence is shown at the same time as the architectural setting that specifies such relationships. This convention—which I label simultaneous angle of view, in that it combines a physically impossible conjuncture of perspectives—effectively solves the problem I posed, as it did for pre-Renaissance attempts to render diagrams of cylinders (Edgerton

[9] Elsewhere Stuart and I develop the argument that the Classic Maya used *ba* to denote not "first," its general translation from some modern Mayan languages, but "top" or "head" (Houston and Stuart n.d.)

Fig. 9 Temple with visitors. Vessel from Tikal (after Coe 1967: 100).

1991:27). The convention also applies to the human body. One Maya vessel, for example, illustrates kneeling figures, with a knee visible at the same time the legs are crossed (Kerr 1992: 437). This cannot be a literal scene, because the position would be exceptionally painful; instead, it depicts a simultaneous angle of view, a finely ordered arrangement of body parts that is probably dictated by gestures insisted on at court.

Another example of "simultaneous view" occurs in the common depiction of houses in Maya art (see Taube, this volume)—in a sense, the scene represents a cross section through the axis of a building, although again at a diminutive and unlikely scale because of the primacy of the body in such imagery, and the existence of architectural cues to sketch context. And, yet, the back wall again doubles as a doorjamb. In the house shown here, the stepped entrance is fully a profile view, whereas the rest of the structure is shown from a frontal perspective. In the few places where pyramids are shown with people, the human actors appear (rather improbably) ascending the broad, stepped platforms to the side, because this movement accords with the lateral "flow" of narrative information and order of precedence; the front stairway is left empty as always (Fig. 9). I speculate that frontal views of pyramids resulted from some protocol of behavior related to the proper approach to such buildings. It is probably relevant that houses linked with gods appear frontally, with both jambs clearly visible (e.g., Kerr 1990: 211, 285).

A related convention is oblique vantage. The vantage point into a palace chamber—a perspective ordained for us by the artist—lies somewhat to the right of the midline axis of a room. By glancing in at an oblique angle, the spectator perceives the left corner of the throne but not the right. Attendants on the right side of the room disappear behind an obscuring doorjamb (Kerr 1990: 255). This vantage has intriguing sociological implications, for the viewer does not enjoy a highly privileged position, being somewhat off axis from the building and some distance from the doorway. Possibly this reflects the artist's

Fig. 10 Column text, Hacienda Chilib, Campeche (after unpublished drawing by Ian Graham).

Fig. 11 Texts on sides of vessel (after Hellmuth 1987: figs. 45 and 46).

a 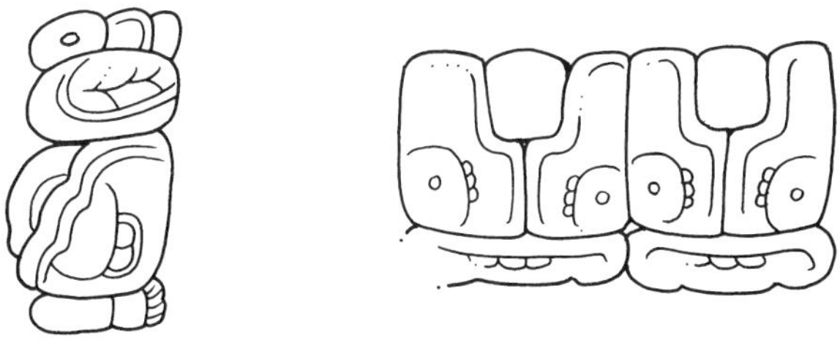 b

Fig. 12 Cross-sectioned glyphs for houses and ballcourts: (a) unprovenanced panel (after drawing by Ian Graham); (b) Tonina unnumbered panel, double ballcourt glyph (after Yadeun 1993: 137).

status or, more to the point, the status deliberately imposed on the viewer. At the same time, however, we should heed a caveat from Samuel Edgerton (personal communication, 1996): the suggestion that Maya tableaux were to be understood as "windows," with a "stage-like space" behind the plane of the image, requires further substantiation.

The emphasis on profile and on sections in some of this art reflects a larger concern in Maya construction with axial and bilateral disposition, a pattern that can be, as in the North Acropolis of Tikal, a preoccupation of considerable longevity, regardless of subsequent modifications to building plan (Coe 1990: fig. 5). This concern with axiality accounts for some peculiarities of reading order, as in a column text from Hacienda Chilib, Campeche, that orients glyphs inward to an invisible line of axis (Fig. 10) (Mayer 1981: 15, pl. 12); ordinarily, the glyphs would all face left. Similarly, an Early Classic vessel has glyphs that are oriented to an invisible line bisecting the object (Fig. 11); it is probably no coincidence that the lid ornament of the vessel aligns with this axis. In depictions of buildings, we see this emphasis very heavily in depictions of temples and less so in palace scenes, which tend to compromise axiality to accommodate a larger number of human figures. That is, when axiality is stressed, it is the building that is important; when it is not, the emphasis is clearly on people. Notably, the hieroglyphs referring to ballcourts and houses tend to be sectioned, as though sliced by an archaeological trench (Fig. 12).[10]

[10] The Maya themselves used a convention to indicate that images of buildings were cross-sectioned: concentric circles, sometimes with two small dots attached. Elsewhere in Maya art this convention signifies that limbs or extremities—a hand or a lower torso—has been severed from the rest of the body. Possibly the Maya applied this corporeal reference to buildings because architectural depictions are only part of a larger whole.

A final convention consists of abbreviation. Rarely do the Classic Maya show anything but a schematic architectural frame. The massive platforms under most palaces and pyramids tend to be omitted; the upper cornices are compressed into flatter shapes. Elongated buildings with multiple doorways are seldom shown, nor does there appear anything more than a few terraces, of which the most ambitious depictions are those in the Bonampak murals (Miller 1985: 191). Actual buildings may be shown and some of their features rendered, but there is little apparent drive to do this with absolute fidelity; buildings have been abbreviated to focus on the portion framing or providing ground lines for human figures.

RECIPROCAL METAPHOR AND ARCHITECTURAL DEPICTION

A fundamental way of understanding architectural depictions is through metaphor, the mapping of a "model in one domain to a corresponding structure in another domain" (Lakoff 1987: 114, 288). Nonetheless, models do not simply move in one direction: rather, they operate as "reciprocal metaphors," because the conceptual mapping may go both ways, the domain being shaped and systematized by one moving back to restructure the other.[11] Ethnography provides numerous examples of such mapping, in which buildings and settlement display an anthropomorphic symbolism and, in the thoroughly studied case of the Batammaliba in Africa, many other levels of metaphor and representation (Blier 1987: 135–139).[12] For instance, a Batammaliba house is dressed "in cloths for funerals and it is cicatrized, like a young girl, towards the end of construction" (Pearson and Richards 1994: 22–23), a pattern generally echoed by Carsten and Hugh-Jones (1995: 39), who note in many cultures an explicitly articulated parallel between the life spans of houses and their occupants. Furthermore, a Batammaliba cemetery is itself "a model of the settlement and the tomb locations mirror the house locations in a village" (Pearson and Richards 1994: 23).

Mesoamerica is equally rich in metaphor. Working with Tzotzil Maya, Robert Laughlin (1993: 101) reports on what he terms a "poetic association" between flora and humans, according to which labels for plant morphology contribute to descriptions of human features, and terms for "human or animal anatomy . . . name plant parts." These reciprocal metaphors shape behavior in analogical ways, so that a farmer may tighten his belt to grow a gourd with a

[11] See King (n.d.) for a similar treatment.

[12] Mary Douglas (1972: 514, 521) was among the first to draw attention to symbolism in domestic space. Her ideas are couched, however, in a cautionary tale that questions the ability of archaeologists to study such matters.

constricted center (Laughlin 1993: 107). Similar beliefs and practices characterize Nahua understandings of the human body (López Austin 1988: 346–347) as well as those of the Mixtec, for whom "the body is a central metaphor for things ranging from orientation in space to social and political arrangements" (Monaghan 1994: 96). A few scholars, from Hume to Guthrie, even presume to view anthropomorphization as central to the religious impulse: through a "strategy of perception" people interpret the nonhuman world as though human (Guthrie 1993: preface, 83).

The House Metaphor

Not surprisingly, reciprocal metaphors shape representations of Classic Maya architecture (see Taube, this volume). One of the most common domains is that of the "house," the features and terminology of which the Maya mapped onto a wide variety of objects and receptacles. The hieroglyphic terms for houses are discussed by David Stuart elsewhere in this volume, but the two relevant labels here are *nah* and *y-otot* or *y-otoch* (depending on the language), the first being a reference to a building and the second, apparently, implying the possession of such a structure, perhaps in the sense of "home" (Barrera Vásquez 1980: 608).[13] A subset of this metaphor includes instances of miniaturization, in which smaller objects used as containers are labeled hieroglyphically and characterized iconographically as "homes." Figure 13 compiles examples of glyphs labeling vessels and dishes as *y-otot,* strongly recalling later Lacandon practice of terming a "god pot" *nahk'uh,* "god house" (Davis n.d.: 223). Of particular interest in the Classic material is a rare expression describing a plate as *u-lak y-otot, u k'inil u chaanil,* "his plate, his house, his sun-thing, his sky-thing," or, in abbreviated form on another plate, "his house, his sun-thing." Here, the reciprocal metaphor probably invoked a cosmological perception of the world as a large plate (Karl Taube, personal communication, 1994). Yet, whatever the context, the linkage of vessels to houses explains some features in Classic Maya ceramic art, ranging from details of roof lids and rims (Coe 1973: pl. 78; Emmerich 1984: pl. 25) to the houselike form of cache vessels, such as those from Quirigua and Guaytan (Fig. 14) (Taube 1994: 652); a separate series of miniature vessels represents the

[13] As David Stuart points out (personal communication, July 1994), there is a perplexing problem with respect to terms for house: although used together in hieroglyphic texts, *na*(*h*) and *y-otot* seem to be mutually exclusive in most lowland Mayan languages, with Cholan using *otot* and Tzeltalan using *na.* The languages that combine both are the Yucatecan, as in Mopan *naj* and *y-otoch* (Ulrich and Ulrich 1976: 149, 297), although Cholti may contain a hint of such usage.

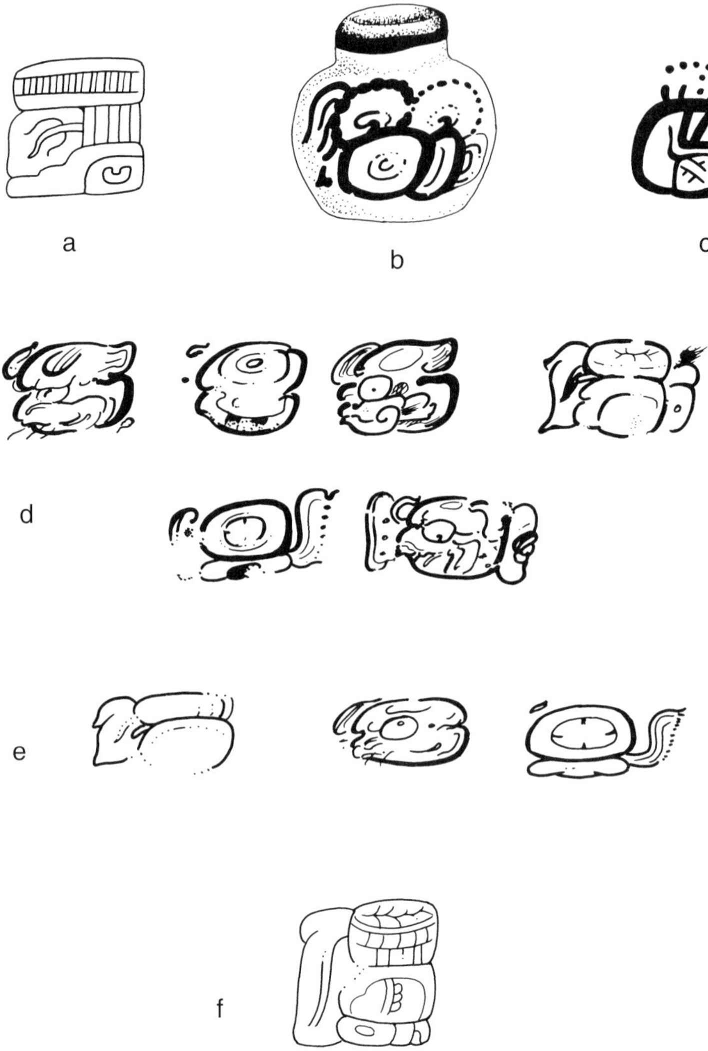

Fig. 13 *y-otot* labels from vessels and other containers: (a) Tikal, fitted lid of blackware vessel (after Kubler 1969: fig. 53); (b) unprovenanced miniature vessel (after Robicsek and Hales 1981: 220); (c) unprovenanced miniature vessel (after Coe 1973: pl. 77); (d) unprovenanced ceramic (after Dumbarton Oaks slide archive dr. 13-LC-p2-162); (e) unprovenanced ceramic (after Dumbarton Oaks slide archive dr. 14-LC-p2-213); (f) unprovenanced, wooden box described as *y-otot* (after preliminary drawing courtesy of David Stuart).

Fig. 14 House model (ceramic box) from Guaytan, Guatemala. Darkened areas indicate paint (after Smith and Kidder 1943: fig. 41c).

sedan chairs of the Classic Maya (Smith and Kidder 1943: fig. 52a).[14] The interplay of cache-vessel imagery and building façades suggests strongly that the house-to-vessel metaphor is fully reciprocal, as is the metaphor of house-to-person (see Taube, this volume; Danziger 1996: 72).

Another subset of reciprocal metaphors appears in tombs, which the Classic Maya consistently describe as "houses" or "homes," in addition to the more explicit terminology of "burials" or, more allusively, "watery holes," probably in reference to the underwater imagery of tombs (Hellmuth 1987: 357; Stuart, this volume). These tombs seem to have had individual names; some even use the term for "house," *nah* (Fig. 15).[15] The metaphor here does not involve miniaturization—a change of scale and dimension—so much as transformation in the nature of the beings that occupy the structure. For example, in the Mixteca

[14] Another reciprocal metaphor, between the human body and ceramic vessels, is explored by Karl Taube in this volume. Lacandon terminology for ceremonial jugs reflects such concepts: the wide opening is called the "head," the side the "face," and clay supports the "feet" (Davis n.d.: 113).

[15] Like a few other signs, the *nah* glyph occasionally violates conventional reading order. Classic scribes preferred to orient the "T" to face to the top or to the left. The examples in Fig. 14 accord with this preference.

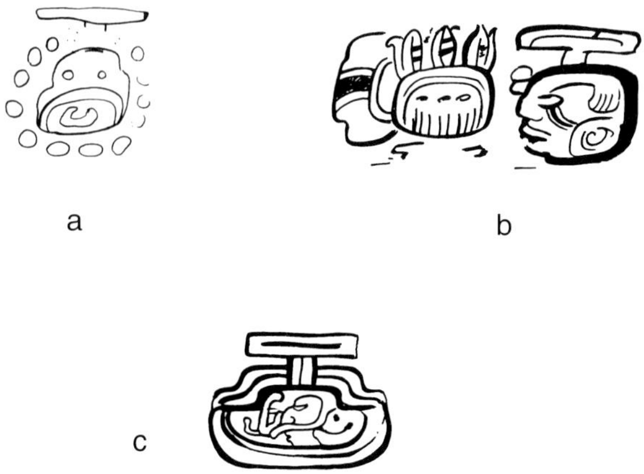

Fig. 15 House names in tombs: (a) Tikal Burial 48 (after Coe 1990: fig. 175); (b) Río Azul Tomb 6 (after drawing courtesy of David Stuart); (c) Río Azul Tomb 23 (after Hall n.d.: fig. 51, with changes from photograph in Adams 1986: 438).

Alta of Mexico, houses often connote moments of transformation and crisis, the house of the dead being the "true house" of the deceased (John Monaghan, personal communication, 1994). Similarly, Classic Maya tombs represent a special kind of house, occupied by entities different in kind from the living. Viewed in this way, the red-painted, vertical glyph bands in some royal tombs may depict doorways, a suggestion strengthened by the fact that the bands, like doorways, usually extend from the floor of the tomb to the springline of the vault (Fig. 16) (Karl Taube, personal communication, June 1994; Chase and Chase 1987: figs. 14 and 23); at Caracol, Belize, such "doorways" appear on the wall opposite the actual entrance to the tomb. Conceivably, the stone house models at Copan embody related concepts. They look like houses and have the same pinched roof and basal platforms as houses, yet the glyphs unambiguously label them as "sleeping places" or "residences" of a god, whose figure fills the doorways in at least two models (Fig. 17) (Andrews and Fash 1992: figs. 16 and 17; Grube and Schele 1990: figs. 2, 3, and 5).

A Cosmological and Political Metaphor

Two other metaphors operate at a broader scale. The first likens the levels of the cosmos—underworld and overworld—to components of buildings, particularly thrones. Most iconographers recognize that thrones may consist of two parts: a sky band on which the ruler or lord sits and, underneath, supports

Fig. 16 Possible representation of doorway at Caracol, Belize, Structure B19-2nd (Chase and Chase 1987: fig. 23).

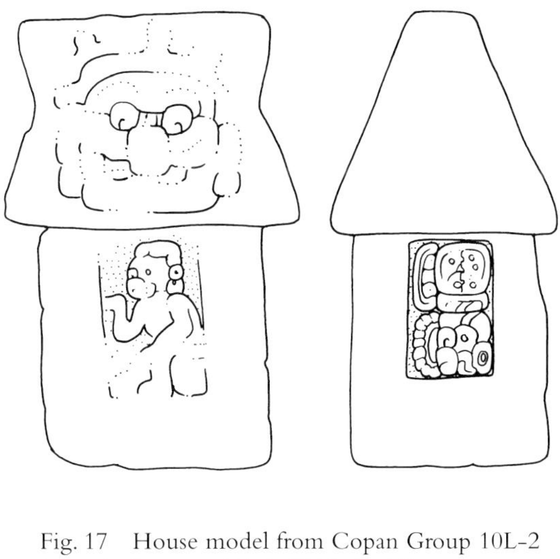

Fig. 17 House model from Copan Group 10L-2 (after Andrews and Fash 1992: fig. 17).

Fig. 18 Pawahtun as house supports. Unprovenanced altar (after drawing by Linda Schele).

in the form of Pawahtun, an Atlantean figure with both aged and youthful aspects and a variety of headdresses. Many of these Pawahtun are associated with the underworld, a connection made especially clear on throne supports from a bench in Copan Structure 9M-146 (Baudez 1994: fig. 112a): the supports appear as firefly Pawahtun, and at least one smokes a cigar, a clear reference to a dark, close, underworld place. An alternative conception of Pawahtun is that they serve as roof supports. An unprovenanced altar in the Dallas Museum of Fine Art and the corners of Structure 11 at Copan show as much (Fig. 18) (Taube n.d.: 113). In explaining this feature, Taube (n.d.: 113) points out that the Classic Maya regard the Pawahtun as the "sustainers of the world." The world-bearers support not only the sky but, through metaphorical extension, the roof of a house or the flat slab of a throne. Again, the symbolism can be

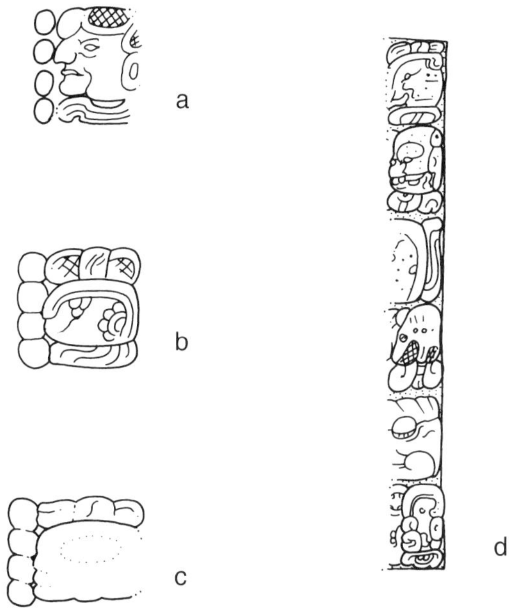

Fig. 19 Pawahtun titles used by subordinate lords. Comparison with text on House E throne support, Palenque: (a) Pomona Panel 1 (after unpublished drawing by Ian Graham); (b) unprovenanced lintel (after materials supplied by David Stuart) ; (c) unprovenanced panel (after Mayer 1978: pl. 53); (d) Palenque House E Throne support, right leg (after photograph in Spinden collection, Peabody Museum, Harvard University, courtesy of David Stuart).

quite elusive. Is the cosmos ordered like a house or the house like the cosmos? The concept of reciprocal metaphor allows us to resolve such questions by acknowledging the indissoluble, almost playful association between semantic domains. To enrich the metaphors further, Maya sculptors injected another dimension by identifying Pawahtun throne supports as specific subordinate lords. A lintel, probably from the vicinity of La Pasadita, Guatemala, shows two such lords, arms upstretched, sustaining two seated figures: Shield Jaguar II of Yaxchilan and his local representative (Mayer 1984: pl. 203). The subordinates have the headdresses of Pawahtun and are explicitly described as such in the accompanying captions (Fig. 19). In using this imagery, the Maya employed another metaphor: the likening of political support by vassals to the role of Pawahtun in buttressing the world (Taube n.d.: 197–200). Similar patterns appear on the throne supports from House E at Palenque that seem quite literally to show subordinate lords impersonating stones (Fig. 19d) (Houston and Stuart 1996: 297–300).

Metaphor in Stairways of Succession

Another reciprocal metaphor is attested in a few hieroglyphic stairways, particularly Hieroglyphic Staxirway 1 from Yaxchilan (Fig. 20), the hieroglyphic stairway of Structure 26 at Copan, and La Amelia Hieroglyphic Stairway 1. All reflect a concern with legitimate succession, insofar as they recapitulate the enthronements of preceding lords (Mathews n.d.: 78–91; Stuart and Schele 1986). The stairways also depict predecessors according to the conventions of ancestral representation, so that some appear within cartouches (Yaxchilan; see McAnany and Houston, this volume), others grasp heads of the god *K'awil* (La Amelia), and still others have smoking tubes in their foreheads (Copan), as though they have come to personify this god. The chronology on two of these stairways—Copan and La Amelia—does not appear to follow a linear time line but rather loops back and forth in blocklike calendrical segments (Stuart and Schele 1986: 10–11). In contrast, the Yaxchilan stairway shows an orderly, sequential arrangement. The latest dates are on the lowest step, and the earliest, clearly referring to the first members of the Yaxchilan dynasty, occur on the top riser. Accordingly, as spectators ascend they move to the beginnings of the royal family; as they descend, they return to contemporary people and events, in a kinetic reexperience of dynastic succession. But how do the stairways involve metaphors? I suspect an explanation may lie in Yucatec sources such as the Motul and San Francisco dictionaries, which document an etymological relationship between *-ts'ak,* "a count of stairs and stairways and other things that go on top of each other" (Motul) or "step or count of steps of parentage or for

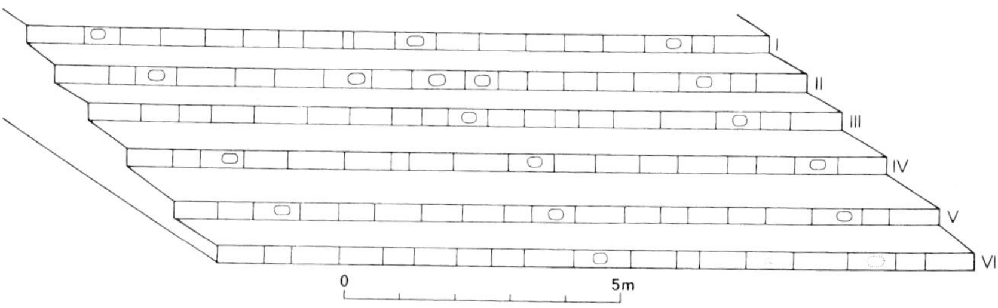

Fig. 20 Axonometric view of Yaxchilan Hieroglyphic Stairway 1. Two medallions on Step II hold ancestral cartouches (after Graham 1982: 141).

things that go on top of each other" (San Francisco) and *ts'akab*, "ancestry, caste, lineage or generation" (Ciudad Real 1984: 123v–124r; Michelon 1976: 455; Barrera Vásquez 1980: 873). Possibly the Maya were making this relationship even more explicit by showing ancestors as stacked stairs.

Conflationary Metaphor in Ballcourt and Stairway Imagery

A final, quite subtle kind of metaphor corresponds to what Mary Miller and I describe as architectural conflation (Houston 1996; Miller and Houston 1987). This metaphor not only establishes a connection between two types of structures but conflates their imagery, producing images that fuse two kinds of building that are involved in two distinct sets of activity. The clearest example is the common depiction of ball playing against stairway risers, possibly the last place to set a latex ball into play, because the ricochet would quickly become uncontrollable. An explanation for this is simply that two related sequences of events—ball playing and the subsequent torture, mutilation, and decapitation of captives—have been merged, along with the architectural setting appropriate to these activities. An especially effective illustration comes from Yaxchilan, Mexico, in which the ball about to be struck by a waiting player contains a flexed, glyphically labeled captive being flung down a stairway. The conflation is metaphorically apt: just as a captive rolls down a stairway, so does a ball carom against the sides of a ballcourt. Another possible example of architectural conflation is the occurrence of apparent symbolic sweatbaths in the Maya lowlands. The heat being generated and the sweat being purged seem to be of an entirely symbolic sort, with the bathers being effigies of gods (Houston 1996). Nonetheless, in this instance the conflation—of sweatbaths and small sanctuaries for the storage and purification of idols—is expressed materially rather than through the device of pictorial convention.

A RANGE OF DEPICTION

With such conventions and metaphors in mind, we can begin to detect—and understand—the principal architectural emphases in the art of the Classic Maya. The largest extant depictions of the built environment comprise clusters of buildings, which may be shown in one of two ways: as three-dimensional models or as frontal views of buildings arranged into plans.[16] Among the best-documented examples of the former is a model of ballcourts, cramped, massed

[16] Representations of cities in murals of Chichen Itza, including those of the Monjas that show attacks on walled cities (Bolles 1977: 202–203), are best left for another study that focuses on later Maya depictions. The same can be said for Post-Classic house models from

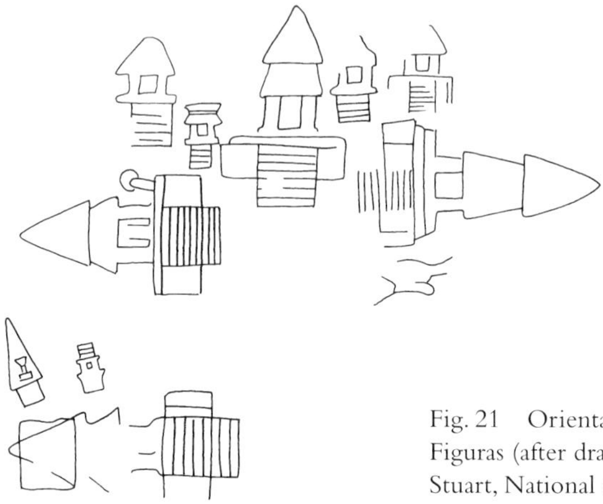

Fig. 21 Orientation plan at Planchon de las Figuras (after drawing courtesy of George Stuart, National Geographic Society).

platforms, chultunes, and access stairways found by Juan Pedro Laporte in the Mundo Perdido complex at Tikal (Laporte and Fialko 1995: fig. 74). It is doubtful that this object records a real landscape or even an architect's model—the grouping of buildings does not correspond to any known configuration at Tikal, and some of the platforms sit improbably close to one another, with one stairway abutting the back of another structure. Of the plans or frontal views, we have the rock carvings at Planchon de las Figuras, Chiapas, Mexico, a large slab of exposed bedrock on the banks of the Lacantun River (Fig. 21) (Bullard 1965: 45–48; Maler 1903: 204–206, fig. 67; Mullerried 1927). According to George Stuart (n.d.), the carvings are rather more than crude productions; their relief is high, and a few have deep depressions in places meant to depict windows.

At Planchon, the arrangement of buildings corresponds to a pattern best described as an orientational plan, which is common to Mesoamerican depictions of courtyards—a good example appears in the colonial Mapa Quinatzin (Radin 1920: pl. 17). Structures flatten out from the center as though viewed from an invisible pivot at the center of a courtyard. Despite the aerial view, the sculptor at Planchon did not stress an accurate depiction from the air so much as a spectator's view at ground level. Samuel Edgerton (1991: 27, 28) notes that such two-dimensional schemata are "natural to the human species," appearing

---

Mayapan (Proskouriakoff 1962: fig. 6) or for depictions of constructional activity—wall plastering and the raising of stone lintels—in the Madrid Codex (pp. 14a, 15a, and 95b). The Madrid provides the only known scenes of construction in the corpus of Maya art: for example, Madrid 14a glosses the image of a deity touching a stone wall as **u-ta-k'(a)/u-sa-s(a),** *u-tak' u sas,* or "he plasters his wall."

in the art of young children as well as many non-Western cultures. Wisely, Edgerton cautions against the use of "naive" to describe such modes of representation, which express not so much "an abstract, uniform system of linear coordinates" (Edgerton 1975: 7)—the essence of renaissance perspective—as an ingenious combination of what James Gibson (cited in Edgerton 1975: 10) describes as the "visual world" and "visual field." These kinds of perception involve different experiences. The visual world recalls our movement and orientation with respect to the ambient environment. It includes what we know to be present, as apprehended and cognized through many senses, not just sight. By contrast, the visual field involves "what we perceive when we fixate with the eyes" (Edgerton 1975: 10). An orientational plan invokes both: glimpses from a fixed vantage point (the "field," the frontal view of a pyramid as seen from the center of a plaza), along with the results of movement and reorientation (the "world," an image combining four different glimpses).[17]

Equally remarkable is a ballcourt model in the northern part of the Planchon slab (Fig. 22a). A groove conducted water from a spring into an I-shaped depression. Another set of petroglyphs from Las Palmas depict ballcourts or depressions, with channels grooved for the flow of water or some other fluid (Fig. 22b; Navarrete, Lee, and Rhoads 1993: figs. 50 and 51). This pattern recalls the drainage lines inscribed on the top of Piedras Negras Altar 4 (Fig. 22c) (Maler 1903: fig. 24), the spiraling conduit on top of a ball effigy at Copan (Baudez 1994: fig. 60), and the ballcourt models from Santoton and Tepancuapan (Navarrete 1984: figs. 89 and 90). Some of the channels connected with ballcourts may reflect the belief, documented in Post-Classic Central Mexico, that the central hole of a court is a "well," a source of water for irrigation (Stern 1949: 65). This is an ancient concept; a rare, Pre-Classic model of a ballcourt from highland Guatemala doubles as a vessel in which water could fill the court and drain into the body of the ceramic (de Borhegyi 1980: fig. 4; Schávelzon 1991: fig. 9). I also speculate that the cupules connected by grooves on the Las Palmas petroglyphs represent the channel and holding tank systems now being documented in Classic Maya cities (Scarborough, Connolly, and Ross 1994: fig. 3). Regrettably, this suggestion is almost impossible to prove, although we can be

[17] Perhaps the most surprising quality of such views is what the Maya chose to represent. For all the modern emphasis on the Classic Maya as denizens of the tropical rainforest, trees or shrubbery seldom appear with images of architecture, which tend to represent a world shaped and domesticated by human artifice. When trees or plants appear, they often occur near scenes of battle, as at Mulchic or Bonampak (Miller 1986: 113, pls. 40, 41; Barrera Rubio 1980: fig. 1). Perhaps this pattern reflects the actual location of battles well outside settled areas, or artists may have associated scenes of strife and discord with uncultivated wilds, in contrast to an orderly landscape occupied by buildings.

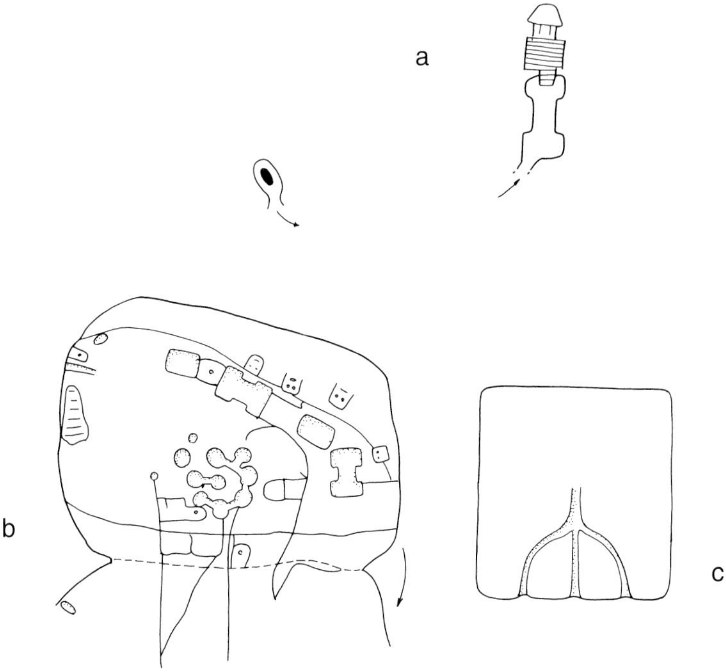

Fig. 22 Ballcourts and conduits for liquids: (a) pecked ballcourt plan, Planchon de las Figuras, Mexico (after drawing courtesy of George Stuart, National Geographic Society); (b) ballcourt petroglyphs, Las Palmas, Mexico (after Navarrete, Lee, and Rhoads 1993: fig. 51); (c) grooves on Piedras Negras Altar 4 (after Maler 1903: fig. 24).

certain that the Lacantun River periodically inundated the Planchon slab, a feature that doubtless attracted the Maya to this spot. One theme stands out in all such evidence: the ritual reproduction or creation of a partly urban, partly agricultural landscape, with particular emphasis on the channeling of fluids. The model terracing and water channels in Post-Classic Central Mexico offer an obvious parallel, as do the grooves and steps in Yucatec caves, where cenote water or solution droplets flow over stepped forms hewn into rock (Miller 1982: figs. 118–120; Thompson 1897: pl. IV).

The next depictions of interest—those recording substructural platforms and ballcourts with stairways—involve a smaller scale than courtyard plans and water systems. Nonetheless, these are the closest the Classic Maya get to showing public spaces with people (the landscapes are completely lacking in human figures). In my opinion, the stepped platforms and ballcourts are profoundly dramaturgical. Erving Goffman (1959) might label these the "fronted" or "inclusive" features of Maya architecture, the places where a dynasty interacts with the outside world in terms set by the court. In many respects, Maya royal stagecraft is precisely the opposite of western practice rooted in Classical theater. Flat areas are the locations for the audience, the ascending levels of a platform mark the place for focal activities, such as the heaping of tribute, the arrangement of visitors or other participants in court ritual, or the display of captive mutilation and sacrifice. The added benefit of such levels is that they place the participants in their appropriate level of verticality vis-à-vis the audience; they also offer concurrent locations for different rituals, so that platforms may show the musical performances and formal address and unwrapping of balls that accompany ball play. Moreover, as Karl Taube (personal communication, 1994) points out, many chambers or passageways near platforms could be interpreted in dramaturgical ways, in that they may have served as dressing chambers or places for the sudden appearance of new actors, as unexpected and crowd-pleasing as any theatrical tricks from the American Northwest coast (Holm 1990: 379, 383). Yet, we should not assign too much weight to the Goffmanesque perspective or dramatic analogy. For one thing, the inner recesses of the palace could hardly be said to lack theatrical aspects or the quality of formal display; they simply hold a reduced number of actors, some of whom also saw the more public spectacles. For another, it could not always have been possible to distinguish rigidly between the actors and members of the audience. Participation, particularly in terms of "structured movement systems" (Kaeppler 1985), probably involved spectators as well, who might have danced in open plazas while dynastic displays took place (Grube 1992; Monaghan 1994: 91).

Most scenes of Maya architecture focus insistently on exterior views, even though interior views may form part of an image. Almost exclusively in use outside permanent buildings were the litters and temporary structures mentioned before. As with many objects, the Maya took pains to indicate the material of construction: some scaffolds with crossbars contain clear hieroglyphic markings of *tah* ("pine"), an appropriately light wood for a portable object; in the same way the Maya would mark a canoe or war dart with the *te* or "wood" sign. But these images are relatively uncommon. The preponderant architectural scene comprises the outlines of a palace room, often placed behind ascending levels of basal platforms. These are the most intimate views of all, for the location is inherently exclusive and the numbers of participants are few. Almost always the viewer is slightly outside the scene, beyond the confines of a palace chamber. Above the throne and most important figures are swagged curtains that define regal space (parasols do not seem to serve the same function, because they tend to accompany musicians). An intriguing fact is the ubiquity of narrative palace scenes in the Late Classic period and their near absence in the Early Classic, when royal figures appear with pillows and thrones but scarcely with any delineation of architecture. I suspect courtly life as an expression of political theater developed to a far greater extent in the Late Classic, a period to which we can date most of the great palace complexes, such as those at Tikal and Palenque. This may also explain the progressive enclosure of space noted by Ledyard Smith (1950: figs. 2–5) in Structure A-V at Uaxactun, where ease of ingress became more difficult through time and, in the jargon of access analysis, the enclosed spaces "deeper" in access diagrams.

The most difficult question about palace scenes has been left for last. Do any depict real buildings or architecturally defined spaces? Despite the formulaic presentations—of rulers and other lordly figures on thrones, with a few platforms levels below them—I suspect that some of the depictions are the regularized and orderly representations of actual buildings. A good illustration of this was excavated by Juan Pedro Laporte in the Mundo Perdido sector of Tikal (Laporte and Fialko 1995: fig. 70): the doorjamb to the side of this dressing scene—doubtless an intimate preparation for a more public event—is described as *ts'ibal-na y-otot bakab,* the "writing house is the house of the bakab." The figures in the scene are clearly historical personages, and the building itself, identified hieroglyphically, is likely to have been an actual location within Tikal or some site nearby. As Mary Miller contends, we can also identify, probably, the location of some of the events depicted on the Bonampak murals of Chiapas, Mexico, because the long, ascending platform levels seem to correspond closely to those fronting the South Acropolis at the site, the locus of the captive mutilation and dances illustrated in Rooms 2 and 3 (Miller 1985). Nonetheless, the scenes have passed through a filter, and it would be a mistake to infer hard architectural data from sanitized and conventionalized imagery.

CONCLUSION

What is clear so far is how imaginative and resourceful the Classic Maya could be in representing their built world. What is just as certain is that layers of reciprocal metaphor, complex pictorial conventions, and historical nuance envelop these images of temples and ballcourts, platforms and palaces. The most common images by far, the palace scenes, exist in architectural settings where the positioning of bodies reflects and verifies the relative ranking of individuals. The palace scenes have little meaning outside of the interactions taking place within them, and it is partly for this reason that architecture seldom appears in anything approaching its true proportions or physical scale relative to the people who used it. In Maya art there exist great limitations to architectural scenes—

a selection carefully made by the Maya themselves, and unlikely to result from problems of modern sampling. The formal variety of Maya architecture—the corridors, the multiroomed buildings, and the complex, involuted basal platforms—is reduced to a surprisingly restricted set of images.

The much-vaunted "naturalism" of Maya art and its attention to details of curtain knots and moldings and specifications of building material belie its essentially formulaic nature, in which idiosyncrasy and deviations from decorum have only a small role. If indulged too far, artistic license would reduce the general intelligibility and garble the lucidity of intended messages about appropriate ritual behavior and relative social station. What remains for the future is to explain the finer points of such decorum and to synthesize available sources for a fuller comprehension of ancient Maya architectural space. Beyond this, our ultimate goal is more ambitious. Depictions may tell us how the Classic Maya saw the built environment, but they provide only one step toward the more vital goal of understanding how that environment was used and why it changed. Other papers in this volume launch toward that goal.

Acknowledgments Elizabeth Boone graciously facilitated the summer seminar and symposium at Dumbarton Oaks that allowed this essay to take shape. During the summer of 1994, the other summer fellows—Nan Gonlin, Tricia McAnany, Karl Taube, and David Webster—contributed immeasurably to the ideas presented here. To Karl Taube go very special thanks for his many insights into Maya iconography; without him this paper could not have been written in its present form. George Stuart of the National Geographic Society showed his usual generosity by sharing his researches at Planchon de las Figuras, as did John Monaghan and John Pohl with their suggestions about Mexican sources, supplemented by comments from two anonymous reviewers. David Stuart was equally generous with his knowledge of Mayan script. Sam Edgerton reminded me of other work on linear perspective and its visual antecedents. The final preparation of this paper was made possible by a grant from the National Endowment for the Humanities (Collaborative Projects, with David Stuart) and with support from Dean Clayne Pope of the College of Family, Home, and Social Sciences, Brigham Young University.

BIBLIOGRAPHY

Adams, Richard E.W.

1986 Río Azul: Lost City of the Maya. *National Geographic* 169: 420–451.

Andrews, E. Wyllys, V, and Barbara W. Fash

1992 Continuity and Change in a Royal Maya Residential Complex at Copan. *Ancient Mesoamerica* 3: 63–88.

Andrews, George F.

1975 *Maya Cities: Placemaking and Urbanization.* University of Oklahoma Press, Norman.

1989 *Comalcalco, Tabasco, Mexico: Maya Art and Architecture.* 2nd ed. Labyrinthos, Culver City, Calif.

Anonymous

1981 Graffito aus Chicanna, Campeche. *Mexicon* 2: 90.

1984 Campeche: Graffiti im Río Bec-Gebiet. *Mexicon* 6: 81.

Aveni, A., and H. Hartung

1986 *Maya City Planning and the Calendar.* Transactions of the American Philosophical Society, vol. 76, pt. 7. Philadelphia.

Barrera Rubio, Alfredo

1980 Mural Paintings of the Puuc Region in Yucatán. In *Third Palenque Round Table, 1978,* pt. 2 (Merle Greene Robertson, ed.): 173–182. University of Texas Press, Austin.

Barrera Vásquez, Alfredo (ed.)

1980 *Diccionario Maya Cordemex: Maya–Español, Español–Maya.* Ediciones Cordemex, Mérida, Yucatan, Mexico.

Baudez, Claude F.

1993 *Jean-Fréderic Waldeck, peintre: le premier explorateur des ruines mayas.* Hazan, Paris.

1994 *Maya Sculpture of Copán: The Iconography.* University of Oklahoma Press, Norman.

Beals, Ralph L., Pedro Carrasco, and Thomas McCorkle

1944 *Houses and House Use of the Sierra Tarascans.* Smithsonian Institution, Institute of Social Anthropology, Publication 1. Washington, D.C.

Billig, Erland

1977 *Spätantike Architekturdarstellungen,* vol. 1. Acta Universitatis Stockholmiensis, Stockholm Studies in Classical Archaeology 10, pt. 1. Stockholm.

Blier, Susan P.

1987 *The Anatomy of Architecture: Ontology and Metaphor in Batammaliba Architectural Expression.* Cambridge University Press, Cambridge.

Bolles, John S.

1977 *Las Monjas: A Major Pre-Mexican Architectural Complex at Chichén Itzá.* University of Oklahoma Press, Norman.

Bullard, William R., Jr.

1965 Ruinas ceremoniales mayas en el curso inferior del Río Lacantun, Mexico. *Estudios de Cultura Maya* 5: 41–51.

Carpenter, Rhys

1962 *Greek Art: A Study of the Formal Evolution of Style.* University of Pennsylvania Press, Philadelphia.

Carsten, Janet, and Stephen Hugh-Jones

1995 Introduction. In *About the House: Lévi-Strauss and Beyond* (Janet Carsten and Stephen Hugh-Jones, eds.): 1–46. Cambridge University Press, Cambridge.

Chase, Arlen F., and Diane Z. Chase

1987 *Investigations at the Classic Maya City of Caracol, Belize, 1985–1987.* Monograph 3. Pre-Columbian Art Research Institute, San Francisco.

Ciudad Real, Antonio de

1984 *Calepino maya de Motul.* 2 vols. Universidad Nacional Autónoma de México, México, D.F.

Coe, Michael D.

1965 *The Jaguar's Children: Pre-Classic Central Mexico.* Museum of Primitive Art, New York.

1973 *The Maya Scribe and His World.* Grolier Club, New York.

1978 *Lords of the Underworld: Masterpieces of Classic Maya Ceramics.* Princeton University Press, Princeton, N.J.

Coe, William R.

1967 *Tikal: A Handbook of the Ancient Maya Ruins.* University Museum, University of Pennsylvania, Philadelphia.

1990 *Excavations in the Great Plaza, North Terrace and North Acropolis.* 6 vols. Tikal Report, no. 14. University Museum Monograph 61. University of Pennsylvania, Philadelphia.

Coggins, Clemency C.

n.d. Painting and Drawing Styles at Tikal: An Historical and Iconographic Reconstruction. Ph.D. dissertation, Harvard University, 1975.

Cook de Leonard, Carmen

1955 Una maqueta prehispánica. *El México Antiguo* 8: 169–191.

Corson, Christopher

1976 *Maya Anthropomorphic Figurines from Jaina Island, Campeche.* Ballena Press, Ramona, Calif.

Danziger, Eve

1996 Parts and Their Counterparts: Spatial and Social Relationships in Mopan Maya. *Journal of the Royal Anthropological Institute* 2: 67–82.

Davis, Virginia D.

n.d. Ritual of the Northern Lacandon Maya. Ph.D. dissertation, Tulane University, 1978.

de Borhegyi, Stephan F.

1980 *The Pre-Columbian Ballgames: A Pan-Mesoamerican Tradition.* Contributions in Anthropology and History, no. 1. Milwaukee Public Museum, Milwaukee, Wis.

DONALDSON, THOMAS L.
1965 *Architectura Numismatica: Ancient Architecture on Greek and Roman Coins and Medals.* Argonaut, Chicago.

DOUGLAS, MARY
1972 Symbolic Orders in the Use of Domestic Space. In *Man, Settlement and Urbanism* (Peter Ucko, Ruth Tringham, and G. W. Dimbleby, eds.): 513–521. Duckworth, London.

DOXIADIS, CONSTANTINOS A.
1972 *Architectural Space in Ancient Greece* (J. Tyrwhitt, trans. and ed.). MIT Press, Cambridge, Mass.

EDGERTON, SAMUEL Y., JR.
1975 *The Renaissance Rediscovery of Linear Perspective.* Basic Books, New York.
1991 *The Heritage of Giotto's Geometry: Art and Science on the Eve of the Scientific Revolution.* Cornell University Press, Ithaca, N.Y.

EGGEBRECHT, ARNE (ED.)
1987 *Les Azteques: Trésors du Mexique ancien.* 2 vols. Roemer- und Pelizaeus-Museum, Hildesheim, Germany.

EKHOLM, GORDON F.
1946 The Probable Use of Mexican Stone Yokes. *American Anthropologist* 48: 593–606.

EMMERICH, ANDRÉ
1984 *Masterpieces of Pre-Columbian Art from the Collection of Mr. & Mrs. Peter G. Wray.* André Emmerich Gallery and Perls Galleries, New York.

FEELEY-HARNIK, GILLIAN
1985 Issues in Divine Kingship. *Annual Review of Anthropology* 14: 273–313.

FOSTER, SALLY M.
1989 Analysis of Spatial Patterns in Buildings (Access Analysis) as an Insight into Social Structure: Examples from the Scottish Atlantic Iron Age. *Antiquity* 63: 40–50.

GARZA TARAZONA, SILVIA
1970 *Nomencladores: Catálogo de representaciones arquitectónicas en códices mixtecos.* Antropología Matemática 16. Museo Nacional de Antropología, México, D.F.

GAY, CARLO, AND FRANCES PRATT
1992 *Mezcala: Ancient Stone Sculpture from Guerrero, Mexico.* Balsas Publications, Geneva.

GOFFMAN, ERVING
1959 *The Presentation of Self in Everyday Life.* Doubleday, New York.

GOLDSTEIN, MARILYN M.
1980 Relationships between the Figurines of Jaina and Palenque. In *Third Palenque Round Table, 1978,* pt. 2 (Merle Greene Robertson, ed.): 91–98. University of Texas Press, Austin.

GRAHAM, IAN
1982 *Corpus of Maya Hieroglyphic Inscriptions,* vol. 3, pt. 3: *Yaxchilan.* Peabody Museum of Archaeology and Ethnology, Harvard University, Cambridge, Mass.

GRAHAM, IAN, AND ERIC VON EUW
1977 *Corpus of Maya Hieroglyphic Inscriptions,* vol. 3, pt. 1: *Yaxchilan.* Peabody Museum of Archaeology and Ethnology, Harvard University, Cambridge, Mass.

GRUBE, NIKOLAI
1992 Classic Maya Dance: Evidence from Hieroglyphs and Iconography. *Ancient Mesoamerica* 3: 201–218.

GRUBE, NIKOLAI, AND LINDA SCHELE
1990 *Royal Gifts to Subordinate Lords.* Copán Note 87. Copán Mosaics Project, Instituto Hondureño de Antropología e Historia, Copan Ruinas, Honduras.

GUTHRIE, STEWART
1993 *Faces in the Clouds: A New Theory of Religion.* Oxford University Press, Oxford.

HALL, GRANT D.
n.d. Realm of Death: Royal Mortuary Customs and Polity Interaction in the Classic Maya Lowlands. Ph.D. dissertation, Harvard University, 1989.

HANKS, WILLIAM F.
1990 *Referential Practice: Language and Lived Space among the Maya.* University of Chicago Press, Chicago.

HARTUNG, HORST
1980 Certain Visual Relations in the Palace at Palenque. In *Third Palenque Round Table, 1978,* pt. 2 (Merle Greene Robertson, ed.): 74–80. University of Texas Press, Austin.
1984 El tablero de Oaxaca: Notas sobre un elemento arquitectónico precolombino. *Cuadernos de Arquitectura Mesoamericana* 2: 67–74.

HELLMUTH, NICHOLAS M.
1987 *Monster und Menschen in der Maya-Kunst: Eine Ikonographie der alten Religionen Mexikos und Guatemalas.* Akademische Druck- u. Verlagsanstalt, Graz, Austria.

HENIG, MARTIN
1990 A House for Minerva: Temples, Aedicula Shrines, and Signet Rings. In *Architecture and Architectural Sculpture in the Roman Empire* (Martin Henig, ed.): 152–162. Oxford Committee for Archaeology, Monograph 29. Oxford.

HERMES, B., AND G. GALINDO
1993 Investigation of Structure 216 of Yaxhá. *Mexicon* 14 (4): 66–67.

HOHMANN, HASSO
1995 *Die Architekture der Sepulturas: Region von Copan in Honduras.* Akademische Druck- u. Verlagsanstalt, Graz, Austria.

HOLM, BILL
1990 Kwakiutl: Winter Ceremonies. In *Handbook of North American Indians,* vol. 7: *Northwest Coast* (Wayne Suttles, ed.): 378–386. Smithsonian Institution Press, Washington, D.C.

HOUSTON, STEPHEN D.
1996 Symbolic Sweatbaths of the Maya: Architectural Meaning in the Cross Group at Palenque, Mexico. *Latin American Antiquity* 7: 132–151.

HOUSTON, STEPHEN D., AND DAVID STUART
1996 Of Gods, Glyphs, and Kings: Divinity and Rulership among the Classic Maya.

Antiquity 70: 289–312.

n.d. The Presentation of Self in Royal Life: Personhood and Portraiture among the Classic Maya. Manuscript on file, Department of Anthropology, Brigham Young University.

JONES, CHRISTOPHER

1985 The Rubber Ball Game: A Universal Mesoamerican Sport. *Expedition* 27 (2): 44–52.

KAEPPLER, ADRIENNE

1985 Structured Movement Systems in Tonga. In *Society and the Dance* (Paul Spencer, ed.): 92–118. Cambridge University Press, Cambridge.

KERR, JUSTIN

1989 *The Maya Vase Book: A Corpus of Rollout Photographs of Maya Vases,* vol. 1. Kerr Associates, New York.

1990 *The Maya Vase Book: A Corpus of Rollout Photographs of Maya Vases,* vol. 2. Kerr Associates, New York.

1992 *The Maya Vase Book: A Corpus of Rollout Photographs of Maya Vases,* vol. 3. Kerr Associates, New York.

KING, MARK B.

n.d. Reconstructing Mixtec Ideology: The Symbolism of Gender and Agriculture. Paper presented at the Fifty-Ninth Annual Meeting of the Society for American Archaeology, Anaheim, April 1994.

KOWALSKI, JEFF K.

1987 *The House of the Governor: A Maya Palace at Uxmal, Yucatan, Mexico.* University of Oklahoma Press, Norman.

KRICKEBERG, WALTER

1969 *Felsplastik und Felsbilder bei den kulturvölkern Altamerikas mit besonderer berücksichtigung Mexicos,* vol. 2: *Felsbilder Mexicos als historische, religiöse und Kunstdenkmäler.* Verlag von Dietrich Reimer, Berlin.

KUBLER, GEORGE

1969 *Studies in Classic Maya Iconography.* Memoirs of the Connecticut Academy of Arts and Sciences, vol. 18. New Haven.

LAKOFF, GEORGE

1987 *Women, Fire, and Dangerous Things: What Categories Reveal about the Mind.* University of Chicago Press, Chicago.

LAPORTE, JUAN PEDRO, AND VILMA FIALKO

1995 Reencuentro con Mundo Perdido, Tikal, Guatemala. *Ancient Mesoamerica* 6: 41–94.

LAUGHLIN, ROBERT M.

1993 Poetic License. In *The Flowering of Man: A Tzotzil Botany of Zinacantán,* vol. 1 (Dennis E. Breedlove and Robert M. Laughlin): 101–108. Smithsonian Contributions to Anthropology 35. Smithsonian Institution Press, Washington, D.C.

LAWRENCE, DENISE L., AND SETHA M. LOW

1990 The Built Environment and Spatial Form. *Annual Review of Anthropology* 19: 453–505.

LEACH, ELEANOR W.

1988 *The Rhetoric of Space: Literacy and Artistic Representations of Landscape in Republican and Augustan Rome.* Princeton University Press, Princeton, N.J.

LEHMANN, HENRI

1964 Maisons de céramique (Nayarit, Mexique). *Objets et Mondes* 4 (2): 107–118.

LEYENAAR, TED J. J., AND LEE A. PARSONS

1988 *Ulama: The Ballgame of the Mayas and Aztecs, 2000 B.C.–A.D. 2000: From Human Sacrifice to Sport.* Spruyt, Van Mantgem, and De Does, Leiden, Netherlands.

LÓPEZ AUSTIN, ALFREDO

1988 *The Human Body and Ideology: Concepts of the Ancient Nahuas,* vol. 1. University of Utah Press, Salt Lake City.

MALER, TEOBERT

1903 *Researches in the Central Portion of the Usumatsintla Valley.* Memoirs of the Peabody Museum of Archaeology and Ethnology, vol. 2, no. 2. Harvard University, Cambridge, Mass.

MATHEWS, PETER L.

n.d. The Sculpture of Yaxchilan. Ph.D. dissertation, Yale University, 1988.

MAYER, KARL HERBERT

1978 *Maya Monuments: Sculptures of Unknown Provenance in Europe.* Acoma Books, Ramona, Calif.

1981 *Classic Maya Relief Columns.* Acoma Books, Ramona, Calif.

1984 *Maya Monuments: Sculptures of Unknown Provenance in Middle America.* Verlag Karl-Friedrich von Flemming, Berlin.

MEIGHAN, CLEMENT W. (ED.)

1976 *Monumenta Archaeologica,* vol. 2: *The Archaeology of Amapa, Nayarit.* Institute of Archaeology, University of California, Los Angeles.

MICHELON, OSCAR (ED.)

1976 *Diccionario de San Francisco.* Bibliotheca Linguistica Americana, vol. 2. Akademische Druck- u. Verlagsanstalt, Graz, Austria.

MILLER, ARTHUR G.

1982 *On the Edge of the Sea: Mural Painting at Tancah-Tulum, Quintana Roo, Mexico.* Dumbarton Oaks, Washington, D.C.

MILLER, MARY E.

1985 The Architectural Backdrops of the Murals of Structure 1, Bonampak. In *Fourth Palenque Round Table, 1980* (Elizabeth P. Benson, ed.): 185–191. Pre-Columbian Art Research Institute, San Francisco.

1986 *The Murals of Bonampak.* Princeton University Press, Princeton, N.J.

MILLER, MARY E., AND STEPHEN D. HOUSTON

1987 The Classic Maya Ballgame and Its Architectural Setting: A Study of Relations between Text and Image. *RES: Anthropology and Aesthetics* 14: 46–65.

MONAGHAN, JOHN

1994 The Text in the Body, the Body in the Text: The Embodied Sign in Mixtec Writing. In *Writing without Words: Alternative Literacies in Mesoamerica and the Andes* (Elizabeth H. Boone and Walter D. Mignolo, eds.): 87–101. Duke

University Press, Durham, N.C.

Mullerried, Federico K. G.
1927 El llamado planchon de las figuras, en el estado de Chiapas. *Revista Mexicana de Estudios Históricos* 1 (6): 235–243.

Navarrete, Carlos
1984 *Guía para el estudio de los monumentos esculpidos de Chinkultic, Chiapas.* Universidad Nacional Autónoma de México, México, D.F.

Navarrete, Carlos, Thomas A. Lee, Jr., and Carlos Silva Rhoads
1993 *Un catálogo de frontera: Esculturas, petroglifos y pinturas de la región media del Grijalva, Chiapas.* Universidad Nacional Autónoma de México, México, D.F.

Orrego Corzo, Miguel, and Rudy Larios Villalta
1983 *Reporte de las investigaciones arqueológicas en el grupo 5E-11.* Parque Nacional Tikal, Instituto de Antropología e Historia de Guatemala, Ministerio de Educación, Guatemala City.

Pearson, Michael Parker, and Colin Richards
1994 Ordering the World: Perceptions of Architecture, Space and Time. In *Architecture and Order: Approaches to Social Space* (Michael P. Pearson and Colin Richards, eds.): 1–37. Routledge, London.

Pedley, John G.
1987 Reflections of Architecture in Sixth-Century Attic Vase-Painting. In *Papers on the Amasis Painter and His World* (A. P. A. Belloli, ed.): 63–80. J. Paul Getty Museum, Malibu, Calif.

Pendergast, David M.
1969 *Altun Ha, British Honduras (Belize): The Sun God's Tomb.* Art and Archaeology, Occasional Paper 19. Royal Ontario Museum, Toronto.

Pérez Campos, Elizabeth M. (ed.)
1992 *Comalcalco.* Instituto Nacional de Antropología e Historia, México, D.F.

Pincemin, Sophia, and Mauricio Rosas
1985 Representaciones arquitectónicas en los códices mayas. *Cuadernos de Arquitectura Mesoamericana* 6: 87–90.

Price, Martin J., and Bluma L. Trell
1972 *Coins of Greece, Rome, and Palestine.* Vecchi, London.

Proskouriakoff, Tatiana
1962 Part 4: The Artifacts of Mayapan. In *Mayapan, Yucatan, Mexico* (H. E. D. Pollock, ed.): 321–442. Carnegie Institution, Publication 619. Washington, D.C.

Radin, Paul
1920 *The Sources and Authenticity of the History of the Ancient Mexicans.* University of California Publications in American Archaeology and Ethnology, vol. 17, no. 1. Berkeley.

Richter, Gisela M. A.
1969 *A Handbook of Greek Art.* Phaidon, London.

Robertson, Donald
1959 *Mexican Manuscript Painting of the Early Colonial Period: The Metropolitan Schools.*

Yale University Press, New Haven, Conn.

Robicsek, Francis, and Donald M. Hales
1981 *The Maya Book of the Dead: The Ceramic Codex.* University of Oklahoma Press, Norman.

Roys, Ralph L. (trans.)
1965 *Ritual of the Bacabs.* University of Oklahoma Press, Norman.

Ruppert, Karl, and John H. Denison, Jr.
1943 *Archaeological Reconnaissance in Campeche, Quintana Roo, and Peten.* Carnegie Institution, Publication 543. Washington, D.C.

Scarborough, Vernon L., Robert P. Connolly, and Steven P. Ross
1994 The Pre-Hispanic Maya Reservoir System at Kinal, Peten, Guatemala. *Ancient Mesoamerica* 5: 97–106.

Schávelzon, Daniel
1991 Nuevas consideraciones sobre representaciones mayas de arquitectura. *Cuadernos de Arquitectura Mesoamericana* 15: 75–87.

Schávelzon, Daniel (ed.)
1982 *Las representaciones de arquitectura en la arqueología de América,* vol. 1. Universidad Nacional Autónoma de México, México, D.F.

Schele, Linda, and Mary E. Miller
1986 *The Blood of Kings: Dynasty and Ritual in Maya Art.* George Braziller, New York, and Kimbell Art Museum, Fort Worth, Tex.

Smith, A. Ledyard
1950 *Uaxactun, Guatemala: Excavations of 1931–1937.* Carnegie Institution, Publication 588. Washington, D.C.

Smith, A. Ledyard, and A.V. Kidder
1943 *Explorations in the Motagua Valley, Guatemala.* Contributions to American Anthropology and History, no. 41. Carnegie Institution, Washington, D.C.

Smith, Mary E.
1973 *Picture Writing from Ancient Southern Mexico: Mixtec Place Signs and Maps.* University of Oklahoma Press, Norman.

Solís Olguín, Felipe
1982 *La civilización azteca.* Museo de Nagoya, Nagoya, Japan.
1992 Evidencias arqueológicas de la prática del juego de pelota en la antigua México-Tenochtitlan. In *El juego de pelota en Mesoamérica: Raíces y supervivencia* (María Teresa Uriarte, coord.): 143–155. Colección América Nuestra, América Antigua, 39. Siglo Veintiuno, México, D.F.

Stern, Theodore
1949 *The Rubber-Ball Games of the Americas.* Monographs of the American Ethnological Society, no. 17. University of Washington Press, Seattle.

Stuart, David, and Linda Schele
1986 *Interim Report on the Hieroglyphic Stair of Structure 26.* Copan Note 87. Copán Mosaics Project, Instituto Hondureño de Antropología e Historia, Copan Ruinas, Honduras.

STUART, GEORGE
n.d. Letter to Flora Clancy, November 11, 1986. Manuscript on file, National Geographic Society, Washington, D.C.

TAUBE, KARL A.
1988 A Study of Classic Maya Scaffold Sacrifice. In *Maya Iconography* (Elizabeth P. Benson and Gillett G. Griffin, eds.): 331–351. Princeton University Press, Princeton, N.J.
1994 The Birth Vase: Natal Imagery in Ancient Maya Myth and Ritual. In *The Maya Vase Book,* vol. 4 (Justin Kerr, ed.): 652–685. Kerr Associates, New York.
n.d. The Ancient Yucatec New Year Festival: The Liminal Period in Maya Ritual and Cosmology. Ph.D. dissertation, Yale University, 1988.

THOMPSON, EDWARD H.
1897 *Cave of Loltun, Yucatan.* Memoirs of the Peabody Museum of American Archaeology and Ethnology, vol. 1, no. 2. Harvard University, Cambridge, Mass.

TOWNSEND, RICHARD F.
1992 *The Aztecs.* Thames and Hudson, London.

TRIK, HELEN, AND MICHAEL E. KAMPEN
1983 *The Graffiti of Tikal.* Tikal Report, no. 31. University Museum Monograph 57. University of Pennsylvania, Philadelphia.

ULRICH, MATEO, AND ROSEMARY DE ULRICH
1976 *Diccionario bilingüe: Maya Mopán y Español, España y Maya Mopán.* Instituto Lingüístico de Verano, Guatemala City.

VALLOIS, H.
1908 Etude sur les formes architecturales dans les peintures de vases grecs. *Revue archéologique* 11: 359–390.

VON WINNING, HASSO, AND OLGA HAMMER
1972 *Anecdotal Sculpture of Ancient West Mexico.* Ethnic Arts Council of Los Angeles, Los Angeles.

WAUCHOPE, ROBERT
1938 *Modern Maya Houses: A Study of Their Archaeological Significance.* Carnegie Institution, Publication 502. Washington, D.C.
1940 Domestic Architecture of the Maya. In *The Maya and Their Neighbors: Essays on Middle American Anthropology and Archaeology* (C. L. Hay et al., eds.): 232–241. Appleton-Century, New York.

YADEUN, JUAN
1993 *Toniná.* El Equilibrista, México, D.F.

"The Fire Enters His House": Architecture and Ritual in Classic Maya Texts

DAVID STUART
HARVARD UNIVERSITY

HIEROGLYPHIC INSCRIPTIONS were frequent embellishments on Maya architecture. At Palenque, to cite a familiar example, nearly all the extant texts come from wall panels, piers, façades, or stairways. At Copan, as well, few buildings of the principal acropolis were without some sort of inscription. Prominent texts on stelae and altars, usually placed before structures or in ceremonial courtyards, were themselves integral components of the built environment. It is therefore reasonable to suspect that the monumental texts might have something to say about the activities that took place in and around buildings and about the conceptions the Maya themselves held about their own social and ritual space. The present paper analyzes many of the architectural references in Maya texts and pays particular attention to the records of building dedications and their associated ceremonies.

The present discussion is necessarily limited to those sites with hieroglyphic texts, but it should be remembered that numerous Maya centers of the Classic period, particularly in the north and central areas, show an apparent disinterest in public inscriptions. The varied distribution of texts may well reflect different cultures of scribal behavior, with some places simply less concerned, for whatever reason, with the public display of writing and its associated iconography. Alternatively, the differences might simply be because of poor preservation. Chenes-style buildings of the central lowlands, for example, were sometimes painted with hieroglyphic texts, as I observed in 1991 on the west side of Structure II at Chicanna—oddly, the glyphs are not mentioned by Potter (1977: 65–68). The destruction of the thin plaster veneers on these structures conceivably could have obliterated a great many glyphs. It also must be remembered that many texts from northern sites occur on door lintels or columns, and others may await discovery with further architectural excavation. The text-rich southern centers of Palenque, Yaxchilan, Piedras Negras, and Copan, among others, have a great many well-preserved architectural inscriptions, and they will naturally be a focus of the present study.

In a telling passage from his *Relación de las cosas de Yucatán,* Bishop Landa describes the preconquest Maya custom of placing written texts on buildings:

> In either of the two months of Chen or Yax and on the day which the priest set, they celebrated a festival, which they called *Oc Na,* which means the renovation of the temple in the honor of the Chacs, whom they regarded as the gods of the cornfields; and in this festival . . . they renewed their idols of clay and their braziers; for it was the custom that each idol should have its little brazier in which they should burn their incense to it; and, if it was necessary, they rebuilt the house, or renovated it, and they placed on the wall the memorial of these things, written in their characters. (Tozzer 1941:161)

Few of the inscribed "memorials" Landa mentions have survived from the Post-Classic era, although the painted glyphs from the façade mural of the "Las Pinturas" temple at Coba may be one well-preserved example (Fettweiss 1988: pl. VIII). Nevertheless, as I hope to demonstrate with the aid of new decipherments, numerous Classic period texts seem to commemorate rites of house renewal and renovation, much as Landa describes.

THE PRIMACY OF DEDICATION TEXTS IN MAYA INSCRIPTIONS

Despite the numerous regional styles and genres of Maya writing, most surviving inscriptions of the Classic period can be classified as "dedication texts," meaning those inscriptions that, in part or as a whole, record or commemorate the ownership or manufacture of venerated things (Stuart n.d.a). For example, short inscriptions on stelae usually commemorate the erection of these monuments, called *lakamtun,* or "banner stone," in the singular (Stuart and Houston 1994: 30, 37). Glyphs on pottery seem to be similarly oriented, referring to the function and manufacture of vessels and naming their owners (Stuart 1989; Houston, Stuart, and Taube 1989). The essential function of such dedication texts is to mark the political, social, or ritual activation of an object or monument.

To claim that dedicatory texts constitute the true emphasis of Classic Maya inscriptions contradicts much received wisdom. The ancient documents, it is often said, served primarily as vehicles for royal political history and little else

(Marcus 1992). Although records of life events of rulers and their associates are commonplace in the texts, we would be mistaken to conclude that the commemoration of royal life history was the only reason for composing public inscriptions. Rather, looking at the internal structure of inscriptions, it becomes apparent that texts usually single out a particular event or episode as a narrative focus (Josserand 1991, 1995), very often placed at the end of a text. These highlighted passages and the featured events are usually statements of dedication, with other historical information providing a context for the culminating dedicatory event. I venture to suggest, therefore, that the essential purpose of most monumental texts of Classic times was not simply to record royal life history but rather to record the activities surrounding the placement, creation, and activation of ritual things and spaces. Instead of relegating "history" to a secondary concern of the texts, however, it might be more precise to say that, within Maya perceptions of historical reality, dedication events were among the most important of events worthy of permanent record (Stuart n.d.a).

Perhaps the best known and largest category of dedication texts is the formulaic inscription painted or carved on pottery, what Coe (1973) originally called the "Primary Standard Sequence," or PSS (Stuart 1989). As noted above, most pottery texts, in their most common form, work as simple ownership statements, "so-and-so's drinking vessel for fruity cacao" being a typical example (Stuart 1989; Houston, Stuart, and Taube 1989). Other types of objects and monuments, ranging from bone needles to stelae to temple pyramids, are "owned" by named persons or supernaturals in much the same way. The famous inscribed bones from Burial 116 at Tikal, for example, carry a variety of different texts, but many share the essential statement "the bone of Hasaw Kaan K'awil (Ruler A)." The marking of personal property, it would seem, was a major concern among Classic Maya elites.

But dedicatory texts were often more than simple name tags. In many instances, a verb or verb phrase is usually part of such texts, specifying the ritual acts performed on or around the object, monument, or building. Many of these so-called dedication events have remained difficult to decipher, perhaps the most important being the God N or "step" verb of the PSS (MacLeod 1990), to be discussed below at some length. Other glyphs are more transparent, such as the common event deciphered by Grube (1990) as *ts'ap,* with the Cholan meaning "to plant in the ground." This is routinely used to refer to the dedications of stelae, as in the oft-repeated phrase *ts'ap-ah u-lakamtun,* "his banner stone (stela) is planted." Other dedicatory events probably refer in a similar fashion to the physical placement or positioning of an object or monument. Others, as I hope to demonstrate below, describe the more ritualistic activities performed to sanctify them. Such hieroglyphic statements, with their strong affinities to ethnographically recorded customs, are important in the study of many aspects of ancient Maya political, economic, and ritual behavior.

"HOUSE" GLYPHS AND OTHER ARCHITECTURAL TERMS

Before delving into the meanings of architectural dedication ceremonies as recorded in the inscriptions, it is first necessary to review some essential features of Maya architectural vocabulary from the Classic period. Numerous terms have been identified over the past several years, many of which are little different from words in modern Mayan languages. Needless to say, this Classic terminology forms an essential backdrop for the study of how the Maya defined and conceived of their own built environment.

First and foremost are two widespread words for "house," *nah* and *otot* (as they were apparently pronounced in Classic times). Today, some languages use only one or the other as a general reference for house, as in Greater Tzeltalan *na* and Cholan *otot.* Yucatecan languages, however, use both, with some distinction in their usage (Hanks 1990: 91). *Nah* is by far the more general term, meaning "building" or "structure" (as in *popol nah,* "council building"), although it may often carry the specific meaning "house" or "household group" (*u-nah-il Pedro,* "Pedro's house"). Yucatec *otoch,* cognate to Cholan *otot,* more specifically conveys the notion of "dwelling" or "domicile," for it is an inherently possessed noun, meaning that it is always prefixed by a possessive pronoun—*inw-otoch,* "my home," *(u)y-otoch-ob,* "their homes," etc. Significantly, the inscriptions of the Classic period employ both terms *nah,* "structure," and *otot,* "dwelling," in very much the same way as found in Classical and modern Yucatec (Classical Cholti may have used both terms as well, but this has to be confirmed). The general distinction between *nah* and *otot* is found also in Nahuatl, where *calli,* sometimes "house," carries the broader significance "structure" (*petla-calli,* "basket," literally a "mat-structure"; *a-calli,* "boat," literally a "water-structure"), and *chantli* is the specific, inherently possessed term for "home, dwelling."

As with most words appearing in Maya inscriptions, terms such as *nah* and *otot* may be spelled by means of a variety of hieroglyphic signs. The word sign (logograph) for **NAH** is a youthful head with a barlike element protruding from the front of the face, but this is customarily abbreviated by omitting the head altogether (Fig. 1, top row). This sign, as one might expect, is commonly used in designations and proper names for structures, such as **NIK-TE'-NAH,** for *nikte' nah,* literally "flower building," a name for a type of council house or community structure mentioned in several Late Classic sources (Stephen Houston, personal communication, 1991). Sometimes we find the **-hi** syllable as an

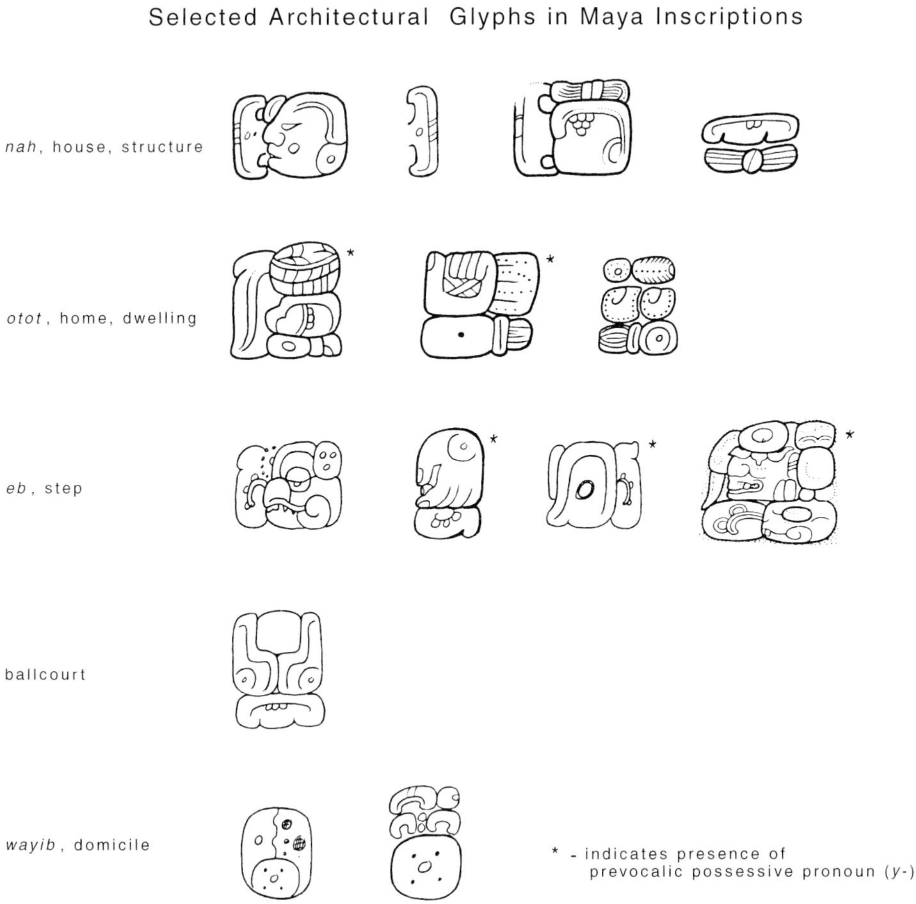

Fig. 1 Architectural glyphs and related terms.

optional phonetic complement, producing **NAH-hi.** Also, in later texts, the word may be spelled with the two phonetic signs (each in various forms) **na-hi.**

Likewise *otot* has its many variants (Fig. 1, second row). The basic form is a representation of a thatched structure atop a squat platform, much like "house" glyphs from Central Mexico (Stuart 1987). The straightforward iconic origin of the glyph is most clear in early examples, for by Late Classic times the form of the glyph came to be less naturalistically rendered and ultimately reanalyzed into rather abstract-looking elements.[1] Prefixed to the **OTOT** logograph, both

[1] In previous discussions of the **OTOT** glyph, the lower platform element has been mistaken as a separate phonetic sign. Fox and Justeson (1984: 63), for example, interpreted

in early and late examples, is the syllable **yo-** (Stuart 1987). The initial *y-* provides the prevocalic pronoun for *y-otot,* "his/her home." On very rare occasions in Early Classic texts, the prefix to this house glyph is **ya-,** indicating an alternative pronunciation *y-atot,* a form found in Proto-Mayan **atyooty* (Kaufman and Norman 1984: 127). Also common is the complementary suffix **-ti,** which also occurs in the fully phonetic versions spelled **yo-to-ti,** found at Palenque and Chichen Itza, among a few other sites. Finally, one spelling, **yo-to-che** from Xcalumkin (Column 4, A3a) probably indicates the Yucatec form *(u)y-otoch.* If this reading is correct, it would represent one of only a handful of cases in which phonological distinctions between Maya languages are reflected in ancient spellings.

The term *otot* is ubiquitous in Classic texts, and, given its literal significance as "home, dwelling," the natural temptation exists to interpret the buildings with which it is directly associated as elite residential structures. Although this may be a correct inference in a few select cases, it generally is not possible to assume such an interpretation. To cite one example, House E of Palenque Palace, apparently known in ancient times as the Sak Nuk Nah, "White Big House," is specificed as the *otot* of the great ruler K'inich Hanab Pakal (or "Pakal," as he is often known) in the inscription of the Tablet of the 96 Glyphs. House E was, in fact, a throne room associated with this king and several of his successors, even though it was called Pakal's bulding long after his death. Nonresidential structures of specialized ritual function, it would seem from this and other cases, were dubbed *otot* and were seemingly "owned," over the course of centuries, by the individuals who built them. Several other *otot* structures in the Palenque Palace are linked to Pakal's name.

Aside from the two common terms for "house," a number of more specific types of architectural terms occur in the inscriptions. The apparent glyph for "ballcourt" was identified some years ago by Houston (Miller and Houston 1987). There can be little doubt of its significance, as the sign represents the two sides of a playing alley (Fig 1, fourth row), although the phonetic reading of the sign remains unclear. Select cases of the sign have the suffixes **-na** and **-ni,** indicating a word ending in *-n.* The ballcourt sign occurs in a variety of texts, many of which, again, label ballcourts or architectural features likened to ballcourts with the name of its owner. One such text from Tonina, Monument

---

the platform as the syllabic element **to,** whereas Lounsbury (1973: 119) suggested it read **cho** in the codical versions of the glyph. The gradual abstraction of the original pictographic form gave rise to this confusion, reinforcing the necessity to consult early examples when possible.

141, states that a playing alley known as the "Three Enemies(?) Court"—perhaps an allusion to the frequent association of ballcourts and captives—is the ballcourt of the local ruler named K'inich Baknal Chaak (Ruler 3).

Related to ballcourts are ceremonial stairways (Miller and Houston 1987), the glyph for which sometimes resembles one-half of a ballcourt sign (Fig. 1, third row). This was surely pronounced *eb,* "step," for it sometimes takes the additional signs **e-bu,** serving as clues to its reading. This phonetic spelling often stands alone in place of the iconic "step" glyph, and its possessed form is spelled **ye-bu,** for *y-eb,* "his steps." An example of the spelling **ye-ba-la** (*y-eb-al,* "his step") on a stair at Yaxchilan may represent a slight linguistic difference at this site.

Some architectural terms appear to be very specialized. Yaxchilan Lintel 23 mentions the word **U-pa-si-li,** or *u-pas-il,* "its opening," apparently in reference to a door of the structure. The same term may also be used at Chichen Itza, where the front of Lintel 1 of the Temple of the Three Lintels opens with **U-PAS,** written with the "sun-at-horizon" logograph, read **PAS.** Another very specific item in ancient Maya architectural vocabulary may have been *nuch',* spelled **nu-ch'a** on the eaves of House C in Palenque Palace. This might be cognate with Tzotzil *nuk',* "roof ledge."

In addition to the simple terms of reference like house or step, most categories of Maya-owned objects, from monuments, to buildings, to specific architectural features could bear proper names (*k'aba'*). For example, a passage from Stela C of Copan states that *?-chah tun-k'oh? u-k'aba' u-lakamtun,* or "the '? stone image'(?) is the name of his banner stone" (Fig. 2a).[2] This sort of statement often is preceded by a certain dedicatory action or event like those already described (in this case *ts'ap-ah*), which would necessarily come first according to the proper verb–subject word order of Mayan languages. In architectural inscriptions, as we shall see, the statements are very similar. Lintel 23 of

[2] The suggested value **K'OH,** meaning "substitute, representation, mask," for the glyphic element suffixed to **TUN-ni** is very tentative. This sign is to be distinguished from the similar **li** syllable by the interior parallel lines of the sign, which loop back on themselves rather than continue across the same space, as in **li.** The **K'OH** reading is suggested only by circumstantial evidence, for it occurs in the possible **spelling U-K'OH?-ba-hi-li,** *u-k'oh-bah-il* on Copan Stela 4 after the dedication verb *ts'ap-ah* (Grube 1990), where it must somehow refer to the stela. *K'ohba(h)* is glossed in Yucatec as "image," which may be appropriate in this context. The combination *x-tun-k'oh,* "x stone representation," seems, moreover, a fitting basis for stela names, as on Stela C. The term *k'ohbah* is in fact attested in other Classic inscriptions, where it is spelled phonetically, as on the circular altar from near Structure 10L-30 at Copan, where it is used in the first glyph (Andrews and Fash 1992; fig. 15b), spelled **k'o-ho-ba.** Alone, the putative **K'OH** sign is sometimes prefixed to deity names, where it may work to specify the image of the god named.

a

b

Fig. 2 Examples of monument names: (a) Copan Stela C; (b) Yaxchilan Lintel 23 (after Graham 1982: 136).

Yaxchilan includes the passage shown in Fig. 2b, which reads *? u-k'aba' y-otot,* or "? is the name of his/her home." The name of the owner then follows, in this case a royal woman of the Yaxchilan dynasty. Again, this phrase follows a special dedicatory statement (the "rattles-fire" glyph) that will be discussed at length below.

Building names are specified in the inscriptions of many other sites, with Palenque perhaps having the most examples. Translating the proper names of ancient buildings could potentially open an interesting window on architectural function and Maya perceptions of their built environment, but, unfortunately, many of the structure names are difficult to read. Usually the names appear to be descriptive, written with various adjectives attached to the base-*nah,* or alternatively with some term incorporating the locative ending *-nal.*[3] A few of these structure names are cited below in the discussion of dedicatory passages in the inscriptions; others are listed in Stuart and Houston (1994: fig.

[3] The use of the *-nal* suffix on hieroglyphic place names is discussed in Stuart and Houston (1994: 21). Its locative function is reconstructed on the basis of the ancient sources, and it is largely absent in modern languages. Vestiges may still be seen, however, in the Yucatec term *muk-nal,* "tomb" (literally "bury place"). It also appears in some historically documented place names, such as *Uuk-hab-nal,* an ancient toponym for Chichen Itza in the native chronicles of Yucatan. The locative *-nal* suffix may be derived from *na(h),* "house," and the -V*l* suffix sometimes used on collective nouns, producing **na-al* "a cluster of houses"—perhaps an appropriate ending for place names. A similar transformation can be seen in Chol *te'-el,* "forest," from *te',* "tree."

104). Even where readily translatable, however, such as the Bolon Ahaw Nah ("Nine Ahaw House") mentioned on Tikal Altar 5, their meanings remain obscure.[4] For example, the inner sanctuary of the Temple of the Sun at Palenque was possibly named K'inich Paskab, "Sunny," as recorded on the inscribed balustrades of that structure published by Schele and Mathews (1979: no. 334). Descriptive names for buildings may not say so much about function, but it may be possible to connect them to historically known labels. A newly found hieroglyphic text inscribed on a throne at Tonina notes that Ruler 8 of that site "sat in the *nikte' nah* (**NIK-TE-NAH-hi**)," which literally means "flower (plumeria) building." In Yucatec, *nikte'il na* is a documented name for a type of community house, or "casa donde se hace junta" (Barrera Vásquez 1980: 570; see Houston 1993: 111). It is possible that this building at Tonina, decorated with imagery of flowers, serpents, and captives, served such a purpose.

RECORDS OF ARCHITECTURAL CONSTRUCTION

A great many dedication texts from the Classic period record the building of structures or smaller architectural features. The hieroglyph commonly used on these occasions (Fig. 3a-b) is a verb long considered to fall under the general class of dedication verbs (Schele 1982: 297). It has sometimes been called a "house" event (Schele 1982: 131), because the main sign seems to be a representation of a thatched covering as in the glyph **OTOT,** "house." However, the phonetic value of the glyph has thus far been difficult to determine.

In several inscriptions, the syllabic sign **ta** is added to the basic "roof" sign, seemingly functioning as a phonetic complement, which would indicate that the root ends in *-t* or *-at* (Fig. 3c). Customarily the verbal inflection includes a positional ending (MacLeod 1984), either *-lah* (as seen most often at Palenque) or *-wan* (common at Copan). In the inscriptions of Copan, where phonetic spellings are common, the verb *pat-wan,* "is built," is spelled **pa-ta-wa-ni,** and it behaves very much like the "house" event (Fig. 3d). From the parallel structures of the texts concerned, I believe it likely that **pa-ta-wa-ni** and "HOUSE"-**ta-wa-ni** are variations on the same term, "is built." That is, the main sign representing a pole-and-thatch structure with a superfixed element is a word sign with the value **PAT.** The verb root *pat* (and its cognates throughout western Mayan languages) means "to make, do" and in Proto-Cholan it is specifi-

[4] It is unclear what Tikal structure is being referred to by the name "Nine Ahaw House" on Altar 5 (at Block 18). It seems to specify the location of a burial, for the verb *muk-ah,* "is buried," occupies the preceding glyph block. The name can be interpreted either as calendrically based ("Nine Ahaw House") or possibly as referring to a "nine lords house." The same name may have been applied to Structure 10L-22A at Copan (Fash et al. 1992: 435).

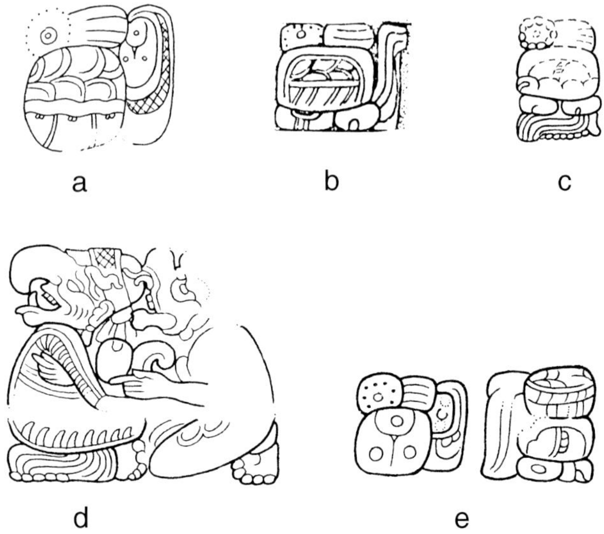

Fig. 3 Spellings using the verb *pat* "to build, make": (a) **PAT-la-ha,** from a hieroglyphic panel from the Palenque area; (b) **PAT-wa-ni,** from the Palace Tablet, Palenque (drawing by Linda Schele); (c) **PAT-ta-wa-ni** from Altar U at Copan; (d) **pa-ta-wa-ni** from the Temple Inscription, Copan; (e) **PAT-la-ha yo-OTOT-ti,** "his dwelling was built," from an inscribed wooden box of unknown provenience (redrawn from photograph in Coe 1974).

cally glossed as "to build a house" (Kaufman and Norman 1984). This meaning is confirmed by one text from the environs of Tortuguero (Coe 1974: 57), which includes the phrase **PAT-la-ha yo-OTOT-ti,** or *pat-l-ah y-otot,* "his dwelling is built."

Examples of "building" recorded in the inscriptions include many from the site of Palenque. There, as a part of a phrase that often closes wall-panel inscriptions, the *pat* verb appears along with other architectural and geographical terms. For instance, on the hieroglyphic stairway of House C of the Palenque Palace (Fig. 4a), the following sequence of signs is used to close the inscription: **ET?-NAH yo-OTOT PAT-la-ha LAKAM-HA',** or *et-nah y-otot, pat-l-ah Lakamha',* "The 'Companion Building' is his house, it is built at Lakamha."[5] In the pre-

[5] The value **ET** for the sign in the house name was first tentatively proposed by Stephen Houston (personal communication, 1991) and is included here with a query. The sign is very commonly prefixed by **ye** in other examples, and the combination **ye-te,** recalling Yucatec *yéetel,* "with, and" seems to be functionally equivalent. If a logograph, **ET,** based on the root for "companion," seems a good possibility. Interestingly, the tomb within the Temple

Fig. 4 "House Building" records from Palenque: (a) the hieroglyphic stairway of House C, Palenque; (b) sanctuary jamb of the Temple of the Foliated Cross.

ceding passage, the stairway inscription commemorates the display of several captives whose full-figure portraits grace the basal platform, seen today on the western face of the East Courtyard (Robertson 1985: 66–69). The naming of the building and the recording of its construction, as in so many Maya texts, are the culminating events of the entire inscription.

In another Palenque inscription, found on the doorjamb of the inner sanctuary of the Temple of the Foliated Cross (Fig. 4b), the inscription records the "entering" of the shrine (as further discussed below), and closes with the phrase **8-("DAY")-8-WINAL?-hi-ya u-to-ma 8-AHAW 8-IK'-K'AT CHUM-TUN-ni 13-"K'ATUN" PAT-la-ha LAKAM-HA',** loosely translated as "it was 8 days and 8 winals before 8 Ahau 8 Uo, the seating of the *tun,* the thirteenth K'atun, that it (the shrine) was built at Lakamha'."

The *pat* verb also can refer to the building of staircases, called *eb* in the ancient texts as they are today. Hieroglyphic Stairway 1 from Itzan, Guatemala, includes the phrase **PAT-ta-wa-ni ye-bu,** for *pat-wan y-eb,* "his steps were

---

of the Inscriptions may be called a **9-ET-NAH,** or a "Nine Companions House," referring to the nine stucco portraits on its walls (Stephen Houston, personal communication, 1991). This name appears on the east tablet of the temple, at position T11.

Fig. 5 A record of stairway construction on Hieroglyphic Stairway 1, Itzan (drawing based on photograph by Ian Graham).

built" (Fig. 5). The same phrase appears at distant Copan, where on Step 38 of the great hieroglyphic stairway it refers to construction of the monument's final, upper phase under Ruler 15 of that site (Stuart n.d.b).

It is perhaps significant that *pat* forms the base for the word *pat-an,* meaning "tribute, service" in numerous Mayan languages. *Patan* is attested in the Classic inscriptions (Fig. 6), spelled **pa-ta**, sometimes with the addition of a numerical prefix to specify amounts of tribute, as in **18-pa-ta** for "eighteen tribute items" (Stuart n.d.a). Save for context, references to "make, build" and "tribute" are indistinguishable in the ancient inscriptions. It is possible, although highly speculative, that *pat* once had a more specific meaning connected in some way with the production of tribute and the rendering of labor service. If so, we should entertain the notion that the hieroglyphic passages discussed thus far convey the idea that buildings were constructed out of service or tribute to their high-ranking owners.

If nothing else, this brief overview of the hieroglyphic uses of *pat* suggests that the commemoration of actual building construction was a feature of Classic Maya texts. The purpose of these inscriptions was not only to record the date and location of a structure's completion but sometimes also to establish the ownership of "houses" and "steps" and other kinds of architectural features. Fortunately, however, inscriptions were not always limited to simply labeling buildings with dates and names. A great many dedication texts shed considerable light on the dedication rites themselves and thus lead us into some broader considerations of ancient and modern Maya ceremonialism.

THE FIRE-ENTERING RITE

Lintel 56 from Yaxchilan displays yet another representative example of an architectural dedication inscription (Fig. 7). However, rather than simply recounting the construction of the building in which it was housed (Structure 11, most likely) and the name of the owner, the dedicatory event phrase associated with the "his/her house" glyph offers much more information. An initial series begins the text: 9.15.6.19.1 7 Imix 19 Zip. As written, the date is a scribal error (19 *winals* is a mathematical impossibility). Rather it is clear that

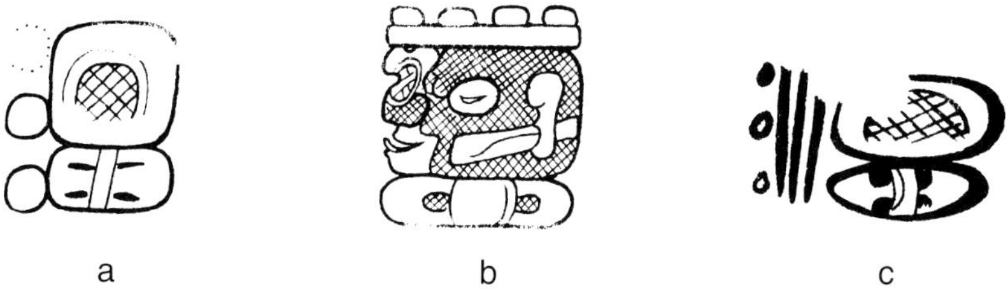

Fig. 6 Tribute glyphs: (a) **3-pa-ta,** *ox patan,* "three (items of) tribute, service," from Chichen Itza (drawn from Coggins 1992: fig. 5.43); (b) **9-pa-ta,** *bolon patan,* "nine (items of) tribute, service," from Machaquila (redrawn from Graham 1967: fig 39c); (c) **18-pa-ta**, *waxaklahun patan,* 18 (items of) tribute," from Tikal, miscellaneous text.

the intended date was 9.15.6.13.1 7 Imix 19 Zip, involving the subtraction of 6 from the *winal* position. This long count and the associated discussion of the moon age occupy about a third of the entire text, up to block G1, leaving the rest to record the event and the persons connected with it. As with nearly all sentences, the word order is verb–subject. Several imbedded parenthetical statements of relationship exist throughout this inscription, but it is essentially a record of a single ritual episode.

The principal verb phrase of this sentence, from blocks H1–H2, exemplifies what is perhaps the most frequent of all architectural dedication statements. The combination in block H1 has two parts—a "fire" glyph preceded by a sign representing the tail of a rattlesnake. The reading of the fire glyph as **K'AK',** "fire" has long been established (Kelley 1968), although at times it might also read **BUTS',** "smoke" (Stuart 1987). The meaning of the rattles sign is less clear, although Kelley (1976: 122), following Knorosov, has suggested the reading **TSAB,** meaning "snake rattle." This particular decipherment has two limi-

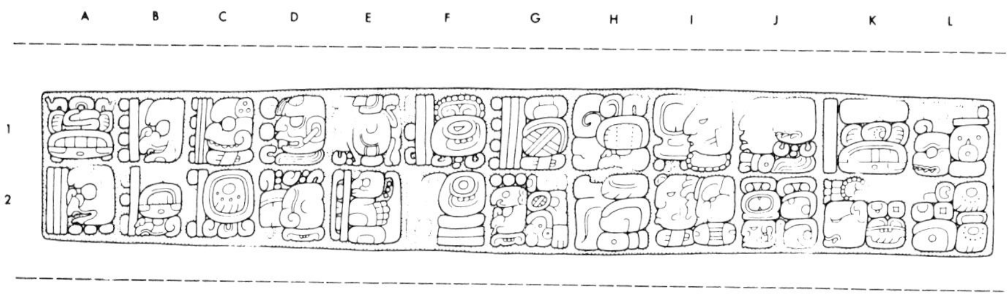

Fig. 7 Yaxchilan Lintel 56 (after Graham 1979: 121).

tations, however. The first troubling aspect of the reading is the lack of phonetic indicators, such as syllabic complements or full substitutions (**tsa-ba**) by syllabic signs. Second, and perhaps most significantly, the "rattles" sign must alone represent the verb of the sentence, because it occurs immediately after the inscription's date, and every other word of the passage has been shown to be a noun. Known meanings of *tsab* make little sense as a verb in this context. It may be unusual to have a single sign represent a verb without any inflectional morphemes indicated, but, given the occasional tendency to abbreviate or underrepresent spellings in the Maya script, it is not without precedent (Stuart and Houston 1994: 13–18). We will return to the rattles-fire verb glyph momentarily after discerning more of the structure of this particular inscription.

The next glyph in the lintel inscription again has two parts. The first is not readily recognizable, but the second is familiar as **U-K'ABA',** "his/her/its name."[6] Two glyphs after the rattles-fire combination is the glyph for "his house," *y-otot* (**yo-OTOT**), which is, in turn, followed by the woman's name, Ix Sak Biyan (**IX-SAK-bi-ya-ni**), and several of her titles and other terms of reference, including **ch'o-ko IX-ki,** for *ch'ok ixik,* "young woman."[7] The *u-k'aba' y-otot* combination before her name establishes that the unknown glyph following the rattles-fire event compound is the proper name of "her house." As with the passage from Yaxchilan, Lintel 23, described above, this is yet another case of a dedicatory passage featuring the proper name of the object or monument that is ritually initiated or activated.

[6] The evidence behind the reading **K'ABA'** is largely unpublished, although it has been cited extensively (Schele and Freidel 1990; Harris and Sterns 1992). My own arguments for the reading were circulated in a letter to Stephen Houston in 1987. The evidence is straightforward and involves both contextual and phonetic lines of argument. The contexts are well illustrated by the examples discussed here, but the most telling clues are the frequent phonetic complements **-ba-** and **-a** and the fuller phonetic form **k'a-ba-a** found in the inscriptions of Chichen Itza and on an unprovenanced vessel from the Naranjo area (Coe 1973: 103). At precisely the same time I posited this decipherment, Nikolai Grube arrived at a similar understanding, and although he rejected the precise value **K'ABA'** at that time (letter to Stephen Houston, 1987), he soon accepted it (Nikolai Grube, personal communication, 1988).

[7] The prefix to female names is here read as **IX-**, not **NA-** as often supposed (see Justeson 1984: 359). The head sign is certainly syllabic **na** or **NAH** in numerous contexts (Lounsbury 1984), but sometimes it appears that an additional logographic value is indicated. A hieroglyphic panel from Bonampak seems to refer to a woman whose name is prefixed not by the customary female head but instead by the phonetic combination **i-xi.** *Ix-* is the widespread prefix on female names in Mayan languages (far more common than *na-*) and was initially suggested as a reading for the glyphic prefix by Berlin (1959: 6). In the texts of Yaxchilan, we occasionally find the female head with the purely optional suffix **-ki,** probably reading **IX-ik,** for *ixik,* "woman."

Thus far, most of the dedicatory inscription on Lintel 56 is readable save for the rattles-fire compound. Because this is the principal verb phrase of the entire inscription, however, its opacity leaves a conspicuous gap. How do we decipher it? As with most decipherments, we must rely on visual evidence (its representational aspects), contextual evidence (its "behavior" relative to other glyphs), and, most importantly, phonetic evidence in the form of syllabic complements and substitutions.

Variations on the rattles-fire glyph can be recognized in parallel passages of many other inscriptions and offer vital clues to the decipherment. A good example occurs on Lintel 31 of Yaxchilan (Fig. 8). There, as in many texts, a

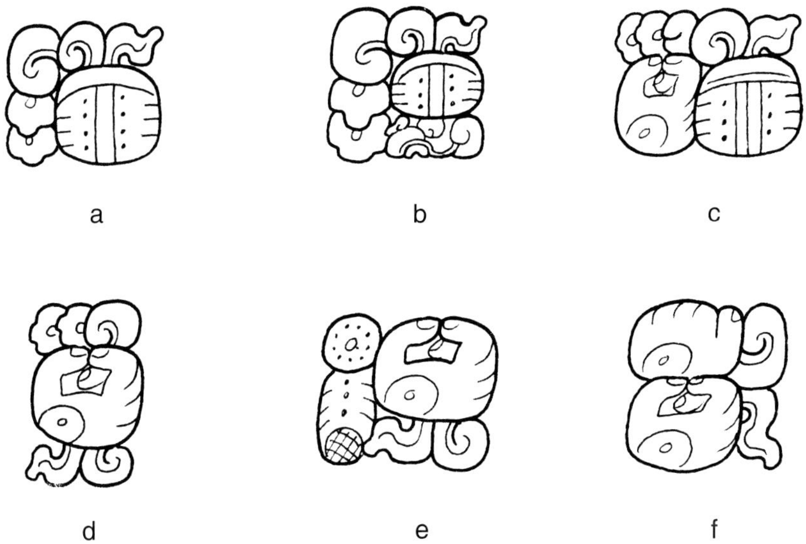

Fig. 8 Alternative forms of the *och k'ak'* glyph.

dedication statement closes an inscription—in this case, it runs across three different lintels (29, 30, and 31)—and thus is the culmination of the historical narrative. The fire glyph is visible in its simplified form (without the long-nosed head attachment seen on Lintel 56), and the rattles glyph precedes as the main verb. Intervening, however, is the syllable sign **chi.** As this optional sign cannot modify the fire glyph, read **K'AK',** it most likely serves to complement the rattles element. In other words, the reading of the rattles sign most likely ends in *-ch*.

a b c

Fig. 9 Other glyphs with *och,* "enter": (a) *och bih,* to die; (b) *och ha'*; (c) *och k'in.*

At Palenque, where numerous cases of the rattles-fire glyph also appear, we find another telling variation. The event phrase that concludes the text of the Palace Tablet, apparently another house dedication record, includes *y-otot,* and the preceding verb contains three signs: **o-chi-K'AK'** (Fig. 8). That is, the fire sign has been reduced to its "flames" abbreviation, and the **chi** is again present. However, here an **o-** syllable replaces the rattles sign found in other examples. These are surely not simple substitutes, because we know that the rattles element must serve as a logograph. Rather, there is good reason to surmise that the **o-chi** sequence is functionally equivalent to the rattles glyph. From this, we can test the hypothesis that the rattles sign is to be read **OCH.**[8]

The most obvious support for reading this sign as **OCH** is that Yucatec *och* means "rattlesnake rattles." In some glyphs, the rattles element can be replaced by a fist sign (Fig. 8f); and, significantly, the Yucatec word for "fist" is none other than *ok* (phonologically cognate to *och*). Parallels with "fist" may occur in other languages as well, but poor sources on Cholan languages make this difficult to confirm. *Och* as a verb meaning "enter" is widespread in Cholan and Tzeltalan languages (Kaufman and Norman 1984: 127), and I suggest this meaning is to be applied to most examples of the rattles sign. In Yucatec, the cognate root for "enter" is *ok,* strongly indicating that the spellings found in the Classic texts reflect more the Cholan and Tzeltalan pronunciation. In a particularly widespread glyphic expression (Lounsbury 1974), the putative **OCH** sign possibly combines with **BIH** or **bi-hi** to form the metaphor for death *och bih,* literally, "to go on a road, to enter a road" (Fig. 9a). Another verbal glyph associated with death is possibly *och ha',* "to go in the water" (Fig. 9b).[9] Moreover, the fist variant of the "enter" verb occurs with **K'IN** in the Classic period variant of

[8] The **OCH** decipherment was circulated to fellow epigraphers in 1990 but first saw publication elsewhere (Freidel, Schele, and Parker 1993: 76).

[9] One example of **OCH-HA'** occurs on Tikal, Stela 31, at D23. *Ok ha'* is today a term for "baptize" in Yucatec.

the glyph for "west," producing **OCH-K'IN** or **OK-K'IN** (Fig. 9c). *Okol k'in* ("sun entering") is a word for "sunset" in Yucatec, with cognate forms in other languages. Reading the rattles-fire combination as *och k'ak'* leads to a possible full translation of the dedicatory phrase as "enters the fire." On the Tablet of the 96 Glyphs at Palenque (Fig. 10), the full phrase would therefore read *och k'ak' ta-y-otot,* "the fire enters into his house."

Fig. 10 *Och k'ak'* with the locative phrase *ta-y-otot.*

This idea immediately recalls Landa's mention of the *ok nah,* or "house entering" dedication ritual, for the verb used in Landa's account is identical to what is found in the glyphs: Yucatec *ok* and Cholan *och,* "to enter." Landa was explicit in his mention of fire and braziers in the house renewal ceremony, leading to the natural conclusion that the *ok nah* rite may be a later manifestation of the Classic period *och k'ak'* ceremony. Unfortunately, the details of the earlier ritual, as with so many Classic period rites, have not been provided in the inscriptions, and so the extent of the parallel I have drawn must remain a matter of some speculation.

THE "CENSER" GLYPH

There exists in the inscriptions a separate event phrase that is in many ways parallel to the aforementioned fire-entering ritual (Fig. 11). The verb itself can take a variety of forms, but the essential components are a bowl-like element with a *k'in* infix followed by **-NAH** (Fig. 11a-c). The "*k'in* bowl" sign, with smoke or fire volutes emanating from it in some examples, almost certainly represents the top of the zoomorphic incense burner portrayed in numerous examples of Maya art (Fig. 11d) (see Taube, this volume). Occasionally, also, a **-le** sign is suffixed to the burner, leading Stephen Houston (personal communication, 1992) to suggest that the indicated verb root is *el* or *elel,* used in various terms for "to burn" in Yucatec. The **-NAH,** of course, is "structure" or "house," resulting in the phrase "house burning," or perhaps more specifically, "house censing." Because of the uncertainty of the phonetic decipherment of

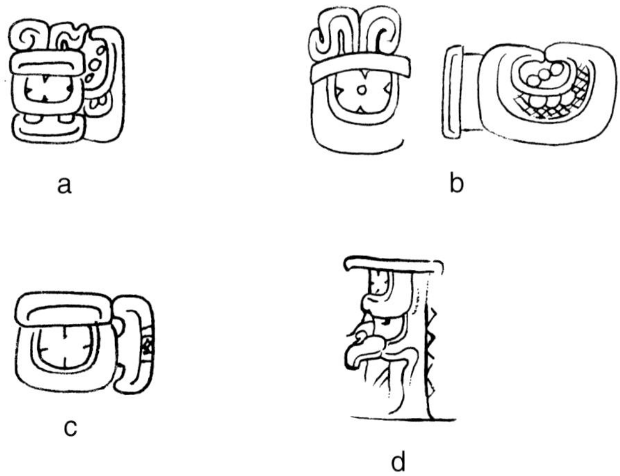

Fig. 11 The "censing" verb: (a) Piedras Negras Panel 4; (b) Tonina Monument 141; (c) Piedras Negras Throne 1; (d) effigy censer (after Taube 1994: fig. 8e).

the root, I simply refer to this phrase, possibly read *el-nah,* as "house censing."

A simple example of the house censing event within the context of a larger inscription comes from Throne 1 of Piedras Negras (Fig. 11c). The inscription is fragmentary but, as discussed in more detail below, seems to celebrate the transport and delivery of a "bundle" to or by the soon-to-be installed Ruler 6. The text continues with a record of his accession and then finally a notation of the period ending 9.17.15.0.0 5 Ahau 3 Muan. The verb here is house censing, followed by a building name, Chahuk Nah, "Lightning House"(spelled **cha-hu-ku-NAH**), and then *y-otot* with the name of Ruler 6.[10] Taken together, the dedication phrase reads "5 Ahau 3 Muan (is) the '15'-*tun,* (is) the 'house-censing,' Chahuk Nah is the home of 'Ruler 6'."

We find at Yaxchilan a nearly identical phrase on the underside of Lintel 21 (Fig. 12). Here the initial series date is 9.0.19.2.4 2 Kan 2 Yax, far earlier than the style of the inscription itself. The event associated with the early date is again house censing, followed by the house name and then *y-otot,* with the name of the seventh ruler of the Yaxchilan dynasty ("Moon Skull"). The narra-

[10] The designation Ruler 6 here refers to Proskouriakoff's (1960) "Series 7" ruler, folowing the revision by Houston (1983). The reading of the Throne 1 text as presented here is based on the event recorded on the front of the left support, *hul-i ikats k'ohbah(?),* "it arrived, the bundle, the image," followed by the name of Ruler 6.

Fig. 12 Yaxchilan Lintel 21 (from Graham 1977: 59).

tive then jumps forward nearly three centuries to record a seating ceremony involving the noted Late Classic ruler Bird Jaguar IV in the same house on 9.16.1.0.9, only nine days after his formal inauguration as king. The inscription was clearly composed at or near this second date, which is far later than the other two Early Classic lintels of the same structure. It seems likely, therefore, that the censing event recorded on Lintel 21 was an original dedication event, associated with construction of the building, and not a renewal ceremony.

Such attention to the chronology of dedication events has obvious significance for archaeology and the dating of elite architectural stratigraphy. Dates of ritual dedications are not commemorated for all buildings at all sites, but clusters of such dates on buildings at the same site, or even in the same architectural complex, allow for reconstruction of very precise building sequences. Table 1 presents an example, with several dedication dates inscribed on buildings at Palenque.

TABLE 1. A SELECTION OF BUILDING DEDICATIONS FROM PALENQUE

Date	Building/Feature	Dedication Event
9.14.8.15.18 6 Etznab 6 Zac	House A-D	*och k'ak*
9.12.19.14.12 5 Eb 5 Kayab	Cross Group	*och nah; pat-l-ah; och k'ak'*
9.11.15.14.19 4 Cauac 7 Tzec	House A	(missing)
9.11.6.16.11 7 Chuen 4 Ch'en	House C, east steps	*pat-l-ah*
9.11.2.1.11.9 Chuen 9 Mac	House E	*och k'ak'*
9.8.16.10.19 4 Cauac 2 Pax	House C, eaves	*och nah*

The "censer" sign, showing occasional volutes of fire or smoke rising from its top, is clearly related to the hieroglyph for "east" in the Classic inscriptions. Here, the same *k'in*-bowl sign rests atop **K'IN** in the spelling **LAK-K'IN,** for *lak'in,* "east" (Justeson n.d.). *Lak* is "plate," as it apparently was in Classic times (Houston, Stuart, and Taube 1989), but it was also a term used in the inscriptions for incense burners, a meaning no doubt reflected in the colonial meaning for *lak,* "ídolo de barro" (Barrera Vásquez 1980: 433). At Copan, numerous cylindrical stone vessels used as containers for clay censers were called *saklaktun,* "false-stone *lak.*" The hieroglyphic labels for these objects make use of **LAK** signs representing spiked censers. The strong association between the *k'in*-bowl sign and the word *lak* reiterates the theme of incense burning in these house dedication rites.

Two important dedication expressions have thus far been identified: "fire entering" and "house censing." Both are strongly related thematically and occupy the same position in architectural inscriptions. Their functions are so similar, in fact, that one might suspect that they represent two different ways of expressing the same thing, perhaps simply reflecting distinct languages in use at different sites. It is true that the "censing" expression is far more numerous at Piedras Negras than it is at Yaxchilan, for example, but both censing and fire-entering co-occur at several different centers. For the present, suffice it to say that the two rituals are very closely connected as the principal means of recording architectural dedicatory rites but that there probably existed subtle distinctions between them.

SOME ETHNOGRAPHIC PARALLELS

The vague descriptions of "fire-entering" dedication rites treated thus far bring to mind similar kinds of ceremonies in modern Mesoamerica. Among the Tzotzil Maya of Zinacantan, the Ch'ul Kandela ("Holy Candle") ritual takes place soon after a new house is built, "to give the house a 'soul' " (Vogt 1969: 461). The ritual involves several steps, beginning with erection of a small cross outside the structure, before which candles and incense are burned. Inside, the ritual continues with prayer to the Earth Lord over a table with six candles set upon it. Candles and pine boughs are then planted in the four corners of the house, and chicken broth is poured into these locations as well as in the center of the house. This last step appears to be considered an act of feeding the new structure, and more broth and liquor are poured over the rafters of the roof (Vogt 1969: 461–465). In neighboring Chenhaló, a very similar house dedication ceremony described by Guiteras-Holmes (1961: 26) includes lighting of the first hearth fire by an elderly couple to "tame" the new "wild" house.

The "feeding" of the corner posts and roof is a very widespread feature of new house ceremonies in other Maya communities and throughout Mesoamerica. Redfield and Villa Rojas (1964: 146–147) describe a new house ceremony from northern Yucatan similar to that of the Tzotzil. Whittaker and Warkentin (1965: 79–84) provide a native Chol description of what seems to be the same rite as documented among the nearby Tzotzil. Interestingly, the parallels can be traced to the Pre-Hispanic Aztec, specifically to the ceremonies accompanying the renewal of temples and in the construction of residences (Durán 1971: 149). These ceremonies were called *calmamalihua,* or "house drilling." In addition to feeding the house corners, Durán (1971: 149) notes that "the host himself takes a newly lighted firebrand and points it in one direction and in another, thus taking possession of the home he built." Among modern Nahuatl speakers, the same ceremony is called *caltlacualiztli*, "feeding the house" (Sandstrom 1991: 30). Some essential parallels can be extended as far as the American Southwest, where house dedication rites include placement of various items under the four corners of the house and subsequent "feeding" of the roof (Saile 1977).

Interestingly, the Ch'ul Kantela ceremony described by Vogt goes by another name, *'och kantela,* "candle-entering," which is glossed by Laughlin (1975: 65) as "dedicate new house." The same ceremony is also called *'och limuxna na,* literally "offerings entering a house." Of course, this terminology is closely related to Yucatec *ok nah*. The act of "entering" and the meanings that surround it seem to be extremely important in modern Maya ritual speech and ceremonial life. *Och* and *ok* are found throughout Mayan languages not only as "enter" but also as "become" or "begin," referring to changes in states of being. It is specifically used in several languages to refer to the assumption of new political or religious offices (Schele 1984: 301–302).[11]

Several aspects of modern Lacandon ceremonial life may also be closely related to the Classic period fire-entering and censing of buildings. McGee (1990) and Bruce and Perera (1982: 29–31) describe at some length the rites revolving around "god pots" (*u-läk-il k'uh*), small effigy incense burners designed also for holding offerings, food, and drink for supernatural entities. These and other rituals take place in the local *y-atoch k'uh,* "god house." The notion of feeding and sustaining the gods is central to all these rituals, for incense, *pom,* "is the principal foodstuff given to the gods" (McGee 1990: 44). It is possible that the entrance of fire and the burning of incense in Classic Maya architectural rituals had similar meanings tied to the symbolic "feeding" of structures or

[11] In her discussion of heir-apparency rites at Palenque, Schele (1984) suggests the reading **OCH** for the animal head element that appears in the event phrase associated with young kings-to-be. This animal is otherwise used as the tenth day sign (Oc), and a meaning of "enter" would seem appropriate given the cognate forms *ok* and *och*. However, there is reason to believe that the animal sign is **OK,** "leg, foot," and not **OCH.** In these passages from the tablets of the Cross Group, the animal sign is combined with **-TE,** probably for **OK-TE,** as in the deity name Bolon (Y)okte'. The same animal is sometimes suffixed by **-ko** or can be replaced by the syllabic combination **yo-ko** (Grube and Stuart 1987). In the recently discovered stucco frieze from Tonina, the same animal sign appears in the name caption of a death god: **a-ka-OK KIMI-ya,** or Ak Ok Kimi, "Turtle-Foot Death." This unusual name is explained by the turtle shells on the feet of his portrait. The rattles **OCH** and the animal **OK** seem to have been kept separate in texts of the Classic period, suggesting that Schele's "enter" reading in the Palenque texts is incorrect.

were part of a complex of ceremonials incorporating "feeding" rites.

The widespread practice of "feeding" houses reflects the essential idea that dwellings are animate beings in some sense (see Taube, this volume). Architectural terminologies in Mayan languages consistently reflect this notion by referring to parts of buildings as parts of "bodies." Thus, in Tzotzil, a door is *ti' na* or "house mouth"; a thatch roof is *holol* or "head of hair" (Laughlin 1975). Essentially the same words are found throughout all Mayan languages (e.g., Yucatec *chi' na'* for "door" and *pol na* for "roof"). As we have seen, the rituals associated with architectural dedication in many indigenous communities hinge on perceptions of buildings as living beings, and the frequent house-building rituals commonly serve to spiritually activate the living space. In addition, throughout Mesoamerica, four-cornered houses are often considered to be small-scale replicas of the cosmos (Vogt 1976, 1993; Lok 1987). Building and dedicating a house thus becomes an act of cosmic renewal within the intimate social setting of the family. Houses may be universes in miniature, but the reverse is also true. Schele's seminal identification of the "First Hearth Place" as the cosmogony site of Classic Maya mythology demonstrates that the universe was considered a house (see Freidel, Schele, and Parker 1993; Taube, this volume). Carlsen and Prechtel (1991: 39) also state that the conception of the world as a house is fundamental to both modern and ancient Maya cosmology.

The larger cosmological significance of the Classic dedication rituals described thus far may be symbolized in part by the "censer" glyph, where a *k'in* or sun symbol appears inside the censer bowl. Such imagery suggests that the ritual fire created was somehow equated with the sun and that, by extension, the dedication of structures and other censer rituals involved the continual creation of numerous "new" suns, the elemental source of heat and life. Perhaps the placement of a "sun" within a newly constructed building not only gave life to that space but also affirmed its cosmological symbolism.

We have seen in our perusal of some Classic terms and dedication statements that monuments were often given proper names. The great importance of bestowing names on ritual objects and monuments is apparent from such commemorations, and it might be said that the giving of names to things was sometimes an essential part of dedication rituals. Throughout Mesoamerica, names are explicitly considered labels, not of the individual but of one's soul, or part of one's soul (Guiteras-Holmes 1961: 111). The part of the soul called *tonal* among some Maya groups, and *tonalli* among the Mexica Aztec (Nahuatl for "a thing that is warm"), was labeled with the day of one's birth, which then came to be a personal name. Bestowing names was thus often considered a creative,

[12] That naming something bestows it with some special quality or status may seem in-

life-giving act, even upon what we consider to be inanimate objects.[12] Among the Tzotzil, people as well as many objects of ritual and daily life possess souls called *ch'ulel*: houses, candles, and images of saints (Vogt 1969: 370–371). In an interesting soul connection, the red color of ritual objects and monuments from the Classic period probably represents blood, where the soul is believed to reside, thus lending them a certain animate and precious quality (McGee 1990). The naming of buildings, sculptures, and ritual implements during Classic times may have functioned in much the same way.

TOMB-RENEWAL CEREMONIES

The *och k'ak'* ritual is not solely associated with the dedication of "houses" or those structures designated by the general term *otot*. We find in several examples, for instance, that the fire-entering event phrase sometimes precedes a distinctive glyph whose main sign is an unusual "stepped" element holding a

Fig. 13 An *och k'ak'* dedication phrase from a Tonina monument (redrawn from Yadeun 1993: fig. 14).

human skull within its outline (Fig. 13). Cross-hatching, presumably indicating darkness, often surrounds the skull element. Typically the prefix to this is **tu-**, and **-il** and **-NAL** are common suffixes. The prefix here no doubt represents the preposition *t-* before the possessive pronoun *u-*, and the *-il* serves as the nominal suffix on the possessed noun. Thus, the skull-in-step main sign presumably must refer to the architectural feature into which the "fire enters."

A vital clue to the meaning of the skull-in-step sign comes from inscriptions at Tonina. The precise same combination of signs, with the **tu-** prefix and all,

---

trinsically obvious, yet we find in several sources that invoking a thing or person by name was itself an act of creation. A well-known example comes from the Popol Vuh, when the primordial gods invoke, and thus create, the world: "And then the earth arose because of them, it was simply their word that brought it forth: For the forming of the earth they said 'earth'" (Tedlock 1985: 73). By understanding that names were traditionally labels for souls in Mesoamerican belief, it follows that lending a name to someone or something invests that person or object with life. Perhaps it is significant that the Yucatec verb phrase *pat k'aba'* "to name something" makes use of the verb *pat*, which otherwise means "to make or build." As we shall see, this idea is very important in understanding ancient house-dedication ceremonies.

Fig. 14 Tonina Monument 69 (after Becquelin and Baudez 1982: fig. 141).

appears on several small disc altars from that site (Fig. 14). Interestingly, these disc altars served to commemorate the 260-day anniversaries of the deaths of those portrayed on them. The text of Monument 69, for example, notes the death of a noble I will call "Sky-Fire" and, at the close of the text, commemorates its 260-day anniversary. The anniversary phrase includes the skull-in-step with its customary **tu-** prefix, and its "owner" is explicitly named as the recently deceased "Sky-Fire." Given the suppositions that the sign is somehow architectural in its reference, that the image of a skull within a step is significant, and that the "owners" of the objects are dead, I argue that the skull-in-step sign signifies a tomb or burial. As noted above, some examples of this putative burial glyph have the locative suffix **-NAL.** The word for "tomb" in Yucatec Maya is *muknal, muk* being the widespread Mayan root for "bury." There seems good reason, therefore, to propose a full phonetic decipherment of the dedication phrase as *och-i k'ak' t-u-muk-il,* "the fire entered his/her tomb."

Let us look at one example of this phrase from an inscription at Seibal (Fig.

Fig. 15 A burial rite from Seibal Tablet 5 (after Graham 1996: 59).

15). The hieroglyphic panels of Structure A-14 constitute the longest single inscription from Seibal (Graham 1996: 57–61) and include seven dates. Recorded twice is the day 9.15.16.7.17 6 Caban 10 Kankin, which seems to be the focus of the historical narrative. The first example of the date, on Tablet 5, is followed by the illustrated statement *och-i k'ak' t-u-muk-nal-il* (unfortunately, the events with the second example of the 6 Caban 10 Kankin date are missing). The name of the tomb occupant is K'an Mo' Balam ("Yellow Macaw-Jaguar"), the Holy Lord of Seibal. Being the one interred, K'an Mo' Balam is of course not the contemporaneous ruler of the polity; other portions of the inscription clearly indicate that one Yich'ak Balam ("Jaguar Claw") is the current king, and indeed he is named further on in the tomb dedication phrase as the overseer of the ritual (Tablet 6, EE1–EE2). Interestingly, Tablets 7 and 8 recall events of the Early Classic period before once again mentioning the 6 Caban 10 Kankin date, although the inscriptions are difficult to read. I therefore offer the suggestion that K'an Mo' Balam was an Early Classic ruler of Seibal, whose tomb, presumably somewhere in Structure A-14-Sub, was entered for a renewal ceremony some 300 years later. There is no archaeological evidence of the existence of this tomb, but I predict that once Structure A-14 is more completely excavated, a significant Early Classic burial may be found.[13]

The rite described by the hieroglyphic phrase "fire entering the tomb" may appear somewhat unusual, for there has been, until recently, little said in the archaeological literature concerning postinterment ritual activities. However,

[13] Smith (1982: 63–77) offers a detailed description of the excavations in Structure A-14, which were mostly superficial. The latest construction phase is far later than the date of the inscribed tablets, which may have been reset from an earlier version of this building. If, however, the tablets originated from another locale, then the location of the posited Early Classic tomb of K'an Mo' Balam is unknowable.

there is ample archaeological evidence of ritual burning within burials. Coe (1959: 127) notes that Burial 10 of Piedras Negras was opened and burned in antiquity. Two recently investigated tombs at Copan, Burials XXXVII-8 (William Fash, personal communication, 1993) and the so-called Margarita burial (Robert Sharer, personal communication, 1993) show evidence of considerable burning. The first Copan case is clearly intrusive, the bones having been jumbled before the tomb "firing," after which the tomb was resealed. These are but a few of many examples known from both archaeological reports and recent investigations in the field.

The "censing" event also occurs in close connection to tombs, as shown by several inscriptions from the area of Piedras Negras. Many of the small wall panels from this site, such as Panels 3 and 4, may have served as tomb markers of a sort, for they often end with a record of a tomb-censing ceremony. The original placement of these stone panels is not certain, but at least some may have been set into the front of outset platforms on stairways, as shown in Proskouriakoff's (1963: 25) reconstruction of Structure K-5. Whether or not tombs were placed beneath these platforms at Piedras Negras is open to question, but similar outsets at other sites, such as on Structure A-1 at Altun Ha, suggest the possibility. In any event, as Proskouriakoff suggests in her drawing, censers were probably placed on these platforms (see Taube, this volume). The tomb censing mentioned on many of these panels may therefore refer to the burning of ceremonial censers outside of tombs rather than inside.

SOME OTHER ARCHITECTURAL FORMS

Another architectural term is *way-ib,* "dormitory," a location for still another type of firing ritual that occupies the same place in the *och k'ak'* phrase as *y-otot* and *u-muk-nal.* Typically, a preposition is added to the possessed form of this noun, producing **tu-WAY[bi]-li,** or *t-u-way-ib-il,* "in his domicile" (Houston and Stuart 1990). The **WAY** sign is otherwise used as the term for "animal companion spirit" or "co-essence," particularly as part of captions for supernatural figures painted on Maya polychrome ceramics. *Way* is not only an attested word for animal companion or *nagual* but also for the verbs "sleep" and "dream." In this context, the instrumental suffix *-ib,* produces *way-ib,* with "bed" or "dormitory" as possible translations (it is possible that the instrumental suffix here is *-ab,* as there are some ambiguities in the glyphic spelling convention used).

The hieroglyphic expression *och k'ak' t-u-way-ib-il,* "the fire entered his dormitory," is somewhat rare, but it appears to refer to the dedication of a very specialized type of religious structure (Fig. 16). Rather than a designation for

Fig. 16 Fire entering a *way-ib,* from Tonina Fragment 91 (after Bequelin and Baudez 1982: fig. 132).

Fig. 17 Caption on a *way-ib* house model from Copan (after Andrews and Fash 1992).

the sleeping places of people, *way-ib* in this context seems to refer to places where the images of gods or supernatural images "resided" or were kept in relative seclusion. Significantly, in all known examples of the *way-ib* glyph (**WAY** with a **bi** infix), including those found in contexts outside of the fire-entering rite, it is possessed by supernatural beings. Several examples of the glyph come from a series of miniature house models from Copan (Fig. 17), all of which are labeled **U-WAY[bi]-li K'UH,** or *u-way-ib-il k'uh,* the "dormitory of the god." As Taube (this volume) points out, each house model includes a seated image of God C (the *k'uh,* "god," glyph) inside its door, and small holes in the roof above were used to suspend a covering that was lowered when the god was considered to be "asleep." Similarly, a lintel inscription from Ikil, Yucatan (Andrews and Stuart 1975), labels the inner wall niche of Temple 1 as a *way-ib* (here spelled **U-wa-ya-bi-li**), and rings placed above the niche may have been used to hang a covering of some sort. Other textual references to *way-ib* structures are less easy to fathom, as on the Tablet of the Sun at Palenque, where a "burning" at the *way-ib* of a member of Palenque Triad is recorded. This burning ritual appears to be connected in some way to sweatbath rites described in similar passages on the Tablets of the Cross and Foliated Cross (Houston 1996). Whatever the precise event being described it would seem, nonetheless, that *way-ib* was the term for some sort of temple repository or shrine for sacred images.[14]

An inscribed stone panel from the Usumacinta area, possibly the site of La

[14] Duncan Earle (personal communication, 1990) notes that the Classic period *way-ib* structures may be related to certain lineage shrines used among the modern Quiche, called *warabal ja,* a "sleeping house." Freidel, Schele, and Parker (1993: 188–193) have extended this connection. It remains unclear, however, whether we should view the Classic *way-ib* as lineage shrines, for a more general function is certainly possible.

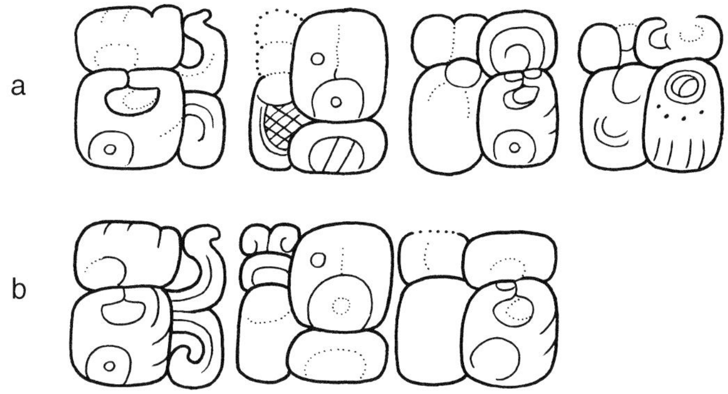

Fig. 18 Repetition of a fire-entering ritual in the *way-ib* of a local deity, from a looted panel (inked after preliminary sketch by Ian Graham).

Mar, carries several records of *way-ib* entering rites (Fig. 18a-b). According to its text, one such event took place on 9.6.10.13.17 12 Caban 5 Ceh, and another occurred nearly a century and a half later on the period ending 9.13.15.0.0 13 Ahau 18 Pax. In both instances, the *way-ib* is owned by the same god or supernatural (also named on Stela 1 from La Mar), indicating that the same structure was rededicated at the later date or, perhaps more likely, that a new "domicile" was constructed on the second date.

Finally, I would like to add to the list of architectural types an even more specialized and rare glyph that appears so far only at Palenque and nearby Tortuguero. On the so-called Death's Head monument from the Cross Group at Palenque (Fig. 19), we read that on the day 5 Eb 5 Kayab, **OCH-K'AK tu-pi-bi-NAH-li,** or *och k'ak' t-u-pib-nah-il,* "fire entered into his *pibnah*." I have

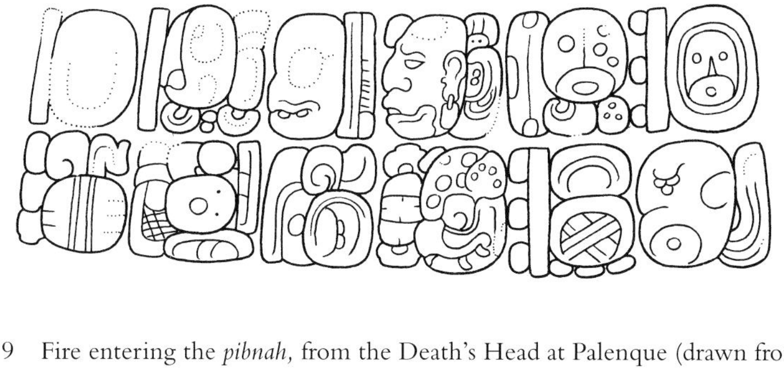

Fig. 19 Fire entering the *pibnah,* from the Death's Head at Palenque (drawn from an unpublished photograph by Teobert Maler, courtesy of the Peabody Museum of Archaeology and Ethnology, Harvard University).

briefly discussed this term before (Stuart 1987: 38), suggesting that it refers to the interior sanctuaries of the Cross Group, possibly as sweatbaths—an alternative meaning of *pib,* "oven," in Yucatec. As alluded to above, Houston (1996) greatly expands on the sweatbath interpretation of the Cross Group sanctuaries, noting that an alternative term was *chitin,* also "oven" (Yucatec *kitin*). *Pibnah* is used throughout the dedicatory texts of the Cross Group in direct reference to the inner sanctuaries of each temple, which were individually given proper names as well (see Stuart and Houston 1994: fig. 104).[15]

The dedicatory verb for most of the *pibnah* structures (all on 5 Eb 5 Kayab, or 9.12.19.5.12) is not *och k'ak'* but another glyph seemingly based on *och* (Fig. 20). The other components include a stepped sign resembling the platform in **OTOT,** and the frequent suffix **-NAH**. The two readable signs **OCH** and **NAH** produce a verbal phrase identical to Yucatec *ok nah,* "house entering." It is quite possible that these dedication statements in the Cross Group involved precisely what Landa described for the house-entering ritual of pre-Conquest Yucatan: a renewal of idols and braziers within the temples, with the inscriptions being "commemorations of these things, written in their characters." The parallel becomes even more striking when we consider that the dedication texts may specifically refer to the "entering" of the "god" into the sanctuary, possibly in the form of renewed effigy figures or elaborate incense burners. If this interpretation is correct, it is essentially the same as the modern Lacandon renewal ceremony for effigy "god pots."

NOTES ON MAYA FIRE RITUALS

As reflected in many of the hieroglyphic passages examined thus far, acts of ceremonial burning or censing were of great importance in ancient Mesoamerican and Maya religion, as of course they remain today among numerous indigenous communities. Indeed, fire or incense seems to be at the center of the architectural rites discussed in the Classic inscriptions. The archaeological evidence of burning rites, mainly in the form of ceramic censers of one type or another, is the most visible indication we have of the ubiquity of these ceremonies throughout Mesoamerica before the Conquest. Ethnohistorical accounts are also fundamental sources for understanding fire rituals, perhaps the most detailed of which are Sahagún's records of "New Fire" ceremonies among the Aztec of Tenochtitlan (Anderson and Dibble 1953). Despite the vast archaeological, artistic, and now hieroglyphic evidence that the Maya took part

[15] My decipherments of these dedication phrases in the Group of the Cross at Palenque have been discussed elsewhere by Schele (1990) and by Freidel and Schele (1989).

Fig. 20 A verb possibly reading *och nah,* "house entering."

in the ritual burning of sacred objects, we tend, I think, to consider these as not so common as bloodletting or at least secondary in importance to bloodletting as a ritual practice. However, I have reached the conclusion that the inscriptions and art of the Classic period are in fact replete with records of ceremonial burning and that these are, not surprisingly, intimately tied to sacrificial rites and other ceremonies associated with dedication and important stations in the Maya calendar. Thus, burning and bloodletting went hand-in-hand as modes of spiritual and ritual expression.

Several years ago Houston (1988) provided the phonetic decipherment for the verb **ho-ch'o** or **ho-ch'a,** for *hoch',* "to drill," usually followed by **K'AK'** with the more specific meaning "to drill fire" (Fig. 21). Scenes depicting fire

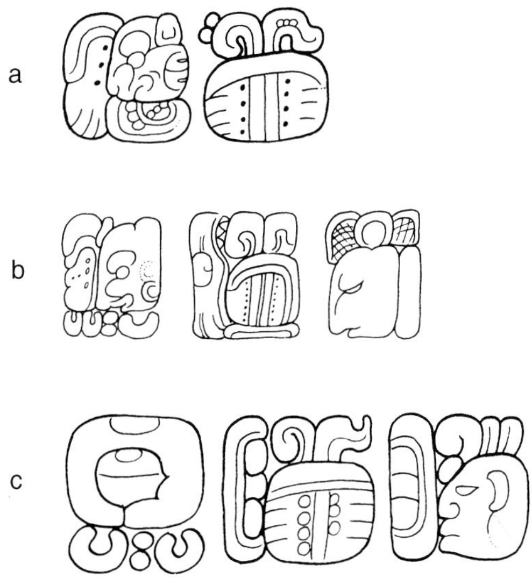

Fig. 21 Drill glyphs: (a) *hoch'-ah k'ak'* from a provenanced lintel (after Stuart and Houston 1994: fig. 89); (b) Yaxchilan Lintel 29 (after Graham 1979: 67); (c) Yaxchilan Stela 1 (after an unpublished field drawing by Ian Graham, Corpus of Maya Hieroglyphic Inscriptions, Harvard University).

drilling have long been known in the Dresden and Madrid Codices, yet the importance of the ritual in Classic times was apparently profound, for records of the *hoch' k'ak'* ritual are widespread in the monumental inscriptions of the southern lowlands. For example, a sculpted lintel from the area of Yaxchilan portrays a drilling scene rather like those from the manuscripts and is captioned by the phrase *hoch'-ah k'ak',* "the fire was drilled" (Stuart and Houston 1994: fig. 89). At Yaxchilan, also, drilling records are included as part of the supplementary series after initial series dates. On Lintel 29 (Fig. 21b) we read that the birth of Bird Jaguar, dated by an initial series, occurred six days (?) after "the fire of God N-Possum was drilled" (see Taube [1989] for a discussion of this particular supernatural). On Stela 1 of Yaxchilan (Fig. 21c), the period ending 9.13.10.0.0 occurred six days after "the fire of the Maize God was drilled." In this last case, the verb is spelled with a logographic sign that, by its parallel behavior, almost surely is the word sign for **HOCH'.**

Many other fire-drilling rituals are recorded in the eastern Peten area at the sites of Sacul and Naranjo. Stela 9 from Sacul (Fig. 22) depicts a standing ruler dressed as the Jaguar God of the Underworld and holding a long, knotted staff and miniature "shield." The inscription above this image gives the long count date for the monument, 9.18.0.0.0 13 Ahau 18 Mac, and a single action, *hoch' k'ak',* "fire drilling." The name of the Maize God follows in the next glyph, probably designating him as the "owner" of the fire.[16] The presence of this lone verb above the scene suggests that the staff held by the ruler may be a ceremonial drill, too large for practical application but symbolic of the rite itself.

Stela 30 from Naranjo offers an excellent example of a ruler in similar ritual attire, also with a probable ceremonial drill (Fig. 23). He wears the facial markers of the Jaguar God of the Underworld and is specifically named as his impersonator in the accompanying text (Houston and Stuart 1996). The knotted staff is the same as that on the Sacul monument and is delicately inscribed with records of the current period ending date and, above, at least one earlier *tun* ending.[17] In his other hand, the ruler holds a distinctive tridentlike flint object.

[16] The deity names associated with fire rituals in the supplementary series do not conform to any discernible pattern, yet the Maize God seems most frequent. In addition to Yaxchilan Stela 1 and Sacul Stela 9, he is the fire owner on Naranjo Stela 13 (Block E9). Stela 2 from Motul de San José names Chak Xib Chaak after *til-k'ak',* "fire burning," as might also Stela 17 from Itzan. A parallel statement on Stela 8 from Naranjo may specify the Headband Gods described by Coe (1989). The overall significance of drilling fires on behalf of gods is not clear, but it may somehow refer to the renewal of fires within temples or shrines associated with these deities. In this way, it may be conceptually related to the entering dedicatory rituals described above.

[17] The two discernible dates inscribed on the drill or staff are 9.13.10.0.0 7 Ahau 3 Cumku (L1-L2) and 9.14.3.0.0 7 Ahau 18 Kankin (Lp19-Lp20). The shared 7 Ahau may account for their unusual pairing.

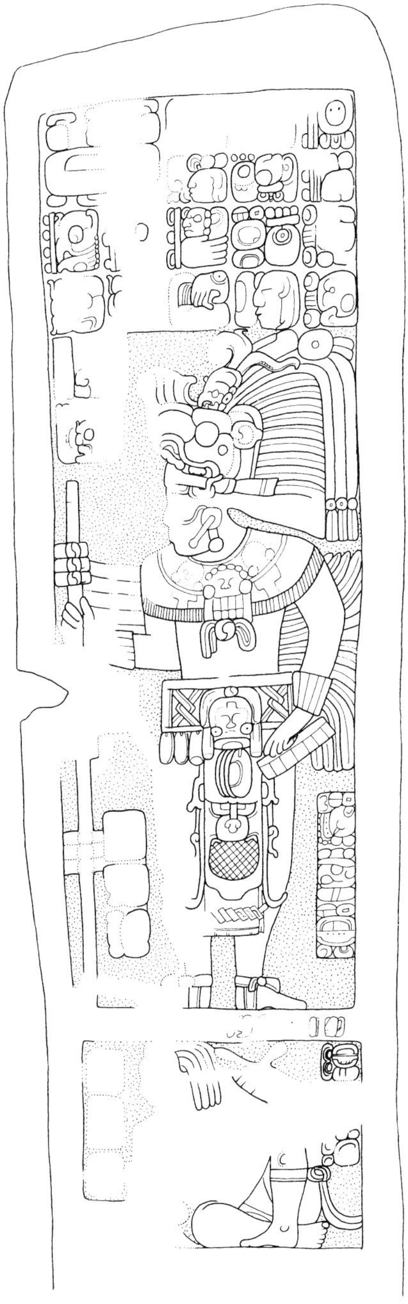

Fig. 22 Sacul Stela 9. The inverted hand glyph above the ruler's headdress is *hoch' k'ak',* "drill fire" (inked from a preliminary field drawing by Ian Graham, Corpus of Maya Hieroglyphic Inscriptions, Harvard University).

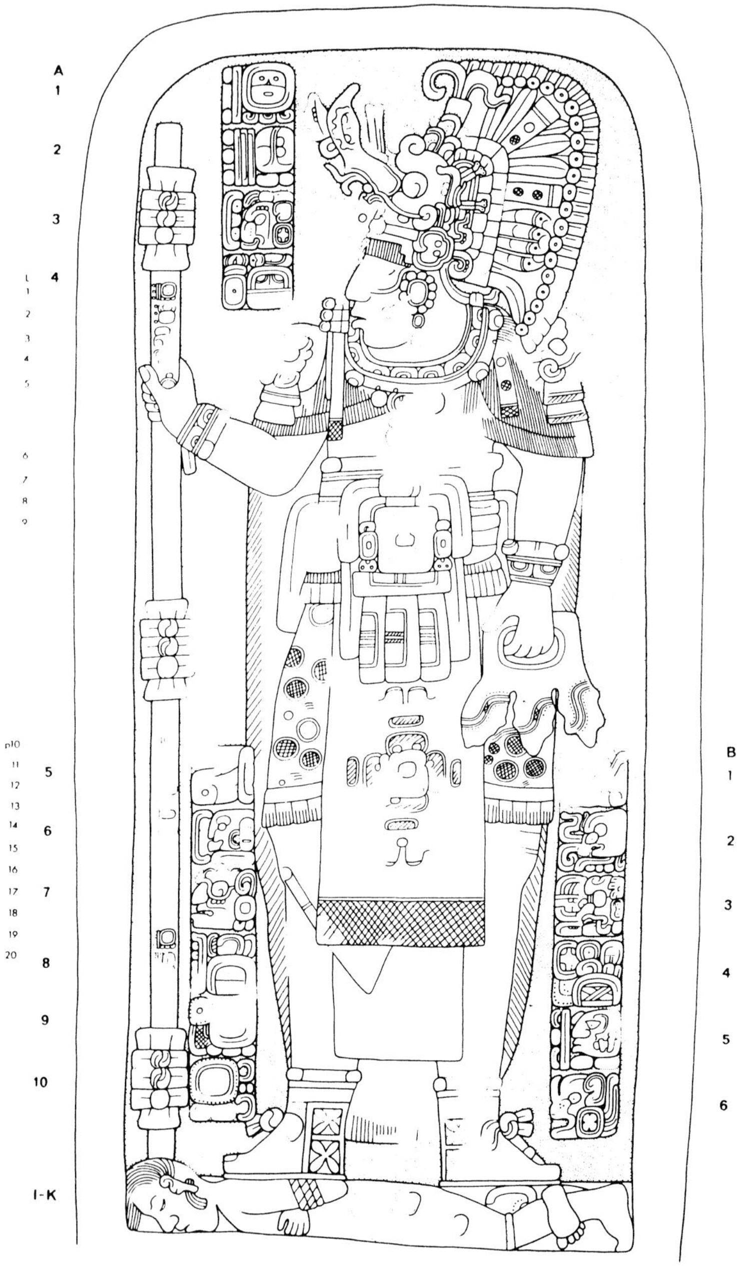

Fig. 23 Naranjo Stela 30 (after Graham 1978).

The inscription does not include the "drill" verb but merely states that *u-bah ti-ak'ab,* "his person(?) (is) in darkness." Drilling rituals among the Aztec, such as in the new fire ceremony, occurred at night (Anderson and Dibble 1953: 25).

The distinctive costume assemblage combining Jaguar God characteristics, long drill staffs, and sometimes the trident flint can be traced to several different monuments (Kubler 1977: 15–16), one of the more interesting perhaps being Altar 5 from Tikal (Fig. 24). Here two kneeling impersonators holding possible drill staffs wear the Jaguar God facial markings. The figure on the left holds the trident flint. Between them lie a stack of long bones topped by a human skull. The inscription of the altar identifies the bones as that of a woman, named in the line of glyphs below the figures. Furthermore, we read that the bones and skull were "opened" (*pas-ah*) on the day 9.13.19.16.6 11 Cimi 19 Mac, presumably referring to the opening of the woman's tomb (according to an earlier passage, as already discussed [see note 4], this woman was buried some eight years previously in the "Nine Ahaw House"). Thus, once more there is an

Fig. 24 Tikal Altar 5 (after Jones and Satterthwaite 1982: fig. 23).

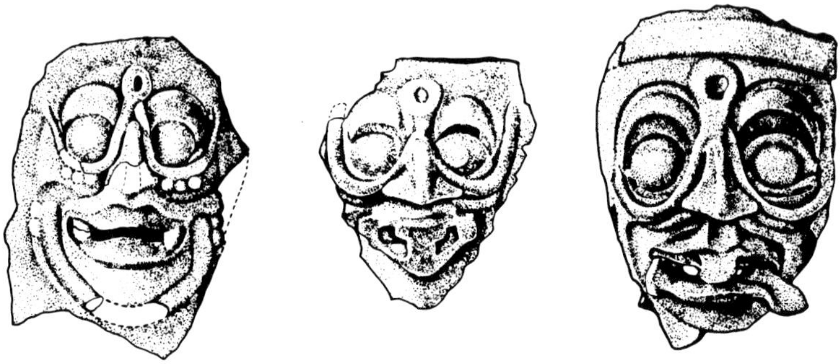

Fig. 25 Incense burner fragments from Seibal with visages of the Jaguar God of the Underworld (after Sabloff 1975: figs. 217–219).

association between tomb reopenings and fire making, recalling the *och k'ak'* rituals mentioned in other texts. Interestingly, excavations under Stela 16, with which Altar 5 is associated, "uncovered a human skull and bones as additional cache elements" (Jones and Satterthwaite 1982: 37). These are almost surely the bones depicted on the altar.

Thus far we have seen that jaguar imagery is strongly associated with the fire-drilling ritual, specifically as part of the costume of the rulers who performed these nocturnal rites. Even more frequent is the visage of the Jaguar God of the Underworld on ritual incense burners found throughout the Maya area (Fig. 25). In addition, Taube (1992) has pointed to several other connections between jaguars and fire symbolism. What is this relationship between jaguar imagery, specifically night-jaguar imagery, and fire? I suggest a simple though speculative answer may be that the Jaguar God of the Underworld, possibly as a manifestation of the night sun, was the supernatural patron of fire and fire making. On Stela 10 of Yaxchilan, an image of the Jaguar God of the

Fig. 26 Detail of ruler's headdress from Yaxchilan Stela 10, showing Jaguar God of the Underworld with fire glyph forehead.

Underworld wearing a large *k'ak'* hieroglyph as his forehead, might lend some credence to this interpretation (Fig. 26).

This brief digression into the symbolism of Maya fire-drilling ceremonies may seem removed from considerations of Maya architecture and its functions, but the dedication and renewal events described in the ancient sources demonstrate the central role of burning and censing in ancient Maya house rituals.

THE "STEP" VERB

Before concluding this review of architectural themes in the inscriptions, it is important to mention another hieroglyph that, although indirectly related to the burning and censing rituals already discussed, is nonetheless important to understanding aspects of Classic Maya architectural function. This is the so-called step verb, which, along with its "God N" head variant, appears to work as the most common type of dedicatory verb in Maya texts (Fig. 27). It customarily takes the suffixed sign **-yi,** a common feature on many intransitive verbs known from the inscriptions. This verb is perhaps most familiar as a component

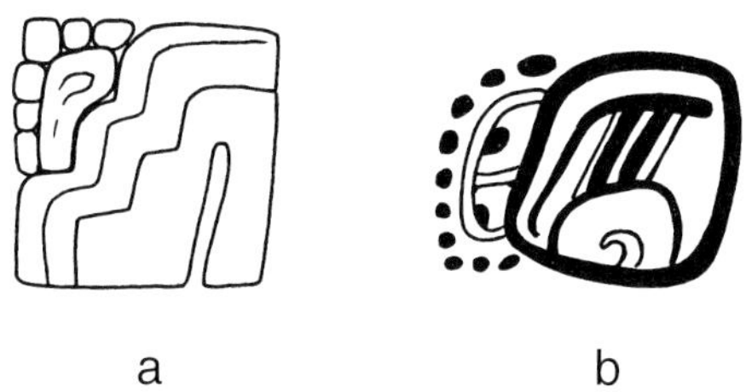

Fig. 27 The "step" verb ("ascend, go up"?) in its early (a) and late (b) variants.

of the PSS "formula" on pottery and other portable objects (Coe 1973). Like other dedicatory verbs discussed thus far, it is customarily followed by the term for the object or monument on which it is inscribed, such as *y-uch'-ib,* "his vessel," or, in architectural inscriptions, *y-otot,* "his house."

MacLeod (1990) has offered the most detailed discussion of the step verb and its variants, suggesting that its reading is *huy* or *hoy,* "to bless." There is reason to doubt this reading, however. The supposed phonetic indicator **hu-**, attached to the front of the step form, derives in fact from a representation of a human footprint shown ascending the steps, as is clearly visible in the Early Classic examples (Fig. 27a). Over time, this prefixed footprint "devolved" into or came to be reanalyzed by Maya scribes as the familiar syllabic character **hu** (as noted earlier, the **OTOT** sign underwent a similar process of graphic abstraction over time). The original footprint form of the prefixed element on the step sign casts significant doubt on the *huy* reading.

The early forms of the step glyph and the contexts of its appearance in the inscriptions provide a number of telling clues about its possible meaning. Both the step glyph and its God N equivalent commonly appear as part of large, extended "name tags" on pottery or other portable elite objects, including jewelry and cloth. When found in monumental texts, the step verb nearly always appears in intimate architectural spaces as a part of inscribed staircases, benches, wall panels, and door lintels; only rarely does it appear as a dedicatory verb on stelae. One noteworthy example appears on Throne 1 from Piedras Negras (Fig. 28), where the step verb follows the sentence *u-kuch-wa ikits,* "he carries the cargo." The step seems to initiate an appended sentence and is followed by the undeciphered name of a building, ending in *-nah,* "house." The physical setting of the text and its reference to a building name links the step verb to the architectural environment. Given the visual origin of the step verb, such an association is not necessarily surprising, but, in light of its associated sentence on Throne 1, it may be possible to narrow the possible significance of the step verb. *Ikits* or *ikats,* "cargo," is the object of the preceding sentence; significantly, because no subject follows the step glyph, it might be understood that *ikats* is again the topic of discussion.

Fig. 28 Piedras Negras Throne 1 support.

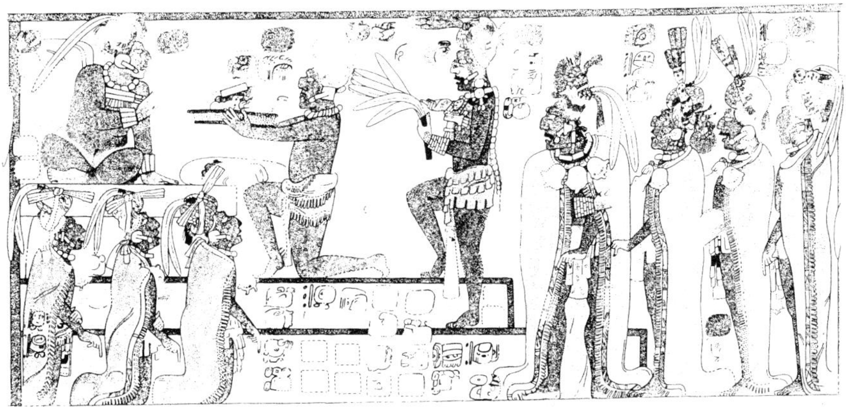

Fig. 29 Vessel depicting gift presentation with stairway, from Burial 116 at Tikal (after Culbert 1993).

Let us assume for the moment that the foot-ascending-steps glyph is a close representation of the action being expressed, as is found with several other verbs of the script such as "scattering" or "to see." The image depicted by a glyph is not always a reliable indicator of meaning, but, given the architectural association of the step in this instance, our assumption may not be unwarranted. The meaning might therefore revolve around concepts such as "ascend, rise, go up," or something generally similar (the verb, whatever its meaning, is marked as intransitive). Significantly, perhaps, tribute scenes found on Maya ceramics take place before thrones or benches at the tops of stepped platforms (Fig. 29); the presentation of gifts or tribute (the distinction is sometimes unclear) is sometimes explicitly shown in connection with these staircases and the persons ascending them. A fine example of the stair ascension theme appears on cylinder 4P-8/2 from Tikal, a stuccoed drinking vessel from Burial 116 (Fig. 29). Two figures step up to the enthroned noble or ruler; one holds a large plate or dish in his outstretched arms, and the other holds a quetzal feather bundle. More dramatic representations of "tribute ascension," as one might call it, come from a painting in Naj Tunich cave. Here in Drawing 5 (Stone 1995: 136) a cloth manta bundle with quetzal feathers is shown atop a tall flight of steps, presumably having been presented by the figure who gazes up at it (Fig. 30). The associated text (Drawing 6) although badly effaced, does include the glyph for *ikats,* "cargo." This painting appears on the surface of a pyramid-shaped rock in the cave (Stone 1995: 190), and the drawing may well have alluded to the stone as an artificial pyramid.

Fig. 30 Tribute presentation scene (?) on stairway, from Naj Tunich cave, Guatemala (drawing based on photograph by George Stuart).

As noted, the foot-ascending-steps verb and its God N equivalent are among the essential features of the PSS on ceramics and other objects. Plates, drinking vessels, cloth, and other portable objects are commonly inscribed with self-referential tags expressing ownership (i.e., "the plate of so-and-so"), and the verb in question must refer to some action involving these objects. From the contexts of its use and the court imagery discussed, it stands to reason that the verb makes reference to the presentation of the objects on which it is found, usually in connection with tribute. The "ascension" of vessels, cloth, and other objects to a ruling noble or king indicates that the direction of flow for these gifts or tribute was, at least in their initial transfer, from subordinates to those of higher rank or office.

Another significant example of tribute imagery occurs in a miniature panel fragment recently unearthed at Palenque (Fig. 31). The scene is very incomplete, but a kneeling figure bearing a heavily loaded tumpline is clearly visible in the lower portion of the extant image. Behind the large bundle stands a tall figure named in the accompanying glyphic caption as the Palenque ruler Akul

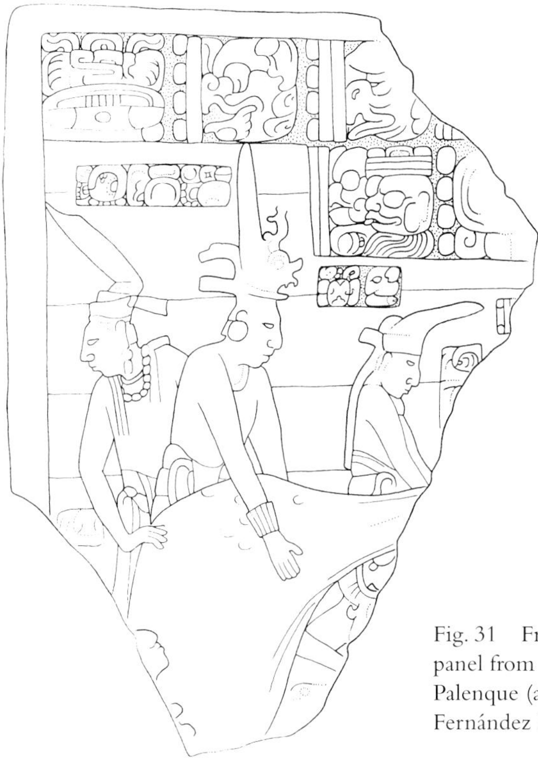

Fig. 31 Fragment of miniature wall panel from the fill of Temple 21 at Palenque (after González Cruz and Fernández Martínez 1994).

Anab III, otherwise known as "Chaacal III." Interestingly, his name here lacks the otherwise customary honorific prefix *K'inich*. The date inscribed on the stone (9.14.19.10.17 4 Caban 10 Zip) falls nine years into the reign of this king but also within a "hiatus" period when no other monuments were carved at this site. Shortly before his inauguration, the previous Palenque ruler K'inich K'an Hok' Chitam (K'an Xul II) was captured by Tonina, as shown on Monument 122 of the latter center. The ensuing political disruptions at Palenque were cited by Peter Mathews (personal communication, 1984) as a probable cause for the lack of sculptural output until about A.D. 730, when the first major monument of Akul Anab's reign was carved.[18] The new fragment is significant not only for falling within this supposed gap but also for its highly unusual subject matter. The Palenque ruler appears modestly costumed, with a

[18] The Tablet of the Slaves, commissioned, actually, by his subordinate Chak Suts' (Schele 1991).

simple cloth headdress and a few jewels. Moreover, Akul Anab seems to be helping unload the tumpline cargo—seemingly an odd activity for a Holy Lord to undertake. An explanation for this highly unusual scene may be found in the background, where regularly spaced horizontal lines represent what are surely the steps of a platform or pyramid. As with the vases and the Naj Tunich painting already discussed and illustrated, the Palenque panel may relate the theme of tribute presentation. Given the historical context of the carving during the years after Palenque's possible conquest by Tonina, the stone may have commemorated a "payment" of goods by the Palenque king at the steps of a Tonina lord. This interpretation is largely speculative, of course, but the association of cargoes, steps, and warfare in this fragmented panel is particularly noteworthy.

The association of steps with scenes of presentation allows us to return to the text from Piedras Negras Throne 1 (Fig. 28), where the "step" verb followed a reference to the "carrying" of a cargo. There may be enough evidence now to tentatively read the entire passage as "he carries the cargo, (and) it ascends the so-and-so house." It is probably no accident that such a statement appears on a royal throne or bench, which on the basis of scenes painted on ceramics was the major setting for the presentation of tribute goods and gifts.

In an intriguing inscription, the "step" verb appears three times on the back of Naranjo Stela 12 (Fig. 32), in each case in direct association with a record of warfare provided by the so-called "axe" event. Following the step glyphs, in turn, is a different possessed object, as indicated by the distinctive **U-** and **ya-** prefixes, but unfortunately the terms themselves are impossible to read with assurance. It is reasonable to interpret these "step" references as records of the presentation or delivery of exacted goods. As indirect support for this interpretation, one can point to the direct mention of **9-pa-ta,** "nine items of tribute," later in this same text, at block E2a. Also tantalizing are the glyphs at G1b and F2a, spelling **yi-ka-tsi,** for *y'ikats,* "his cargo" and the title of the conquered Yaxha lord (Stuart n.d.a).

The association between warfare and monumental staircases is well-known from the archaeology of the Classic period. Peter Mathews (personal communication, 1983) suggested that hieroglyphic staircases in particular were sometimes constructed by victorious groups at conquered sites. Hieroglyphic Stairway 1 at Naranjo, with its Caracol inscription, is a clear example of such a monumental statement of conquest and domination. Not all hieroglyphic staircases can be interpreted in this way, yet it is true that warfare and captives are dominant themes of inscriptions on steps. It stands to reason that the importance of steps in the symbolism of tribute or gift delivery goes far toward explaining the nature of these and other inscribed steps at Maya centers. Caracol's conquest

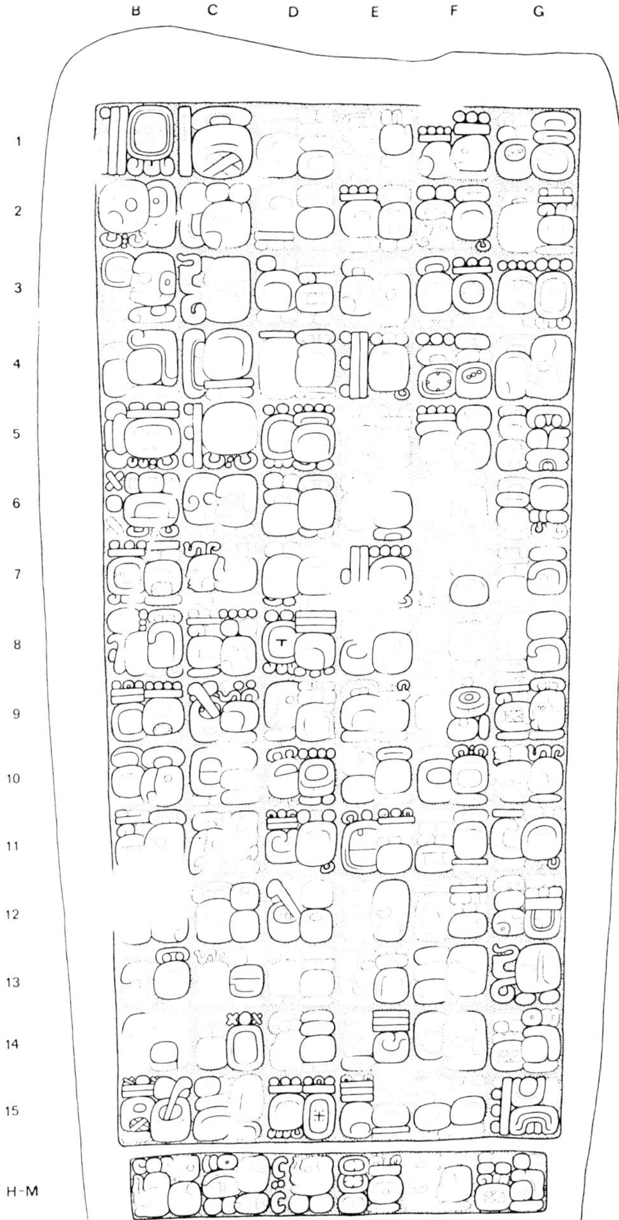

Fig. 32 Naranjo Stela 12. "Step" and "God N" verbs are at C12a, E1a, E9a, and D14a (after Graham and Von Euw 1975: 36).

stairway at Naranjo may well have been constructed as a delivery point for the tribute and goods extracted from the local subject population. It is interesting to note that this stairway was subsequently vandalized in antiquity; the steps were rearranged in a meaningless sequence of inscribed blocks. This may have occurred with the renewed independence of Naranjo in the early years of the Late Classic period. Similarly, steps relating themes of war and capture at Dos Pilas and elsewhere may have been conceived as locales for the presentation of tribute by neighboring victims. This scenario may help account for the extremely large size of some preserved staircases, such as that on the north face of Temple 11 at Copan, which often may have been designed more for the display of goods and prisoners than for any practical purpose of access (see Houston, this volume).

An important usage of the "step" or "God N" verb has yet to be mentioned. In several architectural inscriptions it precedes *y-otot,* "his house," much as it combines with the words for possessed objects in the dedicatory texts of the PSS on portable objects. With "house," the foot-ascending-steps glyph must somehow work also as a general dedicatory statement. A good example of this use comes from the bench inscription of Structure 9N-82 at Copan—the so-called House of the Bacabs (Webster 1989) (Fig. 33). There a full-figure version of the God N "head variant" of the step verb follows an initial date and is followed by **yo-OTOT** and then, in turn, by the name of the house's owner. If we pursue the supposed significance of the step event as something like "ascend," what would the dedicatory statement be saying? It is perhaps doubtful that a "house" would be presented as a gift or tribute in the same manner as a ceramic vessel, but it remains possible that the parallel usages allude to the building of the structure with tribute labor (recall the use of *pat,* "make, build houses," in *pat-an,* "service, tribute"). Perhaps a more simple interpretation, however, would read the bench text as "his house went up," referring to its actual construction.

It must be mentioned, however, that despite the speculative discussions on the significance of the step verb, its phonetic reading still evades us. The evidence for its meaning revolving around concepts of "ascend" or "go up" is based on the context of the verb's usage and the visual image it originally represented, but the final confirmation must come, of course, from phonetic clues of its reading. Two inscriptions from Yucatan may be important in testing this reading, for they appear to be phonetic variants of the step or God N glyph. In the PSS text of Structure 1 at Ikil (Andrews and Stuart 1975), the verb is **?-ba-yi,** suggesting that the root may end in *-ab.* The text on Capstone 2 of Uxmal (Graham and von Euw 1992: 141) makes use of the same glyph, with

Fig. 33 Initial phrase from the text of the hieroglyphic bench from Structure 9N-82, Copan, Honduras.

the telling addition of the **hu**-like prefix that was originally the foot of the step verb. This may help establish the equivalence with the step glyph. If so, it is interesting that the Cholan root *t'ab* carries precisely the meaning suggested here: "go up, ascend" (Kaufman and Norman 1984). The sign above the **ba** in these glyphs is difficult to read, and any **t'a** value would need to be tested against an independent sample of occurrences

CONCLUDING REMARKS

Nearly all Maya architecture was, at one time or another, ritual space. This was true not only for conspicuous elite constructions but also probably for humble dwellings as well, if the ethnographic sources cited here are any indication. The ceremonial role of ancient Maya architecture was no doubt as varied as the forms and scales we witness in the archaeological record; yet, as I have attempted to show in this paper, the rites of dedication were of paramount interest to those who composed Maya documents. Commemorative inscriptions recounting fire entering and other rituals in houses, tombs, and shrines were no small part of Maya history as they chose to present it.

The "fire entering" expression and its relatives were specific dedicatory expressions for buildings, and although we have explored somewhat the ideas of "entering" and the ethnographic parallels of new house ceremonies, the significance of fire in these ceremonies deserves further comment. Taube (this volume) has expanded greatly on the iconographic symbolism of fire in Maya architecture, and following his arguments I suggest that placing a fire within a new building figuratively makes it a home by creating a "hearth," thereby investing the space with heat and strength. Among many modern Maya and Mesoamerican groups, heat is widely held to be a reflection of one's strength or vitality, of one's soul (Gossen 1974; Villa Rojas 1980; López Austin 1988). Perhaps by bringing the heat of fire into a building, the space is vivified and invested with its own soul. The existence of this same ritual in tomb-renewal ceremonies, as we have seen at Seibal and other sites, may represent the occasional desire to "revivify" the *muknal,* the dwelling of the deceased ancestor. Surely the tomb ceremonies involved more complex actions as well, such as the inexplicable removal and redeposition of bones as described and depicted on Tikal, Altar 5. Indeed, the sources on ancient Maya mortuary ritualism are rich and varied enough that they warrant a more thorough study than I can provide here.

These details aside, it now seems very clear from ancient architectural inscriptions that the Maya had much to say about their own built environment. These texts do not necessarily tell us all we would like to know of the everyday activities in temples and palaces, but they do allow us to explore with more precision the functions of buildings and their perceptions of "houses" as social, political, and ritual spaces. Moreover, the texts agree remarkably well with Landa's brief mention of the written "memorials" of house renewal rites involving ceremonial braziers—rites that have their descendants throughout modern Mesoamerica.

As discussed at the beginning of this essay, the extant Maya inscriptions, when viewed as a whole, appear to focus on the history of dedicated things and monuments and less on the recounting of personal royal deeds than is often claimed. The built environment, even when not the topical focus of textual records, was at the very least a primary setting for the dedicatory rites and other events that shaped the Maya historical record.

BIBLIOGRAPHY

Anderson, Arthur J. O., and Charles E. Dibble (trans.)

1953 *The Florentine Codex: Book 7—The Sun, Moon, and Stars, and the Binding of the Years*. School of American Research, Santa Fe.

Andrews, E. Wyllys, IV, and George E. Stuart

1975 The Ruins of Ikil, Yucatan, Mexico. In *Archaeological Research in the Yucatan Peninsula*. Middle American Research Institute, Publication 31. Tulane University, New Orleans.

Andrews, E. Wyllys, V, and Barbara W. Fash

1992 Continuity and Change in a Royal Maya Residential Complex at Copan. *Ancient Mesoamerica* 3: 63–88.

Barrera Vásquez, Alfredo

1980 *Diccionario Cordemex: Maya–Español, Español–Maya*. Ediciones Cordemex, Mérida, Yucatan, Mexico.

Becquelin, Pierre, and Claude F. Baudez

1982 *Tonina: une cité maya du Chiapas,* vol. 3. Mission archéologique et ethnologique française au Mexique, Paris.

Berlin, Heinrich

1959 Glifos nominales en el sarcófago de Palenque. *Humanidades* 2 (10): 1–8.

Bruce, Robert D., and Victor Perera

1982 *The Last Lords of Palenque*. Little, Brown, Boston.

Carlsen, Robert S., and Martin Prechtel

1991 The Flowering of the Dead: An Interpretation of Highland Maya Culture. *Man* 26 (1): 23–42.

Coe, Michael D.

1973 *The Maya Scribe and His World*. Grolier Club, New York.

1974 A Carved Wooden Box from the Classic Maya Civilization. In *Primera Mesa Redonda de Palenque,* pt. 2 (Merle Greene Robertson, ed.): 51–58. Robert Louis Stevenson School, Pebble Beach, Calif.

1989 The Hero Twins: Myth and Image. In *The Maya Vase Book*, vol. 1 (Justin Kerr, ed.): 161–184. Kerr Associates, New York.

Coe, William R.

1959 *Piedras Negras Archaeology: Artifacts, Caches, and Burials*. University Museum Monographs. University of Pennsylvania, Philadelphia.

Coggins, Clemency Chase (ed.)

1992 *Artifacts from the Cenote of Sacrifice, Chichen Itza, Yucatan*. Memoirs of the Peabody Museum of Archaeology and Ethnology, vol. 10, no. 3. Harvard University, Cambridge, Mass.

Culbert, T. Patrick

1993 *The Ceramics of Tikal*. Tikal Report, no. 25. University Museum, University of Pennsylvania, Philadelphia.

Durán, Fray Diego

1971 *Book of the Gods and Rites and the Ancient Calendar* (Fernando Horcasitas and Doris Heyden, trans.). University of Oklahoma Press, Norman.

Fash, Barbara, William Fash, Sheree Lane, Rudy Larios, Linda Schele, Jeffrey Stomper, and David Stuart

1992 Investigations of a Classic Maya Council House at Copán, Honduras. *Journal of Field Archaeology* 19: 419–442.

Fettweis, Martine

1988 *Coba et Xelha: Peintures murales mayas.* Institut d'ethnologie, Musée de l'homme, Paris.

Fox, James A., and John S. Justeson

1984 Polyvalence in Mayan Hieroglyphic Writing. In *Phoneticism in Mayan Hieroglyphic Writing* (J. S. Justeson and L. Campbell, eds.): 17–76. Institute for Mesoamerican Studies, State University of New York, Albany.

Freidel, David A., and Linda Schele

1989 Dead Kings and Living Temples: Dedication and Termination Rituals among the Ancient Maya. In *Word and Image in Maya Culture* (William F. Hanks and Don S. Rice, eds.): 233–243. University of Utah Press, Salt Lake City.

Freidel, David A., Linda Schele, and Joy Parker

1993 *Maya Cosmos: Three Thousand Years on the Shaman's Path.* William Morrow, New York.

González Cruz, Arnoldo, and Gerardo Fernández Martínez

1994 Inscripciones calendáricas encontradas en Palenque. *Arqueología Mexicana* 2 (8): 60–62.

Gossen, Gary H.

1974 *Chamulas in the World of the Sun: Time and Space in a Maya Oral Tradition.* Harvard University Press, Cambridge, Mass.

Graham, Ian

1967 *Archaeological Explorations in El Peten, Guatemala.* Middle American Research Institute, Publication 33. Tulane University, New Orleans.

1977 *Corpus of Maya Hieroglyphic Inscriptions,* vol. 3, pt. 1: *Yaxchilan.* Peabody Museum of Archaeology and Ethnology, Harvard University, Cambridge, Mass.

1978 *Corpus of Maya Hieroglyphic Inscriptions,* vol. 2, pt. 2: *Naranjo, Chunhuitz, Xunantunich.* Peabody Museum of Archaeology and Ethnology, Harvard University, Cambridge, Mass.

1979 *Corpus of Maya Hieroglyphic Inscriptions,* vol. 3, pt. 2: *Yaxchilan.* Peabody Museum of Archaeology and Ethnology, Harvard University, Cambridge, Mass.

1982 *Corpus of Maya Hieroglyphic Inscriptions,* vol. 3, pt. 3: *Yaxchilan.* Peabody Museum of Archaeology and Ethnology, Harvard University, Cambridge, Mass.

1996 *Corpus of Maya Hieroglyphic Inscriptions,* vol. 7, pt. 1: *Seibal.* Peabody Museum of Archaeology and Ethnology, Harvard University, Cambridge, Mass.

Graham, Ian, and Eric von Euw

1975 *Corpus of Maya Hieroglyphic Inscriptions,* vol. 2, pt. 1: *Naranjo.* Peabody Museum of Archaeology and Ethnology, Harvard University, Cambridge, Mass.

1977 *Corpus of Maya Hieroglyphic Inscriptions,* vol. 3, pt. 1: *Yaxchilan.* Peabody Museum of Archaeology and Ethnology, Harvard University, Cambridge, Mass.

1992 *Corpus of Maya Hieroglyphic Inscriptions,* vol. 4, pt. 3: *Uxmal, Xcalumkin.* Peabody Museum of Archaeology and Ethnology, Harvard University, Cambridge, Mass.

GRUBE, NIKOLAI

1990 Die Errichtung von Stelen: Entzifferung einer Verbhieroglyphie auf Monumenten der Klassichen Mayakultur. In *Circumpacifica: Festschrift für Thomas Barthel* (B. Illius and M. Laubscher, eds.): 189–215. Peter Lang, Frankfurt.

GRUBE, NIKOLAI, AND DAVID STUART

1987 *Observations on T110 as the Syllable* ko. Research Reports on Ancient Maya Writing 8. Center for Maya Research, Washington, D.C.

GUITERAS-HOLMES, CALIXTA

1961 *Perils of the Soul: The World View of a Tzotzil Indian.* Free Press of Glencoe, New York.

HARRIS, JOHN F., AND STEPHEN K. STEARNS

1992 *Understanding Maya Inscriptions: A Hieroglyph Handbook.* The University Museum, University of Pennsylvania, Philadelphia.

HANKS, WILLIAM

1990 *Referential Practice: Language and Lived Space among the Maya.* University of Chicago Press, Chicago.

HOUSTON, STEPHEN D.

1983 On "Ruler 6" at Piedras Negras, Gautemala. *Mexicon* 5: 84–86.

1988 The Phonetic Decipherment of Mayan Glyphs. *Antiquity* 62: 126–134.

1989 *Hieroglyphs and History at Dos Pilas: Dynastic Politics of the Classic Maya.* University of Texas Press, Austin.

1996 Symbolic Sweatbaths of the Maya: Architectural Meaning in the Cross Group at Palenque. *Latin American Antiquity* 7: 132–151.

HOUSTON, STEPHEN D., AND DAVID STUAR

1990 *The Way Glyph: Evidence of "Co-essences" among the Classic Maya.* Research Reports on Ancient Maya Writing 30. Center for Maya Research, Washington, D.C.

1994 *Classic Maya Place Names.* Studies in Pre-Columbian Art and Archaeology 33. Dumbarton Oaks, Washington, D.C.

1996 Of Gods, Glyphs, and Kings: Divine Rulership among the Classic Maya. *Antiquity* 70: 289–312.

HOUSTON, STEPHEN D., DAVID STUART, AND KARL A. TAUBE

1989 Folk Classification of Classic Maya Pottery. *American Anthropologist* 91: 720–726.

JONES, CHRISTOPHER, AND LINTON SATTERTHWAITE

1982 *The Monuments and Inscriptions of Tikal: The Carved Monuments.* Tikal Report, no. 33, pt. A. University Museum, University of Pennsylvania, Philadelphia.

JOSSERAND, KATHRYN

1991 Narrative Structure of Hieroglyphic Texts at Palenque. In *Sixth Palenque Round*

Table, 1986 (Virginia M. Fields, ed.): 12–31. University of Oklahoma Press, Norman.

1995 Participant Tracking in Maya Hieroglyphic Texts: Who Was That Masked Man? *Journal of Linguistic Anthropology* 5 (1): 65–89.

JUSTESON, JOHN S.

1984 Interpretations of Maya Hieroglyphs. In *Phoneticism in Mayan Hieroglyphic Writing* (J. S. Justeson and L. Campbell, eds.): 315–362. Institute for Mesoamerican Studies, State University of New York, Albany.

n.d. An Interpretation of the Classic Maya Hieroglyphic Spelling of "East." Manuscript on file, Peabody Museum, Harvard University, Cambridge, Mass., 1982.

KAUFMAN, TERRENCE S., AND WILLIAM M. NORMAN

1984 An Outline of Proto-Cholan Phonology, Morphology, and Vocabulary. In *Phoneticism in Mayan Hieroglyphic Writing* (J. S. Justeson and L. Campbell, eds.): 77–166. Institute for Mesoamerican Studies, State University of New York, Albany.

KELLEY, DAVID H.

1968 Mayan Fire Glyphs. *Estudios de Cultura Maya* 7: 141–157.

1976 *Deciphering the Maya Script*. University of Texas Press, Austin.

KUBLER, GEORGE

1977 *Aspects of Classic Maya Rulership on Two Inscribed Vessels.* Studies in Pre-Columbian Art and Archaeology 18. Dumbarton Oaks, Washington, D.C.

LAUGHLIN, ROBERT M.

1975 *The Great Tzotzil Dictionary of San Lorenzo Zinacantan*. Smithsonian Contributions to Anthropology, no. 19. Smithsonian Institution Press, Washington, D.C.

LOK, ROSSANA

1987 The House as a Microcosm: Some Cosmic Representations in a Mexican Indian Village. In *The Leiden Tradition in Structural Anthropology* (R. de Ridder and J. Karremans, eds.): 211–223. E. J. Brill, Leiden, Netherlands.

LÓPEZ AUSTIN, ALFREDO

1988 *The Human Body and Ideology: Concepts of the Ancient Nahuas.* 2 vols. (T. Ortiz de Montellano and B. Ortiz de Montellano, trans.). University of Utah Press, Salt Lake City.

LOUNSBURY, FLOYD G.

1973 On the Derivation and Reading of the "Ben–Ich" Prefix. In *Mesoamerican Writing Systems* (Elizabeth P. Benson, ed.): 99–143. Dumbarton Oaks, Washington, D.C.

1974 The Inscription on the Sarcophagus Lid at Palenque. In *Primera mesa redonda de Palenque,* pt. 2 (Merle Greene Robertson, ed.): 5–19. Robert Louis Stevenson School, Pebble Beach, Calif.

1984 Glyphic Substitutions: Homophonic and Synonymic. In *Phoneticism in Mayan Hieroglyphic Writing* (J. S. Justeson and L. Campbell, eds.): 167–184. Institute for Mesoamerican Studies, State University of New York, Albany.

MacLeod, Barbara
1984 Cholan and Yucatec Verb Morphology and Glyphic Verbal Affixes in the Inscriptions. In *Phoneticism in Mayan Hieroglyphic Writing* (J. S. Justeson and L. Campbell, eds.): 233–263. Institute for Mesoamerican Studies, State University of New York, Albany.
1990 The God N/Step Set in the Primary Standard Sequence. In *The Maya Vase Book*, vol. 2 (Justin Kerr, ed.): 331–347. Kerr Associates, New York.

Marcus, Joyce
1992 *Mesoamerican Writing Systems: Propaganda, Myth, and History in Four Ancient Civilizations.* Princeton University Press, Princeton, N.J.

McGee, R. Jon
1990 *Life, Ritual, and Religion among the Lacandon Maya.* Wadsworth, Belmont, Calif.

Miller, Mary Ellen, and Stephen D. Houston
1987 The Classic Maya Ballgame and Its Architectural Setting: A Study of Relations between Text and Image. *RES: Anthropology and Aesthetics* 14: 47–66.

Potter, David F.
1977 *Maya Architecture of the Central Yucatan Peninisula.* Middle American Research Institute, Publication 44. Tulane University, New Orleans.

Proskouriakoff, Tatiana
1960 Historical Implications of a Pattern of Dates at Piedras Negras, Guatemala. *American Antiquity* 25: 454–475.
1963 *An Album of Maya Architecture.* University of Oklahoma Press, Norman.

Redfield, Robert, and Alfonso Villa Rojas
1964 *Chan Kom: A Maya Village.* University of Chicago Press, Chicago.

Robertson, Merle Greene
1985 *The Sculpture of Palenque,* vol. 1: *The Temple of the Inscriptions.* Princeton University Press, Princeton, N.J.

Sabloff, Jeremy
1975 *Excavations at Seibal,* no. 2: *Ceramics.* Memoirs of the Peabody Museum of Archaeology and Ethnology, vol. 13. Harvard University, Cambridge, Mass.

Saile, David G.
1977 Making a House: Building Rituals and Spatial Concepts in the Pueblo Indian World. *Architectural Association Quarterly* 9 (2, 3): 72–81.

Sandstrom, Alan R.
1991 *Corn Is Our Blood: Culture and Ethnic Identity in a Contemporary Aztec Indian Village.* University of Oklahoma Press, Norman.

Schele, Linda
1982 *Maya Glyphs: The Verbs.* University of Texas Press, Austin.
1984 Some Suggested Readings of the Event and Office of Heir-Designation at Palenque. In *Phoneticism in Maya Hieroglyphic Writing* (J. S. Justeson and L. Campbell, eds.): 287–305. Institute of Mesoamerican Studies, State University of New York, Albany.
1990 House Names and Dedication Rituals at Palenque. In *Vision and Revision in Maya Studies* (F. Clancy and P. Harrison, eds.): 143–157. University of New

Mexico Press, Albuquerque.

1991 The Demotion of Chak-Zutz': Lineage Compunds and Subordinate Lords at Palenque. In *Sixth Palenque Round Table, 1986* (Virginia M. Fields, ed.): 6–11. University of Oklahoma Press, Norman.

Schele, Linda, and David Freidel

1990 *A Forest of Kings: The Untold Story of the Ancient Maya.* William Morrow, New York.

Schele, Linda, and Peter Mathews

1979 *The* Bodega *of Palenque, Chiapas, Mexico.* Dumbarton Oaks, Washington, D.C.

Smith, A. Ledyard

1982 Major Architecture and Caches. In *Excavations at Seibal, Department of Peten, Guatemala* (Gordon R. Willey, ed.): v–263. Memoirs of the Peabody Museum of Archaeology and Ethnology, vol. 15. Harvard University, Cambridge, Mass.

Stone, Andrea J.

1995 *Images from the Underworld: Naj Tunich and the Tradition of Maya Cave Painting.* University of Texas Press, Austin.

Stuart, David

1987 *Ten Phonetic Syllables.* Research Reports on Ancient Maya Writing 14. Center for Maya Research, Washington, D.C.

1989 Hieroglyphs on Maya Vessels. In *The Maya Vase Book,* vol. 1 (Justin Kerr, ed.): 149–160. Kerr Associates, New York.

n.d.a A Study of Maya Inscriptions. Ph.D. dissertation, Vanderbilt University, Nashville, Tenn., 1995.

n.d.b The Texts of Temple 26: The Presentation of History at a Maya Dynastic Shrine. In *Copan: The Rise and Fall of a Classic Maya Kingdom* (William L. Fash and E. Wyllys Andrews V, eds.). School of American Research Press, Sante Fe. (In preparation.)

Stuart, David, and Stephen D. Houston

1994 *Classic Maya Place Names.* Studies in Pre-Columbian Art and Archaeology 34. Dumbarton Oaks, Washington, D.C.

Taube, Karl

1989 Ritual Humor in Classic Maya Religion. In *Word and Image in Maya Culture* (William F. Hanks and Don S. Rice, eds.): 351–382. University of Utah Press, Salt Lake City.

1992 *The Major Gods of Ancient Yucatan.* Studies in Pre-Columbian Art and Archaeology 32. Dumbarton Oaks, Washington, D.C.

1994 The Birth Vase: Natal Imagery in Ancient Maya Art and Ritual. In *The Maya Vase Book,* vol. 4 (Justin Kerr, ed.): 652–675. Kerr Associates, New York.

Tedlock, Dennis (trans.)

1985 *Popol Vuh.* Simon and Schuster, New York.

Tozzer, Alfred M. (trans.)

1941 *Landa's relación de las cosas de Yucatán.* Papers of the Peabody Museum of Archaeology and Ethnology, vol. 18. Harvard University, Cambridge, Mass.

Villa Rojas, Alfonso

1980 La imagen del cuerpo humano según los mayas de Yucatán. *Anales de Antropología* 17 (2): 31–46.

Vogt, Evon Z.

1969 *Zinacantan: A Maya Community in the Highlands of Chiapas.* Belknap Press of Harvard Univerity Press, Cambridge, Mass.

1976 *Tortillas for the Gods: A Symbolic Analysis of Zinacanteco Rituals.* Harvard University Press, Cambridge, Mass.

n.d. Zinacanteco Dedication and Termination Rituals. Manuscript on file, Department of Anthropology, Harvard University, Cambridge, Mass., 1993.

Webster, David (ed.)

1989 *The House of the Bacabs, Copan, Honduras.* Studies in Pre-Columbian Art and Archaeology 29. Dumbarton Oaks, Washington, D.C.

Whittaker, Arabelle, and Viola Warkentin

1965 *Chol Texts of the Supernatural.* Summer Institute of Linguistics, Norman, Okla.

Yadeun, Juan

1993 *Toniná: El laberinto del inframundo.* Gobierno del Estado de Chiapas, México, D.F.

The Jade Hearth: Centrality, Rulership, and the Classic Maya Temple

KARL TAUBE
UNIVERSITY OF CALIFORNIA AT RIVERSIDE

WITH THEIR MASSIVE platforms and frequently elaborate superstructures, temple pyramids are among the most striking and resonant images of the ancient Maya. Whether to house the gods or the honored dead, these imposing structures form the core and center of Maya sites, serving as pivotal links between the living and the divine. In addition, temple buildings are not only some of the earliest public architecture known for the ancient Maya but also the initial focus of complex art, whether in the form of massive platform masks or stone monuments directly oriented to the buildings. But despite the central role of the temple in ancient Maya society and culture, there has been relatively little interest in its underlying function and meaning. The basic metaphoric theme explored in this study is the temple as a house, both as a dwelling place of gods and as a model of the universe. The symbolism of the three-stone hearth constitutes an essential theme of temple ritual and imagery. As symbols of the *axis mundi,* hearths in the form of temple censers served as a means of conjuring and communicating with the divine. It will be seen that the Classic Maya elite elevated the humble domestic hearth into a precious symbol of royal power. The jade Jester God, a major emblem of Maya kings, evoked the concepts of the hearth and world center. At sites such as Tonina, Quirigua, and Copan, Maya rulers portrayed themselves in terms of temples and their attendant urns—that is, as sacred, pivotal intermediaries between supernatural beings and the mortal plane.

THE TEMPLE AS A HOUSE

Since the nineteenth-century dawning of Maya archaeology, scholars have noted the similarity of recent Maya houses to Classic monumental architecture.

In 1844, the artist Frederick Catherwood (cited in Wauchope 1938: 149–150) first suggested that Maya masonry temples derived from the pole-and-thatch Maya house, a basic feature of Maya life to this day. In the early twentieth century, Edward Thompson (1911) argued that many traits seen in Classic monumental architecture represent conservative survivals of original wood-and-thatch houses. In his classic analysis of modern Maya houses, Robert Wauchope (1938: 150–151) also acknowledged the presence of commoner domestic traits in elite Classic architecture. However, to Wauchope, these features do not derive from a conservative, unconscious bowing to tradition. Instead, he considered them to be intentionally adopted for purposes of style and decoration. But, although deliberate, the translation of everyday domestic architecture into stone and stucco is not only decorative but has important symbolic value as well. The evocation of the basic Maya house defines the temple as a dwelling place, albeit of gods rather than mortals. The four-sided house also serves as a model for perceiving and structuring the universe. By adopting the cosmic house metaphor, the Classic Maya temple embodied and channeled some of the most essential and powerful principles of the cosmos.

The concept of the temple as a deity house is by no means limited to the ancient Maya. Bruce Trigger (1990: 121) notes that ancient temples were commonly regarded as god houses in many regions of the world:

> the temples of the early civilizations were usually designed to be the earthly dwellings of gods rather than assembly places for communal worship. Much of the cult was conducted in seclusion inside these buildings, which in many cultures were called literally "gods' houses." (Trigger 1990: 121)

This is precisely the case for the ancient Maya; in colonial Yucatec, the common term for temple is *k'u na,* meaning "god house" (Barrera Vásquez 1980: 423), and similar meanings can be readily found in early colonial dictionaries of other Mayan languages (e.g., Acuña 1983: 544; Laughlin 1988: 373). Following initial epigraphic insights by David Kelley (1976: 133), David Stuart (1987: 33–39) notes that in both the Post-Classic codices and Classic Maya monuments, temples are referred to as *otoch* or *otot,* a term meaning "house" in Mayan languages. In ancient Maya temple scenes, gods frequently appear in their thatched houses, and the representations of thatched buildings on Maya structures probably denote them as dwelling places of gods (e.g., see Fig. 2b). At Late Classic Copan, there are in-the-round forms of this motif, here as rectangular temple models containing a seated God C figure (see Houston, this volume). Grube and Schele (1990) note that accompanying texts describe these temple models as *u waybil k'u,* signifying "the sleeping place of god." Just as humans require privacy and rest, so too is it with gods in their temple houses.

For at least one of the Copan temple models, a pair of curtain holes occurs on the roof above the central doorway (see Andrews and Fash 1992: fig. 17). Commonly found in palace and temple structures, these holes supported cloth or mat hangings that served as the Maya version of doors (Fig. 1a–e; see Anderson 1985). Such curtains were the principal means to secure privacy within domiciles and temples alike. In Early Post-Classic murals at Chichen Itza, doorway curtains occur in both temples and domestic structures (Fig. 1a–b). Just as a covered household doorway could signal for privacy, the temple curtains probably were also used to indicate states of the god housed within. In terms of the Copan temple models, a curtain-covered doorway probably indicated that the god was asleep in his resting place, or *waybil.*

At times, actual Maya temples are represented with false, curtain-covered doorways. The earliest instance occurs on the Late Pre-Classic Structure H-X at Uaxactun. Both sides of the real doorway are flanked by niches marked with mat designs, denoting curtain-closed doorways (Fig. 2a). A similar situation occurs on Structure 2 at the Terminal Classic Chenes site of Hochob. Elongated representations of thatched houses frame the sides of the central zoomorphic doorway, and, in both cases, the false house doorways are covered by hanging mats (Fig. 2b). Flanking false doorways also occur with roughly contemporaneous Río Bec structures (see Gendrop 1983: figs. 12d, 31a–b, 35, and 45b). Here the doorway niches are covered by checkered patterns representing woven cloth or matting (Fig. 2c). The false-curtained temple doorways may have denoted divine occupancy, signaling to the observer the proper decorum of caution and respect, much as if one were approaching a palace.

Aside from serving as god houses, temples were also models of the cosmos. The house metaphor for the world is well-attested in contemporary Maya lore. In the *ch'a ch'aac* ceremonies of contemporary Yucatan, the four-legged wooden altar represents the world, with the altar surface being the earth and the overarching crossed saplings representing the heavens (Sosa n.d.: 346). The modern Chorti believe the world to be supported by four corner posts. Fought (1972: 377–379) notes that the Chorti term for the cosmic corner post is *oi,* "one of the tree trunks set in the ground to support the roof and walls of a house." According to one Zinacanteco Tzotzil informant, the universe is "like a house, like a table" (Vogt 1976: 11). Both the Tzotzil and Tojolabal Maya consider the universe to be a quadrangular structure supported at its corners by supernatural beings (see Holland 1963: 92; Ruz 1982: 55; Vogt 1976: 15–16). Among the Tzotzil of San Andrés, the immortal world bearers are termed *yoyal*

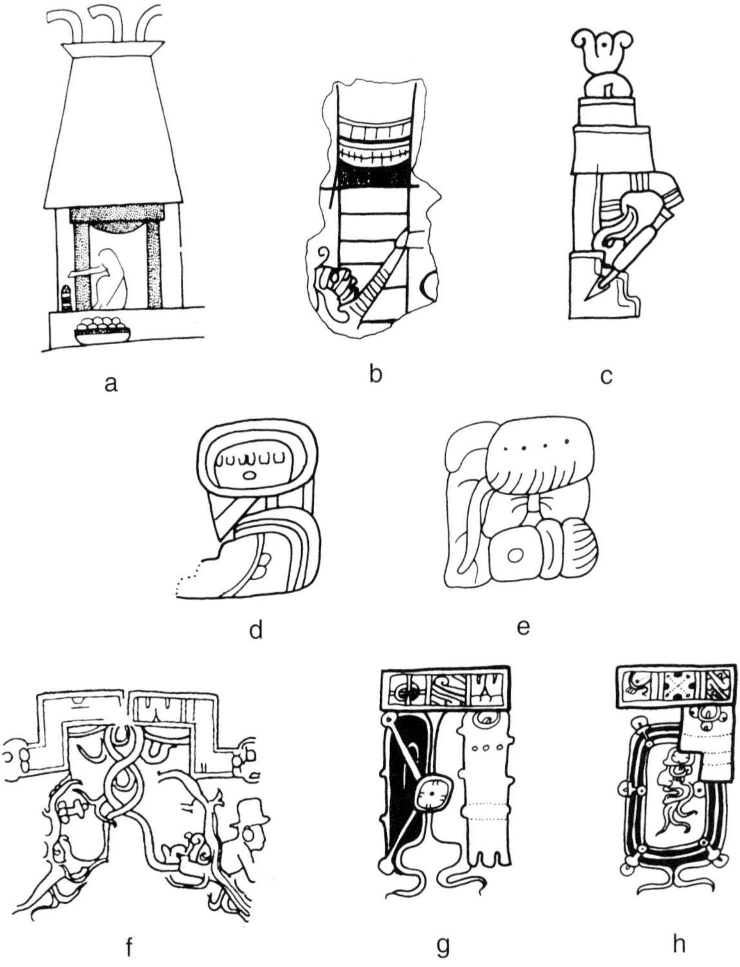

Fig. 1 Doorway curtains in ancient Maya domestic and sacred architecture: (a) curtain suspended in doorway of Early Post-Classic Maya house, detail of mural from Upper Temple of the Jaguars, Chichen Itza (after Coggins and Shane 1984: fig. 17); (b) temple doorway covered by curtain, detail of mural from Temple of the Warriors, Chichen Itza (after Morris, Charlot, and Morris 1931: pl. 168d); (c) curtain in temple doorway (Codex Grolier: 5); (d) Early Classic temple logograph with triangular curtain element (after Mayer 1984: pls. 26–27); (e) Late Classic temple logograph with bound doorway curtain, Tablet of the Cross, Palenque; (f) curtain and serpentine birth rope suspended from sky band, Caracol Stela 3 (from Taube 1994a: fig. 3b); (g and h) Post-Classic depictions of eclipses, sky curtains covering the sun (Codex Dresden: 54b, 55a).

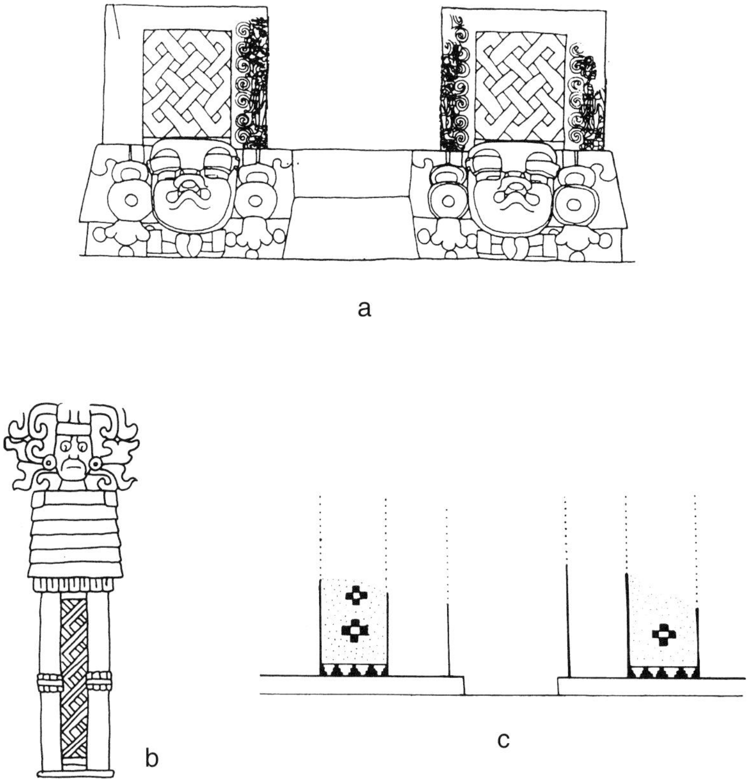

Fig. 2 False-curtained doorways in ancient Maya architecture: (a) false curtains marked with mat designs, Structure H-X, Uaxactun, Late Pre-Classic period (drawing by Linda Schele); (b) one of two false structures flanking central doorway of Hochob Structure 2 (after Gendrop 1983: fig. 73c–d); (c) false-curtained doorways flanking actual entrance, Structure IV, Becan (after Gendrop 1983: fig. 12d).

balumil, with *yoyal* signifying the vertical house beam, or *horcón* (Delgaty and Sánchez 1978: 234).

The contemporary Maya concept of four corner posts supporting a cosmic structure can be readily traced to the colonial and pre-Hispanic periods. In the colonial Yucatec Books of the Chilam Balam of Chumayel, Mani, and Tizimin, one of the world trees erected after the flood is termed the *yocmal caan,* or the "housepost (*horcon*) of the sky" (Craine and Reindorp 1979: 119; Edmonson 1982: 48; Roys 1933: 100). In these Yucatec accounts, these world trees are not grown, but "stood up" (*ualhi*), much like raising the corner posts of a house.

Similarly, the four columnar world trees in the Dresden New Year pages are accompanied by a verb that Nikolai Grube (1990) reads as *ts'apah,* or "is erected." The contemporary highland Maya concept of supernatural beings supporting the world derives from the pre-Hispanic Pawahtuns, the four aged beings supporting the corners of the universe (see Taube 1992b: 94). Like the four world trees, the Pawahtuns serve as the corner beams supporting the cosmic house (see Fig. 20e). This theme of the cosmic world bearers supporting a temple roof also appears on actual temples at Copan and Chichen Itza (see Schele and Miller 1986: 122; Taube 1994b: 214–216).

Whether as growing trees or aged men, the corner posts of the cosmic house support the heavenly roof. Many of the horizontal sky bands in the upper portion of Maya scenes probably represent the roof of the world house. The sky band on Caracol Stela 3 displays a doorway curtain, thereby denoting the sky band as the roof and ceiling (Fig. 1f). When unfurled over the door, the hanging curtain of the cosmic house could well refer to darkness and the night. On pages 54b and 55a of the Dresden codex eclipse pages, eclipses are depicted as hanging sky curtains covering the sun within the house (Fig. 1g–h).

THE THREE HEARTHSTONES

In the cosmic house model, the four corner posts represent directional trees supporting the heavens. However, traditional Maya houses lack a central post for the *axis mundi* from which the directions radiate. Instead, the middle place is represented by the three-stone hearth, known as *k'oben* in Yucatec; *yoket* in Chol, Tojolabal, and Tzeltalan languages; and *xkub* in Quiche (Wauchope 1938: 119; Barrera Vásquez 1980: 406; Attinasi n.d.: 342; Lenkersdorf 1979, 1: 421; Delgaty and Sanchez 1978: 233; Laughlin 1975: 451; Acuña 1983: 241, 275).[1] As the first central place, the simple three-stone hearth may well constitute the original construction of creation, antedating even the erection of the four corner posts.

In a cross-cultural discussion of architecture and world view, Pearson and Richards (1994: 12) note that the domestic hearth commonly represents the world center. In comparison to the four-cornered house model, the hearth

[1] The etymology of the Mayan terms for hearthstones is varied. Quite possibly, the Yucatec term *k'oben* is related to the word *k'oba,* which signifies "lake or river stone" (Barrera Vásquez 1980: 406). Water-tumbled rocks would be especially suited for the gently rounded contours of hearthstones. Whereas the Tzeltalan term *yoquet* probably derives from the term for leg or foot (*oq*), the Quichean *xkub* may well be a contraction of *ox kub,* or three *kub,* with *kub* signifying "stone" (Edmonson 1965: 62). In the colonial Cholti Moran dictionary, the hearth (*tenamaste*) is glossed as *chubentun* (Moran 1935: 64). At present, there is still no phonetic reading for the Classic three hearthstone sign.

more closely reflects a circular plan and thus serves as a more appropriate model for concepts of concentricity and centrality. According to Post-Classic Central Mexican thought, the old fire god Xiuhtecuhtli-Huehueteotl resides in a hearth at the world center. The *Anales de Cuauhtitlan* explicitly defines this place as three sacred hearthstones, each personified by a specific god (Bierhorst 1992: 23).[2] The Florentine Codex describes this locus as the circular earth navel, or *tlalxicco*: "mother of the gods, father of the gods, who resideth in the navel of the earth, who is set in the turquoise enclosure, [enclosed] with the waters of the lovely cotinga, enclosed with clouds—Ueueteotl, he of Ayamictlan, Xiuhtecuhtli" (Sahagún 1950–82, 6: 88–89). In this account, the earth navel is a place of duality, embodying both the male and female creative principles. In addition, it is a place of clouds and water, hardly what one would expect in an actual fiery hearth. This evocation of dualistic principles seems to describe the hearth as a place of creation. However, as the *axis mundi,* the hearth is also a conduit between the levels of earth, sky, and underworld. Similarly, it will be seen that, for the Classic Maya, the sacred hearth is also portrayed as a watery place and frequently fuses with the verdant ceiba, or *yax che,* also marking the world center. Some of the curious anomalies to be discussed—such as tree censers, caiman mouth hearths, jade hearthstones, and vegetal smoke—probably derive from this profound grafting of tree and hearth.

Recent pioneering investigations by Freidel, Schele, and Parker (1993: 65–71) have revealed that the placing of the hearthstones constitutes a major mythological act at the creation of the current Maya Baktun cycle—that is, the

[2] It appears that the three hearthstones constituted an important part of Mixtec creation mythology. Linda Schele (personal communication, 1994) notes that the tree birth scene on Selden page 2 illustrates the three stones in profile. An even more striking scene occurs on page 17 of the Nuttall Codex, which, according to John Pohl (personal communication, 1994), concerns the gods creating the first new fire. The three stones occur twice: first, as seats for three gods petitioned by Lady 3 Flint, and second, in the scene illustrating the fire ceremony. Two appear on mountains flanking the central pyre, and a third occurs in the structure above. Painted with the black facial markings of Central Mexicans, the two individuals seated on the mountains are named 4 Motion and 7 Reed. It will be recalled that at the sacrificial pyre at Teotihuacan, Nanahuatzin was transformed into the fifth sun, Nahui Ollin, or 4 Motion. Moreover, according to the *Historia de los reinos de Culhuacan,* 7 Reed was a name for the moon (Caso 1959: 91). Nanahuatzin and the cowardly Tecuciztecatl did penance on two hills, the Pyramids of the Sun and the Moon (see Sahagún 1950–82, 7: 4–5, 44–46). The pyre lies within a low, crenelated U-shaped enclosure of light blue color, recalling one of the Aztec terms for the sacrificial pyre at Teotihuacan, *xiuhtetzaqualco,* meaning "turquoise enclosure" (Sahagún 1950–82, 1: 84). I believe that this scene represents a Mixtec interpretation of the creation of the fifth sun, with the two gods seated on their mountains on either side of the sacrificial pyre. It will be subsequently seen that, for the Classic Maya, the jade hearth was also identified with rebirth and apotheosis.

13.0.0.0.0 4 Ahau 8 Cumku event of 3114 B.C.[3] In their work, entitled *Maya Cosmos,* the authors note that Quirigua Stela C provides a detailed account of the 4 Ahau 8 Cumku setting of this three-stone hearth, here qualified by the sign *yax,* meaning green, first, and by extension, center. Each stone is identified with a specific god, recalling the Central Mexican *Anales de Cuauhtitlan* account. Far from being restricted to Quirigua, the 4 Ahau 8 Cumku event also appears on Late Classic monuments from Copan, Palenque, Dos Pilas, and Piedras Negras (Schele 1992: 121). But although Freidel, Schele, and Parker seem to have defined one of the fundamental acts of Maya creation mythology, a great deal of the argument hinges on the identification of the three-stone glyph (Fig. 3a). Also the main sign of the Seibal emblem glyph, this sign looks suspiciously like a pile of rocks. Nonetheless, in examples from Tonina, Naranjo, Copan, and Salinas de los Nueve Cerros, the three stones emit smoking volutes, lending considerable support for the hearth identification (Fig. 3c–g).

The widespread appearance of the three-stone hearth in Maya inscriptions suggests that it was a basic feature of Classic Maya households. However, although three-stone hearths are widely documented for contemporary Maya peoples, there is surprisingly little evidence for their presence during the Classic period.[4] As Pyburn (1989: 334) notes, pre-Hispanic hearths are not only rare but tend to be poorly documented in the archaeological literature.[5] According to Wauchope (1938: 117), contemporary Maya commonly reuse hearthstones from abandoned houses. Rounded and relatively large, averaging some 30 cm in diameter (Wauchope 1938: 117), such stones are fairly rare and valued objects and were probably reused in antiquity as well. It is noteworthy that one of the few archaeological instances of the three-stone hearth occurs at the site of Ceren (Sheets 1992: 55, fig. 4.6). Here, stone retrieval and reuse was precluded by the cataclysmic eruption of the Laguna Caldera volcano and the resulting deposition of ash.

Aside from actual hearths, three-pronged *incensarios* probably also indicate the widespread occurrence of three-stone hearths by at least Late Formative

[3] Although not presented in the published volume *Maya Cosmos,* Linda Schele (personal communication, 1994) has independently noticed several of the observations mentioned in this paper, most notably the three-stone place at Izapa and the hearthstone jade cache at Seibal.

[4] Edward H. Thompson (1892: 262) reports the widespread occurrence of three-stone hearths during his archaeological research in the vicinity of Labna, Yucatan. However, the presence of pre-Hispanic *k'oben* hearths in the Puuc region has not been corroborated by later researchers.

[5] For excavated Post-Classic hearths from highland Guatemala, including a three-stone example, see Fauvet-Berthelot (1986: 126–127, 195–198).

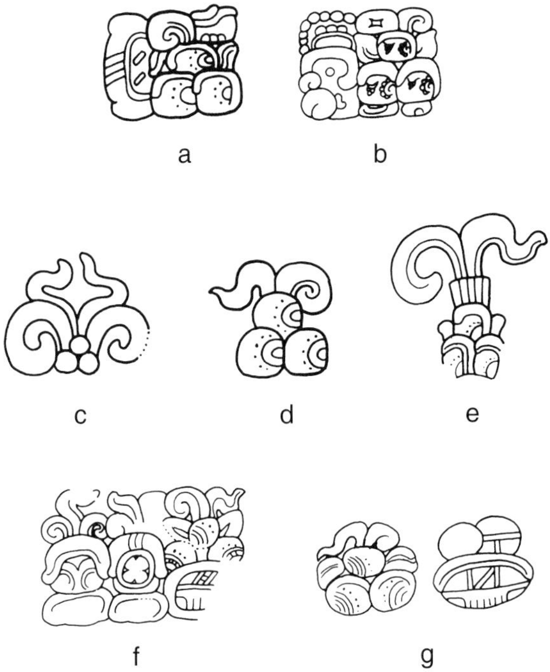

Fig. 3 The three hearthstones in Classic Maya epigraphy and art: (a) the green hearthstone place, Quirigua Stela; (b) the Seibal emblem glyph, Tablet 4 of Hieroglyphic Stairway, Seibal; (c) three smoking hearthstones, Monument 74, Tonina; (d) one of a series of smoking hearthstones on headdress of ruler, detail of recently excavated stela, Tonina; (e) three stones with burning wood, Naranjo Stela 30; (f) smoking sky hearthstones with glyphs for Tikal Paddlers, Stela 16, Copan; (g) smoking hearthstones with sky *ahau* glyph, Stela 1, Salinas de los Nueve Cerros.

times (see Fig. 10a–b). Occurring at such early sites as Chiapa de Corzo, Izapa, and Kaminaljuyu (Lowe 1965), these censers function much like portable three-stone hearths. Like the stones supporting the cooking vessel, the three prongs hold the incense bowl above the central fire. The placement of three stones in bowls, reported for such sites as Uaxactun, Zaculeu, Copan, and K'axob, probably constitutes an intermediate form, with actual stones serving as supports for the fire offering (for examples, see Fash 1991: 90–92; Ricketson and Ricketson 1937: 72; Woodbury and Trik 1953: 27, 113).[6]

[6] David Webster (personal communication, 1994) called my attention to the three-stone vessel from the Early Classic Burial VIII-36 and further suggested that another badly fragmented vessel also may have contained three stones, but because of its placement at the

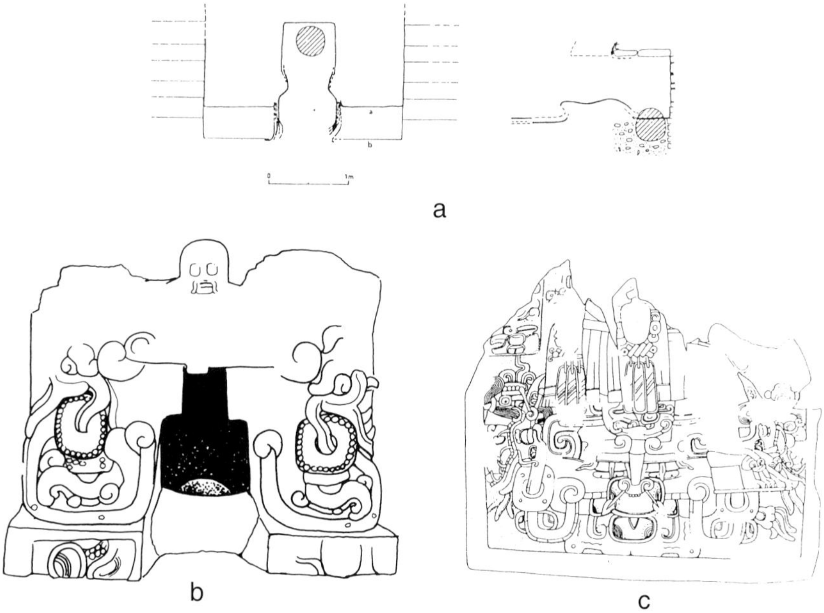

Fig. 4 The hearthstone stairway shrine at Tonina: (a) plans of stairway shrine, with stone represented by hachure (after Becquelin and Baudez 1979–82, 1: fig. 38); (b) drawing of front of shrine with stone in gullet of *wits* monster; note two representations of stones at lower left and right (after Becquelin and Baudez 1979–82, 1: fig. 40c); (c) lower portion of Tonina Monument 106; three stones in *wits* monster mouth (after Becquelin and Baudez 1979–82, 3: fig. 175).

Although Ceren provides the only well-documented Classic three-stone kitchen hearth in situ, large, worked stone spheres have been found over much of the Maya area, including Kohunlich (Romano Pacheco, Navarette, and Pinto 1981: pl. 206), Tonina (Becquelin and Baudez 1979–82, 1: 37), and Zaculeu (Woodbury and Trik 1953: 224–225), and in the southern piedmont region at Tonala (Ferdon 1953: 91, pl. 23), Izapa (Norman 1976: 262–265), Bilbao, and El Castillo (Parsons 1969: 79).[7] Dating from the Late Pre-Classic to the Terminal

---

extreme eastern edge of the burial, only two were retrieved. Patricia McAnany (personal communication, 1994) notes that a lip-to-lip vessel cache containing three stones was recently excavated at K'axob, Belize.

[7] At times, the stone spheres are decorated with the face of the Fat God (e.g., Parsons 1986: fig. 133; Ekholm 1970: 94–95). I suspect that the Fat God, the same entity commonly appearing on Piedmont "potbelly" sculptures, is the god of the kitchen hearth. In a number

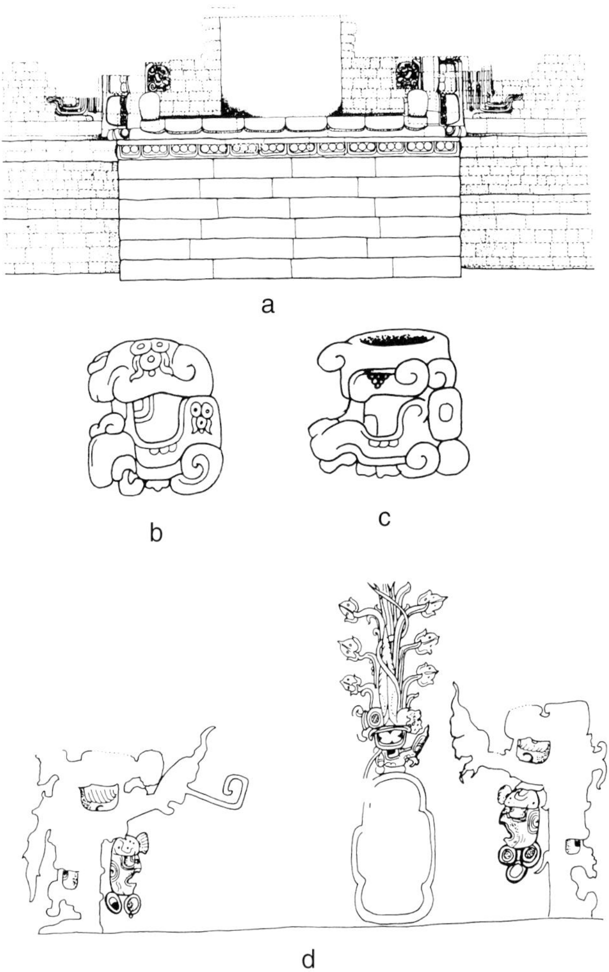

Fig. 5 Copan Structure 22 and hearthstones in *wits* monster maws: (a) *wits* monster doorway with pair of zoomorphic *tun* signs at sides of mouth, Copan Structure 22 (after Hohmann and Vogrin 1982: fig. 319); (b) detail of *tun* sign from doorway maw of Copan Structure 22; (c) zoomorphic censer reportedly found by Maudslay within Copan Structure 22 (after Maudslay 1889–1902, 1: pl. 12); (d) schematic drawing of red background vessel with *tsuk* stones in *wits* monster mouths; note censer bowl atop quatrefoil cave in center of scene (after Coe 1978: vessel 16).

---

of instances, he appears in groups of three, not only as stone sculpture but also as the tripod feet of food vessels (see Parsons 1986: 92; Brainerd 1958: fig. 88). For a possible Late Classic Seibal example of three Fat Gods supporting an altar, see Fig. 7b).

Classic periods, these stones probably marked actual or symbolic hearths. During the excavation of Tonina Structure E5-5, Becquelin and Baudez (1979–82, 1: 37) uncovered a stairway shrine containing a single sandstone ball approximately 70 cm in diameter (Fig. 4a–b). Set into the center of the shrine chamber, the stone protruded some 15 cm above the stucco floor. The shrine façade portrays an elaborate *wits* monster, or zoomorphic mountain, with the interior chamber constituting its open gullet. On each side of the open mouth, a rounded *tun* stone is carefully delineated in stucco (Fig. 4b). Together, the two flanking stucco representations and the actual stone ball represent the triangularly arranged hearth in the mouth of the zoomorphic mountain. Becquelin and Baudez (1979–82, 1: 37) report that the shrine chamber bears evidence of soot, and it will be noted later that such axial stairway shrines are important places for fire offerings.

At the side of Structure E5-5 stands Monument 106, an Early Classic stela displaying a *wits* monster virtually identical to that appearing on the adjacent shrine (Fig. 4c). In addition to displaying a similar pair of serpents projecting through earspools, the stela example has three triangularly placed stones in its open maw. This stela probably portrays the ruler sitting atop the neighboring stairway shrine.

During the Classic period, *wits* monsters often display round stones in their mouths, and it could be argued that the Tonina stela simply illustrates the stony quality of *wits* monster teeth. However, Copan Structure 22 indicates that the placement of *tun* stones in *wits* monster mouths was neither casual nor fortuitous (Fig. 5a). Two large zoomorphic *tun* signs are prominently placed on the sides of the *wits* monster maw serving as the temple doorway (Fig. 5b). But if this pair of *tun* signs constitute flanking stones, where is the third and central stone? Maudslay (1889–1902, 1: 29) reports finding two zoomorphic stone censers within Structure 22. The example illustrated by Maudslay is simply a zoomorphic *tun,* comparable in scale to the *tun* profiles in the doorway mouth (Fig. 5c). Axially oriented to the doorway during fire offerings, such a censer would serve as the third central stone, here containing the burning offering. A Late Classic vessel illustrates the use of such a censer as the central stone (Fig. 5d). In this case, a pair of inwardly facing *wits* monsters hold the flanking stones in their mouths. The stones are forms of the *tzuk* head defined by Grube and Schele (1991), who interpret it as a symbol of cosmic world partitions. I suggest that the *tsuk* head defines and ultimately represents the center, whether it is placed equidistantly in groups of four, three, or simply a single head as the *axis mundi*. Between the two *tzuk* stones stands the zoomorphic censer.[8] Contain-

[8] A kin-marked bowl constitutes the top of this censer; Stephen Houston (personal com-

ing a world tree and situated directly above a quatrefoil cave, the censer constitutes an *axis mundi* offering access to both the heavens and the underworld.

The caiman, the *axis mundi* creature *par excellence,* also appears with the hearth in its mouth. The early colonial Yucatec *Ritual of the Bacabs* describes the head of the earth caiman, Itzam Cab, as the three stone *k'oben,* with the flames being its tongue (Roys 1965: 50). In another passage, the *pib* sweatbath serves as the mouth of this being (Roys 1965: 61).[9] A stucco relief from Copan apparently illustrates an Early Classic form of this concept. The sculpture portrays a caiman with a series of round stones in its teeth, quite possibly the three-stone hearth (see Fash 1991: fig. 40). Similarly, the Late Classic Copan Altar T depicts a splayed caiman with three *tsuk* stones projecting from its mouth (see Maudslay 1889–1902, 1: pls. 95 and 96).

One of the most ambitious monumental programs dedicated to the three-stone hearth occurs at the Late Pre-Classic site of Izapa. On the central axis of Mound Group B, three massive stone balls were placed on pillars (Fig. 6a). Known as Miscellaneous Monuments 6, 8, and 10, the spheres average some 65 cm in diameter. The slightly larger central stone and pillar project south of the flanking monuments, creating a triangle. Thus, like the Structure E-5 shrine at Tonina, this monumental group represents the three-stone place in the center of the primary temple stairway. Directly south of the central stone and pillar lies Throne 1, the top of which displays a crossed band sign within a crenelated cartouche (Fig. 6a–b). A similar juxtapositioning of crossed bands with the column and ball occurs on the Late Formative Shook Panel, here capping the head of the central figure (Fig. 6c). It will be subsequently noted that, for the Late Pre-Classic and Classic Maya, certain jade ornaments worn in this position denoted the *axis mundi.* When seated atop the crossed bands directly in front of the three raised hearthstones, the Izapa ruler was enthroned in the center of the cosmos.

A possible portrayal of Throne 1 occurs on Stela 8, one of the three stelae directly behind the raised stone spheres of Group B (Fig. 6e). Noting the similarity of this profile rendering to Throne 1, Norman (1976: 105) points out that the Stela 8 scene also displays a crenelated device closely resembling the upper surface of the actual throne. In a quatrefoil on the back of a turtle, the Stela 8

---

munication, 1994) notes that, epigraphically, the kin-marked bowl may be read *el* or *elel,* signifying "to burn" in Mayan languages.

[9] Although Roys (1965) interprets this incantation as a reference to a *pib* earth oven rather than the sweatbath, the text explicitly describes the creation of steam through water striking a stone referred to as a *zintunil.* In the early colonial Motul and San Francisco dictionaries, *sin tun* is glossed as "piedra de baño" (Barrera Vásquez 1980: 730).

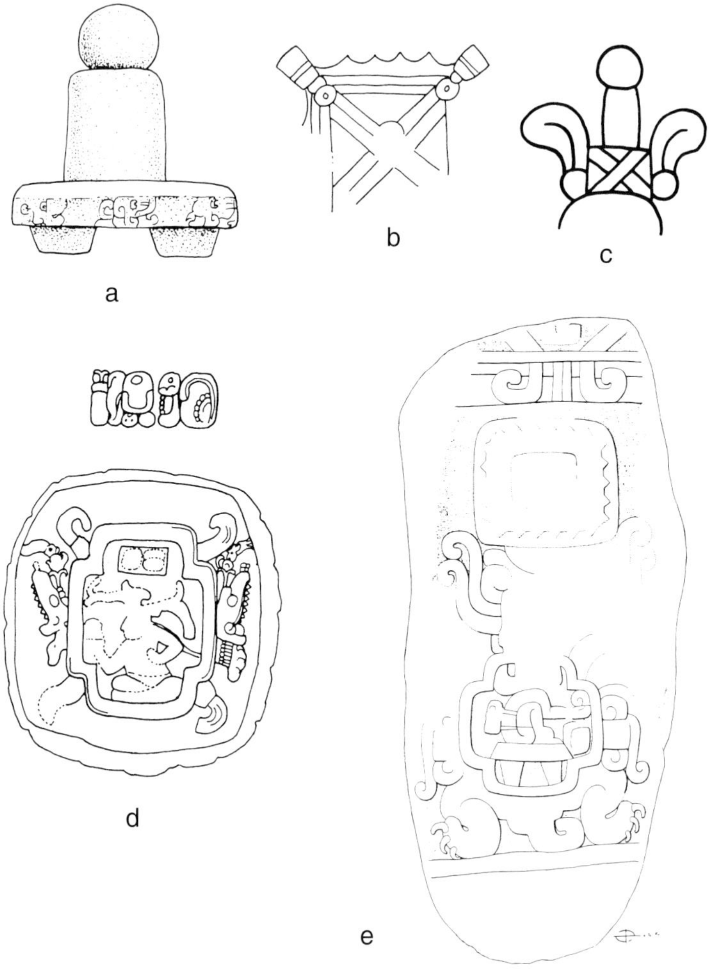

Fig. 6 The three-stone group at Late Pre-Classic Izapa: (a) schematic drawing of Throne 1 backed by central ball and pillar (after Norman 1976: fig. 5.32); (b) design from upper surface of Throne 1, Izapa (after Norman 1973: pl. 63); (c) ball and column atop crossed bands; detail of head ornament from Shook Panel, Late Formative (after Fields 1991: fig. 9; (d) seated ruler in center of turtle quatrefoil, accompanying text reads *tuyol ak,* or "at the heart of the turtle," El Peru altar (drawing courtesy of Linda Schele); (e) ruler seated on throne inside quatrefoil turtle, Izapa Stela 8, Late Pre-Classic period (drawing courtesy of James Porter).

throne is strikingly similar to Machaquila Altar 1, which portrays a Late Classic ruler seated in another quatrefoil turtle (Fig. 6d). Stephen Houston (personal communication, 1991) notes that the accompanying text describes the scene as *tuyol ak,* or "at the heart of the turtle." Citing an identification by Matt Looper, Freidel, Schele, and Parker (1993: 82) note that on Madrid page 71a, the three hearthstones appear on the back of a turtle. The authors interpret this scene as representing stellar constellations and in support note that the contemporary Quiche place a three-hearthstone constellation near another star group denoted as a turtle. Although identification of a turtle with the hearth may well be illustrated in the night sky, the association probably derives from their shared meaning of centrality. As a circular model of the earth (see Taube 1988), the turtle embodies the same concepts of concentricity and centrality found with the three-stone hearth. At Izapa Mound Group B, the throne of kingship appears with crossed bands, three stones, and the turtle, all signifying the pivotal *axis mundi.*

As a sign of the middle place, the three hearthstones appear with radial stairway pyramids, structures that in their very design refer to the axis and center. During the burial of the Late Pre-Classic E-VII-Sub at Uaxactun, a lip-to-lip vessel cache was placed on the stucco floor near the top of the principal stairway. The sole contents were three simple stones, possibly a three-stone censer (see Ricketson and Ricketson 1937: 72, fig. 33). Among the most striking examples of a radial stairway pyramid is Structure A-3 at Seibal, the site epigraphically labeled as the three-stone place (Fig. 3b). The interior temple floors bore considerable evidence of burning, particularly in association with Stela 21, placed in the very center of the structure (Smith 1982: 24). This monument represents a figure dressed as the Jaguar God of the Underworld, or JGU, a deity that David Stuart (personal communication, 1993) suggests may be the Classic Maya god of fire.[10] The cache directly below this pivotal monument contained three jade boulders weighing from 6.25 to 10 pounds (Smith 1982: fig. 18, 241; Willey 1978: 100). For Terminal Classic Seibal, these three boulders constituted the central three-stone place, a hearth of green jade.

Structure D5-1, one of the most imposing buildings at Tonina, is another example of a radial stairway building.[11] Like Seibal Structure A-3, a carved stela stood in the temple interior. This Early Classic stela, Monument 74, depicts a

[10] The strange twisted "cruller" atop the nose of the JGU probably refers to fire making. In Teotihuacan and later Aztec iconography, similarly twisted elements appear in depictions of fire drilling, evidently alluding to the tightly twisted rope of the pump drill.

[11] I am indebted to Stephen Houston for calling my attention to Tonina Structure D5-1 as an example of a radial stairway pyramid.

ruler with three smoking hearthstones in his headdress (Fig. 3c). The wooden staff and costume of knotted and hanging paper of this figure recalls Late Classic monuments from Naranjo (e.g., Naranjo Stelae 11, 30, and 33). Dressed as the JGU, the Naranjo ruler also wears knotted paper and wields the wooden staff. One of these monuments, Naranjo Stela 30, displays the three hearthstones in the headdress, in this case supplied with burning *ocote* wood (Fig. 3e). David Stuart (personal communication, 1993) suggests that the staff wielded by the Tonina and Naranjo lords represents a symbolic fire-making stick. In view of the abundant fire iconography and identification with the three-stone hearth, Classic Maya radial stairway structures were clearly important loci for fire-making rituals.

According to Coggins (1987: 476), Seibal Temple A-3 and the Castillo at Chichen Itza were radial pyramids used for new fire ceremonies. At the time of its discovery, the jade jaguar throne within the inner Castillo bore a burned turquoise mirror with three large jade pendants and smaller beads on its back (Erosa Peniche 1947). Both Coggins (1987) and I (Taube 1992a: 184–187) note the identification of mirrors with fire and hearths in Mesoamerican thought. On Codex Borgia page 63, a petaled turquoise mirror—quite similar to the actual El Castillo example—serves as the fiery hearth for a cooking vessel. Like the radial pyramids at Uaxactun, Seibal, and Tonina, the Castillo is probably also identified with hearths and fire.

Aside from radial structures, certain round altars were also identified with fire-making rites and the three-stone hearth. In Maya inscriptions, the glyph for altar frequently accompanies the logographic sign for temple pyramid (see Chase, Grube, and Chase 1991: fig. 5). Composed of three stones, the altar glyph is notably similar to the three-stone hearth sign, save that the upper stone tends to be larger, denoting the altar surface supported by smaller stone supports. It appears that circular altars supported with three feet denoted the hearth, much like a flat griddle on three cooking stones. One such monument is Piedras Negras Altar 1, which contains an epigraphic reference to the 4 Ahau 8 Cumku event and the green hearthstones (Fig. 7a). The recently discovered El Cayo Altar 4 is another example of a three-legged altar (Fig. 7d). The top of this remarkable monument represents such a legged altar in use; rendered in profile, a large spiked censer occupies the center of the depicted altar. A miniature model of a three-stone altar represents the stone disk with three spherical supports, much like the spheres serving as Classic hearthstones (Fig. 7c). A prone jaguar atop a censer occupies the center of the altar, again reinforcing the theme of jaguars, fire, and centrality. Seibal Altar 1 depicts a similarly positioned jaguar supported by three seated human figures (Fig. 7b).

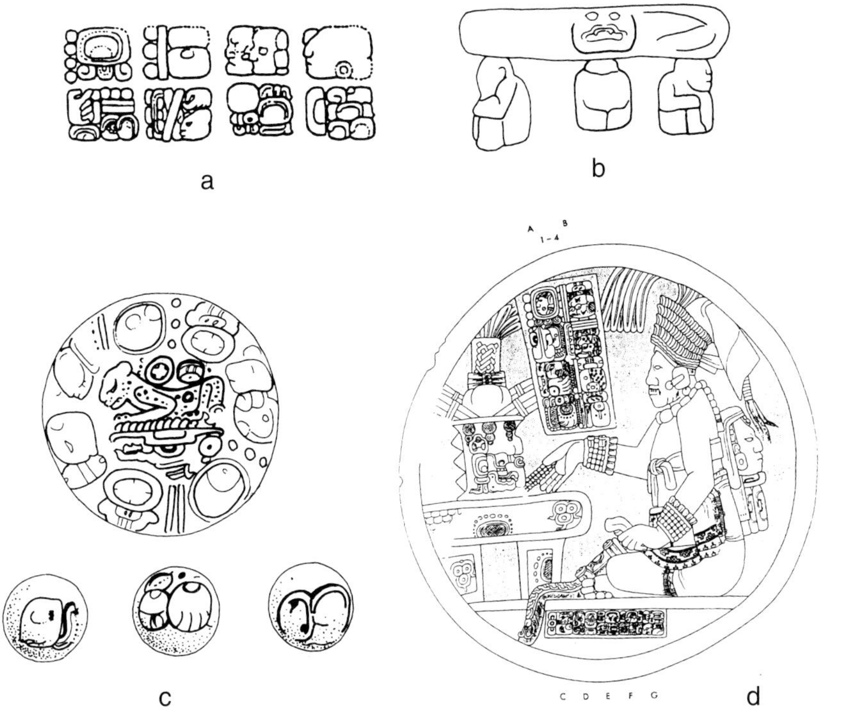

Fig. 7 Three-legged altars and hearth symbolism: (a) detail of Piedras Negras Altar 1 text, referring to the green hearthstones and the 4 Ahau 8 Cumku event (drawing courtesy of Linda Schele); (b) Seibal Altar 1, jaguar altar supported by three seated figures (after Smith 1982: fig. 140b); (c) painted and incised stone altar model with three spherical supports; note jaguar atop censer in center of altar scene (after Robicsek and Hales 1981: fig. 62b); (d) altar fire offering represented atop actual three-legged altar, El Cayo Altar 1 (drawing courtesy of Peter Mathews).

Two Late Classic vessels epigraphically label a particular water jaguar, *ha hix,* as the *way* of the *ahau* three-stone place, that is, the hearth of kings (Fig. 8a–b). In both scenes, the roaring jaguar is surrounded by a cartouche marked with the "stacked canoes" water sign. A similar roaring jaguar appears on the Late Classic codex-style "Cosmic Plate" (see Fig. 8c). Although the qualifying term accompanying the *hix* compound is eroded, it may well be the Imix water sign, again referring to the water jaguar *way.* Below the jaguar lies a horizontal band of water marked with the "stacked canoes" sign. In addition to the roaring jaguar and standing water, the three hearthstones are also present. Rendered in

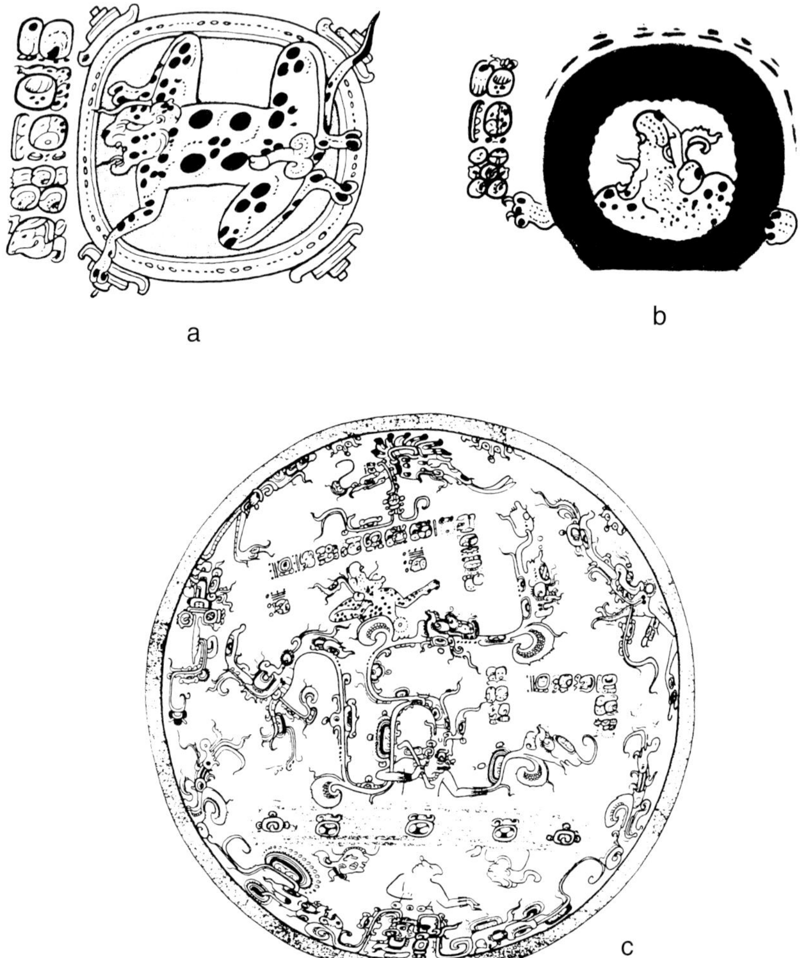

Fig. 8 The roaring water jaguar and the Ahau hearthstone place: (a) water jaguar epigraphically labeled as *way* of Ahau hearthstones, detail of codex-style vase (from Houston and Stuart 1989: fig. 3); (b) water jaguar as *way* of Ahau hearthstones, detail of polychrome vessel (after Reents-Budet 1994: fig. 5.10); (c) interior of Cosmic Plate, roaring jaguar at upper center of scene with three hearthstones in profile at base of scene (drawing courtesy of James Porter).

profile, they appear at the base of the scene (Figs. 8c and 9a). Both of the flanking heads are stony *tsuk* heads, marking the central head as the middle place.

Fig. 9 Hearthstone and fire iconography: (a) detail of three hearthstones at base of Cosmic Plate scene, note God C on forehead of central stone (see Fig. 8c); (b) hearthstones in profile, crossed bands and Caban curl element possibly referring to *tan yol kab,* the world center (after Robicsek and Hales 1981: table 3a); (c) smoking head at tip of serpent tail, Abaj Takalik Stela 5, Late Pre-Classic (detail of drawing courtesy of James Porter); (d) Early Classic smoking head on serpent tail, Altar 12, Tikal (after Jones and Satterthwaite 1982: fig. 59a); (e) smoking head on serpent tail, Lintel 3 of Temple IV, Tikal (drawing courtesy of Linda Schele); (f) smoking head on serpent tail, Lintel 14, Yaxchilan (after Graham and von Euw 1977: 37); (g and h) smoking heads on serpent tails, details from codex-style vases (after Kerr 1992: 389; 1990: 224).

A codex-style vase portrays a very similar profile rendering of the three stones; in this case, the flanking heads face outward, thereby framing the central head in a symmetrical arrangement (Fig. 9b). In both scenes, the central head displays a profile God C face on its brow. This particular entity commonly appears on the ends of serpent tails, a curious convention originating in Late Pre-Classic Maya iconography (Fig. 9c–h). Smoke, frequently with jade beads, exudes from the top of the head, identifying this element as a fire-related object, quite possibly a zoomorphic censer. The pair of curling smoke volutes is frequently serrated and beaded, thereby bearing a close resemblance to plant growth, such as the *nal* maize signs sprouting out of earspool assemblages (e.g., Fig. 9e and g). At times the God C brow is represented face on, revealing that it is essentially the T533 stylized Ahau face (Fig. 9c and h). The smoking capped Ahau sign commonly appearing in male parentage statements and on the ends of jaguar tails is probably a simplified form of this device. The tops of Late Pre-Classic three-pronged *incensarios* are depicted with volutes strikingly similar to those appearing with the capped Ahau (Fig. 10a–b). In terms of the two vessel scenes, the central heads seem to represent smoking censers, with the pair of outpouring volutes simultaneously referring to both vinelike growth and roiling smoke. In Late Classic Maya iconography, censers frequently exude similar symmetrical coils of plantlike smoke (Fig. 10d–g).

URNS OF THE TEMPLE

As the essential means of burning offerings or "food" for divine beings, censers form an obvious thematic link to the three-stone kitchen hearth. Simply put, incense burners are the kitchen hearths of the gods and ancestors.[12] In *Maya Cosmos,* the authors note that Classic offering vessels—namely, censers and the related cache vessels—denote the central place and serve as portals between the human plane and the divine (Freidel, Schele, and Parker 1993: 214–218, 241). According to Freidel, Schele, and Parker (1993: 454) spiked censers allude to the thorny ceiba trunk and, by extension, represent the *axis mundi.* In addition, Copan cache censers often display cacao pods on their sides as if they are growing trees laden with cacao (see Strömsvik 1941: figs. 15d,

[12] In contemporary Maya belief, fire offerings constitute the cooked maize sustenance or *wah* of divine beings (see Taube 1989: 38). The Kekchi, who describe *pom* incense as *xwa Qaawa,* or "tortilla of our father," use incense as a means of communication with the supernatural: "Pom carries the prayers upwards into the mouth of the Tzuultaq'a who consumes the smoke and the messages with it" (Wilson n.d.: 91). Whereas contemporary highland Maya copal commonly appears as small disks, resembling miniature tortillas, the ancient Maya typically offered copal balls, the same form as the favored Classic maize food, the tamale.

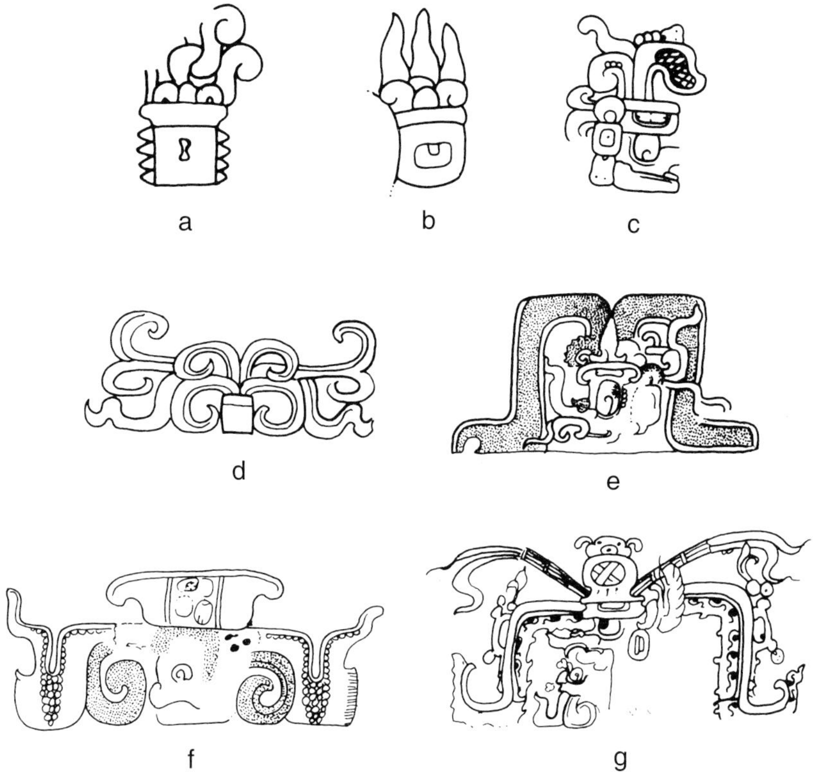

Fig. 10 Censers in Late Pre-Classic and Classic Maya iconography: (a) three-pronged censer with burning offering, Izapa Stela 24 (after Norman 1973: pl. 29); (b) burning three-pronged censer, Abaj Takalik Monument 62 (after Orrego Corzo 1990: pl. 29); (c) burning zoomorphic censer with *k'in* bowl on brow, Yaxha Stela 31 (after drawing by Ian Graham); (d) burning vessel with symmetrical coils of smoke (after Robicsek and Hales 1981: vessel 18); (e) burning zoomorphic censer (after Kerr 1989: 54); (f) zoomorphic censer with flanking plantlike coils (after Kerr 1992: 415); (g) zoomorphic censer with burning torches and inverted vessel (after Robicsek and Hales 1981: vessel 168).

17a–b, and 20c). However, aside from representing the central world tree, censers and cache vessels are also inextricably tied to temple architecture and iconography.

During the Classic period, Maya offering vessels frequently display the same iconographic formats found on stucco temple façades, that is, frontal faces framed by elaborate earspool assemblages with outwardly facing zoomorphic profiles. Although the similarities are particularly striking in Early Classic Maya art (see

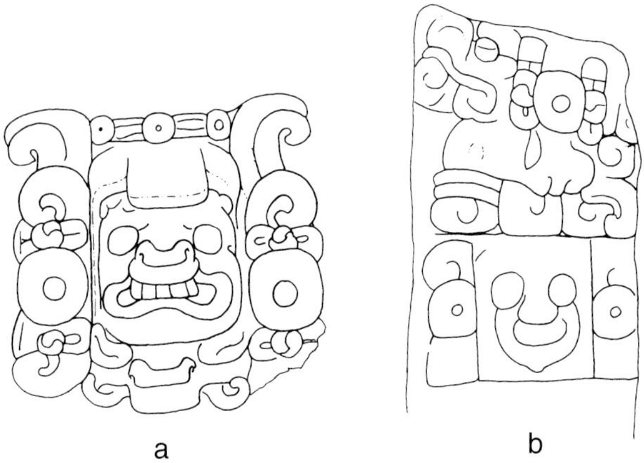

Fig. 11 Late Pre-Classic Maya censers: (a) early ceramic censer in Peten style, Denver Art Museum (after photograph in the Foundation for Latin American Anthropological Research [FLAAR] slide archive, Dumbarton Oaks, slide EC-cc4-46/1); (b) descending ancestor consuming offering from burning censer, detail of El Mirador Stela 18 (after drawing by Stephen Houston).

Hellmuth 1987), certain Late Pre-Classic censers also resemble temple façades. One censer in the collections of the Denver Art Museum bears a visage strikingly similar to Late Pre-Classic stucco façades from Uaxactun and El Mirador (Figs. 2a and 11a). The frontally facing mask of El Mirador Stela 18 probably denotes such a censer, here placed below an ancestral face with volutes of clouds or smoke (Fig. 11b).

The prevalence of static, frontally facing masks on Classic censers and cache vessels is not because the early Maya were incapable of narrative art. Highly anecdotal scenes can be readily found in the Late Pre-Classic and Early Classic periods as well as in Late Classic Maya art. Instead, these masks mark censers and cache vessels as ritual urns of the temple. However, the vessels resemble temple façades for yet another reason. During particular ritual acts, these urns essentially became miniature temples, the seat and dwelling place of gods. I have recently noted that for the Classic Maya, lidded four-sided vessels frequently denote houses, with the sloping lid representing the thatch roof (Taube 1994a: 652; see Houston, this volume). Although I focused my discussion on cache vessels, this is also true for four-sided censers. One Late Classic censer lid is clearly portrayed as a temple roof topped by three burning heads (Labbé 1982: 24). A similar censer, here with the rectangular lower portion still intact, was discovered in the Cueva de los Andasolos, Chiapas. Like the previous example, the lid is topped with three heads, quite possibly the three stones in profile (Navarrete and Martínez 1977: figs. 18–21). For those familiar with Teotihuacan art, the identification of censers with temples should come as no surprise. As early as 1922, Manuel Gamio (1922: 29) noted that Teotihuacan censers appear to represent miniature temples.

Fire offerings were a central component of Classic Maya temple ritual. David Stuart notes that a primary event recorded in Classic dedication rites was *och k'ak'*, meaning "the fire entered" (Stuart, this volume). Fire was the medium by which individuals conjured the gods through the offering of blood, copal, and other precious substances. These fire rites involved a ritual process that could be best described as *focusing,* a term derived from the Latin *focus,* meaning "hearth." During the ceremony, there was a focusing of scale and attention from the temple to the place of fire itself, which became the specific point of communication with the divine. In this context, censers became the concentrated embodiment of the temple and served as the house and seat of the conjured being. This ritual process of focusing continues in contemporary Lacandon censer rites, the primary means by which the Lacandon communicate with their gods. Contained within the temple god house, or *yatoch k'u,* the anthropomorphized god pot censers sleep until awakened for offerings of food and incense. When burning, the god pot and the precious jade stone inside become the *nah k'uh* or house of the god, and it is through this vessel that the ritual participants communicate with the deity (Davis n.d.: 22, 72–74, 77, 223).[13]

For ancient Maya temples, axial stairway altars were used for fire offerings, the same region as the three stone shrines of Tonina Structure E5-5 and Izapa Group B. Another Izapa Group B structure, Mound 30i, displays a probable Late Pre-Classic form of the *wits* monster in the center of the stairway. Near this monument were the remains of two ceramic incense burners, indicating that this area was a locus of fire offerings (Lowe 1965: 57). Writing of Late Pre-Classic Tikal, Ferree (n.d.: 13–14) notes that censers were primarily at the front and base of temples. For all of the Classic phases of Zaculeu Structure 1, major fire offerings were centered at the base of the upper stairway (Woodbury and Trik 1953: 28–30). At Late Classic Seibal, a four-sided stone slab hearth was placed at the base of the Structure 79 stairway (Smith 1982: 165).

[13] Tozzer (1907: 87–88) notes that the Lacandon place a highly prized jade or other stone in the censers below the copal offering. The placement of jade in braziers is clearly pre-Hispanic in origin. At the highland site of Zaculeu, a Late Classic stone effigy censer contained a rounded jade cobble (Woodbury and Trik 1953: 218, fig. 178a–b). An Early Classic cache at Tikal contained a burned jade boulder with copal incense adhering to its upper surface (Coe 1990: 355). In this ritual deposit, the boulder seems to have functioned as a jade hearth.

Aside from material evidence of burning, the texts and iconography associated with stairway shrines also provide important clues regarding their use and significance. At Chichen Itza, a tenoned stone disk was discovered in the stairway shrine of the Terminal Classic Caracol temple. The monument clearly portrays a fire ritual, with a brazier occupying the center of the scene (see Ruppert 1935: fig. 169). Similarly, a Late Classic vessel depicts a burning censer atop a skull-shaped stairway block (see Fig. 13a).

Many of the epigraphic references to fire ceremonies occur on square or rectangular panels, and many of these probably served as facings for stairway blocks placed on the central axis of temples (see Stuart, this volume). This is certainly the case for the so-called Lintel 5 of Piedras Negras, which was found on the stairway slope of a temple lacking a vaulted superstructure (Satterthwaite 1936). Depicting a standing figure holding a spear, this monument is notably similar to a panel in the collections of Dumbarton Oaks (Fig. 12a–b). On both panels, the long glyphic texts are stepped above the figure, creating a vaulted effect to suggest that the individual is standing within a chamber. As facings on projecting stairway blocks, these panels probably were shrines for the honored dead, who would be conjured during fire rituals atop these miniature houses. On the temple towers of the Río Bec–style Structure II at Hormiguero, the false stairway blocks are rendered as miniature houses, quite possibly with thatched roofs (see Gendrop 1983: fig. 40a–b). The *wits* monster stairway shrine of Tonina Structure E5-5 is simply a more developed form of this concept, with the open mouth representing the interior of the pyramidal mass (Fig. 4).

In the modern Quiche town of Chichicastenango, a stone slab stairway block occurs at the base of the Santo Tómas church (see Robicsek 1978: pl. 4). Used by Quiche day keepers for fire offerings and prayer, this stairway altar is much like a glorified public version of the semiprivate ancestral shrines. Known as *warabalja* or "sleeping houses," the rectangular stone slab ancestral shrines are like houses for the dead, who are awakened and seated in the shrine with prayer and incense (see Tedlock 1992: 76–77).

At times, Classic stairway blocks display frontal masks that closely resemble actual incense burners. An excellent Early Classic example from Tikal portrays the JGU, the probable Classic Maya god of fire (Fig. 13b). William Coe (1990: 352) notes that this sculpture was clearly used in fire rituals: "The entire surface of stairblock U. 29, found practically calcified, obviously became a special stage for burning." The Jaguar Stairway at Copan portrays a Late Classic version of a JGU stairway block, and it is likely that this example was also used in fire offerings (Fig. 13c). Another axial stairway block mask occurs at Comalcalco, a sculpture that strongly suggests a ceramic incense burner translated into stucco (Fig. 13d).

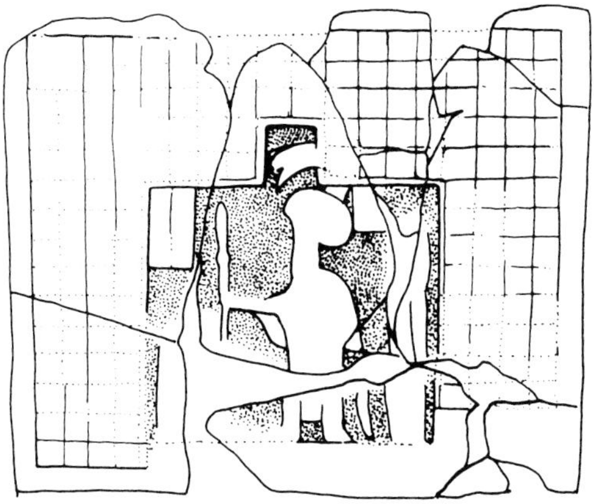

a

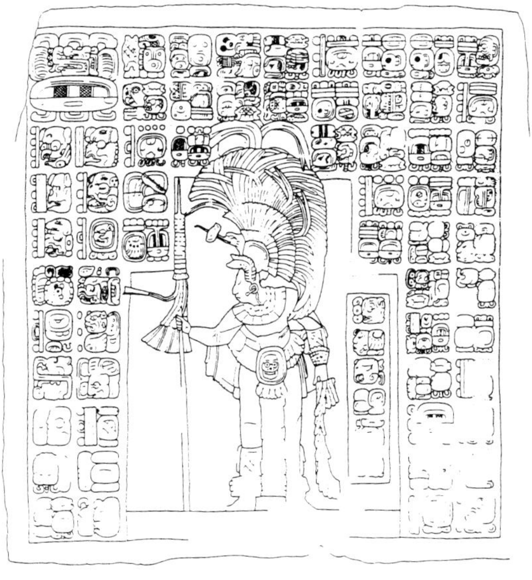

b

Fig. 12 Probable stairway block panels from the Piedras Negras region depicting lords standing in vaulted chambers: (a) Piedras Negras Lintel 5, panel from Structure R-3, Piedras Negras (after Morley 1937–38, 5: pl. 126b); (b) unprovenienced panel in the collections of Dumbarton Oaks (drawing by Stephen Houston).

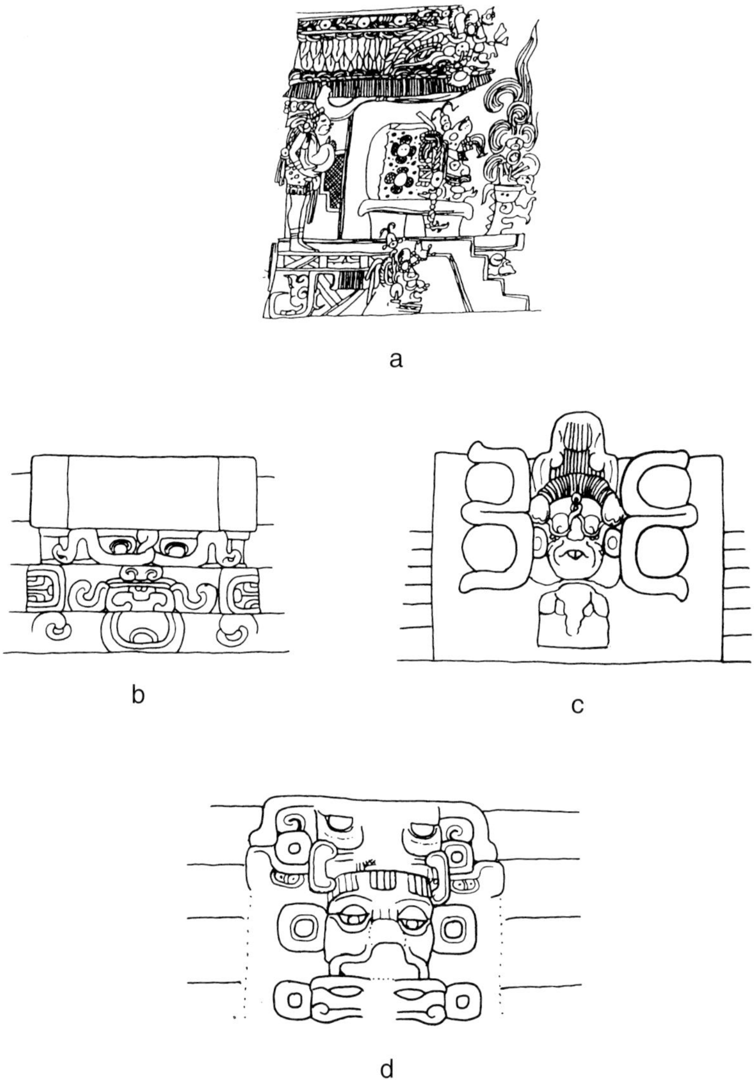

Fig. 13 Stairway blocks in Maya art and architecture: (a) stairway block supporting burning censer, detail of incised vase (from drawing courtesy of Linda Schele); (b) Early Classic stairway block with face of Jaguar God of the Underworld, Structure 5D-22-3rd (after Coe 1990: fig. 97a); (c) Late Classic Jaguar God of the Underworld stairway block from the Jaguar Stairway, Copan (after Anton 1970: pl. 36); (d) sculptured stucco stairway block, Temple VI, Comalcalco (after Andrews 1989: fig. 89).

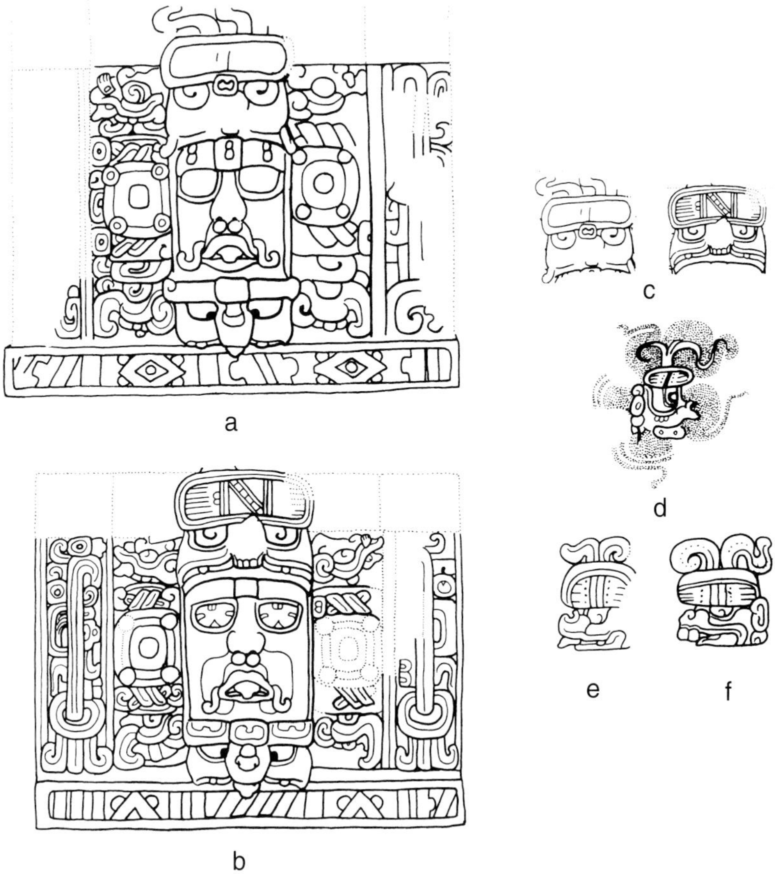

Fig. 14 The Early Classic façades from Kohunlich and fire iconography: (a and b) two of the Kohunlich panels depicting Sun Gods wearing skeletal fire headdress—note smoke emanating from upper example (after Romano Pacheco, Navarette, and Pinto 1981); (c) detail of two skeletal fire sign headdresses; (d) burning skeletal fire sign, probably a censer, detail from Late Classic vessel (after Reents-Budet 1994: fig. 5.10); (e and f) skeletal fire glyphs, Copan Altar K, Seibal Stela 9.

If the large masks on stairway blocks represent censers, then what of the many stucco masks that emblazon the sides of temple platforms? There is evidence that censers were lined along the edges of temple platforms. A fragmentary mural from Chichen Itza depicts such a series of ceramic braziers on a temple platform (Morris, Charlot, and Morris 1931: fig. 168c). Excavations at the Palenque Temple of the Cross have revealed that elaborate flanged Palencano censers were ranged along the temple terraces (González 1993). In both appearance and iconographic meaning, the great platform masks at Early Classic Kohunlich are very much like the Late Classic Palencano censers (Fig. 14a–b). In addition, the Kohunlich masks wear skeletal headdresses topped by smoking fire signs (Fig. 14c). In one Late Classic scene, this same skeletal head serves as a burning brazier and is identical to zoomorphic examples of the fire logograph (Fig. 14d–f). The Kohunlich masks are representations of burning censers placed on the temple platforms.

THE JESTER GOD AND THE JADE HEARTH

Recent iconographic research by Kent Reilly (1990) and Freidel, Schele, and Parker (1993: 132–139) has established that Formative Olmec and Classic Maya rulership was closely tied to the concept of the world center—that is, the kings were frequently portrayed as the living embodiment of the *axis mundi*. This theme of centrality was graphically portrayed by the jewelry and costume worn on the royal body. For the Maya, an item of jade placed at the central crown of the head symbolized the world axis. Coined the Jester God by Schele (1974: 49), this device commonly displays the themes of the world tree and the jade hearth.

Richard Hansen (n.d.: 147–148) notes that the Classic Maya Jester God frequently bears the visage of the Principal Bird Deity, the pre-Hispanic form of Vucub Caquix. In support, Hansen cites a Late Classic Jester God displaying both avian and vegetal imagery (Fig. 15i). The conflation of the monster bird with growing trees can be readily traced to the Late Pre-Classic Kaminaljuyu Stela 11 and the Dumbarton Oaks plaque, which portray rulers wearing Principal Bird Deity trees atop their heads. Both examples display three circles, quite probably the hearthstones in profile (Fig. 15b–c). Schele and Miller (1986: 120) identify these headdress elements as personified forms of the *axis mundi*. However, foliated Jester Gods frequently appear in identical contexts in Classic Maya art. In addition to crowning the tops of heads, they often display the face of the Principal Bird Deity (Fig. 15d–i). On the Leiden Plaque, the tree above the bird head supports three balls, probably the same three spheres appearing on the trunk of the cited Late Pre-Classic examples (Fig. 15d). The blending of the monster bird and tree to represent the *axis mundi* is entirely apt, because this creature is the archetypal denizen of the world tree. Pre-Hispanic scenes of the bird being shot out of the tree are well-known and can be traced back to as early as the Late Pre-Classic period (see Coe 1989). In one Late Classic vessel scene illustrating this episode, a growing tree tops the head of the monster bird

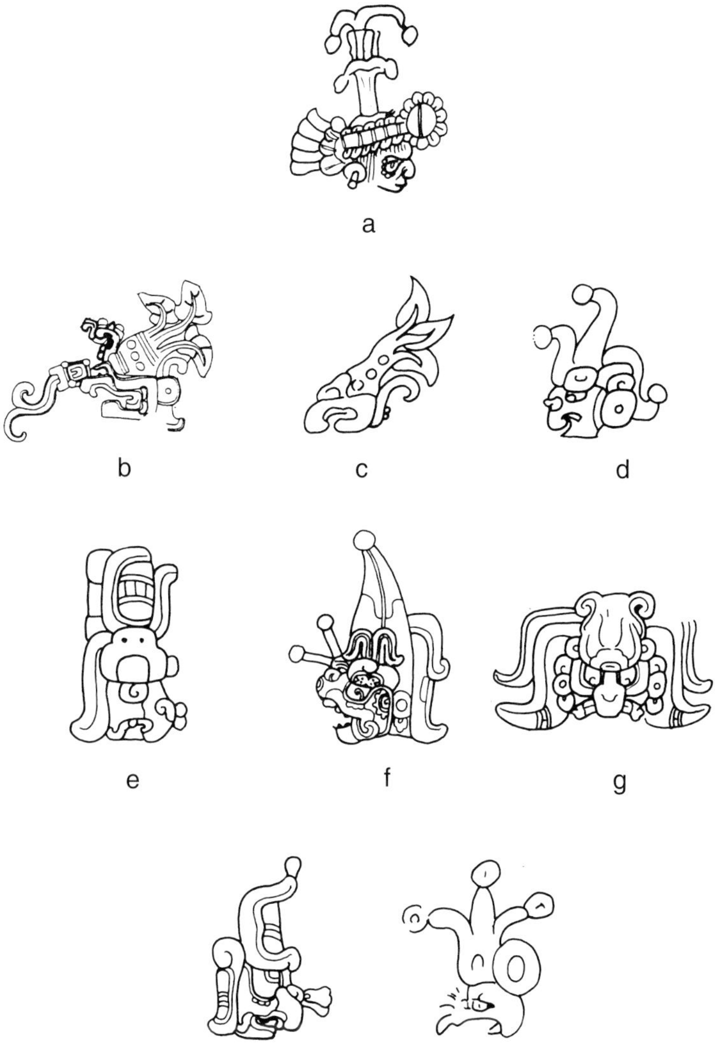

Fig. 15 The aviform jade Jester God as the world axis: (a) anthropomorphic form of the Principal Bird Deity wearing world tree at crown of head (after Hellmuth 1987: fig. 719); (b) Jester God world tree with three balls on trunk, Stela 11, Kaminaljuyu (from Schele and Miller 1986: pl. 32a); (c) Jester God world tree with three balls on trunk, Dumbarton Oaks plaque (after Coe 1966: figs. 2 and 7); (d) Jester God world tree with three balls on branches, Leiden Plaque (after Schele and Miller 1986: pl. 33b); (e) Early Classic avian Jester God (after Miller 1986: pl. 20); (f) smoking Jester God, Lamanai Stela 9 (after Reents-Budet 1988: fig. 1); (g) avian Jester God with flanking foliation, Copan Stela P (after Fash 1991: fig. 50); (h) Late Classic aviform Jester God, Temple of the Inscriptions sarcophagus, Palenque (after Schele and Miller 1986: fig. 1.3i); (i) aviform Jester God as world tree (after Hansen n.d.: fig. 117g).

(Fig. 15a). Once severed from the defeated bird, this head would constitute the same form of the Jester God, a bird head sprouting a verdant tree.

The Jester God not only occurs as single jade atop the head but also as a set of three encircling the brow. In this context, the three jades denote the *axis mundi* hearth. Richard Hansen (n.d.: 146, 148) notes that La Mojarra Stela 1 depicts a Late Pre-Classic version of the triple-stone headband, here as flaming Principal Bird Deity heads (Fig. 16e). Hansen (n.d.: 146, 148) compares this headband to a Late Classic example from the Oval Palace Tablet at Palenque (Fig. 16f). In fact, the triple Jester God headband is very common in Classic Maya iconography and appears in the monumental art of such sites as Machaquila, Seibal, Xultun, Yaxchilan, and Naranjo (Fig. 16g–i).[14] In addition, epigraphic references to the triple Jester God occur in texts from Early Classic Tikal and Yaxchilan as well as Late Classic Copan and Palenque (Fig. 16a–d). One Late Classic Palenque ruler, Lord Xoc, adopted the triple Jester God as his name (Fig. 16d). In the Palace Tablet scene illustrating this accession and naming, the protagonists are seated on three thrones marked with the heads of a jaguar, fish, and serpent (see Schele 1979: 52). In the Quirigua Stela C account of the 4 Ahau 8 Cumku creation event, the three stones are described as jaguar, water, and serpent thrones (see Freidel, Schele, and Parker 1993: fig. 2:5), a series virtually identical to the Palenque scene. The three Palenque thrones probably allude to the three precious stones embodied in the name of this king.

Rather than being limited to royal headbands, the triple Jester God also occurs in scenes to delineate the middle place. Three Early Classic Jester Gods appear on the walls of Tomb 19 of Río Azul (Fig. 16j). The heads are that of the Principal Bird Deity topped by a tree. Each of the central tree trunks supports a large bead, much like the ball and columns from the three-stone group at Izapa. Whereas Río Azul Tomb 12 concerns the four directional sides of the cosmic house, Tomb 19 depicts the jade hearth and the middle place. In the Late Classic murals of Bonampak Structure 1, the triple Jester God hovers in the sky above the Room 1 accession and coronation (Fig. 16k). At times, the triple Jester God can be united as a single stone representing both the flanking profiles and the middle frontal face (Fig. 16l). This convention reveals that the zoomorphic *yaxhal wits nal* or "greening maize mountain" depicted on the Tablet of the Foliated Cross at Palenque is actually the three-stone place from which the Maize God emerges.

[14] For examples aside from those illustrated, see Naranjo Stelae 12 and 14; Yaxchilan Lintel 58; Xultun Stelae 10 and 23; and Machaquila Stelae 3, 4, and 8. An Early Classic censer provides an in-the-round view of a triple Jester God headband worn by a monkey scribe (see Berjonneau, Deletaille, and Sonnery 1985: pl. 365).

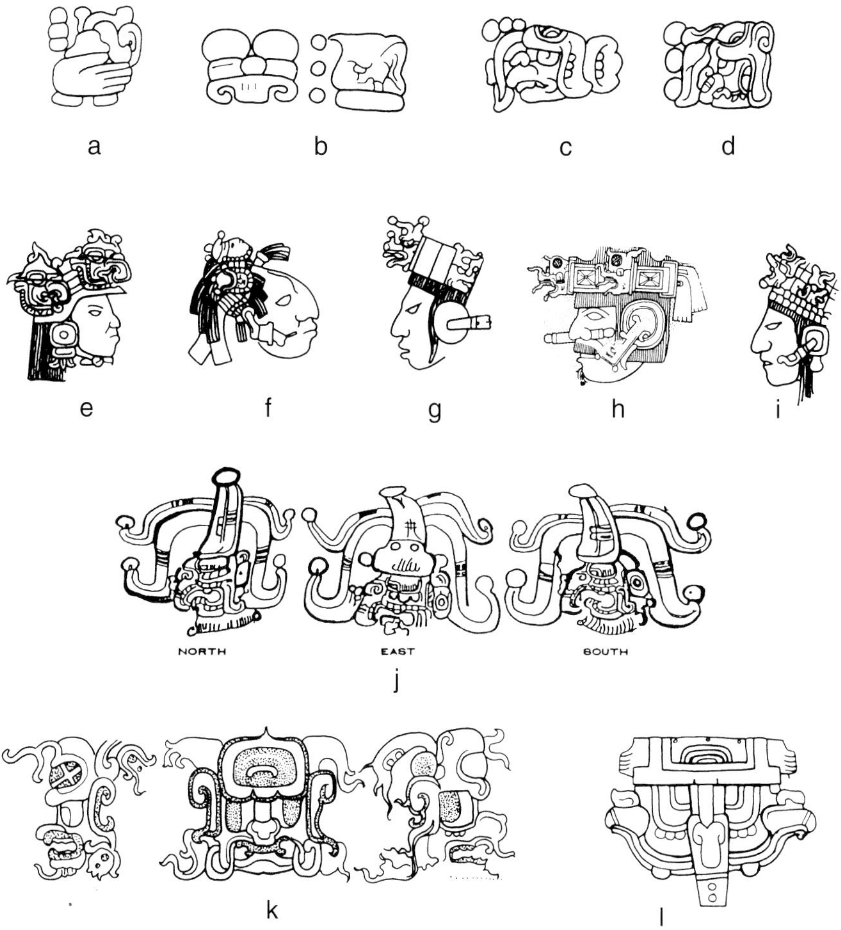

Fig. 16 The triple Jester God in Maya epigraphy and art: (a) triple Jester God in accession expression, Tikal Stela 4 (after Jones and Satterthwaite 1982: fig. 5b); (b) triple Jester God preceded by *hun ahau* compound, Yaxchilan Lintel 20 (after Graham and von Euw 1977: 47); (c) triple Jester God, possibly read *ox hun,* Copan Stela J (after field drawing by Barbara Fash); (d) Lord "Xoc" appellative, Palace Tablet, Palenque (after Schele 1979: fig. 10); (e) Proto-Classic ruler with triple Jester God headdress, La Mojarra Stela 1 (after Winfield Capitaine 1988: fig. 7); (f) triple Jester God headdress, Oval Palace Tablet, Palenque (after Schele 1979: fig. 8); (g) triple Jester God headdress, Machaquila Stela 7 (after Graham 1967: fig. 57); (h) triple Jester God headdress, Seibal Stela 10 (detail of drawing by James Porter); (i) triple Jester God headdress, Xultun Stela 3 (after von Euw 1978: 15); (j) three Jester Gods painted on walls of Tomb 19, Río Azul (after Hall n.d.: fig. 15); (k) three Jester Gods in sky band of Room 1, Bonampak (after Miller 1986: pl. 1); (l) conflated triple Jester God (after Berjonneau, Deletaille, and Sonnery 1985: pl. 397).

Although Jester God images tend to be relatively small articles of adornment, massive examples do exist. Carved from jade boulders, these may well have served as the sacred, precious hearthstones of the community. Stephen Houston (personal communication, 1989) notes that the massive, round jade boulder from the Sun God's tomb at Altun Ha is actually a Jester God (Fig. 17a). If spread out, the design can be identified readily as the head of the Principal Bird Deity topped by the world tree (Fig. 17b). As Pendergast (1982: 48, 73) notes, this same entity appears as stucco masks on the sides of Structure B-4, the temple containing the tomb (Fig. 17c). Projecting out from the upper stairway Structure B-4, the Sun God's tomb is a massive stairway block, much like the aforementioned stairway blocks used in fire offerings. Both the tomb roof and the adjacent round altar on the open temple summit bear evidence of burning, and clearly fire was an important ritual focus of Structure B-4 (Pendergast 1982: 46, 72, 110, 117). Although it is not known whether the Jester God boulder was actually used in fire rituals, this spherical jade carving probably represented a sacred hearthstone.

Aside from the Altun Ha boulder, other massive carved jades can be cited as probable sacred hearthstones. An Early Classic jade statuette depicting the Maize God with a Jester God headdress may also be a symbolic hearthstone (Fig. 17d). This large jade—as well as similar examples from Copan and other sites (e.g., Fash 1991: pls. VIII, IX; Kelemen 1969: pl. 242a, b)—was probably the prized contents of a sacred bundle. The Tablets of the Cross and Foliated Cross at Palenque portray images of large Jester Gods in the center of unwrapped cloth bundles (Fig. 17e). A Late Classic polychrome represents another unwrapped Jester God bundle, here placed before God D, the anthropomorphic counterpart of the Principal Bird Deity (Fig. 17f). Portrayed as a rounded skull, the bundle image is capped with the same jeweled tree commonly found with Jester Gods, including the Altun Ha example. In the accompanying text, the head is qualified with the *sak* or "white" prefix, in probable reference to *sak hunal,* a Classic term for the Jester God (Schele 1991).

In early colonial Quiche accounts, the sacred bundle carried and cared for by the temple priests is explicitly described as a fire (*gagal*) bundle. The *El título de los señores de Totonicapán* describes the contents of the *Giron-Gagal* bundle as a sacred stone (Recinos 1950: 205, n. 3).[15] In the Late Classic Vase of the Seven

[15] The identification of bundles with fire ritual and the three hearthstones is not restricted to the Maya. John Pohl (personal communication, 1994) notes that the Mixtec sacred bundles typically appear with the fire drill and stick. As part of the nose-piercing accession rite illustrated on Codex Nuttall page 52, the Mixtec king 8 Deer stands before a sacred bundle. Byland and Pohl (1994: 140–148) note that the accompanying priest 4 Jaguar is portrayed

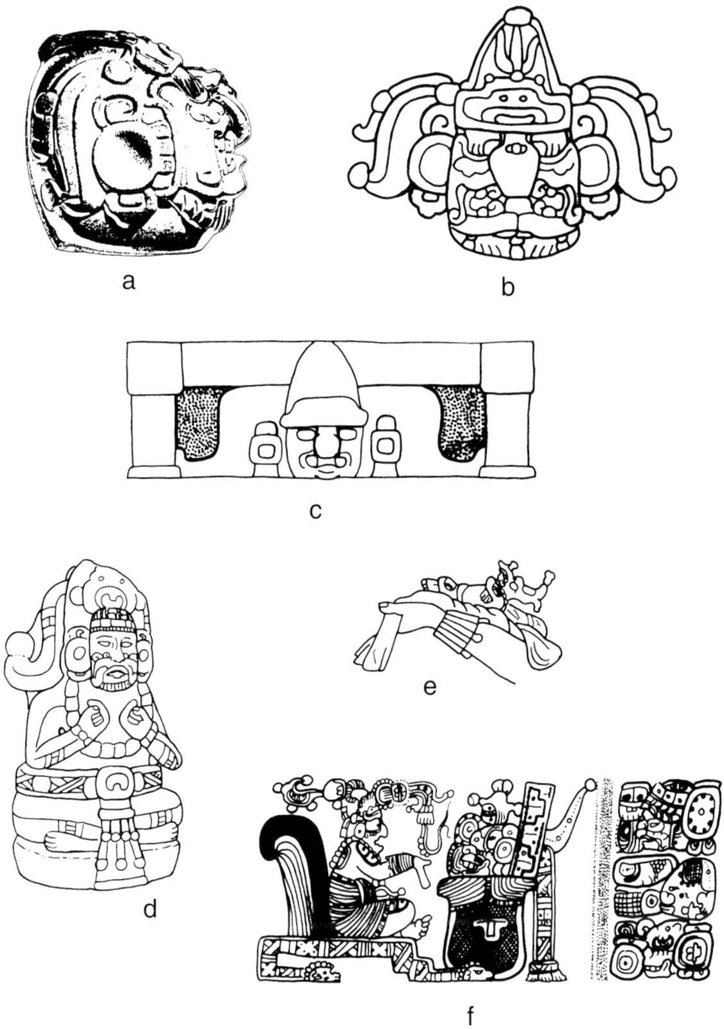

Fig. 17 Massive Jester God jades: (a) jade avian Jester God boulder from Tomb B-4/7, Altun Ha (after Pendergast 1982: fig. 33b); (b) rollout drawing of carved design on jade boulder (after Pendergast 1982: fig. 33a–c); (c) Jester God stucco façade from Structure B-4, Altun Ha (after Pendergast 1982: fig. 40); (d) Jester God jade boulder in the form of Maize God (after Hellmuth 1987: fig. 25); (e) Jester God statuette as contents of unwrapped sacred bundle, Tablet of the Cross, Palenque (after Schele 1979: fig. 6b); (f) massive Jester God in unwrapped bundle, accompanying text refers to Hunahpu as the taker of the *sak hunal* stone (after Reents-Budet 1994: 14–15).

Gods scene illustrating the 4 Ahau 8 Cumku event, God L sits on a jaguar throne surrounded by three bundles, quite probably containing the three stones of the 4 Ahau 8 Cumku creation event (see Freidel, Schele, and Parker 1993: fig. 2:6). Another Late Classic polychrome portrays an actual king seated on a throne above two large bundles; next to the throne, there is a rotund stone image of approximately the same rounded shape and dimensions as the nearby bundles (see Kerr 1992: 370).[16] Like the Izapa three-stone group and the Vase of the Seven Gods, this scene probably illustrates the throne accompanied by the three sacred stones of rulership, here with one unwrapped from its enclosing bundle. It is quite likely that such sacred hearthstones were passed through generations of kings as statements of sovereignty and territory, in terms not of a simple house but of an entire political domain.

The aforementioned scene illustrating God D with the unwrapped Jester God bundle is a mythical corollary of elite dynastic behavior (Fig. 17f). The accompanying text states that the spotted headband twin, Hunahpu, is the taker of this stone, and both Hunahpu and his father, the Maize God, also appear on this vessel (see Reents-Budet 1994: 14–15). Along with serving as the personified form of the day name Ahau, meaning "king" or "lord," Hunahpu embodies the proper roles and behavior of Maya kings (Coe 1989). One of the major mythical tasks performed by this god is carrying and placement of the sacred hearthstones (Kerr 1994: 549; Taube n.d.: figs. 72, 74).[17] A large and finely carved Early Classic limestone sphere—quite probably a sacred hearthstone—portrays Hunahpu carrying such a stone above his head (Fig. 18a) (see Hellmuth 1987: fig. 29).

The carrying and setting of the hearthstones by the Hero Twins introduces the apparent climax of the Classic Popol Vuh epic, the resurrection of their

as a Chichimec and suggest that the nose-piercing scene concerns ritual ties to peoples of Central Mexico. Along with the nose-piercing rite of accession, the sacred bundle was an essential ritual component of Chichimec rulership. In the *Anales de Cuauhtitlan,* after Itzpapalotl introduces the Chichimec to the three sacred hearthstones, her body is burned and a sacred bundle is made from her remains (Bierhorst 1992: 23). In the immediately preceding scene on Nuttall pages 51 and 52, 8 Deer appears with three stones placed on mountains. It appears that, like the Chichimec *Anales de Cuauhtitlan* episode of the Itzpapalotl bundle, 8 Deer is shown gathering the three sacred stones used in the sacred bundle ceremony.

[16] In another Late Classic vessel scene, an enthroned king is portrayed with three bundles. As in the previous example, the scene concerns the arraignment of captives (see Kerr 1994: 550).

[17] One particular Classic *way* illustrated on the Altar de Sacrificios vase appears as Hunahpu carrying a large, rounded stone. The same *way* character occurs on a stylistically very similar vase surrounded by three stones (see Reents-Budet 1994: 174).

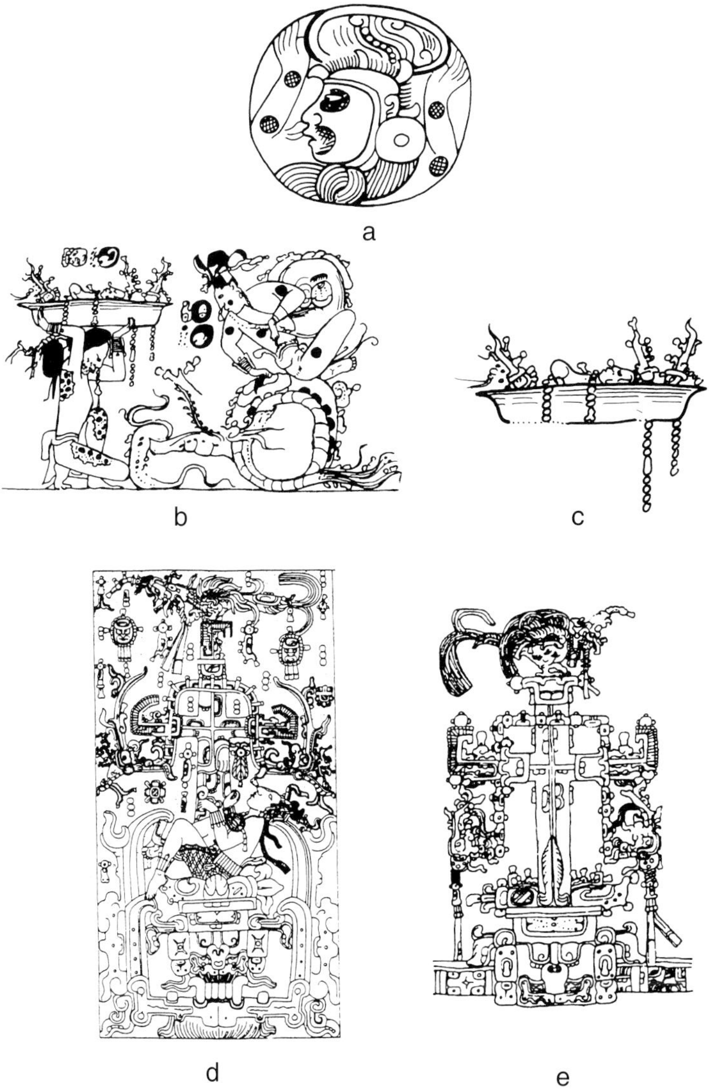

Fig. 18 The placing of the three sacred stones in Maya mythology: (a) Hunahpu carrying probable hearthstone, incised cartouche from probable Early Classic sacred hearthstone (drawn from photograph in the FLAAR slide archive at Dumbarton Oaks, slide EC-st. V-1/11); (b) the Hero Twins with the regalia of their father (detail of drawing by Linda Schele); (c) detail of bowl carried by Hero Twin Xbalanque, containing three Jester God jewels and probable jade statuette of Maize God (after Robicsek and Hales 1981: vessel 186); (d) world tree on sarcophagus lid, Palenque; note three serpent jewels on branches of tree (detail of drawing by Merle Greene Robertson); (e) the *wakah chan* world tree with three trefoil Jester God stones at ends of branches (drawing by Linda Schele).

father, the Maize God. In one now well-known resurrection scene, the Maize God rises out of the middle of a turtle shell marked by a burning skull hearth (see Taube 1993: cover, 77). Much like the accession scene in Bonampak Room 1, Hunahpu seems to be dressing his father in his jade finery. Another Late Classic codex–style vessel represents the Hero Twins carrying the sacred bundle and a bowl filled with the jade of their father (Fig. 18b–c). The contents are three beaded serpent jewels—the form of the Jester God worn by the Maize God—and a seated image, quite probably one of the aforementioned Maize God jade statuettes (Fig. 18b). Whereas the accompanying text mentions the Maize God entering the water (*och ha*) as the *wak ahau* or raised-up lord, a closely related bundle and jade dressing scene describes him as entering a road, or *och bil* (see Robicsek and Hales 1981: vessel 82). The same reference to entering the road occurs on the sarcophagus text of Pacal, who in the accompanying scene is portrayed as the Maize God at the base of the world tree (Fig. 18d) (Freidel, Schele, and Parker 1993: 76–77). The tree branches are tipped by the same three serpent Jester God jewels carried by Xbalanque in the aforementioned scene (Fig. 18b–c).

The authors of *Maya Cosmos* note that the world tree on the Palenque sarcophagus lid is the same *wakah chan* or "raised-up sky" tree depicted on the Tablet of the Cross (Freidel, Schele, and Parker 1993: 71, 77–78). In addition to the serpent jewels on the two lower branches, the ends of all three tree limbs are tipped by a trefoil device (Fig. 18e). This form is commonly found with Jester Gods and, in the case of the Late Pre-Classic Dumbarton Oaks plaque, serves as the glyph for the Jester God headband (Coe 1966: figs. 11, B3). Moreover, as jeweled world trees rising out of avian censers, the two Palenque trees are strikingly similar to examples of Jester Gods (Fig. 15d–i). The texts of both the Palenque Temple of the Cross and Quirigua Stela C state that the three green hearthstones were lifted into the sky by the *wakah chan* tree (Freidel, Schele, and Parker 1993: 67, 71–72). It appears that the *wak chan ahau,* or lord of this tree, was the Maize God (Freidel, Schele, and Parker 1993: 73). Freidel, Schele, and Parker (1993: 418, n. 21) note that, in this context of resurrection, the Maize God is a personified version of the world tree.[18] By wearing the three jade jewels, the resurrected Maize God became the world tree supporting the three green hearthstones. When the king placed the triple Jester God on his head, he reenacted this basic creation event, the raising of the green hearth and the *axis mundi* into the sky.

[18] Virginia Fields (1991) makes a compelling case that a great deal of the Jester God imagery concerns maize and can be traced back to Middle Formative Olmec iconography. However, in her study, Fields focuses specifically on maize rather than the broader significance of the Jester God as the world axis.

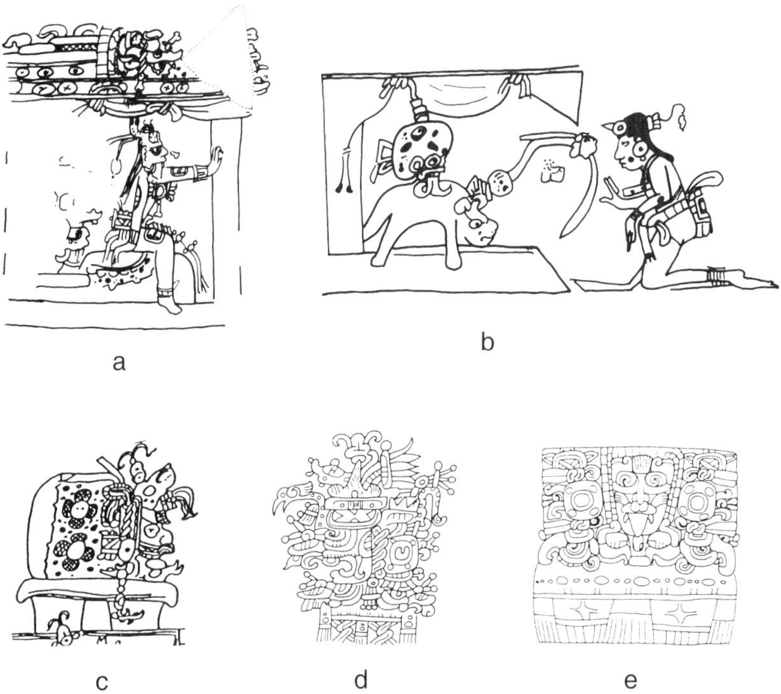

Fig. 19 Enthroned headdresses in Classic Maya art: (a) detail of Late Classic vessel scene illustrating probable headdress behind enthroned Pax God (after Kerr 1992: 378); (b) Hunahpu facing Tlaloc headdress on jaguar throne (after Kerr 1990: 192); (c) enthroned headdress (see Fig. 13a); (d) Early Classic representation of headdress atop jaguar cushion throne with Pop signs (from Hellmuth 1987: fig. 82); (e) Early Classic depiction of GI face and headdress atop jaguar cushion throne with *po* signs (after Hellmuth 1987: fig. 115).

THE TEMPLE AND THE KING

Classic Maya temples were by no means aloof and impersonal objects divorced from the human plane. Not only are rulers portrayed on temples, but they were directly involved with the temple rites; the vast majority of stelae and other Classic Maya monuments are oriented to temples, not palace structures. One of the most common themes on Classic monuments is ritual impersonation and dance, an essential component of temple worship. Certain headdresses used in these dances were prized and sacred articles of the temple. In Late Classic vessel scenes, headdresses appear on thrones within temples, as if sentient embodiments of the divine being (Fig. 19a–c). In one revealing scene, the spotted twin Hunahpu approaches such an enthroned headdress as if greeting an omnipotent lord (Fig. 19b). This convention of placing headdresses on thrones is not limited to Late Classic art; it also occurs on Early Classic censers and cache vessels (Fig. 19d–e).

In Classic Maya art, it is often difficult to distinguish between temple headdresses and censers (e.g., Fig. 19a and c–e). The similarity partly serves to group both as temple items, but the relationship between censers and headdresses goes further. Classic vessel scenes show headdresses with burning censers, as if they were part of fire-conjuring rites (e.g., Fig. 13a) (Coe 1973: 82; Kerr 1990: 192; Kerr 1992: 378). Like censers, headdresses become the seat or house of the divine being during ritual impersonation. As symbolic homes and mediums for the divine, dance headdresses are much like "censers in motion," and possibly for this reason the Maya elite—especially women—often wear symbolic "Quadripartite Badge" censers as headdresses (e.g., Tikal Stela 2, Yaxchilan Lintels 14 and 32, Naranjo Stela 24).

As a form of reciprocal metaphor (see Houston, this volume), headdresses are not only compared to miniature temples or god houses, but temples themselves frequently evoke the qualities of ritual headdresses. As repositories of divine spirit, temples were considered much like living beings. In one remarkable Tikal graffito, a temple is personified as a seated man, with the roof serving as its head, the supporting platform as the lower legs and body, and the stairway as the loincloth (Fig. 20a). Among the Maya, the temple roof constitutes the symbolic headdress of the building. This same concept can be observed in Teotihuacan style *incensarios*. Although Gamio (1922: 29) suggested that the composite ceramic censer represents a miniature temple, the interior space contains not an entire figure but, rather, a large single face, creating an architectonic headdress out of the surrounding assemblage (see Berlo 1984). On the aforementioned Quirigua Stela C and the closely related Stela A, jaguar figures wear temple roofs and surmounting birds as headdresses, as if they are dancing personified temples (Fig. 20b–c). Stephen Houston (personal communication, 1994) notes that the great jaguar litter figure of Lintel 2 of Tikal Temple IV wears a thatched temple roof on its head, much as if it were a headdress (Fig. 20d). The roof element is partially obscured by a triple Jester God headband. The three *wits* monster heads frequently ranged along the lower front portions of temple roofs are probably architectonic versions of the triple Jester God headband (Fig. 20e).[19]

[19] Other examples of three *wits* heads on the lower front of temple façades occur on Tikal Temples I and II, Yaxchilan Structures 20 and 33, and Bonampak Structure 1. Although

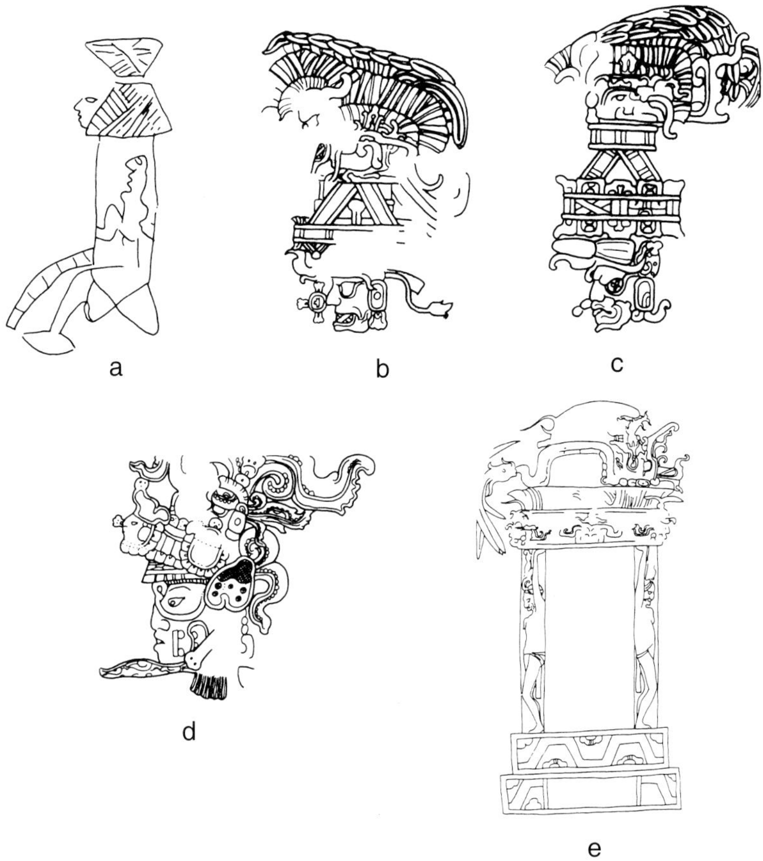

Fig. 20 Anthropomorphized temples in Late Classic Maya iconography: (a) Tikal graffito depicting temple as seated male, with the roof as the head, the temple platform as the legs and hips, and the stairway as the loincloth (after Trik and Kampen 1983: fig. 15b); (b) dancing Jaguar God with temple roof topped with bird serving as headdress, Quirigua Stela C (after Maudslay 1889–1902, 2: pl. 20); (c) dancing Jaguar God with temple roof and bird as headdress, Quirigua Stela A (after Maudslay 1889–1902, 2: pl. 8); (d) Jaguar God wearing temple roof and triple Jester God in headdress, Lintel 2 of Tikal Temple IV (after Jones and Satterthwaite 1982: fig. 73); (e) temple with three foliated stones in roof, detail of Late Classic altar (drawing by Linda Schele).

additional *wits* heads tend to continue on the flanking sides, the consistent appearance of three heads on the frontal façades suggests that the triadic grouping constitutes the central and essential message.

The overlapping themes of temple, censer, and headdress are frequently portrayed on Classic Maya frontal stelae (Fig. 21a–b). The frontal stelae of Copan, Quirigua, and Tonina display an elaborate concern with headdresses, frequently formed of stacked heads and earspool assemblages accompanied by outwardly facing profiles. When wearing these headdresses in ritual, the kings would appear as animated versions of temple and censer iconography. At certain sites, there are stone monuments depicting only the head and headdress, intermediate forms between stelae and censers. Although major stone monuments, the "stelae" of Salinas de los Nueve Cerros are strikingly like flanged censers (Fig. 21c). Moreover, elaborate texts cover the sides and backs of Palenque stone censer supports, as if these monuments constituted the Palenque version of stelae (see Schele and Mathews 1979: nos. 281, 282, 303, 391). But perhaps the most striking example of the ambiguity between frontal stelae, temples, and censers is Structure 1 at the Chenes site of Nocuchich. Some 5 m in height, it is a solid masonry tower displaying a massive frontal face (Pollock 1970: 43–44). Originally supplied with broad flanges on its sides, Structure 1 is a unique blending of censer, stela, and temple.

Schele and Freidel (1990: 90–91) note that Classic stelae frequently portray kings as the world tree to denote the *axis mundi*. However, aside from tree imagery, frontal stelae also evoke the concepts of temples and their censers to describe the middle place. In terms of Maya cities, this use of temple imagery in costume is especially evocative, as it not only places the king in the world axis but also unites him to the sacred architectural landscape. Flora Clancy (1988: 209) contrasts the static quality of the full-frontal stelae of Copan and Quirigua with profile representations of rulers: "the full-frontal figures may be understood as representing the godlike or herolike qualities of Maya rulership, and the asymmetrical representations narrate the ruler's actions and deeds." The same can be said of the great frontal masks and figures displayed on temple buildings. By wearing temple costume and motifs, the king becomes the living embodiment of the temple and its divine occupants.

CONCLUSIONS

In their seminal identification of the three hearthstones in Classic Maya inscriptions, Freidel, Schele, and Parker (1993) have opened up entirely new vistas for interpreting Maya architecture and cosmology. In this study, I have stressed that the hearth is a central motif of temple architecture, ritual, and iconography. As the vitalizing centers of temples, censers symbolized the basic three-stone hearth of the Maya household. Through the ritual process of focusing, censers constituted the house and seat of conjured gods. In addition to

Fig. 21 Examples of Maya frontal stelae: (a) Monument 26, Tonina (after Mathews 1983: 61); (b) recently discovered stela, Tonina (after Yadeun 1993: 88); (c) Stela 1, Salinas de los Nueve Cerros (after line drawing by Ian Graham).

actual censers, temple stairway block shrines and three-legged altars also evoked the three-stone hearth. As plans of the *axis mundi,* radial stairway temples were closely identified with the central hearth and appear to have been important places for fire-making rituals.

The recognition of the three hearthstones in profile has intriguing implications for the interpretation of Maya architecture and iconography. When the hearthstones are in profile, the central stone represents the middle place, flanked and framed by the other two stones. Freidel, Schele, and Parker (1993: 140) note that the plan of certain triadic architectural groupings reflects the three stones as if seen from above. However, it is quite possible that series of three linearly oriented temples, such as found with Classic E-Groups, also allude to the three stones, albeit not in plan but in profile. In this regard, David Stuart (personal communication, 1994) has called my attention to such a grouping at Dos Pilas Structure L5-49. The middle structure of this three-temple platform contained Panel 18, which mentions the 4 Ahau 8 Cumku event and the green hearthstones (see Houston 1993: 23, fig. 4-4). Stuart notes that this monument is epigraphically labeled as a "fire stone" and suggests that it may have been used in fire-making rituals.

In this study, I have stressed that the frontal mask panels and profile earspool assemblages constitute references to temples and related objects, whether these be censers, headdresses, or even the body of the king. Along with the temple, they also served as symbolic *axes mundi*—conduits and temporary "homes" for conjured beings. With the outwardly facing profile heads, the frontal masks themselves embody the concept of centrality. Much like the hearthstones in profile, the flanking profile heads on the headdress and earspool assemblages frame the central frontal face (Fig. 21a–c). In the Classic frontal representations, the smaller profile masks qualify the central face, which serves as the active and dominant image. A similar pattern can be discerned for many of the temple façades discussed in this study. Here the sculptures on the sides of central axis frame and qualify the "real" events and players. Thus, at Late Pre-Classic Uaxactun and Late Classic Hochob, false doorways flank the actual central passage. For the Tonina stairway shrine, false stucco hearthstones frame an actual central hearthstone, whereas at Copan, zoomorphic *tun* stones may have flanked a similarly appearing *tun* censer placed on the central axis. A similar case could be made for the great masks on the sides of the central stairway, which serve to qualify and frame the burning censers and costumed impersonators moving along the stairway and central axis of the building.

As localized embodiments of the sacred world axis, both rulers and temples are frequently portrayed with similar accoutrements and iconography. As early as Late Pre-Classic Izapa, the throne of kingship was identified with both the world axis and the temple. The three raised hearthstones behind this throne were also worn as precious jades on the brow of the king. When wearing the triple Jester God headband, the king was a living embodiment of the *axis mundi,* as both a verdant tree and a jade hearth. The three *wits* forms commonly found on the lower front of temple façades are probably architectonic versions of this triple-stone headband. But, although striking, the many symbolic parallels between the living kings and temples fade in comparison to funerary temples, which serve as the homes and embodiment of the deceased king. Much as Clancy suggests for frontal stelae, the static and archaistic nature of temple façades serves to portray what is enduring and constant in Maya kingship and religion, linking the generations of the living to the honored dead.

Acknowledgments This study is the direct result of my participation as a summer fellow in Pre-Columbian Studies at Dumbarton Oaks. I wish to thank both Elizabeth Boone and Richard Diehl for their support during my stay at Dumbarton Oaks. I am also indebted to Carol Calloway and Nicholas Hellmuth for their assistance with the Foundation for Latin American Anthropological Research slide archive at Dumbarton Oaks. As a summer fellow, I benefited greatly from the many insights and contributions generously provided by the other four seminar members—Nancy Gonlin, Stephen Houston, Patricia McAnany, and David Webster—as well as David Stuart, who visited us during the summer seminar. I also wish to thank Stephen Houston, Peter Mathews, James Porter, and Linda Schele for generously allowing me to publish their line drawings. Lastly, I would like to thank Stephen Houston for his editorial suggestions during the preparation of this manuscript.

BIBLIOGRAPHY

Acuña, René (ed.)

1983 *Thesaurus verborum: Vocabulario de la lengua Cakchiquel y Guatemalteca, nuevamente hecho y recopilado con sumo estudio, trabajo y erudición* (Fray Tomás de Coto). Universidad Nacional Autónoma de México, México, D.F.

Anderson, Michael

1985 Curtain Holes in the Standing Architecture of Palenque. In *Fourth Palenque Round Table, 1980* (Merle Greene Roberston, gen. ed.): 21–27. Pre-Columbian Art Research Institute, San Francisco.

Andrews, E. Wyllys, V, and Barbara Fash

1992 Continuity and Change in a Royal Maya Residential Complex at Copan. *Ancient Mesoamerica* 3: 63–88.

Andrews, George F.

1989 *Comalcalco, Tabasco, Mexico: Maya Art and Architecture.* 2 vols. Labyrinthos, Culver City, Calif.

Anton, Ferdinand

1970 *Art of the Maya.* Thames and Hudson, London.

Attinasi, J. J.

n.d. Lak T'an: A Grammar of the Chol (Mayan) Word. Ph.D. dissertation, University of Chicago, 1973.

Barrera Vásquez, Alfredo (ed.)

1980 *Diccionario Maya Cordemex: Maya-Español, Español-Maya.* Ediciones Cordemex, Mérida, Yucatan, Mexico.

Becqueln, Pierre, and Claude F. Baudez

1979–82 *Tonina: Une cité maya du Chiapas (Mexique).* 3 vols. Mission archéologique et ethnologique française au Mexique, Mexico City.

Berjonneau, Gerald, Emile Deletaille, and Jean-Louis Sonnery

1985 *Rediscovered Masterpieces of Mesoamerica: Mexico–Guatemala–Honduras.* Editions Arts, Boulogne.

Berlo, Janet

1984 *Teotihuacan Art Abroad: A Study of Metropolitan Style and Provincial Transformation in Incensario Workshops.* British Archaeological Reports, International Series 199. Oxford.

Bierhorst, John

1992 *History and Mythology of the Aztecs: The Codex Chimalpopoca.* University of Arizona Press, Tucson.

Brainerd, George W.

1958 *The Archaeological Ceramics of Yucatan.* Anthropological Records, no. 19. University of California, Berkeley.

Byland, Bruce, and John M. D. Pohl
1994 *In the Realm of 8 Deer.* University of Oklahoma Press, Norman.

Caso, Alfonso
1959 Los nombres calendáricos de los dioses. *El México Antiguo* 9:77–110.

Chase, Arlen, Nikolai Grube, and Diane Chase
1991 *Three Terminal Classic Monuments from Caracol, Belize.* Research Reports on Ancient Maya Writing, no. 36. Center for Maya Research, Washington, D.C.

Clancy, Flora S.
1988 The Compositions and Contexts of the Classic Stelae at Copan and Quirigua. In *The Southeast Classic Maya Zone* (Elizabeth Hill Boone and Gordon R. Willey, eds.): 195–221. Dumbarton Oaks, Washington, D.C.

Coe, Michael D.
1966 *An Early Stone Pectoral from Southeastern Mexico.* Studies in Pre-Columbian Art and Archaeology 1. Dumbarton Oaks, Washington, D.C.
1973 *The Maya Scribe and His World.* Grolier Club, New York.
1978 *Lords of the Underworld: Masterpieces of Classic Maya Ceramics.* Princeton University Press, Princeton, N.J.
1989 The Hero Twins: Myth and Image. In *The Maya Vase Book,* vol. 1 (Justin Kerr, ed.): 161–184. Kerr Associates, New York.

Coe, William R.
1990 *Excavations in the Great Plaza, North Terrace and North Acropolis of Tikal.* 6 vols. Tikal Report, no. 14. University Museum Monograph 61. University of Pennsylvania, Philadelphia.

Coggins, Clemency
1987 New Fire at Chichen Itza. In *Memorias del primer coloquio internacional de Mayistas:* 427–484. Universidad Nacional Autónoma de México, D.F.

Coggins, Clemency C., and Orrin C. Shane III
1984 *Cenote of Sacrifice: Maya Treasures from the Sacred Well at Chichen Itza.* University of Texas Press, Austin.

Craine, Eugene R., and Reginald C. Reindorp
1979 *The Codex Pérez and the Book of Chilam Balam of Mani.* University of Oklahoma Press, Norman.

David, Virginia Dale
n.d. Ritual of the Northern Lacandon Maya. Ph.D. dissertation, Tulane University, 1978.

Delgaty, Alfa Hurley de, and Agustín Ruíz Sánchez
1978 *Diccionario Tzotzil de San Andrés con variaciones dialectales.* Instituo Lingüístico de Verano, México, D.F.

Edmonson, Munro S.
1965 *Quiche–English Dictionary.* Middle American Research Institute, Publication 30. Tulane University, New Orleans.
1982 *The Ancient Future of the Itza: The Book of Chilam Balam of Tizimin.* University of Texas Press, Austin.

Ekholm, Gordon F.
1970 *Ancient Mexico and Central America.* American Museum of Natural History, New York.

Erosa Peniche, José A.
1947 Descubrimiento y exploración arqueológica de la subestructura del Castillo en Chichen-Itzá. In *Vigesimoséptimo Congreso Internacional de Americanistas,* vol. 2: 229–248. Instituto Nacional de Antropología e Historia, México, D.F.

von Euw, Eric
1978 *Corpus of Maya Hieroglyphic Inscriptions,* vol. 5, pt. 1*: Xultun.* Peabody Museum of Archaeology and Ethnology, Harvard University, Cambridge, Mass.

Fash, William L.
1991 *Scribes, Warriors and Kings: The City of Copán and the Ancient Maya.* Thames and Hudson, London.

Fauvet-Berthelot, Marie-France
1986 *Ethnopréhistoire de la maison maya (Guatemala, 1250–1525).* Centre d'etudes mexicaines et centraméricaines, Mexico City.

Ferdon, Edwin N., Jr.
1953 *Tonala, Mexico: An Archaeological Survey.* Monographs of the School of American Research, no. 16. Santa Fe.

Ferree, Lisa
n.d. The Pottery Censers of Tikal, Guatemala. Ph.D. dissertation, Southern Illinois University, 1972.

Fields, Virginia
1991 The Iconographic Heritage of the Maya Jester God. *In Sixth Palenque Round Table, 1986* (Merle Greene Roberston, gen. ed.): 167–174. University of Oklahoma Press, Norman.

Fought, John G.
1972 *Chorti (Mayan) Texts.* University of Pennsylvania Press, Philadelphia.

Freidel, David, Linda Schele, and Joy Parker
1993 *Maya Cosmos: Three Thousand Years on the Shaman's Path.* William Morrow, New York.

Gamio, Manuel
1922 *La población del valle de Teotihuacan,* vol. 1. Secretaria de Agricultura y Fomento, México, D.F.

Gendrop, Paul
1983 *Los estilos Río Bec, Chenes, y Puuc en la arquitectura maya.* Universidad Nacional Autónoma de México, México, D.F.

González, Arnoldo
1993 El templo de la cruz. *Arqueología Mexicana* 1 (2): 39–41.

Graham, Ian
1967 *Archaeological Explorations in El Peten, Guatemala.* Middle American Research Institute, Publication 33. Tulane University, New Orleans.

GRAHAM, IAN, AND ERIC VON EUW

1977 *Corpus of Maya Hieroglyphic Inscriptions,* vol. 3, pt. 1: *Yaxchilan.* Peabody Museum of Archaeology and Ethnology, Harvard University, Cambridge, Mass.

GRUBE, NIKOLAI

1990 Die Errichtung von Stelen: Entzifferung einer Verbhieroglyphe auf Monumenten der Klassichen Mayakultur. In *Circumpacifica: Festschrit für Thomas S. Barthel* (Bruno Illius and Matthias Laubscher, eds.): 189–215. Peter Lang, Frankfurt.

GRUBE, NIKOLAI, AND LINDA SCHELE

1990 *Royal Gifts to Subordinate Lords.* Copan Note 87. Copan Acropolis Archaeological Project and the Instituto Hondureño de Antropología, Tegucigalpa, Honduras.

1991 *Tzuk in the Classic Maya Inscriptions.* Texas Notes on Pre-Columbian Art, Writing, and Culture, no. 15. Center for the History and Art of Ancient American Culture, University of Texas, Austin.

HALL, GRANT D.

n.d. Realm of Death: Royal Mortuary Customs and Polity Interaction in the Classic Maya Lowlands. Ph.D. dissertation, Harvard University, 1989.

HANSEN, RICHARD

n.d. The Archaeology of Ideology: A Study of Maya Preclassic Architectural Sculpture at Nakbe, Peten, Guatemala. Ph.D. dissertation, University of California at Los Angeles, 1992.

HELLMUTH, NICHOLAS

1987 *Monster und Menschen in der Maya-Kunst: Eine Ikonographie der Alten Religionen Mexikos und Guatemalas.* Akademische Druck- u. Verlagsanstalt, Graz, Austria.

HOHMANN, HASSO, AND ANNEGRETE VOGRIN

1982 *Die Architektur von Copan.* 2 vols. Akademische Druck- u. Verlagsanstalt, Graz, Austria.

HOLLAND, WILLIAM R.

1963 *Medicina maya en los altos de Chiapas: Un estudio del cambio socio-cultural.* Colección de Antropología Social, vol. 2. Instituto Nacional Indigenista, México, D.F.

HOUSTON, STEPHEN D.

1993 *Hieroglyphs and History at Dos Pilas: Dynastic Politics of the Classic Maya.* University of Texas Press, Austin.

HOUSTON, STEPHEN D., AND DAVID STUART

1989 *The* Way *Glyph: Evidence for "Co-essences" among the Classic Maya.* Research Reports on Ancient Maya Writing, no. 30. Center for Maya Research, Washington, D.C.

JONES, CHRISTOPHER, AND LINTON SATTERTHWAITE

1982 *The Monuments and Inscriptions of Tikal: The Carved Monuments.* Tikal Report, no. 33, pt. A. University Museum, Monograph 44. University of Pennsylvania, Philadelphia.

KELEMEN, PÁL

1969 *Medieval American Art: Masterpieces of the New World before Columbus.* 3rd ed., 2 vols. Dover Publications, New York.

KELLEY, DAVID HUMISTON
1976 *Deciphering the Maya Script.* University of Texas Press, Austin.

KERR, JUSTIN
1989 *The Maya Vase Book,* vol. 1. Kerr Associates, New York.
1990 *The Maya Vase Book,* vol. 2. Kerr Associates, New York.
1992 *The Maya Vase Book,* vol. 3. Kerr Associates, New York.
1994 *The Maya Vase Book,* vol. 4. Kerr Associates, New York.

LABBÉ, ARMAND J.
1982 *Religion, Art and Iconography: Man and Cosmos in Prehispanic Mesoamerica.* Bowers Museum Foundation, Santa Ana, Calif.

LAUGHLIN, ROBERT M.
1975 *The Great Tzotzil Dictionary of San Lorenzo Zincantan.* Smithsonian Contributions to Anthropology, no. 19. Smithsonian Institution Press, Washington, D.C.
1988 *The Great Tzotzil Dictionary of Santo Domingo Zinacantan.* 3 vols. Smithsonian Contributions to Anthropology, no. 31. Smithsonian Institution Press, Washington, D.C.

LENKERSDORF, CARLOS
1979 *Diccionario Tojolabal–Español.* 2 vols. Editorial Nuestro Tiempo, México, D.F.

LOWE, GARETH
1965 Desarollo y función del incensario en Izapa. *Estudios de Cultura Maya* 5: 53-64.

MATHEWS, PETER
1983 *Corpus of Maya Hieroglyphic Inscriptions,* vol. 6, pt. 1: *Tonina.* Peabody Museum of Archaeology and Ethnology, Harvard University, Cambridge, Mass.

MAUDSLAY, ALFRED P.
1889–1902 *Archaeology.* Biologia centrali-americana. 5 vols. Porter and Dulau, London.

MAYER, KARL HERBERT
1984 *Maya Monuments: Sculptures of Unknown Provenance in Middle America.* Karl-Friedrich von Flemming, Berlin.

MILLER, MARY ELLEN
1986 *The Murals of Bonampak.* Princeton University Press, Princeton, N.J.

MORAN, FRAY PEDRO
1935 *Arte y diccionario en lengua Choltí: A Manuscript Copied from the Libro Grande of Fr. Pedro Moran of about 1625.* Maya Society, Baltimore.

MORLEY, SYLVANUS G.
1937–38 *The Inscriptions of the Peten.* 5 vols. Carnegie Institution, Publication 437. Washington, D.C.

MORRIS, EARL H., JEAN CHARLOT, AND ANN AXTELL MORRIS
1931 *The Temple of the Warriors at Chichen Itza.* Carnegie Institution, Publication 406. Washington, D.C.

NAVARETTE, CARLOS, AND EDUARDO MARTÍNEZ
1977 *Exploraciones arqueológicas en la cueva de los Andasolos, Chiapas.* Universidad Autónoma de Chiapas, Tuxtla Gutiérrez, Mexico.

Norman, V. Garth
1973 *Izapa Sculpture,* pt. 1: *Album.* Papers of the New World Archaeological Foundation, no. 30. Brigham Young University, Provo, Utah.
1976 *Izapa Sculpture,* pt. 2: *Text.* Papers of the New World Archaeological Foundation, no. 30. Brigham Young University, Provo, Utah.

Orrego Corzo, Miguel
1990 *Investigaciones arqueológicas en Abaj Takalik.* Instituto Nacional de Antropología e Historia de Guatemala, Guatemala City.

Parsons, Lee Allen
1969 *Bilbao, Guatemala: An Archaeological Study of the Pacific Coast Cotzumalhuapa Region.* Publications in Anthropology 12. Milwaukee Public Museum, Milwaukee, Wis.
1986 *The Origins of Maya Art: Monumental Stone Sculpture of Kaminaljuyu, Guatemala, and the Southern Pacific Coast.* Studies in Pre-Columbian Art and Archaeology 28. Dumbarton Oaks, Washington, D.C.

Pearson, Michael Parker, and Colin Richards
1994 Ordering the World: Perceptions of Architecture, Space, and Time. In *Architecture and Order: Approaches to Social Space* (Michael Parker and Colin Richards, eds.): 1–37. Routledge, London.

Pendergast, David M.
1982 *Excavations at Altun Ha, Belize, 1964–1970,* vol. 2. Royal Ontario Museum, Toronto.

Pollock, H. E. D.
1970 Architectural Notes on Some Chenes Ruins. In *Monographs and Papers in Maya Archaeology* (William R. Bullard, Jr., ed.): 1–87. Papers of the Peabody Museum of Archaeology and Ethnology, vol. 61. Harvard University, Cambridge, Mass.

Pyburn, K. Anne
1989 Maya Cuisine: Hearths and the Lowland Economy. In *Prehistoric Economics of Belize.* Research in Economic Anthropology, suppl. 4 (Patricia McAnany and Barry L. Isaac, eds.): 325–344. JAI Press, Greenwich, Conn.

Recinos, Adrian
1950 *The Popol Vuh: The Sacred Book of the Ancient Quiche Maya* (Delia Goetz and Sylvanus G. Morley, trans.). University of Oklahoma Press, Norman.

Reents-Budet, Dorie
1988 *The Iconography of Lamanai Stela 9.* Research Reports on Ancient Maya Writing, no. 22. Center for Maya Research, Washington, D.C.
1994 *Painting the Maya Universe: Royal Ceramics of the Classic Period.* Duke University Press, Durham, N.C.

Reilly, F. Kent
1990 Cosmos and Rulership: The Function of Olmec-Style Symbols in Formative Period Mesoamerica. *Visible Language* 24 (1): 12–35.

Ricketson, Oliver G., and Edith B. Ricketson
1937 *Uaxactun, Guatemala: Group E, 1926–1931.* Carnegie Institution, Publication 477. Washington, D.C.

ROBICSEK, FRANCIS

1978 *The Smoking Gods: Tobacco in Maya Art, History, and Religion.* University of Oklahoma Press, Norman.

ROBICSEK, FRANCIS, AND DONALD M. HALES

1981 *The Maya Book of the Dead: The Ceramic Codex.* University of Virginia Art Museum, Charlottesville.

ROMANO PACHECO, CARLOS NAVARETTE, AND VICTOR SEGOVIA PINTO

1981 *Kohunlich: Una ciudad maya del clásico temprano.* San Angel Ediciones, México, D.F.

ROYS, RALPH L.

1933 *The Book of Chilam Balam of Chumayel.* Carnegie Institution, Publication 438. Washington, D.C.

1965 *Ritual of the Bacabs.* University of Oklahoma Press, Norman.

RUPPERT, KARL

1935 *The Caracol at Chichen Itza, Yucatan, Mexico.* Carnegie Institution, Publication 454. Washington, D.C.

RUZ, MARIO HUMBERTO

1982 *Los legítimos hombres: Aproximación antropológica al grupo Tojolabal,* vol. 2. Universidad Nacional Autónoma de México, México, D.F.

SAHAGÚN, FRAY BERNARDINO

1950–82 *Florentine Codex: General History of the Things of New Spain* (A. J. O. Anderson and C. E. Dibble, trans.). School of American Research, Santa Fe.

SATTERTHWAITE, LINTON

1936 *A Pyramid without Temple Ruins.* Piedras Negras Preliminary Papers, no. 5. University Museum, University of Pennsylvania, Philadelphia.

SCHELE, LINDA

1974 Observations on the Cross Motif at Palenque. *In Primera mesa redonda de Palenque,* pt. 1 (Merle Greene Roberston, ed.): 41–61. Robert Louis Stevenson School, Pebble Beach, Calif.

1979 Genealogical Documentation on the Tri-Figure Panels at Palenque. In *Tercera mesa redonda de Palenque,* vol. 4 (Merle Green Robertson, ed.): 41–70. Herald Printers, Monterey, Calif.

1991 *Workbook for the 1991 Workshop on Maya Hieroglyphic Writing, with Commentaries on the Group of the Cross at Palenque.* University of Texas Press, Austin.

1992 *Workbook for the Sixteenth Maya Hieroglyphic Workshop at Texas, with Commentaries on the Group of the Cross at Palenque.* University of Texas Press, Austin.

SCHELE, LINDA, AND DAVID FREIDEL

1990 *A Forest of Kings: The Untold Story of the Ancient Maya.* William Morrow, New York.

SCHELE, LINDA, AND PETER MATHEWS

1979 *The* Bodega *of Palenque, Chiapas, Mexico.* Dumbarton Oaks, Washington, D.C.

SCHELE, LINDA, AND MARY ELLEN MILLER

1986 *The Blood of Kings: Dynasty and Ritual in Maya Art.* George Braziller, New York, and Kimbell Art Museum, Fort Worth, Tex.

SHEETS, PAYSON
1992 *The Ceren Site: A Prehistoric Village Buried by Volcanic Ash in Central America.* Harcourt Brace Jovanovich, Fort Worth, Tex.

SMITH, A. LEDYARD
1982 Major Architecture and Caches. In *Excavations at Seibal* (Gordon R. Willey, gen. ed.). Memoirs of the Peabody Museum of Archaeology and Ethnology, vol. 15, no. 1. Harvard University, Cambridge, Mass.

SOSA, JOHN ROBERT
n.d. The Maya Sky, the Maya World: A Symbolic Analysis of Yucatec Maya Cosmology. Ph.D. dissertation, State University of New York, Albany, 1985.

STRÖMSVIK, GUSTAV
1941 *Substela Caches and Stela Foundations at Copan and Quirigua.* Contributions to American Anthropology and History, no. 37. Carnegie Institution, Washington, D.C.

STUART, DAVID
1987 *Ten Phonetic Syllables.* Research Reports on Ancient Maya Writing, no. 14. Center for Maya Research, Washington, D.C.

TAUBE, KARL A.
1988 A Prehispanic Maya Katun Wheel. *Journal of Anthropological Research* 44: 183–203.
1989 The Maize Tamale in Classic Maya Diet, Epigraphy, and Art. *American Antiquity* 54: 31–51.
1992a The Iconography of Mirrors at Teotihuacan. *In Art, Polity, and the City of Teotihuacan* (Janet C. Berlo, ed.): 169–204. Dumbarton Oaks, Washington, D.C.
1992b *The Major Gods of Ancient Yucatan.* Studies in Pre-Columbian Art and Archaeology 32. Dumbarton Oaks, Washington, D.C.
1993 *Aztec and Maya Myths.* British Museum Press, London, and University of Texas Press, Austin.
1994a The Birth Vase: Natal Imagery in Ancient Maya Myth and Ritual. In *The Maya Vase Book*, vol. 4 (Justin Kerr, ed.): 650–685. Kerr Associates, New York.
1994b The Iconography of Toltec Period Chichen Itza. In *Hidden among the Hills: Maya Archaeology of the Northwest Yucatan Peninsula* (Hanns J. Prem, ed.): 212–246. Verlag von Flemming, Möckmühl, Germany.
n.d. The Ancient Yucatec New Year Festival: The Liminal Period in Maya Ritual and Cosmology. Ph.D. dissertation, Yale University, 1988.

TEDLOCK, BARBARA
1992 *Time and the Highland Maya.* Revised ed. University of New Mexico Press, Albuquerque.

THOMPSON, EDWARD H.
1892 The Ancient Structures of Yucatan Not Communal Dwellings. *Proceedings of the American Antiquarian Society* 8: 262–269.
1911 The Genesis of the Maya Arch. *American Anthropologist,* n.s. 13: 501–516.

TOZZER, ALFRED M.
1907 *A Comparative Study of the Mayas and the Lacandones.* Archaeological Institute

of America. MacMillan, New York.

Trigger, Bruce G.
1990 Monumental Architecture: A Thermodynamic Explanation of Symbolic Behavior. *World Archaeology* 22: 119–132.

Trik, Helen, and Michael E. Kampen
1983 *The Graffiti of Tikal.* Tikal Report, no. 31. University Museum Monograph 57. University of Pennsylvania, Philadelphia.

Vogt, Evon Z.
1976 *Tortillas for the Gods: A Symbolic Analysis of Zinacanteco Rituals.* Harvard University Press, Cambridge, Mass.

Wauchope, Robert
1938 *Modern Maya Houses: A Study of Their Archaeological Significance.* Carnegie Institution, Publication 502. Washington, D.C.

Willey, Gordon R.
1978 Artifacts. In *Excavations at Seibal* (Gordon R. Willey, gen. ed.). Memoirs of the Peabody Museum of Archaeology and Ethnology, vol. 14, no. 1. Harvard University, Cambridge, Mass.

Wilson, Richard
n.d. Mountain Spirits and Maize: Catholic Conversion and Renovation of Traditions among the Q'eqchi of Guatemala. Ph.D. dissertation, London School of Economics, University of London, 1990.

Winfield Capitaine, Fernando
1988 *La estela 1 de La Mojarra, Veracruz, México.* Research Reports on Ancient Maya Writing, no. 16. Center for Maya Research, Washington, D.C.

Woodbury, Richard B., and Aubrey S. Trik
1953 *The Ruins of Zaculeu, Guatemala.* 2 vols. Byrd Press, Richmond, Va.

Yadeun, Juan
1993 *Toniná.* Citibank, México, D.F.

The Iconography of Maya Architectural Façades during the Late Classic Period

LINDA SCHELE†
UNIVERSITY OF TEXAS AT AUSTIN

THE FAÇADES of Maya architecture served as a stage front for ritual and carriers of important religious and political symbolism from the beginnings of public art in the Late Pre-Classic period. These fundamental roles of public architecture remained throughout the history of the Classic period and beyond, into the Post-Classic period. From the beginning of Maya public architecture, the builders favored the substructure of buildings as one of the principal locations to display symbolic and narrative information. This emphasis on the substructural terraces may be the result of historical accident, because only in rare cases have elements of the temples above the substructures been preserved in buried buildings. Excavations in Group H at Uaxactun by Juan Antonio Valdés (1988, 1989) indicate that Late Pre-Classic buildings also had architectural sculpture on the entablature of the temples on top of sculpted platforms. This pattern of use continued throughout the Classic period, and by the Early Classic period builders also used vertical bearing walls as sites for imagery. The repertoire of locations, thus, included the terraces of substructures, vertical bearing walls in the form of both solid walls and piers, the entablature above the bearing walls, and roof combs. I suspect Pre-Classic buildings also sported roof combs, but, to my knowledge, no archaeological evidence for them has yet been uncovered.

Late Classic buildings continued to use these same zones, although sculptors rarely used all of these surfaces in any one building, and artists at different sites came to favor particular decoration patterns because of local architectural and historical traditions. For example, Palenque's buildings usually have sculpture on the front piers, on the eaves, on the four entablatures, on the roof combs, and more rarely on the balustrades and substructural terraces. At Tikal, sculptors favored the entablatures and especially emphasized the huge roof combs; they more rarely used the terraces on the pyramidal substructures. Thanks to Barbara Fash's excellent work with the disarticulated sculpture of Copan and to recent excavations by the various projects in the Copan Acropolis Archaeological Project, we can now identify its pattern as one incorporating pairs of small window slits into sculptural sequences arranged on the vertical bearing wall. Copan sculptors also modeled the corners of buildings and regularly used the entablatures, roof combs, stairways, and speakers' platforms projecting from the stairs. Earlier buildings inside the acropolis have plaster mask sculptures on the substructural terraces in the central Peten tradition, although this practice was abandoned by the Late Classic period. The builders of Yaxchilan and Bonampak concentrated on stairways, entablatures, and roof combs.

In the Chenes and Río Bec regions, builders treated the entire front façade of the building as a single sculptural sequence, with the image of a huge mask flowing from the vertical walls onto the entablature. Sculptors at Copan also used this kind of masked façade on Temples 11 and 22, and at Uxmal it appears on the upper temple on the west face of the Pyramid of the Magician. The Puuc and Northern Yucatecan styles of architectural decoration used all of the areas discussed above but tended to emphasize the balustrades of stairways instead of the substructural terraces. The prominent exception to this pattern is the Osario at Chichen Itza. Peter Schmidt has found that the upper three of the seven terraces on this building carried sculptural panels on all four sides of the building. The *tableros* (panels) of the Temple of the Warriors hold relief panels, as do most of the platforms and many of the benches at Chichen Itza.

These sculptural programs were rendered in one of two major techniques: plaster modeled over stone armatures or relief mosaic sculpture covered with a thin layer of plaster. Sculptors used two techniques in the second kind of sculpture: to sculpt the stones before they were set in the wall or to carve in the relief after the stone was set in the wall. At Copan, it seems clear that some of the very deep relief and three-dimensional forms were sculpted before the stones were set in the wall, with the fine detailing done after the wall was set. Copan offers the only well-documented example of the sustained use of both techniques. Most of the architectural sculpture on buildings buried inside the acropolis was modeled in plaster, whereas the sculpture of later building (after approximately A.D. 650) used stone relief. Most of the buildings at sites in the Peten, Chiapas, and Belize have modeled stucco relief, whereas the use of stone mosaic relief is characteristic of Copan, Quirigua, the Chenes and Puuc regions, and Northern Yucatan.

In preparing this paper, I assembled every published drawing or photograph of Late Classic architecture decoration that I could find and then sorted them into types on the basis of the programs of symbolism their builders used. Obviously, in a paper like this, I cannot discuss every one of these sculptural programs, but as I worked with the corpus of examples I had assembled, I detected repeated themes and strategies that appeared at many different sites. I concentrate on the most important and dominant of these programs as they appear in their various forms. Although this inventory is not intended to be exhaustive, it will provide a useful look at the kinds of functions and meanings that can be documented for the architectural sculpture of the Classic period.

THE MASK PROGRAMS

The most ancient and widespread of all architectural decoration in lowland Maya architecture are the mask façades, so named because they depict heads without bodies under them. Such façades are known from the beginning of the Late Pre-Classic period until the architecture of Tulum at the time of the European invasion. The earliest versions of the masked façade were created from plaster modeled over stone armatures, but by the Late Classic period they were also rendered in stone mosaics, especially in the Chenes and Puuc regions as well at Copan and Quirigua.

Although sculptors represented many different supernatural beings in these images, they used a standard template for the presentation that varied little after its first appearance in the third century B.C. The main head could be a historical portrait, an anthropomorphic supernatural, or a zoomorphic supernatural, but regardless of the particular being represented, the images set around it were usually the same. A set of earflares with appended accoutrements including maize foliation, flowers and associated foliation, knots, mat signs, mirrors, and other symbols are normally found in these assemblages. Often the most critical element is the headband or headdress worn by the mask, because many mask heads, including the famous "long-nosed god," are anonymous without the detail of the headgear or earflares.

On the north façade of the Palenque Palace, the mask very probably represented K'an Hok' Chitam, a historical ruler. In an unusually complex representation of the theme, the central head is flanked by the heads of a serpent bar (Fig. 1), with K'awils emerging from its mouths. Late Pre-Classic and Early Classic examples of similar masks have framing bands with double-headed serpents, but in the Palenque example, the Cosmic Monster holds this structural position. Elsewhere, I (Schele 1992; and Freidel, Schele, and Parker 1993) have identified the double-headed serpent as the ecliptic and the Cosmic Monster as

Fig. 1 Restoration drawing of the panels from the north façade of the Palenque Palace (restored areas are stippled).

one form of the Milky Way. The presence of either symbol in the contexts of the mask façade located the contexts as that of the heavens. Many Early Classic examples of the anthropomorphic heads are now known to represent one or the other of the Hero Twins in their roles as planets, but representations of the Principal Bird Deity, a jaguar god, mountain monsters, and many others also occur.

The masked substructure that was particularly characteristic of the Late Pre-Classic and Early Classic architecture became less popular during the Late Classic period. Instead, Late Classic buildings concentrated on using the mask on the superstructures in new and imaginative ways. The most extraordinary development was in the Río Bec, Chenes, and Puuc regions (Gendrop 1983). One of the most impressive techniques was to treat the entire façade as a great monster head with the door as its mouth, as on Homiguero Structure 5 and the Pyramid of the Magician at Uxmal (Fig. 2a). People entering such buildings appeared to be walking into the gullet of the monster. At Chicanna and Dzibilnocac, builders combined profile views of the eye and forehead on the side of the door with a front view of the head above it. The effect was the same. Other styles, such as at Xkickmook and Chicanna, limited the mask components to the entablature so that the head did not have a lower jaw. Many of these façades

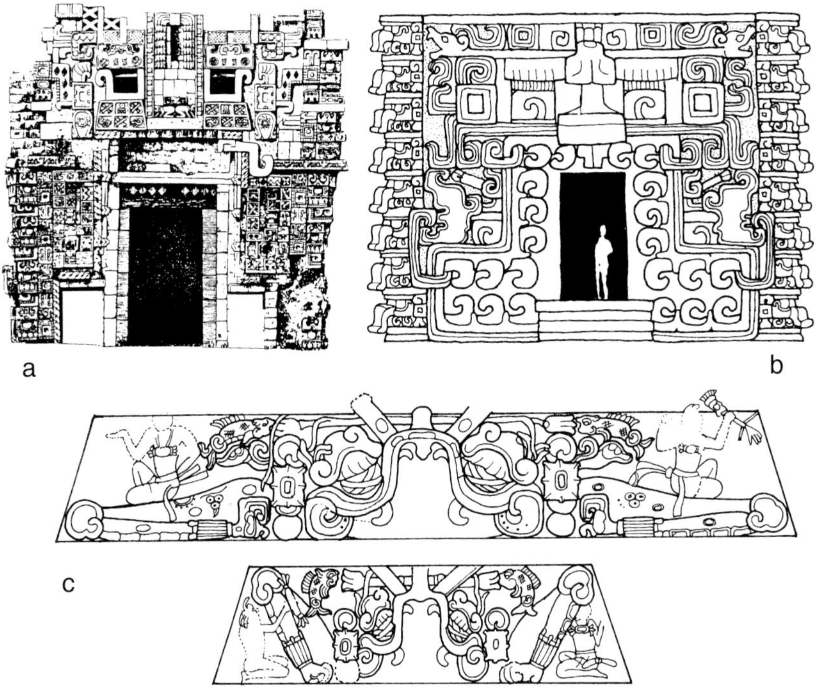

Fig. 2 (a) West façade of the Magician at Uxmal, with a front view of monster head (after Seler 1917); (b) façade at Tabascaño, combined front and side view monsters; (c) entablature of the Temple of the Cross at Palenque.

combine the main door mask with stacks of smaller masks, flanking the main head or decorating corners. The most elaborate development occurred in the Codz Pop at Kabah, where the entire northern façade of the building is covered with earflare to earflare stacks of mask heads.

Who Was That Masked Building?

The identity of the masks on these façades is the most misunderstood and understudied problem in Late and Terminal Classic architecture. Since Seler first associated the long-snouted façades of Uxmal with God B and God K, these identifications have been widely accepted (Kowalski 1987: 187–202), with a special place given to Chaak, the rain god. The evidence has rested primarily on the resemblance of the snouts of the masks to representations of these gods in the codices rather than to specific iconographic features of the masks. In my own study, I have not identified Chaak unless the image contains either his diagnostic shell earflares or his shell diadem. By applying this limitation, I found only a single stack of masks at Chicanna with the required identification feature. On the other hand, diagnostic features that I could recognize pointed to other deities or to places in the sacred landscape.

Mountains

David Stuart's (1987) work with the Copan inscriptions identified the stack of mask heads on the corner of Temple 22 as *wits*[1] "mountain" personifications. The front façade of that temple also presented the door as the mouth of the mouth—or a cave (Schávelzon 1980). I suspect that most of the door monsters in the northern styles are also mountain monsters, but the diagnostic traits that marked mountain images of the south usually are not present in the north. Some of these mountains can be identified directly with creation iconography as the mountain that held the grain of maize that was used to create the first human beings. Those masked façades that do not have distinctive identifying traits depend on context for their identity.

Sky Dragons

However, not all of the masked façades represented mountains and caves, or, if they are mountain façades, they incorporated other iconography. At Palenque the Temple of the Cross (Fig. 2c) has a crocodilian monster model. The creature has "cauac" markings and eyelids consistent with a mountain monster, but it has water lilies and fish surrounding its head. This combination of signs is distinctive of the front head of the Cosmic Monster at Copan and Quirigua.

The reconstruction of Kabah Structure 1A1 shows sky bands flanking the center door masks, and the corner masks are linked by entwined serpent bodies. The same sky band and twisted snakes characterize the western temple on the Pyramid of the Magician at Uxmal. Arthur Miller's (1974) identification of these twisted serpent cords as the *kuxan sum* or "living cord" that connected Maya rulers to the heavens has been confirmed by new interpretations of the Classic period myth of creation (Freidel, Schele, and Parker 1993: 59–122). These twisted snakes also mark the creation location called Na Ho Kan, so that façades with twisted snakes may very well represent this location or the *kuxan sum* descending to earth. This category of monster façades may represent the

[1] This paper was written using the unified alphabet of the Academia de Lenguas Mayas of Guatemala, an orthography that also has been accepted in the latest publications of Yucatec dictionaries by government and university organizations in Yucatan. The editor of this volume did not allow this decision and has imposed his own orthographic conventions.

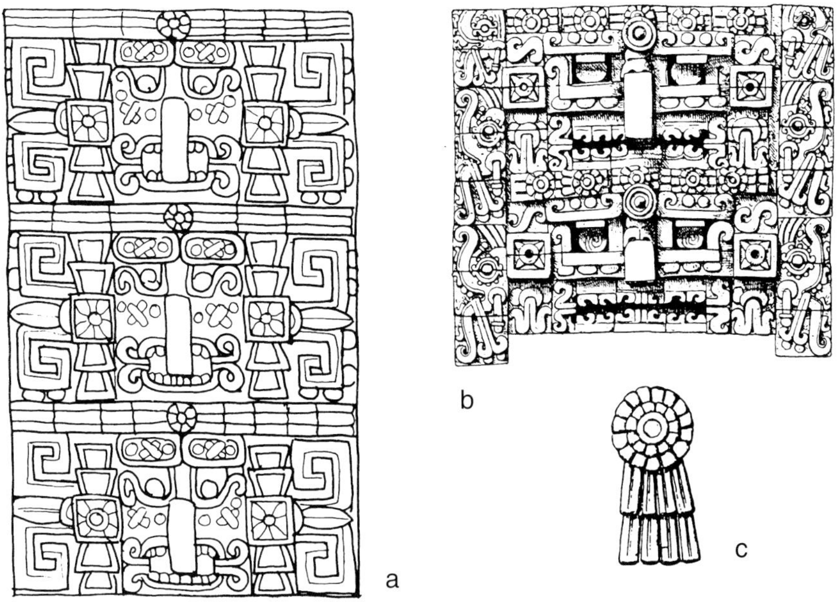

Fig. 3 (a) Mask stack from the Temple of the Warriors at Chichen Itza; (b) mask from the West Building of the Nunnery Quadrangle; (c) *its* signs from the Nunnery Quadrangle at Uxmal (b and c, after Seler 1917).

front head of the Cosmic Monster in these cases, although this monster overlapped mountain imagery and could merge both concepts. There is good evidence that the Maya saw a complete landscape in the sky.

Itzamna

The masks on the Temple of the Warriors (Fig. 3) at Chichen Itza have always been identified as Chaaks, but they have flower headbands as their principal diagnostic marker (Freidel, Schele, and Parker 1993: 158). Schele (n.d.a; Freidel, Schele, and Parker 1993: 410–412) identified this headband as the iconic version of the *its* glyph. The headband is the characteristic marker for God D (Taube 1992a: 31–40), whose name has been deciphered as Itsamna, and of the cosmic bird that sits on top of the world tree. Its name, Itsam Yeh, Itsam Kah, or Mut Itsamnah,[2] was written using the same flower sign. *Its* is the word for

[2] Schele (Freidel, Schele, and Parker 1993: 41–412) based the name of the bird on an occurrence on a pot that has the head of God D followed by what she took to be a *ye* sign. Since then, Grube, Martin, Houston, and others have pointed out that the "ye" sign has a

flower nectar but also for what David Freidel (Freidel, Schele, and Parker 1993: 210–213) calls the "cosmic sap"—the sacred and magical substances that seep from the objects of the world. *Its* is also "sorcery" and "enchantment" so that *itsam* is one who enchants and does magic. Itsamna of the codices and Itsamhi of the Classic inscriptions was the first sorcerer of this creation.

In the summer of 1994, Peter Mathews and I examined a great many of the long-nosed gods at Chichen Itza. We did not look at every example, but we did check most of the masks in the main group, the Osario, and around the Monjas. Only the heads on the *iglesia* lack this flower headband. The vast majority of long-snouted heads in Chichen Itza represent the latched-beaked bird of Itsam Yeh, the great bird that Taube (1992b: 80) identified as the *nawal* of Itsamna. Nikolai Grube (personal communication, 1994) reminded me that the word *itsa* very likely means "water sorcerer." The ubiquitous presence of the Itsam Yeh bird on Chichen architecture may have been more than a device to mark the buildings as magic places: they also may have referred to the *itsa* who built the site.

However, *its* signs and long-nosed gods with flower headbands occur with equal frequency at Uxmal. In fact, three of the four buildings in the Nunnery Quadrangle[3] have *its* signs distributed along the superior molding (Fig. 3b). Furthermore, all of the mask stacks on the west, north, and east buildings have the same flower headband. Perhaps more telling are the house images on the west building—they combine the *itsam* head with the image of a house to form the iconic representation of the name Itsam Na, "Sorcery House."[4] The famous god of Yucatan was not a crocodile or iguana house as Thompson (1970) proposed, but it was a house for sorcery. The north building had its own way of making this identity. Its house images have vision serpents emerging from their

---

hook in its interior. Grube and Martin (in Schele and Grube 1994: 18) identified the second sign in the bird name as *kah* and suggested that the name was Itzam Kah, "Town Sorcerer." I have checked this sign in photographs but have not seen the original pot. If it is their *ka* sign, then their reading of the name would be the better one. Because I have used the Itsam Yeh name in several other publications, I will retain it until a general consensus is achieved. David Stuart also pointed out two examples from Xcalumkin that have the bird's name as Mut Itsamnah. There were at least two names for this bird during the Classic period.

[3] All of the observations concerning the iconography of the Nunnery Quadrangle were made in collaboration with Peter Mathews in preparation for a book we will be publishing.

[4] This area of the entablature of the west building was reconstructed by Mexican archaeologists, but Jeff Kowalski, Peter Mathews, and I have examined records of the Instituto Nacional de Antropología e Historia on these restorations and feel that there was reasonably good evidence for the entablature as restored.

summit. Like the west building, it was a place where the lords of Uxmal traveled to the otherworld and called forth creatures and ancestors from that world. The entire Nunnery Quadrangle is an Itsam Nah.

Other buildings in the north are similarly marked. A doorway in a building at Sisila has *its* signs surrounding it and I suspect that the masks on the north side of the Codz Pop at Kabah are also flower-banded Itsamnas. Most importantly, the Itsam Yeh bird stands over the door to the inner sanctuary of the three temples in the Group of the Cross at Palenque. The same image of bird-surmounted houses appears on pots and on the ascension stelae of Piedras Negras. But perhaps the most stunning example is the encased temple known as Rosalila at Copan. It is covered with the Itsam Yeh bird. All of these buildings are Itsam Nah. Moreover, the Palenque buildings are named glyphically as *pib na* and *kunul*. The first term means "underground house" and the second is "seat-conjuring place." *Kun* has been identified by Barbara MacLeod (personal communication, 1992) as the term for "seat" and *kunul* by Schele (1987) as a "place for conjuring." Thus, all of the names for these special houses refer to them as a place where conjuring and magic are done.

Other kinds of buildings were also marked as houses, *nah*, through symbolic imagery. The towers of the Río Bec style have long been recognized as model images of the pyramid temples of cities further to the south like Tikal. House images without specific markings as to their functions also graced buildings at Chicanna, Kabah, and Hochob. Houston (in his editorial comments) suggested that Río Bec towers were "abbreviated, synechdochic precincts" with both pyramid and palace combined into one architectural symbol.

CREATION IMAGERY

Recent insights (Freidel, Schele, and Parker 1993: 59–122) into the creation myth of the Classic period have provided a template that explains many architectural arrangements and imagery programs of the Classic period. The myth of Creation describes the setting up of a series of structures by the principal actors, who include the Maize God, the Paddlers, Itsamna, and God L. The structures they created included three thrones that formed the first cosmic hearth, a turtle or peccary that Chaak cracked open to allow the rebirth of the Maize God, a house made up of four sides and four corners, a cosmic tree called Wakah Chan, a maize tree called the K'an te Na, a ballcourt made of a cleft, and finally a mountain. Most of the structures have analogs in the constellations and other patterns of the sky. These actions took place at a series of supernatural locations including, among others, Na Ho Kan ("House-Five-Sky"), Matawil (???),

Kab Kun ("Earth seat"), Yax Hal Wits ("First True Mountain"), Ho Hanab Wits ("Five-Flower Mountain"), Ek' Nab ("Black Sea"), K'a[5] Chan ("Lying-down or Closed Sky"), K'a Nab ("Lying-down or Closed Sea"), Wak Chan ("Six or Raised-up Sky"), Wak Nabnal ("Six or Raised-up Sea"), etc.

One of the major strategies of Late Classic builders—in fact, throughout Maya history—was to create analogs of these objects and locations in their architecture. One of the most central of these symbols was the three stones of creation. According to Stela C at Quirigua, the three stones consisted of a jaguar throne stone, a snake throne stone, and a shark (or *xok*) throne stone. Like a hearth in a Maya house, these "stones" were typically arranged in a triangle. This arrangement is a very ancient and familiar pattern in Maya architecture, and it continued to play a major role during the Classic period. The Group of the Cross at Palenque created the three stones as a way of centering the world and establishing the place of creation. I think the last remodeling of the main plaza at Tikal by Ruler A created analogs of the three stones with Temple 33 and the North Acropolis at one point of the triangle, and Temple I and Temple II at the other two points. There are many other examples found at many different sites. The imagery placed on or within these groups could reflect the identities of the three stones or be independent of them.

The turtle and the trees appear less directly in the imagery, although they are still there. At Uxmal, the House of the Turtles located above the ballcourt may be a reference to the turtle of creation. At Copan, the west façade of Structure 26 depicts the history of the site emerging up the stairs from the inside of the inverted head of a vision serpent. The top of the altar, which is also the roof of the serpent's mouth, has an image of the maize tree emerging from the crack in the turtle's back (Fig. 4). The trees of creation could be symbolized in poles and images, but they were not made into buildings—at least not to my knowledge.

However, buildings were sometimes named for them. David Stuart (personal communication, 1987) was the first to realize that Temple 16 at Copan and the Temple of the Foliated Cross at Palenque have the same name—Na K'an Te. The inscription on Tikal Stela 31 records another building of the same name—but we do not know which one it was. Temple 16 is the most complete of these: it had great Pawahtuns on the corners supporting a roof that had a sky serpent arching across. Below on the front steps were a great maize plate, band

[5] In Freidel, Schele, and Parker (1993), I used the value *ch'a* for T128. However, new substitution patterns have shown that this sign was *k'a* or *k'al* (MacLeod n.d.; Schele and Looper 1996). These two locations would have been K'a Kan, "Lying-down Sky," (or K'a[l] Kan, "Closed sky") and K'a Nab or K'al Nab, "Lying-down Sea" or "Closed Sea," with both forms probably referring to the sky and sea before they were separated.

Fig. 4 The altar at the base of the hieroglyphic stairs at Copan. Drawing above appears on the top surface of the altar.

with earth signs, and another with a zigzag band with *le* signs. This last image marks the place of creation on many pots. Matthew Looper's (1995, n.d.) work on nearby Quirigua has shown that the entire site reproduces the geography of creation. He has identified Stelae A and C along with zoomorph B as the three stones of creation. Earlier, Grube, Schele, and Fahsen (1991) had identified the

Fig. 5 Copan West Court, south façade of Temple 11.

main plaza as the Ek' Nab, and Matthew Looper (personal communication, 1994) has identified at least one building on the acropolis as the Ho Hanab Wits. David Freidel[6] identified the West Court in the acropolis at Copan as the Ek' Nab because the level of the first terrace is marked as the surface of water by a huge stone shell on the south façade of Temple 11, by crocodile heads on the platform on the west side of the court, and by the reviewing stand depicting Chaak rising from the waters (Fig. 5).

Na Ho Kan

According to the text of Quirigua Stela C, Na Ho Kan was the place where the jaguar throne stone was set up by the Paddler Gods. Along with the other two thrones, the cosmic hearth was put in place so that the turtle could be cracked open by Chaak. The hearth and the turtle have been identified in the constellation of Orion just below one of two points where the ecliptic crosses

[6] David Freidel made this identification in a portion of *Maya Cosmos* (Freidel, Schele, and Parker 1993) that we eliminated for editorial reasons. His major evidence is that the reviewing stand shows Chaak rising from the watery underworld in an image analogous to the Cosmic Pot (Schele and Miller 1986: pl. 122). The inscription on that pot identifies the location as the Ek' Waynal Ek' Nabnal.

Fig. 6 Pot showing the supernatural location called Na Ho Kan. Photograph by Justin Kerr.

the Milky Way. In the ritual of the Bacabs, the Maya called this location the place of the four roads (Schele 1993). Maya painters left us a picture of Na Ho Kan on a black-background pot (Fig. 6), where they recorded the location as Na Ho Kan Wits Xaman, "House-Five-Sky Mountain North." Entwined serpents representing the *kuxan sum* meander through the space and surround the gods who are being born.

The Maya seem to have used these entwined serpents and sometimes entwined cords to mark buildings they meant to represent Na Ho Kan. These cords mark the main pyramid at Xunantunich (Fig. 7) as this sacred location. Deity representation of *te'*, "tree," and moon signs sit in the lower register amid enframing runs of entwined cords. The second level has sky bands entwined around Pawahtuns and a now-destroyed central figure. The upper register is nearly destroyed, but it appears to have stepped frames arranged side by side in a row. Nikolai Grube (personal communication, 1995) and I believe that this frieze represents Na Ho Kan and that the entire pyramid is the Na Ho Kan Wits. The same Na Ho Kan mountain also may be represented at Hochob, which has twisted snakes above its monster door, and at Payan, which has twisted snakes emerging from the sides of its monster door.

The east façade of the Monjas at Chichen Itza (Fig. 8) is one of the most interesting representations of the creation. Its lower zone and the area above the medial molding has stacks of Itsam Yeh heads with the heads of gods emerging

a b

Fig. 7 Twisted cord/snakes of Na Ho Kan at (a) the main pyramid at Xunantunich and (b) Pyramid of the Magician at Uxmal.

above their beaks. At least one of these gods is a paddler. The medial molding has the twisted cords of the *kuxam sum* and the stepped frame from Xunantunich. The door has the teeth of the cave monster set in the serrated contour of the lip. A sky band with planetary signs that represent the signs on the ecliptic sits about the door. Snakes with zigzag bodies surround a feathered opening. The figure inside the opening may represent the owner of the house, but Nikolai Grube (personal communication, 1995) and I believe it also refers to the Maize God who sits at the place of creation unfolding the path of the planets along the ecliptic. The upper molding consists of corner snake heads joined by an angular pattern with serrated edges. This pattern is particularly prevalent on the west building of the Nunnery Quadrangle at Uxmal, where flowers fill the spaces between the lattice. The upper side of this snake has the upper bands that occur on the Venus bundles on the platforms in the Main Group and the Osario Group. This symbol is part of the Tlaloc-Venus war complex. Thus, creation unfolded here in association with war and politics.

The Creation Mountain

The most pervasive images from creation mythology is the creation mountain. It was represented in two ways: as the Yax Hal Witsnal and as the snake mountain. The first of these two kinds of mountains appears in its most informative iconic form on the Tablet of the Foliated Cross at Palenque (Fig. 9a),

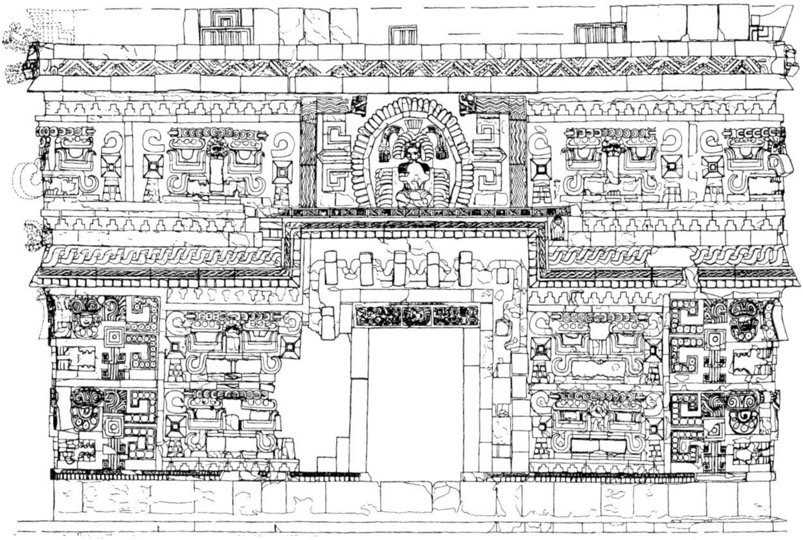

Fig. 8 Chichen Itza, the east façade of the Monjas. Drawing by John S. Bolles.

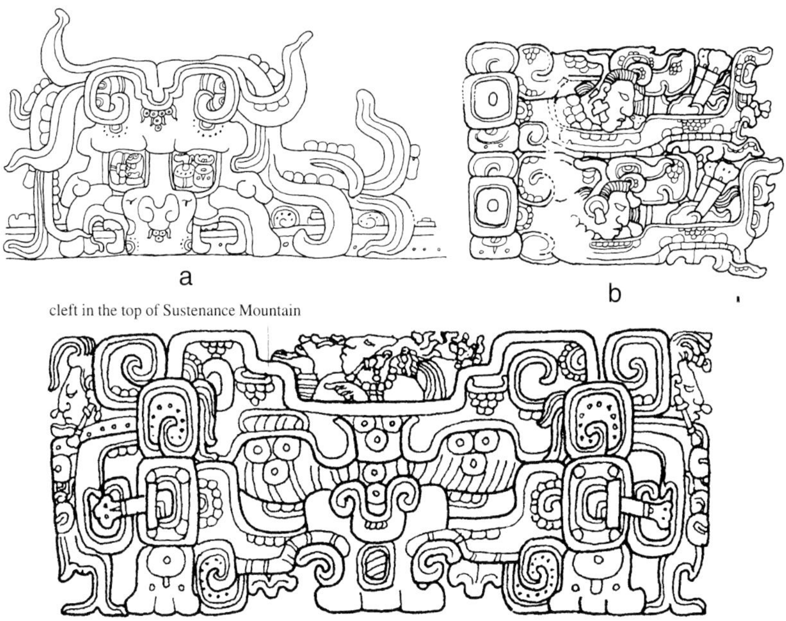

Fig. 9 Mountain monsters from (a) Palenque, Tablet of the Foliated Cross, Yax Hal Wits; (b) Tikal Temple IV, Lintel 3; and (c) Bonampak Stela 1.

where its name, Yax Hal Witsnal ("First True Mountain-place"), occurs in its eyes (Schele and Freidel 1991). Other forms appear on the base of Bonampak Stela 1 (Fig. 9c) and Lintel 3 of Temple IV at Tikal (Fig. 9b). All three versions have a stepped cleft in the forehead, out of which emerges maize in the form of either the plant or the god. I think this mountain was portrayed on the roof comb of the Temple of the Sun. The mountain is surrounded by sky bands and Pawahtuns holding strange tubes extending from the mountain. This scene may show the Maize God or some other deity sitting in the mountain cleft as he lays out *kuxan sum*.[7] I suspect the figure sitting on top of the mountain as he holds the double-headed serpent bar is Kan Balam in the role of the Maize God. The creation mountain also occurs at Chicanna, where it has maize rising from its cleft and a person sitting inside its maw.

This Yax Hal Witsnal appears in full architectural form at several sites. The most impressive example of the Yax Hal Wits comes from Copan in the form of Temple 22. Although its very complex iconography has yet to be put together, some elements are well known. The front door was the mouth of a huge monster, and although we have recovered only a fraction of the pieces, we have found the eyelids and the molars are marked with "cauac" signs (Schele 1986). Both are signs of the *wits* monster. The stacks are corner masks that are clearly mountain monsters, and the entablatures had Maize Gods emerging from other symbols that included huge maize leaves, Venus glyphs, and portraits of the king.

A related image appears on Temple 5D-33-2nd at Tikal. The lower mountain image has a person sitting inside the maw with snakes emerging from the sides of the mountain. This is both the Yax Hal Witsnal and the snake mountain. The middle level mountains also combine an emerging head and maize images with snakes emerging from the mouth, and the top level on the bearing wall of

[7] The Paris Codex, as well as several pots, such as the Acasaguastlan Vase, show deities, usually the Maize God or the Sun God with snakes flowing outward from the crooks of their arms or extending outward from their navels or wounds in the torso. The Paris Codex new year's pages show the twisted cords of the Maize God's umbilicus (and its analog in the intestines of a sacrificial victim) flowing through several successive scenes of creation that climaxes with the laying out of the ecliptic in the sky and all its constellations. Taube, Grube, and I interpret this new year's image as a replay of the unfolding of the sky order at creation. In terms of the Classic period creation story, this action took place at the Orion nexus where the Maize God was reborn. Orion sits near one of the two locations in the sky where the ecliptic crosses the Milky Way. The second location is also represented in Maya art in images of the king holding the Double-headed Serpent Bar as he wears the costume of the world tree. This image corresponds to the nexus at Scorpio. I take the snakes in all these compositions—whether represented as a twisted umbilicus or a ceremonial bar—to represent the ecliptic.

Fig. 10 Stucco from Uaxactun Structure G-X-Sub 3. The lower head represents the Yax Hal Wits sitting in the Primordial Sea. The upper head represents a human-made mountain with a snake penetrating it from side to side. This is the earliest representation of snake mountain in Mesoamerica.

the temple itself depicts an open-mouthed crocodile with vegetation, perhaps maize, growing from its back.

Presentation of different versions of the mountain on different levels is also a feature of the Late Pre-Classic façade from Group H at Uaxactun (Fig. 10). The largest platform on the upper level of the acropolis had a stack of mountain monsters flanking the main stairs. The lower mountain has a double cleft and vegetation emerging from its side. It sits in water scrolls filled with fish. This image is a perfect representation of the creation mountain of the Popol Vuh myth—"split mountain–bitter water." It is also the Yax Hal Wits.

I think the upper mountain in this image is the human-built mountain of the city. The head variant in its mouth is *tsuk,* the sign that usually marks the nose of mountain monsters. A vision serpent penetrates through the mountain to make it snake mountain. I believe this snake mountain is a very early version of the symbol that became the famous Coatepec of the Aztec founding myth. Sites where "snake mountains" appeared may well have considered themselves to be "Places of the Cattail Reed" or Tollan, in the nomenclature of the Aztec.

The most impressive snake mountain in Maya architecture is the Castillo of

Chichen Itza. Most interpretations of this pyramid have identified the snakes on the balustrades and in the doorway above as Kukulcan or Quetzalcoatl. The heads at the base of the pyramid (Fig. 11a) certainly are feathered, but I do not think the main reference is to the Post-Classic god Quetzalcoatl. Feathered serpents have a long and ancient history in Maya art—and almost all of the examples from both Early and Late Classic contexts are vision serpents. At Chichen, feathered serpents are also war serpents—as Karl Taube's (1992b) work has shown. In the image of snake mountain at Uaxactun, the serpent penetrates the pyramid from side to side. At Chichen Itza, both balustrade and doorway serpents appear head down in the position of descent, in contrast to vision serpents that normally rear in head-up position. This contrast in position is a critical difference.

The balustrades of the Osario and the Caracol and the moldings of buildings throughout Chichen depict serpents entwined in a twisted pattern. Sometimes they are feathered serpents twisting around flowers or eyes as in the Great Ballcourt. At other times they are marked with feathers, flowers, clouds, jade disks, and other jewels. All but the flowered snakes have a long history in Maya art, but the twisting of these snakes into cords (Fig. 11b) marks them as the *kuxan sum*. They are the umbilicus that descends to connect the sacred space of Chichen to the Milky Way and the heavens. This theme was particularly favored in the north.

The Cleft

One of the most prominent characteristics of the creation mountain is the cleft in its head. In the Popol Vuh and at Yaxchilan, the word for ballcourt is *hom,* which is also the word for "abyss, chasm, hole." Moreover, the stepped sides of the ballcourt match the shape of the cleft in the mountain top (Schele and Freidel 1991: 308; Gutierrez 1994). Ballcourts were programmed to reflect this identity.

At Copan, the ballcourt carries images of the prideful bird of the last creation in his full glory as the red macaw (Kowalski and Fash 1991). He is shown before the Hero Twins defeated him (Freidel, Schele, and Parker 1993: 362–372). The markers in the floor of the Ballcourt IIb show the Hero Twins engaged in the ball game of the Popol Vuh myth. At Chichen, the imagery of creation was presented with a slightly different twist (Freidel, Schele, and Parker 1993: 374–385), but it was creation nevertheless. The ball-game scenes show the teams playing with a skull ball as in the creation myth and the sacrifice of the loser generates a gourd vine. This vine is found throughout Chichen, but on the upper register of the piers of the Lower Temple of the Jaguar, the vine

a

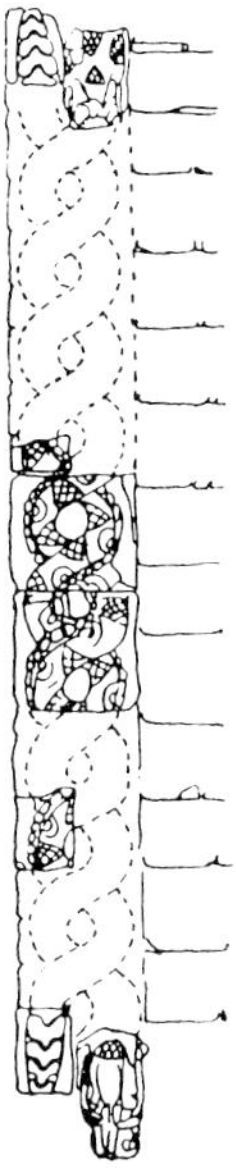

b

Fig. 11 (a) Feathered snake head at the base of the stairs of the Castillo; (b) twisted snakes from the Caracol (after Marquina 1950: fig. 273).

emerges from the head of old gods who sit in the ends of the creation turtle as the Maize God is reborn. In the north building this vine makes a lattice around poles represented on the center piers. The Maize God lies in the lower register with feathered serpents emerging from his belly like an umbilicus. The inner scenes depict the transfer of political power within the context of the ball game. Other ballcourts emphasized the role of the ball game in war, alliance making, and as a portal that allows communication with the ancestral dead. Tonina and Yaxchilan both show the ancestral dead on the ballcourt markers.

The cleft had other manifestations in the façades of buildings, especially in the north. The double-stepped cleft represents the mountain cleft in its most reduced form. It is used on an interior wall of House B in the Palenque Palace (Fig. 12). At Tonina, the mountain cleft was built into one of the lower terraces to mark the whole mountain as a place of creation. The cleft signs are placed base-to-base as if one is the reflection of the other. This sign also became a prominent theme in the mosaic façades of the north. It is part of the entablature design on the Palace of the Governors at Uxmal and on Structure 1 at Xlabpak, among many other buildings.

The stepped frame I have already pointed out in northern architecture may also represent a mountain. This frame also occurs with some frequency in

a

b

c

d

Fig. 12 (a) Mountain cleft from House B at Palenque; (b) mirrored clefts from Tonina; (c) cleft symbol from Xlabpak Structure 1; (d) cleft from Structure 1A2 at Kabah (c and d, after Pollock 1980).

Teotihuacan art, where Parsons (n.d.) tentatively associated it with mountains. The most extraordinary use of this frame in the Maya area is at Acanceh in a building that many associate with the Teotihuacan style (Miller 1991). Huge birds fold around the corners of the entablature as two rows of these stepped frames stretch out between them. Inside the frames sit a series of animals, including birds, bats, snakes, and various land animals. The upper band has a cloud band with hanging feathered shells. The medial molding is compartmented with alternating braids and *po* signs. I have unsuccessfully tested these animals as constellations, but the presence of the birds on the corners suggests we are looking at something associated with the sky.

The same stepped frames show up on Yaxchilan Temple 33. Here the façade had three niches with figures sitting on thrones. I do not have photographs or drawings showing the detail of the thrones, but I wonder if they do not represent the three thrones of creation. Between them sit two of the stepped frames with a stafflike vertical between them. The staff widens in the top where it divides into four partitions. I suspect these are either *xukpi* bird staffs like those carried by Yaxun Balam in his dances or they are world trees. Because the step in front of this building carries images of the ball game with direct references to the game of creation, I suspect this is yet another façade using creation imagery as part of the supernatural sanction for political history.

These stepped frames also show up at Copan in several contexts, including in the Cementerios Group where they have infixed "cauac" signs or aged supernaturals emerging from within. In general, they seem to mark a particular kind of location—that may or may not have been associated with mountain locations by the Classic Maya.

MAT AND FLOWER HOUSES

Barbara Fash (Fash et al. 1992) brought to our attention the existence of Popol Nah or "mat house" in Classic period architecture. Mat houses were places where the councils of nobles and other leaders met. Similar houses discussed in the ethnohistorical and ethnological literature (Fash et al. 1992: 434–436) describe various kinds of functions, including feasting, dancing, and the meeting of councils. Mat signs distributed across its façade mark Structure 22a (Fig. 13) as a Popol Nah. Its symbolism includes 9 Ahaw glyphs, and it may display images of the lords constituting the council. According to Barbara Fash's restoration drawing, there was a roof comb with a lord sitting on a double-headed jaguar throne.

Stephen Houston (personal communication, 1992) also pointed out that the Cordemex dictionary of Yucatec Maya equates *nikteil nah* or "flower house"

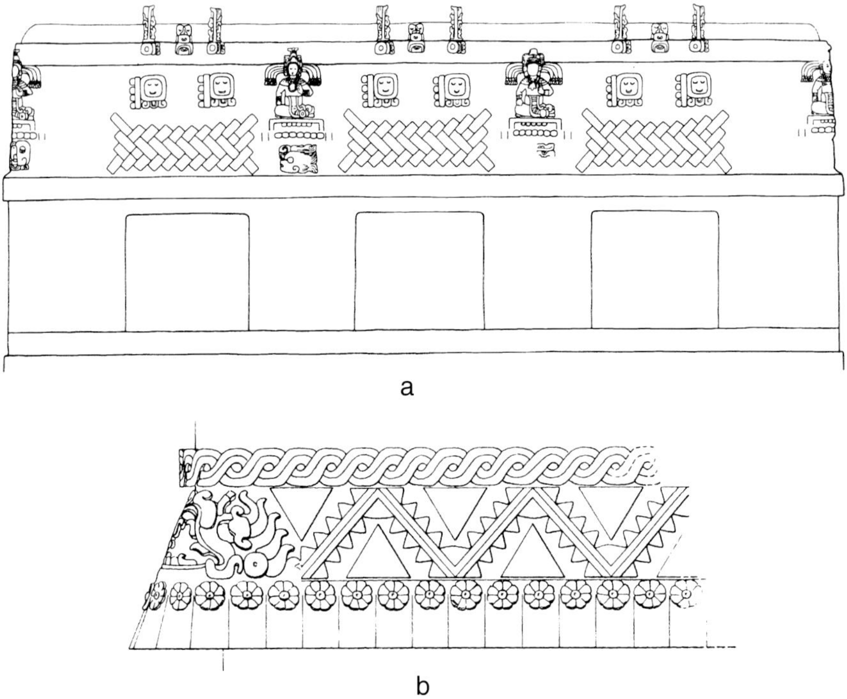

Fig. 13 Mat and flower houses: (a) Copan Temple 22 and (b) detail from the Codz Pop at Kabah (after Pollock 1980).

with *popol nah*. The most amazing of these flower houses is House E at Palenque. It is the only building within the palace that had no evidence of a roof comb, and, at least in its final version, it had rows of flowers painted in rows on the west façade. Texts and images inside the building belong to the reign of Pakal, Akul Anab III, and Balam K'uk'. These images included the accession of Pakal on the Oval Palace Tablet, its throne with references to Pakal, Kan Balam, K'an Hok' Chitam, and Akul Anab III. Other sculptures and paintings depict the Cosmic Monster, the White-Bone Snake, and a procession of lords moving toward the Oval Palace Tablet. The proximity of steambaths suggests that the Southwest Court, which borders on the flower façade, was used for vision rites and contacting ancestors.

The Tablet of the 96 Glyphs dates Pakal's dedication of House C to 9.11.2.1.11 9 Chuen 9 Mac (Nov. 1, 654). The dedication phrase calls the building the Sak Nuk Nah, "White Grand House." Quiche friends in Guatemala have told me that they call their council houses *sak jah,* their cognate of the lowlands Maya *sak nah.* This gives us three names for council houses—*popol nah, nikteil nah,* and *sak nah.*

At Chichen Itza, there is at least one other kind of council house—the Temple of the Warriors and the Temple of the Chacmol below it (Freidel, Schele, and Parker 1993: 157–160; Schele and Freidel 1990: 364–370). This council house is not marked as a mat, flower, or white house. Instead it depicts the council on the piers inside the temple structure above (or in portraits on the wall above the bench in the Temple of Chacmol). On the piers in front of the substructure a procession of warriors, priests, lords, and captives converge on the stairs so that a ritual of governance is forever frozen in process. Above sits a Chacmol statue, which Mary Miller (1985) identified as a theme derived from depictions of captives in the southern lowlands. The recent discovery of a nude Chacmol has proven her right.

Like other important buildings in Chichen, the temple described above has feathered serpents as the main columns in the entry door. Their heads are down in the position of the *kuxan sum* snakes, and the upper panel below the lintel carries images of Pawahtun holding up the sky. Other Pawahtuns stand on the doorjambs leading into the temple with the squash vine from the ball-game scene rising beside them. The outer walls have stacks of masks, which have the flower headband of the Itsam Yeh bird (Freidel, Schele, and Parker 1993: 158). The Temple of the Warriors and very probably the Temple of the Chacmol are *itsam nahob,* "conjuring houses."

Between the stacks of Itsam Yeh heads sit panels with feathered serpents, but, in these images, the bird dominates the design. The head has the bifurcated tongue and other anatomical features of a snake, but the body has the legs of a bird. This creature wears a collar and has arcs of small and large feathers circling its upper body. It truly is a serpent bird, or, more likely, it is the front view of legged serpents known at Copan and Cacaxtla and in the Xiuhcoatl of Central Mexico. In its mouth sits the head of a man wearing a stepped nose ornament. I believe this image descends from the Tlaloc warrior images prominent at Teotihuacan and earlier warrior images from the southern lowlands.

Other buildings in Yucatan combine the Itsam Nah imagery of the Temple of the Warriors with the themes of flowers. I have already discussed the west building of the Nunnery Quadrangle at Uxmal as an Itsam Nah, but both the west and north buildings intersperse reversed frets that I believe to be *muyal,* "cloud," signs with a lattice pattern (Fig. 14). The lattice has zigzag edges, and it is filled with flower images. I suggest that this flower lattice represented a real kind of temporary structure made for ritual use, like the *nikte* arches so promi-

a b

Fig. 14 (a) Flower lattice and *muyal* symbol from the north building of the Nunnery Quadrangle and (b) detail of the flower lattice.

nent in Yucatecan ritual today. However, it also marks these houses as *nikteil nah.* This flower lattice is also prominent on the Monjas at Chichen Itza, which may be another flower house.

Most importantly, the Codz Pop of Kabah is covered on one side with stacks of masks. I suspect they are Itsam Yeh birds for many have flower headbands, but the medial moldings have serpents made of the same zigzag lattice. Twisted cords ride above the serpent bodies, and a row of flowers is below it. The flowers continue onto the other side of the building, where the entablature had a row of standing figures. I suspect these may be the equivalent of the precinct lords shown on Structure 22a of Copan.

Finally, Structure 1 of Labna interweaves many of these themes into a tapestry of symbolism defining the many functions of the council house. The south façade of the center wing has *pop,* "mat," signs on its lower walls. The south façade has the double-stepped frets that identify the mountain cleft, but here with stacks of flowers and *its* signs filling the empty spaces. The west façade also has *its* signs on it. This building is marked as an *itsam nah,* a *nikteil nah,* and the cleft in the mountain of creation.

WAR IMAGERY

The Nunnery Quadrangle and the Temple of the Warriors discussed above have direct war imagery included within the symbolism of the flower council house. At Chichen, it consists of the warriors and captives included in the procession colonnade on the west side. The terraces on the south side also have images of reclining warriors wearing mosaic headdress and goggle eyes. They carry smoking staffs with a mirror attached as jaguars and eagles sit between

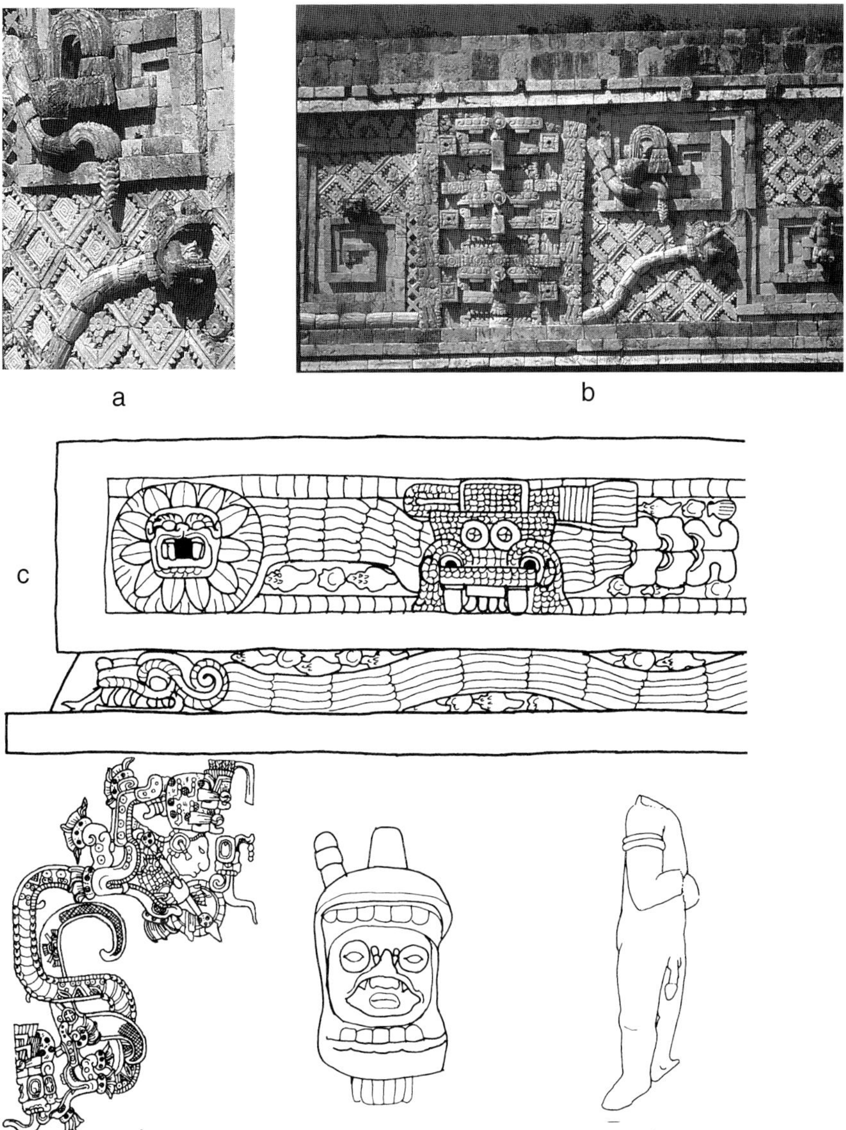

Fig. 15 (a and b) Detail of the west building of the Nunnery Quadrangle. Photographs by MacDuff Everton; (c) detail of the Temple of Quetzalcoatl, Teotihuacan; (d) War Serpent with goggle-eyed headress and emerging founder from Yaxchilan Lintel 25; (e) person emerging from the Uxmal serpent; (f) captive from the rear of the north building of the Nunnery Quadrangle.

them chewing on sacrificial hearts. Exactly this combination of imagery recurs on the platform of jaguars and eagles.

In the Nunnery Quadrangle at Uxmal, the war imagery occurs in two forms. On top of the Itsam Yeh stacks on the north building sit goggle-eyed Tlaloc (Fig. 15a) bundles associated with war and sacrificial imagery in the southern lowlands as early as the Tikal–Uaxactun war of A.D. 378. The nude figures on the rear of this building are also bound as captives. The west building is even more extraordinary. There are two feathered serpents (Fig. 15b) that loop across the façade with their bodies intertwining. Only one head survives, but it has a human wearing a *xok* fish mask emerging from its open maw. Peter Mathews (personal communications, 1995–97) and I assume the other head was similar. Both tails are complete with rattles, but a feathered object rides on the tail above the rattles. Upon close examination of this object, Mathews and I realized it is the Uxmal version of the drum major headdress associated with war and accession at Palenque (Schele and Villela 1992). More importantly, this combination of feathered serpent and headdress is the exact image (Fig. 15c) on the Temple of Quetzalcoatl—the primary war monument at Teotihuacan (Taube 1992b; Parsons 1985). That feathered serpent of war floats in the primordial sea, whereas at Uxmal it floats among clouds and flowers, but the effect is the same—the war serpent is sanctioned by supernatural space.

Closely related imagery occurs on the Venus Platform in the Main Plaza at Chichen. There the upper molding of the platform has an undulating rattlesnake body attached to a three-dimensional head emerging from the top of the balustrade in an image (Fig. 15e) that is even closer to the Teotihuacan original. Instead of shells, the Chichen artists depicted fish around the body to show it is in the primordial sea. The temptation is to suggest that the artists of Uxmal and Chichen Itza copied the Temple of Quetzalcoatl at Teotihuacan, but by the time the Maya constructed their buildings, Teotihuacan was long-abandoned. Moreover, even before the abandonment of Teotihuacan, the Temple of Quetzalcoatl had been encased in a later temple that did not carry this symbolism. The image of the snake bearing the headdress of war had to be a much more widely distributed and understood symbol than its representation at Teotihuacan.

War iconography is also associated with the Upper Temple of the Jaguars at Chichen. Freidel, Schele, and Parker (1993: 374–384) identified its imagery as associated with *ox ahal* places that celebrated victory in war. They proposed that the inner murals represented the founding wars of the Itsa and the exterior showed intertwined war serpents, shields, and jaguars surmounted by *tok' pakal,* the symbol of war for the Classic Maya. Recent examinations of the east façade identified the objects resting between the entwined serpent bodies as flowers. Flower serpents are also prominent in the buildings newly excavated at the Court of the Thousand Columns under the direction of Peter Schmidt.

War imagery and its association with ballcourts also abound further south. Barbara Fash's (W. Fash 1991: 145) work with the fallen sculpture of Temple 26 reconstructed huge Tlaloc masks on the upper temple, and David Stuart (n.d.) has shown that the inner inscription records the dedication of the building and the dynasty history in what he calls Maya and Teotihuacan "fonts." The façade includes portraits of Copan's warrior kings, who also appear in Tlaloc war costumes on the hieroglyphic stairway rising to the temple above. Temple 16 and the West Court can also be identified with this imagery. Built by Yax Pasah, the last great king of Copan, the stones fallen from its upper temple and substructure include Tlaloc imagery of all sorts as well as skulls, ropes, and other associated themes. Excavation under the oversight of Alfonso Morales on the temple described above found glyphs referring to K'inich Yax K'uk' Mo' as the founder. William Fash (1991) first identified a huge headdress from this upper façade as combining a *k'uk' mo'* image with Tlaloc features, and he and Barbara Fash have suggested that the figure that once sat in a quatrefoil portal inside the building was also a portrait of the founder manifesting the quetzal as his *way* or *nawal.* The ancestral theme is reinforced by the presence of the 16 members of the dynasty on Altar Q below the stairs.

Finally, the south end of the West Court has two low altars dedicated many years earlier by Smoke-Imix-God K. Most interesting, the small building between them has an effigy drum and banner stones lying in front of it. The presence of banner stones here suggests the scaffold sacrifice discussed by Taube (1988) and the banner ritual of Panquezlitztli that is so prominent in the imagery and architecture of El Tajin, the Mixtec codices, and the founding myths of the Aztec (Koontz n.d.). Similar banner stones were found in association with Group 6 at Cerros (Kathryn Reese-Taylor, personal communication, 1994) and with the Early Classic temple at Copan nicknamed Papagayo. That building is directly associated with the ballcourt, as is its successor, Temple 26.

At Tikal, the major war imagery I have observed occurs in the Group of the Seven Temples. The stuccos on the rear of the central temple include cartouche shields that appear on skirts worn in period-ending rituals in Late Classic Tikal. This same design also marks the headdress of the God of Zero, who is one of the main protagonists in the ball-game imagery at Copan. These cartouches lie between images of crossed bone awls like those used in bloodletting rites. Interestingly, these seven temples are associated with a triple ballcourt.

HISTORICAL IMAGERY AND NARRATIVES

At Tikal, two buildings related historical narratives in particularly dramatic ways. The Temple of Inscriptions relates an extraordinary history of Tikal beginning at 5.0.0.0.0 and concerning not only its rulers but a supernatural entity named with a *sak* sign and a *hix*-faced bird. The dedication phrase for this building names it a *waybil,* a term that is related to the modern Quiche term for their lineage shrines—*waribal.* The interior of the building with its many graffiti seems to have been a place where members of the lineage spoke with their ancestors in vision rites.

A captive display narrative was modeled in stucco on the entablature of Structure 5D-57. The scene shows the ruler named Hasaw Kan K'awil holding a prisoner at the end of a rope in an event called *nawah,* "he was ornamented [as a sacrifice]." Hasaw Kan appears in a Tlaloc-Venus war costume. The recorded date places this event 13 days after he captured Jaguar Paw, the ruler of Calakmul. Recently, Simon Martin (personal communication, 1994) recognized Jaguar Paw's name among the glyphs in the text to the right of the figures.

At Palenque, the same *nawah,* "ornamentation," event is shown on the substructure of House A, where nine captives kneel or stand waiting for their fate. The texts on the inner two captives say that they are being ornamented as the captives (*yahal*) of the king. On the opposite side of the court, six additional captives are depicted on the substructure. Each has his name next to him and is mentioned in the text on the central stairs in association with building dedication rituals (Schele 1994). The sculptures on the piers and entablatures of these buildings do not survive in the detail necessary to reconstruct the full program, but surviving fragments suggest there were standing figures on the piers around the court—especially House C and D. The entablatures show supernatural heads among which human figures danced.

The west side of House C has seated portraits of rulers, of which at least one can be identified as Pakal. The outer piers of House A and AD displayed other portraits of kings, although their identities do not survive on House D. I have taken these portraits to represent the kings of the succession with their mothers and fathers seated below them, although the particular identities of any of them must remain speculative in the absence of glyphic names. Merle Robertson (1985: 4–5) argued that House D was early and assigned it to the reign of Kan Balam, whereas I have always felt that Houses A, D, and AD were one building and thus dated to the time of the latest-named king—K'an Hok' Chitam. I have recently reviewed the inscriptions on pier a and above the piers on this building and think that they may record its dedication and the day on which the gods entered the house. At least one of these dates is readable as 9.11.15.14.19 4 Cauac 7 Tzek, and the date above the piers appears to fall within the same k'atun. Because prisoners on the west substructure carry the date 9.11.9.10.13, I now think House A may belong to these dates, while reserving the possibility that the dedication dates may refer to a building below the present structure. If House A is this early, the identity of the pictured figures will have to be reevaluated.

The shattered piers on the north (House AD) have few remnants left, but at least one figure holding a spear and wearing a peccary headdress has the name K'an Hok' Chitam next to his head (Robertson 1985: figs. 252–253). We cannot tell much more about the images on these northern piers, but it seems likely that all of them represented images of the king as warrior. These images stood above the substructure that had K'an Hok' Chitam represented in a series of masks surrounded by doubled-headed serpents and a Cosmic Monster frame. Little has survived of the entablature, but this façade and the substructural decoration that turned to the corners focused on K'an Hok' Chitam as warrior and center of the cosmos.

Only the piers of the Temple of the Sun (Fig. 16) have survived with enough detail to tell us something of that program, but I think it hints at the strategy used for all three temples. The plain substructures had alfardas with texts that linked the births of the Palenque triad god associated with each temple to the ritual in which they entered the temple on 9.12.19.14.12 5 Eb 5 Kayab. This date and event was repeated on Piers A and D of the Temple of the Sun. Piers B and C represented frontal standing figures presumably engaged in this house-entering ritual. Only the feet of Pier B survive, but another figure sits inside the maw of a white bone snake on its northern side. There may have been a matching figure on the inside of Pier C, but it did not survive; however, much of the outer figure did. It represents a man dressed in elaborate gear carrying a Tlaloc shield. The reference seems to be to Tlaloc-Venus warfare.

The same association of war with house dedication ritual appears on Temple 18 of Copan (Fig. 17a). David Stuart (personal communication, 1987) first suggested to me that the only date recorded for the four figural piers possibly corresponds to 1 Cib 19 Ceh (9.17.2.12.16), the dedication date of Temple 11. If he is right, and I think he is, then these four piers record the dedication rituals of an earlier building that took place in the West Court, probably on the south façade of Temple 11. The texts on the two eastern panels identify the figure as Yax Pasah, whereas the western texts have no surviving personal name.

The location of the dance is probably the West Court that I have already associated with the Lying-down Sea, Tlaloc-Venus war and founder's rituals,

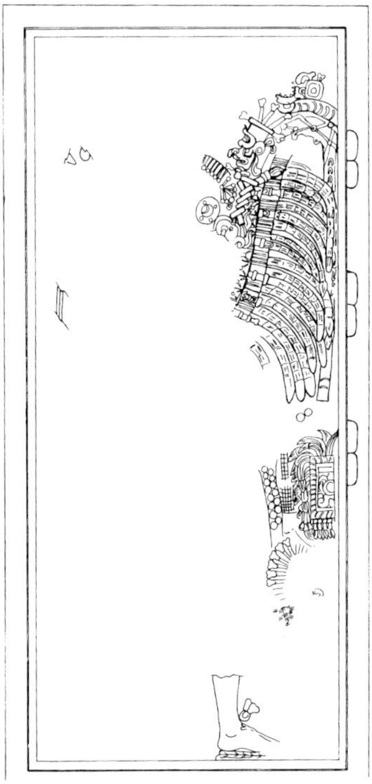

Fig. 16 Palenque, Temple of the Sun, Pier C.

and scaffolding and banner rituals. The stairway at the base of Temple 11 was long ago identified by Miller (1988) as a false ballcourt with Chaak emerging from the sea. Grube and Schele (1990) also identified it as a Wak Ebnal, a "Six-Stair-Place," of the kind associated with ball-game sacrifice. Its dedication text names it as both the *yol,* "the portal of," and the ballcourt of Yax Pasah.

The ritual shows Yax Pasah and his companion dancing on the sign of a plaza or a mountain. The dancers wear trophy heads and one has a stuffed body hanging on his back. All are festooned with ropes and three of them carry shields and spears. The fourth dances with skull rattles. This feature is very important because it associates this ritual with that on a pot.

The pottery scene (Fig. 17b) centers on a small *itsam nah* that holds a bundle, a censer with a baby sacrifice, and two headdresses. Six naked figures dance before the bundle with their penises perforated and bound with paper. Three of them hold serpent bars with flints in the mouths of the snakes. Two of them hold the skull rattles and bundles. The sixth holds a bundle, and the seventh

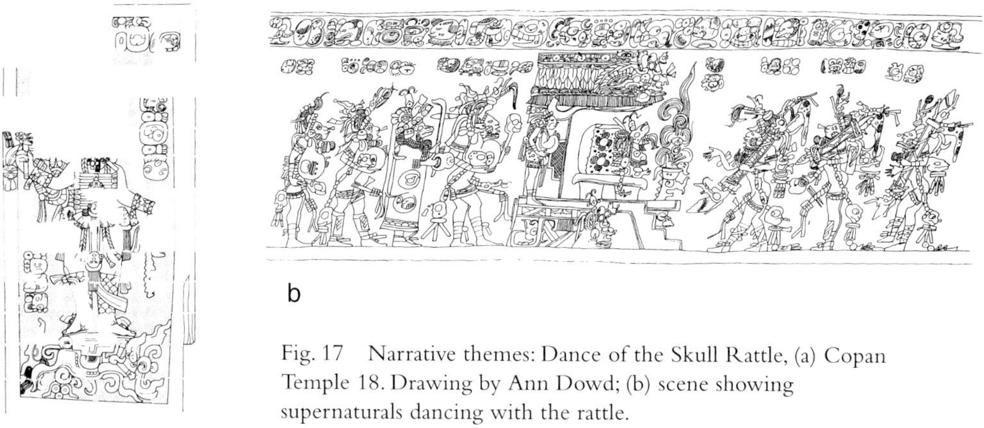

a

b

Fig. 17 Narrative themes: Dance of the Skull Rattle, (a) Copan Temple 18. Drawing by Ann Dowd; (b) scene showing supernaturals dancing with the rattle.

wears the guise of the *way* named Sak Ox Ok or "White-Three-Dog." I know of at least two other pots that show this ritual, and the dance in Room 3 at Bonampak has performers who wear the same chest belts and knots. All of these narrative images apparently depict this ecstatic dance.

Tonina is the site that emphasized the display of captives most forcefully. Not only are captives extremely prominent in the imagery of the stone sculptures, but recent excavations by Juan Yadeun (1992, 1993) have revealed captives, many of them named as historical individuals, rendered in stucco on the buildings built on terraces 5, 6, and 7, and another building straddling the fourth and fifth terraces has a bench with legs representing trilobed flints. Its backrest depicts Venus with a peccary resting in its folds. I (Schele n.d.b) have suggested that this represents Venus in Gemini, which corresponds to its northernmost extension.

Yadeun (1993) has discovered the depiction of yet another ritual at Tonina. Rendered in a stucco frieze, the scene (Fig. 18a) shows *wayob* and characters from the creation myth cavorting within a huge feathered (or foliated) scaffold mounted with skull and trophy heads. Justin Kerr has two pots in his archive showing the same ritual. Pot 4924 (Fig. 18b) depicts two scaffolds—one with skulls and the other with a person seated on a throne inside each frame. At least one of them has the face marking of God A', so that I am not sure if they are humans, humans transformed into *wayob,* or supernaturals. The Tonina scene has a box frame sitting in front of it. And as at Tonina, *wayob* cavort around the scaffold as skeletal *nawals* dance with severed heads and human attendants bring battle banners into the scene.

This same relationship between myth and its ritual reenactment may also

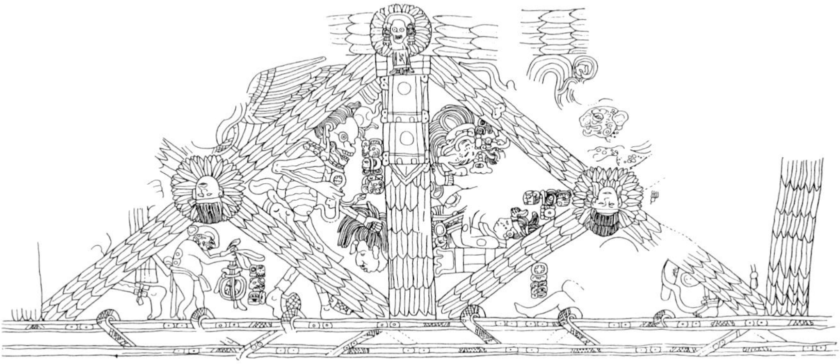

a

b

Fig. 18 (a) Tonina, stucco panel, and (b) pottery painting depicting the Tonina ritual. Photograph by Justin Kerr.

explain the piers of House D on the Palace at Palenque. Pier B depicts a decapitation scene that may be the sacrifice of one twin by another. Freidel, Schele, and Parker (1993: 273–274, 280–281) have identified Pier C as the redressing of the Maize God after his resurrection. He holds the Wakah Chan, the tree he will soon erect at the center of the world. They also identified the scene on Pier D as a snake dance performed by First Father and First Mother after his redressing. He wears a Tlaloc around as he dances. Pier E is too damaged to be read, but Pier F shows another decapitation scene in which the Maize God is the aggressor. I suspect this scene represents the final punishment of the Xibalbans. Finally, the surviving text on Pier G records the birth of First Mother in a form directly related to the same information in the Group of the Cross. A second clause included *u chukwa,* the verb for "capture" inflected for the transitive. I suspect this text continued from Pier A and that the full text described the episodes of the myth of creation as depicted on the piers.

Of course, these scenes may be purely mythical, but Coe (1989) published an excerpt from a Kekchi source discovered by Estrada Monroy (1979). This part of the document describes a town-founding ceremony conducted by Ah Pop'o Batz'. The heart of the ceremony was a dramatic reenactment of the Popol Vuh myth in the tradition of the modern Dance of the Conquest and other pageants of the Guatemalan highlands. Coe (1989) used this account and comparative data from other cultures to propose that the Popol Vuh story had always been performed in great public dramas. I propose that the piers of House D depict exactly this kind of performance. If I am right, then the scenes there are both mythical and historical.

CONCLUSIONS

In a relatively short study such as this, it was not possible to include a complete survey of all the strategies of decoration used by the Maya during the Late Classic period. For example, I did comment on the programs that have been documented on the residential architecture for both royal and elite households in the Copan Valley, at Tikal, at Palenque, and elsewhere. At Copan, at least, the imagery used in elite households shares the imagery and compositional pattern with royal households. A detailed comparison between the two sets of imagery might distinguish motifs and symbols that were restricted to royal versus elite context, but to my knowledge nothing of this sort has so far been identified by any researcher. Distinctions in rank or status seem to have been signaled by scale, quality of craftsmanship, materials, and quantity but not by restrictions of imagery or composition.

Gathering material for this paper also yielded surprises. For example, I did not anticipate that so many buildings in Yucatan would have flower, mat, and *its* symbols to mark them as community and conjuring houses. The unexpected prevalence of this symbolism may reflect the prominence of the *multepal* form of government in the north (Schele and Freidel 1990: 356–376; Grube 1994). And although I knew that the long-nosed heads on the Temple of the Warriors at Chichen Itza represented Itsam Yeh, I did not expect this image to be so ubiquitous in the architecture of the north. The symbolism of many northern buildings marks them as *itsam nah.* The architecture of the southern lowlands did not use Itsam Yeh in mask stacks but placed the full-bodied bird on various parts of the building.

Finally, one of the most pervasive strategies used by Late Classic builders was to construct analogs of locations and landscape features associated with the creation of the fourth world. Many architectural programs functioned to center the world in the time and space of creation (Freidel, Schele, and Parker, 1993: 123–172, 362–372). This strategy was not unique to the Maya; it can be documented throughout Mesoamerican history. Reilly (1994, n.d.) has identified much of the same symbolism in architecture at La Venta, and Bernal-Garcia (n.d.) has traced the imagery of creation through the art and architecture of major cultural traditions of Mesoamerica. García Zambrano (1994) has documented the cosmology of Pre-Columbian rituals of foundation and their associated cosmology as they survived into the early colonial period.

Perhaps the best documented example of creation symbolism in public architecture is the Templo Mayor and the sacred precinct of Tenochtitlan. Townsend (1979, 1992: 108–154) has discussed the use of cosmology in Aztec art and architecture with great detail and subtlety. The Templo Mayor is a replica of snake mountain where the patron god of the Aztecs, Huitzilopochtli, was born from his mother Coatlicue (Matos Moctezuma 1987; Broda, Carrasco, and Matos Moctezuma 1987) and materializes the great foundation myth at the heart of the Aztec state (León-Portilla 1987). The caches (Broda 1987) around its base helped identify its location as the primordial sea at one level and as the swampy lake around Coatepec on the other. Other offerings reflect its meaning as the sustenance mountain (Taube 1986). Finally, Koontz (n.d.) has shown that the people of El Tajin materialized the same cosmology of mountain, ballcourt, water source, and founding in the architecture of their city. For Mesoamericans, the city and the architectural sequences in it were the earthly manifestation of creation and founding throughout their history. Like a great cultural fugue, the many different traditions replayed these themes with variation and changing emphasis. Maya builders constructed their buildings within that tradition.

BIBLIOGRAPHY

BERNAL-GARCÍA, MARÍA ELENA

n.d. Carving Mountains in a Blue/Green Bowl: Mythological Urban Planning in Mesoamerica. Ph.D. dissertation, University of Texas, 1993.

BRODA, JOHANNA

1987 The Provenience of the Offerings: Tribute and Cosmovision. In *The Aztec Templo Mayor* (Elizabeth Hill Boone, ed.): 211–256. Dumbarton Oaks, Washington, D.C.

BRODA, JOHANNA, DAVID CARRASCO, AND EDUARDO MATOS MOCTEZUMA

1987 *The Great Temple of Tenochtitlan: Center and Periphery in the Aztec World.* University of California Press, Berkeley.

COE, MICHAEL

1989 The Hero Twins: Myth and Image. In *The Vase Book: A Corpus of Rollout Photographs of Maya Vases*, vol. 1 (Justin Kerr, ed.): 161–184. Kerr and Associates, New York.

ESTRADA MONROY, AGUSTÍN

1979 *El mundo k'ekchi' de la Vera-Paz.* Editorial de Ejército, Guatemala City.

FASH, BARBARA, WILLIAM L. FASH, SHEREE LANE, RUDY LARIOS, LINDA SCHELE, JEFFREY STOMPER, AND DAVID STUART

1992 Investigations of a Classic Maya Council House at Copán, Honduras. *Journal of Field Archaeology* 4: 419–442.

FASH, WILLIAM L.

1991 *Scribes, Warriors and Kings: The City of Copán and the Ancient Maya.* Thames and Hudson, London.

FREIDEL, DAVID, LINDA SCHELE, AND JOY PARKER

1993 *Maya Cosmos: Three Thousand Years on the Shaman's Path.* William Morrow, New York.

GARCÍA ZAMBRANO, ANGEL J.

1994 Early Colonial Evidence of Pre-Columbian Rituals of Foundation. In *Seventh Palenque Round Table, 1989* (Virginia M. Fields, ed.; Merle Greene Robertson, gen. ed.): 217–227. The Pre-Columbian Art Research Institute, San Francisco.

GENDROP, PAUL

1983 *Los estilos Río Bec, Chenes y Puuc en la arquitectura maya.* Universidad Nacional Autónoma de México, México, D.F.

GRUBE, NIKOLAI

1994 Hieroglyphic Sources for the History of Northwest Yucatan. In *Hidden among the Hills: Maya Archaeology of the Northwest Yucatan, Peninsula* (Hanns Prem, ed.): 316–358. Acta Mesoamericana 7. Verlag Von Flemming, Möckmühl, Germany.

GRUBE, NIKOLAI, AND LINDA SCHELE

1990 *Six-Staired Ballcourts.* Copán Note 83. Copán Mosaics Project and the Instituto Hondureño de Antropología e Historía, Copan, Honduras.

GRUBE, NIKOLAI, LINDA SCHELE, AND FEDERICO FAHSEN

1991 Odds and Ends from the Inscriptions of Quirigua. *Mexicon* 13: 106–112.

GUTIERREZ, MARY ELLEN

1994 *Ballcourts: The Chasms of Creation.* Texas Notes on Precolumbian Art, Writing, and Culture, no. 53. Center for the History and Art of Ancient American Culture, Department of Art, University of Texas, Austin.

KOONTZ, REX ASHLEY

n.d. The Iconography of El Tahin, Veracruz, Mexico. Ph.D. dissertation, University of Texas, Austin, 1994.

KOWALSKI, JEFF K.

1987 *The House of the Governor: A Maya Palace at Uxmal, Yucatán, México.* University of Oklahoma Press, Norman.

KOWALSKI, JEFF KARL, AND WILLIAM L. FASH

1991 Symbolism of the Maya Ball Game at Copán: Synthesis and New Aspects. In *Sixth Palenque Round Table, 1986* (Virginia M. Fields, ed.; Merle Greene Robertson, gen. ed.): 59–68. University of Oklahoma Press, Norman.

LEÓN-PORTILLA, MIGUEL

1987 The Ethnohistorical Record for the Huey Teocalli of Tenochtitlan. In *The Aztec Templo Mayor* (Elizabeth H. Boone, ed.): 71–95. Dumbarton Oaks, Washington, D.C.

LOOPER, MATTHEW

1995 The Three Stones of Maya Creation Mythology at Quirigua. *Mexicon* 17: 24–30.

n.d. The Sculptural Programs of Butz'-Tilwi, an Eighth-Century King of Quirigua, Guatemala. PhD. dissertation, University of Texas, Austin, 1995.

MACLEOD, BARBARA

n.d. T128: The Next Generation. North Austin Hieroglyphic Hunches, no. 11. Manuscript on file, Department of Art, University of Texas, Austin, 1995.

MARQUINA, IGNACIO

1950 *Arquitectura prehispánica.* Instituto Nacional Autonoma de México, México, D.F.

MATOS MOCTEZUMA, EDUARDO

1987 Symbolism of the Templo Mayor. In *The Aztec Templo Mayor* (Elizabeth Hill Boone, ed.): 185–210. Dumbarton Oaks, Washington, D.C.

MILLER, ARTHUR

1974 The Iconography of the Painting in the Temple of the Diving God, Tulum, Quintana Roo: The Twisted Cords. In *Mesoamerican Archaeology: New Approaches* (Norman Hammond, ed.): 67–186. University of Texas Press, Austin.

MILLER, MARY E.

1985 A Re-examination of Mesoamerican Chacmool. *The Art Bulletin* 68: 7–17.

1988 The Meaning and Function of the Main Acropolis, Copan. In *The Southeast*

Classic Maya Zone (Elizabeth Boone and Gordon Willey, eds.): 149–195. Dumbarton Oaks, Washington, D.C.

MILLER, VIRGINIA

1991 *The Frieze of the Palace of the Stuccoes, Acanceh, Yucatan, Mexico.* Dumbarton Oaks, Washington, D.C.

PARSONS, MARK

n.d. Three Thematic Complexes in the Art of Teotihuacán. Manuscript on file, Department of Art, University of Texas, Austin, 1985.

POLLACK, H. E. D.

1980 *The Puuc: An Architectural Survey of the Hill Country of Yucatan and Northern Campeche, Mexico.* Memoirs of the Peabody Museum of Archaeology and Ethnology, vol. 19. Harvard University, Cambridge, Mass.

REILLY, KENT

1994 Enclosed Ritual Space and the Watery Underworld in Formative Period Architecture: New Observations on the Function of La Venta Complex A. In *Seventh Palenque Round Table, 1989* (Virginia M. Fields, ed.; Merle Greene Robertson, gen. ed.): 125–136. The Pre-Columbian Art Research Institute, San Francisco.

n.d. Visions of Another World: Art, Shamanism, and Political Power in Middle Formative Mesoamerica. Ph.D dissertation, University of Texas, Austin, 1994.

ROBERTSON, MERLE GREENE

1985 *The Sculpture of Palenque,* vol. 3: *The Late Buildings of the Palace.* Princeton University Press, Princeton, N.J.

SCHÁVELZON, DANIEL

1980 Temples, Caves or Monsters? In *Third Palenque Round Table, 1978* (Merle Greene Robertson, ed.): 151–162. University of Texas Press, Austin.

SCHELE, LINDA

1986 *Interim Report on the Iconography of the Architectural Sculpture of Temple 22 (from the 1986 Field Season).* Copán Note 19. Copán Mosaics Project and the Instituto Hondureño de Antropología e Historía, Copan, Honduras.

1987 *Workbook for the Maya Hieroglyphic Workshop at Texas, with Commentaries on the Group of the Cross at Palenque.* Department of Art, University of Texas, Austin.

1992 *Workbook for the Sixteenth Maya Hieroglyphic Workshop at Texas, with Commentaries on the Group of the Cross at Palenque.* Department of Art, University of Texas, Austin.

1993 *Creation and the Ritual of the Bakabs.* Texas Notes on Precolumbian Art, Writing, and Culture, no. 57. Center for the History and Art of Ancient American Culture, Department of Art, University of Texas, Austin.

1994 Some Thoughts on the Inscriptions of House C. In *Seventh Palenque Round Table, 1989* (Virginia M. Fields, ed.; Merle Greene Robertson, gen. ed.): 1–11. The Pre-Columbian Art Research Institute, San Francisco.

n.d.a The Principal Bird Deity as Itzam Yeh, the Avatar of Itzamna. Paper presented at the Symposium for "Mexico: Splendors of Thirty Centuries" at the Los Angeles County Museum of Art, 1991.

n.d.b Creation, Cosmos, and the Imagery of Palenque. Paper prepared for the Seventh

Round Table of Palenque, June 1993.

SCHELE, LINDA, AND DAVID FREIDEL

1990 *A Forest of Kings: Untold Stories of the Ancient Maya.* William Morrow, New York.

1991 The Courts of Creation: Ballcourts, Ballgames, and Portals to the Maya Otherworld. In *The Mesoamerican Ballgame* (Vernon Scarborough and David Wilcox, eds.): 289–317. University of Arizona Press, Tucson.

SCHELE, LINDA, AND NIKOLAI GRUBE

1994 *The Workbook for the Eighteenth Maya Hieroglyphic Workshop at Texas, with Commentaries on the Tlaloc-Venus Wars from A.D. 378 to 730.* Department of Art, University of Texas, Austin.

SCHELE, LINDA, AND MATTHEW LOOPER

1996 *Workbook for the Texas Forum on Maya Hieroglyphic Writing, with Commentaries on the Inscriptions of Quirigua and Copan.* Department of Art, University of Texas, Austin.

SCHELE, LINDA, AND MARY ELLEN MILLER

1986 *The Blood of Kings: Dynasty and Ritual in Maya Art.* George Braziller, New York, and Kimbell Art Museum, Fort Worth, Texas.

SCHELE, LINDA, AND KHRISTAAN VILLELA

1992 *Some New Ideas about the T713\757 "Accession" Phrases.* Texas Notes on Precolumbian Art, Writing, and Culture, no. 27. Center for the History and Art of Ancient American Culture, Art Department, University of Texas, Austin.

STUART, DAVID

1987 *Ten Phonetic Syllables.* Research Reports on Ancient Maya Writing, no. 14. Center for Maya Research, Washington, D.C.

n.d. The Texts of Temple 26: The Presentation of History at a Maya Dynastic Shrine. In *Copan: The Rise and Fall of a Classic Maya Kingdom* (William L. Fash and E. Wyllys Andrews V, eds.). School of American Research Press, Santa Fe. (In preparation.)

TAUBE, KARL A.

1986 The Teotihuacan Cave of Origin: The Iconography and Architecture of Emergence Mythology in Mesoamerica and the American Southwest. *RES: Anthropology and Aesthetics* 12: 51–82.

1988 A Study of Classic Maya Scaffold Sacrifice. In *Maya Iconography* (Elizabeth Benson and Gillett Griffin, eds.): 331–351. Princeton University Press, Princeton, N.J.

1992a *The Major Gods of Ancient Yucatan.* Studies in Pre-Columbian Art and Archaeology 32. Dumbarton Oaks, Washington, D.C.

1992b The Temple of Quetzalcoatl and the Cult of Sacred War at Teotihuacan. *RES: Anthropology and Aesthetics* 22: 53–87.

THOMPSON, J. ERIC S.

1970 *Maya History and Religion.* University of Oklahoma Press, Norman.

TOWNSEND, RICHARD

1979 *State and Cosmos in the Art of Tenochtitlan.* Studies in Pre-Columbian Art and

Archaeology 20. Dumbarton Oaks, Washington, D.C.

1992 *The Aztecs*. Thames and Hudson, London.

Valdés, Juan Antonio

1988 Los mascarones preclásicos de Uaxactún: El caso del grupo H. In *Primer simposio mundial sobre epigrafía maya:* 165–181. Asociación Tikal, Guatemala City.

1989 El grupo H de Uaxactún: Evidencias de un centro de poder durante el preclásico temprano. *Memorias el segunda coloquio international de mayistas,* vol. 1: 603–624. Universidad Nacional Autónoma de México, México, D.F.

Yadeun, Juan

1992 *Toniná: El laberinto del inframundo.* Gobierno del Estado de Chiapas, Yucatan, México, D.F.

1993 *Toniná*. Citibank, México, D.F.

Finding Function and Meaning in Classic Maya Architecture

STEPHEN D. HOUSTON
BRIGHAM YOUNG UNIVERSITY

> Lastly, there is the problem of relating the architecture to the ancient culture, of determining its position and function in the life of the people. This, in a sense, is the ultimate goal of architectural research, and until the problem is solved, we cannot feel that the remains possess full meaning, or that they rest in their true historical setting. (Pollock 1940: 200)

MORE THAN fifty years ago H. E. D. Pollock (1940) posed two important problems: how did the ancient Maya use buildings, and how did they invest them with meaning? Recent work brings us closer to solving these questions, perhaps in ways that would have surprised Pollock. In the first place, Mayanists now enjoy better "contextualization," to use David Webster's term. Careful, focused archaeology helps us understand the architectural energetics, ancestral memorials, lineage and site-oriented rituals, and long-term dynastic themes discussed in this volume. As William Fash stresses, expensive, deep excavation—not test pitting—allows us to study such things, although, to be sure, shallow excavations widen our sample. In the second place, fresh interpretations of glyphs and imagery enable us to consider a new set of issues, including levels of metaphor, encoding social hierarchy, performance, and the vital forces thought by ancient Maya to animate their buildings. Few contributors could have written the same essays even five years ago. Third, students of Maya architecture increasingly find themselves in dialogue with specialists from regions and disciplines with which we have had little contact. Mayanists may now draw upon innovative studies of buildings in Suffolk, Tenochtitlan, Chan

Chan, and Madagascar. Some comparisons will prove misleading or poorly conceptualized, or our information may be inadequate for the job (see Johnston and Gonlin). At the least, though, the extended range of possibilities pries us away from accustomed paths and rutted thinking.

THINGS SAID

The papers in this book go far in establishing the contours of future debate on Maya architecture. One group of papers shows how regional variation and idiosyncratic emphases interplay with broad commonalities of belief. For example, the "hearth" theme discussed by Taube appears throughout the Classic Maya region but expresses itself in a great variety of ways. Its subtle, multilayered meanings accord with the notion that "meaning is not a single or unitary thing" (Johnson 1993: 31). Maya designers, builders, and sculptors make rich and imaginative linkages of the general to the particular, or the mythological to the tangible, and then back again: a "water house" occurs both in mythological time and space and, apparently, as particular buildings at Comalcalco, Copan, and perhaps Altun Ha; a grouping of smooth cobbles is at once a heap of worn stones and the *fons et origo* of creation.[1] Furthermore, Fash and Schele document the widespread distribution of certain types of ritual building, such as "mat" or "flower houses," whose elaborate, sculpted façades reflect their intended use.[2] None of these structures, however, copies slavishly from other buildings but instead uses similar elements in new combinations or, as Miller puts it, "a vocabulary that was both universally Maya and simultaneously local."

[1] See Jameson (1990: 106) for comparable levels of hearth metaphor in ancient Greece.

[2] We have only just begun to understand such thematic buildings. Structures associated with disembodied skulls and crossbones occur in several contexts, ranging from supernatural depictions on pots (López and Fahsen n.d.: fig. 10.6) to Structure 5D-96 at Tikal (Coe 1967: 89) and probably the platforms in the Cementerio Group at Uxmal (Graham 1992: 121–133). Parenthetically, the platforms at Uxmal may have been used for specific offerings, because one glyph of uncertain context records the Yucatec word for "tobacco," **k'u-?tso,** *k'uts*—Graham (1992: 131, B1). This recalls later practice at Coba, where a structure apparently specifies ritual offerings and their supernatural recipients—Houston (1989: 30). Similarly, "water houses" appear in a number of sites, including Comalcalco (Andrews 1989: fig. 20), unprovenanced vessel in the Denver Museum of Natural History (personal observation), El Peru and vicinity (Houston, this volume, fig. 18), Temple 11 at Copan (Karl Taube, personal communication, 1994), and Structure A-2 at Altun Ha (Pendergast 1979: pl. 17). Another type would be the "Teotihuacano" or "Tula" house connected to the mythogenic "otherness" of royal famlies (David Stuart, personal communication, 1994). Good examples include those at Tikal (Laporte Molina n.d.: 133–148). The salient question is, Do these represent types of structures codified by the Classic Maya? William and Barbara Fash are currently working out some of these details in their research at Copan, including the detection of possible "charnel houses" and "founder's temples" (personal communication, 1996).

Additional work needs to be done to determine where and when such buildings appear and what their local attributes might be. Research by Hansen (this volume) and others (Valdés 1992a: 28–29) indicates that some features linked to the Classic period in fact originate long before.

The themes of metaphor and personification appear throughout the volume, especially in papers by Houston, Stuart, and Taube. As in many cultures (Carsten and Hugh-Jones 1995: 22–23, 42–44; Littlejohn 1967), the ancient Maya projected the concept of "house" into many domains, often through the device of "reciprocal metaphor" (see Houston, this volume). Taube shows that the sun or moon could be eclipsed by a figurative doorway curtain; a constellation represents the hearth of a house writ large across the nighttime sky.[3] The motivation for such metaphoric projections is not hard to find. Familiar forms, whether of the house or human body, provide an immediate basis of ideas for organizing the world (Pearson and Richards 1994: 10). Their familiarity makes them especially suitable for "structural replication" (Vogt 1969: 571–581; Jamison n.d.: 133), which acquires force through repetition and by its intelligibility to a large number of people.

Personification, too, is seen widely in Maya architectural symbolism. The Classic Maya explicitly liken buildings to human beings and not only in a metaphoric sense. Just as people consume food, so do the heat and smoke of incense burners activate and vitalize architecture (see Stuart, this volume). To put this another way, the Maya regarded some, if not all, buildings as animate entities. In this respect, Maya buildings strongly evoke architectural concepts in southeast Asia (Waterson 1990: 115–137), where, in a "two-way mapping," the house objectifies the body and the body personifies the house (Carsten and Hugh-Jones 1995: 43).[4] The fact that such parallels occur is relatively uninter-

[3] An inscription from Tamarindito further suggests that royal ancestors were defined in terms of "houses" (Houston 1993: fig. 4–17), perhaps analogous to the *na* or localized patrilineages of the Tzotzil Maya (Laughlin 1975: 245; Vogt 1983: fig. 6.4). In this text appear the names of mother and father, the first linked to something that can be partially deciphered as *nikte nah* (**? NIK-te na-hi**) or "flower house," the father to the "maize" or "8 house" (**AH-?-na na-hi**). However, we do not know precisely what these terms mean: the pairing of house labels is unique to this inscription. Future research should evaluate the potential of Lévi-Strauss's model (1987) of "house-based societies" or *sociétés à maison*. These consist of "a hybrid, transitional form between kin-based and class-based social orders" in which the "house as name, concept or building . . . (offers) . . . an image or demonstration of the unity achieved" between conflicting forces (Carsten and Hugh-Jones 1995: 8, 10).

[4] Africanists also emphasize the presence of "house souls," often of a complex sort, and the wide use of body metaphors to describe house and community (Blier 1987: 118–119, 131; Griaule and Dieterlen 1954).

esting—after all, body/house metaphors are close to universal. What concerns us more are the specifics, how such metaphors relate to indigenous theories of the human body. Regrettably, our knowledge of Maya theories is poor in comparison to knowledge about ancient Nahua belief (López Austin 1988).

Other essays present a growing understanding that buildings are both receptacles for, and participants in, ritual activity. In this way, architecture serves as rather more than a billboard for emotive "key symbols" (Ortner 1973), "models for"/"models of" reality (Geertz 1973: 93; see also Jamison n.d.: 100–103, 122–124), or "canonical symbols" (Blanton 1994: 8–13), although these surely come into play. Few visitors to Maya cities can miss the obtrusive, formal emphasis on architectural verticality and social rank, palatial and social exclusivity, centralized ancestral precincts, and dynastic exaltation. The building façades discussed by Schele make bold statements about the way the world is, the way it was, and the way it should be. Nonetheless, in very practical terms, the shape and layout of buildings permit certain activities to take place. Monumental stairways, for example, do many things beyond allowing people to move up or down a building or platform. Iconographic and textual data show that stairways or terraces can display tribute, booty, and captives. By sitting at various levels, the Maya establish or confirm relative social ranking; by ascending stairways, they move back in time and retrace dynastic succession.[5]

Proskouriakoff (1963: 120) pointed out long ago that the Maya manipulate space in ways that can serve more than aesthetic needs. Classic buildings not only create mass but define and enclose space (see also Kubler 1985: 249). Participants in processions move through them in predetermined ways to create what de Certeau calls a "spatial story" (de Certeau 1984) that "weave(s) time and space together into a kind of narrative" (Thomas 1993: 81). The audience perceives such activities as mediated by the dramaturgical qualities, sight lines, and acoustical properties of spaces (see Upton 1979). Progressive enclosure, additional doors, corridors, and rooms change the meaning of a space by making it more difficult to get to, so that, in David Pendergast's words (1992: 62–63), openings and plazas go from "unrestricted" to "claustral" in their layout, perhaps with implications for the "ever widening gulf between rulers and ruled" (see also Awe, Campbell, and Conlon 1991). We see this at Palenque. A

[5] In a sense, such stairways exemplify Anthony Gidden's (1989: 276) notion of time/space relations, developed in turn from Heidegger's point that "*time does not exist*" but rather "is expressed in the nature of how things are, their persistence and change" (italics in original). Stairways are places where the "flow of action"—ascent and descent—takes place in "time-space" contexts, instantiating "rules and resources which have no time-space existence (save as memory traces)" (Giddens 1989: 275). That is, action triggers dynastic memory in a publicly charged manner.

cursory "access analysis" of the "Palace"—in fact, a series of distinct structures of varying date and function—suggests that an unremarkable sector of small rooms to the southeast was the least accessible—techniques from Hiller and Hanson (1984); data from Robertson (1985a, 1985b). Presumably this pattern reflects room or building function, although, as Johnston and Gonlin (this volume) argue, we cannot glibly equate diminished accessibility with increased "privacy," a culturally loaded term.

Another theme in the papers is the discussion of individual regal wishes in the design of buildings. William Fash demonstrates for Copan that there is much less innovation than one would think, with rulers renewing "tried and trusted religious themes" by renovating and expanding the structures that exemplify them. However, when good evidence is in place, particularly from earlier and later rulers, some patrons stick out as "visionaries," to use Fash's term. They cause large shifts to take place in architectural mass and orientation of site cores. Something, perhaps an impetus even greater than individual aggrandizement, made all of this activity worthwhile. Whether such changes result from the ebb and flow of dynastic interaction and symbolic affiliation remains unclear (e.g., Jamison n.d.: 105–115).

The historical setting of Maya architecture is taken up by Mary Miller (this volume). She delves deeply into the design of meaning in Classic architecture and stresses the multivocality of architecture. In terms of discourse, this means that many stories or "narratives" can be read into Maya buildings, some reporting, perhaps, on what went through the minds of the patrons in commissioning such works. Many of us believe that such stories can be convincing, even though, to some, they call for an unacceptable degree of "*verstehen* and empathy" (Watson 1991: 269). Glyphs allow us to identify patrons or "possessors of buildings," in more precise Maya parlance. With varying success, we can place constructions within an historical context of war and alliance and a more impersonal framework of ritual, building function, and house nomenclature (see Houston, Stuart, this volume). But this should not be undertaken lightly or in a spirit of overconfidence. Glyphs offer the welcome possibility of understanding in small part historical agents and their motivations (Bourdieu 1990: 41), of seeing that, "(h)ouses are built and rebuilt by individuals . . . who have their own view of the work, even if that view is a rereading or restatement of the dominant or socially accepted view" (Johnson 1993: 32). Yet they also tempt us into making too much of our narratives. In this, Mary Miller would probably accept one aspect of the so-called postprocessualist critique, if not its other epistemological anarchies: many stories can be told about Maya buildings and why they were built, but we should not blur the distinction between multiple, ancient perceptions and tales of our own invention, whatever their usefulness in organizing data (Johnson 1994: 176).

One final point. Most of the studies here examine what might be called the *architecture of expectation,* a term bearing on the difficult questions of function and meaning. The contributors study and in part reconstruct what the designers expected the buildings to signal and how they expected the buildings to function. As Webster (this volume) indicates, at stake here are, among other things, potent issues of control and power. Designers devised "dominant locales" as places "to which subjects repeatedly return" (Thomas 1993: 77) to "generate the major structural principles implicated in the constitution of different types of society" (Gregory 1989: 209). Not for a minute, though, should we believe that those expectations dominated or monopolized the use and perception of buildings: "meaning does not inhere in the structure of space: it has to be invoked in the practice of reading . . . (through) . . . a tradition of interpretation" (Thomas 1993: 76)—that is, we should not neglect the role of viewers in interpreting Maya buildings.[6]

Other rituals, such as ballcourt feasting, evidently took place on a planned or ad hoc basis (Fox n.d., 1996), and we may imagine many behaviors and meanings not explicitly advertised by the shape and ornament of buildings. Indeed, there is little reason to believe that structures were ritually autonomous, that continuous behaviors were restricted to a single building. Nor is there reason to think that Maya royal architecture exists apart from a "discursive field of kingship," in which factions perceive the landscape according to their own political agenda (Duncan 1993: 247). This is where studies of artifacts (in themselves problematic) (see Johnston and Gonlin), depictions of the built environment (Houston, this volume), and shifts in architectural programs become relevant, for they suggest alternative possibilities not sketched in formulaic glyphic texts, building façades, or structure plans.

UNFINISHED BUSINESS

Only a deluded optimist would claim that this book addresses all there is to say about Classic Maya architecture. Hardly: for want of time, many points could not be discussed in the two days allotted for the symposium, and many

[6] Thomas (1993: 92) develops an intriguing argument that "the escalation of architectural complexity within the megalithic tombs was an attempt to ensure that the 'correct' reading was made of them." Maya architecture, too, seems guided by a desire to reduce semantic ambiguity. Contrast the relatively spare, if physically impressive, iconography of the Pre-Classic with the explosion of building ornament in the Late Pre-Classic/Early Classic (see Hansen, this volume; also Laporte Molina n.d.: 269–278; Valdés 1992b: pls. 34–38).

others have yet to be aired in any forum. I have selected two for broader consideration: the application of Euroamerican concepts to Classic Maya architecture and the identity of Maya builders.

Vernacular Architecture and the Classic Maya

A very substantial body of literature exists on the subject of "vernacular" architecture, especially in England and the United States (Hall 1972; Marshall 1981). But what is vernacular architecture, and how does it apply to the Classic Maya? Many definitions, particularly traditional ones, sit firmly in the Euroamerican tradition, which defines vernacular buildings mostly in terms of what they are not: they are not created by professional architects, they are neither "high-style" nor monumental, and they do not result from individual genius (Upton and Vlach 1986: xv). Nikolaus Pevsner (1963: 15) says it all: "A bicycle shed is a building; Lincoln Cathedral is a piece of architecture."

Implicit in many of these studies is the notion that "stylistic innovation starts at the top of the social scale and then 'filters' down" (Johnson 1993: 8) in crude, almost passive imitation of elite, high-style buildings (Hubka 1986: 427). To phrase this differently, "vernacular architecture . . . (is) . . . the local version of a widespread academic style" (Upton and Vlach 1986: xvi). But there are other, almost contradictory definitions of the vernacular that suggest a different origin for ornament and overall design. One somewhat older view stems from the perspective of partial environmental determinism: vernacular buildings respond in an immediate and direct way to local economic needs or environmental setting. The builders are often the owners, who construct their dwellings and ancillary structures with a kind of "naive spontaneity" unconditioned by cultural patterns or by long-standing mental templates or "generative grammars" of architecture (Glassie 1975; Hubka 1986: 428). Another view is more cultural and "structuralist" (in Johnston and Gonlin's sense, this volume). The vernacular reflects a "strong popular or social identity" roughly equivalent to Robert Redfield's "little tradition" (Redfield 1960: 42). Undiluted by "extensive outside contact," it serves the needs of "conservative people . . . attached to older, precedented, local architecture" (Upton and Vlach 1986: xvii). A populist sensibility tends to envelop this approach. Buildings are thought to express the people's requirements rather than the tyrannies of elite fashion and social control.

Such approaches have come in for a good deal of thoughtful criticism. Environmental determinism and its watered-down, economic cousins seem increasingly out of favor, because they ignore compelling cultural features of building design (Johnson 1993: 9–12). The view that vernacular tradition develops apart from high style, or that the vernacular responds passively to design changes of an elite sort, fails to take into account the "variety and dynamics of societies" (Jamison n.d.: 96–97), the great complexity of interaction between different builders, their techniques, and varied needs and motivations. Even in Euroamerica, the folk builder in a folk society isolated from "modernizing processes" seems to be a caricature (Holdsworth 1993: 102; Hubka 1984: 204). In an insightful monograph, Rapoport (1990: 17) softens the analytic distinction between vernacular and high style by suggesting a more subtle, interwoven relationship between the two. He emphasizes—correctly, in my view—the need to look at entire cultural landscapes, albeit with increasing discrimination of their parts (Rapoport 1990: 14, 18–19). This is something we have been unable to do in this book; our gaze has focused instead on the "parts" that constitute such landscapes.

Nonetheless, Rapoport believes we should maintain certain fundamental distinctions. To him, change occurs more rapidly in high-style architecture, with greater evidence of jagged discontinuities with past practice (Rapoport 1990: fig. 2.4). Moreover, we should pay attention to the difference between vernacular and "primitive" traditions. The primitive is unspecialized, homogenous, isolated from "great traditions" (Rapoport 1969: 4). In contrast, greater specialization and heterogeneity characterize the vernacular tradition, which lies closer to high style on the continuum of building traditions. Implicit in this discussion is a connection between societal and building types. Primitive societies create "primitive" buildings, but vernacular or high-style societies do not exist per se. They form part of the same collectivity, and their buildings exist within the same society.

Clearly, there is something inconsistent in this formulation, which compares things (primitive, vernacular, high style) that are defined by different criteria (societal type and social station). To place these ideas on a more coherent basis, Kent (1990: 129) examines linkages between "categories of sociopolitical complexity" and the "use of space (behavior) and the built environment (cultural material)," which "becomes more segmented or partitioned as a group's culture becomes more segmented and complex." Broadly speaking, her "Category V" consists of peasant societies integrated into larger political and economic systems. Yet it is hard for Mayanists to draw instructive conclusions from this study. As Kent admits, her results are qualitative, with distinctions like "little/some/much" segmentation or partitioning. What is even less helpful, and somewhat surprising from a processualist, is the lack of attention to internal variability. What do we learn from the demonstration that Maya, past and present, segmented space and the built environment more than, say, the Kikuyu or Kapauku? Is it prudent to view such "traditional forms . . . (as) . . . changeless" (Upton and Vlach 1986: xx)? Even if we look solely at "domestic" architecture, the dwellings and connected spaces that seem to grip most students of traditional building, what, in complex societies, are the varieties of such architecture, and why do they come into existence?

At the least, by using terms such as "vernacular" scholars acknowledge that social and economic distinctions within a society generate different kinds of buildings. This is useful. What is less healthy is the perpetuation of rigid distinctions between so-called high-style buildings and vernacular, "low-style" structures. Supposedly, high style is nontraditional, unresponsive to pressing local needs, uninfluenced by the "owner"; instead, high style is "young," "nonconservative," "unprecedented," even nonfunctional.[7] I doubt that Mayanists are well served by the Euroamerican connotations of these terms or by the questionable divisions they reify (see also Webster, this volume). The available literature on vernacular buildings tends to cleave modest dwellings from palaces or "great houses" (Brunskill 1978: 22), a humble chapel from a cathedral. High-style buildings—Pevsner's "architecture"—form the preserve of other disciplines, such as art history. For our purposes, this is poor anthropology. We need sound theory that will relate elite to nonelite architecture and establish better understandings of Maya systems of design, patronage, and construction. Performance theory may refine ideas about how behavior shapes, and is shaped by, space and its multiple, contingent definitions (Schechner 1990: fig. 2.1).[8] The great advantage of studying Classic Maya architecture—its historical setting and abundant documentation—also represents its drawback, for detailed evidence and particularistic explanation potentially obscure more profound truths about Maya buildings. The comparative approach will alert us to alternative perspectives and more subtle interpretations.

[7] Vernacular research shows a keen awareness of modern changes in labor, materials, and design. In Brunskill's (1978: 29) terminology, "polite" architecture—an objectionable, snobbish term—has logarithmically displaced the vernacular. Such curves or thresholds are irrelevant to the Maya, where change has to be understood apart from the increasing influence of professional architects or their hunger for "internationalism" and aesthetic innovation (Brunskill 1978: 25).

[8] Schechner's "performance event-time-space chart" expresses some of the nuances of performances and their shifting locales. A classification of space (e.g., "multispace") intersects with a general kind of performance ("sacred ritual") to define an event ("pilgrimage"). The behavioral complexity of the chart underscores the futility of attempting a simple functional classification of Classic Maya buildings. It is instructive to consider Juan Pedro Laporte's exquisitely detailed reconstructions of palatial sequences at Tikal. Within a single class of building—the "palace"—occur numerous, shifting patterns of doorway access and room layout (Laporte Molina n.d.: 149–157), suggesting high diversity of room use through time.

There is another point to be made about Maya architecture, particularly with respect to modern examples that may elucidate past practices. Despite a smattering of work, we know relatively little about such buildings, a situation shared with other parts of Mesoamerica, where documentation is dated by concerns of another era (Beals, Carrasco, and McCorkle 1944). Compare this with the state of knowledge of historic architecture in North America. Work by Kniffen (1986) builds on decades of systematic, descriptive research. And despite a number of legitimate criticisms (Johnson 1993: 35–38; Stone 1988), Henry Glassie's influential work on folk housing in Virginia remains a classic, at once provocative and stimulating. We are less favored in the Maya region. Amazingly, Wauchope's (1938) monograph on "modern Maya houses" (see also Wauchope 1940) remains our basic source. Superb and pathbreaking for its time, it cannot meet—nor should it be asked to meet—modern standards of descriptive rigor and theoretical sophistication. More recent research involves ethnoarchaeological programs with a behavioral emphasis (e.g., Fauvet-Berthelot 1986: 235–263; Lee and Hayden 1988; Smyth 1991); their detail obliges localized, restricted study. In my view, there is an urgent need to prepare a comprehensive survey or atlas of indigenous Maya buildings. This is not only because present knowledge is incomplete, but because native technologies and their practitioners, ritual mediations (see Stuart, this volume), building styles, systems of labor organization, use of materials, and nomenclature are swiftly disappearing in some areas. Environmental pressures and the impermanence of Maya building materials (thatch, wattle-and-daub, wicker) mean that the buildings themselves will disappear rapidly. Standards of recording have been set elsewhere: measured, scale drawings showing structural detail and ancillary structures (Brunskill 1965–66, 1978; Mercer 1975); careful selection of study regions (Fox and Raglan 1951); attention to adequate samples, either judgmental or statistical (Johnson 1993: 24); and a sensitivity to historical and ethnic setting (Vlach 1986). This is an ambitious project that cannot wait long. If undertaken wisely, it will contribute crucial, contrastive evidence to discussions of traditional architecture.

The Identity of Maya Builders

We have spoken about agency—the people who commissioned the pyramids. Next to nothing is known, however, about the individuals who actually designed these structures, although Abrams (1994: 97–101) has provided an excellent summary of possible systems of labor organization. To our misfortune, not one building has an unambiguous "name tag" denoting architectural authorship. As David Stuart shows in this volume, structures display not direct records of building but statements of patronage, ownership, and ritual sponsorship. In fact, the limited and hedged nature of these statements almost suggests that rulers were not involved in the details of design—otherwise, one presumes, they would have let us know! The only representations of construction in the corpus of Maya art come from the Madrid Codex (Webster, this volume). Accompanying texts appear to say, *u tak' u sas k'u*: "he plasters the wall with the god's clay," or, more likely, "the god plasters the wall with white clay." In either case, the construction is being done by a most unusual builder and does not bear on the status or identity of Classic architects. (Parenthetically, elsewhere in the Madrid Codex gods engage in many prosaic activities, so building is not privileged as a special, godlike activity.)

Colonial dictionaries of Mayan languages do describe builders and architects and hint at their status. Colonial Tzotzil, for example, contains expressions for "official builder," *jch'ubajel* or *ch'ubavil,* "man who makes walls" (Laughlin 1988, 1: 201); a similar terms exists in Colonial Tzeltal (Calnek 1988: table 3). However, a consideration of the term "official" in its colonial usage leads to the conclusion that it corresponds to an artisan rather than a holder of high office or an intrinsically important person. Susan Miles's report (1957) on Colonial Pokomam occupations makes its clear that "master architect," *ah noah,* was a skill open to all, to be lumped with masons, potters, and fisherman; strangely, though, this term was also applied to "authors." Similar terms, assigned to builders, masons, and quarriers of stone, can be found in the "calepino"—a comprehensive dictionary—of Coto, an early Cakchiquel source (Coto 1983: 22–23, 176). Although not quite Colonial in date, being compiled from a variety of sources of varying age, the Pío Pérez dictionary of Yucatec Maya also attests to a term for "architect" or "mason," *pak'bal,* "maker of walls" (Barrera Vásquez 1980: 626). Here, too, the feeling one gets is of skilled craftsmen not clearly linked with great learning or high status (Eaton 1991).[9] Earlier still, Bishop Landa comments that "common people built at their own expense the houses of the lords" (Tozzer 1941: 86, 171), an observation mirrored by a statement in a *Relación* of 1579, in which commoners were said to have "made and repaired (a lord's) house" (Tozzer 1941: 287 ff). From such remarks, builders (or even master builders) would seem not to have been socially prominent in pre-Colonial times. Rather, they were concerned—so the sources emphasize—with the skillful shaping of stone walls into permanent constructions. The danger in using this evidence is the debatable assumption of continuity with Classic practice, al-

[9] See also Andrews and Rovner (1973: 91) for a specialized, possibly Late Classic tool kit. My thanks to Karl Taube for this reference.

though some data do suggest high levels of skill and presumably specialization in such activities (Woods and Titmus 1996: 487–488).

My prediction for the Classic period is this: Maya builders will probably remain as anonymous to us as the great architect of Chartres is to medievalists, although, as with some Maya sculptors, distinctive "signatures" of style and design may mark their buildings, if not in a manner that is easily verifiable.[10] In Gothic France, the glory of Bishop and God obscured and supplanted the architect's identity (Stoddard 1972: 179). Among the Classic Maya, it was perhaps the centrality of gods and kings that drew a similar, concealing veil. Data on building practices, such as construction bins or segmented walls, suggest glimmerings of labor gangs; their social positions remain unknown, but it is a fair chance that they belonged to groups highly conversant with building techniques (Jamison and Wolff n.d.: 26). So here is a paradox: our volume reports in detail on the function and meaning of Maya buildings but proposes nothing conclusive about the identities of planners and builders, the architects who made new shapes out of a well-established, often ancient vocabulary of form. In the absence of such knowledge, can we speak meaningfully of royal programs, of royal intention in architectural planning and practice? Can we understand the process, the chain of decision making, by which platforms and pyramids, palaces and plazuelas were transformed from idea to material form? Can we know how architectural knowledge was transmitted, whether openly or through the "gatekeeping" of apprenticeship, in "which skilled individuals create their own competitors" (Coy 1989: 9, 10)? These and other questions await us in the next decade, when Maya epigraphy, archaeology, and ancillary fields promise to achieve a mature, self-reflective status.

Things to Do

Until that time we have much to do. Architects with an interest in the physics of Maya buildings, their conflicting mass and stress, need to go beyond the early studies of Roys (1934). Broader landscapes should be incorporated into our research on individual buildings. Where possible, the symbolics of masonry and water courses deserve examination to the standard pioneered by Andeanists (Niles 1987: 207–232; Protzen 1993); work at Caracol, Belize, suggests exciting advances in this direction (Arlen Chase, personal communica-

[10] A sculptor at Aguateca and Dos Pilas carved glyphic finials into a distinctive "trumpet shape" (personal observation, with David Stuart). The appearance of this attribute on most sculptures of the time reflects the low number of first-rank sculptors working in this kingdom. However, the very complexity of building design, at several removes from the designer's intention, will make it difficult to identify architectural "hands."

tion, 1995). The politically charged issue of architectural reconstruction requires further discussion about its aims and methods—what is being said by such work, who is the expected audience, what will happen to such reconstructions through time (Fowler and Houston 1991: 63; Quintana 1992)? Epigraphers need to wring every last datum out of Maya texts about systems of building nomenclature and historical explanations for why certain structures were renovated. Iconographers, too, must reevaluate accepted ideas about building façades, as Fash and his colleagues are now doing at Copan. From this will come a heightened understanding of places as points of communication between the living and the dead or the natural and the supernatural (see McAnany, this volume; McAnany 1995: 26–55; Ray 1977: 373). Finally, we must look to other regions, other approaches, if with a utilitarian perspective: how do cross-cultural comparisons illuminate our data, and, more to the point, how do we go about discerning such parallels and contrasts in a persuasive manner? It is hard to imagine a more auspicious time to study ancient Maya buildings. May this volume express a little of that promise, and may it open new ways of looking at function and meaning in Classic Maya architecture.

Acknowledgments My thanks go to Elliot Abrams, John Clark, John Hawkins, John Monaghan, and David Webster for commenting on this paper.

BIBLIOGRAPHY

Abrams, Elliot M.
1994 *How the Maya Built Their World: Energetics and Ancient Architecture.* University of Texas Press, Austin.

Andrews, E. Wyllys, IV, and Irwin Rovner
1973 *Archaeological Evidence on Social Stratification and Commerce in the Northern Maya Lowlands: Two Mason's Tool Kits from Muna and Dzibilchaltun, Yucatan.* Middle American Research Institute, Publication 31. Tulane University, New Orleans.

Andrews, George F.
1989 *Comalcalco, Tabasco, Mexico: Maya Art and Architecture.* 2nd ed. Labyrinthos, Culver City, Calif.

Awe, Jaime J., Mark D. Campbell, and Jim Conlon
1991 Preliminary Analysis of the Spatial Configuration of the Site Core at Cahal Pech, Belize, and Its Implications for Lowland Maya Social Organization. *Mexicon* 13 (2): 25–30.

Barrera Vásquez, Alfredo
1980 *Diccionario Maya Cordemex: Maya–Español, Español–Maya.* Ediciones Cordemex, Mérida, Yucatan, Mexico.

Beals, Ralph L., Pedro Carrasco, and Thomas McCorkle
1944 *House and House Use of the Sierra Tarascans.* Institute of Social Anthropology, Publication 1. Smithsonian Institution, Washington, D.C.

Blanton, Richard E.
1994 *Houses and Households: A Comparative Study.* Plenum, New York.

Blier, Suzanne P.
1987 *The Anatomy of Architecture: Ontology and Metaphor in Batammaliba Architectural Expression.* Cambridge University Press, Cambridge.

Bourdieu, Pierre
1990 *The Logic of Practice.* Stanford University Press, Stanford, Calif.

Brunskill, Ronald W.
1965–66 A Systematic Procedure for Recording English Vernacular Architecture. *Transactions of the Ancient Monuments Society* 13: 43–126.
1978 *Illustrated Handbook of Vernacular Architecture.* Faber and Faber, London.

Calnek, Edward E.
1988 *Highland Chiapas before the Spanish Conquest.* Papers of the New World Archaeological Foundation 55. Brigham Young University, Provo, Utah.

Carsten, Janet, and Stephen Hugh-Jones
1995 Introduction. In *About the House: Lévi-Strauss and Beyond* (J. Carsten and S. Hugh-Jones, eds.): 1–46. Cambridge University Press, Cambridge.

Coe, William R.
1967 *Tikal: A Handbook of the Ancient Maya Ruins.* University Museum, University of Pennsylvania, Philadelphia.

Coto, Fray Thomás de

1983 *Vocabulario de la lengua cakququel v guatemalteca, nuevamente hecho y recopilado con summo estudio, trauajo y erudición* (R. Acuña, ed.). Universidad Nacional Autónoma de México, México, D.F.

Coy, Michael W.

1989 *Apprenticeship: From Theory to Method and Back Again.* State University of New York Press, Albany.

de Certeau, Michel

1984 *The Practice of Everyday Life.* University of California Press, Berkeley.

Duncan, James

1993 Representing Power: The Politics and Poetics of Urban Form in the Kandyan Kingdom. In *Place/Culture/Representation* (J. Duncan and D. Ley, eds.): 232–248. Routledge, London.

Eaton, Jack D.

1991 Tools of Ancient Maya Builders. In *Maya Stone Tools: Selected Papers from the Second Maya Lithic Conference* (Thomas R. Hester and Harry J. Shafer, eds.): 219–228. Monographs in World Archaeology 1. Prehistory Press, Madison, Wis.

Fauvet-Berthelot, Marie-France

1986 *Ethnopréhistoire de la maison maya.* Etudes mésoaméricaines 13. Centre d'études mexicaines et centraméricaines, México, D.F.

Fowler, William R., Jr., and Stephen D. Houston

1991 Excavations at Tikal, Guatemala: The Work of William R. Coe. *Latin American Anthropology Review* 3 (2): 61–63.

Fox, Sir Cyril, and Lord Raglan

1951 *Monmouthshire Houses: A Study of Building Techniques and Smaller House-Plans in the Fifteenth to Seventeenth Centuries.* National Museum of Wales, Cardiff, United Kingdom.

Fox, John G.

1996 Playing with Power: Ballcourts and Political Ritual in Southern Mesoamerica. *Current Anthropology* 37: 483–509.

n.d. Feasts, Ballgames, and Ritual Process in Mesoamerica. Paper presented at the Sixtieth Annual Meeting of the Society for American Archaeology, Minneapolis, May 1995.

Geertz, Clifford

1973 Religion as a Cultural System. In *The Interpretation of Cultures: Selected Essays by Clifford Geertz:* 87–125. Basic Books, New York.

Giddens, Anthony

1989 A Reply to My Critics. In *Social Theory of Modern Societies: Anthony Giddens and His Critics* (D. Held and J. B. Thompson, eds.): 249–301. Cambridge University Press, Cambridge.

Glassie, Henry

1975 *Folk Housing in Middle Virginia: A Structural Analysis of Historic Artifacts.* University of Tennessee Press, Knoxville.

GRAHAM, IAN

1992 *Corpus of Maya Hieroglyphic Inscriptions,* vol. 4, pt. 2: *Uxmal.* Peabody Museum of Archaeology and Ethnology, Harvard University, Cambridge, Mass.

GREGORY, DEREK

1989 Presences and Absences: Time-Space Relations and Structuration Theory. In *Social Theory of Modern Societies: Anthony Giddens and His Critics* (D. Held and J. B. Thompson, eds.): 185–214. Cambridge University Press, Cambridge.

GRIAULE, MARCEL, AND GERMAINE DIETERLEN

1954 The Dogon. In *African Worlds* (D. Forde, ed.): 83–110. Oxford University Press, London.

HALL, SIR ROBERT DE Z.

1972 *A Bibliography on Vernacular Architecture.* David and Charles, London.

HILLIER, BILL, AND JULIENNE HANSON

1984 *The Social Logic of Space.* Cambridge University Press, Cambridge.

HOLDSWORTH, DERYCK

1993 Revaluing the House. In *Place/Culture/Representation* (J. Duncan and D. Ley, eds.): 95–109. Routledge, London.

HOUSTON, STEPHEN D.

1989 *Reading the Past: Maya Glyphs.* British Museum, London.

1993 *Hieroglyphs and History at Dos Pilas: Dynastic Politics of the Classic Maya.* University of Texas Press, Austin.

HUBKA, THOMAS C.

1984 *Big House, Little House, Back House, Barn: The Connected Farm Buildings of New England.* University Press of New England, Hanover, N.H.

1986 Just Folks Designing: Vernacular Designers and the Generation of Form. In *Readings in American Vernacular Architecture* (Dell Upton and John M. Vlach, eds.): 426–432. University of Georgia Press, Athens.

JAMESON, MICHAEL H.

1990 Domestic Space in the Greek City-State. In *Domestic Architecture and the Use of Space: An Interdisciplinary Cross-Cultural Study* (Susan Kent, ed.): 92–113. Cambridge University Press, Cambridge.

JAMISON, THOMAS R.

n.d. Symbolic Affiliation, Architecture, and Settlement Patterns in Southern Belize: Nim Li Punit and Xnaheb during the Late Classic. Ph.D. dissertation, State University of New York, Albany, 1993.

JAMISON, THOMAS R., AND GREGORY A. WOLFF

n.d. Excavations in and around Plaza A-I and Plaza A-II. In *Xunantunich Archaeological Project: 1994 Field Season* (R. M. Leventhal, ed.): 25–47. Manuscript on file, Department of Anthropology, University of California, Los Angeles.

JOHNSON, MATTHEW

1993 *Housing Culture: Traditional Architecture in an English Landscape.* Smithsonian Institution Press, Washington, D.C.

1994 Ordering Houses, Creating Narratives. In *Architecture and Order: Approaches to*

Social Space (Mike P. Pearson and Colin Richards, eds.): 170–177. Routledge, London.

Kent, Susan
1990 A Cross-Cultural Study of Segmentation, Architecture, and the Use of Space. In *Domestic Architecture and the Use of Space: An Interdisciplinary Cross-Cultural Study* (Susan Kent, ed.): 127–152. Cambridge University Press, Cambridge.

Kniffen, Fred B.
1986 Folk Housing: Key to Diffusion. In *Readings in American Vernacular Architecture* (Dell Upton and John M. Vlach, eds.): 3–26. University of Georgia Press, Athens.

Kubler, George A.
1985 The Design of Space in Maya Architecture. In *Studies in Ancient American and European Art: The Collected Essays of George Kubler* (T. R. Reese, ed.): 242–255. Yale University Press, New Haven, Conn.

Laporte Molina, Juan Pedro
n.d. Alternativas del clásico temprano en la relación Tikal-Teotihuacan: Grupo 6C-XVI, Tikal, Péten, Guatemala. Ph.D. dissertation, Universidad Nacional Autónoma de México, 1989.

Laughlin, Robert M.
1975 *The Great Tzotzil Dictionary of San Lorenzo Zinacantán.* Smithsonian Contributions to Anthropology 19. Smithsonian Institution, Washington, D.C.
1988 *The Great Tzotzil Dictionary of Santo Domingo Zinacantán.* Smithsonian Contributions to Anthropology 31. Smithsonian Institution, Washington, D.C.

Lee, Thomas A., Jr., and Brian Hayden
1988 *Ethnoarchaeology among the Highland Maya of Chiapas, Mexico.* Papers of the New World Archaeological Foundation 56. Brigham Young University, Provo, Utah.

Lévi-Strauss, Claude
1987 *Anthropology and Myth: Lectures, 1951–1982.* Blackwell, Oxford.

Littlejohn, John
1967 `The Temne House. In *Myth and Cosmos: Readings in Mythology and Symbolism* (J. Middleton, ed.): 331–356. Natural History Press, New York.

López, Francisco, and Federico Fahsen
n.d. Nuevas referencias sobre cerámica códice en contexto arqueológico en el sitio de Nakbe. In *Investigaciones arqueológicas en Nakbé, Petén: El resumen de la temporada de campo de 1993* (Richard D. Hansen, ed.): 284–299. Manuscript on file, Department of Anthropology, Brigham Young University.

López Austin, Alfredo
1988 *The Human Body and Ideology: Concepts of the Ancient Nahuas.* 2 vols. (T. Ortiz de Montellano and B. Ortiz de Montellano, trans.). University of Utah Press, Salt Lake City.

Marshall, Howard W.
1981 *American Folk Architecture: A Selected Bibliography.* Publications of the American Folklife Center, no. 8. Library of Congress, Washington, D.C.

McAnany, Patricia A.
1995 *Living with the Ancestors: Kinship and Kingship in Ancient Maya Society*. University of Texas Press, Austin.

Mercer, Eric
1975 *English Vernacular Houses: A Study of Traditional Farmhouses and Cottages.* Her Majesty's Stationery Office, London.

Miles, Susan
1957 The Sixteenth Century Pokom-Maya: A Documentary Analysis of Social Structure and Archaeological Setting. *Transactions of the American Philosophical Society* 47: 733–781.

Niles, Susan A.
1987 *Callachaca: Style and Status in an Inca Community.* University of Iowa Press, Iowa City.

Ortner, Sherry B.
1973 On Key Symbols. *American Anthropologist* 75: 1338–1346.

Pearson, Mike P., and Colin Richards
1994 Ordering the World: Perceptions of Architecture, Space and Time. In *Architecture and Order: Approaches to Social Space* (Mike P. Pearson and Colin Richards, eds.): 1–37. Routledge, London.

Pendergast, David M.
1979 *Excavations at Altun Ha, Belize, 1964–1970,* vol. 1. Royal Ontario Museum, Toronto.
1992 Noblesse Oblige: The Elites of Altun Ha and Lamani, Belize. In *Mesoamerican Elites: An Archaeological Assessment* (Diane Z. Chase and Arlen F. Chase, eds.): 61–79. University of Oklahoma Press, Norman.

Pevsner, Nikolaus
1963 *An Outline of European Architecture.* 7th ed. Penguin Books, Harmondsworth, United Kingdom.

Pollock, H. E. D.
1940 Sources and Methods in the Study of Maya Architecture. In *The Maya and Their Neighbors: Essays on Middle American Anthropology and Archaeology* (C. L. Hay et al., eds.): 179–201. Appleton-Century, New York.

Proskouriakoff, Tatiana
1963 *An Album of Maya Architecture.* University of Oklahoma Press, Norman.

Protzen, Jean-Pierre
1993 *Inca Architecture and Construction at Ollantaytambo.* Oxford University Press, New York.

Quintana, Oscar
1992 Probleme der Konservierung von Maya-Ruinen. In *Die Welt der Maya: Archäologische Schätze aus drei Jahrtausenden* (E. and A. Eggebrecht, eds.): 139–141. Verlag Philipp von Zabern, Mainz am Rhein, Germany.

Rapoport, Amos
1969 *House Form and Culture.* Prentice-Hall, Englewood Cliffs, N.J.
1990 *History and Precedent in Environmental Design.* Plenum, New York.

RAY, BENJAMIN

1977 Sacred Space and Royal Shrines in Buganda. *History of Religions* 16 (4): 363–373.

REDFIELD, ROBERT

1960 *Peasant Society and Culture*. University of Chicago Press, Chicago.

ROBERTSON, MERLE G.

1985a *The Sculpture of Palenque,* vol. 2: *The Early Buildings of the Palace and the Wall Paintings.* Princeton University Press, Princeton, N.J.

1985b *The Sculpture of Palenque,* vol. 3: *The Late Buildings of the Palace.* Princeton University Press, Princeton, N.J.

ROYS, LAWRENCE

1934 *The Engineering Knowledge of the Maya.* Carnegie Institution, Publication 436, 6: 27–105. Washington, D.C.

SCHECHNER, RICHARD

1990 Magnitudes of Performance. In *By Means of Performance: Intercultural Studies of Theatre and Ritual* (R. Schechner and W. Appel, eds.): 19–49. Cambridge University Press, Cambridge.

SMYTH, MICHAEL P.

1991 *Modern Maya Storage Behavior: Ethnoarchaeological Case Examples from the Puuc Region of Yucatan.* Memoirs in Latin American Archaeology, no. 3. University of Pittsburgh, Pittsburgh.

STODDARD, WHITNEY S.

1972 *Art and Architecture in Medieval France.* Icon Editions, New York.

STONE, G. W.

1988 Artifacts Are Not Enough. In *Documentary Archaeology in the New World* (M. C. Beaudry, ed.): 68–77. Cambridge University Press, Cambridge.

THOMAS, JULIAN

1993 The Hermeneutics of Megalithic Space. In *Interpretative Archaeology* (C. Tilley, ed.): 73–97. Berg, Providence, R.I.

TOZZER, ALFRED M.

1941 *Landa's relación de las cosas de Yucatán: A Translation.* Papers of the Peabody Museum of American Archaeology and Ethnology, vol. 18. Harvard University, Cambridge, Mass.

UPTON, DELL

1979 Toward a Performance Theory of Vernacular Architecture in Tidewater Virginia. *Folklore Forum* 12 (2–3): 173–196.

UPTON, DELL, AND JOHN M. VLACH

1986 Introduction. In *Readings in American Vernacular Architecture* (Dell Upton and John M. Vlach, eds.): xiii–xxiv. University of Georgia Press, Athens.

VALDÉS, JUAN ANTONIO

1992a El crecimiento de la civilización maya en el area central durante el preclásico tardío: Una vista desde el grupo H de Uaxactún. *U tz'ib* 1 (2): 16–31.

1992b Von der ersten Besiedlung bis zur Späten Präklassik. In *Die Welt der Maya:*

Archäologische Schätze aus drei Jahrtausenden (E. and A. Eggebrecht, eds.): 22–40. Verlag Philipp von Zabern, Mainz am Rhein, Germany.

VLACH, JOHN M.

1986 The Shotgun House: An African Architectural Legacy. In *Readings in American Vernacular Architecture* (Dell Upton and John M. Vlach, eds.): 58–78. University of Georgia Press, Athens.

VOGT, EVON Z.

1969 *Zinacantan: A Maya Community in the Highlands of Chiapas.* Belknap Press of Harvard University Press, Cambridge, Mass.

1983 Ancient and Contemporary Maya Settlement Patterns: A New Look from the Chiapas Highlands. In *Prehistoric Settlement Patterns: Essays in Honor of Gordon R. Willey* (E. Z. Vogt and R. M. Leventhal, eds.): 89–114. University of New Mexico Press, Albuquerque, and Peabody Museum of Archaeology and Ethnology, Harvard University, Cambridge, Mass.

WATERSON, ROXANA

1990 *The Living House: An Anthropology of Architecture in Southeast Asia.* Oxford University Press, Kuala Lumpur, Malaysia.

WATSON, PATTY JO

1991 A Parochial Primer: The New Dissonance As Seen from the Midcontinental United States. In *Processual and Postprocessual Archaeologies: Multiple Ways of Knowing the Past* (R. W. Preucel, ed.): 265–274. Occasional Paper 10. Center for Archaeological Investigations, Southern Illinois University, Carbondale.

WAUCHOPE, ROBERT

1938 *Modern Maya Houses: A Study of Their Archaeological Significance.* Carnegie Institution, Publication 502. Washington, D. C.

1940 Domestic Architecture of the Maya. In *The Maya and Their Neighbors: Essays on Middle American Anthropology and Archaeology* (C. L. Hay et al., eds.): 232–241. Appleton-Century, New York.

WOODS, JAMES C., AND GENE L. TITMUS

1996 Stone on Stone: Perspectives on Maya Civilization from Lithic Studies. In *Eighth Palenque Round Table, 1993* (Martha J. Macri and Jan McHargue, eds.; Merle Greene Robertson, gen. ed.): 479–489. Pre-Columbian Art Research Institute, San Francisco.

Index

Italic numbers indicate figures.